SEXUALITY REPOSITIONED
DIVERSITY AND THE LAW

Sexuality Repositioned: Diversity and the Law

Edited by

BELINDA BROOKS-GORDON
LORAINE GELSTHORPE
MARTIN JOHNSON
ANDREW BAINHAM

For the Cambridge Socio-Legal Group

·HART·
PUBLISHING

OXFORD – PORTLAND OREGON
2004

Hart Publishing
Oxford and Portland, Oregon

Published in North America (US and Canada) by
Hart Publishing c/o
International Specialized Book Services
5804 NE Hassalo Street
Portland, Oregon
97213-3644
USA

Distributed in the Netherlands, Belgium and Luxembourg by
Intersentia, Churchillaan 108
B2900 Schoten
Antwerpen
Belgium

Hart Publishing is a specialist legal publisher based in Oxford, England.
To order further copies of this book or to request a list of other
publications please write to:

Hart Publishing, Salter's Boatyard, Folly Bridge,
Abingdon Road, Oxford OX1 4LB
Telephone: +44 (0)1865 245533 or Fax: +44 (0)1865 794882
e-mail: mail@hartpub.co.uk
WEBSITE: http//www.hartpub.co.uk

British Library Cataloguing in Publication Data
Data Available
ISBN 1–84113–489–9 (paperback)

Typeset by Hope Services (Abingdon) Ltd.
Printed and bound in Great Britain on acid-free paper by
TJ International Ltd, Padstow, Cornwall

Preface

This collection of essays is the fourth book by the Cambridge Socio-Legal Group. The chapters in this book comprise a series of papers which were either presented during, or arose from, a three-day residential seminar held by the Cambridge Socio-Legal Group at Pembroke College. We are especially grateful to Frances Murton who skilfully sub-edited the whole manuscript. The final stages of the book benefited from the incomparable efficiency of Jill Brown at the Centre for Family Research. We thank the discussants who contributed to the lively debates which, continuing into the evenings, made the seminar such an intellectual pleasure.

The Editors
Cambridge, January 2004

Contents and Discussants

Notes on Contributors and Discussants

Andrew Bainham is Reader in Family Law and Policy at the University of Cambridge, a Fellow of Christ's College and the current Chair of the Cambridge Socio-Legal Group. He is editor of the *International Survey of Family Law* and author of the textbook *Children: The Modern Law*, the third edition of which is published in 2004. Among his most recent projects has been the writing of a research report with Clem Henricson of the National Family and Parenting Institute funded by the Joseph Rowntree Foundation on the division between family policies and policies directed specifically at children.

Charlotte Bilby is a lecturer in Forensic Psychology at the University of Leicester where she leads the postgraduate courses in the Assessment and Treatment of Sex Offenders. Her main area of research interest is evaluation of central government crime reduction and prevention initiatives. These activities focus on the effectiveness of offending behaviour programmes, including those for sexual offenders, and the implications for future policy development and practice.

Belinda Brooks-Gordon is a University Lecturer at Birkbeck College, University of London where she is Director of the Family and Systemic Therapy Programme. Her research addresses questions on human sexuality, sex work, and also sexual offences. This includes the human rights issues involved in sexual labour, the clients who pay for it, and the officers who police it. A key area of her research activity into sexual offences includes the effectiveness of sexual offending behaviour programmes, evaluation of clinical treatment delivery, and the implications for future policy development and practice.

Pak-Lee Chau is a staff research scientist at the Pasteur Institute, Paris. He read medicine, and did research in physics and pharmacology at Cambridge. He was a supervisor in physiology and pharmacology at New Hall, Cambridge, for seven years. He has collaborated with Jonathan Herring on five papers on medico-legal aspects of reproductive physiology.

Marc Desautels currently works at the Forensic Section of the School of Psychology at the University of Leicester and is also a course tutor in counselling at the Institute of Continuing Education at the University of Cambridge. He is currently doing a PhD at the University of Leicester on group process and the therapeutic relationship in the treatment of sexual offenders. He has worked for a number of years as a counsellor in private practice and for various agencies.

Michael Freeman is a Professor of English Law at University College London. He is the author of books including *Violence In The Home—A Sociological Study*, *The Rights And Wrongs Of Children*, *The Moral Status of Children*, and *Introduction to Jurisprudence* (now in its seventh edition). He is the editor of the *International Journal of Children's Rights* and the new *International Journal of Law In Context*.

Roger Ingham is Reader in Health and Community Psychology at the University of Southampton, and Director of the Centre for Sexual Health Research. The Centre has been established for a number of years, and carries out quality research in the field of sexual conduct in the UK and in other countries; it is a multidisciplinary centre, involving psychology, statistics, geography, sociology, medicine, and other disciplines. These studies have included sexual behaviour amongst young people, contraception use and decision making, risk perception, attitudes to services and sex education in school settings, and other related topics. Studies have also been carried out in other European countries, and the Centre currently runs a large DFID funded programme to extend work into developing countries across the world.

Roger Ingham has worked in this area for many years. During this time he has published widely on relevant topics and worked closely with policy makers in this country and abroad. He has been a consultant for the World Health Organisation's AIDS programme, and currently co-ordinates a large DFID funded programme on sexual health in poorer countries. He was a member of the Department of Health's Sexual Health and HIV Strategy core group, and is currently a member of the Government's Independent Advisory Group for the Teenage Pregnancy Unit and of the Teenage Magazine Arbitration Panel.

Julie Jessop is a Senior Research Associate at the Centre for Family Research, University of Cambridge. She has worked on various research projects connected with the sociology of the family, including divorce and post-divorce parenting, interventions for children of divorce, adolescents and bereavement, as well as the development of sexuality. She is currently working on part of a three year Wellcome Trust funded bio-ethics project looking at issues surrounding human tissue collection in the UK. She is the co-ordinator of the Women's Workshop on Qualitative Family/Household Research, and has recently co-edited a book on *Ethics in Qualitative Research* (Sage, 2002).

Martin Johnson is Professor of Reproductive Sciences at the University of Cambridge and Visiting Professor in the Department of Physiology at the University of Sydney, Australia. He was for 6 years until 1999 a member of the Human Fertilisation and Embryology Authority, and is a former Chair of the British Society for Developmental Biology. He is the author of numerous works on reproductive and developmental science and medicine, on bioethics and on medical education. He is co-author of the standard undergraduate teaching text on mammalian reproduction *Essential Reproduction* (Blackwell, 1999, 5th Edition).

Loraine Gelsthorpe is Senior Lecturer in Criminology at the Institute of Criminology, University of Cambridge and a Fellow at Pembroke College, Cambridge. Her research interests include feminist perspectives in criminology, gender, crime and justice, the exercise of discretion and discrimination in the delivery of criminal justice, the links between crime, social exclusion and social justice since the 1950s, and youth justice. She has written extensively on these and related issues. Her current research revolves around probation and community penalties, especially in relation to 'what works' and women. Loraine Gelsthorpe chairs the British Society of Criminology's Professional and Ethics Committee. She is also a psychoanalytical psychotherapist.

Jonathan Herring is a Fellow of Exeter College and University Lecturer in Law at the University of Oxford. He is author of *Family Law* (Pearson 2004), *Criminal Law: Text, Cases and Materials* (OUP: 2004) and *Criminal Law* (Macmillan, 2002). He writes on criminal, family and medical law issues. He is also an advisory editor for the *Family Court Reports*.

Liat Levanon is a PhD student at the Law Faculty, University of Cambridge, writing her thesis about the offence of rape. She acquired her first degree in law at the Hebrew University of Jerusalem. She was a member of the editorial board of the Hebrew University Law Review (Mishpatim), served as an Articled Clerk at the Israeli Supreme Court, and was a teaching assistant in Criminal Law at the Academic College of Law in Ramat-Gan, as well as a research assistant in this College and in the Israeli Democracy Institute in Jerusalem. Her publications (with Professor Mordechai Kremnitzer of the Hebrew University) relate to different aspects of criminal law, mainly the offence of sexual harassment, the offence of bribery, incitement to violence, and aid in committing an offence.

Craig Lind is a Lecturer in Law at the University of Sussex. His research interests range across the whole of family law. He is one of two coordinators of the Children and Young Person's Research Group at Sussex and is currently arranging an interdisciplinary conference on the Regulation of Childhood. His publications are principally in the areas of family law, sexuality and culture. At present he is working on a major project which considers the cultural contexts surrounding the export and import of sexualities.

Linda McDowell is Professor of Geography at University College London. She is author of numerous books and papers about labour market restructuring and gender divisions of labour including *Redundant Masculinities?* (Blackwell 2003). She is currently working on a study of European migrant labour in postwar Britain for a book provisionally entitled *Hard Labour* (UCL Press).

David Pearl started his career as an academic, first in Cambridge and then at the University of East Anglia where he was Professor of Law and Dean of the Law School from 1989–1994. He was appointed a Circuit Judge in 1994 and served as Chief Adjudicator of the Immigration Appellate Authority from 1994–1997.

He was the President of the Immigration Appeal Tribunal from 1997–1999 and then became the Director of Studies of the Judicial Studies Board. He was responsible for organising and implementing the training of the judiciary on the Human Rights Act. Since 2002, he has been President of the Care Standards Tribunal, a newly constituted Tribunal that hears appeals arising out of the regulatory decisions made by the Secretary of State, the National Care Standards Commission (and its successors), the General Social Care Council, OFSTED, and the National Assembly for Wales. He is a contributor to Hoggett and Pearl *The Family Law and Society: Cases and Materials* now in its fifth edition, and Pearl and Menski *A Textbook on Muslim Family Law* now in its 3rd edition, as well as numerous other publications. He is a Bencher of Gray's Inn and a Life Fellow of Fitzwilliam College Cambridge.

Kerry Petersen is an Associate Professor in the School of Law and Legal Studies, La Trobe University, and a barrister and solicitor of the Supreme Court of Victoria. In 1995–96 she was a Senior Research Fellow at the Law School, University of Glasgow, Scotland. She has published widely in the fields of medical law and human reproduction law. Recently, she co-edited *Controversies in Health Law* with Ian Freckelton (The Federation Press 1999) and *Regulating Reproductive Technologies* with Margaret Coady (Special Issue: *Journal of Law and Medicine* Vol 9 2002). She is currently working on an Australian study analysing the views of clinicians on the regulation of assisted reproductive technologies.

Joanna Phoenix is Lecturer in Sociology at the Department of Social and Policy Sciences, University of Bath. Her research interests include gender and crime, prostitution and youth justice and punishment. She has published widely on issues relating to women's and young people's involvement in prostitution. She is currently completing *Illicit and Illegal: Sex and Social Control* for Willan Publishing. In 2003, she completed the first independent, national research examining the social and welfare provision for young people in prostitution. Her most recent project examines professional discourses of Orisk1 and Oneed1 in the context of young lawbreakers.

Zoë-Jane Playdon was educated at the universities of Newcastle on Tyne, Leicester and Warwick, and at Henley Management College. Zoë-Jane holds doctorates in contemporary Irish literature and in participative management. Formerly a National Coordinator at the Department of Education and Science, and subsequently head of Continuing Vocational Education at the University of Warwick, at present she is Regional Education Adviser at Kent, Surrey and Sussex Department of Postgraduate Medical and Dental Education, at the University of London. She has worked in GLTB civil liberties for fifteen years, advising a variety of government and other agencies, is co-Chair of the Gay and Lesbian Association of Doctors and Dentists and co-founder, with Dr Lynne Jones MP, of the UK Parliamentary Forum on Transsexualism.

Ken Plummer is Professor of Sociology, University of Essex and a regular Visiting Professor of Sociology at the University of California at Santa Barbara. He is author of many books and articles including *Telling Sexual Stories, Documents of Life-2*, and *Intimate Citizenship: Private Decisions and Public Dialogues* to be published later this year by the University of Washington Press. He is also the founder editor of the journal *Sexualities*, and co-author of *Sociology: A Global Introduction* (2nd ed, 2002).

Martin Richards is Director of the Centre for Family Research and Professor of Family Research at the University of Cambridge. His research interests include marriage, divorce and family life and psychosocial aspects of new genetic and reproductive technologies. His books include *Sexual Arrangements: Marriage and Affairs* (with Janet Reibstein, Heinemann/Charles Scribners Sons 1992), *The Blackwell Companion to the Sociology of Families* (editor with Jackie Scott and Judy Treas, Blackwell, 2003) and he is co-editor of three of the Cambridge Socio-Legal Group volumes—*What is a Parent?* (2001), *Body Lore and Laws* (2002) and *Children and their Families: Contact, Rights and Welfare* (2003). He is currently working on a book on historical and contemporary uses of reproductive and genetic technologies.

Lynne Segal is Anniversary Professor of Psychology and Gender Studies at Birkbeck College, University of London. Her books include *Is the Future Female? Troubled Thoughts on Contemporary Feminism; Slow Motion: Changing Masculinities, Changing Men; Straight Sex: The Politics of Pleasure; Why Feminism? Gender, Psychology, Politics.*

Andrew Webber is Senior Lecturer in German at the University of Cambridge and a Fellow of Churchill College. He has published widely on the construction of identity and culture in modern German literature and film. He is currently completing a Cultural History of the European Avant-garde for Polity Press.

Jeffrey Weeks is Professor of Sociology and Executive Dean of Arts and Human Sciences at London South Bank University. He is the author of some twenty books, and numerous articles, mainly on the history and social organisation of sexuality and intimacy. His most recent books include *Making Sexual History* (Polity Press 2000), *Same Sex Intimacies* (with Brian Heaphy and Catherine Donovan, Routledge 2001) and *Sexualities and Society: A Reader* (with Janet Holland and Matthew Waites, Polity Press 2003).

Helena Willén is senior lecturer in Public Health at the Nordic School of Public Health in Göteborg, Sweden. Her PhD work in psychology concerned reproductive decision-making, while later research interests have been focussed on aspects of individual and family decision-making, such as divorce decisions, parental decision-making in the everyday life of post-divorce families, and health and lifestyle decision-making among adolescents. Helena is currently coordinator of the MPH programme at the Nordic School of Public Health, and teaches psycho-social dimensions of health at post-graduate level.

1

Introduction: Sexuality Repositioned

LORAINE GELSTHORPE*

INTRODUCTION

WE ARE BOMBARDED with images of sexuality on a daily basis through newspapers, through the visual media, and through public advertisements and unsolicited email. These images heighten sexual excitement and interest, but also raise sexual fears, whether about a growing slave trade in young men, women and children for sex, access to pornography on the internet, the powers of Viagra for male potency and female orgasm, or penis size. We have also become attuned to regular health warnings about AIDS and teenage pregnancy. There has been a huge increase in new sexual knowledges too, arising from debates in different quarters: feminist, lesbian and gay (queer) politics, and other sexual movements. At the same time there have been media and public inspired campaigns to further the criminalisation and increase the punishment of sex offenders, to establish ever more extensive registers of known sex offenders, and to change the laws so as to protect more assuredly potential victims. More than this, sexuality is often used to denote who and what we are, and what we can become. Even as I write, the Church of England and the Anglican community worldwide are embroiled in bitter debate about the possibility and impossibility of gay priests taking high office within the 'body of Christian unity' and the Vatican has issued uncompromising and controversial statements on sexuality in relation to marriage, reproduction and parenthood.

This book focuses on perspectives on sexuality in contemporary social life against this backcloth of developments and debates. The title of the book: *Sexuality Repositioned: Diversity and the Law* emerged after long discussion about the focus and direction of the seminar in the Spring of 2003. In essence, much of the book concerns boundaries between disciplines, competing perspectives and tensions between the social realities of sexualities and state interests as

---

* With thanks to my colleagues Andrew Bainham, Belinda Brooks-Gordon and Martin Johnson for their helpful inputs to this chapter.

reflected in the law. In this way, the book makes a significant contribution to an understanding of controversies concerning sexual positions in the late twentieth and early twenty-first centuries. But before describing the content of the book, it is worth dwelling on the development of knowledges about sexualities over time. Detailed descriptions of the historical development of sexual knowledges have been eloquently given elsewhere, of course (see Chapters Two and Three this volume; Weeks, Holland and Waites, 2003; Weeks, 1985). Suffice to say here, that questions as to what sexuality is, how it develops, what it means, what symbolic import it carries, and how it shapes our everyday interactions with each other are crucial questions. And indeed, we have witnessed huge revolutions in knowledge about sexuality over time.

CHANGING PERSPECTIVES ON SEXUALITY

Early attempts to understand sexuality drew from the natural sciences; it was perceived to be logical to want to put it on a scientific basis. European sexological pioneers such as Austrian psychologist van Krafft-Ebing, and Havelock Ellis in Britain, made moves to put sexuality on a scientific footing by seeking to establish what have been described as the 'laws of nature' (see Weeks, 1985).

There were simultaneous sociological reflections from August Comte, Max Weber and Emile Durkheim amongst others (and here the main concern was with the 'laws of society'; Weeks, 1985). They looked for the social characteristics of individuals' sexualities, and patterns of sexuality and sexual relationships. Further contributions from anthropologists such as Edward Westermarck revealed interest in differential cultural perceptions, understandings and laws concerning the body and the erotic. British sexologist, Havelock Ellis, pursued strong interests in the notion of cultural variations of sexual behaviour. It is important to mention, too, the work of Sigmund Freud who was concerned with both developmental aspects of sexuality and with the relationship between sexuality and civilisation (see, for example, Freud, 1905; 1908; 1930). Freud's contributions have been widely read and widely criticised. At his worst, Freud's notions of sexuality merely reflect the interests of the late nineteenth century and early twentieth century bourgeoisie; at his best, however, Freud managed to chart complex fields regarding gendered divisions and recognised the role of the unconscious in individuals' daily struggles in defining, identifying and negotiating sexuality (a theme which is taken up by Susie Orbach, 1999, amongst others, writing about the impossibility of sex). American sexologist Alfred Kinsey *et al.* (1948; 1953) continued the application of a scientific zeal to human sexual behaviour. His systematic examination of the variety of sexual patterns in the USA in the 1940s and beyond ultimately challenged what was thought to be 'deviant' and to be 'normal' and, as Weeks, Holland and Waites (2003) suggest, this paved the way for late twentieth century social scientific explorations of sexuality and its meaning in society.

The 'sexual revolution' of the 1960s and 1970s—invoking notions of liberation from biological science and 'natural phenomena'—represented a potential realm of freedom to feminists (Firestone, 1971; Millett, 1971) and lesbian and gay writers and activists (Altman, 1971; Katz, 1976; 1995) amongst others. Gagnon and Simon (1973) and Foucault (1979) and Plummer (1995) continued this critical line of questioning regarding sexuality by looking at how society has continually changed the contours of sexuality and invested sexuality with its import and significance. Signs that the sexual revolution continues include the raft of proposed legislation tackling issues on which UK governments have been previously tentative: gay and lesbian couples to be allowed to register their unions as 'civil partnerships', transsexuals to be issued with new birth certificates, and the repeal of Section 28 of the Local Government Act are all reforms which follow public opinion. Elsewhere in Europe, North America and Australasia, Government legislation is expanding the legitimacy of varied sexualities, and the social values on which this change is based are also permeating traditionally conservative societies such as China. The fact that television programmes and other media fora can now be led by gay men and women with little comment (for example, gay personalities Anna Nolan and Brian Dowling on *Big Brother*, comedians Sue Perkins and Rhona Cameron on the celebrity versions of *Big Brother* and *I'm a Celebrity Get Me Out of Here!*) has exploded traditional stereotypes for the public, and suggests further liberalisation and tolerance if not positive approval of diversity. By the end of 2003, the Conservative Party had selected its first ever openly gay Parliamentary candidate for a constituency. In the same year, Commander Brian Paddick of the Metropolitan Police was awarded a large settlement from the *Mail on Sunday* following media intrusion into his personal life, successfully arguing that the fact that he is gay is irrelevant. Thus the limits of outrage are perhaps being steadily and stealthily redrawn.

One attempt to understand the notion of sexuality and its relationship to society has come from sociologist Anthony Giddens (1992). In an exploration of sexuality and modern cities, Giddens examines how 'sexuality' comes into being and what connections it has with the changes that have affected personal life on a more general level. He introduces and recognises as a late modern phenomenon the notion of 'plastic sexuality' depicting a sexuality freed from the constraints of reproduction (as a consequence of modern contraception and new reproductive technologies alongside notions of new identities in which sexuality is 'decentred'). Thus 'plastic sexuality' frees sexuality from 'the rule of the phallus, from the overweening importance of male sexual experience' (1992: 2). Jeffrey Weeks (1995) has similarly explored sexual values in an age of uncertainty in the face of the collapse of traditional sexual and gender certainties. His insightful reflections on the need for a democratising sexual ethics are telling of the opening up of new conceptions of sexuality.

Modern conceptions of sexuality, however, are not necessarily reflected in legal narratives, notwithstanding signs of liberation in the law. On the contrary, law reflects the tensions inherent in the relationships between sexuality, identity and society. Historical and legal records outline ways in which legal categories of sexuality have at once both lagged behind contemporary sexuality and challenged traditional conceptions of sexuality. Despite the advent of new knowledge about sexuality, new perspectives, and new experiences even, we do not *routinely* or *habitually* reflect on the interface of social and legal dimensions of sexuality. Rather, the law is periodically reviewed in response to some crisis or campaign. The idea for this book thus came from awareness that it is important to explore some of the social and moral censures and contours that shape and mark the boundaries of sexuality. The production of the book has coincided with the first major overhaul of sexual offences for fifty years, which has itself attempted to clarify an inordinately complex and controversial legal realm, and this makes the book especially timely. So, too, the fact that the book heralds a further review of sex laws concerning prostitution in order to address the possibility of safety zones and the licensing of prostitution as well as tackling the involvement of organised crime in prostitution, and its links with heroin and crack cocaine abuse. Both these events have fuelled our concerns and make our socio-legal explorations of different sexual positions significant.

It is worth dwelling on one further aspect of sexuality at this point. This concerns the surveys of sexual behaviour in Britain in 1994 and 1999.

SEXUAL SURVEYS

The first National Survey of Sexual Attitudes and Lifestyles was commissioned in 1987 and published in 1994 (Wellings, Field, Johnson and Wadsworth, 1994). The impetus for such a study was the HIV epidemic, and the attendant concern to assess and control its spread heralded a new era of sexual research throughout the world. The advent and spread of AIDS and HIV brought about a major shift, not only in terms of public awareness of sexually transmitted diseases and hitherto taboo or hidden sexual practices, but also in the extent to which government felt that it could legitimately intervene in order to contain anxiety. Prior to the 1980s, politicians in Britain tended to avoid involving themselves too publicly in matters of sexual health, while the public, as shown by the British Social Attitudes Survey, was becoming less and less censorious of people's differing sexual preferences. Widespread concern about AIDS changed this picture. Government now intervened with some vigour, sponsoring television commercials to promote the use of condoms, while at the same time, the public became more homophobic.

Mrs Thatcher famously withdrew the promised funding from the national survey in its early stages, marking the political, as well as intellectual and scientific challenges that it represented, but the Wellcome Trust stepped into the breach. The result was a survey of almost 19,000 adults (aged between 16–59), which shed light on patterns of sexual behaviour. Indeed, the survey explored the relationships between sexual lifestyles and reproductive and sexual health by collecting data on personal relationships, sex education, reproductive health and careers and other related information. The survey yielded unparalleled amounts of information on trends in teenage pregnancy, influences on teenage fertility, and trends in the timing and phasing of major life events such as first sexual experiences, first live-in relationships and the birth of the first child.

In 1999 a repeat survey of sexual attitudes and lifestyles was begun (funded by the Medical Research Council and Department of Health); its principal aim being to measure changes in sexual behaviour over the previous decade or so. This second survey was informed by concerns and records of relatively high rates of teenage conception and sexually transmitted infection among young people in Britain in particular. In the first survey there had been indications of a decline in age at first intercourse in successive age groups, and a significant increase in condom use among the youngest age cohort in the sample. Analysis of responses to this second survey from over 11,000 participants (aged 16–44) indicated that the proportion of women reporting first intercourse before 16 years increased up to, but not after, the mid-1990s. The authors (Wellings *et al.*, 2001) also report that there has been a sustained increase in condom use and a decline in the proportion of men and women signalling no contraceptive use. Importantly, only a small minority of teenagers have unprotected first inter-course.

This second National Survey of Sexual Attitudes and Lifestyles also provides updated estimates of sexual behaviour patterns—in relation to patterns of heterosexual and homosexual partnerships, for instance. Based on the same sample of over 11,000 respondents, the authors suggest that the findings here relating to increases in homosexual relationships, and the number of sexual relationships engaged in and payment for sex (notably men paying for sex), are consistent with changing cohabitation patterns and rising incidence of sexually transmitted infections (Johnson *et al.*, 2001). Differences in the findings between the two national surveys, a decade apart, are thought to reflect not only improved survey methodology, but also the emergence of more tolerant social attitudes.

These two surveys, combined, provide a wealth of information on sexual atti-tudes and behaviour and it is against this background that we have seen moves in the UK to change the legislative focus.

THE CONTENT OF THE BOOK

The essays in this book explore some of the vexed questions that inhabit the bor-derlands of social and legal debates about sexuality. Contributors bring exper-tise from a wide range of disciplines: law, sociology, psychology, criminology, German literature, and reproductive biology included. Following the tradition of our earlier socio-legal explorations (*What is a Parent? Body Lore and Laws* and *Children and their Families: Contact, Rights and Welfare*) the idea has been to weave together different perspectives, not to identify a single thread within the tapestry of ideas, nor indeed to impose a uniform pattern, but to juxtapose different textures of debate and intellectual contours. Thus the book is 'socio-legal' in broad conception. Much of the discussion is at a 'social' level, some of the discussion concerns developments in law, and some concerns social and legal tensions. But there is no single dominating theme within; rather, the book offers a rich display of contemporary and cutting-edge thinking about different sexual positions.

The book is divided into three sections: 1) Sexuality and Society—which sets out broad conceptual, theoretical and political developments over time, outlines key areas of discrimination and different positions on rights (the right to be different, for example), and broadly sets the scene for the discussion which follows; 2) The Development of Sexuality—which explores the place of the science of sexuality in a social context, challenges some of the assumptions underlying scientific, social and legal perspectives and discusses psychological and health positions on the development of sexuality, and 3) 'Problematic' and Prohibited Sexualities—which addresses the boundaries of the acceptable and the unacceptable in law (as depicted in the Sexual Offences Act 2003), explores the contestation of boundaries between public and private spheres, legitimate and illicit acts in film representations of sexuality, claims to sexual freedoms versus protectionist policies, and looks at the law in practice by focusing on the provision of treatment of sex offenders. There is some overlap between these sections, but also some differentiation in focus.

PART ONE: SEXUALITY AND SOCIETY

In **Chapter Two,** Jeffrey Weeks offers a major overview of thinking about sexuality so far, and also proposes ways to develop our conceptual understanding of sexualities. His suggestions for rethinking the sexual go far beyond notions of sex as a fundamental instinctive drive; indeed, he acknowledges the sexual and the erotic as highly socially malleable and socially contextualised. Weeks argues that there are no rights and wrongs in sexuality *per se*, but that to understand the sexual and the erotic we must grasp the complexity of social forces which shape such things in their socially and historically contingent contexts. In a powerful analysis of the implications of this realisation, Weeks selects five particular themes: the problematisation of sexuality and the institutionalisation of heterosexuality, gendering sexualities (as social practices), new subjectivities (new sexual identities), globalisation (in which western categorisations of sexuality interact and interpenetrate with those operating in other sexual cultures, and in which the nature and experience of risk has changed for instance), and finally, a conflict of values. Here, Weeks argues that in a world that is simultaneously globalised and challenged by emergent differences and new fundamentalisms, questions of values and ethics come to the fore. As with Lynne Segal (see Chapter Four), Jeffrey Weeks argues that the new voices from evolutionary psychology, which echo earlier biological perspectives on sexuality as straightforward human evolution, provide merely false and hopeless promises of security. Recognition of the contingent and arbitrary nature of sexuality however, brings its own problems in that we are left to decide upon social and sexual arrangements; for if there is no genetic imprint that will tell us how to live, we have to make moral and ethical decisions. It is for this reason that Weeks turns to the language of human rights and of sexual or intimate citizenship as a way of creating an iterative framework through which we can try to decide upon minimum standards to respect each other's differences and common humanity.

Further contribution to our understanding of discourses on sexuality comes from Ken Plummer's rich analysis in **Chapter Three** of the social worlds in which different sexuality theorists have flourished, announced and pronounced on sexuality. This is to suggest that academic worlds have 'their own spaces, languages, memberships and identities', their own social worlds and intellectual memories. Plummer charts various disciplinary 'sex wars' focusing particularly on paradigm ruptures, epistemological crises and the emergence of new critical sexualities theories. Critical theory, feminism, multiculturalism, discourse theory, standpoint theory, queer theory, critical realism, post-colonialism, constructionism, interpretive ethnography and critical humanism, for instance, have all challenged traditional theories of sexuality. Plummer notes how core issues of social exclusion and difference which highlight ethnicity, class, gender, age, disabilities, and nation, have been introduced to sexual agendas and how new items such as the cyber-worlds of sexualities (cyber-porn, cyber-dating and cyber-sex, for instance) have been added too. But he also notes certain ironies in the development of theories; the ways in which 'the body' has disappeared from theory from time to time (with small but notable exceptions) for example. Thus he argues that there is need to bring 'lust' and the body back into sexuality studies. More than this, Plummer embarks on an agenda-setting exercise in which he identifies a new range of sensitising concepts and questions that might be developed into grounded theories. How can we talk of establishing intimate encounters with self and others, how do we produce sexual feelings, how do we organise sexual worlds and how can we understand these things in the light of a wider sexual order reflecting patriarchy, compulsory heterosexuality, and homophobia for instance, and in a wider world of time and space regarding situation, networks, public spheres, society and global space? Thus Plummer suggests an analytical framework that at once encompasses a social psychology of sexuality and a political economy. But he rightly acknowledges that many sexuality theorists are activists and that the charting of new understandings will be insufficient to the task of changing the sexual order at both personal and political levels. For this reason he goes on to outline potential forms of sexual suffering linked to sexuality which require social (not just clinical or sexological) analyses: the sufferings of desire and sexual excitement, the sufferings of

relationships, the sufferings of coercion and violence, the sufferings of reproduction and the sufferings of disease. All of these sufferings can be seen as
personal, yet they may be compounded by sexual stigmas and social inequalities. From this point Plummer presents differing futures. The one is optimistic,
tolerant, and individualisation is celebrated. The other future envisaged is
overshadowed by social inequalities and social exclusion and a clash of sexual
civilisations.

In a discursive, lively and politically charged essay (**Chapter Four**) Lynne
Segal reflects on the intertwining of the biological, medical, psychological and
political dimensions of sexuality. She discusses the renewed interest in what is
seen as the biological foundations and future of human sexuality and concludes
that the more we are promised simple pathways to 'earthly delights' the easier
prey we become as objects of manipulation. In a trenchant critique of the selective reasoning of some advocates of evolutionary psychology in particular, Segal
argues that it is infuriating to have to do battle with those who pit science
against culture or else attempt to colonise it. An equally critical eye is cast over
the powerful attempts of pharmaceutical industries to bypass cultural dynamics
and suggest that sex is nothing more than a medical function, analogous to
breathing or ingestion. Thus health workers and the public learn of new sexual
priorities from those companies who have a vested interest in marketing cures
for erectile dysfunction (a condition rarely mentioned in the first half of the
twentieth century; one might ask why, but surmise that this was not because it
didn't exist, but because it was too shameful to raise—so to speak—the subject).
Following this exposé, Segal outlines pharmaceutical moves to medicalize
women's sexual needs and concludes that the battle over sexual bodies continues, for both ideological and commercial ends, both arriving within freshly
coined biological discourses.

Turning from these broad disciplinary debates and questions about how best
to theorise sexuality towards contemporary practises of sexuality, Linda
McDowell (**Chapter Five**) focuses on sexuality, desire and embodied performances of sexuality in the workplace. In enlightening fashion, McDowell explores
the relationships between contemporary transformations in the economy and
the social construction of identity by discussing the ways in which sexualised
identities have been theorised in recent work on the labour market by, *inter alia*,
sociologists, geographers and feminist scholars. Picking out the rise of consumer
societies, the shift from manufacturing to service economies and the expansion
of women into the visible work force, she identifies the impact on gendered
assumptions within job descriptions, and gendered differences in the occupational structure of the workplace. McDowell also draws attention to the
increasing significance of the everyday 'performance of sexuality' as an integral
component of the job description. Drawing on a range of illustrative empirical
studies involving sexuality and sexualised work practices, she highlights the way
in which idealised images and versions of the embodied, sexually desirable
masculinity and femininity of potential and actual employees, have shaped

performance of sexuality and body work. McDowell concludes that 'body work', in both the sense of working on one's own body and working on the bodies of others (caring work, health and fitness work as well as body image specialists such as beauticians) is an increasingly significant element of the social relations of waged labour in contemporary industrial societies such as the UK. All of this, of course, implicitly raises questions about the uses of law to regulate sexualised social relations in the workplace.

In **Chapter Six**, Craig Lind draws us close to the law in his insightful discussion of sexuality and same-sex relationships. Lind not only charts and questions the legal regulation of same-sex relations, but very usefully draws out the implications of discussion here for the parameters of family law. Indeed, he introduces arguments that serve to undermine any attempt to use same-sex sexuality as justification for unequal or unfairly discriminatory treatment. His underlying argument is that same-sex couples should be entitled to exactly the same rights as different sex couples in the regulation of their relationships. This makes interesting reading in the light of Queen Elizabeth II's speech at the opening of Parliament on 26th November, 2003, when she emphasised a commitment to equality and the intention to bring forward legislation on the registration of civil partnerships between same sex couples. Elsewhere, matters appear to be moving in a rather different direction. In his State of the Union address on January 20th, 2004, USA President George Bush emphasised the sanctity of marriage and strong resistance to redefining marriage as anything other than a union of a man and a woman.

In **Chapter Seven**, Zoë-Jane Playdon explores themes relating to discrimination in the UK against lesbians, gay men and trans people—lumped together as a perceived 'homogenous undesirability' whilst in reality being a heterogeneous population facing both shared and specific issues. Unlike some of the other chapters within the book, which are firmly rooted in theory, Playdon approaches her subject through a dual lens of practical 'activism' and theory, charting challenges to regulation and the development of civil liberties. Playdon records how active pressure for civil status has intersected with the law and medicine and the educational establishment, showing the role of each of these institutions in defining, resisting, and facilitating change. She draws examples from gay, lesbian and trans history, to illustrate what is common and what is special, and how the theoretical and activist relationship among and within each of these groups has developed historically. Her commentary on trans issues is especially informative. Transexualism was not acknowledged as a distinct medical category until 1968. Sectioning under the mental health legislation, aversion therapy and electro-convulsive therapy (ECT) were used in its treatment, while as late as 2002 exorcism was advocated as a possible 'cure' by a practising psychiatrist. Playdon goes on to outline the problems and inequalities created by Section 28 of the Local Government Act 1988, which effectively removed teaching about gay, lesbian and trans issues from schools. Noting recent legislative developments which include a Gender Recognition Bill to allow trans people to gain legal recognition in their 'real' gender and employment protection for gay men and lesbians, there is wry analysis which points to a resurgence of opposition to the removal of Clause 28 as if society always needs a scapegoat to assuage its (hetero) sexual anxiety. In a concluding section to the essay, drawing in references to the European Court of Human Rights as well as recent forms of activism, Playdon presses the case for resistance to pragmatic activism which might well emphasise the diffuse, contentious and fragmentary nature of debates concerning gay men, lesbian women and trans people. It is suggested that there is much to be gained by maintaining communality and group identity as a whole whilst recognising separate people and groups, separate sexual positions we might say.

PART TWO: THE DEVELOPMENT OF SEXUALITY:
CONTEMPORARY DEBATES

Martin Johnson opens the discussion in **Chapter Eight** by offering an important reflective exploration of how human sexuality has been studied by biomedical scientists. He notes different fashions in scientific methods and the production of particular categorisations and analytical frameworks in order to place 'science' in its 'social' context. Thus, far from rehearsing the 'truths' of scientific endeavour, he explores the limitations and possibilities of biomedical approaches which revolve around natural selection, sexual selection and both genetic and epigenetic influences. Of central concern here traditionally has been what causes sexuality? But this question is often expressed more narrowly in terms of what causes 'aberrant sexuality' as though what is deemed 'aberrant' is self-evident and what is deemed non-aberrant has no 'cause'. As Johnson suggests, however, such an approach is strongly influenced by the social and cultural context which has shaped not only the question, but the scientific method too.

Chapter Nine introduces engagement with the law again. Authors Pak-Lee Chau and Jonathan Herring explore the assumption of sexual classification as male or female by focusing on the intersex state (or pseudohermaphrodite state as it is sometimes known) and then the legal implications of this. Such a state poses a radical challenge to the long-standing social and legal assumption that everyone can be categorised as either male or female. Having carefully distinguished between sex and gender (an important point since so many people either use the terms interchangeably as if there is no difference or simplistically assume that sex is an 'objective fact' and gender a 'social construction'), Pak-Lee Chau and Jonathan Herring critically review the biological evidence on the origins, development and nature of intersex states and argue that, in the light of a proper understanding of intersexuality, the present law is unsupportable. Challenging medical approaches to intersex states, which so often have involved 'corrective' surgery on children so as to be able to classify individuals into one of two sexes (often primarily for parental or social benefit rather than for the individual child), they consider ways in which the law could approach definition by sex so as to accommodate intersex states. Thus, here, the authors propose a radical change to the contours of the law.

In **Chapter Ten** Julie Jessop continues this critical theme concerning understandings of the development of sexuality with a review of different psychological perspectives. She argues that for a good part of recorded history the development of all things 'sexual' has been regarded as unproblematic, based on 'natural' biological processes of human development and the need to reproduce. Commentaries on the development of sexuality have thus revolved around 'normal' and 'natural' patterns of sexual behaviour. Awakenings to the social context and significance of sexuality, however, have led to different forms of study and this chapter focuses primarily on the growing number of empirical studies which take a qualitative approach to the subject of sexuality. That many of these studies have been based on adolescents and on heterosexual relationships becomes part of a critical theme within the chapter as a number of theoretical and methodological problems are exposed. Importantly, both chapters present implicit challenges to the law by drawing attention to the uncertainties surrounding the development of sexuality.

In one of five essays in the book which revolve around children and young people, Roger Ingham discusses a number of issues relating to young people's sexual health in **Chapter Eleven.** Ingham initially discusses conceptions of 'sexual health' which involve not only the avoidance of negative physical effects (sexually transmitted infection and early and unplanned pregnancy, for example) but which include positive psychological aspects of sexuality such as mutuality and respect. He then goes on to illustrate how wider legal and policy contexts have significant implications for individuals' sexual health. Critical of the limited gaze of psychology as a discipline, arguing that traditional approaches within the discipline have failed to address the wider contexts that lead to conditions of vulnerability, and drawing on studies from other countries as well as UK based studies, Ingham offers a selection of research examples which *do* throw light on sexual health and which have implications for policy development. The unifying characteristic of such research is its emphasis on drawing data from young people themselves; qualitative analysis of interviews with young people both in the UK and elsewhere thus provides the basis for a grounded understanding of sexuality amongst young people. From this, in what is clearly an innovative approach, Ingham sets out the case for a dynamic processual analysis of factors to be taken into account in attempts to understand and develop appropriate policy. More than this, Ingham presses argument for cultural change towards greater openness towards sexuality and increased emphasis on the values of mutuality and respect rather than on religious and cultural dogma to constrain young people's sexuality.

In **Chapter Twelve** Andrew Bainham and Belinda Brooks-Gordon provide an extensive and challenging critical overview of the social and legal debates surrounding recent legal reforms on sexual offences encapsulated in the Sexual Offences Act 2003. Setting the reforms in context and describing the debates that led up to recent legislation, Bainham and Brooks-Gordon acknowledge that the Act gives effect to some much-needed reforms. The explicit recognition now being given to the seriousness of non-penile penetrations, the shift towards gender-neutrality in sexual offences and the legitimate concern about child sexual abuse and the abuse of other vulnerable people, are all welcomed. At the same time, the authors argue that the 2003 Act offends, in a fundamental way, a number of key precepts of the criminal law including the principles of minimum criminalization, maximum certainty and fair warning. They suggest that the Act represents a dangerous departure from the usual requirements of subjective mental culpability for serious offences, and brings about an unwarranted proliferation of criminal liability where no identifiable harm has yet occurred. Indeed, the tenor of their essay is that the 2003 Act is fundamentally flawed and will serve no one well.

Andrew Webber also considers the role of the law in his chapter on sexuality, film and the law (**Chapter Thirteen**). Here, Webber focuses on the triangular relations between sexuality, film and law, as illustrated by selected cinematic performances of homosexuality. The material used to provide a focus for the discussion was produced in Germany and France between the 1920s and the 1980s, a period in the West which is widely acknowledged to have witnessed moves towards more liberal censorship regimes. The examples discussed emerge from different historical and cultural circumstances, generating different forms of scandal and different codes of control or retribution. But there is a unifying theme that centres on the contestation of the boundaries between public and private spheres, legitimate and illicit acts, social reality and representation. Contemporary debates about obscenity and censorship, pornography and paedophilia, suggest that these issues are still very much alive.

Michael Freeman writes about the sexual abuse of children in **Chapter Fourteen**. Drawing on his vast experience of writing and researching in this field, he describes the development of legal interventions over time and the way in which legal responses have been slow to recognise children as legal subjects. Touching on both definitional and measurement problems, as well as outlining possible explanations for child sexual abuse, Freeman then critically explores various models that have been employed to support children. He argues that power analyses have perhaps been neglected in explanations of child sexual abuse and that family support models have merely situated the welfare of the child in the 'shadow of the welfare of the family'. Freeman goes on to suggest that if we are to create a 'protected environment' we must make it unlawful to hit children and that the law must be used to spell out parental responsibilities more clearly.

In **Chapter Fifteen**, David Pearl discusses the work of the Care Standards Tribunal. The Protection of Children Act 1999 provided for a specialist Tribunal to hear appeals brought by individuals who had been placed on the statutory lists of those deemed unsuitable to work with children. Closely informed by the practice of such Tribunals (over which David Pearl has presided in his role as a Judge), the essay focuses on issues that arise when the Tribunal struggles to create a balance between the protection of children and assessment of risk and the human rights of the individual to work with children in his or her chosen field.

Chapter Sixteen by Kerry Petersen also focuses on children. The chapter revolves around claims to sexual freedoms versus protectionist policies. It is an essay in which there is acknowledgement that whilst at a general level laws regulating sexuality are based on moral values, cultural assumptions and gender issues, in the case of young people these matters are compounded by competing claims to personal autonomy, parental responsibilities and the state's duties and powers. Focusing on voluntary consensual sexual activity amongst young people, Peterson draws on both her knowledge of common law developments in family law and medical law in the Australian States and Territories and of legal developments concerning children and young people in England and Wales (including the famous case of *Gillick v West Norfolk and Wisbech Area Health Authority* for instance) to illustrate some of the tensions between the different parties involved. Given that sexual activity amongst young people in the UK generally starts at an earlier age than elsewhere (according to national surveys such as those mentioned above), the discussion offered here is clearly important to our understanding of what might be appropriate levels of protection and freedom.

Joanna Phoenix continues the theme of protection for young people in **Chapter Seventeen** where she discusses young people, prostitution and policy reform. In particular she argues that contemporary constructions of 'childhood' and 'sex' render silent the paradox of using child protection methods for young people engaged in prostitution who are at (or close to) the age of sexual consent. In an informative and challenging essay, Phoenix provides an up to date account of the innovations and reforms that have led to contemporary youth justice policy, outlines various ambiguities and partialities within the policy field, and sets out the case for legislation which more accurately reflects the lived realities of the young people whom the law is meant to serve.

Finally, in **Chapter Eighteen**, Belinda Brooks-Gordon, Charlotte Bilby and Tracey Kenworthy consider the application of treatment for sex offenders within the criminal justice system. That the Sexual Offences Act 2003 will have implications for responses to sex offenders, of course, is beyond doubt, but this essay focuses on possible treatment effects. The essay firstly describes some of the difficulties in assessing evidence on treatment effects but emphasises the importance of systematic reviews. The authors then report on the findings from a systematic review of psychological treatments for sex offenders before concluding with a critical and helpful examination of what they call 'facilitators and barriers to treatment'. This is an important discussion in the context of heightened fears about sex offenders and the need to maximise the efficacy of treatment in order to assuage both public fears and address issues relating to the ethicality and legitimacy of interventions.

The book does not pretend to be comprehensive. Issues relating to globalisation and sexualities (sexual tourism, for example), and more systematic analysis of cross-cultural perspectives on sexuality and the law would all be relevant to our purpose in examining the interface of the social and the legal. But the discussions of the intersections between the social (encompassing psychological perspectives) and the legal within the book, reflect state of the art debate within the UK and thus serve as a foundation for other trans-cultural and trans-legal debates.

REFERENCES

ALTMAN, D, *Homosexual: Oppression and Liberation* (London, Allen Lane, 1971).

FIRESTONE, S, *The Dialectic of Sex* (London, Cape, 1971).

FOUCAULT, M, The *History of Sexuality, Volume I: An Introduction* (London, Allen Lane, 1979).

FREUD, S, 'Three Essays on the Theory of Sexuality' (trans. J Strachey, 1905). (*On Sexuality*, vol 7, edition compiled and edited by A Richards, Harmondsworth, Middlesex, Penguin, 1991).

—— '"Civilised" Sexual Morality and Modern Nervous Illness' (trans. J Strachey, 1908). (*Civilisation, Society and Religion*, vol 12, edition compiled and edited by A Richards, Harmondsworth, Middlesex, Penguin, 1991).

—— 'Civilisation and Its Discontents' (trans. J Strachey, 1930). (*Civilisation, Society and Religion*, vol 12, edition compiled and edited by A Richards, Harmondsworth, Middlesex, Penguin, 1991).

GAGNON, J and SIMON, W, *Sexual Conduct: the Social Sources of Human Sexuality* (London, Hutchinson, 1973).

GIDDENS, A, *The Transformation of Intimacy. Sexuality, Love and Eroticism in Modern Societies* (Cambridge, Polity Press, 1992).

JOHNSON, A, MERCER, C, ERENS, COPAS, A, McMANUS, S, WELLINGS, K, FENTON, K, KOROVESSIS, C, MACDOWELL, W, NANCHAHAL, K, PURDON, S, and FIELD, J, 'Sexual Behaviour in Britain: Partnerships, Practices, and HIV Risk Behaviours', 2001, *The Lancet*, vol 358, December 1, pp 1835–42.

KATZ, J, *Gay American History: Lesbians and Gay Men in the USA* (New York, Thomas Y Crowell, 1976).

—— *The Invention of Heterosexuality* (New York, NAL/Dutton, 1995).

KINSEY, A, POMEROY, W and MARTIN, C, *Sexual Behaviour in the Human Male* (Philadelphia and London, WB Saunders, 1948).

KINSEY, A, POMEROY, W, MARTIN, C and GEBHARD, P, *Sexual Behaviour in the Human Female* (Philadelphia and London, WB Saunders, 1953).

MILLETT, K, *Sexual Politics* (London, Hart-Davis, 1971).

ORBACH, S, *The Impossibility of Sex* (London, Allen Lane, The Penguin Press, 1999).

PLUMMER, K, *Telling Sexual Stories. Power, Change and Social Worlds* (London, Routledge, 1995).

WEEKS, J, *Sex, Politics and Society. The Regulation of Sexuality Since 1800* (London, Longman, 1981).

—— *Sexuality and Its Discontents: Myths, Meanings and Modern Sexualities* (London, Routledge and Kegan Paul, 1985).

—— *Invented Moralities. Sexual Values In An Age Of Uncertainty* (Cambridge, Polity, 1995).

—— HOLLAND, J and WAITES, M, (eds), *Sexualities and Society* (Cambridge, Polity, 2003).

WELLINGS, K, FIELD, J, JOHNSON, A and WADSWORTH, J with BRADSHAW, S, *Sexual Behaviour in Britain, the National Survey of Sexual Attitudes and Lifestyles* (Harmondsworth, Middlesex, Penguin, 1994).

—— NANCHAHAL, K, MACDOWELL, W, MCMANUS, S, ERENS, B, MERCER, C, JOHNSON, A, COPAS, A, KOROVESSIS, C, FENTON, K and FIELD, J, 'Sexual Behaviour in Britain: Early Heterosexual Experience', 2001, *The Lancet*, vol 358, December 1, pp 1843–50.

Part 1
Sexuality and Society

2

The Rights and Wrongs of Sexuality

JEFFREY WEEKS

A SPECTRE IS HAUNTING the world of sexuality: the fact of sexual diversity. The question of how we learn to live with diversity is now high on the political and cultural agenda across the divides of east and west, north and south. There are controversies arising from diversity across the western world, on everything from lesbian and gay parenting to gays in the military, from same sex marriages to surrogacy, from the needs of lone mothers to the rights of transgendered people, from immigration rights to welfare entitlements. In other parts of the world the concerns are often more basic: how to survive if your way of life, your sense of yourself, or your everyday sexual practices do not fit into traditional or neo traditional patterns. Think of the fundamentalist preoccupations with the body, and with gender and sexual conformity (Bhatt, 1997). Think of the stoning to death of (women) adulterers and of homosexuals. Think of the still fearful response to HIV/AIDS even in countries like South Africa (Altman, 2001). To an unprecedented degree the question of how we live with sexual diversity has become a key issue about the way we live today. All this in turn impacts on questions of rights and responsibilities, social inclusion and exclusion, belonging and citizenship, that may take different forms in different cultures, but are contributing to a global discourse on the rights and wrongs of sexuality.

Recognising the fact of diversity is not of course the same as valuing diversity as a good in itself. Many prefer to affirm the norm and castigate the abnormal. Nor should a recognition of sexual variation preclude debate about how to evaluate the myriad forms of diversity, demarcating the acceptable from the unacceptable, the harmful from the harmless. We might all easily agree that sexual activities involving force and coercion, and abuse of the young and vulnerable are wrong. But how do we evaluate consensual sado-masochistic practices, or other 'extreme' forms of erotic pleasure. To respond to these we must inevitably draw on ethical standards that are largely external to our perception of the erotic. Awareness of the existence of diverse sexualities does not in and of itself tell us how we can intervene to promote the benign and prevent the perverse (both of which are themselves contested terms). There are of course those who offer a fundamentalist defence of 'traditional values'—usually, in practice, offering a reinvention of tradition—and we cannot underestimate their influence in some jurisdictions. There are others, interestingly from all parts of the political spectrum, who believe that all questions about the relative merits of erotic practices are complicit with forms of power and prefer to stake out a libertarian position. More often than not, however, such questions tend to get buried whenever moral panics sweep over us, as they all too frequently still do, suggesting we are still desperately uncertain in confronting the complexity of contemporary mores. But the fact that sexual issues are now transparently central to the political, social and cultural agenda, in ways they were not barely half a generation ago, underlines that profound shifts have taken place in our cultural landscape, and in our individual and collective priorities—and the need to find guidelines for learning to live with diversity (Weeks, 1995).

This preoccupation with the impact of sexual diversity is the result, I will argue, of a dual transformation. In the first place, for a variety of reasons I will explore later, what has historically been regarded as peripheral or marginal to the central direction of societies is now seen as at the heart of social concerns: *sexuality matters to society*.

Secondly, there has been a revolution in our understanding of sexuality in recent years. We can no longer understand the sexual, despite the best efforts of some contemporary theorists influenced by the new genetics (see chapters by Johnson, and by Segal, this volume; also Lancaster, 2003), as a fundamental instinctive drive, wired into our genes, to which the social must react. Rather we can see the erotic as highly socially malleable, shaped by permissions and inhibitions, interventions and non interventions, definitions and self definitions, which create sexual categories, hierarchies, meanings and subjectivities (Plummer, this volume). *Society matters to sexuality*.

As sex goes, so goes society. As society goes, so goes sexuality.

RETHINKING THE SEXUAL

This dual recognition is relatively new. When I began researching and writing about sexuality in the 1970s there was a complete dearth, not of writing about sex, but of writing that made sense to me in trying to understand the changing erotic landscape. Ken Plummer (1975) lamented the lack of a serious sociology of sexuality, and few could gainsay him. Writing about sex, Plummer also suggested, makes you 'morally suspect'. That was certainly the experience of the pioneering sexologists who sought from the late nineteenth century to put the understanding of sexuality on a *soi disant* scientific basis. The founding father of sexology, the Viennese physician Richard van Krafft Ebing, found it tactful to clothe the more explicit case histories in his publications in the decent obscurity of a dead language, that is, Latin. The great British sexologist, Havelock Ellis, faced the indignity of having his pioneering study of 'sexual inversion' banned in a famous court case as lewd and obscene in the 1890s. He reacted by thereafter publishing future volumes of his great work on the psychology of sex only in the USA. Freud, of course, was pilloried for trying to bring sex into everything. The German sexologist, and campaigner for homosexual rights, Magnus Hirschfeld, had his library burnt by the Nazis soon after they came to power, and he died in exile (Weeks, 1985). Writing about sex could be dangerous.

The next generation learnt the lesson, by striving for a would be positivistic objectivity (Simon, 1996)—which did not of course fool their morally conservative critics. Alfred Kinsey made his reputation as a student of the gall wasp before venturing into human sexual behaviour. The most famous of his successors, William Masters, of Masters and Johnson notoriety, was told to make his scientific reputation in another field, and to wait 15 years before venturing in the realms of sex—advice he religiously followed (Weeks, 1985).

What a transformation! Today, sexual studies are one of the fastest growing areas of the curriculum. A recent survey I read said that courses on sex and gender are the largest speciality in sociology in the USA. At least 90% of UK undergraduate sociology courses have modules on sexuality, lesbian and gay studies, queer studies and the like. Queer theory in particular has been one of the most significant influences on literary and cultural studies in the USA and elsewhere over the past decade.

Book shelves groan. All mainstream publishers have lists on sexual and gender studies. Conferences proliferate. The recent book by Dennis Altman (2001) proclaims the necessity of understanding *Global Sex*. We are in a different world.

I have suggested we can see this as a result of two interlocked shifts, in thinking about the importance of sexuality to society, and in thinking about the significance of society to sexuality. The first is a result of what can be described as a long, but unfinished sexual revolution, which began in the early twentieth century, went public in the 1960s, and which has accelerated in the past couple of decades at an unprecedented pace. It is, in a globalising world, a global revolution but its epicentre remains in the advanced industrialised, late modern societies of the west. We can relate it to the gender revolution, the emergence of new sexual subjects and identities, to what Anthony Giddens (1992) calls the 'transformation of intimacy', to the increasing separation of sex and reproduction, to the consumer society, to growing individualisation. All these factors are crucial, and interconnected. They have contributed to a pluralisation of social and sexual worlds, to a challenge to traditional values, to a secularisation of values, and an individualisation of choices. It is, inevitably, an uneven revolution. Oppressions, sexual hierarchies, uneven divisions of labour, exploitations, bigotry, sex related diseases and violence survive, which is why we can describe the revolution as unfinished. But that there has been a profound transformation cannot to my mind be denied.

The second shift, in our theoretical understanding of the interconnections between the social and the sexual, may be less obvious, but is equally profound, especially for those of us with an academic bent. The comments by the American sexologists, John Gagnon and William Simon (1973) in the early 1970s, that sexuality, far from being the most resistant to social influences was in fact the most malleable, the most sensitive transmitter of social shifts, heralded a paradigm shift of major proportions. They suggested that at some stage society may have needed to invent the importance of sexuality. This paved the way to Michel Foucault's (1979) famous comment in the first volume of his *History of Sexuality*, that sexuality was a historical deployment, or in the English translation, an 'historic construct', a discursive unification of bodies, organs, desires and meanings which had no intrinsic or necessary connection.

Foucault's work particularly had a huge impact on our thinking about the sexual. But it should now also be clear that he was building on new forms of sexual knowledge already in development. These were in turn being heavily influenced by radical social movements including second wave feminism and the gay liberation movement which emerged from the late 1960s. The work of young scholars inspired by these movements began to develop critical social scientific approaches to sexuality. Already by the mid-1970s feminists were questioning the basic categories of sexuality, and a number of pioneering lesbian and gay historians were interrogating the fixity of the heterosexual-homosexual dichotomy to show that this apparently fundamental binary divide had a relatively recent history (see Weeks, 1977). If the homosexual identities we took for granted were indeed a historical construction, then so could the norm of heterosexuality be seen as something that was invented (Richardson, 1996). In a similar way the sharp distinction that some of the pioneering sexologist writers on sexuality had drawn between 'civilised' and 'uncivilised' patterns of behaviour could also be challenged. Racialised western assumptions about the closer to nature, 'primitive' aspects of other societies, could now be seen in the burgeoning post-colonial literature as reflecting the way in which both western and non-western behaviours had been constructed in the imperial encounters of the nineteenth and twentieth centuries.

In other words, sexuality, far from being the domain of the given, the natural, the biological, was pre-eminently historical, social, and moreover shaped in relations of power (see articles in Phillips and Reay, 2002). Traditional patterns of male power over women constructed female sexuality as subordinate, reactive, rooted in the maternal. The power of the heterosexual norm, which itself was historically specific, was central to the construction of the sexual 'other', of homosexuality. The racist and orientalist ideologies which emerged in the context of Western imperialism and colonialism had constructed non-western peoples and sexualities as fundamentally different, often inferior and lower down the evolutionary scale, or as exotic, over-sensuous or decadent. In his introductory volume to *The History of Sexuality*, Foucault (1979) hinted at all these elements, and provided a research agenda, which has been enormously creative. But work was already going on, and many other influences were already at play, from the post-Kinsey traditions of sexological research, and the new history influenced by the new social movements, to a radical sociology, and subsequently new critical, queer, postcolonial and post-structuralist approaches within cultural studies and the humanities.

One index of the changed perspectives may be seen in a radical shift in the language used to discuss sexuality. The most characteristic metaphors used in early sexological writings (and in 1960s liberatory writings) revolved around Manichean conflicts: between the sacred and the profane, sex and society, suppression and release, repression and liberation. Today the most common metaphors in writing about sexuality and sexual identities are 'invention', 'construction', 'embodiment', 'social practices', 'fictions', 'narratives', 'performance'—all emphasising the ways in which sexual meanings, identities, enactments are cultural artefacts, and culturally specific. There are no rights and wrongs in sexuality *per se*. To understand the erotic we must grasp the complexity of social forces which shape it.

THE IMPLICATIONS

What are the implications of this? I shall pick on five.

The Problematisation of Sexuality

I have already suggested in broad terms the significance of this. We can no longer easily see sexuality as a given and constant nexus of instincts, drives and desires with automatic effects on individual and social lives. Rather we need to see the erotic as always and necessarily given meaning only through the social. Sex is always tangled up in language, and it is, as Plummer (1973) suggested, only given sexual meaning through naming: nothing is sexual until naming makes it so. That means inevitably that to find the sexual we always need to look for its specific local manifestations, and the forces that structure it. The early sexological theorists sought the laws of nature that would explain sexuality as a universal phenomenon (Weeks, 1985). Today we need to understand the social organisations of sexualities in all their diverse forms. There may be a relatively limited range of possible bodily conjunctions and pleasures, but different societies on a global scale, and different cultures and subcultures within any particular society, organise the erotic in a variety of different ways.

We therefore need to speak not of sexuality but of sexualities, not of sex and society but of sexual cultures.

To understand sexual cultures today we need to understand the diverse contexts in which meanings are attributed to intimacy and eroticism, and the complex social interactions which shape the erotic cultures of different societies.

But recognition of the diversity of sexual forms should not give rise to an easy pluralism, which assumes their happy coexistence. Sexualities are hierarchically organised, with some forms dominant while others are subordinate and marginalised, and are shaped by complex relations of power. The most familiar of these relate to gender, class, age, race and ethnicity (Rubin, 1984, Weeks, 2003). In recent years there has also been an increasing recognition that sexualities in the west at least have been organised into institutionalised forms of heterosexuality, leading to critiques of 'compulsory heterosexuality', 'heterosexism', the 'heterosexual panorama', the 'heterosexual assumption', 'heteronormativity'—the phrases vary, but the effort put into formulating these concepts underlines the importance many people give to questioning our taken for granted assumptions (Butler, 1990, Warner, 1993, Weeks, Heaphy and Donovan, 2001.) These formations intersect with a host of other factors, high amongst which are religion and the traditional patterns of life which shape cultures.

Gendering Sexualities

The complex ways in which gender is constructed, and reinforced and set in patterns of dominance and subordination through the institutionalisation of heterosexuality, is central to our developing understanding of sexualities and sexual cultures. Some feminist theorists have indeed argued that gender constitutes sexuality, and that female sexuality is shaped and organised through the mechanisms of male domination. Other theorists have argued for a significant distinction between the domains of sexuality and gender, regarding their relationship as more complex and contingent than is often thought (see discussion in Jackson, 1999, Adkins, 2002). The important point we always have to bear in mind, however, is that masculinity and femininity are always relational: they are constituted by their mutual relationship not by an eternal essence. The relationship inevitably shifts over time and over the life course of individuals in particular cultures. But in most societies masculinity and femininity have been organised hierarchically, with masculinity as the unspoken but assumed norm, and this has tended to shape everyday interactions—and sexual theory.

But of course, the existence of a hierarchy does not determine in an absolute way. If that was the case, there could be no change. On the contrary, it provides the necessary condition for resistance, and for sexual politics. The impact of feminism since the 1960s has simultaneously sharpened our awareness of the arbitrary nature of gender divisions, and increased the possibility of changing them. In recent years gender has increasingly been seen not simply as lived, but as 'performed' through the constant iteration and re-enactment of what are regarded as the essential characteristics of both sex (male and female) and gender (Butler, 1990, 1993).

There have been remarkable changes in the organisation of gender over the past generation. This is not simply an ideological shift, but also reflects a shift in the whole economic and social basis of gender. In most western countries, women have been increasingly incorporated into the work force, and legislation has formally recognised the equality of men and women. This in turn has influenced ongoing debates in non-industrialised and recently industrialised societies. But what is also increasingly clear is that whatever the moves towards formal equality, and whatever the local successes of both long term economic and social shifts and ideological transformations, the traditional assumptions about the social meanings of masculinity and femininity remain deeply embedded. This is the basis for the understanding of heterosexuality as institutionalised not only in formal structures but in our minds—what Holland *et al* (1998) call 'the male in the head'.

We must now see gender and sexuality, as Connell (1995) argues, as 'social practices', and studies such as his have revealed the variety of structured social practices which have defined masculinity, femininity and attitudes to sexuality. These practices give rise to dominant and subordinate forms, and challenges to hegemonic forms of masculinity and femininity in recent years have involved processes of re-making the self for women and many men—but always against heavy institutional, and psychological, barriers.

New Subjectivities

Sexualities are organised and institutionalised in different ways, including the systematic patterning of forms of subjectivity. A crucial aspect of this is the way we organise our sense of self, our identities, around our sexual desires. The extent to which sexuality is central to people's sense of self is itself historically specific, as the first volume of Michel Foucault's (1979) *The History of Sexuality* powerfully suggested. Foucault argued that sex became increasingly central to understandings of the self and the construction of a sense of being in modern western societies from the seventeenth century onwards. The most clear cut example of this is in the emergence of distinctive homosexual identities, beginning from the seventeenth century but developing into recognisably modern forms from the late nineteenth and early twentieth centuries.

In a culture in which a particular form of sexuality was either denied or punished, it was inevitable that people organised their sense of self around their sexuality in various forms of resistance—through what Foucault described as a 'reverse discourse'. Historians have increasingly sought to understand the dynamics of push and pull, definition and self-definition which have shaped the emergence of non-orthodox sexual identities. It is significant that in the sexological writings of the late nineteenth century, the terms referring to same-sex behaviour emerged before the language of heterosexuality. It was those with sexual desires who were socially stigmatised and regarded as deviant and who needed to assert their sense of self in relation to sexuality by claiming as their own the perverse sexological categories made available to them—often, interestingly, in informal dialogue with the sexologists themselves, as Oosterhuis's (2000) study of

Krafft-Ebing demonstrates. Of course, as societies have developed complex responses to sexual diversity and non-conformity over the last hundred years, these identities have themselves become complex and overlapping, and in some instances have become focal points for challenges to the very notion of fixed sexual identity, as the queer insurgency illustrates (Warner, 1993).

Identities are usually seen as basic to who or what we are, and in relation to sexual identities, it has been traditional to see an automatic relationship between desire and self-description, self and social identity. But the evidence for this has always been problematic, as the work of Kinsey and his colleagues in the 1940s made dramatically clear (see Weeks, 1985, Simon, 1996). They recognised both the spectrum of sexualities, and the disjunction between sexual behaviour and sexual identity. This issue has become the focus of considerable debate since the 1970s, and given rise to political mobilisation. For many socially marginalised groups the assertion of distinctive sexual identities has been a critical aspect of the struggle for freedom of choice. For lesbians and gays in particular, but also for bisexuals, transgendered people and a proliferation of even more marginalized groups, it has been critical to assert the significance of organising a sense of self around a sense of one's needs and desires (see Playdon, this volume). Identities have been struggled for, often against extremely forceful and imposed norms. In the modernist project, of which in some ways the sexual movements of the 1970s were heirs, it was taken for granted that the historical distinction between heterosexuality and homosexuality would be reflected in homogeneous identities, of for example, heterosexuals, lesbians, and gays. In recent years this has met a dual challenge. The emergence from the late 1980s of 'queer' political movements radically challenged the homogeneous nature of the identities that existed, and constituted a self-conscious refusal of identity on the part of many younger people. An even more significant challenge has come from a growing recognition that the meanings developed around sexual identity in the West were of little relevance to many marginalized people from minority ethnic communities within the western world, or to many people in other cultures. The complexity of the relationship between the development of western norms and the experience of colonialism has given rise to a more sophisticated and complex post-colonial theorisation of sexual identities (see, for example, Altman, 2001, Parker 1991, 1999). The export of sexual identities from the developed to the developing world must now be assessed in the context of an understanding of neo-colonial power relations, though without seeking to idealize those identities associated with pre-colonial traditions and indigenous cultures, nor dismissing the significance of the emergent new identities (see Alexander, 2003, Phillips, 2003.)

Globalisation

This is closely related to a recognition of the growing importance of globalisation in relation to the organisation of sexualities (Altman, 2001). A globalised world is one in which western categorisations of sexuality increasingly interact and interpenetrate with those operating in other sexual cultures, and in which new categorisations emerging worldwide—whether being universalised or asserted in opposition to one another—are increasingly interconnected across cultures (see Weeks, Holland and Waites, 2003). Globalisation is not of course new in the field of sexuality any more than it is in wider economic and cultural relations. It is often forgotten that in the earlier part of the twentieth century an international discourse had emerged around common sexual issues. Magnus Hirschfeld's World League for Sexual Reform brought together people not only from the industrialised countries in Western Europe and America but also from Asia, Africa and Latin America. The agenda that then developed—for example over the sexual exploitation of young children, the recognition and rights that should be accorded self-defined homosexuals, sexual disease, birth control and abortion, marriage and divorce—strikingly resembles the issues that are central to contemporary debates about globalisation and sexuality (Weeks, 1977: 139–42).

A globalised world, it may be argued, is a world in which the nature and experience of risk has changed. The spread of the HIV/AIDS epidemic since the 1980s to become a global pandemic is a vivid and tragic illustration of this. Sexual behaviour has of course always been associated with risk: the risk of unwanted pregnancy, of disease, of exploitation, of prejudice and oppression. These risks did not disappear with the emergence of a new discourse of sexual rights since the 1960s. But the risks have changed their forms, giving rise to new forms of conflict—over, for example, the rights and roles of women in non-industrialised societies, and the responsibility of the developed world to the South in relation to matters such as the population explosion. These often become central to political differences on a global scale, such as the postulated conflict between western and Islamic values. Conflicts over sexuality have become integral to the emergence of fundamentalist politics both within western societies and elsewhere around the world (Bhatt, 1997). Fundamentalism, it has been suggested, is about the refusal of dialogue, the declaration of absolute values in relation to a perceived relativism. The relativisation of sexual values has accompanied the recognition of a plurality of sexualities in western societies, and this has led to issues of the family, traditional gender relations, sex education and homosexuality becoming central preoccupations of fundamentalist movements. Many of these movements are trans-national with identities organised around the great religious faiths such as Hinduism and Islam that have bridged divisions between the north and the south in global terms. And yet processes of engagement between cultures and movements on an international scale have in turn given rise to new discourses of human rights on a global scale, which are already having a significant impact on sexual politics within specific countries. I think, for example, of the impact that Britain's involvement in the European Union is having on debates on sexuality in the United Kingdom, in relation to a common heterosexual/ homosexual age of consent or same sex partnership rights (Weeks, Heaphy and Donovan, 2001, Wintermute and Andenaes, 2001). Or we can refer to the globalisation of concern with child sex abuse (Reavey and Warner, 2003), leading to international campaigns and inter-governmental collaboration against sex tourism. We can also cite the global fight against AIDS.

The HIV/AIDS epidemic provides a vivid case study of the processes at work. Seeing AIDS through the prism of globalisation throws new light on the epidemiology of a sex-related set of diseases; on the processes of mobilisation which have combated the epidemic on a trans-national scale; and on the dominance of certain ways of understanding the epidemic which are gendered, ethnicised and embody certain assumptions about sexuality (Altman, 1994, 2001). AIDS provides a reminder of the uneven development of societies, and the necessity for both international and specific local responses that this engenders. Through these, sexual behaviours and identities are being contested and reconstructed— and the rights of people living with HIV and AIDS are being articulated.

And yet struggles over human rights are themselves not unproblematic. A recognition of the human rights of women, for example, does not mean that as yet it is possible to develop a common assumption about what those rights mean in practice, as controversies over the legitimacy of women wearing the veil, enforced or arranged marriages, access to birth control and the like underline. The work on international campaigns about reproductive rights suggests that there is a double push in this global movement: for bodily integrity and the right of women to control their own body; but also for challenging wider social, economic and cultural inequalities, without which rights may become meaningless. While a common discourse on reproductive rights is emerging, particularly in the language of international human rights, the meanings vary across different societies, dependent on different traditions, circumstances, and relations of power (for example, see Petchesky and Judd, 1998.)

This is true of all claims to specific rights as well as ambitious assertions of universalistic or human sexual rights. If sexual cultures are multifarious and have specific historical formations, how do we distinguish those claims to rights that have a universal resonance, and those which are highly culturally specific— and possibly distasteful to large numbers of citizens around the globe? One answer lies in the realisation that human rights do not exist in nature. They are not there to be discovered written on tablets of stone. They have to be invented, in complex historical conjunctures and contestations, as part of the making of minimal common values (Weeks, 1995). And in a divided, often violently polarised world, that is not an easy task.

Conflict of Values

This pluralistic, diverse world is subject to unavoidable conflict of values that can neither be wished away, nor easily resolved, either by a resort to absolute standards, science, history, tradition, or to the assumed moral righteousness of our own positions, whatever they may be. In a world that is simultaneously globalised and challenged by emergent differences and new fundamentalisms, the question of values and ethics inevitably comes to the fore. Sexuality may always have been an arena of moral and cultural conflict, but in contemporary societies sexuality is becoming an increasingly central and explicitly debated issue in mainstream cultural conflicts and political debates over values and citizenship. Debates about who and what we are, what we need and desire, how we should live, are to a striking degree also debates about sexuality. It is not surprising therefore that debates over sexuality display anxiety and uncertainty. The fear aroused by the HIV/AIDS epidemic was more than simply concern about a new and possibly incurable disease; it also underlined our uncertainty about contemporary moral stances (Weeks, 1995). The frequent waves of fear about the prevalence of the abuse of children (Freeman, this volume; Reavey and Warner, 2003) reflect uncertainty about the relations between adults and children in the contemporary world, the erosion of traditional sources of authority, and the problems of combating exploitation and protecting the vulnerable.

Advances in science only serve to compound the general air of uncertainty (Johnson and Segal, both this volume). How for example should we react to the possibilities opened up by embryological research? What are the implications for sexual values and ethics of the internet revolution? In a world where traditional sources of authority such as religion and the patriarchal family are under intense pressure, and heightened individualism is increasingly the norm, it is difficult to see how there can ever be agreement on a fixed set of values, or categorical list of rights and responsibilities, to which everyone can readily adhere. The challenge, to my mind, is to find a balance between a recognition of individual needs and desires, mutual responsibilities, sensitivity to difference, and at least a minimum agreement on common human standards. And that is not easy.

For many people, as I have suggested, advances in science do hold the key, and they seek a new security in the genetic revolution, asserting that differences of gender or sexuality are a result of adaptive patterns laid down in the course of human evolution (Lancaster, 2003). This approach, offered by the new evolutionary psychology, seems to me a false and hopeless promise. There is no reason to think that speculations about what might have happened in the early stages of human existence amongst our common ancestors on the African savannah can in any way resolve contemporary dilemmas. At the same time, however, the social and historical perspectives on the making of sexualities that I have outlined do not in themselves carry any set moral or political values. The usefulness of seeing sexuality as shaped in culture is that it allows us to recognise the contingency and arbitrariness of our own social arrangements. It does not, however, tell us how we should live today.

It is for this reason, I suggest, that the language of human rights and of sexual or intimate citizenship has come to the fore (Peteschky, 2000, Plummer,

1995, 2003, Richardson, 2000; see also Chau and Herring, this volume), It provides a discursive form through which the necessary debates can be carried on in working out what is and is not possible. It provides an iterative framework through which we can try to agree the minimum standards we need to attain to recognise simultaneously each other's differences and common humanity.

As Peteschky (2000) observes, prior to the early 1990s, sexuality was absent from international human rights discourse. The international argument began to emerge with the Vienna conference on Human Rights in 1993, the UN declaration of the Elimination of Violence against Women later that year, the world population conference in Cairo in 1994, and the women's conference on Beijing in 1995. But of course, the ground work had been going on quite clearly since the 1970s, with the various campaigns of second wave feminism and the internationalising of the lesbian and gay movement. The global HIV/ AIDS epidemic helped force sexuality onto the international sexual agenda. And as I mentioned above, the precursor movements were much older, going back at least to the early twentieth century. But as Peteschky (2000) again notes, while the claim to rights can be enabling, it can as easily lead to a conflict of rights. We need some agreed values to guide us through the thickets.

In an earlier work I argued that the very malleability of sexuality allows it to express a variety of human potentialities. The erotic offers a space of possibility for exploring and positively affirming the different ways of being human. But these possibilities must be tempered by two fundamental principles that constitute a minimum universal standard: the right to life, and the right to liberty. These principles require in turn that we reject actions which involve domination, coercion, force and violence (Weeks, 1995: 63–4). What follows from this, I suggest, is a recognition of the need to delineate the factors that make for autonomy and choice, and I outline three basic 'rights of everyday life' which can help guarantee that: the right to difference, the right to space, and the rights of exit and of voice (Weeks, 1995: 142–54).

I do not pretend that these in and of themselves answer our dilemmas. They provide at best guidelines to rethink the ways we live our sexual lives today. I refer to them here to illustrate my main point: that in order to make use of the emerging discourse on sexuality and human rights, we need to clarify our values, to say where we are coming from. In doing so we should not claim that these are the only values, the necessary starting points, the settled Truth. On the contrary, we live in a world of many, and conflicting truths. We can only move forward, towards creating agreed minimum standards dialogically with those who might disagree with us, if we know where we stand, which are our truths. That is the best response to the accusations of relativism frequently thrown at those who espouse the value of sexual diversity.

LIVING WITH UNCERTAINTY

Sexual rights (and wrongs) can be said to be concerned with three sets of practices: practices of identity (for example, male/female/transgendered, straight/gay/bisexual, etc); erotic practices (same sex, heterosex, 'normal' and transgressive etc); and practices of relating (marriage, adulterous etc). Each produces its own uncertainties in a world of rapid change. But it is not, perhaps, surprising that a great deal of contemporary debate focuses on the family and intimate relationships because it is here that identities and sexual activity are crystallized, and given meaning. The well advertised 'crisis of the family' that conservative thinkers and politicians have recurrently alluded to over the past couple of generations, is not simply about changes in domestic patterns. It is fundamentally about the changing relationships between men and women, men and men, women and women, adults and children. This leads to some profound questions. Has there really been, as Giddens (1992) and Beck and Beck-Gernsheim (1995) suggest, a basic shift in the relationship of men and women towards new patterns of egalitarian intimacy? To what extent does the emergence of non-heterosexual families of choice represent an augury of more egalitarian and chosen lifestyles (Weeks, Heaphy and Donovan, 2001; see also Lind, this volume)? To what extent are the sharp dichotomies between heterosexuality and homosexuality dissolving in a post-familial world?

Each of these requires a study in its own right. What is clear, to me at least, is that debates about sexual rights and wrongs must in the end be debates about relationships, about intimacy, and about the values, and rights (and wrongs), as I have suggested, of everyday life. Whatever the fantasies about the erotic possibilities of the internet and of cybersex, sexuality is always ultimately about interaction with flesh and blood others. It is through that interaction that the meanings of sexuality are shaped, and what we know as sexuality is produced. And in the process we are producing new stories about the types of relationships we want, narrative frameworks which articulate and configure emerging values.

I have argued that the recognition of the role of the social in constituting what we regard as the sexual provides a focus for political and cultural confrontations. The emergence of an explicit and increasingly mainstream political and cultural discourse around sexuality since the 1960s, is no accident. It is a product of the disruption of settled patterns of sexual life under the impact of profound social change on a global scale. Traditionalists aspire in vain to a restoration of stability. New voices articulate the aspiration for recognition of new identities and new ways of being. A cacophany of sexual narratives, of old and new 'sexual stories' (Plummer, 1995) compete to be heard. And an apparent paradox emerges. New sexual subjects seek ever more the right to privacy in their sexual and relational choices, and yet engage in a proliferating public discussion of their needs and desires, their rights and responsibilities. The growing 'sequestration' or privatisation of sexual life that Giddens (1991) noted as a characteristic of modern western erotic experience has been balanced by an explosion of discourses about intimate life, which have profoundly redefined what we understand as sexuality on a global scale. The ways in which we talk about sexuality and intimate life help to shape them.

Humans, as Plummer (1995, 2003) argues, are storytelling beings, and through stories we create our world. There has been a proliferation of sexual stories since the eighteenth century, but only since the late twentieth century have these stories gained a mass audience. The sexual stories we tell are deeply implicated in moral and political change, and shifting stories of self and identity carry the potential for radical transformations of the social order. Over the past generation we have seen a change in the forms and organisation of the stories we tell each other, and late modern stories reveal and create a multiplicity of new projects, new constituencies, new possibilities for the future. These are stories of human life chances, of emotional and sexual democracy, of pluralistic forms of sexual life, opening the way for a new culture of intimacy and what Plummer describes as 'intimate citizenship'.

Is this a vain optimism? I know that around the world, in various countries, sex radicals despair of ever breaking through against what I call the heterosexual assumption (see Weeks, Heaphy, and Donovan, 2003), with all its institutionalised power. Local gains are often countered by national losses, especially when conservative political forces resume power. Similarly, national gains can be thwarted by local resistances. As befits a long revolution, two steps forward are followed by one step backwards. Uneven development takes its toll. Yet it seems to me undeniable that the past couple of generations have seen an unprecedented and almost certainly irreversible shift in values and practices at the level of everyday life (for example, Laumann *et al.*, 1994, Wellings *et al.*, 1994, Johnson *et al.*, 2001).

This is manifested in different ways in different countries. The moral conservatism fuelled by religious fervour that shapes the culture wars in the United States is much less obvious in western Europe and Britain, despite the fervour with which specific legislative changes in a liberal direction are fought over. In fact, there is evidence that, in Britain at least, unlike the 1960s, where liberal reforms led public opinion, now public opinion is in advance of legal reform, which is often mired in the sclerotic legislative processes (see Bainham and Brooks-Gordon, this volume). The delay of marriage, the rise of co-habitation which has now become a norm before marriage, the rapid rise of single households, the emergence of new patterns of intimacy, such as lesbian and gay "families of choice", are indices of major shifts in behaviour, and increasingly of beliefs as well (McRae, 1999; Lewis, 2001; Weeks, Heaphy and Donovan 2001). We can rightly make a series of necessary qualifications about these developments. Most people still marry and then re-marry. The average number of partners is relatively low. Serial monogamy is the norm. Cohabitation before marriage may now be routine, but most offspring of such unions are still registered by both parents. Homosexual relations may be more tolerated, the age of consent has been equalised, and the recognition of same sex partnerships may be imminent, but culturally the heterosexual assumption remains strong. Similarly, despite the 'transformation of intimacy' that Anthony Giddens (1992) has proclaimed, there are still great inequities in the relationship between men and women (Jamieson, 1998).

But at the same time there is no doubt that by and large the British population has become more tolerant in its attitudes towards sexual diversity, especially amongst younger people (Johnson *et al.*, 2001). And whatever the difficulties, the continuing patterns of inequality, violence and struggle and the continuing inequities between men and women, new patterns of life and new values are emerging. There is plentiful evidence, for example, which suggests a widespread acceptance of the merits of companionate and more equal relationships, even as we fail to achieve them. As Giddens (1992) argued, the egalitarian relationship has become a measure by which increasing numbers of people feel they must judge their own individual lives. At the centre of this ideal is the fundamental belief that love relationships and partnerships should be a matter not of arrangement or tradition, but of personal choice based on a balance of attraction, desire, mutual trust and compatibility. Again, one must qualify this by recognising that Britain has become an increasingly diverse society and has a variegated pattern of values and domestic organisation. But this is surely the point: it is no longer possible to see Britain as a homogenous society, with a single moral standard. It is well on the way to becoming a pluralistic society not simply in cultural and ethnic terms, but also in attitudes to the family and sexuality.

The new stories of intimacy that are now increasingly shaping our culture can be seen as examples of a new or accentuated individualism in most Western societies. The economic and cultural changes in the past generation have tended to exalt the individual over the collective. The triumph of economic liberalism since the 1970s has tended to elevate individual self-expression and material well being, and undermine many of the traditional sources of solidarity such as the trade unions and other collective forms. This individualism in turn has had its effect on family and sexual life. The 1990s demonstrated, that whatever the social authoritarian efforts of people like Reagan in the United States and Thatcher in the UK, the triumph of economic liberalism has tended to undermine traditional patterns. This new individualism has aroused extreme anxieties amongst moral conservatives (Phillips, 1999). It has left more generally an underlying sense of unease, which is manifest in recurrent 'moral panics' around sexual issues (Weeks, 2000: chapter 12). Yet whatever the undercurrent of uncertainty (Weeks, 1995), it has also provided greater opportunities than ever before for individuals to explore their own needs and desires, to become more autonomous in their chosen ways of life. Most people, perforce, have to negotiate the rapids of change without recourse to a transcendent value system, or tradition, and by and large they surf the waters successfully.

People are not particularly interested in politics or the politics of family and sexuality in particular. They do not have grand visions of new ways of living, even as at an every day level they do necessarily engage in 'experiments in living' (Giddens 1992; Weeks, Heaphy and Donovan 2001). There is both a pragmatism in the adaptation to changes in every day life, and a new contingency as people have, in a real sense, to create values for themselves. Their liberalism may well be limited to a form of live and let live morality. There is no positive endorsement of different ways of life. Yet there are very few households in Britain, which are not touched by the transformations of everyday life. Most people know single parents. Most people know a member of their family who may be lesbian or gay, or a member of an interracial partnership. Most households have experienced divorce, re-marriage, cohabitation, broken families, reconstituted families. This surely is one of the major reasons why attempts during the 1980s and 1990s to return to Victorian, or 'basic' values, were dismal failures. We are in the midst, as I have argued, of a genuine social revolution. The revolution is unfinished, partial, uneven in its impact. But we all now have to live with the consequences and implications. And the evidence surely is that most people adapt extremely well.

THE FRAMEWORK OF CITIZENSHIP

The lesson of the past generation is that the dramatic changes with regard to family and sexual life have not been led by the political elite but by grassroots shifts which are subject to a whole variety of long term social trends. Governments, of course, have to respond, but they inevitably do so in a variety of different ways, depending on political traditions, the prevailing balance of cultural forces, the nature of the political institutions, the day to day crises which force some issues to the fore, and the pressure from below, whether from conservative or fundamentalist resistance to change, or from radical social movements. By and large legislators prefer to follow trends in public opinion, and in a changing social geography, rather than lead them.

There is, inevitably, a wider argument to be had, over whether these tentative, ambivalent, usually reactive responses from governments are enough. I suspect that in most cases they do reflect a public mood that generally seems to be saying: 'let well alone' unless some spectacular abuses or contradictions come to light. The contradictory elements revealed in the Sexual Offences Act in 2003 (Bainham and Brooks-Gordon, this volume)—on the one hand getting rid of anachronistic laws which penalised male homosexuals particularly, on the other hand seeking, without any clearly defined principles, to define new areas of sexual harm—perhaps reflect a public opinion which is simultaneously more tolerant of homosexuality and increasingly intolerant of anything which can be described as abuse or sexual harm, especially of young people. In the process new restrictions may emerge. Respect for privacy and the urge for protection vie for hegemony in a changing world of sexuality.

The debate over same sex partnerships, marriage and chosen families, further illustrates some of the tensions and ambiguities that claims to sexual or intimate citizenship inevitably involve. Is same sex marriage necessary because it will mark the full integration of lesbians and gays into society, as gay conservatives argue? Or desirable because it mimics, undermines and transgresses the hetero-sexual institution, as queer activists might argue? Should gay families be acknowledged because we all need families, or because they subvert the concept of the traditional family as the foundation stone of society? (see debates in Sullivan, 1997; Wintermute and Andenaes, 2001; Merin, 2002; Weeks, Heaphy and Donovan, 2001).

The reality is that across the world many thousands are making choices about how they want to live on a day by day basis. Most of them are not particularly preoccupied by theoretical disputes. They are concerned, however, that they can live their chosen lives with openness and legitimacy, that indeed they have the full freedom to choose, so that they can live their lives with a sense of mutual care, responsibility, respect, and transparency.

Through their voices, in the variety of individual and collective stories, we see new claims being articulated, circulated and re-circulated, creating new communities of knowledge and empowerment, new realities. Through the vicissitudes of everyday, intimate life, new ways of living, life experiments, are being constructed. And slowly, often painfully, with due hesitation, principle and pragmatism hopelessly confused, with two steps forward, one step backwards, our societies, I would argue, are learning at last, to live with sexual diversity.

REFERENCES

ADKINS, L, *Revisions: Gender and Sexuality in Late Modernity* (Buckingham, Open University Press, 2002).

ALEXANDER, M J, 'Not Just (Any) Body can be a Citizen: The Politics of Law, Sexuality and Postcoloniality in Trinidad and Tobago and the Bahamas' 2003, in J Weeks, J Holland and M Waites (2003) 174–82.

ALTMAN, D, *Power and Community: Organizational and Cultural Responses to AIDS* (London and Bristol, Taylor and Francis, 1994).

—— *Global Sex* (Chicago, University of Chicago Press, 2001).

BECK, U and BECK-GERNSHEIM, E, *The Normal Chaos of Love* (Cambridge, Polity Press, 1995).

BHATT, C, *Liberation and Purity: Race, New Religious Movements and the Ethics of Postmodernity* (London, University College London Press, 1997).

BUTLER, J. *Gender Trouble: Feminism and the Subversion of Identity* (London and New York, Routledge, 1990).

—— *Bodies that Matter: On the Discursive Limits of Sex* (London and New York, Routledge, 1993).

CONNELL, RW, *Masculinities* (Cambridge, Polity Press, 1995).

FOUCAULT, M (1979) *The History of Sexuality, Volume 1: An Introduction* (London, Allen Lane).

GAGNON, J and SIMON, W, *Sexual Conduct. The Social Sources of Human Sexuality* (London, Hutchinson, 1973).

GIDDENS, A, *Modernity and Self-Identity* (Cambridge, Polity Press, 1991).

—— *The Transformation of Intimacy: Sexuality, Love and Eroticism in Modern Societies* (Cambridge, Polity Press, 1992).

HOLLAND, J, RAMAZANOGLU, C, SHARPE, S, and THOMSON, R (eds), *The Male in the Head*, (London, The Tufnell Press, 1998).

JACKSON, S, *Heterosexuality in Question* (London, Sage, 1999).

JAMIESON, L, *Intimacy: Personal Relationships in Modern Societies* Cambridge, Polity Press, 1998).

JOHNSON, AM, MERCER, CH, ERENS, B *et al*, 'Sexual Behaviour in Britain: Partnerships, Practices, and HIV Risk Behaviours' (2001), *The Lancet*, vol. 358 (9296) 1 December 2001, 1835–1842.

LANCASTER, R, *The Trouble with Nature: Sex in Science and Popular Culture* (Berkeley, Los Angeles and London, University of California Press, 2003).

LAUMANN, EO, MICHAEL, RT, GAGNON, JH and MICHAELS, S, *The Social Organization of Sexuality: Sexual Practices in the United States* (Chicago, University of Chicago Press, 1994).

LEWIS, J, *The End of Marriage? Individualism and Intimate Relations*, (Cheltenham and Northampton. MA, Edward Elgar, 2001).

MCRAE, S, (ed), *Changing Britain: Families and Household in the 1990s* (Oxford, Oxford University Press, 1999).

MERIN, Y, *Equality for Same Sex Couples*, (Chicago, Chicago University Press, 2002).

OOSTERHUIS, H, *Stepchildren of Nature: Krafft-Ebing, Psychiatry and the Making of Sexual Identity* (Chicago and London, University of Chicago Press, 2000).

PARKER, R, *Bodies, Pleasures and Passions: Sexual Culture in Contemporary Brazil* (Boston, Beacon Press, 1991).

—— *Beneath the Equator: Cultures of Desire, Male Homosexuality and Emerging Gay Communities in Brazil* (London and New York, Routledge, 1999).

PETCHESKY, R, 'Sexual Rights: Inventing a Concept, Mapping an International Practice' in R Parker, RM Barbosa and P Aggleton (eds), *Framing the Subject: The Politics of Gender, Sexuality and Power* (Berkeley, University of California Press, 2000) 81–103.

—— and JUDD, J, (eds). *Negotiating Reproductive Rights: Women's Perspectives Across Countries and Cultures* (London, Zed Books, 1998).

PHILLIPS, M, *The Sex-Change Society: Feminised Britain and Neutered Male* (London, The Social Market Foundation, 1999).

PHILLIPS, O, 'Zimbabwean Law and the Production of a White Man's Disease' in J Weeks, J Holland and M Waites, *Sexualities and Society: A Reader* (Cambridge, Polity Press, 2003) 162–73.

PHILLIPS, KM, and REAY, B, (eds), *Sexualities in History: A Reader* (London and New York, Routledge, 2002).

PLUMMER, K, *Sexual Stigma: An Interactionist Account* (London, Routledge and Kegan Paul, 1975).

—— *Telling Sexual Stories: Power, Change and Social Worlds* (London and New York, Routledge, 1995).

—— *Intimate Citizenship* (Seattle, University of Washington Press, 2003).

REAVEY, P, and WARNER, S, (eds), *New Feminist Stories of Child Sexual Abuse: Sexual Scripts and Dangerous Dialogues* (London and New York, Routledge, 2003).

RICHARDSON, D, (ed), *Theorising Heterosexuality: Telling it Straight* (Buckingham and Philadelphia, Open University Press, 1996).

—— *Rethinking Sexuality* (London and Thousand Oaks, Sage, 2000).

RUBIN, G, 'Thinking Sex: Notes for a Radical Theory of the Politics of Sexuality' in CS VANCE (ed), *Pleasure and Danger. Exploring Female Sexuality,* (London and Boston, Routledge and Kegan Paul, 1984).

SIMON, W, *Postmodern Sexualities* (London and New York, Routledge, 1996).

SULLIVAN, A, (ed), *Same Sex Marriage: Pro and Con—A Reader* (New York, Vintage, 1997).

WARNER, M, (ed), *Fear of a Queer Planet: Queer Politics and Social Theory* (Minneapolis and London, University of Minnesota Press, 1993).

WEEKS, J, *Coming Out: Homosexual Politics in Britain from the Nineteenth Century to the Present* (London, Quartet Books, 1977).

—— *Sexuality and its Discontents: Meanings, Myths and Modern Sexualities* (London, Routledge and Kegan Paul, 1985).

—— *Invented Moralities: Sexual Values in an Age of Uncertainty* (Cambridge, Polity Press, 1995).

—— *Making Sexual History* (Cambridge, Polity Press, 2000).

—— *Sexuality*, Second Edition (London and New York, Routledge, 2003).

—— and HOLLAND, J (eds), *Sexual Cultures: Communities, Values and Intimacy* (Basingstoke and London, Macmillan, 1996).

—— HEAFHY, B and DONOVAN, C, *Same Sex Intimacies: Families of Choice and other Life Experiments* (London and New York, Routledge, 2001).

—— HOLLAND, J and WAITES, M, (eds), *Sexualities and Society: A Reader* (Cambridge, Polity Press, 2003).

WELLINGS, K, FIELD, J, JOHNSON, AM and WADSWORTH, J, *Sexual Behaviour in Britain: The National Survey of Sexual Attitudes and Lifestyles* (Basingstoke and London, Macmillan, 1994).

WINTERMUTE, R and ANDENAES, M, (eds), *Legal Recognition of Same-sex Partnerships: A Study of National, European and International Law,* (Oxford and Portland, Oregon, Hart Publishing, 2001).

3

Social Worlds, Social Change and the Rise of the New Sexualities Theories

KEN PLUMMER

. . . all discourses of sexuality are inherently discourses about something else; sexuality rather than serving as a constant thread that unifies the totality of human experience, is the ultimate dependent variable, requiring explanation more often than it provides explanation . . . (Simon, 1996)

. . . This is the real mark of what is different about the late twentieth century: those who used to be spoken of are now struggling in various ways, using different, often hesitant or incoherent languages to speak for themselves. The result is inevitably confusing, but enormously significant. We are here in a world where the imperatives of history, nature and science are being displaced by the norm of sexual choice, and where a master narrative is being displaced by a multiplication of new narratives, each claiming its own truth . . . (Weeks, 2000)

INTRODUCTION: THE SOCIAL WORLDS OF STUDYING SEXUALITY

THE STUDY OF human sexualities now has at least a century of research and thinking behind it. As with all study and research, it congeals into various 'social worlds', which often have little connection with each other (Clarke, 1998; Strauss, 1984). One world—such as 'evolutionary thinking'—will have its own history, language, 'gurus', journals, conferences, ideologies and may have little contact with another—such as 'queer theory'—which will also replicate its own history, language, gurus, journals,[1] and conferences. What may be called

---

[1] There are now many journals in the field. But as the editor of one of them, I do wonder if there is much cross-fertilization. Certainly, and perhaps wrongly, I do not feel the need to read across all the journals but just make the occasional perusal to ensure that I really am not missing anything. See (inter alia) *Journal of Sex Research, Archives of Sexual Behavior, Australian Journal of Sex, Marriage and the Family, British Journal of Sexual Medicine, Culture, Heath & Sexuality, International Journal of Sexuality and Gender Studies* (formerly the *Journal of Gay, Lesbian, and Bisexual Identity), Journal of Sex Research Sex Education, Sexual and Marital Therapy,* and of course, *Sexualities!*

'social world theories of science', then, suggests that academic worlds have their own spaces, languages, memberships, identities, histories, and technologies which are always in dynamic process: shifting, changing, interpenetrating and, these days, increasingly global. They set boundaries of who is in and who is out of the debate; who can be listened to and who ignored; they fashion out 'publics' and 'counter-publics' (Hess, 1997; Warner, 2002).

The social worlds of sexuality studies can and often do overlap, but in the main they function more or less autonomously. They will have their own sexual study habitus and will assemble their own shared histories and intellectual memories. Some may be lofty and elite; others much more mundane and open. Some may claim 'science' and seek objectivity; others may be much more avowedly political. Many will depend upon the creation of enemies to function: the debates they generate spearheaded by the creation of a counter-public. Tensions across worlds may be so great that they will not even look at what each other is interested in (except perhaps to attack it). Thus, to juxtapose some of the writings from *GLQ* alongside the *Archives of Sexual Behavior* would be to enter different planets (ironically, Warner's book is called *Queer Planet*). It might be an odd, even marginal, person who would read both! Or to take another instance: a recent analysis of 'theory in sexuality research' by David L. Weiss brings together some 25 'classics of sexual theory' for the *Journal of Sex Research* (1998). (The listing is reproduced as Table 1, but see also Geer and O'Donahue 1986). This journal is one of the leaders of 'the field', but it provides what some might consider a generally odd listing. Despite the major contributions of feminist and queer scholars to the emergence of recent theory, with the exception of Foucault and Tieffer, they all seem to be ignored. What we are left with is a curious North American and 'sexological bias', which reflects the different social worlds I have described above.

Table 1. 25 classic works of sexual theory (as designated by David L Weiss in *The Journal of Sex Research*, 1998 Vol 35 No 1).

Authors	Date	Contribution
Ellis (Havelock)	1901/1936	Non-judgmental approach to analysis of sexuality, explored various sexual concepts, early conceptualization of sexual orientation.
Freud	1905/1957	Early presentation of specific theoretical framework, theory of sexual development.
Malinowski	1929	Early Anthropology.
Mead	1935	Early Anthropology, concept of gender.
Pitts	1964	Review of Structural-Functionalism, concept of social control of sexuality.
Broderick	1966	Mini-theory on childhood sexual development.
Reiss	1967	Mini-theory combining research and theory, formulation of specific propositions, concept of sexual permissiveness.

Authors	Date	Contribution
Trivers	1972	Evolutionary perspective, concept of parental investment.
Gagnon & Simon	1973	Concept of sexual scripting, early social constructionism.
Beach	1976	Concepts of proceptivity and receptivity, female selection.
Foucault	1976/1980	Early social constructionism, critique of positivism.
Byrne	1977	Affect-reinforcement theory, causal model.
Symons	1979	Evolutionary perspective.
Fox	1980	Anthropological approach, incest.
Herdt	1981	Anthropological approach, development of sexual orientation.
Maltz & Borker	1983	Patterns of communication, concept of male and female cultures.
Maddock	1983	Family systems theory, focus on non-pathological family dynamics.
Van Wyk & Geist	1984	Sexual development processes, sexual orientation.
Green	1985	Causal model, childhood and adolescent experiences.
Reiss	1986	Cross-cultural meta-analysis.
Allgeier	1987	Causal model of sexual orientation.
Geer & O'Donohue	1987	Metatheoretical approach to numerous sexual theories.
Levine & Troiden	1988	Analysis of concept of sexual addiction.
Tiefer	1991	Feminist critique of various sexological concepts.
Laumann, Gagnon, Michael & Michaels	1994	Testing theoretically derived hypothesis with national probability sample.

All these scientific social worlds themselves are also riddled with their own splits and tensions. Thus, the 'sex wars' within academic feminism are well known and formidable and in their time have been well documented (e.g. Vance, 1984). But likewise, to look at the *Journal of Homosexuality* and then *GLQ* would not reveal much consensus. Worlds of research around HIV and AIDS are also notoriously at odds with each other on a global level. Assumptions, languages, histories, referential communities are in tension. There is a continuing academic 'Rhetorical War Over Sexuality' (Smith and Windes, 2000).

Whilst there are already some interesting histories of researching and theorizing the sexual, an account of their social worlds and the tensions therein must be awaited. Paul Robinson's *The Modernization of Sex* (1976) is now a classic and details the work of Kinsey, Masters and Johnson and Ellis in terms of both their content and their social impact. More recently, Kath Weston's *Long slow burn: sexuality and social science* (1998) Janice Irvine's *Disorders of Desire* (1990), and Julia Eriksen's *Kiss and Tell* (1998) have provided major critical reviews (though again strongly tied to the US traditions). Other works have brought together some of the key 'sexual documents' of our time (including the works by Jeffreys, 1987; Porter and Hall, 1995; Bland and Doan, 1998). We do have starts then in looking at the histories and social worlds of sex research and theory and it is clear that there are both massive data and secondary sources for such a project. But it is a huge undertaking and way beyond the aims of this short chapter. Nevertheless, as a nod in this direction, I could perhaps itemize some of the key players and positions. All have their own histories and all are around today.

First there are the *fieldworkers*—ethnographers, anthropologists, travellers. These include the early writers who brought back accounts of the sexual in 'foreign parts'; and whose contemporary counterparts are the anthropologists and the 'urban ethnographers'. Many of these have recently been criticized for their interest in exotic specimens and bringing a kind of colonialist type of mentality to the study of sexualities (e.g. Weston, 1998). Some have now re-surfaced as ethnographers of the queer (e.g. Halberstam,1998).

Next are the *clinicians*—from Krafft-Ebing and Freud to the more contemporary work of the late Bob Stoller(1976) and a legion of others. These bring back accounts of the workings of the inner psyche and its turmoils (cf. Oosterhuis, 2001).

By contrast are the *biologists* and *physiologists* who start to specialise in the reproductive sciences (Clarke, 1998), and who generate eventually the science of sex: sexology.

Of growing current concern are the *socio-biologists* and *evolutionary psychologists*, whose work suggests how much sex is shaped by the key adaptive biological differences between men and women.

Then there are the *sex surveyors*—symbolised by Kinsey (1948, 1953), though he was far from being the first, whose task seemed to be to tell the tale of who does what to whom how often. These range enormously from the large scale but solitary works of Shere Hite (1976) to the funded researches which many countries conducted in the wake of the HIV /AIDS pandemic such as those by Wellings (1994) in the UK and Laumann (1994) in the US.

The *symbolic interactionist theorists* are a relatively small group, spearheaded by Gagnon and Simon (1973). They were closely allied with the urban ethnographers above and became the forerunners of what is now known as social constructionism.

The academic *political activists*—notably the Women's Movement and the Gay/Lesbian Movement—started to challenge many orthodoxies of the worlds of sex research from the 1970s onwards, producing their own analyses of sexuality, gender and power. Some of them also brought Marxist/materialist accounts.

Since the 1980s we have seen the arrival of *research* into the social worlds of *AIDS/HIV;* a world wide pandemic which has had the curious consequence of generating a major global programme of sex research and international conferencing. It has been dubbed The AIDS Industry.

And at about the same time, we started also to see what I have called the *Foucauldian Deluge*—work which followed in the wake of Michael Foucault's extraordinarily influential book *The History of Sexuality (1980)*, and which led to sexualities being seen as a discursive formation. Many of these social worlds (and there are others) function in relative ignorance of each other.

THE EMERGENCE OF NEW CRITICAL SEXUALITIES THEORIES

Moving under various (often contradictory and contested) guises over the past few decades we have seen a paradigmatic shift, a continuous attack and sustained critique on the orthodoxies of our time. Critical theory, epistemological anarchism, feminism, multiculturalism, discourse theory, constructionism, standpoint theory, queer theory, critical realism, critical humanism, postcolonialism, interpretive ethnography and other stances have all made their challenges. At their hearts, they have made traditional 'knowledge' about social life much more problematic. Indeed, the social theorist Ulrich Beck refers to 'Zombie knowledge' from the past—knowledge which simply hasn't taken on board the rapidly changing times we live in. And he cites the importance of locating all our old 'knowledges' nowadays in a global frame—we have always to think beyond the local. Our social theorizing is embedded in moral and political structures which need to be made much more explicit and part of our work. Our methodologies suffer from what Norman Denzin has called 'a triple crisis of representation, legitimation and praxis' (Denzin, 1997: 3). Moreover, our epistemologies may have suffered from too grand a claim for the search for *the* truth. Grand claims for finding a single way have been replaced by a language of pluralized truths, multiple pathways, and fragments. And all of this must affect the ways in which we now study—think, argue, theorize, research and act—around the fields of sexualities.

Although it would be hard to locate a specific time, place or people who worked to challenge some of the dominant assumptions of many of the schools of sex research that were prominent in much of the twentieth century, there can be no doubt that there has been considerable growth over the past fifty years or so. From a few papers in mid century that were relatively underdeveloped in both their theory and analysis, there was a major explosion of work in all directions. Spearheaded by AIDS research, the gay movement, the women's movement, and many wider social changes such as globalization, by the early 1990s there were many people working in the field that helped to re-shape it and provide 'New Agendas for Sexual Research' (Segal, 1997). From a number of differing strands dating from the late 1960s, a momentum gathered during the

1970s, became very prominent in the 1980s, and achieved almost cult status towards the end of that decade and the start of the 1990s. Its hey day in the UK was perhaps the very successful conference on Sexuality organized by the British Sociological Association in 1994[2] and the conference organized at Middlesex University around that time (Segal,1997). More recently, the whole position has become canonical in terms of texts, journals and readers (e.g. Abelove, Barale & Halperin (eds), 1993); Jackson and Scott (1996); Lancaster and di Leonardo (1997); Nardi and Schneider (1998); Parker and Aggleton (1999); Plummer (2002); Stanton ed. (1992); Weeks, Holland and Waites (2002); Williams and Stein (2002)). But there are also now some small signs of it attracting less interest. Indeed, in one recent study, Kath Weston (Weston, 2002, pp 1–2)—admittedly talking more about gender suggests that this research has 'passed its glory days' and is now haunted by a 'sense of intellectual exhaustion'. This is probably a very common life cycle for a social world of research.

The most formative influence for me was the trail blazing work of William Simon and John Gagnon. Both worked at the Kinsey Institute for Sexual Behaviour in the 1960s, collecting and unearthing mounds of empirical data, yet felt the need to theorise sexuality more adequately—to remove the data from the simple realm of the biological, the 'natural' and the merely factual and to place it squarely in the realms of the social, the symbolic and the theoretical. Starting in 1966, a highly fruitful partnership emerged which produced over 30 articles and linked books which culminated in *Sexual Conduct* (Gagnon and Simon, 1973). Drawing on the work of Kenneth Burke, their Chicago based training in symbolic interactionism and especially the dramaturgical metaphors of Erving Goffman, they argued that sex, far from being natural, was located well within the realms of the social and the symbolic. They introduced the key idea of scripting, an idea that has never to this day been fully exploited.

But I am being personal and biased. There are many entrances into this new thinking, and whichever path taken, they have much in common. At the heart of this would be challenging the view that sexuality is far from a given natural and is always for humans at the intersections of the social and cultural. As I have remarked elsewhere:

> . . . their prime aim is to sense the ways in which human sexualities are social through and through, and to claim that any analysis which does not recognise this must be seriously flawed. Sexuality, for humans, never just is. It has no reality *sui generis*, and any concern with 'it' must always harbour wider social issues : human sexualities have to be socially produced (no human can ever just do it), socially organised, socially maintained and socially transformed (Plummer, 2002: 1).

---

[2] The British Sociological Association's Annual Conference was held in 1994 on 'Sexualities in Social Context'; over 250 papers were presented—mainly by young British sociologists. This was surely a coup on the parts of the organisers: to take over the major agenda of British sociology. See: the three volumes published as *Sexual Cultures, Sex and Sensibility,* and *Sexualizing the Social* (Weeks et al, 1996). I review these volumes in *Signs* Vol 24 No 1.

What could perhaps be called proponents of 'Critical Sexual Theory' or, better, 'The New Sexualities Theorists' would all probably agree that what matters in understanding human sexualities is not so much the raw bodily elements, but the mapping of meanings between body and culture (what Gagnon and Simon refer to as cultural, inter and intra-psychic scripting—but others use other terms). They would all emphasise the diversity of sexualities with a vigorous critique of unitary models and the presumption of any fixed, given, universal heterosexuality. The concern is with how sexualities have changed (and may change)—whether it is women's sexuality, gay sexuality, sexuality linked to HIV etc, and that such changes have both long term and short-term dimensions. There is also a constant return to the ways in which sexuality increasingly becomes a political focus—with many conflicts—from those over pornography in the women's movement to those over gay male sexuality (the so called 'sex panic' debates) in the gay movement.

Here a space emerges for new kinds of sexualities and a time when the Grand Narrative of Sexuality has come to an end. 'Sex' is no longer the source of truth, as it was for the moderns with their strong belief in science. Instead, human sexualities become destabilised, decentred and de-essentialised: the sexual life is no longer seen as harbouring an essential unitary core locatable within a clear framework (like the nuclear family) with an essential truth waiting to be discovered : there are only fragments. As Jeffrey Weeks remarks:

> the imperatives of history, nature and science are being displaced by the norm of sexual choice, and where a master narrative is being displaced by a multiplication of new narratives, each claiming its own truth (Weeks, 2000: 238).

So now, at the start of the twenty first century, there is a proliferation of books, readers, conferences, journals, and research into social aspects of sexuality. The situation seems radically different from when I started out in this field some thirty years ago: no longer is it a minority, or even stigmatizing, business. It is true that some of this new work I find problematic. (For example, some of it is fast sending itself into a self-made ghetto; some of it continues to suffer from the old illusions of the search for a fixed truth; some of it engages eccentrically with just one or two 'texts'; some of it continues in time worn ways of uncritical empirical fact gathering; some of it wallows in a theoretical obscurantism of the sexual world; and some of it remains too firmly wedded to a Freudianism with a dark history and too many problems). Nevertheless, compiling a partial check list (a very postmodern tool!) in no particular order of importance of some of the issues on the agenda of sexual theorists at the start of the twenty first century is to sense something of the vibrancy of this field. (I have decided not to clutter this list with references).

—The continuing challenges of feminism, anti-racism, the LGBT movements, post-colonialism, multi-culturalism and anti-ageism—most of whom continue to provide full blown critiques of theory, method and substance in the study of sexualities. Closely allied has been the call for a return to seeing the role of materiality in sexualities—the return of what has been called a 'political economy of sexualities'[3]

—The continuing significance of AIDS/HIV and its role in galvanizing research, politics and new world wide debates about the meaning of sexualities and the nature of sexual acts. Much of this has been directly linked to the gay movement and more recently much of it has raised issues of globalization and the plight of low income societies.

—The problematisation of 'heterosexuality'. Assumed and taken for granted in much early research, activists within feminism and within the queer movement have started to chart the history of this idea (it appears after homosexuality) and the ways in which its binary split with homosexuality tends to become an organizing assumption of much western thought.

—The importance of the post-modern as a challenge to any unitary theory of the truth. Although post-modernism may now be less 'fashionable' than it was in the 1980s and the 1990s it has left its legacy both on sexual analysis (where there is no longer a Grand Truth of the Sexual—'King Sex has been dethroned') and indeed on the social organization of sexualities themselves (where they are now more likely to be seen in their multiplicities, diversities and local embedded contexts).

—The much clearer positioning of reproductive politics and reproductive health within the field. The rise of new reproductive technologies in particular has severed the presumed link with biological sex, and has instigated new practices of reproduction without 'genital sexual activities'. This starts to shift around centuries old understandings of the purpose of sexual activities and reproductive methods.

—The concern with both the *performativity*, the *doing* of gender and the nature of sexualities conceived as 'doing things together'. In removing a broad essentialism from the study of the sexual, we turn more and more to daily practices of doing sex.

—An interesting return to, and problematization of, the body and the corporeal, seeing the need to bring 'lust' and the body back into sexuality studies whilst not overstating it. Much of the new constructionism played down the body, or reduced it to a text. New trends suggest this is changing.

---

[3] Although probably more recognized by anthropologists and historians than sociologists, there are also signs of a contrasting mode of analysis which highlights 'political economy'. The reader by Roger Lancaster and Micaela di Leonardo (*The Gender/Sexuality Reader* 1997) gathers essays which 'contextualize . . . gender, sexuality, and human bodily experience within the historical vicissitudes of colonialism, imperialism and class stratification' (p 4), and approving citing William Roseberry's definition of political economy as: 'The attempt to constantly place culture in time, to see a constant interplay between experience and meaning in a context in which both experience and meaning are shaped by inequality and domination (and the) attempt to understand the emergence of particular peoples at the conjunction of local and global histories, to place local populations in the larger current of world history' (p 4) . . . Williams Roseberry's *Anthropologies and Histories* (New Jersey: Rutgers UP 1990).

—The persistent concern with boundaries, borders, differences and who is inside/outside. More than anything, this now seems to be the function of the established skirmishes around 'queer theory'. Whilst many patterns of same sex relations are becoming normal, others remain subject to taboo and stigma. The case studies of the paedophile and child sexualities will prove instructive here. There are also core issues of social exclusion and difference which highlight ethnicity, class, gender, age, disabilities, and nationality and are gradually becoming more focused.

—The power of the media, representation and what has been called 'the media-zation of sexualities'. Sexual lives are increasingly lived in worlds of mediated forms—from hip-hop worlds to reality television. Most centrally here has been the rise of cyber-worlds of sexualities—which come with a whole new language and series of issues. Here we have a new language that maybe mirrors new forms of sexualities—*cyber-porn, cyber-queer, cyber-dating, cyber-stalking, cyber-rape, cyber-victim, cyber-sex*.

—The centrality of the process of globalization and its impact upon sexualities, as some groups have more and more, and others less and less. Access to, and exploitation by, sexual markets is highly differentiated by class, ethnicity and gender. There is the global clash of sexual civilizations: important schisms over gender and sexualities between fundamentalist worlds (Christian, Muslim and others) and non-fundamentalist worlds.

—Issues of power and sex continue to be important, and along with this come new political debates identified as 'the sexual citizenship debates', especially as they move more and more into a global concern with human sexual rights.

Two things strike me as significant about this listing. The first is the sheer range of new issues on the agenda. The list is not at all complete but it pushes us to question the very foundations of much earlier thinking. It challenges us to look at the rapidity of change taking place in this field today. And it makes us confront the ways in which the sexual is embedded in a matrix of inequalities—of class, nations, race, gender, and age alongside processes of marginalization, exclusion and domination.

The second significant feature about such a listing is just how little input has come from the traditional social worlds of research into sexuality: sexology. And indeed just how different would be a similar listing of issues raised by them. In one major sense, nearly all the listing above comes from *activists in the academy*. Their agendas are not at all neutral and their goals have been radically to transform the sexual scene and the linked gender regimes. In all of this we see that the simple study of sex *as sex* has gone. This means that any understanding of the critical development of the new thinking on sexuality has to engage with the ideas of these new social movements: the understanding of new sexualities theories was profoundly shaped by ideas from both the lesbian and gay movement and the women's movement.

Bringing the Body (Back) In

One of the ironies of these new 'social' developments, however, has to be the ways in which in their quite proper zeal to show that the sexual was not a simple matter of bodily sex drives, but social through and through, the new theories started to study sexuality with little attention to bodies. There were exceptions—Martin Weinberg's early work on nudism looked at the management of bodies and moralities (Weinberg, 1970/2) and Foucault's (1980) work talked about bodies a great deal (but only in discourses). But in general, for some twenty-five years or so, the lusty, corporeal body went missing!

So now there is a need to bring 'lust' and the body back into sexuality studies (cf. Plummer, 2002/3; Dowsett, 1996; 2000).[4] This may seem an odd claim because the original claims of constructionism were to get away from too bodily a focus on sex—to weaken the 'drive' and biological essentialist models. And it is odd too because one of the major developments within social science thinking over the past twenty years or so has been the social theorizing over the body: there has been much recent work on the 'sociology of bodies' by which 'the body' has moved centre stage.[5] It remains a bit perplexing that the new literatures on sexualities and bodies somehow remain disconnected. So whilst it is true that *the gendered body* has been much discussed, *the sexualized or eroticised body* has received much less attention. When it is discussed it is usually in the form of the sexualized text or representation and not the fleshy, corporeal body. But the body, surely, is both a central site of concern for the *practice*s of sex as well, of course, as the symbolism. Hence whilst we can see the body as an erotically charged symbol swamped with sexual meanings, we must surely also see it as a series of material practices of embodiments. It is both bodily sign and bodily project. Since more is known of the former than the latter, let me suggest some themes around the idea of sexual body projects. Here we can start to think of commingled skins, of being inside another's body or having another's body invade the self: to penetrate and be penetrated, to invade and be invaded, to engulf or be engulfed, to take or be taken. What too of a sociology of embodiments around the erotic activities surrounding the mouth, the vagina, the anus, the breast, the toe? The corporeal body needs bringing into the new sexuality studies.

We might start to speak of *the embodiment of sexual practices; of doing body work around sex.* 'Sexualities' here will involve social acts through which we 'gaze' at bodies, desire bodies, taste (even eat) bodies, smell bodies, fashion and adorn bodies, touch bodies, hear bodies, penetrate bodies, and bring bodies to

---

[4] The next three paragraphs are drawn from a paper published in the Italian Journal of sociology, and hitherto not published in English (Plummer, 2002a).

[5] Indeed, by 1998 the British Sociological Association could organise its annual conference around the theme of 'Making sense of the Body', and just a year earlier the journal *Body and Society* was launched.

orgasm. These bodies can be our own or those of others. 'Doing sex' means 'doing erotic body work'. *Sex body projects* could entail, at the very least, the following: *presenting and representing* bodies (as sexy, non-sexy—on the street, in the gym, in the porno movie); *interpreting* bodies and body parts ('the gaze' and the 'turn ons' and 'turn offs'—sexual excitements of different kinds from voyeurism to stripping); *receiving* bodies; *manipulating* bodies (through the use of fashion. cosmetics, prosthetics); *penetrating* bodies (all kinds of intercourses from body parts like fingers and penises to 'sex toy objects'); *transforming* bodies (stages of erotic embodiment, movements towards orgasms); *commodifying* bodies (in sex work, live sex acts, stripping, pornography and the like); *ejecting and ejaculating* bodies as all kinds of bodily fluids—semen, blood, sweat, saliva, even urine and fecal matter—start to commingle; *possessing* bodies (as we come to own or dominate others bodies); *exploiting* bodies (as we come to abuse or terrorise them); *transgressing* bodies (as we go the extremes in the use of our erotic bodies) and *desiring* bodies.

From this we could also start to talk about 'the new body technologies of sexuality'. These new technologies include at one extreme how erotic bodies are (and have been for some time) managed through medical interventions. I think here not only of the long histories of birth control, but of the more recent medical interventions such as Viagra which work to engorge the body with eroticism, with transgender realignment surgery which helps refashion the genitalia; with the new methods of assisted conception (artificial insemination (AI), in vitro fertilization (IVF), embryo transfer (ET), gamete intra-fallopian transfer (GIFT)) which further separate out acts of sex, reproduction, gestation, and childrearing: sexed bodies, genetic bodies, nurturing bodies, gestating bodies; and with the multi-billion dollar industry of the cosmetic industry, where the breast, the face, the body becomes transformed through medical procedures often for a sexual end. These are but instances of technology at work to shift the sexualizing body. And they also start to suggest an iceberg tip of such transformations. The body is being reconstituted for post modern times and we are entering the age of the post-human and the cyborg (Haraway, 1991). This also means new modes of (dis) embodied sexualities such as may be found in the worlds of the seemingly rapidly growing cybersex. Through telephone sex, on line porn, sex chat rooms, web cam erotics, virtual realities etc, new disembodied sexual worlds may be in the making. Masturbation, solitariness and isolation may be one hallmark of such a world. But accessibility to sexual imagery on a global scale and a permanent supply of partners is another.

All this suggests the importance of *the changing erotic body*: how the erotic use of the body has changed over time. If we follow the tradition of Norbert Elias, we may see bodies as becoming more and more 'civilized'. Schilling summarises this as a 'progressive socialisation, rationalisation and individuation of the body' (1993: 163–4). By contrast, if we follow Foucault, we may see them becoming more and more 'disciplined'. Whichever interpretation is given, they become more bounded and with that more open to inspection as embodied citizens with rights and duties. Medical interventions—from Viagra to the huge sex therapy industry, from AIDS education to transgender, along with cyber-worlds may be seen as micro-circuits of power, ever more finely regulating and modifying aspects of erotic embodiment.

Fragments of Sexual Theorisations: Accounting for Sexual Actions

Although post-modern sensibilities tell us that the days of 'Grand Theory' and 'Total Systems' are over, we can, I think, see with some clarity now the 'fragments' that we now need to take on board in sexuality studies which we did not some thirty years ago. We know of course that we must always talk about the local communities and specificities being studied; grand ahistorical, sweeping claims are ruled out. But we can surely also start to talk now about how the many fragments, organising themes and sensitising concepts which we do par-tially understand may be brought into play. Many of these fragments can be framed with the classic action-structure debates of social theory; raising on the one hand the issue of a wider social and sexual order that constrains sexual life; and on the other the micro-processes of sexual action through which sexuality is accomplished or achieved.[6]

One useful way of thinking about a theory of sexuality should be to start with a grounded theory of *sexual action*. Through a range of close empirical tools (from grounded and queer ethnographies to self stories and queered life histor-ies), a set of mini concepts appear[7] which suggest tools for determining what actually goes on in everyday socialised sexual life. At the heart of this will lie human agency, albeit always one constrained by the contingencies of its every-day habitus. We start with the living and breathing, sweating and pumping, sen-suous and feeling world of the emotional, fleshy body acting in the world as I have suggested above. We start, where we can, albeit with some difficulty, with the actual *doings of sexualities*—that bodily charged messy business when we get right down to it! It won't do simply to see it as the release of various drives and hormones: we know now that it is deeply articulated through the social and can only happen when the social erupts. Nor will it do to see it as a simple reper-toire of orgasms and behaviours. We need to home in on the elements of this social act through which sex gets done, to locate it in biographies and contexts; and to see it as a 'continual permutation of action' (Strauss, 1993). Here are some phrases—or sensitising concepts—that may well be worth expanding upon into partial, grounded theories.

---

[6] This is a constant preoccupation in social theory and recent attempts to provide such a theory include those of Anthony Giddens, Margaret Archer and Rob Stones. For me, a useful point of entry is to be found in connections to the work of the late Anselm Strauss.

[7] On this, I have found the work of Robert Prus to be valuable.

Can we talk—and if so, how?—of

1. Establishing intimate encounters with self and others
2. Being 'turned on' by who, what, where, when and why?
3. Getting sexually excited
4. Handling sexual excitement
5. Doing sex acts
6. Embodying eroticisms

And moving on to consider:

1. Making sexual scriptings
2. Producing sexual feelings
3. Performing sexualities
4. Constructing sexual meanings
5. Evolving sexual habitus
6. Organizing sexual subjectivities
7. Sustaining sexual commitments
8. Enacting sexual identities
9. Narrating sexual stories

And moving on to:

1. Making sex codes
2. Organizing sexual worlds
3. Making sexual networks
4. Building sexual cultures

And then locating them within the elements of a wider sexual order:

1. Patriarchy
2. Compulsory Heterosexuality
3. Sex Negativism
4. Sex Hierarchy
5. Homophobia and heterosexism

And finally locating them in the wider worlds of time and space

1. Situation
2. Network
3. Community—Public Spheres
4. Society
5. Global space

Built into these last series of concepts are much wider concerns of social order—
and we might, following Strauss (1993), start thinking about the idea of '*a negotiated sexual order*'. These link to the broadest matters of social organisation,
social hierarchies and ultimately matters of power and social exclusion. It has
been well demonstrated through a mass of (mainly historical) studies that human

sexuality is bound up with basic social institutions of family, religion, economy, and polity; and enmeshed in stratification systems such as age, ethnicity, class and gender as well as its self generated systems of dominance and exclusion organised through patriarchy, compulsory heterosexuality, sexual violence, homophobia, and sex-negativism. We might see sexualities as *embedded* or *nested* in such emergent orders. Nearly twenty years ago, Jeffrey Weeks established a broad context for all this in his classic small study *Sexuality* (1986) where he outlines a framework of key social institutions in which sexualities are inevitably embedded and nested (although he does not use these terms). These are kinship and family systems, economic and social organisation, social regulations and control, political interventions, and cultures of resistance. He seems to overlook religion, which must also play a key role. All of these connect to power. No society accepts a sexual free for all: all societies have rules. And patterns of power become congealed in rules—overt or hidden—which guide the acceptability of different forms of sexualities. Amongst the concepts developed over the past few decades which help capture some of this are: *patriarchy*, which organizes sexualities around the key axis of male power and domination and the gender order which more widely suggests the gendered nature of sexualities (Connell, 1995). *Compulsory heterosexuality*, which suggests the primacy given to heterosexual forms of sexualities (Rich, 1978). *Sex negativism*, which organizes sexuality in a climate usually of fear and negativity (Davis, 1983). *Sex hierarchy* which more broadly suggests how sex is valorized positively and negatively for certain experiences (Rubin, 1984). A *Continuum of Sexual Violence* which suggests how much sexuality becomes embroiled with power and violence (Kelly, 1988). *Homophobia* which suggests the negative stances given usually to same sex patternings (Adam, 1998). And *sex stratification* which suggests hidden and almost 'secret' ways in which love and passion swirl through societies and provides a hierarchy based on 'emotional overcomeness' (Zetterberg, 1966).

Sexual Suffering and Sexual Justice in an Unjust World: Making the World Safe for Sexualities

Developing new theories of sexualities will however never be enough for the new sexualities theorists. As I have suggested above, their raison d'être has never been solely academic: many of their ideas have clear political origins and purposes. The social worlds in which they are grounded are largely those of the new social movements, and they do not want just to theorise the sexual world, but to change it.[8] There can be little doubt that the tacit (and sometimes not so tacit) agenda of the new critical sexualities theories has been to make the world a better world for our sexualities. And this is not quite the same wish as those who work in the field of sexology etc who wish to make our sexualities better (better

---

[8] I apologise for putting this into a Marxist cliché, but I just could not resist it!

orgasms and better intercourse, 'good sex' and 'safe sex') but who do not see such concerns as so profoundly bound up with cultural meanings and social inequalities.

In looking at this, it might be helpful to suggest five potential (or putative) forms of *sexual suffering* linked to sexuality, which need social and not just clinical or sexological analyses. Briefly I can summarise them as:[9]

1. *The Sufferings of Desire and Sexual Excitement.* This is the issue of who and what is found sexually exciting—what 'turns you on'? This is the classic problem of the nineteenth century—from Krafft Ebing to Freud—focused upon the nature of our sexual desires. Just who do we wish to have sex with (sexual orientation) and how often (the issues of addiction and lack of desire). Traditionally, these have been seen as the issues of men, with women suffering a lack of desire; though in recent times, there are many signs of change here.

2. *The Sufferings of Relationships.* How do we integrate (or not) our sexual life into our relationships with others? This ranges all the way from not relating (as in masturbation) to those where the relation is transitory (as in casual sex, and maybe 'promiscuity') to those held sacred within stable patterns of relationships such as the family and the couple (monogamy etc). Traditionally, religion has played a major role in structuring this.

3. *The Sufferings of Coercion and Violence.* This is the issue of handling sexual acts when they are unwanted and often violently imposed. Here sexuality is experienced as unwanted and coerced. The patterns move from simply disliking sex with a partner who imposes it upon you to more extreme versions of abuse, pressured sex, rape and even sexual murder. Again, there is usually a strong gender pattern to this, with men predominantly the aggressors.

4. *The Sufferings of Reproduction.* Here sexuality is experienced as a means of having children or not; and the issues it brings in its wake are linked to abortion, infertility, impotence, illegitimacy, being single, and family size. The ideology of pronatalism plays a major role in all this.

5. *The Sufferings of Disease.* Here sexuality is linked to diseases of all kinds. Some have conventionally been called the 'venereal diseases' or the 'sexually transmitted diseases' (from syphilis to herpes); others such as AIDS have been connected more widely; and still others such as impotence and frigidity, sex addiction and low drive, have become the province of sexological experts.

It is true that all these 'issues' can be found as personal sufferings. They are experienced as frustrations, fears, anger, pain, loneliness, hysteria, and just

---

[9] This brief listing is derived from Plummer (2004) where I also distinguish between personal, social and sociological problems and go on to develop further the ideas that such problems become part of a system of claims and social constructions.

plain 'common unhappiness' linked to emotional and embodied worlds. And they may require personal, therapeutic work. Yet these problems are also deeply shaped by the social times in which we live. Thus, the problems are frequently compounded by sexual stigmas and social inequalities. For instance, much of modern medical science has spent considerable time sorting out the different desires and dysfunctions of desires and arranging them into a kind of stigmatizing sex hierarchy (Rubin, 1984). Indeed, the nineteenth century was a major period for the creation of all kinds of sexual clinical taxonomies and perversions which did not simply label 'neutrally' but which served also to evaluate and exclude. Today, some still remain totally taboo—paedophilia for instance; whilst others such as homosexuality have become significantly more acceptable, been removed from the list of medical complaints and incorporated into prime T.V. sit-coms like *Will and Grace*. Likewise some relationships like the family couple are strongly supported while others are less accepted (the spinster was long a suspicious character in the past (Jeffreys, 1985)). Some violence and coercion is accepted: marital rape has only very recently been recognized as a crime in the West, and in many countries throughout the world all kinds of sexual indignities still seem to be imposed legitimately on women or gays with full approval of the society and its religious leaders. 'Having children through coitus' is nearly always the most acceptable reproductive strategy, whilst other patterns of sexuality are often condemned. Contraception is often taboo, and indeed, this becomes more and more controversial as we enter the world of new reproductive technologies. Finally, of course, most diseases carry a degree of stigma subject to social exclusion: AIDS is only the most recent instance of this.

Sexual sufferings are also linked to social divisions and inequalities. In a now classic study, Iris Marion Young describes the five faces of oppression as exploitation, marginalization, powerlessness, cultural imperialism and violence (Young, 1990). All the problems above are open to such processes. Some sexual sufferings arise from exploitation of other's bodies (much sex work, some forced and arranged marriages, indeed many relationships). Some desires can be ignored and marginalized (e.g. those of gays, fetishists, or the trans-gendered). Some people find themselves in sexual acts where they hold no power (the simple consensual sm. act often means the masochist does indeed hold power: I am talking more about the elements of sex when it has to be done but it is really not desired by one of the doers). Cultural imperialism and sexual problems may be found when certain desires and identities (e.g. western gay identity) are presumed to be universal, or when reproductive strategies differ across societies (e.g. cultural versions of abortion, new reproductive technologies, birth control programs). And violence is universally found in sexualities through abuse, rape, hate crimes and the like.

Sexual Utopias/Sexual Dystopias

It might help to close this essay by suggesting the need to think a little more about the ways in which sexual sufferings and problems may be shaped by wider social contexts in the immediate future. As Table 2 suggests, in one image, the world goes brutal: intimacies become subject to continuing polarized inequalities and ideological positioning—strong disagreements, massive exploitation, damaged lives everywhere. In the other, the world goes democratic: intimacies become subject to equalities, acceptance of differences, openness.

Table 2. Sexualities in a runaway world: utopian and dsytopian challenges

the '**tragic**' 'dystopian' view	the romantic 'utopian' view
abject sexualities—poverty, inequalities, divisions	luxuriant sexualities—higher standards of living
violent/exploitative sexualities	democratic sexualities
fragmented sexualities; the balkanization of sexualities	pluralized sexualities: differences celebrated
hi tech intimacy	hi tech sexualities
impersonal sexualities a world of strangers	new 'communities' of sexualities and communication
cyborgs as monster intimate narcissism and intimate egoism	cyborgs as helpers 'individuated sexualities'
intimate unsichereit	sexual openness
mcdonaldization of sexualities	globalization of sexualities
commercialization and commodification of sexualities	'real' sexual choices
the dumbing down of sexuality	reflexivity sexual self awareness
moral decline & sexual incivility	intimate citizenship, new ethics, moral effervescence
entrenched hierarchies of sexual exclusion	the democratization of personhood & relationships
intimate tribalism	intimate dialogue
uncertainty, chaos, a world out of control, risk, runaway world	chance for 'a new world order', human rights, a new politics

Source: Plummer, 2003.

At one end of possibilities then, are optimistic scenarios of the sexual future suggesting we are witnessing the appearance of a cosmopolitan and diverse array of sexual cultures of choice, located within an active civil society, and organized increasingly through a 'democratizing of democracy' throughout all institutions, all relationships and all sexualities. This 'democratising of sexualities' is found in Gidden's own much criticized ideas of plastic sexuality and pure relationships (Giddens, 1992; 1999; Jamieson, 1998; 1999). It is to be found in the optimism of some early gay activists who argue that discrimination against gays has been significantly weakened in the past thirty years and has led to gays and lesbians now having 'a place at the table' (Bawer,1993). It has led Jeffrey Weeks and others to champion new families of choice and new social experiments in living (Weeks, 1998; Weeks, Donovan and Heaphy, 2001). Important too have been (some of) the post modern theorisations which recognize the diversities of gender and sexuality—which speak of *masculinities*, *femininities* and, indeed, *genders*—as pathways to a future where grand narratives have broken down. Whereas the past spoke of sexuality, now there is recognition of *sexualities*. And much of this newer debate has been linked to the development of a new language of sexual identities, sexual rights, and intimate citizenship. Indeed, my own recent work looks at the need for a dialogic intimate citizenship where people may be able to talk through their contrasting intimacies and sexual differences (Plummer, 1995, 2003; see also Evans, 1993; Weeks, 1998; Bell and Binnie, 2001)). And now, new social movements come to play roles in doing just this on an international scale—witness the recent struggles of women in the United Nations for Sexual Rights discourses around human sexual rights and the sexual citizen (Nussbaum, 1999; Richardson, 2000, 2000a; Petchesky, 2000;).[10] Table 3 suggests some of these new rights being championed.

Table 3.   A sampler of ' sexual rights' proposals

Diane Richardson has suggested the following: The Rights

1. *To various forms of sexual practice*
   - The right to participate in sexual activity (usually found -when -in age of consent type debates; where—in public/private debates; with whom—orientation debates—what kind of sex etc)
   - The right to pleasure
   - The right to sexual and reproductive self determination(eg rape and the rights to say 'no')

2. *To the development of identities*
   - The right to sexual self definition
   - The right to self-expression e.g Don't ask/ Don't tell
   - The right to self realization

---

[10] Rosalind Petchesky suggests that sexual rights are 'the newest kid on the block in international debates about the meanings and practices of human rights' (Parker et al, 2000: 13).

3. *To rights within social institutions*
   • The right of consent within relationships
   • The right to freely choose our sexual partners
   • The right to publicly recognized sexual relationships

Martha Nussbaum has suggested the following lesbian and gay rights:
1. The right to be protected against violence, and in general, the right to equal protection under the law
2. The right to have consensual adult sexual relations without criminal penalty
3. The right to nondiscrimination in housing, employment and education
4. The right to military service
5. The right to marriage and/or its legal benefits
6. The right to retain custody of children and /or to adopt

Sources: Diane Richardson (2000) 'Constructing Sexual Citizenship' *Critical Social Policy* Vol 20 (1) p 105–35. Martha C. Nussbaum *Sex and Social Justice* 1999, Chapter 7 'A Defense of Lesbian and Gay Rights'.

Still others have noted the role that *individualization* is playing in all this. As many people are increasingly released from the traditional (especially gender) roles prescribed by industrial society and instead are encouraged to 'make their own lives'—relationships inevitably become more self conscious, more disclosed and discussed, and more negotiated. Individualization means 'the disembedding of industrial society ways of life' and the 're-embedding of new ones, in which the individuals must produce, stage and cobble together their biographies themselves'. The individual is 'actor, designers, juggler and stage director of his own biography, identity, social networks, commitment and convictions' (Beck: 1997: 95). Indeed, Ulrich Beck has commented that:

> We live in an age in which the social order of the national state, class, ethnicity and the traditional family is in decline. The ethics of individual self-fulfillment and achievement is the most powerful current in modern society. The choosing, deciding, shaping human being who aspires to be the author of his or her own life, the creator of an individual identity, is the central character of our time. It is the fundamental cause behind changes in the family and the global gender revolution in relation to work and politics. Any attempt to create a new sense of social cohesion has to start from the recognition that individualism; diversity and skepticism are written into Western Culture. (Beck, 2000: 165)

Much of this may sound like the good news but there is also a major downside. I am glad that Ulrich Beck says—finally, in his last two words—'Western Culture'. Some of this new thinking and theorizing speaks of 'the world' whilst ignoring the vast majority of it. Whilst this is certainly an important issue for many, it is not an issue for most. Too many studies of the sexual conceal the sheer global inequalities of the contemporary world. Just what kinds of sexual meanings do people bring to the third and fourth worlds, to low-income societies? As Manuel Castells comments:

... a new world, the Fourth World, has emerged made up of multiple black holes of social exclusion throughout the planet. (It) comprises large areas of the globe, such as much of Sub-Saharan Africa, and impoverished rural areas of Latin America and Asia. But it is also present in literally in every country and every city in this new geography of social exclusion. It is formed of American inner-city ghettos, Spanish enclaves of mass youth unemployment, French banlieues warehousing North Africans, Japanese Yoseba quarters and Asian mega-cities' shanty towns. And it is populated by millions of homeless, incarcerated, prostituted, brutalized, stigmatized, sick and illiterate persons . . . . . Everywhere they are growing in number . . . . (1996–8. Vol. 3, p 161–5).

This is a world where one billion people cannot satisfy their most basic needs; where around 4.4 billions have no access to basic infrastructures—accommodation, water, sanitation; and where, at the same time, the three richest men in the world have private assets greater than the national product of the 48 poorest countries combined! As Thomas Pogge says:

> People so incredibly poor are extremely vulnerable to even minor changes in natural and social conditions as well as to many form of exploitation and abuse. Each year, some 18 million of them die prematurely from poverty related causes. This is one third of all human deaths—50,000 everyday, including 34,000 children under age five. (2002: 2).

These are also usually societies with high reproductive rates, high prostitution rates, high rates of HIV and AIDS so we must assume that a considerable amount of sex is going on. *But just what kind of sex is this?* There are many hints from the HIV/AIDS research that there is a significant gender imbalance within it, and whilst men follow traditionally perceived roles, women become passive receptors, but also spending much time in child bearing, and witnessing the deaths of many of their children.

Certainly the world of cyber sex is not their everyday experience! For as Zillah Eisenstein has so powerfully shown, this is often linked to the polarization of vast groups with no access at all to cyberworlds, what Eisenstein calls 'the information haves and have-nots' (1998: 72). Talk of 'virtual sex' makes little sense to huge populations that do not even have access to basic water, medication, or shelter.

The Culture Wars and the Clash of Sexual Civilizations

Alongside these inequalities are also the cross cultural struggles and conflicts over how life should be lived. This is not just dissent and conflict within cultures, but across cultures. Speaking across cultures there are major disagreements on issues such as child marriage, sex work and sex markets, homosexuality and gay rights, genital mutilation and circumcision, women's sexual rights, marriage and the family, abortion and contraception—all of which suggest what we might call a clash of sexual civilizations. Whilst traditional values of the personal life are championed by some, for others they raise issues of major dissent and conflict on a world wide stage. Can they co-exist, and if so how? What are the possible relationships of different positions to each other? Ultimately, we enter here many of the classic problems of contemporary political philosophy—where issues of democracy, freedom, community, participation, empowerment, equality, and justice come to the forefront. Likewise, the persistent traditionalizing roles of religion work against any development of new sexualities—either in theory or practice. Detecting major divides, I suggest at least five broad kinds of arguments being made and positions being taken.[11] Briefly these are:

—*Traditionalism:* seeking a return to the past, usually based on a religion. At its extreme, this position can become fundamentalist.

—*Progressivism:* recognizing the significance of contemporary change and trying to make the world adjust to it.

—*Relativism:* adopting a 'do your own thing' mentality and arguing that anything goes which does not directly harm others.

—*Critical positions:* transcending the whole society/system and offering critiques from beyond.

—*Dialogism:* rejecting one stance and a monologic position and trying to foster a mutuality of voices.

I can personally align myself with all but the first position. But this is the most difficult one to confront in a late or post-modern world. With varying emphases, all traditionalists see chaos around them and seek a return to an old order with a clear authority and firm moral structure. The extreme version of this is fundamentalism and a number of major ideological features of this way of thinking can be detected.[12] Fundamentalist arguments are always concerned 'with the erosion of religion and its proper role in society': they react to what they sense to be its marginalization. Fundamentalists usually become highly selective in the issues they promote and in those they choose to ignore. They see the world as 'uncompromisingly divided into light which is identified with the world of the spirit and the good, and darkness which is identified with matter and evil'. For them, there is an absolute (and usually literal) belief in the sacredness of key texts. And finally, there is a belief in millennialism and messianism—'a miraculous culmination. The good will triumph over evil, immortality over mortality; the reign of external justice will terminate history'. Fundamentalist groups tend to have a clear, chosen membership, sharp boundaries, an authoritarian organisation and strict behavioral requirements. The issues they focus upon are also usually very clear: the reinstatement of 'a unified faith, race, reason, gender duality, normal sexuality, nation and or territory that never was secure' (Marty and Appleby 1995).

---

[11] In my book *Telling Sexual Stories*, 1995 I detected three positions; two more are now added here.

[12] In this I draw from the key work by Marty, Martin E and R Scott Appleby *Fundamentalisms Comprehended* 1995. I quote especially from Almond, Sivan and Appleby 'Fundamentalism: Genus and Species' pp 405–8.

But, as William Connolly has suggested, fundamentalism may well go further than we think; in one sense it resides almost everywhere. Even those who champion 'difference' and 'pluralization' may find that their own positions 'rest upon fundamentals more or less protected from internal interrogation' (Connolly 1995: xii; xvi; 105–6). All positions, must carry an element of foundational belief—and with that some weaker version of fundamentalism. We have then to be very careful for we may all turn out to be creeping fundamentalists at heart. Without being fundamentalists proper, the seeds of fundamentalism may be found in many arguments; how can we move beyond their limiting constraints? We are led back to ask impossible questions: *can we ever find a common ground? Can we ever just sit down and talk with our enemies? Is it all impossible, since fundamentalisms in different guises may be lurking everywhere? How can we create bridges, find connections, make links across divides?* These are key questions for a future political theory of sexuality to answer.[13]

IN CONCLUSION

This essay has worked on a number of fronts and can be seen both as a review and agenda setting. I started by arguing the need to see sex research as composed of many diverse, fragmenting, conflictual and global social worlds each busy constructing their own histories and rhetorics and by and large not engaging with each other. Some of these worlds have grown out of new social movements since the 1970s and have brought with them contested views of sexualities that nevertheless give much greater prominence to the social and the political than they do to the presumed natural and biological views of an essential sex. I have tried to piece together a provisional version of the bits needed for theorising some of this—but in a highly schematic way. Most centrally, I have turned to conflicting political messages. I am personally caught in ambivalence: with the good news of a possible democratic sexuality and open dialogic intimate citizenship on one side. And a painful world of growing intimate inequalities and tribal sexual clashes on the other. We do not live in easy times.

REFERENCES

ABELOVE, H, BARALE, MA & HALPERIN, D, (eds), *The Lesbian and Gay Studies Reader* (New York: Routledge, 1993).

---

[13] These last two paragraphs have previously appeared in Plummer (2003), which starts to explore some answers to such questions. Major sections of this essay are reworkings of my introduction to Plummer (2002). Since this particular volume is for a very specialised and targeted market/audience, and its print run is small, the introduction is unlikely to have a wide readership. I therefore feel at liberty to draw from it. Nevertheless, the organization of this essay is new and there are new sections.

ADAM, B, 'Theorizing Homophobia' *Sexualities* (1998) Vol 1. No 4 pp 387–404.

ALLGEIER, ER, 'Coercive versus Consensual Sexual Interactions' in VP Makosky (ed), *G Stanley Hall Lecture Series*, volume 7 (pp 9–63). (Washington DC: American Psychological Association, 1987).

ALTMAN, D, *Global Sex: Chicago*: (University of Chicago Press, 2001).

BAWER, B, *A Place at the Table: The Gay Individual in American Society*, (New York, Poseidon Press, 1993).

BEACH, FA, 'Sexual Attractivity, Perceptivity, and Receptivity in Female Mammals.' (1976) *Hormones and Behavior*, 7, pp 105–38.

BECK, U, *The Reinvention of Politics: Rethinking Modernity in the Global Social Order*, (Cambridge, Polity, 1997).

—— 'Living your own life in a runaway world: Individualization, Globalisation and Politics' (2000) in W Hutton and A Giddens (eds), *On the Edge: Living with Global Capitalism* (London, Vintage) pp 164–74.

BELL, D and BINNIE, J, *The Sexual Citizen: Queer Politics and Beyond* (Cambridge Polity, 2000).

BLAND, L and DOAN, L, *Sexology Uncensored: The Documents of Sexual Science.* (Cambridge, Polity Press, 1998).

BRODERICK, CB, 'Sexual Behaviour Among Pre-Adolescents' (1966) *Journal of Social Issues* 22, 6–21.

BROWNING, G, HALCLI, A and WEBSTER, F, (eds), *Theory and Society: Understanding the Present* (London, Sage, 2000).

BYRNE, D, 'Social Psychology and the Study of Sexual Behavior.' (1977) *Personality and Social Psychology Bulletin*, 3, pp 3–30.

CASTELLS, M, *The Information Age* 3 Volumes, (Oxford, Blackwell, 1997).

CLARKE, A, *Disciplining Reproduction.* (Berkeley, University of California Press, 1998).

CONNELL, R, *Masculinities* (Cambridge, Polity, 1995).

CONNOLLY, W, *The Ethos of Pluralization.* (NJ: Princeton, 1995).

DAVIS, MS, *Smut: Erotics, Reality and Obscene Ideology* (Chicago, University of Chicago Press, 1983).

DENZIN, N, *Interpretive Ethnography.* (London, Sage, 1997).

DOWSETT, G, 'Bodyplay: Corporeality in a Discursive Silence' in R Parker, RM Barbosa and P Aggleton (eds), *Framing the Sexual Subject :The Politics of Gender, Sexuality and Power* (Berkeley, University of California Press, 2000) pp 29–45.

DOWSETT, G, *Practicing Desire: Homosexual Sex in an Age of AIDS.* (California, Stanford Press, 1996).

EISENSTEIN, Z, *Global Obscenities: Patriarchy, Capitalism and the Lure of Cyberfantasy* (NY, New York University Press, 1998).

ELLIS, H, *Studies in the Psychology of Sex*, Volumes 1–4 (New York, Random House, 1936). Originally published in 1901.

ERIKSEN, J, *Kiss and Tell* (Cambridge, Mass, Harvard University Press, 1998).

EVANS, D. *Sexual Citizenship* (London, Routledge, 1993).

FOUCAULT, M, *The History of Sexuality, Volume 1: An Introduction* (R HURLEY, trans), (New York, Vintage Books, 1980). Originally published in 1976.

FOX, R, *The Red Lamp of Incest* (New York, Dutton, 1980)

FREUD, S, 'Three Essays on Sexuality' in J STRACHEY (ed and trans), *The Standard Edition of the Complete Psychological Works of Sigmund Freud, Volume 7.* (pp 123–243). (London, Hogarth Press, 1957). Originally published in 1905.

GAGNON, JH and SIMON, W, *Sexual Conduct: The Social Sources of Human Sexuality.* (Chicago, Aldine, 1973).

GEER, JH & O'DONOHUE, WT (eds), *Theories of Human Sexuality.* (New York, Plenum, 1987).

GIDDENS, A, *The Transformation of Intimacy.* (Cambridge, Polity Press, 1992).

GIDDENS, A, *Runaway World: How Globalization is Shaping Our Lives.* (London, Profile Books, 1999).

GREEN, V, 'Experiential Factors in Childhood and Adolescent Sexual Behavior: Family Interaction and Previous Sexual Experiences' (1985) *The Journal of Sex Research*, 21, 157–82.

HALBERSTAM, J, *Female Masculinity* (Duke UP, 1998).

HALPERIN, DM, 'Is there a history of sexuality?' in H ABELOVE, M BARALE and D HALPERIN (eds), *The Lesbian and Gay Studies Reader* (London, Routledge, 1993).

HARAWAY, DJ, *Simians, Cyborgs and Women: The Reinvention of Nature* (London, Routledge, 1991).

HERDT, G, *Guardians of the Flute: Idioms of Masculinity*, (New York, McGraw-Hill, 1981).

HESS, DJ, *Science Studies: An Advanced Introduction* (NY, New York University Press, 1997).

HITE, S, The *Hite Report: A Nationwide Study of Female Sexuality* (New York, Dell, 1976).

HUTTON, W and GIDDENS, A, *On The Edge: Living with Global Capitalism* (London: Jonathan Cape, 2000).

IRVINE, JM, *Disorders of Desire: Sex and Gender in Modern American Society* (Philadelphia: Temple University Press, 1990).

JACKSON, S and SCOTT, S (eds), *Feminism and Sexuality: A Reader* (Edinburgh, Edinburgh University Press, 1996).

JAMIESON, L, *Intimacy: Personal Relationships in Modern Societies*, (Cambridge Polity, 1998).

—— 'Intimacy Transformed: A Critical Look at the "Pure Relationship"' (1999) *Sociology* 33: 3.

JEFFREYS, S (ed), *The Sexuality Papers* (London, Routledge, 1987).

—— *The Spinster and Her Enemies* (London, Women's Press, 1985).

KELLY, L, *Surviving Sexual Violence* (Cambridge, Polity, 1988).

KINSEY, A, POMEROY, W, MARTIN, C, GEBHARD, P *et al*, *Sexual Behaviour in the Human Male* (WB Saunders, Philadelphia and London, 1946).

—— *Sexual Behaviour in the Human Female* (WB Saunders, Philadephia and London, 1953).

LAUMANN, EO, GAGNON, JH, MICHAEL, RR and MICHAELS, S. *The Social Organization of Sexuality: Sexual Practices in the United States.* (Chicago, The University of Chicago Press, 1994).

LANCASTER, R and DI LEONARDO, M (eds), *The Gender/Sexuality Reader* (London, Routledge, 1997).

LEVINE, MP and TROIDEN, RR, 'The Myth of Sexual Compulsivity' (1988) *The Journal of Sex Research* 25, 347–63.

MADDOCK, JW, 'Sex In the Family System'. (1983) *Marriage and Family Review*, 6(3/4), 9–20.

MALINOWSKI, B, *Sexual Life of Savages in North-Western Melanesia.* (New York, Halcyon House, 1929).

MALTZ, DN and BORKER, RA 'A Cultural Approach to Male-Female Miscommunication' in JJ GRUPERZ (ed), *Language and Social Identity* (pp 195–216). (New York, Cambridge University Press, 1983).

MARTY, ME and APPLEBY, RS, *Fundamentalisms Comprehended* (Chicago, University of Chicago Press, 1995).

MEAD, M, *Sex and Temperament in Three Primitive Societies* (New York,William Morrow, 1935).

NARDI, PN and SCHNEIDER, BE (eds), *Social Perspectives in Lesbian and Gay Studies* (London, Routledge, 1998).

NUSSBAUM, M, *Sex and Social Justice* (Oxford, Oxford University Press, 1999).

OOSTERHUIS, H, *Stepchildren of Nature: Krafft-Ebing, Psychiatry and The Making of Sexual Identity* (Chicago: University of Chicago Press, 2001).

PARKER, R and AGGLETON, P (eds), *Culture, Society and Sexuality: A Reader* (London: Taylor and Francis, 1999).

PETCHESKY, R, 'Sexual Rights: Inventing a Concept, Mapping an International Practice' in R Parker *et al* (eds), *Sexual Subject: The Politics of Gender, Sexuality and Power,* Ch 4, pp 81–103 (Berkeley, University of California Press, 2000).

PITTS, J, 'The Structural-Functional Approach' in HT CHRISTIANSON (ed), *Handbook of Marriage and the Family*, pp 51–124 (Chicago, Rand McNally, 1964).

PLUMMER, K, *Telling Sexual Stories: Power, Change and Social Worlds* (London, Routledge, 1995).

—— 'Intimate Choices' in G Browning, A Halcli and F Webster (eds), *Theory and Society: Understanding the Present.* (London, Sage, 2000).

—— *Documents of Life–2: An Invitation to a Critical Humanism.* (London, Sage, 2000a).

—— *Sexualities: Critical Assessments. Four Volumes.* (London, Routledge, 2002).

—— 'Rethinking the Sexual in Sociology: Bringing the Body Back In' (2002a) *Rassegna Italiana di Sociologia*, 487–501.

—— *Intimate Citizenship: Private Decisions and Public Dialogues.* (Seattle, University of Washington Press, 2003).

—— 'The Sexual Spectacle: Constructing a Culture of Sexual Problems Talk' in G RITZER, (ed), *International Handbook of Social Problems.* (London, Sage, 2004).

PORTER, R, and HALL, L, *The Facts of Life: The Creation of Sexual Knowledge in Britain 1650–1950* (New Haven CT, Yale University Press, 1995).

POGGE, T, *World Poverty and Human Rights.* (Cambridge: Polity, 2002).

REISS, IL, *The Social Context of Pre-Marital Sexual Permissiveness* (New York, Holt, Rinehart & Winston, 1967).

REISS, IL, *Journey into Sexuality: An Exploratory Voyage* (New York, Prentice Hall, 1986).

RICH, A, 'Compulsory Heterosexuality and Lesbian Existence' in *Blood, Bread and Poetry.* (London: Virago, 1978).

RICHARDSON, D, *Rethinking Sexuality* (London, Sage, 2000a).

—— 'Constructing Sexual Citizenship: Theorizing Sexual Rights' (2000) *Critical Social Policy* Vol 20, No 1, pp 105–35.

ROBINSON, P, *The Modernization of Sex* (London, Elek, 1976).

RUBIN, G, 'Thinking Sex' in C Vance (ed), *Pleasure and Danger* (London, Routledge, 1984).

SCHILLING, C, *The Body and Social Theory* (London, Sage, 1993).

SEGAL, L (ed), *New Sexual Agendas*. (NY: New York University Press, 1997).

SIMON, W, *Postmodern Sexualities*. (London, Routledge, 1996).

SMITH, R and WINDES, RR, *Progay/Antigay: The Rhetorical War Over Sexuality* (London, Sage, 2000).

STANTON, DC (ed), *Discourses of Sexuality: From Aristotle to AIDS* (Ann Arbor: The University of Michigan Press, 1992).

STRAUSS, A, 'Social Worlds and their Segmentation Processes' in NK DENZIN (ed), *Studies in Symbolic Interactionism*. p 125–39 Vol 4 (Greenwich, CT, JAI Press, 1984).

—— *Continual Permutations of Action*. (New York, DeGruyter, 1993).

STOLLER, R, *Perversion: The Erotic Form of Hatred*. (NY, Pantheon, 1976).

SYMONS, D, *The Evolution of Human Sexuality* (New York, Oxford University Press, 1979).

TIEFFER, L, 'Historical, Scientific, Clinical and Feminist Criticisms of 'The Human Sexual Response Cycle' model' (1991), *Annual Review of Sex Research*, 2, 1–24.

TRIVERS, RL, 'Parental Investment and Sexual Selection' in B CAMPBELL (ed), *Sexual Selection and the Descent of Man 1871–1971*, (pp 136–79). (Chicago, Aldine, 1972).

VANCE, CS, (ed), *Pleasure and Danger*. (London: Routledge, 1984).

VAN WYK, PH and GEIST, CS, 'Psychosocial Development of Heterosexual, Bisexual and Homosexual Behavior' (1984) *Archives of Sexual Behavior*, 13, 505–44.

WARNER, M, *Publics and Counterpublics*, (New York, Zone Books, 2002).

WEEKS, J, *Sexuality* (London, Routledge, 1986).

—— 'The Sexual Citizen' (1998) *Theory, Culture and Society* Vol 15, no 3–4, pp 35–52.

—— *Making Sexual History* (Oxford, Polity, 2000).

WEEKS, J, HOLLAND, J and WAITES, M (eds), *Sexualities and Society*. (Cambridge, Polity Press, 2002).

WEEKS, J, DONOVAN, C and HEAPHY, B, *Same Sex Intimacies* (London, Routledge, 2001).

WEINBERG, MS, 'The Nudist Management of Respectability' (1970) in J DOUGLAS (ed), *Deviance and Respectability. The Social Construction of Moral Meanings*. (NY: Basic, 1970).

WEISS, DL, 'Classics of Sexual Theory' (1998) *Journal of Sex Research* (35) 1.

WELLINGS, K, FIELD, J, JOHNSON, AM and WADSWORTH, J, *Sexual Behaviour in Britain: The National Survey of Sexual Attitudes and Lifestyles*. (London, Penguin Books, 1994).

WESTON, K, *Longslowburn: Sexuality and Social Science*. (London, Routledge, 1998).

—— *Gender in Real Time*. (London, Routledge, 2002).

WILLIAMS, CL and STEIN, A (eds), Sexuality *and Gender* (Oxford, Blackwell, 2002).

YOUNG, IM, *Justice and the Politics of Differences* (New Jersey, Princeton UP, 1990).

ZETTERBERG, HL, 'The Secret Ranking' (1966) *Journal of Marriage and Family Life* 28, pp 134–42.

4

New Battlegrounds: Genetic Maps and Sexual Politics

LYNNE SEGAL

Fully four decades on from the moment when so many celebrated its emancipation, trouble still lurks all around sex and sexuality:

> Sexual intercourse began
> In nineteen sixty-three . . .
> Between the end of the Chatterley ban
> And the Beatles first LP. (Larkin, 1974)

Larkin, perhaps, should not have regretted—however playfully—that sexual freedom came too late for him, when sorry, secret moments, punitive public sanctions, violent fantasies and remorse, relentless commercial marketing and suspect enticements, surround our sex lives still.

LOVE HURTS

The more things change, the more it seems fresh obstructions or incitements arise to trouble the joys or consolations we might seek in intimacies with others. Where the multiplicity of sexual pleasures and identities has been most strenuously insisted upon, theorized and catered for, in the USA, we have the starkest portrayals in fiction or film of the cunning perils of its pursuit. Massively popular with its readers and audiences, portrayals of the pains of sex and relationships are evidently eagerly consumed: whether in the hysterically fear laden, unhappy, violent sexual obsessions of a Thomas Pynchon character, Don Dellillo's isolated, fragmented men and women for whom pleasure is always combined with anguish or, most hideously ritualistic, in Brett Ellis's conjuring up of a new anti-hero from the USA. In *American Psycho*, Patrick Bateman's obsession with ravenous, murderous sex can only ever trigger a hunger for even more sadistically murderous, dismembering, encounters:

> My pain is constant and sharp and I do not hope for a better world for anyone. In fact I want my pain to be inflicted on others. I want no one to escape. (Pynchon, 1991; DeLillo, 1998; Easton, 1991: 377).

In the social sciences, one of the founders of Men's Studies in the USA, the sociologist Harry Brod, addresses men's sexual discontents generally, while writing of his own sexual discomforts and anxieties, mourning:

> There have been too many times when I have guiltily resorted to impersonal fantasy because the genuine love I felt for a woman wasn't enough to convert feelings into performance (Brod, 1989).

He blamed contemporary culture, the pin-ups of Playboy, for indoctrinating him with desires that could never be fulfilled. Women's continuing sexual sorrows, at least according to one strand of feminism—one that perhaps surprisingly became rather influential in the Social Sciences—were projected firmly on to men. Those same centre-folds were also held to blame for culturally constructing men's sexuality as predatory, if not sadistic: 'With lovers like men—who needs torturers?', British feminist literary scholar, Susanne Kappeler, asked in 1986 (Kappeler, 1986: 214).

Increasingly, in the closing decades of the 20th century, ever more diverse and innovative therapies have flourished in the self-help arena, designed to treat the newly coined 'sex-addiction', with its ten definitive attributes, a national treatment centre for its cure in California, and support groups dotted across the landscape from New York to Nashville and Los Angeles. Those not suffering from 'sex-addiction', however, may be incubating an alternative 'disorder of desire', including the 15% of men overall said to report lack of sexual interest, the 'tragic' 50% of men over 40 years reported by drug companies to be suffering from some form of erectile dysfunction, reaching, we learn, a 'catastrophic' near 70% in men over 70: all in all, as many as 30 million men, it is estimated, may be suffering from this new sexual 'disease' in the USA alone (Feldman *et al.*, 1994).

The sexual frustrations and miseries described in literature, women's studies, sociology or the psychotherapeutic domain, all tended to be attributed to hierarchical gender regimes or a general cultural malaise attending the frantic consumerism of 'late' capitalism. However, the medicalisation of sexuality associated with diagnoses of erectile dysfunction represents a return to biology in the sexual domain. Indeed, in many areas, culture itself is being newly subsumed back into biology in an upsurge of Darwinian teleology, especially in my own first discipline, psychology. The propagation of evolutionary psychology, which has been especially admired in popular science journalism, has tended to provide confirmation of traditional blueprints for sexual difference. It has refocused attention on the presumed stability of gendered polarities of sexual behaviour, just when the visible shifts and complexities of desire and sexual practices would seem to give us every reason to reject them. But, 'if sex is that straightforward Darwinian project', as the astute psychoanalyst Adam Phillips asks, 'why does it give us so much trouble?' Why indeed? More provocatively still, Phillips adds, 'Freud shows us how if we are *not* in trouble we are not having sex' (Phillips, 2003). Uniquely, Freud, and his psychoanalytic legacy, right up to the present day, has rarely failed to emphasise a pessimistic vision of the ineluctable dangers and disappointments of sex. Although via a different theoretical route, in the early years of sexology—now more than a century ago—Freud's contemporary, and the founding father of sexology, Krafft-Ebing, had also stressed the perils of perversion, when the sexual instinct, for a variety of congenital causes or self-indulgently induced degeneracies, failed to follow the 'natural' or nonpathological course of its biological substratum. However, in the twentieth century, especially in the wake of the 1960s, the now increasingly welcomed science of sexology tended to stress the multiple pleasures of sex, once men and women learned to overcome their 'psychologic inhibitions' and all acquired the appropriate skills for giving and receiving full orgasmic satisfaction. With pleasure-seeking in the air, in the post-Fifties 'American'-led Western world, there was an explosion of behaviouristic sex therapy available, launched by Masters and Johnson (Masters and Johnson, 1966; Masters and Johnson, 1970).

In a new twist, today there is less emphasis on the acquiring of skills, technique and appropriate sex-positive attitudes (though these ideas persist), but they are overlaid by a somewhat different return to biological and chemical basics. Here, it is not so much our ancestral past, although knowledge of the human genome is seen as crucial, but rather the rise of the professional molecular biologist who will help determine our sexual futures. New genetic dreams of a cure for all that ails us, both physically and emotionally, has fuelled the extraordinary rise in the medicalization of sexual anxieties, nowhere more so than in the attention paid to the auditing of men's penile performance. Sexual dysfunctions that were hardly known to exist till recently are diagnosed in tandem with the medical solutions designed to alleviate them, as pharmaceutical corporations increasingly set the contemporary sexual agenda.

This chapter will therefore survey the renewed interest in what is seen as the biological foundations and future of human sexuality, but only after placing it in the context of the highly conflictual struggles that were waged in the name of sexual liberation and sexual politics in the closing decades of the 20th century. These struggles, as many others here have written, illuminate the power relations never far removed from human sexuality. Aspects of power occur across the broadest spectrum of sexually imbued practices, even those not recognised as such: from the personal investments we have in our sexual identities, to the high levels of both coercion and constraint, incentives and seductions, that surround sexual life, as well as the institutional arrangements and cultural discourses which guide and give meaning to our most intimate encounters, dreams, fears and frustrations. It is these struggles which turn our bodies into battlegrounds, on which, as the outstanding French anthropologist, Maurice Godelier, comments: 'it is not so much sexuality which haunts society, but society which haunts the body's sexuality' (Godelier, 1881: 17).

The latest return to biological basics boosted by pharmaceutical interests in administering to our body's sexual proclivities and possibilities is, in my view, testimony to one main thing: the more we are promised simple pathways to earthly delights, the easier prey we become as objects of manipulation, eager to escape realities where love hurts and sexual pleasure eludes us. This is all hardly surprising, if we believe we live in times when people are increasingly uprooted and unsettled, too often bereft of confirmatory meaning and social belongings, in cities that become dumping grounds for globally created problems and changes, as Zygmunt Bauman, Ulrick Beck, and numerous other sociologists of everyday life from the late twentieth century have been arguing (Bauman, 2000 Bauman, 2000; Beck and Beck-Gernscheim, 1995; 2001). But let me look back a generation.

SEXUAL LIBERATION AND THE RISE OF SEXUAL POLITICS

The cultural and legislative shifts of the 1960s in much of the metropolitan 'Western' world, at a time of full employment, rising wages and increasing equality, really did transform the sexual landscape, shifting the ways the world impinges upon our sexual lives.[1] If sex is always somewhere at the centre of society, the space it occupied emerged more visibly, with far greater insistence upon its own centrality and significance, than it ever had before. With huge success, young people set out to overturn the sexual hypocrisy of the previous decade, celebrating the importance of sexual openness, indeed, the importance of sex as pleasure, sex for its own sake alone. '*Make love. We must make love. Instead of making money*', the popular poet, Adrian Mitchell, summed up the decade: *instead of making war, competing for status, committing any other transgression or iniquity*, he might well have added, in that hedonistic utopian moment. It was a little more complex for women. The legacy of that tumultuous decade, when for some prosperity and transformation seemed equally pervasive, is now a battleground. It arouses fondness or loathing, but mostly moralistic dismissal as the last moment of irresponsible, self-absorbed, dreamers. Feminist historian, Sheila Rowbotham, in her memoir of the 'Sixties', *Promise of a Dream,* depicts herself as a confused teenager in the late 1950s, determined (with all her close friends) to break out of the invasive patterns of passivity and hypocrisy, though still surrounded by silence, ignorance and prejudice, without the least guidance, resources or protection for doing so. Although determined to recover from the ordeal of an attempted rape (while still a virgin at seventeen), by engaging in freely chosen sexual contact, she remained, she recalls, for several years comprehensively ignorant about everything to do with sex, still wondering what exactly it was several years after becoming sexually active within the beatnik Bohemian haunts of London and Paris: 'I was not the only one steering without a compass between the dreaded Scylla of frigidity and the humiliating Charybdis branded "nymphomania"' (Rowbotham, 2000: 48).

---

[1] Wages rose by 72%, prices by only 45%, between 1951 and 1963, (Hewison, 1986: 6).

Incongruously, for those anti-materialists wishing to subvert the old order, a booming commercial market was itself suddenly promoting the hedonistic youth movement of emancipation, sex and pleasure: Che Guevara T-shirts for all, 'armed love' on the high streets. Nevertheless, in these years when the notion of 'sexual politics' came to the fore, political struggle against exploitation and oppression, on the home front and abroad, was increasingly seen as inseparable from personal liberation. The term itself was borrowed from Wilhelm Reich's Sex-Pol years, when he had tried to combine Freudian and Marxist perspectives to offer practical advice on sexual matters back in 1920s inter-war Berlin. By the end of the Sixties, whether citing Herbert Marcuse, Norman O. Brown, Allen Ginsberg or David Cooper, throbbing to the beat of rock, dazed by drugs, dazzled by the underground press or simply influenced by the stylish liberalism of the day, sexual pleasure was widely seen as a progressive force, one capable of transforming human relations, however divergently people saw such progress.

Furthermore, for all the new snares, anxieties and terrors sex might still hold for them, it was women who gained most from the many legislative reforms on contraception, abortion, divorce and, later, equal pay and recognition of violence against women, especially policy reforms enacted between 1967 and 1975. Women could now be sexually freer and begin challenging the hitherto ubiquitous double standards (hailing young men's sexual prowess as his entry into 'manhood', while desiring 'virginity' in single women) with the marketing of the (then rather dangerously high-dosage) contraceptive pill from 1961—made available free on NHS prescription from 1967. Women did have far more sexual autonomy.[2] The marketing of the pill also made sex newsworthy, inciting endless public debate. Sex was now a new medium of pleasure for almost everybody on achieving adulthood, the route to social recognition and identity, long before marriage—if it came. Moreover, from quite early on, and although feeding new forms of virulent machismo, it was also clear that men, despite perhaps mouthing applause for women's new sexual freedom, often felt threatened by it. That old chauvinist cheerleader, Norman Mailer, sounded an early alarm: now that women have gained control over reproduction, he lamented, a man might have to bow out 'to the vibrations of his superior, a vibrator' (Mailer, 1972: 126). (His words would prove prophetic, at least for a few feminists, for a short while). Meanwhile, it was only gay men who benefited directly from the partial decriminalisation of consenting homosexual activity in the Sexual Offences Act of 1967.[3]

With feminism hovering in the wings, it would not take long for women to move on from hearing sex celebrated as liberation to seeking 'liberated sex'. In the counter-culture flourishing in the late Sixties, surrounded by demeaning images of themselves in ever more blatant, indeed increasingly sadistic, sexist iconography, militancy was being forced upon women. Meeting together, they

[2] See Rowbotham, 2000; Segal, 1994, chapter 1.
[3] See Hall, 1980.

would soon begin speaking of women's active sexual choice and agency, first of all, in the context of a highly politicised, egalitarian, protest milieu (with the Vietnam war, and female guerrilla fighters, its backdrop). The birth of Women's Liberation and a specifically feminist sexual politics was now ineluctable. Newly born feminists, alongside the gay men and lesbians of early Gay Liberation (lesbians would soon leave Gay Liberation to join Women's Liberation), quickly saw that pleasure was as much a social and political as a personal matter, one they analysed then as hitherto defined and regulated in ways that served the interests of the state and the capitalist market. (This was before the discovery of Michel Foucault, and his genealogy of the multiple cultural institutions and discourses dictating the norms and regimes of 'sexuality'.) It was seeing and hearing the everyday language and iconography of the joys of sex focussed on the power and activity of straight men, while subordinating and disparaging straight women (as 'chics'), lesbians and gay men (as 'queers'), that inspired the women's and the gay liberation movements into a battle against both sexism and, soon, 'heterosexism' and 'homophobia' as well. This radical sexual politics had yet to become more sensitive to race, or to place sexual exploitation in its global context, which is at the heart of the most progressive sexual agendas today.[4]

The dismissive disdain for the frivolities of 'sexual liberation' and the 'sexual politics' it triggered is widespread nowadays, even within feminist scholarship. Yet, it was the ramifications of that battle that led all the way onwards from confronting sexism, to opposing all gender hierarchies as well as challenging the dominant understanding of both 'sexuality' and 'gender'. From the far-reaching, still ongoing debate about the care and treatment of women in relation to all aspects of fertility control and childbirth, the continuing pressure on men to share the responsibilities of household tasks and parenting, campaigns against violence against women and child sexual abuse, to the celebration of diverse or multiple sexualities and the highly successful 'safer sex' strategies pioneered by gay communities against the spread of HIV and AIDS, the struggle for sexual liberation would play *a*, if not *the*, key role in changing patterns of life in Western countries. Indeed, it was the repression of any movements of sexual liberation in the former Eastern European 'state socialist' countries that constituted the prime source of the oppression of women in those regimes. Despite greater access to childcare facilities and extensive participation in the workforce, Eastern Europe saw almost no politicisation of interpersonal relationships or sexual experience, making sexism, violence against women and exclusive maternal responsibility for childcare and housework as unchallenged as it was ubiquitous (Einhorn, 1991).

Nevertheless, trouble soon stalked feminist sexual politics specifically, and feminists fell out with each other as early dreams of the significance of their new-found sexual freedoms unravelled. The persistence of men's sexual coerciveness

---

4   See Lancaster and di Leonardo (1997).

and violence towards women was the first obstacle, contaminating and eventually silencing straight feminists' talk of liberation. Alternative visions of feminist sexual practices, supposedly freeing desire from fantasies of power, submission or other echoes of phallocentrism, bred new forms of feminist prescriptiveness, quite at odds with the ambiguous dynamics of sexual pleasures, fantasy and desire itself. Some feminists, appropriating both Freud and Foucault for their own ends, did move on to analyse the fuller complexities, ambivalences and unsettling elements of power and submission present in all desire—female as well as male.[5] But there was an overall retreat in mainstream feminism to one situating women as comprehensive victims of men's lust and violence, in need of protection from the 'degrading' images of pornography which fanned them (Dworkin, 1981; MacKinnon, 1987). The 1980s would prove a decade of 'sex wars' between feminists, continuing to this day. In my view, some level of confusion is quite inevitable when re-thinking women's sexual agency, given the crucible of contradictions at the heart of sexual desire, which might position us as defenceless and passive at the very same time as we feel most assertive and powerful, or the opposite, and everything in between. In sex we attempt to relieve narcissistic wounds which carry the traces of all our earlier frustrations, hurts and humiliation or, simply, the losses of time passing. All this can be captured easily in fiction, but rarely if ever in traditional measuring tools of the social scientist, although recent narrative analysis at times brings us closer.

In the wider world, well beyond feminist contention, new sexual anxieties were soon triggered by a change in the political climate. As governments of the Right were firmly installed in power in the UK and USA in the 1980s, recession, unemployment and other set-backs meant that the time was now ripe for all kinds of backlash against the recent sexual 'permissiveness', as social anxieties all too easily find displaced expression in sexual scaremongering. An emerging moral Right launched new attacks against women's economic independence (said to be at the expense of men), against single mothers and homosexual practices, massively reinforced when HIV-AIDS struck down its first sufferers (in the West, most visible amongst gay men). For women, a retreat from early feminist dreams of a freer, compassionate world was always likely to accompany the defeat (despite many partial successes) of overall attempts to build a more equal society. Simply finding the time and space for exploring the ambivalent structures of intimacy proved more difficult in less secure times, at least according to many North American and British commentators observing the increasingly busy and fragmented lives of 'late modernity'.[6]

---

[5] See Vance (1984); Snitow *et al* (1994).
[6] See, for example, Beck and Beck-Gernsheim (1995); Dunant and Porter (1996).

CONSERVATIVE RETRENCHMENTS: BIOLOGICAL TALES

As the German philosopher Theodor Adorno was already arguing back in the 1920s, it is inconceivable that any object or concept could be viewed from a single all-encompassing standpoint, least of all, we should now be well aware, confronting the elusive topic of sexuality. His 'negative dialectic' called for a notion of 'open thinking' to throw light upon the endless array of potentially new perspectives obscured or hidden behind familiar conceptions (Adorno, 1973). However, one of the founding metaphors of Western science, surviving three centuries of just such critique, is the exact opposite: the fantasy that the explanation of all life, from the molecular to the social, can be explained in terms of a few single overarching laws.[7] No scientists have pursued this goal more assiduously than those hoping to bring order to the unruly domain of gender, sex and sexuality. It is to sustain belief in some such underpinning simplicity, beneath the disarming complexity of life, that we find again the most flagrant misappropriations of Darwin's legacy, overturning much that we seemed to have already worked out long ago. Thus does Britain's foremost science promoter, Richard Dawkins, battle to defend the classic ideology of science, asserting as its first axiom: 'Plants and animals alike are all—in their immensely complicated, enmeshed ways doing the same fundamental thing, which is propagating genes.'[8]

However, this time around, Darwinian notions of descent through natural selection are usually not, as they were in the beginning, used to confirm racial hierarchy—then seen as intertwined with sexual hierarchy (racism usually arrives culturally freighted nowadays) but rather to shore up the ever more ambiguous blueprint for sexual difference. Whatever the contingencies of identity stressed in feminist philosophies, like that of Judith Butler (1989), we are told, scientific law and order comes from the sex cells: 'the "gametes" of males are smaller and more numerous than the gametes of females', Dawkins explains, 'it is possible to interpret all other differences between the sexes as stemming from this one basic difference. . . . Female exploitation begins here', he declared in 1976 (Dawkins, 1976, p 153; 162). All human behaviour, his American counterpart, EO Wilson, echoed, 'faithfully' obeys this *one* biological principle:

> It pays males to be aggressive, hasty, fickle [and] undiscriminating . . . females to be coy, to hold back until they can identify the male with the best genes' (Wilson, 1978: 552).

When first propounded in the 1970s, this new 'Sociobiology' was deeply embattled. Critics emerged from both the biological and social sciences (Lewontin, 1993; Sahlins, 1977) In the 21st century, with US-led corporate capital aggres-

---

[7] See Dupré, (1993: p 2).
[8] Cited in Colin Hughes, (1998: 6).

sively hegemonic globally, and rampant individualism triumphant, it has been more successfully rebranded as 'Evolutionary Psychology'.

On the rise throughout the 1990s within my own discipline of psychology, and well beyond, evolutionary psychology is eager to stress that it recognises the role of culture, which produces individual and cultural differences, although such variations are not the objects of its concern. But the apparent respect for culture is misleading, when that domain itself is newly biologized—seen as flexible superstructure to the more fundamental cognitive, neural base. As John Tooby and Lena Cosmides spell out, evolutionary psychology can provide us with the elemental 'building blocks out of which cultures themselves are manufactured' through 'content-specific evolved psychologies' (Tooby and Cosmides, 1992: 207). The notion of 'content-specific evolved psychologies', advocated by all leading evolutionary psychologists from Tooby and Cosmides, to Plotkin, Pinker or Dawkins, suggests that culture is passed on as particles or packages of heritable information (sometimes described as 'memes') consisting of rules or representations for the production of appropriate behaviour when our cognitive structures resonate with the demands of specific environments. These 'evolved architectures' of the mind can be specified quite independently of any particular social contexts or practices, and the meanings we collectively bring to them. The social anthropologist Tim Ingold is just one of the forceful critics who reject this misleading portrayal of culture:

> what people do is embedded in lifelong histories of engagement, as whole beings, within their surroundings, and is not the mechanical output of interaction between pre-replicated instructions (whether genetic or cultural) and pre-specified environmental conditions (Ingold, 2000: 2). See also D'Andrade (1981); Rose and Rose (2000).

Like sociobiology before it, evolutionary psychology dismisses all that is unique, culturally diverse and individually specific about human behaviour, human societies and how we negotiate our way within them. Moreover, when seeking out putative behavioural universals and consigning them to the operation of postulated invariant cognitive modules, depicted as genetic adaptations, it is to gender contrasts they repeatedly return . These prove to be precisely those normative behaviours which are as extremely controversial as they are dramatically contested: sexually dimorphic mating strategies; men's preference for younger mates; women's desire for mates with resources; sex-linked shifts in mate selection across the life span; patterns of spousal and same-sex murder etc.

Sexy Science, devoid of Romance, but overflowing with polemical intent, would be one way of characterising the genre. Throughout the 1990s the best-selling science promoter, Robert Wright, ridiculed feminists seeking equality with men as doomed by their foolish denial of the 'harsh Darwinian truths' about human nature: 'Feminists are right to dread some of the rhetorical [note] resistance Darwinism will abet' (Wright, 1994:34). Expressing specious concern that feminism may falter from its own 'doctrinal absurdities', he challenged us to face up to the evolutionary basis of 'the "natural" male impulse to control female sexuality', 'men's natural tendencies to greater promiscuity', 'natural selection' for men to make 'the Madonna-whore distinction', concluding· 'Human males are by nature oppressive, possessive, flesh-obsessed pigs' (Wright, 1994:36). Put more prudently by David Buss, John Archer and others, assertions of the inevitability of men's predatory chase of attractive young females with large breasts and small waists is indeed one of the most frequent cited explanatory accounts in evolutionary psychology. 'Ask the American President!', or 'Look at the second wives of most academics!', Charles Jencks reports E.O.Wilson concluding his lectures, with a grin and a wink, in 1998 (George Bush and Tony Blair are clearly far from models of the male blue-print).[9] Is this any more than pseudo-scientific pornography? Let me join in the fun, with the help of some recent sociological research.

For her recent field research on family relationships in the USA, leading sociologist Judith Stacey interviewed dozens of couples about their sex lives. And she does indeed produce a file with the title 'Men are Pigs', containing the following descriptions:

> [Unlike me] Lance can't get turned on by someone he respects and loves; he can only have sex with someone he's not emotionally committed to . . . I couldn't tolerate it, so I had to move out

> When I came home from work the other night, Jake . . . was totally in heat. And we had sex. We didn't make love . . . and it's like I woke up the next morning, and it's like, I just felt so . . . *shitty*. Why did I do that? I said it was great, I got off, but I feel rotten. I have felt rotten the last two days.

> Let's face it. When you reach a certain age, men are either already taken or they're looking for someone younger and more beautiful. We all know how men are dogs. Absolute dogs.

And so the less predatory lovers lament. Or sometimes, they get what they want, and celebrate:

> Rob and I just fell like I don't know I've fallen before. He knocks my socks off and its damn near everything I want in a man; he's kind, loving, compassionate, gives of him-self to others and his community . . . (Stacey, 2002).

The lovers? Well, as I suspect you won't be surprised to learn, these all too familiar erotic griefs and desires come with a twist. They may be the clichés of evolutionary psychology, evocative of patriarchal precedent and radical femi-nist, or 'feminazi' slogans, but they are in fact the voices of *men*: the experiences of some men with other men, both gay, all with their chromosomes, primary and secondary biological apparatus, all male—no transsexuals, or intersexed.

Certainly, I could have cited evidence of straight men boasting of their many sexual conquests in the 35 countries David Buss visited, where in line with their

---

[9] Cited in Jencks, (2000: 40).

expected behaviour, they reported three or four times the number of sexual couplings with 'young and attractive' partners compared to the women interviewed around them. For this to be possible, as sceptics have noticed, we need only assume that a tiny minority of enormously hyperactive, young and beautiful women were peculiarly fighting their nature to oblige a huge army of randy men (Einon, 1998).

A more plausible assumption might be to suggest that such self-proclaimed virility measurements indicate a type of shared identity work performed by many men to confirm cultural expectations of sexual dominance, rather than any evolved adaptations. For once we look behind gender cliché, at the broader scope of historical and sexological research, it is hard not to admit that there could hardly be *less* fit between evolutionary predictions and shifting human sexual and reproductive practices. In the West, gender polarised differences are fast diminishing, non-procreative, lesbian and gay sexual practices are flourishing, non-penetrative oral sex has been increasingly popular for many decades, birth rates dropping, single motherhood increasing, same sex parenting on the rise, women cohabiting and marrying, if they do, later in life and more women and men remaining childless.[10] Mr Wright and neo-Darwinians, meet women freer to choose how we want to live, though regretfully, rarely in conditions of our own choosing.

Those who point to the evidence of cultural shifts in gendered sexual patterns are always accused of dismissing biology altogether, unless they are prepared to specify just what bearing biology does have on such behaviour. As Martin Johnson illustrates in his contribution to this book, researchers interested in pinning down the biological basis of human sexuality usually emphasise interaction between environmental and genetic contributions. He argues, as well, that there is more overlap than difference in men's and women's sexual practices, while nevertheless hoping to elaborate the distinct biological and evolutionary underpinning for differing gendered practices and specific sexual orientations.[11] But that is just what is so very hard to isolate if, as it seems, both meaning and context are crucial in how humans react to differing states of arousal, such that human conduct can never be disentangled from the social and symbolic: it has been repeatedly shown, for example, that we cannot predict either a man's or a woman's sexual tastes, desires, or behaviour from any biological measurements.[12] Indeed, whether or not arousal is interpreted as 'sexual', and what people do when sexually aroused, are themselves already saturated with cultural ideas. Meanwhile, the battles over evolutionary psychology, with its belief in a 'universal human metaculture' which underpins traditional sexual and gender contrasts, occurs most usefully *inside* biology itself, where presumably no-one can be accused of ignoring biology. Critics of the new Darwinians are led in this country by Steven Rose and Steve

---

[10] See Laumann (1994); Wellings *et al* (1994).
[11] See in this volume, Johnson (2004).
[12] See Kolodny (1979); Meuwissen and Over (1992).

Jones, who claim that they see their own biological labours mocked by the pseudo-scientific posturing of evolutionary psychology (Rose, 1997; Jones, 2000). They have also hastened to defend Darwin from his eager new followers, insisting that for him evolution was never narrowly, or even primarily, a biological affair, but a slow, heterogeneous, profoundly environmental process (Rose and Rose, 2000). Quite staggering changes in the nature of the world occur with few, if any, ties to genetic change.

PREDATORY MALES AND OTHER BUGS

Despite some feminists rallying to evolutionary psychology, the work making media impact is that which, in the footsteps of Wright, demands a return to a profoundly conservative sexual politics. Most provocative of all, the publication of Thornhill and Palmer's *A Natural History of Rape: Biological Bases of Sexual Coercion* greeted the new millennium, affirming the opposed sexual natures and interests of women and men (Thornhill and Palmer, 2000). Carefully selecting the biological data they handle, they return us to the biology of the male scorpionfly, with an appendage on its abdomen, we learn, for the sole purpose of facilitating 'rape'. Leaving aside their anthropomorphic use of 'rape' (one whose meaning has shifted dramatically in recent years as feminists redefined notions of 'consensual' sex and women's sexual agency), what happened to this 'rape appendage' in evolutionary history? It migrated to become a 'mental' rape adaptation in reproductively frustrated men (Thornhill and Palmer, 2000: 64–5). In support of this hypothesis they assert that infertile women are less likely to be raped than fertile women, and if raped they suffer 'less psychological pain' from it (Thornhill and Palmer, 2000: 192–3). Both claims fly in the face of all that is now known of the extent, and prolonged destructiveness, of child sexual abuse.[13] We are also told that evolutionary science teaches us that the way to prevent rape is to inform men of the enormous 'power of their sexual impulses', and instruct them to learn self-control. This is precisely the message every boy already picks up throughout much of his life, his masculinity constantly policed by other boys in our rape-prone society.[14] Feminist friendly voices—repeatedly ridiculed by Thornhill and Palmer—supply the only counter arguments. Offering an exhaustive critique of these authors 'astonishing tone-deafness' to the theoretical diversity in both recent biological and cultural debate, the feminist anthropologist Emily Martin, for instance, concludes that this book is insidious primarily because 'their protestations to the contrary, their account actually amounts to an incitement to rape' (Martin, 2003: 378).

---

[13] See, e.g., La Fontaine (1990); Saraga, (1993).
[14] See Frosh *et al* (2002).

It is the human pornographic imagination, like that of Brett Easton, which resonates most easily with Thornhill and Palmer's account of the similarity between, for instance, women and the female dung fly:

> Struggling females [i.e. female dung flies] sometimes prevent copulation . . . and the resultant rape when their resistance is overcome by certain males, may be a female adaptation that helps females mate with males of superior phenotypic and genetic quality (Thornhill and Palmer, 2000: 83).

Rape is hardly something to be opposed then, Thornhill and Palmer's quaint paternalism notwithstanding, but significant in the breeding of the superior dung fly.

Meanwhile, those who prefer a different form of anthropomorphic titillation could turn their head from its engagement with flies on the cowpat to survey the mating habits of neighbouring insects. The male praying mantis is frequently eaten by the female he mates, during the sex act itself. However, this doesn't interfere with his mating, as he continues having sex even as his female partner ingests his head entirely, indeed, losing his head is reported to deprive him of all 'inhibitions', sending him into a 'sexual frenzy' (possible inspiration for Nagisa Oshima's next film, perhaps!). A different small bug, the male xylocoris, can be observed raping other males, sometimes when his 'victim' is himself mating with a female. Another of Thornhill and Palmer's chosen species, the redback spider, indulges in even greater 'masochistic' orgiastic practices than the praying mantis, ensuring that he is eaten very, very slowly during prolonged copulating, thereby guaranteeing both that the female spider's eggs are fertilised and that she will lose interest in sex once he is dead. These 'dissident' animal behaviours, which evolutionary psychologists prefer to ignore, are reported by the evolutionary biologist, Tim Birkhead, who likes to celebrate not patriarchal precepts but 'postmodern' diversities, down among the animals. Living up to its title, his book *Promiscuity: An Evolutionary History of Sperm Competition and Sexual Conflict* accumulates evidence to establish that, contrary to what Darwin himself believed and today's evolutionary psychologists cheerfully reiterate, the females of most species actively seek multiple partners for sexual engagement. Few, however, can match the 'nymphomania' of our own closest relative, the female chimpanzee, who will copulate between five hundred and a thousand times for each pregnancy, with many different males, inside and outside their own extended family group.[15]

Clearly, there is fun to be had combating the selective reasoning of evolutionary psychology. Nevertheless, it remains infuriating that we still have to do battle with such accredited researchers as Thornhill and Palmer, on a playing field that, ridiculously, either pits science against culture, or else attempts to colonize it.

---

[15] All examples taken from Birkhead (2000); see also Bagemihl (1999).

PHARMACEUTICAL AGENDAS: SEX REMEDICALIZED

There have been even more powerful attempts in recent years to by-pass cultural dynamics and insist that sex is nothing more than a medical function, analogous to breathing or digestion, coming from the pharmaceutical industries. Nowhere is this more obvious than in its infiltration of the field of sexology and sex coun-selling, evident in all its public manifestations, such as the World Congress of Sexology. The World Association of Sexology (WAS) is supported by the World Health Organization (WHO), and is today expanding rapidly, drawing educa-tors, researchers and practitioners from diverse domains. Its most distinguished members include molecular biologists, urologists, psychiatrists, psychothera-pists, health researchers, policy initiators and providers. As it aims to be, it is a powerful progressive force, promoting sexual wellbeing as essential for the health of individuals and society alike. It also stresses the variety of sexual lives and relationships and the multiple functions of sex. This is all the more import-ant at the moment, given the triumphal rise of the Christian Right in the White House in the USA, with its promotion of 'Abstinence Only' sex education poli-cies, known to give rise to teenage misery and disastrous health outcomes in that country and, given US global hegemony, affecting aid programmes world wide.[16]

However, the overwhelming numbers of academics and practitioners who participate in WAS are direct recipients of funding from the pharmaceutical cor-porations, Pfizer, Lilly, Takeda, Bayer, but above all, Pfizer. These companies do not dictate the outcome of their research, but they do set the agenda for it and, at huge international conferences, they fund participants and orchestrate all the major debates. One point alone sums up the dangers of relying upon the private sector for research funding. At WAS conferences one 'disease' has now pushed to the side-lines all other sexual health issues, world-wide, including the continuing pandemic of AIDS. Pfizer, it is said, had the name of their drug, 'Viagra', before it discovered either a relevant medication (the substance was originally tested for cardiac regulation) or knew the nature of the disease, 'erec-tile dysfunction', now said to be afflicting the global male population in huge numbers. Before the second half of the 20th century, it was a condition that was rarely mentioned; female 'frigidity', not erectile dysfunction dominated the conceptual domain of sexual disorders.[17]

Today, hitherto unknowing health workers learn new sexual priorities from Pfizer-funded researchers:

[16] See, e.g. Levine (2002).
[17] See The Second International Consultation on erectile and sexual dysfunctions, Paris, June 28–July 3, 2003. www.congress-urology.org/index.htm (accessed 12 Dec 2002; *Int. J. Impotence Research: The Special Supplement.* (1998).

many of the adult male patients in your clinical practice undoubtedly suffer from the agonizing effects of erectile dysfunction, a condition that may affect 50% of men over 40 years of age and older [sic]; . . . The tragic reality is that it is estimated that less than 10% of men seek treatments.

It has been left to troublesome feminist critics, headed up in the USA by the sexologist Leonore Tiefer, to analyse and object to the raging marketing of this disease, with its ever-increasing medicalization of sexual desire and the massive funding available for erectile auditing (Tiefer, 2001). It is obvious that sexuality in the private sphere was commodified long ago, with the bulk of advertising relying upon aspects of sexual titillation for marketing purposes and explicit sexual goods and services provided in mushrooming sex shops and the pornographic productions now saturating computer networks on the global Internet. But the commercial world has never before so successfully targeted the academic public sector, nor packaged the latest 'crisis of masculinity' as a readily remedial erectile function.

Not content with many millions of men who have had prescriptions written for Viagra since it was launched in 1998 (with Pfizer reporting sales of $1.5bn in 2001 alone) the search is now on for an equivalent drug for women. *The British Medical Journal* itself recently expressed alarm over this rush to medicalize women's sexual needs, covering the search of drug companies for some clearly defined medical diagnosis for a Viagra equivalent.

The corporate sponsored creation of a disease is not a new phenomenon, but the making of female sexual dysfunction is the freshest, clearest example we have. A cohort of researchers with close ties to drug companies are working with colleagues in the pharmaceutical industry to develop and define a new category of human illness at meetings heavily sponsored by companies racing to develop new drugs (Moynihan, 2003: 5). That illness is female sexual dysfunction (FSD).[18] Researchers are at this moment busy in laboratories studying cultured clumps of tissue from animals' genitalia to see how they contract and relax—rodent slides involving Viagra and rat vaginas are nowadays the most popular.[19]

Determined to resist such aggressive pharmaceutical agendas, a movement in the USA, headed up by the feminist sexologist Leonore Tiefer, has been working tirelessly against enormous odds to combat the trend to invent or medicalize women's sexual problems. Initiating a campaign for 'A New View of Women's Sexual Problems', she takes us all the way back to lessons in fact not so new, learned from feminism in the 1970s (Tiefer 2000; 2001). Her approach begins by stressing the cultural, political, economic and interpersonal aspects of sexual experience within our contemporary gendered world and consciousness. It addresses the importance of broad and imaginative sex education (completely absent in the USA), stresses the inadequate access to information and services

---

[18] See Berman, Berman and Goldstein, (1999).
[19] See Bancroft (2002).

for contraception, abortion and general health care provision (extraordinarily, Viagra for 'erectile dysfunction', unlike contraception, is covered by medical insurance in the USA), raises the need for richer vocabularies to describe desire and sexual experience, while arguing for assistance for those suffering the effects of sexual and domestic violence. Tiefer's campaign, though pursued vigorously, rarely makes it into media reports of the hunt for a 'Viagra' for women, with its simplistic notion of a sexual homology between women's and men's sexual interests and experience. This is a view that became hegemonic in mainstream sexology in the wake of Kinsey's and Masters and Johnson's stress on sexual sameness.[20]

Quite at odds with this emphasis on sexual sameness, Meika Loe recently reported in the magazine, *Sojourner*, that letters to 'Dear Abby' and the Ann Landers columns in the USA from women were for the most part hostile to their male partners taking Viagra, blaming it for coercive sexual pressures from men after years of neglect, and for encouraging husbands to leave wives for younger women (Loe, 2001:10). Placed in a national, let alone global, arena, feminist critics point out, the erroneous emphasis on gender similarities also erases all the other inequalities which interweave with gender, as the fractures of class, ethnicity and geography continue to deepen, while those of sexual orientation become ever more ambiguous. Much more could be said on diverse interests, needs and challenges that women face in the sexual arena, but let me give the last word to that vigorous campaigner, Leonore Tiefer:

> Women's sexuality is just coming into its own, for a lot of different reasons . . . and it breaks my heart to think [of these] sexual possibilities as all of a sudden being strait-jacketed into a narrow model of adequate performance and sexual acts. . . . That's why I see it as a boxing ring. It's not just us versus the pharmaceutical industry. It is a vision of women's sexuality that we're struggling over (Tiefer, quoted in Loe, 2001).

All we need to add to this, is that it is not possible to pursue this battle today anywhere but on the global stage. This means placing women alongside men and children in the particular spaces they occupy, many of them spending much of their life fighting off different forms of catastrophe, even as millions of dollars pour into studying the contractions of rodent erectile tissue.

'*Our bodies should be playgrounds/not just battlefields*': queer theorists used as a slogan to launch their own debates on lesbian, gay, bisexual and transsexual politics back in their heyday in the mid-1990s. They were building upon the work of all those who since the 1970s had been stressing the actual diversities of sexual practices, either hidden or rendered abject by languages or discourses of sexual normativity. They wanted, as well, to return to sexuality as a source of pleasure and play, not just as an object of power and social regulation. They were right to do so. Nevertheless, out there in the wider world it remains appropriate to ponder that earlier slogan displayed on gallery walls by the artist,

---

[20] See Irvine (1990).

Barbara Kruger, in which she tried to crystallise feminist challenges on sexuality from previous decades, YOUR BODY IS A BATTLEGROUND. Today, it is still being fought over, for both ideological and commercial ends, both arriving within freshly coined biological discourses.

REFERENCES

ADORNO, T, *Negative Dialectics* (New York, Seabury, 1973).

BAGEMIHL, B, *Biological Exuberance* (London, Profile Books, 1999).

BANCROFT J, 'The Medicalization of Female Sexual Dysfunction: the Need for Caution' (2002) *Archives of Sexual Behaviour* 31: 451–5.

BAUMAN, Z, *Liquid Modernity* (Cambridge, Polity Press, 2000).

—— *Society Under Siege* (Cambridge, Polity Press, 2002).

BECK, U and BECK-GERNSHEIM, E, *The Normal Chaos of Love* (Cambridge, Polity Press, 1995; 2001).

—— and —— *Individualization: Institutionalized Individualism and Its Social and Political Consequences* (London, Sage, 2001).

BERMAN J, BERMAN L, GOLDSTEIN I, 'Female Sexual Dysfunction: Incidence, Pathophysiology, Evaluation, and Treatment Options' (1999) *Urology* 54: 385–91.

BIRKHEAD, T, *Promiscuity: An Evolutionary History of Sperm Competition and Sexual Conflict* (London, Faber, 2000).

BROD, H, 'Eros Thanatized: Pornography and Male Sexuality' in M Kimmel (ed), *Men Confront Pornography* (Crown, New York, 1989).

BUTLER, J, *Gender Trouble*, (London and New York, 1989).

D'ANDRADE, RG, 'The Cultural Part of Cognition' (1981), *Cognitive Science, 5.*

DELILLO, D, *Underworld,* (London, Picador, 1998).

DAWKINS, R, *The Selfish Gene,* (Oxford, Oxford University Press, 1976).

DWORKIN, A, *Pornography: Men Possessing Women* (London, The Women's Press, 1981).

DUNANT, S and PORTER, R (eds), *The Age of Anxiety* (London, Virago, 1996).

DUPRE, J, *The Disorder of Things* (Massachusettes, Harvard University Press, 1993).

EASTON, B, *American Psycho,* (New York, Vintage Books, 1991).

FELDMAN, HA, GOLDSTEIN, I, HATZICHRISTOU, DJ, Impotence and its Medical and Psychosocial Correlates: Results of the Massachusetts Male Ageing Study' (1994) *Journal Urolology* 151: 54–61.

FROSH, S, PHOENIX, A and PATTMAN, R, *Young Masculinities: Understanding Boys in Contemporary Society* (London, Palgrave, 2002).

HALL, S, 'Reformism and the Legislation of Consent', *Permissiveness and Control: The Fate of the Sixties Legislation,* ed National Deviancy Conference (London: Macmillan, 1980).

HEWISON, R, *Too Much* (London, Methuen, 1986).

HUGHES, C, 'The Guardian Profile, Richard Dawkins: The Man who Knows the Meaning of Life', *The Guardian: Saturday Review*, October 3, 1998, p 6.

GODELIER, M, 'The Origins of Male Domination', (1981) *New Left Review*, no 127, 17.

KAPPELER, S, *The Pornography of Representation* (Polity Press, Cambridge, 1986).

INGOLD, T. 'The Poverty of Selectionism' (2000), *Anthropology Today*, 16 (3) 2.

IRVINE, J, *Disorders of Desire: Sex and Gender in Modern American Sexology* (Philadelphia, Temple University Press, 1990).

JONES, S, *The Language of Genes* (London, Flamingo, 2000).

KOLODNY, RC, KOLODNY, RC, MASTERS, W, and JOHNSON, V, *Textbook of Sexual Medicine* (Boston, Little Brown, 1979).

LA FONTAINE, J, *Child Sexual Abuse* (Cambridge, Polity, 1990).

LANCASTER, R, and MICAELA DI LEONARDO (eds), *The Gender Sexuality Reader: Culture, History, Political Economy* (London, Routledge, 1997).

LARKIN, P, 'Annus Mirabilis' In *High Windows* (London, Faber and Faber, 1974).

LAUMANN, EO, *The Social Organization of Sexuality: Sexual Practices in the United States*, (Chicago, University of Chicago Press, 1994).

LEVINE, J, *Harmful to Minors: The Perils of Protecting Children From Sex* (Minnesota, Univ. of Minnesota Press, 2002).

LEWONTIN, RC, *The Doctrine of DNA: Biology as Ideology* (London, Penguin, 1993).

LOE, M, 'Feminists Fight Drug Companies Over Vision of Women's Sexuality' *Sojourner: The Women's Forum*, March, 2001.

MACKINNON, C, 'Not a Moral Issue' in *Feminism Unmodified: Discourses on Life and Law* (London, Harvard Universty Press, 1987).

MAILER, N, *The Prisoner of Sex*, (London, Sphere, 1972).

MARTIN, M, 'What is "Rape"?—Towards a Historical, Ethnographic Approach' in *Evolution, Gender and Rape* (London and Cambridge, Massachusettes, MIT Press, 2003).

MASTERS, W and JOHNSON,V, *Human Sexual Response* (Boston, Little Brown and Company, 1966).

—— and —— *Human Sexual Inadequacy*, (Boston, Little Brown and Company, 1970).

MEUWISSEN, I and OVER, R, 'Sexual Arousal Across Phases of the Human Menstrual Cycle' (1992), *Archives of Sexual Behavior*, 2, 109–19.

MOYNIHAN, R, 'Female Impotence: Firms Under Fire', *The British Medical Journal*, January 3, 2003.

NIETZSCHE, F, *Thus Spoke Zarathrusta* [1883]; *The Antichrist*.

PHILLIPS, A, 'Bored with Sex?' *London Review of Books*, Vol. 25 No. 5, 6th March, 2003.

PYNCHON, T, *Vineland* (London, Minerva, 1991).

ROSE, H and ROSE, S, (eds), *Alas, Poor Darwin: Arguments Against Evolutionary Psychology*, (London, Jonathan Cape, 2000).

ROSE, S, *Lifelines* (London: Penguin, 1997).

ROWBOTHAM, S, *Promise of a Dream* (London: Penguin, 2000).

SAHLINS, M, *The Use and Abuse of Biology*, (London, Tavistock, 1977).

SARAGA, E, 'The Abuse of Children' in Dallos and McLaughlin (eds), *Social Problems & the Family* (London, Sage, 1993).

SEGAL, L, *Straight Sex* (London, Virago, 1994).

SENNET, R, *The Corrosion of Character* (London, Verso, 2002).

SNITOW, A, STANSELL, C and THOMPSON, S, (eds), *Desire* (London, Virago, 1985).

STACEY, J, 'Marital Suitors Court Social Science Spinsters: Perils and Paradoxes of Performing Public Sociology in Postmodern Society', Talk delivered at Leeds University. 24 June, 2002.

THORNHILL, R and PALMER, C, *A Natural History of Rape: Biological Bases of Sexual Coercion* (London and Cambridge, MA, MIT Press, 2000).

TIEFER, L, 'Sexology and the Pharmaceutical Industry: the Threat of Co-optation' (2000) *J. Sex Res.*, 37: 273–83.

—— (ed), *A New View of Women's Sexual Problems* (Binghamton, NY, Haworth Press, 2001).

TOOBY, J and COSMIDES, L, 'The psychological foundations of culture' in J Barkow, L Cosmides and J Tooby (eds), (1992) *The Adapted Mind: Evolutionary Psychology and the Generation of Culture*, (New York, Oxford University Press, 1992).

VANCE, C, 'Concept Paper' in *Pleasure and Danger: Exploring Female Sexuality*, Carole S Vance (ed), (London, RKP, 1984).

WELLINGS, K, FIELD, J, JOHNSON, AM, and WADSWORTH, J, *Sexual Behaviour in Britain: A National Survey of Attitudes and Lifestyles* (London, Penguin, 1994).

WILSON, EO, WILSON, EO, *On Human Nature,* (Cambridge, MA, Harvard University Press, 1978).

WRIGHT, R, *The Moral Animal* (London, Vintage, 1994).

5

Sexuality, Desire and Embodied Performances in the Workplace

LINDA McDOWELL

INTRODUCTION

NEW QUESTIONS ABOUT pleasure, desire and discipline in the workforce of advanced industrial economies have become significant as increasingly diverse workers enter the social relations of waged labour in expanding service sector occupations. In service jobs and occupations, the embodied performance of workers is a key element in the commodity transaction. As an embodied exchange between the suppliers and purchasers of services is typical, the social attributes and sexed body of employees have moved centre stage in both high status and high wage occupations and in bottom end casualised service employment. The latter forms of work have been termed 'high touch', distinct from the apparently more rational and cerebral 'high tech' work of science and industry (Brush, 1999: 161). I shall argue that in both forms of work the question of embodiment is central, showing how the attributes of sexualised gender identities—sex itself, including questions about sexual harassment, skin colour, age, weight, and accent—are mapped onto different forms of work, which are designated as appropriate for differently sexed and gendered workers.

In this 'new economy', dominated by embodied and sexualised forms of work, social divisions are becoming increasingly polarised, both in terms of the conditions and patterns of work and in rewards and security of employment. A division is opening up between masculinised 'self-programmable' labour, workers with high level skills and credentials in career positions with the prospect of prosperity, on the one hand, and low skilled, often uncredentialised 'generic labour' where workers of both sexes labour under 'feminised' conditions, with low levels of security and poor pay (Castells, 2000). This division is reflected in a growing income inequality and, it seems, a recent reopening of the pay gap between men and women, as well as in widening class and status inequalities.

In this chapter therefore, I explore the relationships between contemporary transformations in the economy and the social construction of identity in the workplace. I focus on the ways in which sexualised identities have been discussed and theorised in recent work on the labour market by, *inter alia*, sociologists, geographers and feminist scholars. First, I consider the definition of and connections between the terms sex, sexuality, gender and the body, before exploring recent labour market changes. I then draw on a range of empirical studies to illustrate some of the key issues involving sexuality and sexualised work practices in a number of occupational sites. Until recently, the sociology of the body and sexuality has tended to neglect the labour market as a site of embodied performance, concentrating in the main on the arenas of leisure and the significance of the growing emphasis on consumption in contemporary societies. If sociologists of sexuality and the body have forgotten, or at best underemphasised, the social relations of employment, then theorists of work and employment have tended to forget the labouring body and its sexual desires and fantasies. However, as feminist theorists of work have long emphasised, the association of femininity with the body and nature, as well as with the 'dirty' work of managing and maintaining bodies, has long influenced the attribution of gender to different tasks themselves, as well as to the workers performing these tasks. Gender, sexuality and desire, as well as class exploitation, are part of the explanation of the production and maintenance of divisions of labour.

THINKING ABOUT SEX, SEXUALITY AND THE BODY

As Rosemary Pringle (1999: 248) has argued, sexuality has a complex relationship to at least three other terms—sex, gender and the body, which are often used in ways that conflate the meaning of all these terms. Furthermore, the terms are often assumed to be gender specific, marking the difference between men and women. The Victorians, for example, referred to women as 'the sex'. Women were embodied and inferior, the 'Other', as de Beauvoir (1972) noted, to the masculine disembodied, rational and cerebral 'One'. For the larger part of the twentieth century, sex was assumed to refer to biological attributes that both distinguished men from women and also mapped onto significant social and psychological differences as a natural consequence of these biological distinctions. The differentiation of the term sex from gender, to allow for the socially constructed rather than natural biological differences awaited the development of second wave feminist theory in the late 1960s and 1970s that insisted on the variety across time and space as well as the fluidity of gendered identities. More recently, a complex debate has developed addressing the interconnections between sex and gender.

The term sexuality, however, has a longer and more complex history, emerging in the late nineteenth century, especially in Freudian theory, to capture the diverse patterns of behaviour associated with sexual activities and expression and, as Pringle argues, has now taken on 'broader meanings related to representation, identity and desire' (1999: 249). Sexualised identities came to be seen as socially constructed, deriving from complex interactions between social relations and discourses of representation, instead of an output of a natural sex drive originating outside the social (Johnson, 2002). Thus, as theorists such as Foucault

(1978) and Butler (1990) have argued, sexuality is a socially constructed set of meanings and behaviours, a set of scripts that have to be learnt and practised, reinforced by powerful social regulations of sexualised behaviour (and see other chapters in this collection, especially those by Johnson, Segal and Plummer). The relationship of sexuality as a performance to the sexed body, however, remains a contentious area of debate. Expanding the definition of sexuality from sexual acts *per se* to include representations, everyday interactions and social regulations as well as ideas of fantasy and desire opened up new areas of research. Investigations of the ways in which notions of desire and pleasure, of acceptable sexualised behaviours in arenas other than the bedroom, have been undertaken, including the performance and regulation of everyday behaviours in the workplace as well as workplace cultures. These new studies range beyond an earlier focus on sexual harassment or consensual sexual relationships in the workplace. Here, Pringle has been a key innovator in drawing on the more recent work on the discursive construction of identity, addressing the relationship between sexuality and workplace identities in both her theoretical and empirical explorations of several occupations, including secretarial work and medicine (Pringle 1988, 1998). I want to explore the history of the development of approaches to gender, sexualised identities and desire in more detail below, before illustrating my arguments with contemporary case studies. In the following section, however, I explain why economic restructuring in recent decades in the UK has placed sexualised bodies at the centre of labour market and workplace culture analyses.

ECONOMIC RESTRUCTURING AND THE TRANSFORMATION OF THE ECONOMY: FROM THE LABOURING BODY TO THE DESIRABLE BODY

As Walkowitz (2002: 497) has recently argued:

> The changed meaning of the 'body shop', from the section of a car factory (or a garage knocking wrecks back into shape) to The Body Shop, a chain of stores selling products to relax and decorate human bodies, signifies shifts in the focus of economic activity linked to the commodification of the body.

This shift in meaning nicely captures the contemporary restructuring of the British economy in the post war era (Amin, 1994; Harvey, 1989; McDowell, 1991). Since the 1950s the British economy has been transformed from one dominated by heavy industrial employment in the main undertaken by men, and which reached its apotheosis in 1955 when more than two thirds of all employment was in the manufacturing sector. In the new post-millennial economy, more than two thirds of all workers, over half of them women, are employed in the service economy. Now, 60 per cent of all men and 82 per cent of women in employment work in the service sector.

Women's growing participation (from one third to half of all waged workers over the second half of the twentieth century) has been mainly in public and private consumer services. It has reduced the older pattern of regional differences that characterised the manufacturing economy, as consumer services are in the main sensitive to local markets and so have expanded across the British space-economy. Countering this trend, however, has been the rapid growth of high status, well-paid producer services (inputs to other parts of the labour process) and associated professional occupations, especially financial and business services, in Greater London and the South East, reflected in a growing regional variation in incomes. Thus the sort of high tech, high status work discussed above is most dominant in the South East, whereas low tech, high touch 'feminised' forms of work are expanding in most towns and cities in the UK. This raises new questions about the relationships between employment, geographical diversity and the social construction of gendered identities, especially masculinity, in areas formerly dominated by heavy, male-dominated industrial jobs. Male dominance—in all arenas of social relations including (hetero)sexuality—is in large part dependent on men's labour market participation and their role as 'breadwinner' in the dominant gender regime that has so far been associated with industrial capitalism (Connell, 1995). This economic transformation raises new questions about gender identities, about responsibilities within the home as well as in the labour market, and the prospects of the transformation of social and sexual relations: what Beck and Beck-Gernsheim (1995) have termed 'the normal chaos of love'. Here, however, I concentrate in the main on the workplace.

This post-war transformation of the type of employment and the gender of employees has fundamentally recast the associations between the social relations of production and the social construction of identity. As Macdonald and Sirianni (1996: 4) astutely noted (despite their assumption that all workers are still men):

> The assembly-line worker could openly hate his job, despise his supervisor and even dislike his co-workers, and while this might be an unpleasant state of affairs, if he completed his assigned tasks efficiently, his attitude was his own problem. For the service worker, inhabiting the job means, at the very least, pretending to like it, actually bringing his whole self into the job, liking it, and genuinely caring for the people with whom he interacts.

Further, the jobs and occupations that are currently expanding, demand a focus on the body. This focus is not only on the bodily performance of its workers but increasingly, as Walkowitz (2002) noted, it also involves work on the bodies of others in the 'care, adornment, pleasure, discipline and cure of others' bodies'. In both aspects of body work, social relations based on sexuality, pleasure, desire and fantasy play an increasingly significant part in the employment relation: in hiring and firing, in accepted workplace performances, in interactions between worker and customer or client, and in the ways in which gendered attributes are accorded to different types of work and so are differentially rewarded.

Despite the economic transformations outlined above, gender remains a fundamental characteristic of workplace segregation. Most men and women in the UK are employed in sectors with workers of predominantly the same sex, and men predominate in higher status occupations. Table 1, below shows the percentage of male and female employees by major sectors in 2001.

Table 1

Major sectors	Women %	Men %
Construction	9	91
Agriculture and fishing	22	78
Energy and water	23	77
Transport, storage and communication	25	75
Manufacturing	26	74
Real estate, renting and business	41	59
Public administration and defence	45	55
Wholesale, retail and motor trade	50	50
Banking, insurance and pension funding	52	48
Hotels and restaurants	59	41
Education	71	29
Health and social work	81	19

Source: Equal Opportunities Commission (2001)

Gender segregation is even greater when industries and occupations are more narrowly defined. Table 2 below shows the percentage of male and female employees in selected occupations.

Table 2

Selected occupations	Women %	Men %
Drivers of road goods vehicles	2	98
Production, works and maintenance managers	7	93
Warehouse and storekeepers	15	85
Technical and wholesale reps	19	81
Computer analysts/programmers	21	79
Marketing and sales managers	29	71
Chefs and cooks	50	50
Secondary school teachers	53	47
Sales assistants	72	28
Book keepers and financial clerks	74	26
Computer and record clerks	76	24
Waiters and waitresses	77	23
Counter clerks and cashiers	80	20
Retail checkout operators	81	19
Cleaners and domestics	81	19
Catering assistants	82	18
Primary and nursery teachers	86	14
Nurses	90	10
Care assistants and attendants	92	8

Source: Equal Opportunities Commission (2001)

In this chapter, however, I want to focus explicitly on the aspects of body work, assessing the significance of sexuality, pleasure and desire in both high tech, high status work and in high touch, low status work. I want to explore the ways in which the production of an embodied performance by employees and the maintenance of other bodies are key parts of contemporary working lives. It is in the high touch/low status types of work in the main that the second meaning of bodywork—as the care for others' bodies—is of greatest significance. In other forms of routine service work, however, the bodily performance of the employees in their interactions with customers (Leidner, 1993) is of key significance. In these occupations—in the fast food industry and the retail clothing trade for example—interactions with clients are highly scripted, regulated and monitored and often depend on the manipulation of the employees' sexualised emotions, including the manipulation of sexual desire. These types of work have been described by Hochschild (1983) as dependent on a 'managed heart' in her now classic study of a range of jobs including airline stewarding in which both hetero- and homo-sexual desire is a significant part of both client-employee interactions and between employees. In high tech occupations—in the high status end of the service sector—the sexed body and sexual desire is paradoxically both present and absent. Although an aestheticised, sexually attractive and sexually conformist (i.e. heterosexual) embodied and interactive performance of individual employees is highly valorised (Bauman, 1998), the status of the work undertaken tends to depend on its cerebral, disembodied nature: attributes which are, of course, traditionally associated with a particular version of hegemonic masculinity (Connell, 1995, 2000).

In this discussion, I focus solely on waged employment. If unwaged work, especially that undertaken in the 'private' arena of the household, more commonly entered the analyses of changes in the nature of work, the emotionalization and aestheticization of work may have a far longer history. As Adkins and Lury (2000: 154) insist, it certainly is not as novel as many commentators on the contemporary labour market suggest. What is of key significance here, however, is the growing commoditisation of a great deal of the emotional and aesthetic/sexualised labour that formerly was undertaken in the home and elsewhere for 'love', with all its connotations of gendered and sexualised relationships between men and women, and between adults and their dependants.

THE RISE OF CONSUMER SOCIETIES AND THE SIGNIFICANCE OF DESIRE

The transition of advanced industrial economies from a mass-society, mass producing a limited range of goods for a relatively differentiated market, to an economy based on the development of a highly differentiated range of products to niche markets has, in large part, been based on the rise of advertising and the manipulation of desire. Bauman (1998: 26) has argued that consumer societies are volatile and temporary; objects of desire must not only be instantly available but must also bring instant satisfaction, which quickly wanes. 'Consumers must be constantly exposed to new temptations in order to be kept in a state of constantly seething, never wilting excitation and, indeed, in a state of suspicion and disaffection.'

He continues to suggest an even more explicit parallel with sexual desire:

> It is often said that the consumer market seduces its customers. But in order to do so it needs customers who are ready and keen to be seduced. In a properly working consumer society consumers seek actively to be seduced. They live from attraction to attraction, from temptation to temptation (1998: 26).

In this type of market, the role of the providers and sellers of goods and services as agents of seduction assumes a high significance in a 'society organised around desire and choice' (Bauman, 1998: 29). In growing numbers of service occupations, the interaction between clients and providers is an exchange, based on the manipulation of emotions and a transaction in which the bodily performance of the server is a key part of the exchange. As du Gay (1996) has shown in his study of fashion retail outlets, a scripted exchange, in this case based on an ideal of youthful equality, rather than the heterosexist interactions Hochschild noted in the airline industry, is common in clothes shops aimed at the teenage market. Here the conventional distinction between the workers and clients is blurred in interactions that depend increasingly on the similarity of the sales staff and the customers and their participation in a sociable, yet scripted, ritual that is based on a false notion of equality and familiarity. In these exchanges, a groomed, trimmed, tamed and toned, sexually desirable body and the capacity for continual self-discipline is an increasingly significant aspect of the employment relationship. Casual flirting is a recognised part of the script.

SEXUALITY AND ORGANISATIONS: WORKPLACE CULTURES

As economies have changed, so too has social theorising of workplace relations and cultures. Perhaps the first challenge to the notion of rational bureaucratic organisations or disembodied non-sexual (and by default masculine) workers, that dominated economic sociology and other associated disciplines, came in work that might be grouped under the heading of 'gender and organisations'. Here Acker's (1990) classic paper challenged the notion that organisations consist of profit-maximising institutions that, through the employment of hierarchies of employees without dependants, achieve market-defined ends. In this view of the world, employees, whose skills and knowledge best fit the goals of the organisation, initially are appointed and then are rewarded and promoted on the basis of an objective evaluation of their performance. Acker argued instead that organisations are seldom rational or objective but that their structures, cultures and everyday practices are riven with essentialist and non-essentialist assumptions about gender and sexuality in ways which consistently benefit certain workers, in the main white heterosexual men. The disadvantaged include the usual cast of 'others': women, people of colour, less physically able workers and people with alternative sexual identities. These 'others' may be excluded or alternatively constructed as less suitable, or inferior, workers and restricted to a narrow range of jobs and occupations that are congruent with their gendered and sexualised identities. In consequence, the division of labour *per se* and organisations and their practices are deeply gendered. Both conscious and unconscious practices produce and maintain gender inequality in the workplace.

Acker's work, and the organisational case-studies that followed it, built on earlier and now classic analyses such as Moss Kanter's (1977) work documenting men's dominance of high status occupations and positions. She showed how this dominance was reliant on women's support services, both in the workplace and the home. Acker also insisted on the significance of the 'lived body' in organisations, identifying the dominance of workers who are male, heterosexual, with minimal involvement in procreation and controlled emotions. A wide range of work has documented the ways in which this sexualised bodily norm is part of the maintenance of gender inequalities, confining women to a narrow group of appropriate occupations, as well as saturating the very definition of different tasks and jobs with gendered attributes. The various ways in which the discursive construction of organisational practices produce and maintain patterns of gendered and sexualised behaviour on the shop floor have begun to be documented. As Ferree *et al* (1999: xxix) noted:

> Not only are there gendered assumptions built into most job descriptions and job assignments, as well as variations in pay scales and occupational ladders/promotion schemes, organisations also sexualise workers—presenting authority and physical labour (and I would add, cerebral rationality LMcD) as testaments to heterosexual masculinity, and good looks, "service with a smile" and covert sexiness as evidence of heterosexual femininity. These norms and expectations are maintained by open and hidden harassment and subtle and blunt sanctions by workers of each other and by bosses of workers under them.

A useful summary of a great deal of this work about gendered organisations may be found in a survey by Martin and Collison (1999: 285). Collinson has also contributed in a significant and substantive way to these debates. With Jeff Hearn (Collison and Hearn, 1996), for example, in empirical analyses of managers in several institutions, he has distinguished the varying ways in which male managers manage and regulate their co-workers by constructing alternative versions of masculine identities, that construct or preclude dissent, through coercive or co-operative strategies. These are variously based on versions of male authority or male trust and co-operation that differentially and unequally position male subordinates and peers, but which also at the same time act to affirm masculine solidarity within organisations by excluding femininity and women. Numerous studies of female–dominated occupations and workplaces, whether factory work or secretarial work, have shown how women workers often draw on alternative, feminised scripts and performances in their discursive construction of identity and in their definition of work roles and relations with co-workers in order to challenge masculinised norms and male domination. They introduce questions about familial obligations, pregnancy and menstruation, for example, in a previously disembodied workplace discourse. In studies of British and Japanese factory workers, Westwood (1984) and Kondo (1990) respectively have demonstrated how women in their workplaces assert their identities as mothers and as carers for others, challenging masculinised dominance of factory spaces but, at the same time, paradoxically reinforcing their own inferiority as workers by emphasising their femininity.

Pringle's (1988) analysis of secretarial work was crucial in identifying the links between gender and sexuality and in showing how workplace-based social relations are based on discourses of desire and pleasure. In her study she argued that employees are not passive objects but instead active agents, whose identity is not fixed as they enter the workplace but is instead open, negotiable, shifting and ambiguous. Gendered sexualised identities are thus constructed and challenged through workplace practices in official and unofficial arenas that are saturated by notions about gender and sexuality. Thus organisations are locations and sites for the construction of identity, in which men and women 'do' gender through everyday interactions in dynamic organisations that are themselves embedded within wider social structures, attitudes and assumptions about gender and sexuality. Pringle showed how the relations between secretaries and their bosses in large part depended on gendered interactions. Female secretaries, for example, drew on a number of gendered and/or sexualised discourses, including the office 'mistress' and the office 'wife', to construct particular power relations between them and their male bosses. Flirting and having fun was a common script for male boss/female secretary interaction, as well as the extension of office duties into 'homemaker' tasks (making coffee, arranging food at meeting, buying flowers for the office or gifts for the boss's household for example). In contrast, between women bosses and women secretaries the social relations were both more straightforward and less deferential and typically confined to more strictly defined office-based and work-related activities.

Drawing on Pringle's path-breaking work, a large number of studies have explored the consequences of theorising gender and sexuality as fluid and mutable in analyses of differential performances in numerous occupations. They draw theoretically on two main sources. Foucault's (1978) arguments about the body as an inscripted surface, in which self-discipline and normalistion based on multiple discourses (temporally- and culturally-specific sets of ideas, images, institutional structures, practices and regulations) are crucial in the production and maintenance of an approved body, and Butler's (1990, 1993) theorisation of gender as a regulatory fiction. Both approaches emphasise the performativity of identity. These studies have demonstrated how conventional attributes of hegemonic gender identity and a dominant version of heterosexuality are performed and confirmed in daily and institutional practices in workplaces in ways that benefit (certain) men. Thus studies of, for example, insurance sale-forces

(Leidner, 1993) and retail banking (Halford, Savage and Witz, 1996) have documented how particular occupations are ring-fenced for men by their association with heroic masculinity or with superior patriarchal knowledge-based notions of an idealised rationality. In both cases, these gendered associations with their concomitant higher financial rewards also proved to be the downfall for male workers in each industry as restructuring and cost-cutting drew on an alternative gendered script to recast and feminise both insurance sales and banking.

In these studies, the concept of an embodied, sexualised performance is key, in which the attributes of a desirable and desiring body play a part. As Young (1990) has argued in her recasting of the structures of inequality into five faces of oppression, the body is a significant dimension of oppression. Ugly, fat, non-white, elderly bodies are inadmissible in the interactive sales/advice-giving industries and occupations that increasingly dominate in advanced industrial societies. In this type of work, as Young argued, 'dynamics of desire and the pulses of attraction and aversion' influence the scope and content of interactions between workers, their peers, superiors, clients and customers. In a study of workplace interactions in three merchant banks in the City of London in the early to mid 1990s (McDowell, 1997), I found that women bank employees were constrained by their construction as a sexualised other, as out of place in the cerebral world of corporate banking as in the masculinised boys' school/sports club carnivalesque atmosphere of the trading floor, in which the conventional assumptions that dominate white collar work are discarded. In a range of ways from derogatory comments to outright sexual harassment, discussed in more detail in the following section, women were marked out both as inappropriately sexual and inferior in the different arenas of investment banking.

INTERACTIVE WORK AND EMOTIONAL LABOUR: SELLING AN APPROPRIATE BODY

Masculinised Interactive Work: Women's Confinement to the Sexualised Body in Top End Service Work

> It could be argued that men don't have bodies at all . . . only the heads, the unsmiling heads, the talking heads, the decision making heads, and maybe a little glimpse, a coy flash of suit. How do we know there's a body under all that discreet pinstriped tailoring? We don't and maybe there isn't (Atwood 1992: 80).

> The British have no bodies. They have only heads (Fleury quoted in Armstrong 1995: 15).

As I noted above, in the 1990s I undertook a piece of work looking at the performance of gendered identities within merchant banks in the City of London. The expansion of high status occupations in the financial services industry was a key element in the rapid economic growth of Greater London and the South East in the late 1980s and late 1990s. While many of these occupations, especially investment banking and the legal profession, have long-established and clear class and gender connotations, their rapid growth led to a change in both recruitment practices and in daily interactions in the banking halls, board rooms and chambers. A challenge was mounted to the notion of that form of 'gentlemanly capitalism' (Auger, 2001) based on trust and established through generations of familial and educational connections. Instead a set of new interactions developed, dubbed the 'Americanisation' of the City (Lewis, 1989). British-owned banks (now an absence in the 21st century City) recruited a wider range of employees from non-elite universities for example, and foreign-owned banks also expanded. The new, more cosmopolitan workforce with different ways of doing things challenged British constraint. As Linda Grant (1993) noted in her book *Sexing the Millennium*, in the 1980s and 1990s—the decades when 'greed is good'- money itself became imbued with desire: 'it was money rather than the body which was suffused with eroticism'. Geographers Thrift, Leyshon and Daniels (1987) were quick to notice that a new 'sexy-greedy' atmosphere had begun to permeate City institutions. The carnivalesque world of city trading floors was pictured in the formerly sober financial pages of the broadsheet press where sweating shirt-sleeved traders replaced the disembodied pinstriped-clad men satirised by Margaret Atwood in the quote above. Indeed, banking escaped entirely from the confines of the serious press to become a subject of West End plays, British television serials (*Capital City*) and Hollywood movies (*Trading Places*, *Wall Street* and *Rogue Trader*—the latter based on the true story of Nick Leeson: the man who brought down Barings Bank). Money was indeed sexy and its associations were transferred to the powerful men of money manipulating the world's stock exchanges for their own benefit. Only in the best Hollywood tradition of morality plays were these 'masters of the universe' (Wolfe, 1988) tricked or humbled by their business and social subordinates. In the real world they were transmogrified into 'fat cats' whose vast bonuses came to be resented as the new millennium ushered in a regime of scandal and corporate collapse. The imagery of a fat-cat is decidedly unsexy, combining a Baconesque obscenity of excess adiposity with the sluggishness of age.[1] The lean, mean, 'lunch is for wimps' image of Martin Sheen in *Wall Street* is replaced by a slothful cat monopolising the cream.

In the earlier atmosphere of rapid change and an emphasis on money as the ultimate object of desire, however, I wanted to explore the ways in which the traditional associations of corporate banking with a bourgeois, cerebral masculinity and trading with an embodied 'barrow boy' masculinity might be disrupted. Would the rapid recruitment of men and women from a wider range of social and educational backgrounds alter these associations between money, desire, sexuality and class background? I therefore interviewed matched pairs of men and women in a range of positions throughout the occupational hierarchy in three merchant banks. I wanted to empirically assess Acker's argument that women succeed in male-dominated organisations and corporations only if they

---

[1] Thanks to Belinda Brooks-Gordon for pointing out this combination with such a vivid image.

adopt an unsexed, masculinised performance in the workplace: 'to be successful women have to become honorary men' (Acker 1990). Through a series of quotes from some of the key informants I want to show how this performance of masculinity was attempted, but ultimately seen as impossible, by women bankers. Many of the women whom I interviewed argued that they remain tied to and excluded by the traditional associations between women, an unacceptable version of 'natural' embodiment, and the construction of femininity on the basis of sexualised attributes.

The Impossibility of Being a Man?

The conventional methods that women adopt to construct a masculinised and asexual performance at work range from the adoption of sombre clothing, the disguise of explicitly female conditions or interests, such as pregnancy and mothering, to the development of masculine mannerisms such as the aggressive use of language or dominating behaviour and attempting to become 'one of the boys' by joining in typically male after-work pursuits such as drinking. Among considerable numbers of the younger women bankers whom I interviewed I found evidence of all these attitudes and behaviours in the construction of self in the workplace. 'I try to be unobtrusive, to look more like a man than a woman.' 'I try to dress so that I never stand out. Not too frumpy but nothing garish and nothing that emphasises the body.' And distinctions between women in different occupational positions in the banking hierarchy are also significant in clothing the body:

> I wear tailored shirts and a jacket. Women must wear a jacket unless they want to be associated with a secretary: that's one of the rules.

Exaggerated forms of masculinised language and behaviour are commonplace in the trading and dealing arenas of banking. Here horse-play, sexualised banter, loud and aggressive talk and forms of sexual harassment are common and women are often forced either into the position of unwilling arbiters of boundaries or less than willing participants in the sexualised banter. Examples of the first position are when women find that male colleagues stop talking when they join a group, or with exaggerated courtesy apologise for their language or ask for permission to continue. In the second case, women find that they too are, by choice or through a desire to fit into the accepted atmosphere, just as likely as their male colleagues to 'talk dirty'. For example, a woman trader told me that 'We (city workers) seem to specialise in rude comments but the women are just as bad as the men', and a male manager noted 'Oh yes, as far as sexual banter, the girls (sic) often give as good as they get.'

But women in the main are visible on trading floors only by their absence. As one male trader told the *Independent on Sunday* in September 2002 (08/11/02) 'as I look around this floor, the only woman I can see is making my tea'. On the floor, especially in bull markets, an aggressive, hetero-sexualised masculine confidence in their own abilities creates an atmosphere inimical to many women, and to gay men, and which in the current bear market, might also lead to poor advice. In a recent study by investment bank Dresdner Kleinwort Wasserstein, analysts James Montier (*The Observer Business*, 23/02/03) noted that 'much of the psychology behind markets has to do with the over-confidence of traders and the tendency to exaggerate their own abilities' and so to under-estimate the impact of a falling market. Men, according to Theodora Zenek, an asset manager in the City of London, 'are aggressive buyers, but that either gives you staggering out-performance or staggering under-performance', in part because as she noted men have a 'tendency to fall in love with their investments' (quoted in the *Independent on Sunday* 08/11/02). As I found in my own inter-views in investment banks, sexualised language is widespread on trading floors and money/investments/positions are often referred to as women/lovers and col-leagues as pricks or as a sonofabitch.

In the more conventional arenas of corporate banking where interaction with business clients is a key part of the work, women tended to be treated with patriarchal courtesy and to be excluded through talk and interactions, based on networks of contacts that depend on 'the old school tie'. Even in this side of banking, however, the body mattered, despite its covering by pin-striped tailor-ing, and male interviewees emphasised the importance of the correct clothes—in quality and colour—as well as the importance of bodily hygiene and keeping weight within certain limits. In this world a certain relatively youthful, male public school form of embodied performance based on rigorously disciplined body was a key issue. Slenderness and an idealised image of youthful hetero-sexuality was most highly valorised and through recruitment practices tended to be largely reproduced from year to year. A casual glance at business pages in the broadsheet press is enough to confirm this hegemonic ideal.

In both these arenas within merchant banks, as many women (especially more senior women) noted, a masculinised performance by women is almost impos-sible. As one senior woman said 'I can never be a man as well as a man is.' She had recently abandoned her masculinised protective clothing and had begun to wear bright colours, a softer hairstyle and to capitalise on her difference from men:

> I decided to use my femininity to stand out, to get noticed in meetings for example, so clients would start to ask for me.

I completed my empirical work in the mid 1990s as the City was beginning to boom again and recruitment was high. In this optimistic atmosphere, women may have felt more able to take risks. Even so, women remained a tiny minority in the higher echelons of merchant banks. At the present time, however, the financial sector is once again experiencing redundancies, and although I hesitate to draw a connection between women's experiences of discrimination and tense working conditions, it is noticeable that a number of high profile cases of harassment and unfair dismissal have recently reached the courts. Most of these cases involve discrimination in salaries, especially in performance-related bonuses, as well as sexist behaviours and practices in the firms. For example, the hiring of escort girls for company parties, a claim made by Kay Swinburne who was awarded a substantial amount in October 2000 after her boss at Deutsche Bank falsely alleged that she had slept with a client. In the broadsheets, as well as in the popular press, women often find their claims treated in ways that emphasise their sexual difference and their inappropriate location as embodied women in the spaces of the City. Thus, Jane Hayes found her case reported by *The Independent* under the headline 'mother wins "sexism in City" payout' (11/11/02). Even Clara Furse, the first woman chief executive of the London Stock Exchange and so the most high profile woman in the City at present, found she was not immune from sexist practices. In early 2003, a report that rumours were circulating the City based on distressing innuendoes about her sexuality hit the papers and other news media (*The Observer Business*, 23/02/03). Furse, according to Allison Pearson (2003), who interviewed a number of City women in 2002 for a novel, had adopted the classic disguise strategy of women in the City 'she became a man'. In a comparison that I particularly relish as a geographer by disciplinary training, she was described by the press as 'having the prim exterior associated with a geography mistress', 'almost devoid of sex appeal'. As Pearson clarified, attempting to unsex themselves in the workplace, many women adopt the same set of rules:

> hair short, business like specs instead of contact lenses. Keep your shirt buttoned up, no flash of bra, no visible panty line. Nothing that reminds them that you are someone they might want to have sex with (Pearson, 2003: 21).

Despite this camouflage, Furse became the subject of sexual innuendo, because as my informant quoted earlier noted, women's masculine masquerades in the workplace are inevitably unsuccessful. Even for extremely successful women 'devoid of sex appeal' (as Furse herself suggested she is in a speech at the UK Society of Investment Professionals annual dinner on 26 February 2003) sexual harassment is a too common occurrence. As Furse noted in her speech, 'city news (with some important exceptions) seems to focus on the odd corporate failure, job cuts and, in the case of the London Stock Exchanges, merger speculation, the colour of my suits and the cut of my hair' (reported by Treanor, 2003).

Women in other types of City employment have also found themselves the victims of inimical workplace cultures. As in investment banking, falling profits and tense working conditions have also been noted as one part of the explanation of reportedly high levels of dissatisfaction at work, especially among women in junior positions in City legal firms. Nearly two-thirds of women lawyers who took part in a survey undertaken by the City of London Law Society in 2002, felt their gender was a disadvantage when being considered for a partnership. Some of the largest and most prestigious City firms were singled out for particular criticism. Slaughter and May, for example, was criticised for its atmosphere of a gentleman's club for (white, male) Oxbridge lawyers. Barristers' chambers were also criticised for their old-fashioned, patriarchal atmosphere and refusal to implement family-friendly policies. Thus, in professional City occupations, women's sexuality is paradoxically both ignored, as family-friendly policies are seldom implemented, and exaggerated in everyday interactions that continue to construct women as inappropriately sexualised bodies and so a challenge to the idealised model of a serious employee.

Feminised Interactive Work: Inappropriate Masculine Bodies and Bottom End Service Work

In the discussion of masculine embodiment in the labour market, a binary distinction is common between the cerebral, disembodied worker that lacks desire, identified by Acker (1990), Witz *et al* (1996: 173) and others in bureaucratic organisations, and the embodied, muscled sweating bodies, and emotional male camaraderie or homosociality that develops between men in often dangerous manual occupations in the primary and manufacturing jobs that formerly dominated men's work in many regions of the UK (McDowell and Massey, 1984). But, as I have shown, this binary distinction remains significant even within high status occupations in the service sector such as banking. I want to turn now, to the other end of the service sector and ask what happens to traditional forms of male working class embodiment in the labour market when those jobs and trades that depend on the second version of masculinity have disappeared. I want to argue that although women are still excluded from many high paid service occupations, out of place as embodied sexual representations of femininity, it is now men, particularly working class men, who find themselves as inappropriately embodied and aggressively sexualised in their search for work in low paid servicing jobs at the bottom end of the labour market.

As I noted earlier, among the fastest growing jobs in many British towns and cities are those that are dependent on a subservient, often routinised exchange between service providers and customers, in which the embodied performance of the former is part of the exchange. This type of work, defined by Leidner (1993) as interactive work, is common in the retail sector, in fast food, in the hospitality sector as well as in the provision of basic services in an office environment. It requires a basic minimum of education but, more significantly, also depends on 'service with a smile', the ability to defer to both clients and superiors, and the presentation of a neat, clean servile body that conforms to conventional norms in terms of weight, height, accent, hirsuteness and decoration. It requires an acceptable workplace performance in terms both of presentation, especially appropriate clothing, and behaviour. The Disney Corporation, when recruiting for EuroDisney for example, specified the exact amount of facial hair permitted among its male recruits, the number of earrings (one for men, two for women and no more) as well as dress codes and regulated norms of social interaction. In Britain, the Ministry of Work and Pensions has recently (in 2002) issued a series of guidelines about acceptable dress at work for employees in JobCentres, many of whom are not in front office jobs and so never meet the public. The suggested guidelines were so specific (no cord trousers, only slim fitting trousers, no fleeces, no T-shirts for men) that the staff in JobCentres initially thought they were a hoax. However, in a case supported by the Public and Commercial Services Union, Matthew Thompson, a backroom claims processor, has taken a case to an industrial tribunal that the guidelines amount to sexual discrimination, as women have a choice of outfits to wear at work but men are limited to one outfit, which must include a tie (Ahmed, 2003).

To fit into these idealised images of acceptable versions of embodied, sexually desirable masculinity and femininity, potential as well as current employees have to perform the type of 'body work' identified by Shilling (1993)—dieting say—to maintain the 'right' kind of body, attention to presentation and the construction of an acceptable set of workplace clothes. But attitudes as well as bodily presentation are also a key element in the performance of service work. The attitudinal and embodied attributes of deference and servility, as well as empathy with others' needs, required in these expanding low status 'servicing' jobs, where engagement with the public as well as colleagues is an essential attribute of the work, have often been associated with the social characteristics of femininity. As a consequence, men, especially working class young men, who have developed a particular version of a tough, aggressive, sexualised street credibility that is inappropriate to servicing types of work, are socially constructed as out of place in many workplaces. In an absorbing study of working class youth in a low-income part of Manhattan in the early 1990s, for example, Philippe Bourgois (1995) vividly documented the ways in which the intersection of local attitudes developed by young men growing up in a previously blue-collar neighbourhood in combination with the shift toward a polarised service-dominated economy in NYC placed these men, especially those from minority communities, at a particular disadvantage in attempting to find work. He showed how their social networks and lack of social capital exacerbated their problems in seeking employment:

> Perhaps if their social network had not been confined to the weakest sector of manu-
> facturing in a period of rapid job loss, their teenage working class dreams might have
> stabilised them for long enough to enable them to adapt to the restructuring of the
> local economy. Instead they find themselves propelled headlong into an explosive con-
> frontation between their sense of cultural dignity versus the humiliating interpersonal
> subordination of service work (Bourgois, 1995: 14).

The sort of tough, even violent, machismo valued on the New York streets ran profoundly counter to main employment opportunities available. If these young men were taken on in the service sector, as photocopiers or messengers, for example, Bourgois found that they quickly lost their jobs as their social and cultural capital was inappropriate in white collar workplaces:

Their interpersonal social skills are even more inadequate than their limited professional capacities. They do not know how to look at their fellow service workers—let alone their supervisors—without intimidating them. They cannot walk down the hallway to the water fountain without unconsciously swaying their shoulders aggressively as if patrolling their home turf. Gender barriers are an even more culturally charged realm. They are repeatedly reprimanded for offending co-workers with sexually aggressive behaviour (1995: 142–3).

In a study that I have recently undertaken of the employment prospects of working class young white men in Cambridge and Sheffield (McDowell, 2003), I found that many of the young men to whom I talked had clear views about the types of work they were prepared to consider, regarding most service sector work as 'women's work' and so beneath their dignity. Even if they were prepared to consider employment in the shops, clubs and fast food outlets that were the main source of work for unqualified school leavers in both cities, they often disqualified themselves as potential employees by their appearance (piercings and tattoos as well as inappropriate clothes) and their attitudes during the recruitment process. Employers read the surface signals of bodily demeanour, dress and language as indicators of the underlying qualities they are seeking, or more typically as characteristics they are careful to avoid. If they do find work, often their sexualised, aggressive embodied interactions, especially with women co-workers and superiors disqualify them, as Bourgois (1995) found, and many of them found it hard to perform the deferential servility required in the service economy.

Several of the young men whom I interviewed found employment in McDonalds and in other fast food outlets, for example, in jobs that demand the performance of an explicit script, under constant surveillance in interactions with customers. As Newman (1999) has argued, based on her own detailed study of fast food employment in New York City, the social characteristics of inner city male youth culture, especially in its celebration of independence and rejection of deference, constructs young men as singularly unsuited to this form of deferential interactive service work. Young women, on the other hand, are more experienced in presenting a modest demeanour and deferential attitudes to adult authority, as well as more able to defuse difficult situations, especially when peers demand preferential treatment, such as free food. As one of the young men I interviewed noted:

> They push people around, management does . . . people often don't last long here. They leave after about two months because they can't handle it. They answer back and that.

Selling fast food and other forms of retail employment demand the construction of deferential attitudes as well as an unobtrusive presentation of the embodied self that is often impossible for the types of young men that Bourgois and I interviewed. Interestingly, as well as deference, issues of desire and attraction, often associated with femininity to the disadvantage of working class men, are also important in expanding forms of 'disembodied' service work such as that in call centres. Here, the allure and intimacy of the voice and the ability to establish a rapid and empathetic connection with the caller is important in telephone selling, whether the product is double glazing or sexual fantasies.

In the penultimate section, I turn more briefly to the other form of 'body work' identified by Walkowitz—working on the bodies of others. It is here that issues of sexuality, gendered identities and embodied performances are most evident, raising complex issues of negotiation in the relationship between employees and clients but also for the researcher interested in new forms of labour process. The intervention of the embodied presence of an observer may have a significant effect on the nature of interactions between clients and employees.

Servicing the Bodies of Others: Old and New Forms of Sexualised and Embodied Work

In the two former sections, body-work has been delineated as the work people do on their own bodies to produce an expected workplace performance. As Adkins and Lury (2000: 152) have noted, this work is central in the production process, emphasising the 'mutual interdependence of the performance of identity and the performativity of economies'. Both employees and economies are re-produced through this work, 'a labour of identity' in Adkins and Lury's term, which is largely dependent on the embodied and sexual characteristic of the labourers. The body matters and it is important to note that however fluid and mutable identities may have become, highly valued performances of identity are not equally possible for all.

But the body also matters in a second sense in contemporary economies: there is an increasing amount of paid work that, as Walkowitz (2002) noted, involves working on the bodies of others and it is here in particular that issues about sexual attraction and desire are unavoidable. While there is a large body of literature, a great deal of it from a feminist perspective, on what is often termed 'caring work' (Gardiner, 1997; Ungerson, 1987), it often focuses on work undertaken in the home by relatives and friends rather than on waged labour. There are also, of course, several excellent studies of, for example, the medical professions, addressing questions about gendered inequalities among doctors, nurses, radiologists, as well as studies of social workers, home helps and so on (Pringle, 1998; Lee-Trewick, 1997; Walby and Greenwell, 1994). It is less common, however, to find analyses of newer forms of body work including beauticians, fitness trainers, alternative health care therapists, sex workers, tattoo artists and body piercers, weightwatchers and exercise class leaders. In part, this is because many of these jobs involve close, intimate and often undignified contact with the messy bodies of clients and so are difficult to observe as research subjects. Some of these expanding body maintenance jobs are less about the explicit caring for others' bodies than the joint production of a slim, sexualised energetic body. In both cases, however, the labour process often involves contact with the supine, sometimes naked bodies of clients. In these forms of bodywork, women, and men too, may be open to harassment as the aim is to please customers, with whom the body worker may be engaged in a one-to-one service exchange and the standard 'service with a smile' may too easily be misunderstood.

The embodied, often highly sexualised, nature of these different forms of caring for the body is also deeply implicated in the gender and racialised divisions of labour that are evident in these jobs and occupations. Almost all are low-status and correspondingly low paid occupations, and are often feminised. Higher status caring occupations—medicine is a good example—tend to be defined as 'technical' and, as Walkowitz (2002) notes, prolonged interaction with the body is limited through the delegation of the more messy or personal work to nurses. However, there is no doubt that the changing composition of the medical workforce is challenging earlier associations. Equal numbers of men and women are now admitted to medical schools and women are finding some ways into the higher ranks of the profession. Changing cultures, however, requires more than numerical equality. An essentialist assumption that the presence of women necessarily ensures a more egalitarian culture or one more susceptible to the exploration of emotions or feelings is challenged by empirical evidence (see Pringle, 1998). In other forms of bodily maintenance and care work, the sexual connotations of the intimate touching of the bodies of others tends to be erased or denied by the construction of comparisons with medicine or therapy—the touch is healing rather than sexual.

In many of these forms of working on the bodies of others, distinct divisions of labour are found in different categories of work. Social constructions of 'race', class and gender are drawn on to define particular categories of the potential labour force as most appropriate. Thus, the body maintenance jobs—in gyms, in yoga classes, in beauty parlours for example—often rely on hegemonic notions of the idealised body as slim, young and white, whether male or female. The 'dirtier work' of caring for sick or elderly bodies or paid domestic labour often draws in a racialised global labour force of migrant workers. In sex work and sex tourism these racialised and gendered divisions are explicitly constructed through stereotypical notions about the sexualities of 'exotic others' but the sexual exploitation of domestic 'servants' is a well-documented historical trend. The employment of minority or working class women as both servants and prostitutes by the middle classes has been widely documented in the USA (McClintock, 1994; Pratt, 1997; Romero, 1992), in the UK (Gregson and Lowe, 1994) and elsewhere in Western Europe (Anderson, 2000). Indeed, the general association of the body and sexuality with dirt and pollution also has a long history. As Davidoff and Hall (1987) have shown in England in the 18th and 19th centuries, it was the body work of working women in both the public arena—in the streets, in pubs, hospitals and brothels—as well as in domestic service in middle class homes that enabled middle class women to be constructed as the pure, disembodied angels of the hearth at the peak of the Victorian hypocrisy about sexuality. In the early 21st century, it might perhaps be argued that it is the 'dirty body work' of the once again expanding numbers of paid domestic workers that allow middle class women in professional occupations at least to attempt a workplace performance of disembodied rationality, unencumbered by the demands of caring themselves for the bodies of others. And it is the 'maintenance body work' that produces the fit, slim and healthy body that is not only a mark of middle class privilege, but as I argued above, is an increasingly key element in the production and reproduction of professional and managerial status and increasingly in routine service occupations.

CONCLUSIONS

Body work, in both the sense of working on one's own body and working on the body of others is an increasingly significant element of the social relations of waged labour in contemporary industrial societies such as the UK. In both cases hegemonic notions of acceptable heterosexual femininity and masculinity dominate the ways in which these jobs are constructed, performed and regulated through institutional structures and practices and everyday interactions within workplaces. As I have argued, many of these expanding forms of service work— both the well-paid high status 'programmable labour' and the low paid unskilled 'generic labour' distinguished by Castells (2000)—are dominated by an embodied aesthetic performance of gendered/sexualised identity in the workplace. I have documented the ways in which these performances are unevenly distributed and unequally valued, leading in extreme cases to complex issues about the boundaries of acceptable sexualisation of everyday interactions in the workplace, and so to definitions of sexual harassment. What I have not addressed here is the extent to which the workplace is also the site of acceptable social and sexual relationships, a place where people engage in pleasurable and supportive interactions and often meet potential sexual partners.

In wider debates about the changing nature of contemporary industrial societies, and its connection to new forms of social interactions between individuals and social groups, notions of both individualisation and detraditionalisation (Lash and Urry, 1994) have been developed to capture supposed changes in the significance of class, gender and racialised social divisions in both the social relations of the family and the labour market. It has been argued, for example, that labour market positions are now less determined by the structural constraints of class and gender and more by individual effort and self-design (Beck, 1992, 1994; Giddens, 1992). Lash and Urry (1994) and Bauman (1998) have noted both the shift towards labour that increasingly draws on workers' self-identity and the significance of the emotional, aesthetic and sexualised aspects of work. As Lash and Urry (1994: 4–5) suggest 'social agents are increasingly "set free" from the heteronomous control of social structures in order to be self-monitoring or self-reflexive'. However, in a critical assessment of these arguments, Adkins (2000) has argued that not only are new divisions of inequality between men and women being constructed in the new economy, but also that the so-called cultural turn by many feminist scholars may be deflecting attention from more materialist or structuralist factors in the explanation of the persistence of gender inequalities. The geographer David Harvey (2000), as well as the feminist theorist Chandra Talpade Mohanty (2003), have both argued that in the new millennium class-based and material inequalities under versions of neo-liberal capitalism are producing a more stark structure of inequality than during the long twentieth century. Furthermore, the return to an economy based on deferential service work, less regulated by trade union membership, may also reflect older patterns of economic inequality that the post-war Keynsian welfare state alleviated.

I want to end, therefore, by suggesting that theoretically the combination of materialist and discursive or cultural forms of analysis is essential. Cultural explanations of labour market change do not detract from materialist explanations but rather are an essential part of the sort of multi-perspective approach that is needed to capture the transformations of economies based on multiple forms of sexualised 'bodywork'. A materialist emphasis on the continuing significance of structural inequalities is important as class and income inequalities widen. But the discursive or cultural focus on issues of meaning and representation is also central to understanding contemporary economic change and its association with issues of sexuality, desire, reflexivity, and embodied performances in the labour market.

REFERENCES

ACKER, J, 'Hierarchies, Jobs, Bodies: A Theory of Gendered Organisations' (1990) 4 *Gender and Society* 139.

ADKINS, L and LURY, C, 'Making Bodies, Making People, Making Work' in L McKie and N Watson (ed), *Organizing Bodies: Policy, Institutions and Work* (Basingstoke, Macmillan, 2000).

AHMED, K, 'Workers' Fury as Men from the Ministry Issue 'Style Bible' (2003) *The Observer* 23 February 7.

AMIN, A (ed), *Post-Fordism: A Reader* (Oxford, Blackwell, 1994).

ANDERSON, B, *Doing the Dirty Work: The Global Politics of Domestic Labour* (London, Zed, 2000).

ARMSTRONG, S, Bodies of Opinion *Media Guardian* (1995) 6 November, p 15.

AUGER, P, *The Death of Gentlemanly Capitalism* (London, Penguin, 2001).

BAUMAN, Z, *Work, Consumerism and the New Poor* (Buckingham, Open University Press, 1998).

BECK, U, *Risk Society: Towards New Modernity* (London, Sage, 1992).

—— 'The Reinvention of Politics: Towards a Theory of Reflexive Modernisation' in U Beck, A Giddens and S Lash (eds), *Reflexive Modernisation: Politics, Tradition and Modernisation in the Modern Social Order* (Cambridge, Polity, 1994) 1.

Beck, U and Beck-Gernsheim, E, *The Normal Chaos of Love* (Cambridge, Polity, 1995).

Bourgois, P, *In Search of Respect: Selling Crack in El Barrio* (Cambridge, Cambridge University Press, 1995).

Brush, L, 'Gender, Work, who Cares?! Production, Reproduction, Deindustrialisation and Business as Usual' in MM Ferree, J Lorber and B Hess (eds), *Revisioning Gender* (London, Sage, 1999).

Butler, J, *Gender Trouble* (London, Routledge, 1990).

—— *Bodies that Matter* (London, Routledge, 1993).

Castells, M, 'Materials for an Exploratory Theory of the Network Society' (2000) 51 *British Journal of Sociology* 5.

Collinson D and Hearn J, (eds), *Men as Managers, Managers as Men: Critical Perspectives on Men, Masculinities and Managements* (London, Sage, 1996).

Connell, RW, *Masculinities* (Cambridge, Polity, 1995).

—— *The Men and the Boys* (Cambridge, Polity, 2000).

Davidoff, L and Hall, C, *Family Fortunes: Men and Women of the English Middle Class* (London, Hutchinson, 1987).

de Beauvoir, S, (in French 1949) *The Second Sex* (Harmondsworth, Penguin, 1972).

du Gay, P, *Consumption and Identity at Work* (London, Sage, 1996).

Equal Opportunities Commission, *Men and Women in the Labour Market* (Manchester, EOC, 2001).

Ferree, MM, Lorber, J and Hess, BB (eds), *Revisioning Gender* (London, Sage, 1999).

Foucault, *The History of Sexuality Volume 1: An Introduction* (London, Allen Lane, 1978).

Gardiner, J, *Gender, Care and Economics* (Basingstoke, Macmillan, 1997).

Giddens, A, *The Transformation of Intimacy: Sexuality, Love and Eroticism in Modern Societies* (Cambridge, Polity, 1992).

Grant, L, *Sexing the Millennium* (London, HarperCollins, 1993).

Gregson, N and Lowe, M, *Servicing the Middle Classes* (London, Routledge, 1994).

Halford, S, Savage, M and Witz, A, *Gender, Careers and Organisations* (Basingstoke, Macmillan, 1996).

Harvey, D, *The Condition of Postmodernity* (Oxford, Blackwell, 1989).

—— *Spaces of Hope* (Edinburgh, Edinburgh University Press, 2000).

Hochschild, A, *The Managed Heart: The Commercialisation of Human Feeling* (Berkley, University of California Press, 1983).

Johnson, MH, 'Male Medical Students and the Male Body' in A Bainham, SD Sclater and M Richards (eds), *Body Lore and Laws* (Oxford and Portland, Hart Publishing Ltd., 2002) 91.

Kanter, RM, *Men and Women of the Corporation* (New York, Basic Books, 1997).

Kondo, D, *Crafting Selves: Power, Gender and Discourses of Identity in a Japanese Workplace* (Chicago, University of Chicago Press, 1990).

Lash, S and Urry, J, *Economies of Signs and Space* (London, Sage, 1994).

Lee-Trewick, G, 'Women, Resistance and Care: an Ethnographic Study of Nursing Work' (1997) 11 *Work, Employment and Society* 47.

Leweis, M, *Liar's Poker: Two Cities, True Greed* (London, Hodder and Stoughton, 1989).

Leidner, R, *Fast Food, Fast Talk: Interactive Service Work and the Routinization of Everyday Life* (Berkeley, University of California Press, 1993).

Martin, PY and Collinson, D, 'Gender and Sexuality in Organisations' in MM Ferree, J Lorber and B Hess (eds), *Revisioning Gender* (London, Sage, 1999).

McClintock, A, *Imperial Leather: Race, Gender and Sexuality in the Colonial Context* (London, Routledge, 1994).

Macdonald, CL and Sirianni, C, (eds), *Working in the Service Sector Society* (Philadelphia, Temple University Press, 1996).

McDowell, L, 'Life without Father and Ford: the New Gender Order of Post Fordism' (1991) 16 *Transactions of the Institute of British Geographers* 400.

—— *Capital Culture: Gender at Work in the City* (Oxford, Blackwell, 1997).

—— *Redundant Masculinities? Employment Change and White Working Class Youth* (Oxford, Blackwell, 2003).

McDowell, L and Massey, D, 'A Woman's Place' in D Massey and J Allen (eds), *Geography Matters?* (Cambridge, Cambridge University Press, 1984).

Mohanty, CT, '"Under Western Eyes" Revisited: Feminist Solidarity through Anticapitalist Struggles' (2003) 28 *Signs* 499.

Newman, K, *No Shame in my Games: The Working Poor in the Inner City* (New York, Vintage Books and Russell Sage Foundation, 1999).

Pearson, A, 'Sex, Secrets and Lies' (2003) 23 February *The Observer* 21.

Pratt, G, 'Stereotypes and Ambivalence: the Construction of Domestic Workers in Vancouver, British Columbia' (1997) 4 *Gender, Place and Culture* 159.

Pringle, R, *Secretaries Talk: Sexuality, Power and Work* (London, Verso, 1988).

—— *Sex and Medicine: Gender, Power and Authority in the Medical Profession* (Cambridge, Cambridge University Press, 1988).

—— 'Sex/Sexuality' in L McDowell and J Sharp (eds), *A Feminist Glossary of Human Geography* (London, Arnold, 1999).

Romero, M, *Maid in the U.S.A.* (London, Routledge, 1992).

Shilling, C, *The Body and Social Theory* (London, Sage, 1993).

Thrift, N, Leyshon, A and Daniels, P, *'Sexy Greedy': the New International Financial System, the City of London and the South East of England* (University of Bristol Department of Geography, Working Papers in Producer Services 8, 1987).

Treanor, J, 'Furse Hits Back at "Frivolous" Media' (2003) 27 February *The Guardian* 26.

Ungerson, C, *Policy is Personal: Sex, Gender and Informal care* (London, Tavistock, 1987).

Walby, S and Greenwell, J, *Medicine and Nursing: Professions in a Changing Health Service* (London, Sage, 1994).

Walkowitz, C, 'The Social Relations of Body Work' (2002) 16 *Work, Employment and Society* 497.

Westwood, S, *All Day, Every Day* (London, Pluto, 1984).

Witz, A, Halford, S and Savage, M, 'Organised Bodies: Gender, Sexuality and Embodiment in Contemporary Organisations' in L Adkins and V Merchant (eds), *Sexualising the Social: Power and the Organisation of Sexuality* (Basingstoke, Macmillan, 1996).

Wolfe, T, *The Bonfire of the Vanities* (London, Jonathon Cape, 1988).

Young, IM, *Justice and the Politics of Difference* (Princeton, Princeton University Press, 1990).

6

Sexuality and Same-Sex Relationships in Law

CRAIG LIND[1]

1. INTRODUCTION

The Nature of 'Relationships'

WHEN YOU READ the phrase 'same-sex relationships' of what do you think? What do you imagine will be the subject under discussion? Do you think of friendship? Or do you think of regular sexual partners? Do you think of relationships involving a particular number of people; are only couples in your contemplation? Is home sharing necessary? Do you include the same-sex liaisons of those who have other significant, possibly even formal, relationships (marriage, for example)? In sum, do you think of any of the great variety of relationships into which same-sex sexual desire leads people? Or has your mind been directed to a narrow band of relationships? Do you avoid thinking of some sexual liaisons as 'relationships'?

I imagine we enter into a subject like this with the expectation of a discussion of 'civil partnership' and 'marriage'. And I intend to meet that expectation. But, at the same time, I would like us to keep in mind the questions posed in this opening. While the phrase 'same-sex relationship' conjures up an image of same-sex couples we should not simply assume that that is all we ought to discuss. It is clear that at least some people would have us discuss something else entirely; some would have us examine the alleged incapacity of same-sex desire to ground stable relationships because of the notorious 'promiscuity' of gay men (Green 1992); others, taking a more positive view of similar empirical information, would prefer us to consider relationships that would challenge social conventions (so, for example, non-monogamous relationships, or non-sexual relationships that are more significant for the partners than their sexual encounters are, or communal sexual relationships (Lehr, 1999)).

[1] I am particularly grateful to the participants at the Sexuality Seminar in Cambridge in March 2003. I would also like to express my gratitude to Conor Butler, Emily Haslam, Rod Edmunds, Gerry Cross, Anthony Manion, Pierre Du Plessis, Otto De Jager and Peter Bocetti (amongst many others) for allowing me to use them to test my thinking on the issues raised in this essay.

While we contemplate couple relationships in this chapter I would like us to be perpetually aware of the fact that we do not reflect on these relationships free from cultural constraints. We think of them in the way we are taught to think of them. And in relation to sexuality the law, like the society it serves, focuses on the adult couple relationships that are, in our tradition, generally acknowledged in society and regulated by the state.

Same-Sex Sexuality and the Problems of Relationship Recognition

This introduction is intended to be provocative because, in the course of this chapter I also want to consider the potential that same-sex relationships may have to transform family relationships and their social and legal regulation. I will, therefore, start by considering, in outline, the ways in which same-sex relationships are recognised in the legal rules that serve as the parameters of family law. I will go on to consider the extent to which I believe those rules to be appropriate in their allocation of rights to same-sex partners. In doing so I will introduce arguments that serve to undermine any attempt to allow same-sex sexuality to serve as a justification for unequal or unfairly discriminatory treatment. The growing acceptance of people with alternative sexualities in our societies will be important considerations in this chapter. My underlying position will be that same-sex couples should be entitled to exactly the same rights as different-sex couples in the regulation of their relationships.

The chapter will, however, go on to question the way in which relationships are regulated in our society. It will question the political wisdom of fighting for relationship recognition equal to heterosexual relationship recognition where that regulation is itself under attack. In this respect the regulation of adult family life itself will be considered and arguments about the potential that same-sex relationship recognition has to transform different-sex relationship patterns will be questioned. My argument will ultimately be that, while transformative potential exists, claims made for it are vastly exaggerated and often optimistically misdirected. Their consequences are unlikely, I will argue, to be anything like the consequences predicted for them. This conclusion will, I hope, be both sobering and inspiring.

2. SAME-SEX RELATIONSHIP REGULATION IN ENGLAND AND WALES

I will start, then, with a consideration of the progress that has been made to bring same-sex relationships into the realms of legal regulation. I do not intend to deal with the detail of statute and case law[2] but with its broad scope. My aim

---

[2] For more detailed analyses of the legal position of same-sex family relationships see Bailey-Harris (2001) and Barlow *et al*, (1999).

is to consider trends in the regulation of adult family life. In the course of this discussion I intend to reflect on the direction being taken in the regulation of same-sex relationships (as well as the relationships of people of different sexes) and to consider the kinds of argument that are put forward to convince us that a particular kind of regulation is to be recommended.

It has only really been in the last decade that same-sex relationships have been attracting legal regulation in England and Wales. Initially that regulation took quite subtle forms; the Family Law Act 1996, for example, included protection from domestic violence for 'spouses', 'cohabitants' (defined heterosexually)[3] and 'associated persons' (defined widely enough to encompass same-sex couples).[4] Positive regulation was also less generous to same-sex couples than to different-sex couples; after an amendment in 1995 the Inheritance (Provision for Family and Dependants) Act 1975,[5] for example, effectively allowed a same-sex partner to make a claim against the estate of her deceased partner but only if dependence immediately prior to death was established;[6] different-sex couples were only required to prove cohabitation with the deceased to succeed in a similar claim.[7] A tiered system of family regulation began to emerge which favoured marriage over heterosexual cohabitation and heterosexual cohabitation over homosexual cohabitation (Lind & Barlow, 1996; Bailey-Harris, 2001). Of course, the absence of recognition in family law did not always act to the detriment of same-sex couples. So, for example, because their relationships were not recognised in law, same-sex couples were (and remain) 'individuals' for the purposes of the calculation of their social security benefits. Those benefits which are reduced for married and cohabiting couples (by virtue of an 'aggregation' rule which acknowledges that living in one household is more economical than living in two) are unaffected in same-sex households.[8]

This hierarchy of relationship recognition was reinforced in the House of Lords in *Fitzpatrick v Sterling Housing Association Ltd*.[9] In that case the majority of their Lordships held that the same-sex partner of the deceased could be treated as a member of his family for the purposes of inheriting an assured tenancy under the Rent Act 1977.[10] However, the gender specific definition of

---

[3] Family Law Act 1996, s 62(1)(a).

[4] Family Law Act 1996, s 62(3); the definition includes a wide variety of people who share or have shared a home, or are or were related as spouses or (different-sex) cohabitants.

[5] s1(1)(ba) and (1A) (as amended by the Law Reform (Succession) Act 1995). See too the Fatal Accidents Act 1976, s 1(3)(b).

[6] See too the Rent Act 1977, sch 1, paras 1–3, *Harrogate BC v Simpson* [1986] 2 FLR 91, and Barlow (2001) p.50. The interpretation of the Rent Act 1977 has already been revised (because of the Human Rights Act 1998): *Mendoza v Ghaidan* [2002] All ER (D) 32, discussed below. Further revision of statutory law is, therefore, likely.

[7] Above note 4. See too ss 30–8, Family Law Act 1996.

[8] Social Security Contributions and Benefits Act 1992, s 137(1) (and s 74A(5)); see Hale *et al* (2002) p 119, and Barlow, 2001, p 85. See too Taxation of Chargeable Gains Act 1992, s 222 and Women and Equality Unit 2003 p 40.

[9] [1999] 4 All E.R. 705.

[10] sch 1, para. 3.

spouse in the statute—requiring a person to be either an actual spouse or 'living with the original tenant as his or her wife or husband'[11]—prevented him from inheriting the more generous statutory tenancy of the home. The relevant section was, the court held, incapable of a non-gendered definition. As such, same-sex couples could not be brought within its terms. They were, therefore, entitled to a lesser title by inheritance than were their different-sex counterparts.

Although this difference in treatment was beginning to be considered to be unacceptably discriminatory under the European Convention on Human Rights (the Convention),[12] British courts had, at that stage, no inherent power to apply the Convention. They could use it as an aid to statutory interpretation but not to avoid a meaning that clearly contravened the Convention.[13] However, once the Human Rights Act 1998 came into effect that would change. The court would be a public body obliged to apply the Convention unless primary legislation clearly prevented it from doing so.[14] And at least one of the Law Lords in *Fitzpatrick* speculated that the issue which arose in that case might have to be revisited once the Human Rights Act 1998 was in force.[15]

The opportunity to reconsider the House of Lords decision in the Human Rights Act era arose when *Mendoza v Ghaidan*[16] came before the English courts. While the trial judge took the view that he had to follow *Fitzpatrick* and that the Human Rights Act 1998 did not require him to revise that opinion,[17] the Court of Appeal unanimously took a different view. It held that, as a public body obliged to interpret legislation to comply with the Convention, it could widen the scope of the phrase used in the schedule to include a same-sex partner.[18] Thus where Mr Fitzpatrick was only able to inherit an assured tenancy, Mr Mendoza could inherit the more generous statutory tenancy of his partner's flat.

In the aftermath of this decision the hierarchy of relationship recognition in English and Welsh law is likely to begin to wane. However, there are some statutes that can bear no alternative interpretation without legislative amendment. Section 62(1)(a) of the Family Law Act 1996, for example, defines cohabitants as 'a man and a woman who, although not married to each other, are living together as husband and wife'. That section cannot, it is submitted, be extended to a man and a man or a woman and a woman who are 'living together as husband and wife' (in the gender neutral era ushered in by *Mendoza*). Thus, the hierarchy of treatment under that statute (and others like it) will remain

---

[11] Rent Act 1977, sch 1, para 2(1) and (2).

[12] See *Salgueiro da Silva Mouta v Portugal* [2001] 1 FCR 653. Cf *Frette v France* [2003] 2 FLR 9.

[13] See *R v Secretary of State for the Home Department, ex parte Brind* (1991) 1 All ER 720.

[14] Human Rights Act 1998, s 3.

[15] Per Lord Slynn of Hadley: 'Whether that result is discriminatory against same-sex couples in the light of the fact that non-married different-sex couples living together are to be treated as spouses so as to allow one to succeed to the tenancy of the other may have to be considered when the Human Rights Act 1998 is in force.'

[16] [2002] All E.R. (D) 32.

[17] *Ibid*, para 4.

[18] *Ibid*, paras 34–5.

intact until the specific legislative traces of explicit discrimination are removed by parliament.[19]

Two recent developments might, however, induce us to believe that a transformation of all discriminatory legislation is soon to occur. In the first instance Parliament has begun to be more unequivocal in its allocation of family rights to same-sex couples; the Adoption and Children Act 2002, for example, made explicit provision for same-sex couple adoption.[20] In the second place, despite having expressed serious reservations about recognising same-sex marriage,[21] the government has begun to address the issue of recognising an alternative form of formalised same-sex relationships. The Women and Equality Unit[22] announced that it would consult on a system of partnership registration[23] which would make accessible to same-sex couples many of the benefits which are currently beyond their power to adopt.[24] One of the distinguishing features of the consultation document was that it proposed a system of registration available exclusively to same-sex couples. If adopted, the system will be a simple same-sex alternative to different-sex marriage. Unmarried and unregistered cohabitation will remain beyond the bounds of formal regulation. If the proposals do become law a different hierarchy of relationship regulation will emerge. At its apex will be heterosexual marriage. Next in that hierarchy will be the registered civil partnerships of same-sex couples. This will be followed by different-sex cohabitation and then same-sex cohabitation.

This proposed hierarchy of regulation is not unusual.[25] A number of (western) jurisdictions have set up systems for the formal recognition and regulation of same-sex relationships. Some have done so by statute;[26] others have done so because of an interpretation given to statutory language by the courts.[27] Two

---

[19] See the Human Rights Act 1998, s 3: legislation can only be read to comply with the European Convention on Human Rights 'so far as it is possible to do so'.

[20] Couples may adopt if they either are married or are 'two people (whether of different-sexes or the same-sex) living as partners in an enduring family relationship': s 144(4), Adoption and Children Act 2002. The Act also explicitly contemplates same-sex couple adoption in section 68(3). See too the Adults with Incapacities (Scotland) Act 2000 (2000 asp 4), s 87(2) amending the definition of 'nearest relative' in the Mental Health (Scotland) Act 1984 to include same sex couples. For more on Scotland see Norrie (2001).

[21] See the answer given by Jack Straw (then home secretary) to a question by Stuart Bell on 25 June 1999 (Hansard, volume 324, column 22) giving an assurance that no legislation suggesting an acceptance of homosexual marriage would be proposed by the Government; See too Lobby Briefing, 11.00am, Friday, 2 November 2001(http://www.pm.gov.uk/output/page2350.asp) and Woman and Equality Unit (2003) para 1.3.

[22] Situated within the Department of Trade and Industry.

[23] Woman and Equality Unit (2003).

[24] These include state ordered material and non-material advantages: for some examples, see the Inheritance Taxes Act 1984, ss 18, and 22, the Taxation of Chargeable Gains Act 1992, s 58, and the British Nationality Act 1981, s 6(2) and Sch 1, para 3. Something like the divorce jurisdiction of the courts (operated under the Matrimonial Causes Act 1973) would also be accessible to same-sex registered partners under this scheme.

[25] See Woman and Equality Unit (2003), p 15–16.

[26] See notes 27–34 below.

[27] See, for example, in Ontario, Canada: *M v H* [1999] 2 S.C.R. 3, and in South Africa: *NCGLE v. Minister of Home Affairs* 2000 (2) SA 1.

broad approaches have been adopted. One establishes a system of partnership registration for same-sex couples which serves as an alternative to marriage (sometimes exclusively for same-sex couples and sometimes open to different-sex couples as well[28]). The system of recognition which distinguishes same-sex registered relationships from marriage, even when different sex couples are admitted to the alternative registration system, accepts the hierarchical approach to the status of family relationships. In 1989 Denmark became the first jurisdiction to adopt such a system,[29] followed by most of the Scandinavian countries,[30] many other European countries,[31] and some North American jurisdictions.[32]

The alternative system of relationship regulation does not impose that hierarchy between heterosexual and homosexual relationship recognition. It simply admits same-sex couples to the institution of state regulated marriage. At present the Netherlands[33] and Belgium[34] are the only two jurisdictions to have done so legislatively. Canada appears to have achieved the same end by virtue of Court decisions.[35] Hawaii and Vermont, in the USA, came close to achieving a similar result before the courts in the 1990s,[36] but subsequent legislative intervention which set up alternative systems of civil registration ended progress towards the simple recognition of same-sex marriage.[37]

[28] See Woman and Equality Unit (2003), pp 15–16.

[29] Law on Registered Partnership, No 372, 7 June 1989.

[30] Norway (Law on Registered Partnership, No 40, 30 April 1993); Sweden (Law on Registered Partnership, 23 June 1994 (SFS 1994:1117)); and Iceland (Law on Confirmed Cohabitation, No 87, 12 June 1996). For texts of these statutes see: http://www.france.qrd.org/texts/partnership/. See too Wintemute and Andenaes (2001), Appendix I and Woman and Equality Unit (2003), pp 15–16.

[31] See, for example, France (Loi no. 99–944 du 15 novembre 1999 relative au pacte civil de solidarité), Germany (Law of 16 February 2001 on Ending Discrimination Against Same-Sex Communities: Life Partnerships), Hungary (Civil Code, Article 685/A (amended by Act No. 42 of 1996)), and the Netherlands (Act of 5 July 1997 amending Book 1 of the Civil Code and the Code of Civil Procedure, concerning the introduction therein of provisions relating to registered partnership, Staatsblad 1997, no 324): see Wintemute and Andenaes (2001), Appendix I and Woman and Equality Unit (2003), pp 15–16.

[32] See, for example, California (Cal.Statutes (Stat.) 1999, ch. 588), Hawaii (Hawaii Revised Stat. (eg. S. 572C-4 (1997)), and Vermont (An Act Relating to Civil Unions, 2000 Vermont Stat. No 91 (26 April 2000)): see Wintemute and Andenaes, 2001, Appendix I and Woman and Equality Unit, 2003, pp 15–16.

[33] Act of 21 December 2000 amending Book 1 of the Civil Code, concerning the opening up of marriage for persons of the same-sex (Act on the Opening Up of Marriage), Staatsblad 2001, no 9.

[34] The Law of 13 February 2003 opening marriage up to persons of the same sex (and modifying some provisions of the Civil Code) was published in French on 28 February 2003 in the Moniteur belge, 3ed, p 9880 (http://www.moniteur.be/index_fr.htm), and came into force on 1 June 2003. I am grateful to Robert Wintemute for this reference.

[35] The most recent was *Halpern et al v. Attorney General of Canada* (File: C39172 and C39174)(decided 10 June 2003); The Canadian Government responded to that decision by announcing that it would bring forward legislation by the autumn of 2003 to recognise same-sex unions in a way that deals with the concerns of the courts. See the statement by the Canadian Prime Minister, Jean Chrétien (17 June 2003): http://pm.gc.ca/default.asp?Language=E&Page=newsroom&Sub= newsreleases&Doc=samesexunions.20030617_e.htm (and reported on BBC News, 'Canada Pushes Gay Marriage' at http://news.bbc.co.uk/1/hi/world/americas/2999270.stm (17 June 2003).

[36] See *Baehr* v. *Lewin* 852 P.2d 44 (Hawaii Supreme Ct, 1993), *Baehr v Miike* 910 P2d 112 (Hawaii Circuit Ct., 1996), and *Baker v Vermont* 170 Vt. 194; 744 A.2d 864 (Vermont Supreme Court, 1999).

[37] See Wolfson (2001) and Bonauto (2001).

The British government's approach is the less dramatic of these two. It intends to allow for the registration of same-sex relationships, but without attributing legal recognition to same-sex marriages. There appears to be no reason to believe that that ambition will not be achieved within a fairly short space of time. A civil registration regime, operating as an alternative to marriage for same-sex couples, is likely to be operating in the United Kingdom before very long.[38]

The overall impression created by this state of affairs is that, while same-sex couples have made considerable progress towards achieving state recognition for their relationships in the United Kingdom, that progress has not yielded—and seems unlikely, in the foreseeable future, to yield—complete parity of treatment with different-sex couples.[39] Furthermore, there are many more states in the world in which prejudice against same-sex desire remains rampant (Hoad, 1998; Lind, 2001) and in which recognition of same-sex relationships is 'still a prize perhaps not yet even open for discussion' (Cameron, 2001). For that reason there is still much to work for. Lesbian and gay political activists around the world have been engaged in this challenge for some time.[40] As with most gains made by those with same-sex sexual desire in the last half century the underlying political plea is for equal treatment, a particularly powerful mantra in the aftermath of the civil rights campaigns which sought appropriate rights for women and minority races during the course of the last century.[41]

3. EQUALITY?

The argument for equal treatment is deceptively, and appealingly, simple. A plea that one person should be allowed to do what another can do is easily understood and, in the age of democracy, popularly embraced. Furthermore, the abolition of the prohibition of mixed race marriages by the US Supreme Court in *Loving v Virginia*[42] has made a parallel assertion based on sexuality difficult to deny. Allowing all people to marry provided they choose a partner of the appropriate sex or race raises suspicion in an age of equality. Separate but equal is not a version of the equality principle that has much political credibility anymore. In an era in which alternative sexualities are much more openly tolerated[43] a plea for equal family recognition seems much more likely to

---

[38] See Women and Equality Unit, 2003.

[39] See Women and Equality Unit, 2003 para 1.3: 'It is a matter of public record that the Government has no plans to introduce same-sex marriage'.

[40] Court based challenges to the exclusion of same-sex relationships from marriage regulation can be traced at least as far back as *Baker v Nelson* 191 N.W.2d 185 (Minn. 1971); (appeal dismissed: 409 U.S. 810 (1972)).

[41] See, for example, Vaid (1995), and Wintemute (2001) at p 2.

[42] 388 U.S. 1 (1967).

[43] See 'Gay couples "to get equal rights"', Friday, 6 December 2002 (BBC News): http:/news.bbc.co.uk/1/hi/uk_politics/2548321.stm and 'Britons support unmarried couples' (BBC News, Panorama): http:/news.bbc.co.uk/1/hi/programmes/panorama/2504815.stm.

succeed.[44] Indeed, as I have already noted, much has happened which indicates that success is being achieved. And, on the basis of this reading of the politics of equality, progress directed towards achieving same-sex marriage and full equality between heterosexual and homosexual cohabitation seems inevitable. But some words of caution should be sounded.

At the outset it as well to acknowledge that equality is not a simple concept. It does not demand simply that people should be allowed to do precisely what others can do. It is both subtler and more seductive than that. In Aristotelian thinking we are required to treat equally situated people in the same way (equally), but are also permitted (and sometimes required) to treat differently situated people differently (unequally) (Cachalia *et al.*, 1994; Bridgeman and Millns, 1998). The latter possibility—that unalike people should be treated differently—complicates any discussion of equality. It allows opponents of any activity being promoted on the basis of equality to claim that the differential treatment at issue is justified by some difference between those claiming the privilege and those who already enjoy it. Thus the absence of same-sex family recognition may be justified in the face of arguments for equality; same-sex couples may legitimately be excluded from marriage because their difference from different-sex couples excuses differential treatment. The justifications might call into play the essentially heterosexual purposes, traditions, and social roles protected by the institution of marriage (Norrie, 2000). This argument has managed to keep family regulation in the United Kingdom almost exclusively heterosexual for some time.

Despite the fact that the exclusivity of heterosexual family regulation is waning, the 'difference' argument remains influential. States that have successfully brought same-sex couples into the realms of legal family regulation began, without exception, by creating alternatives to marriage for same-sex couples. They did not—and most continue not to—admit same-sex couples to the institution of marriage itself.[45] The alternatives provide some protection to same-sex couples without undermining the heteronormative nature of marriage and of family law more generally.

This approach has not been universally decried, even in the realms of homosexual writing (Norrie, 2000). The problem is that there are differences between same-sex couples and opposite sex couples, which arise out of the social norms

---

[44] Some have argued (convincingly, it is submitted) that failure to allow lesbians and gay men to do what straight people can do is a simple breach of the principle of sexual equality (Pannick, 1985, especially in ch 8; Koppelman, 1988, Capers, 1991, Wintemute, 1994, especially at p 497). If a woman loses a privilege or benefit—as in *Grant v South Western Trains* [1998] 3 BHRC 578—because she has chosen a female sexual partner her complaint is that she is being denied that benefit because she is a woman. Had she been a man (choosing a female sexual partner) the benefit would have been extended to her. Although the discrimination might also be categorised as discrimination on the grounds of 'sexual orientation' (see *Salgueiro da Silva Mouta v Portugal* [2001] 1 FCR 653), it is, in this view, a simple matter of sex discrimination, against which discrimination there is already legislation (the Sex Discrimination Act 1975 and the Equal Pay Act 1970).

[45] Only the Netherlands, Belgium and (perhaps) Canada have admitted same-sex couples to marriage. See above.

into which people have been raised. These revolve, largely, around the fact that we live gendered social existences (Gilligan, 1982). A number of reasons have been given for the protection that heterosexual relationships enjoy in law (and in other socially regulatory phenomena) (Wardle, 1998). It is self evident that legal regulation has a material impact upon family stability; it is easier to get into marriage than out of it. Family life is, therefore, under state pressure to be stable. Given the empirically established benefits to children of family stability (Rodgers and Pryor, 1998; Cherlin *et al.*,1991) this aim is not only laudable, but one which a society may legitimately foster. Given the fact that the heterosexual family is much more likely to raise children it is much more likely to need closer state regulation (Wardle, 1998, Norrie, 2000). Different rules are therefore, it is argued, appropriate.

Another related justification relates to the property of individuals within couple relationships. Encouraging spouses to share property—by creating mutual ownership, or by allowing for a structure of redistribution at the end of the relationship—is profoundly important. In the past the ownership of property maintained the dependence of women on men, and discouraged *de facto* divorce (the law prohibited *de jure* divorce). Nowadays, the aim is more salutary. It allows economically unrewarding (or underrewarding) child rearing work to be compensated by a share in the property of one who has not had to take the economic risk of raising children (as women most frequently are under social pressure to do) (Maidment, 1985). If men are likely to maintain wealth and women to lose it in the socially productive enterprise of producing future generations of society, the capacity to control property distribution during and after a relationship is as much the state's business as it is the business of the individuals in relationships. Once again, this is much more likely to be problematic in heterosexual relationships—where gendered roles are important—than in same sex relationships. And once again differential treatment is argued to be justified (Norrie, 2000).

In both cases it is clear that the heteronormative assumptions of marriage regulation are not entirely unfounded. Same-sex couples do not have the capacity (or at least an easy capacity) to reproduce, and property differentials in their relationships are rarely as pronounced as they are in heterosexual relationships. In these circumstances it appears relatively easy to argue that differential treatment—which is 'equal treatment' in Aristotelian terms—is justifiable (Norrie, 2000).

However, the increasing capacity of same-sex couples to have and to raise children undermines this argument (Arnup and Boyd, 1995; Gavigan, 1995). Furthermore, generalising these differences to the lives of people for whom the differences do not actually exist makes an absolute rule against accessibility to family regulation unacceptable.[46] Rigidity sits uncomfortably with family

---

[46] See, for example, the facts of *Fitzpatrick v Sterling HA* [1999] 2 FLR 1027 for an instance in which the fact of dependence is established for good (traditional) family reasons: one partner gives up work to care for the other when he is too ill to look after himself.

regulation. It imports a socially unchanging ideal of equality into lives which are almost always more complex than a generalisation can capture. The exclusion of same-sex couples from the same regulation covering different-sex relationships cannot therefore be adequately justified.

Another historical transformation makes it even more difficult to argue that a different, parallel form of regulation is enough to create equality. The 'separate-but-equal' experiments, particularly in the US[47] and South Africa[48] in the context of racial segregation, ended in ignominy. Although the equality principle permits differential treatment, that difference in treatment still requires proper rationalisation. The difference (or exclusion from similar treatment) must serve, in the phrase of American jurisprudence, 'a compelling state interest'.[49] Furthermore, the difference must be in proportion to the difference that is displayed between individuals. Thus the difference between homosexual and heterosexual identity and behaviour may allow for different treatment but only to the extent that it is necessary to maintain the equal dignity of each.[50] The result is that the difference in treatment should extend only so far as to honour the differences between people. It should not prejudice them. Homosexuals should be able to choose same-sex partners where heterosexuals choose different-sex partners, and the consequences should, except for that difference, be the same for both (Lind, 1995). Same-sex marriage—and every other kind of equal recognition of same-sex couples—becomes inevitable. Anything less would not be equal treatment.

At the political level the power of the equality argument, and the end of 'separate-but-equal' varieties of it, seem destined to succeed in establishing legal parity for same-sex couples in family relationships. Its simplicity, in an era of growing tolerance, is incredibly attractive. This prognosis is bolstered by the fact that political progress in this respect replicates much early work on women's equality (Wilson and Sachs, 1978). People are easily able to think—formalistically—that women's equality is achieved by giving women access to what men can do. Formal equality seems still to be the most readily understood conception of the ideal of equality. In the context of sexuality and family regulation, allowing same-sex couples access to the privileges enjoyed by different-sex couples seems as easily to achieve their equality.

But achieving formal equality in these terms must, it is submitted, be subject to careful scrutiny. Will admission to marriage and other forms of heterosexual family regulation enhance the 'real' equality of lesbians and gay men? For decades a debate has raged on the appropriateness of seeking formal equality in

---

[47] Finally abolished by the US Supreme Court in *Brown v Board of Education of Topeka* 347 US 483 (1954).

[48] See *R v Carlese* 1943 CPD 242 and *R v Abdurahman* 1950 (3) SA 136 (A). The doctrine finally ended (in law) when the Constitution of the Republic of South Africa Act 200 of 1993 came into effect in 1994.

[49] See *Baehr* v. *Lewin* 852 P.2d 44 (Hawaii Supreme Ct, 1993).

[50] See Ackermann, J in *National Coalition Gay and Lesbian Equality v Minister of Home Affairs* 2000 (2) SA 1 (Constitutional Court) 1.

these terms (Stoddard, 1992; Wolfson, 1994; Hunter, 1991; Duclos, 1991; Polikoff, 1993; Ettelbrick, 1992; Eskridge, 2001; Boswell, 1996; Sullivan, 1996). While formal equality is easily conceived as an appropriate subject for political lobbying[51] the extent to which equality will be achieved in the real lives of the people for whom it is being sought remains to be measured and assessed. And much scepticism has been expressed on the likelihood of success (Ettelbrick, 1992, Polikoff, 1993). That scepticism has given rise to a considerable body of socio-theoretical debate about the world which is being created by the pursuit of the legal recognition of same-sex couples (Cooper, 2001; Eskridge, 2001; Halley, 2001; Polikoff, 1993; Ettelbrick, 1992). Many remain unconvinced that the struggle currently being fought will, in the end, have been worth it.

4. FORMAL VERSUS REAL EQUALITY

A different notion of equality begins to emerge in the debate that moves from the formal to the 'real'. And once again the debate that surrounds it is not unlike the debate that occupies those who write about the equality of women (Fineman, 2000; Fineman, 1991; Bridgeman, and Millns 1998; Naffine, 1990; Smart, 1995). For some time women have been living in a world that formally acknowledges their equality.[52] And yet profound disquiet continues to be expressed about the real inequalities that continue to dog the lives of women (MacKinnon, 1989; Smart, 1995; McDowell, this volume). The significant question which arises is: why is it that, while women have formal rights to equal treatment, they are still badly paid and unlikely to rise above certain positions in business and government? Why is it that a 'glass ceiling' seems to prevent women from reaching the heights of success apparently so easily attained by men? [53] The real experience of equality appears to give the lie to claims that because formal equality is legally (and even politically) protected equality is actually achieved.

Feminist scholars have offered sophisticated explanations for the failure to achieve real equality for women. The most convincing reasons assert not simply that men have power and favour men in distributing the benefits of society, but also that the structures and institutions of society are themselves masculine in nature; the standard of successful conduct in society is determined by male norms (Smart, 1995; O'Donovan, 1993; MacKinnon, 1987). Culture itself is patriarchal. In fostering a better world, societies promote idealised qualities in

---

[51] See, for example, the Equality Project (http://www.equality.org.za), the organisation in South Africa that is lobbying to achieve 'equal' recognition of same-sex relationships.

[52] In Britain at least since the Equal Pay Act 1970 and the Sex Discrimination Act 1975.

[53] See 'ILO Director-General Takes aim at "Glass Ceiling" Commits Organisation to Gender Equality in Workplace' (Thursday 8 March 2001) *(ILO/01/08)*, http:/www.ilo.org/public/english/region/ampro/cinterfor/temas/gender/doc/press/glass.htm; and 'Breaking through the glass ceiling: Women in management' (International Labour Organisation) at http:/www.ilo.org/public/english/dialogue/sector/techmeet/tmwm97/tmwm-con.htm

their citizens. The ideals of better living are inscribed with values. These values, it is argued, promote the qualities of men over those of women. In the words of Catharine MacKinnon, '[g]ender neutrality is . . . simply the male standard' (1987: 34) (see too Smith, 1993, Loenen, 1995). That standard is replicated in members of society and is inculcated in them by a thorough process of socialisation.

The family is one of the prime sites performing the work of inscribing masculine and feminine qualities in people (Gilligan, 1982). Families—whether founded on marriage or on unmarried cohabitation—are, it is argued, largely responsible for the disempowerment of women (Fineman, 2000, Smart, 1989a, O'Donovan, 1993). Structurally they encourage women to be financially dependent on men. By fostering the social perception that mothers are better childminders than men, they foster work practices that privilege men's work in the economy over women's work in the family (Smart, 1989b, Olsen, 1983). The family becomes the social prison of women (Fineman, 2000). It is a deeply flawed institution where the ideal of equal citizenship is perpetually undermined (but cf. Wardle, 1998). Pursuing equality through it is, therefore, an inherently flawed project (O'Donovan, 1985). Furthermore, state regulation of the institutions of the family has done little to undermine the continuing subordination of women (McKinnon, 1987; Smart, 1995). Even notionally progressive changes for women—child custody wins by women—have negative consequences for the structure of women's cultural lives (enhancing, as they do, the gendered division of labour) (Carbone, 1996; Watson, 1990; Smart, 1989b).

But how is this relevant to same-sex sexuality and the debate on the legal regulation of same-sex couples? Although the answer is fairly obvious there are some who remain sceptical of its importance. And yet ignoring the lessons of feminism in relation to the problems of relationship regulation is, it is submitted, to enter into a social world blinded by the false promise of equality (Polikoff, 1993; 2000; Fuss 1989). The politics of the lesbian and gay fight for equality—particularly in the context of relationship recognition—is infused with the problems of equality that have been identified by feminist scholars. Those problems revolve around the inherent inequality within the family. In circumstances where feminists would have the family transformed, it seems odd that same sex couples should seek entry to it. We have to wonder whether or not family regulation of same sex relationships will open the doors to the privileges of family life? Will legal regulation bring with it the full benefits of a heteronormative life?

5. SAME-SEX RELATIONSHIPS AND THE TRANSFORMATION OF FAMILY LIFE?

The overarching problem for those who seek legal recognition of same-sex families is that legal (and even political) recognition may not bring with it the full enjoyment of social recognition. 'Normal' family life is unlikely to flow from legal recognition. As feminism has demonstrated, formal and substantial equality are not the same thing. In the way that successful women are often successful *women*, same-sex couples might become *same-sex* cohabitants or *same-sex* spouses. Many—if not most people—will not perceive their relationships to be 'real'. In the words of section 28 of the Local Government Act 1988, they will be 'pretended families'. The binary distinction between same-sex and different-sex families will remain intact. Some might even say that it will be enhanced by having a clearer definition; there will be marriage set against *gay* marriage (Weeks, this volume). Same-sex couples will become simply outsiders within the institutions of family regulation.

But some might argue that that is enough: in the longer term real equality will be achieved. Eventually we will fail to notice the gender of the parties to relationships and a transformed relationship norm will emerge. Same-sex and different-sex couples will begin to live reshaped lives (Eskridge, 2001).

The Radical Critique of Marriage and the Problems of Expanding Access to It

While some kind of transformation seems inevitable (Golombok and Tasker, 1997) we cannot simply assume, however, that the egalitarian ambitions of most feminists will be achieved. Our concern must be with whether or not the new norm of relationships will embrace all kinds of couples? Will the heteronormative family be able to adapt itself to accept diverse family relationships? Once again the feminist analogy is instructive. Do we want a world in which women must perform like men in order to succeed? Or should the qualifications for success themselves be transformed (MacKinnon, 1989)? In the context of same-sex couples, should same-sex couples pursue the normative relationships of heterosexual marriage and cohabitation, or should relationships with a different fundamental ethic be pursued (Lehr, 1999; Cooper, 2001)? The important political question is simply whether or not it is appropriate to aspire to a norm which is inscribed with characteristics over which one group has had no influence or control. Is the resulting norm not always more likely to suit the group for whom it was created than any other group to whom access is extended?

The most fundamental critique of the political project of winning same-sex family recognition, then, concerns the nature of family relationships and the prognosis for same-sex sexuality and the notion of equality should that political project succeed (see, in particular: Halley, 2001; Cooper, 2001; Lehr, 1999; Polifoff, 1993; Ettelbrick, 1992; Herman, 1990). We will examine that critique more closely and then go on to consider two kinds of responses to it.

The critique raises a number of concerns. One focuses on what effect the legal regulation of same-sex relationships will have on the construction of sexuality itself. There is a concern that sexuality will become more sanitised once same-sex families are regulated like different-sex families (Lehr, 1999). The fluidity and diversity of sexuality will be undermined. Legal regulation will normalise certain kinds of sexualised (and socialised) conduct. It will, in effect, create a new policing regime which will attempt to assert regulatory control over the ambit of appropriate sexual behaviour. The scope of freedom will, in this way, be narrowed rather than broadened. The response, it is argued, should therefore be to avoid a political struggle that will tend to undermine an ethic of social diversity (Cooper, 2001). Diversity, it is argued, should not be sacrificed on the altar of assimilation, particularly where assimilation is to an institution which prejudices a greater number than those who seek access to it (Polikoff, 1993). The result would be that a very narrow range of same-sex sexual conduct would be condoned (and then not fully). Put simply, the norm would expand but it would settle to reveal a new binary division between the new norm and the new outsider. In achieving this end, new parameters of control will be established to tame sexual desire and to sanitise same-sex sexual conduct for a world which would prefer that it did not exist.

Furthermore, the social structures which maintain power imbalances (based, in particular, on gender, but also on class, race, geographical location, etc.) will not be appropriately challenged by a strategy which seeks simple inclusion of same sex couples in a ready made social institution (Cooper, 2001). Admission to the powerful social and legal institutions of the family is more likely to transform individual relationships than to be transformed by them. And the transformation of individual life will bring a greater number of people into institutions which are argued to be deeply inegalitarian (Herman, 1992; Ettelbrick, 1992).

The two most general responses to these concerns might be called respectively conservative and liberal.

i. The conservative response

For some (see, in particular, Sullivan, 1996), what distinguishes people with same-sex desire from those with different-sex desire is only their desire. In all other respects lesbians and gay men are 'normal'. Furthermore, their identity is perceived as immutable.[54] And inequality arising out of an immutable, unchosen, characteristic, it is argued, is unjust. The argument goes on to assert that society could easily remedy that inequality by extending the privileges of the majority to the minority. Sexuality should be an irrelevant consideration in legal regulation; in the regulation of family relationships, for example, lesbians and gay men should be able to attract exactly the same legal regulation as different-

---

[54] Even people who believe in the socially constitutive notion of identity acknowledge that it does have an element of immutability about it: see Weeks (1991: 84): '. . . most individuals do not feel "polymorphously perverse". On the contrary they feel their sexual desires are fairly narrowly organised, whatever use they make of those identities in real life. Moreover, a social identity is no less real for being historically formed. Sexual identities are no longer arbitrary divisions of the field of possibilities; they are encoded in a complex web of social practices—legal, pedagogic, medical, moral, and personal. They cannot be willed away'.

sex couples. Society would, in effect, acknowledge the 'normality' of lesbians and gay men by adapting its significant institutions to provide for them. Even amongst those who acknowledge the constructed nature of sexuality there are those who take the view that a socially responsible sexuality is a constrained sexuality (Sullivan, 1996). Fitting same-sex desire into the normal patterns of life is an acceptable way of controlling it so that it becomes socially responsible rather than socially obnoxious. Normalisation of sexuality should occur.

The response of this group to the radical critique of marriage and the problems of lesbians and gay men gaining access to it is simply to disagree with it. Marriage is not the unacceptable institution that radical theorists maintain it to be. Normalisation is regarded positively.

ii. The liberal approach

A slightly different approach accepts the radical critique of marriage but maintains that the achievement of same-sex relationship recognition will contribute to the transformation of the family in society (see, in particular: Leonard, 2002; Eskridge, 2001; Wolfson, 2001). People in this position argue that equality demands full social and legal recognition of same-sex relationships on a par with the recognition of different-sex relationships. But the purpose of access to relationship recognition is not simply to achieve formal (and even substantive) equality. It is also aimed at ushering in an era in which a greater diversity of relationships will be acknowledged in legal regulation. An ethic of choice within a model of diverse family forms will be embraced (Eskridge, 2001). Those who wish to have marriage can choose it, and those who don't can continue to resist marriage by avoiding it.

This view is typically liberal in its idealisation of equal treatment, based on freedom of choice and a notion of individual agency. But its embrace of the creation of a diverse family ethic is also postmodern (Eskridge, 2001). It claims to have, in other words, a radical underbelly. Giving same-sex couples access to ordinary family regulation will, it is argued, go some way (if not all the way) towards addressing the concerns of feminists and others about the patriarchal nature of family regulation. Recognising same-sex relationships will force an internal transformation in the basic tenets of all relationships (Eskridge, 2001). Although the desire to be married is regarded as a conservative phenomenon (Sullivan, 1996) the desire to compel the state to recognise same-sex marriage is radical. It brings into public discourse a different way of being married. Same-sex couples will be bound to behave differently from the norm of marriage (Patterson, 1995). This is particularly true in relation to gendered roles and other unquestioned behavioural patterns in different sex family lives (Weeks *et al* 2001). For this reason same-sex relationships destabilise the ideal of marriage. Same-sex couples introduce a reflective element into expectations of behaviour in relationships. As a result of this characteristic they will, it is argued, reveal different ways of being married. In particular, they will undermine gendered power in relationships. A more equitable family ethic will emerge. Same-sex families will, in effect, live the feminist ambition for a family life characterised by real equality. In doing so they will, in effect, foster its achievement beyond their own families. Ideologically suspect relationships will benefit from the disruption to the norm that normalisation of abnormal relationships will cause.

The tranformative potential is not limited to 'leadership by example', however. The fact that there is debate surrounding same-sex marriages will create (indeed, has created) a discourse around the nature of marriage, adult relationships and state regulation. It has increased the scope and variety of relationships that are socially recognised and the mechanisms that the state is prepared to use to regulate them. It has, in effect, led to a tangible increase in the diversity of recognised family forms in society. This, it is argued, is a radical departure from the married/single binary which has been the dominant feature of modern family life. Same-sex relationship recognition encourages new and fragmented forms of family regulation which, in turn, has the effect of destabilising the idea of a singular normal family structure (Leonard, 2002, Eskridge, 2001).

iii. The problem of group identity

What emerges from the debate about marriage is not simply a recognition of the diversity of family relationships but a realisation that lesbians and gay men, like all people, are complex beings with widely diverging politics. The 'lesbian and gay community' is not a singular entity with a singular ambition for relationship recognition. While a binary distinction has been drawn between same-sex desire and different-sex desire, and that distinction has given rise to a bifurcated sexual identity, that divide obscures as much as it illuminates. Sexuality is not an uncomplicated phenomenon (Weeks, this volume; Plummer, this volume; Cooper, 2001; Lehr, 1999).

Part of the complication arises out of the simple fact that people have multiple identities. They are not simply sexual beings. They are also material, cultural, social, economic, political and religious beings (Smart, 1995; Naffine, 1990). A variety of social and individual characteristics contribute towards the creation of complex individual identities (Weeks, this volume; Plummer, this volume). And what are the important attributes of those identities at any particular moment will be determined by the circumstances of the moment. In some circumstances it is more important that people are women than that they are black, in others their race is more import. At times nationality takes priority, while at others family membership is more significant. Sometimes it is important that they have progressive views, at others their sense of identity is enveloped in their cultural heritage. And so on.

6. THE POLITICS OF LESBIAN AND GAY FAMILY REFORM

These observations begin to explain the source of some of the friction that lies at the heart of the equality debate in lesbian and gay circles. But they do not help to resolve it. Instead the debate is likely to be resolved in an ordinary political way. The fact that people recognise same-sex relationships and acknowledge their value is likely to be more influential than the ideological debate of theorists. But that also means that the transformative potential of same-sex relationship recognition is likely to be constrained by the relationship expectations of those people. Whether or not law allocates the rights of marriage to same-sex couples, people will, it is submitted, incrementally recognise their relationships as something like marriage. Indeed, that process has already begun (Weeks *et al*, 2001; Women and Equality Unit *et al*, 2003).

But that also means that the recognition of same-sex marriage is unlikely to be as transformative of family relations as those who argue for it most vociferously suggest it might be (Eskridge, 2001; Wolfson, 1994; Stoddard, 1992). The radical attribute of what I have called the liberal attitude towards same-sex marriage is unlikely to materialise because it neglects the real power of the symbol and status of marriage in our society. If the judgments in cases like *Fitzpatrick* and *Mendoza* are read carefully it is clear that regulation is being extended to same-sex couples but only in circumstances where those couples conduct themselves (even in the absence of marriage recognition) in ways that replicate (indeed, exaggerate) the qualities of heterosexual marriage of the most traditional kind. It is as if we can only consider the regulation of same-sex relationships when the requirements of idealised different-sex relationships are in evidence. Visible same-sex relationships must be heterosexual in all but sex.

With this observation I return to the beginning of this paper. In the last 20 years same-sex couple relationships have become visible. Both gay[55] and straight news reports[56] seem to celebrate the longevity of some same-sex relationships. Soap operas,[57] dramas[58] and sitcoms[59] often incorporate lesbian or gay characters into their story lines. And many more cultural events occur that seem to acknowledge the value of lesbians and gay men to their communities. But the visibility serves two purposes. And marriage is likely to contribute to these purposes. In the first place it fosters a positive attitude towards those whose sexual practice is unusual. But it is also there to distinguish good from bad people; some same-sex sexual conduct is normalised. We become exposed

---

[55] See, for example, 'Dinner with my elders' *The Texas Triangle Online*, Vol IX Issue 14, January 10, 2003: http://www.txtriangle.com/relationships/29_elders.htm

[56] See, for example, Elaine Monaghan 'You can bless a dog. Why not us' *The Times Online*, 16 October 2003, http://www.timesonline.co.uk/

[57] *Eastenders*, even *Biker Grove*.

[58] *Queer as Folk*; *This Life*.

[59] *Will and Grace*; *Ellen*; *Gimme, Gimme, Gimme*.

to 'normal' and 'abnormal' homosexuals. And we are encouraged to be critical of the 'abnormal' ones—the militant lesbians, the parading, defiant queer activists, or just the socially obnoxious, 'dysfunctional' lesbians and gay men.

The lesbian and gay politics that seek legal recognition of same-sex family relationships must be seen in this light. Family coupling is being fostered now in same-sex relationships as it had always been fostered in different-sex relationships. And alternative ways of living domestic lives are being marginalized by the same process of normalisation. People who are unsuited to these lifestyles remain outsiders in society. And the question we must ask ourselves is whether or not we have really progressed when we have managed to enlarge the group of the privileged and retain our prejudices in relation to others. Have we really progressed when sexual desire has not been released from social regulation? Does a reinvigorated policing regime governing sex and sexuality really enhance freedom? Outsider sexuality had brought a kind of liberation of sexual practices (particularly when the 'outsider' began to be known). The growth of regulatory interest in sexuality is, it seems, inevitably directed towards bringing a measure of control to it. The capacity to remain outside, to resist, will, it seems, be worn away. And the individual freedom that may have been its potential is more likely to be lost than found in this era of closer regulation.

7. CONCLUSION

I have tried to set out the progress that is being made towards the recognition of same-sex relationships in the United Kingdom. I have argued that the process will yield, in the short term, a same-sex alternative to marriage. In the longer term I have indicated that I believe same-sex marriage—formally equal to different-sex marriage—will be achieved. But I have also discussed the different concerns of activists and theorists about the simple recognition of same-sex relationships in the way that different-sex relationships are recognised. I have suggested that assimilation of same-sex relationships into the forms of regulation attached to different-sex relationships will not enhance freedom or diversity in society. The extent to which there is a transformation of family relationships will be minor. Instead the normalisation of some same-sex relationships will reinforce the regulatory prejudice which operates against those who don't fit the 'normal' patterns of relationship regulation. That world may be better than the one we are leaving behind, but it isn't the world that we might have hoped for. That world—one in which relationships are regulated to do justice between the parties and not to privilege form over substance—remains elusive. Once same-sex desire has been incorporated into the norm we will have to find some other bases upon which to challenge the inequities that the rules of family regulation will continue to perpetrate.

REFERENCES

ARNUP, K and BOYD, S, 'Familial Disputes? Sperm Donors, Lesbian Mothers, and Legal Parenthood' in D Herman, and C Stychin (eds), *Legal Inversions: Lesbians, Gay Men, and the Politics of Law* (Philadelphia, Temple University Press, 1995) p 77.

BAILEY-HARRIS, R, 'Same-Sex Partnerships in English Family Law' in R Wintemute. and M Andenaes (eds), *Legal Recognition of Same-Sex Partnerships: A Study of National, European and International Law* (Oxford, Hart Publishing, 2001).

BARLOW, A, *Cohabitants and the Law*, 3rd edn. (London, Butterworths, 2001) p 605.

—— BOWLEY, M, COX, L, BUTLER, G, DAVIES, M, GRYK, W, HAMILTON, A, SMITH, P, WATSON, M. *Advising Gay and Lesbian Clients: A Guide for Lawyers* (London, Butterworths, 1999).

BONAUTO, ML, 'The Freedom to Marry for Same-Sex Couples in the United States of America' in R Wintemute and M Andenaes (eds), *Legal Recognition of Same-Sex Partnerships: A Study of National, European and International Law* (Oxford, Hart Publishing, 2001) p 177.

BOSWELL, J, *The Marriage of Likeness: Same-Sex Unions in Pre-Modern Europe* (London, Harper Collins, 1995).

BRIDGEMAN, J and MILLNS, S, *Feminist Perspectives on Law* (London, Sweet and Maxwell, 1998).

CACHALIA, A, CHEADLE, H, DAVIS, D, HAYSOM, N, MADUNA, P and MARCUS, G, *Fundamental Rights in the New Constitution* (Cape Town, Juta, 1994).

CAMERON, E, 'Foreword' in R Wintemute. and M Andenaes (eds), *Legal Recognition of Same-Sex Partnerships: A Study of National, European and International Law* (Oxford, Hart Publishing, 2001) p V.

CAPERS, B, 'Sexual Orientation and Title VII' (1991) 91 *Columbia Law Review* 1158.

CARBONE, J, 'Feminism, Gender and the Consequences of Divorce in M Freeman (ed), *Divorce : Where Next?* (Aldershot, Dartmouth, 1996) p 181.

CHERLIN, AJ, FURSTENBERG, FF, Jr, CHASE-LANSDALE, PL, KIERNAN, KE, ROBINS, PK, MORRISON, DR and TEITLER, JO, 'Longitudinal Studies of Effects of Divorce on Children in Great Britain and the United States' (1991) 252 *Science* 1386.

COOPER, D, 'Like Counting Stars? Re-Structuring Equality and the Socio-Legal Space of Same-Sex Marriage' in R Wintemute and M Andenaes (eds), *Legal Recognition of Same-Sex Partnerships A Study of National, European and International Law* (Oxford, Hart Publishing, 2001) p 75.

DUBERMAN, MB, VICINUS, M and CHAUNCEY, Jr. G, *Hidden From History: Reclaiming the Gay and Lesbian Past* (London, Penguin, 1989).

DUCLOS, N, 'Some Complicating Thoughts on Same-Sex Marriage' (1991) 1 *Law & Sexuality* 31.

DUNLAP, MC, 'The Lesbian and Gay Marriage Debate: A Microcosm of Our Hopes and Troubles in the Nineties' (1991) 1 *Law & Sexuality* 63.

EEKELAAR, J and NHLAPO, T (eds), *The Changing Family: Family Forms and Family Law* (Oxford, Hart Publishing, 1998).

ESKRIDGE, WN Jr, 'A History of Same-Sex Marriage' (1993) 79 *Virginia Law Review* 1419.

ESKRIDGE, WN, 'The Ideological Structure of the Same-Sex Marriage Debate (and some Postmodern Arguments for Same-Sex Marriage) in R Wintemute and M Andenaes (eds), *Legal Recognition of Same-Sex Partnerships A Study of National, European and International Law* (Oxford, Hart Publishing, 2001) p 113.

ETTELBRICK, PL, 'Since When is Marriage a Path to Liberation?' in S Sherman (ed), *Lesbian and Gay Marriage* (Philadelphia, Temple University Press, 1992) p 20.

FINEMAN, MA, 'Cracking the Foundational Myths: Independence, Autonomy, and Self Sufficiency' (2000) 8 *American University Journal Gender, Social Policy & Law* 13.

—— 'Societal Factors Affecting the Creation of Legal Rules for Distribution of Property at Divorce' in MA Fineman and SW Thomadsen (eds), *At the Boundaries of the Law* (New York, Routledge, 1991) p 265.

FOUCAULT, M, *The History of Sexuality: Volume 1, An Introduction* (London, Penguin, 1978) (translated from the French by Robert Hurley).

FUSS, D, *Essentially Speaking: Feminism, Nature and Difference* (New York, Routledge, 1989).

GAVIGAN, SAM, 'A Parent(ly) Knot: Can Heather Have Two Mommies' in D Herman and C Stychin (eds), *Legal Inversions: Lesbians, Gay Men, and the Politics of Law* (Philadelphia, Temple University Press, 1995) p 102.

GILLIGAN, C, *In a Different Voice: Psychological Theory and Women's Development* (Cambridge, Harvard UP, 1982).

GOLOMBOK, S. and TASKER, FL, *Growing Up in a Lesbian Family: Effects on Child Development* (Guildford, Guildford Press, 1997).

GREEN, S, *The Sexual Dead-End* (London, Broadview, 1992).

HALE, B, PEARL, D, COOKE, EJ and BATES, PD, *The Family, Law and Society: Cases and Materials*, 5th edn. (London, Butterworths, 2002).

HALLEY, J, 'Recognition, Rights, Regulation, Normalisation: Rhetorics of Justification in the Same-Sex Marriage Debate.' in R Wintemute and M Andenaes (eds), *Legal Recognition of Same-Sex Partnerships* (Oxford, Hart Publishing, 2001) p 97.

HERMAN, D, 'Are We Family? Lesbian Rights and Women's Liberation' (1990) 28 *Osgoode Hall Law Journal* 789.

HOAD, N, 'Tradition, Modernity and Human Rights: An Interrogation of Contemporary Gay and Lesbian Rights Claims in Southern African Nationalist Discourses', (1998) 2(2) *Development Update* 32 .

HUNTER, ND, ' Marriage, Law and Gender: A Feminist Inquiry' (1991) 1 *Law and Sexuality* 9.

KENNEDY, I, 'Transsexualism and Single-Sex Marriage' in I Kennedy *Treat Me Right* (1988) (and in 2 *Anglo American Law Review* 112 (1973)).

KOPPELMAN, A, 'The Miscegenation Analogy: Sodomy Laws as Sex Discrimination' (1988) 98 *Yale Law Journal* 145.

LEHR, V, *Queer Family Values: Debunking the Myth of the Nuclear Family* (Philadelphia, Temple University Press, 1999).

LEONARD, AS, 'Ten Propositions about Legal Recognition of Same-Sex Partners' (2002) 30 *Capital University Law Review* 343.

LIND, C, 'Sexual Orientation, Family Law and the Transitional Constitution' (1995) 112 *South African Law Journal* 481–502.

—— and BARLOW, A, 'Family Redefinition under Part III of the Family Law Bill 1996' (1996) *Web Journal of Current Legal Issues,* (Issue 2) http://webjcli.ncl.ac.uk/index.html.

LOENEN, T, 'Comparative Legal Feminist Scholarship and the Importance of a Contextual Approach to Concepts and Strategies: The Case of the Equality Debate.' (1995) 3 *Feminist Legal Studies* 71.

MACKINNON, CA, *Feminism Unmodified: Discourses on Life and Law* (Cambridge, Mass, Harvard University Press, 1987).

—— *Towards a Feminist Theory of the State* (London, Harvard University Press, 1989).

MAIDMENT, S, 'Women and Childcare: The Paradox of Divorce' in S Edwards (ed), *Gender, Sex and the Law* (London, Croom Helm, 1985) p 28.

NAFFINE, N, *Law and the Sexes: Explorations in Feminist Jurisprudence* (Sydney, Allen and Unwin, 1990).

NORRIE, KM, 'Marriage is for Heterosexuals—May the Rest of Us be Saved from It' (2000) 12(4) *Child and Family Law Quarterly* 363.

—— 'Sexual Orientation and Family Law' in J Scoular (ed), *Family Dynamics: Contemporary Issues in Family Law* (London, Butterworths, 2001) p 151.

O'DONOVAN, K, *Sexual Divisions in Law* (London, Weidenfeld and Nicolson, 1985).

—— *Family Law Matters* (London, Pluto, 1993).

OLSEN, F, 'Law and the Market' (1983) 96 *Harvard Law Review* 1497.

PANNICK, D, *Sex Discrimination Law* (Oxford, Clarendon Press, 1985).

PATTERSON, CJ, 'Families of the Lesbian Baby Boom: Parents' Division of Labor and Children's Adjustment' (1995) 31 *Developmental Psychology* 115.

POLIKOFF, ND, 'We will Get what we Ask for: Why Legalizing Gay and Lesbian Marriage will not "Dismantle the Legal Structure of Gender in every Marriage"' (1993) 79 *Virginia Law Review* 1535.

—— 'Why Lesbians and Gay Men should read Martha Fineman' (2000) 8 *American University Journal of Gender, Social Policy and Law* 167.

RODGERS, B and PRYOR, J, *Divorce and Separation: The Outcomes for Children* (York, Joseph Rowntree Foundation, 1998).

RUBENSTEIN, WB, *Lesbians, Gay Men, and the Law* (New York, The New Press, 1993).

SACHS, A and WILSON, JH, *Sexism and the Law: A Study of Male Beliefs and Legal Bias in Britain and the United States* (Oxford, Martin Robertson, 1978).

SMART, C, *Feminism and the Power of Law* (London, Routledge, 1989a).

—— 'Power and the Politics of Child Custody' in C Smart and S Sevenhuijsen (eds), *Child Custody and the Politics of Gender* (London, Routledge, 1989b) p 1.

—— 'New Dimensions to Gendered Power Relations in Families' in J Cook, J Roberts and G Waylen (eds), *Towards a Gendered Political Economy*, (London, Macmillan, 2000) p 188.

—— *Law, Crime and Sexuality* (London, Routledge, 1995).

SMITH, P (ed), *Feminist Jurisprudence* (Oxford, OUP, 1993).

—— 'On Equality: Justice, Discrimination, and Equal Treatment' in P Smith, (ed), *Feminist Jurisprudence* (Oxford, OUP, 1993) p 17.

STODDARD, TB, 'Why Gay People Should Seek the Right to Marry' in S Sherman (ed), *Lesbian and Gay Marriage* (Philadelphia, Temple University Press, 1992).

SULLIVAN, A, *Virtually Normal* (London, Picador, 1996).

VAID, U, *Virtual Equality: The Mainstreaming of Gay and Lesbian Liberation* (New York, Anchor Books, 1995).

WARDLE, LD 'Same-Sex Marriage and the Limits of Legal Pluralism' in J Eekelaar and T Nhlapo (eds), *The Changing Family: Family Forms and Family Law* (Oxford, Hart Publishing, 1998) p 381.

WATSON, S, 'Erratic Bureaucracies: the Intersection of Housing, Legal and Social Policies in the Case of Divorce' in Regina Graycar (ed), *Dissenting Opinions: Feminist Explorations in Law and Society* (Sydney, Allen & Unwin, 1990) p 70.

WEEKS, J, *Against Nature* (London, Rivers Oram Press, 1991).

—— *Sex, Politics and Society: The Regulation of Sexuality Since 1800*, 2d ed (London, Longman, 1989).

—— HEAPHY, B and DONOVAN, C, *Same Sex Intimacies: Families of Choice and other Life Experiments* (London, Routledge, 2001) p 1.

WINTEMUTE, R, 'Introduction' in R Wintemute and M Andenaes (eds), *Legal Recognition of Same-Sex Partnerships: A Study of National, European and International Law* (Oxford, Hart Publishing, 2001).

—— 'Sexual Orientation Discrimination' in C McCrudden and G Chambers (eds), *Individual Rights and the Law in Britain* (Oxford, Clarendon Press, 1994) p 491.

—— and ANDENAES, M (eds), *Legal Recognition of Same-Sex Partnerships: A Study of National, European and International Law* (Oxford, Hart Publishing, 2001).

WOLFSON, E, 'Crossing the Threshold: Equal Marriage Rights for Lesbians and Gay Men and the Intra-Community Critique' (1994) 21 *New York University Review of Law and Social Change* 567.

—— 'The Hawaii Marriage Case Launches the US Freedom-to-Marry Movement for Equality' in R Wintemute and M Andenaes (eds), *Legal Recognition of Same-Sex Partnerships: A Study of National, European and International Law* (Oxford, Hart Publishing, 2001) p 169.

WOMAN AND EQUALITY UNIT *Civil Partnership: A Framework for the Legal Regulation of Same Sex Couples* (June 2003) (London) http://www.womenandequalityunit.gov.uk/discrimination/index.htm.

7

Intersecting Oppressions: Ending Discrimination against Lesbians, Gay Men and Trans People in the UK

ZOË-JANE PLAYDON

The decadent apostles of the most hideous and loathsome vices no longer conceal their degeneracy and degradation . . . They appear to revel in their defiance of public opinion. They do not shun publicity. On the contrary, they seek it, and take a delight in their flamboyant notoriety.[1]

ACTIVISM

I wish to provide an activist perspective on the gaining of gay, lesbian and trans civil liberties and, in particular, to focus on what is held in common by activism in these areas. Activism still depends heavily on voluntary work by community organisations, which require a sense of shared values and purpose in order to coalesce. Equally, though, activism requires internal discussions, fuelled by heterogeneous ideas, in order to progress. The activist dynamic, therefore, is one both of commonality and variety, and charting these characteristics is important. Set against those diverse but cohesive standpoints is the lumping together, in the majority public arena, of lesbian, trans and gay issues as a homogenous undesirability, subjected to generalised exclusions, which elide different minority community identities. This chapter, therefore, is also in part an attempt to moderate that homogenised view taken by majority culture.

As trans activist Stephen Whittle (2002: 62) points out 'Theory and activism are inextricably intertwined bedfellows, especially when it comes to the development of policy and law.' Trans, gay and lesbian activism is played out against and within a variety of theoretical perspectives. To take lesbian feminism as an example, in the 1970s, the notion of the personal being political meant that the

---

[1] 'A Book that must be Suppressed,' *The Sunday Express*, 19 August 1928.

separatist organisation strategy of the Women's Liberation Movement was logically extended to lesbian separatism, as 'the ultimate sign of repudiation of and
withdrawal from male society.' (Simms, 1981: 227–39, 231). Lesbian feminism
developed as heterogeneous, however, and during the 1980s:

> challenges from a number of sources have resulted in the decentring of lesbian femi-
> nism: firstly . . . sex-radical lesbians rejected feminist prescription of sexual behaviour
> . . . secondly, Queer politics challenged the separatist emphasis of lesbian activism . . .
> more indirectly, black feminism challenged all white feminists to examine their racism
> and theorize 'whiteness' . . . lesbian feminism in the 1990s is a self-conscious, intellec-
> tually and politically diverse field which abuts on a wide variety of other discourses,
> including Queer Theory, Chicana Theory and Postmodernism (Andermahr et al.,
> 1997: 123).

Equally, theoretical perspectives may arise from activism, so that, for Whittle,
the origins of Queer Theory were in 'the work done in the late 1960s . . . to gain
that removal from DSM III of homosexuality as a psychiatric disorder,' so that
'Queer Theory arose from this utilitarian mix of activism and academia.' It did
so even though 'at the time, this work would have been recognised not as the
start of a major theoretical movement, but rather as part of the process of political activism.' (Whittle, 2002: 62, 65). More self-consciously, theorisation of
'difference' emerged from the disjuncture between majority culture's homogeni-
sation of gay, trans and lesbian people and the lived experience of individuals
themselves. That discussion has almost been polarised around positions, which
support either a social constructivist approach or an essentialist viewpoint. It
has also been deconstructed into 'différence', using Derridian ideas of the operation of language, to challenge 'the very concept of a coherent identity and a self
from which intellectual and political positions flowed' (Andermahr et al., 1997:
61).

The idea of 'history' thus becomes problematic in these connections. The
chronicling of experiences of trans, lesbian and gay people has only recently
begun. For those engaged in activism, the felt experience and the affinities arising from that are perhaps fore-grounded more than events validated by the
'rules of evidence' of historical science as it is usually conceived. Some matters
remain 'secret history,' the lore and wisdom transmitted inside a minority
group, through which it negotiates its relationships with external groups.
Lesbian invisibility has been countered by oral history projects, the purposeful,
sustained process of collecting, editing and publishing spoken accounts of personal experience from members of a minority group. The purposes of such work
are often valorisation, providing accounts which support the discrete identity
and dignity of a group, through witnessing and through theorisation. This chapter, perhaps, will have more of the character of 'herstory', that is, history told
by women, as a story of *sameness*, valuing emotional engagement and evoking
solidarity (Purkiss, 1996). An activist approach, however, is closer to that of the
bricoleur than the historian:

The *bricoleur* reads widely and is knowledgeable about the many interpretative para-digms . . . works between and within competing and overlapping perspectives and par-adigms.

The *bricoleur* understands that research is an interactive process shaped by his or her personal history, biography, gender, social class, race and ethnicity, and those of the people in the setting. The *bricoleur* knows that science is power, for all research findings have political implications. There is no value-free science. The *bricoleur* also knows that researchers all tell stories about the worlds they have studied . . . The prod-uct of the *bricoleur*'s labor is a bricolage, a complex, dense, reflexive, collage-like cre-ation, that represents the researcher's images, understandings, and interpretations of the world or phenomenon under analysis (Denzin and Lincoln, 1994: 2).

Inevitably, activists have no foreknowledge of the kinds of narratives that will be created from their work. They seek to shape compelling arguments to arouse the awareness of a specific forum or of the public in general, to interest them in their issues, and to arouse them to act. History and historiography are data to be interrogated for what they may yield in the way of approaches, or precedents, or weaknesses in the arguments of the other side. History is essentially some-thing which activists hope to make.

Similarly, personal identity is less important than political identification. In an arena where sweat equity is the major asset, the work that someone is will-ing to take on and complete for the group is crucial, in a way that genealogy is not. Identity politics thus constitute a strategic essentialism: to take forward a legal case of discrimination, it is necessary for the appellant to be gay, or lesbian or trans, but not for their legal team to share that identity. However, there may be an argument to be made for the legal team to have affinities with the emo-tional experiences of the defendant. For example, in the case of *P v S and Another (Sex Discrimination)*,[2] the trans woman P was supported by a lesbian solicitor, Madeleine Rees and a black barrister, Rambi de Mello. She specifically asked for Helena Kennedy as QC in the case, because she believed her to have 'the passion,' the emotional engagement with a struggle for freedom, as a nec-essary concomitant to an intellectual engagement with the legalities of the case.[3] In a different vein, as the chapters by Johnson and by Chau and Herring in this book discuss, identity may also be constructed through biological arguments, which support the idea of essential physiological differences, and which may be decisive for some individuals.

Further, although complex theoretical understandings are a necessary part of the bricolage of activism, less sophisticated viewpoints are also invaluable. Althusser's idea of the Ideological State Apparatus, taken with Foucault's cri-tique of power relationships, still provides a useful, practical way of framing activism, more recent theoretical positions notwithstanding. It brings into clear

---

[2] *P v S and Another (Sex Discrimination)* [1996] 2 FLR 347.
[3] Personal recollections as a member of the team supporting the case.

focus the institutions and their processes, through which social exclusion is created and maintained: pragmatically, the Church, law, medicine and education are, in the end, the arenas in which gay, lesbian and trans liberties are lost or won. From this standpoint, exclusion commenced with a dominant religious ideology defining a particular group as morally bad, continued with the law carrying out specific sanctions against the group's members, and conscripted medicine to 'cure' the social evil and end the moral panic. Finally, education is brought into service to disseminate justifications for these actions, and to suppress the voice of the minority group.

Unpicking and reversing these actions is the practical task of activism. Often, it requires relatively simple messages, to gain attention, and thus there is a difficult balancing act to be maintained in seeking equal civil status in a way that is true to community understandings. The aim is to weigh the experiences and needs of excluded individuals and groups against what is practically achievable in the public arena at any given point. Thus, activist groups may produce homogenised (and sometimes sanitised) versions of their minority community, for the purposes of legal argument and political lobbying. Such strategic essentialisations are actions of political expediency, fundamental to the provisionality which informs the processes of activism. They are hostages to fortune, given to be taken back, and given as reminders of the power inequity that action must change. They represent a nomadic position, a transit in the arc of movement towards freedom, not a final, definitive, resting point.

Activism is also something that is held in general, as well as being the specific preserve of particular specialist groups in minority communities. Three broad activist responses to social exclusion are made in the areas of language, direct action and organising, and while new directions may be discovered and promoted by specific individuals and groups, every community member is able to engage in this agenda. Language and identity will be reclaimed, so that, for example, the abusive terms 'gay', 'queer' and 'dyke' have been reclaimed and used as acts of political defiance, while trans people have refused the pathologised terminology of 'a transsexual' or 'transsexuals' as ways of speaking to or about them. 'We're here, we're queer, get used to it,' is one populist way of expressing this reclamation, with sloganised tee-shirts finding an equally honourable station. Second, relationality and public space is reclaimed, by actions ranging from a woman kissing her girlfriend in the street, to Gay Pride marches, being 'out' at work, and challenges to predominant stereotypes of dress or activity. Third, a pressure for change in civil status will be created, legal remedies will be sought and political lobbying will be combined with wide-ranging educational programmes, through the media, conferences, publications and lectures. As people organise, activist communities will be created, able to provide support to each other, in a variety of ways, apart from politically. Now, the Internet produces new interest groups for gay, trans and lesbian people on almost a daily basis but before them, small ads or word of mouth provided knowledge of clubs, pubs, safe meeting-places, and sources of help, despite all of society's attempts at suppression.[4] Just going to a lesbian, gay or trans pub or club is, in and of itself, at some level an act against social exclusion, a reclaiming of space.

Finally, writing about activism from this standpoint is problematic. Breadth is gained at the expense of depth and in seeking to generalise intersections between trans, lesbian and gay activism, I shall lose particularities. However, what is held in common is relatively broad: action in support of 'that fundamental and inalienable value which is equality.'[5]

SOCIO-LEGAL INTERSECTIONS

All lawyers who have had criminal and divorce practice know that there is in modern social life an undercurrent of dreadful degradation, unchecked and uninterfered with.[6]

A militant, Christian orthodoxy, legitimised by a transcendent male God,[7] was a crucial part of Victorian mind and society. That ideology provided aggressive denunciations of gay, lesbian and trans people, and social exclusion was operationalised through the emerging science of medicine. Early sexologists described three communities interchangeably as, for example, 'constitutional invert', 'sexual intermediacy', or 'psychic hermaphrodite' (King, 1993), thus refusing to recognise the different groups of people (see Chau and Herring, this volume), and denying their rights to debate and define their own identities—a process now called abjection.[8] However, such 'cases' were still only a matter of casual censure, such as the magistrate's comments about Bill [Mary] Chapman in 1835: 'She may be a disorderly and disreputable character, which, in fact, her dressing as a man clearly shows, but I know of no law to punish her for wearing male attire.'[9]

The second intersection in the abjection of gay men, lesbians and trans people, however, is provided by legal debates and actions which took place out of the public gaze, in privileged settings, not subject to public debate. Labouchère's addition to the Criminal Law Amendment Act in 1885, added homosexuality to the list of punishable offences. Instantly, gay men who expressed their sexuality were effectively criminalized, with their future offering a choice of complete secrecy about their sexuality; or prison with hard labour,

---

[4] For example, see Gardiner, J (2003) for an account of the famous Gateways club.

[5] See footnote 2.

[6] Parliamentary Debates (House of Commons), Criminal Law Amendment Bill, 4 August 1921, para. 1799–1806, *Criminal Law Amendment Bill [Lords]*. Cited in Oram and Turnbull (2001: 158).

[7] The political purposes of orthodox, transcendent Christianity are interestingly discussed by Pagels (1979).

[8] By 'abjection' I mean the socio-political processes of casting out that which disturbs identity, order, systems, by denying it a voice or an identity: effectively denying it agency, excluding it from social discourses. For definitions, discussions and further reading see Andermahr et al (1997).

[9] Anon quoted in 'The Sinks of London Laid Open: A Pocket Companion for the Uninitiated,' (Oram and Turnbull, 2001: 23–8, 25).

or a 'cure' by the sexologists. Gay male identity was excoriated, as in Queensberry's notorious, insulting card left 'To Oscar Wilde posing Somdomite' (Ellmann, 1987: 412), and was severely punished if that apparent identity could be linked with gay sexual behaviour. Although since Henry VIII buggery had been punishable by death or life imprisonment, and this act just extended illegality to cover all forms of homosexual acts in private or in public, the change in the law, and Wilde's case in particular, brought gay male sexuality into the public eye as a focus for renewed punishment and panic.

In 1921, a similar attempt to add lesbianism to the Criminal Law Amendment Act was defeated in the Lords, since as Lord Birkenhead warned:

> You are going to tell the whole world there is such an offence, to bring it to the notice of women who have never heard of it, never dreamed of it. I think this is a very great mischief.'[10]

Case-law, rather than statute, operated in the case of trans people. In the case of X,[11] it was decided that no trans people in Scotland could have their birth certificates corrected or receive civil recognition in their sex. However, in 1968, Ewan Forbes, well-known in the trans community as a trans man whose birth certificate had been corrected in 1952, won the case that he, rather than his non-trans male cousin, should follow the male succession and inherit the title from his father Lord Sempill. All records of that case disappeared, to the extent that the Public Records Office in Edinburgh was unable to find any traces of it, until a direct request by Dr Lynne Jones MP, Chair of the Parliamentary Forum on Transsexualism, stimulated its discovery (Playdon, 1996).

Stereotyping provided the third intersection. The trials of Oscar Wilde in 1895, the obscenity case brought against Radclyffe Hall's *The Well of Loneliness* in 1928, and the nullity of the marriage of trans woman April Ashley in 1970 [the case of *Corbett v Corbett*][12] each produced 'a brilliantly precise image' by 'grafting of a narrow set of cultural signifiers' onto an ostensibly homogenous body of people (Doan, 2001: xii). All gay men were witty, elegant aesthetes. Lesbians were mannish unfortunates burdened with Stephen Gordon's 'mark of Cain'. And, in the public imagination, trans people would always be trans women [so that trans men became invisible] and trans women would always be, in the judge's terms, 'a pastiche of femininity', a sort of piss-elegant drag-queen, a kind of figure of fun. Interestingly, all three stereotypes occupied wealthy circles, either the upper-middle class social and literary circles of Wilde and Hall, or the 'jet-set' film and entertainment world of Ashley. The majority of ordinary people were cut off from identification with these powerful public symbols and their cultures, so that access to a gay or lesbian or trans identity was made more problematic for working class individuals, for example.

---

[10] Quoted in Souhami (1998: 112).
[11] *X (Petitioner)* (1957) SLT (Sc Ct) 61.
[12] *Corbett v Corbett (Otherwise Ashley)* [1970] 2 All E.R. 33.

The practical consequence of these changes in social identity provides the fourth intersection of oppressions for trans, lesbian and gay people. Because each was socially abhorrent, each had no employment rights. Even though it was not and is not illegal to be lesbian [apart from in the Armed Services until 1999], 'as lesbianism became a clearer concept during the twentieth century, it was also increasingly associated with a semi-criminal underworld of violence, murder and sexual depravity generally.' (Oram and Turnbull, 2001: 158). This meant that it was considered reasonable to dismiss a woman from employment for being a lesbian, on the grounds that a hypothetical future customer or employee might object to working with them, and that there is no legal redress in employment law. This was redressed in December 2003, with the implementation of the Employment Equality (Sexual Orientation) Regulations although their effectiveness in reducing workplace discrimination has yet to be tested.

In a money-based society, the right to work is the most fundamental right: people should be judged by their economic potential, and denial of employment security is in effect denial of security of home, family and life. This point was argued successfully in 1996 in the European Court of Justice case, *P v S and Another (Sex Discrimination)*, which extended the Sex Discrimination Act to trans people.[13] Similar arguments were used in the European Court of Human Rights to end discrimination against lesbians and gay men in the UK Armed Services in 2000.[14] In both cases, it might be speculated ironically, the moral anxiety of an earlier age had perhaps been offset by Reaganomics and Thatcherism, with the dogma of money redefining people by their utility as production units, rather than by their human need. Consumerism as a social ideology may also have influenced the rise in university programmes in women's studies and gender studies, since, as a colleague running such a programme once put it to me, 'Provided it makes money, the authorities don't seem to care what you teach'.

Viewed holistically, these are degradations of labour, not liberators of it, since consumerism offers only some severely restricted freedoms, which operate to its material advantage. In support of this view, it might be noted that gay, lesbian and trans people still cannot marry and that Section 28 until recently inhibited the teaching of LGT issues in schools in England and Wales. Further, since 1970 it has not been possible for trans people to correct their birth certificates, or to adopt, and only strong community action has prevented trans people being sent to the wrong sex prison, where trans women at least were routinely raped by male inmates and warders alike. In spite of Home Office assurances, the treatment of trans people by the Prison Service continues to be a matter for concern to trans activists, since it often does not provide hormone treatment for trans people in custody and no apparent policy lies behind decision-making.[15]

---

[13] See footnote 2.

[14] *Smith and Grady v United Kingdom* (2000) 29 EHRR 493; *Lustig-Prean and Beckett v United Kingdom* (2000) 29 EHRR 548.

[15] Parliamentary Forum on Transsexualism, *Notes of Meeting 5 June* (Westminster, Dr Lynne Jones MP, 2003).

SOCIO-MEDICAL INTERSECTIONS

'I have seen the plague stalking shamelessly through great social assemblies.'[16]

Contrasting clinical viewpoints provided the first medical intersection in the treatment of lesbians, gay men and trans people. Those represented by Krafft-Ebbing, viewed patients as perverted and degenerate as a result of their inherited vice; and those such as Havelock Ellis, viewed patients as often intellectually and artistically distinguished and experiencing an unavoidable biological disposition to same-sex partnerships. One viewpoint advocated coercive violence while the other advocated corrective understanding. In the first regime, gay men experienced hormone therapy as an alternative to imprisonment (Alan Turing, cracker of the Enigma code and progenitor of computer science, committed suicide after his treatment; Hodges, 1992), aversion therapy, or more extremely in the Third Reich, termination as part of the 'final solution.' Lesbians were committed to mental hospitals—'the asylums are largely peopled by nymphomaniacs and people who indulge in this vice [lesbianism]'[17]—or might be clitorectomised (Dally, 1991). Transsexualism was not recognised as a distinct medical category until 1968, when it appeared as a separate heading in the *Index Medicus* (American Medical Association, 1968). Sectioning into mental hospitals, aversion therapy and ECT were used in its treatment, while as late as April 2002, exorcism was advocated as a 'cure,' by a UK psychiatrist working in the field.[18]

The more benign medical approaches to gay men, poignantly fictionalised in EM Forster's (1971) posthumously published *Maurice,* ranged from denial, to hypnotism, to marriage either as a cure or as a convenient charade. If you did not act as though you were 'cured' then the alternative was to go abroad, as Wilde's friends begged him to do. Lesbianism might be benignly regarded as neurasthenia or as temporary hysteria, and treated with similar 'cures' as gay men, unless, of course, the women concerned were able to live independent social lives and thus escape the concerns of their families. More recently, it has been regarded as a behavioural disorder, and treated accordingly. *The Last Time I Wore a Dress* describes Daphne Scholinski's experience of being placed in a mental hospital at the age of 15, for what her psychiatrist called 'failure to identify as a sexual female,' and being subjected to a regime of compulsory

---

[16] See footnote 1.
[17] Parliamentary Debates (House of Commons), Criminal Law Amendment Bill, 4 August 1921, para. 1799–1806, *Criminal Law Amendment Bill [Lords]*. Cited in Oram and Turnbull (2001: 158).
[18] Royal College of Psychiatrists Educational Meeting, 16 April 2002, London, Royal Society of Medicine. Speaking from the floor, the medical practitioner said that while he did not expect wide acceptance for his viewpoint, he asked that it be taken seriously: in his experience, exorcism had been very effective in treating transsexualism, as had constant prayer.

re-education, which required her to wear makeup, walk with a swing in her hips, and pretend to be obsessed with boys. The confinement and treatment to make her behave 'like a woman' took place from 1981 to 1984 (Scholinski and Adams, 1997). These standards of behaviour are those still required from trans women by medical practitioners, where there remains a reigning medical idea that a major purpose of the real life experience (RLE), is to ensure that trans people will be invisible in society, that they will be able to 'pass.' In some NHS clinics, at time of writing, trans women are obliged to attend wearing a skirt and high heels, or they are told that they are 'not serious' and their healthcare is cancelled. In at least one other clinic, quite bizarrely, trans people are obliged to go before a panel of lay-people, who will contribute to the decision as to whether they should receive clinical care based on their appearance. This is not only a breach of patient confidentiality, but is also not used for access to any other surgical procedure. Some psychiatrists claim that rectal or vaginal examinations are a necessary part of their assessment processes and effectively impose them, in breach of informed consent, to say nothing of common-sense. Certainly as recently as 1993, surgeons required trans women to sign a humiliating form of consent, produced just before treatment, which said 'I . . . of . . . do consent to undergo the removal of the male genital organs and fashioning of an artificial vagina as explained to me by . . . (surgeon). I understand it will not alter my male sex and that it is being done to prevent deterioration in my mental health.'

In 1980, as the main entry for homosexuality was removed from the American Psychiatric Association's third, revised edition of the *Diagnostic and Statistical Manual of Registered Mental Illnesses* (American Psychiatric Association, 1980: 261–4), so transsexualism was entered into it. These classifications provided clear signposting for the need for specialist clinical care for trans people, and in that sense were helpful, more, perhaps, in the USA, where DSM categories were related to claims on private healthcare insurance. Less helpfully, these medical categorisations indicate a second intersection between trans people, gay men and lesbians, the idea that they are 'unhappy with themselves.' Homosexuality remains in the DSM as 'ego-dystonic homosexuality,' a sense of unease with one's sexuality, just as transsexualism, entered as 'Gender Identity Disorder,' is a sense of unease with one's gender. Intrinsically, however, none of these people are mentally ill: their 'discomfort' arises from heterosexist bigotry.

The separation between body and mind, which the DSM propagates, indicates a third intersection, the use of heterosexual genital sex as the baseline for defining relationality, as Chau and Herring discuss elsewhere in this work. In this discourse, lesbians are viewed as usurping male sexual privilege, so that the varieties and possibilities of their relationality are reduced, in the popular phrase, to the question 'what do lesbians do in bed?', a reductionism which emerges as the internalised homophobia 'lesbian bed-death' in populist lesbian writing. Gay male sex is conceptualised as anal sex, and used to elide transwomen's sexual possibilities, since, discussing Ashley's vagina in *Corbett v*

Corbett, the judge declared that 'the difference between sexual intercourse using it, and anal or intra-crural intercourse is, in my judgement, to be measured in centimetres.'[19] The supposed sexual life of heterosexual trans men lies somewhere between these discourses: for example, their female partners are assumed to be 'taken-in' by them, in some instances, while some phalloplasty focuses on developing a prosthetic penis capable of erection, clearly a major patriarchal site of anxiety. Gay trans men still do not exist in the public mind, and interestingly, their assumed absence forms the keystone of the transphobia of pseudo-sociological works such as *The Transsexual Empire* (Raymond, 1979).[20] Like lesbian trans women, gay trans men are a particular source of uncertainty (and thus a particular locus of discrimination) because their circumstances operate immediately, and directly, against the values and assumptions of a viewpoint constructed on the primacy of heterosexual genital sex as the basis for relationality. That these viewpoints are founded in a medical discourse, is demonstrated by the continued existence of sexology as a medical specialty, by the textbooks illustrating 'phenotypes' of gay, lesbian and trans people (the latter still current), and by the research, still being produced, into 'tomboys and sissies' which focuses on modifying children's behaviour rather than seeking to treat parental anxieties, as Johnson discusses in this book.

Leading from this, a fourth intersection, then, lies at questions of etiology. Is it nature or nurture? Are lesbians, gay men and trans people the 'product' of inherited congenital determinants (like having blue eyes or blonde hair) or are they 'creations' of their upbringing and social circumstances? Victorian sexology decided for nature, but in penalising homosexual behaviour in public and in private, the 1885 Criminal Law Amendment Act, seemed to be asserting that homosexuality was espoused behaviour, a matter of choice. Politically, a 'nurture' argument opened up the possibility of a cure by the new discipline of psychiatry, rather than punishment. On the other hand, a congenital etiology offered a powerful argument for reforming the punitive treatment of gay men, lesbians and trans people. Natural justice demands that people are not penalised for that which is beyond their control. Biologists' observations of the animal kingdom were marshalled to support the idea of a 'gay gene,' or a 'brain-sex,' which predisposed individuals to certain forms of behaviour. The choice to follow this predisposition then became a matter of individuals' freedom of expression. Some part of this ideology, at least, informed the work of the Albany Trust, set up in 1958 to inform and educate, alongside the Homosexual Law Reform Society, after government's refusal of the recommendations of the Wolfenden Report that consenting gay sex be legalised for men over 21 years of age (Altman, 1971).

It was also the prevailing medical discourse for trans people, following Harry Benjamin's introduction of the syndrome of transsexualism into the general

---

[19] See footnote 12.
[20] For an analysis of the text see Stone (1987).

medical community in 1954. Throughout the 1950s and 1960s, trans people in the UK were understood to experience a congenitally-based condition. They were entitled to appropriate, if limited, clinical care, had their birth certificates corrected, could marry and adopt and had full civil liberties. The route was not easy; since name changes on social security documents were not available pre-operatively, automatically outing people in anything other than casual jobs. A few prominent people received unwelcome attention from the Press, such as Roberta Cowell, whose father was Surgeon-General to the King, but the vast majority of this tiny minority lived their lives unremarkably and out of the public eye.

Professor John Money's 'John/Joan' case is discussed in detail by Chau and Herring in this volume. Briefly, in 1967, American physician and self-styled 'missionary of sex (Colapinto, 1997: 59),' Professor John Money, announced that he had solved the nature/nurture debate. One of a pair of twin boy babies had accidentally been penectomised during circumcision: he had been reassigned as female, never been told of his reassignment and brought up as a girl. Money announced that, after long-term follow-up, the girl had successfully adjusted to her new role. Thus, it was clearly nurture, not nature, which decided the sex of people. By implication, it might be argued that it was nurture, too, which decided the sexuality of mentally stable people who had no anti-social desires—heterosexuals, in other words—thus further confirming homosexuality as a mental illness and criminal activity. From the point of view of the trans communities, it is not possible to overestimate the influence of this single, highly publicised case. Many of the senior medical practitioners who still provide care for trans people in the UK were Money's students; his work made it to the high street bookshops as pop-science; and he was successful in seeking a high media profile. As one trans activist put it to me:

> You know, I bought that paperback, *Sexual Signatures,* and I thought, right, now I'll find out who I am, now I'll sort out . . . I must have been about nineteen or twenty and I was just exhausted by trying to work out who I was, what I was, whatever. And he told me I was mad. If I'd been brought up properly, and as far as I knew I'd had the same upbringing as my brother, I'd be fine. And I was like so clearly not fine. So I must be insane. I spent years wondering if I'd go madder, years controlling everything I did so no-one would find out I was really mad, wasn't this respectable, intelligent, responsible person but really a crazy person.[21]

Gender reassignment programmes were closed and the same set of 'therapies' that had been used on gay men and lesbians were transferred wholesale for use on trans people. This new pathologisation was followed by a new disenfranchisement of trans people in the UK, through the 1970 case of *Corbett v Corbett*, in which medical evidence of congenital disposition, which had formerly been accepted in courts of law, was now ignored.[22] From that point on, civil identity

---

[21] Personal discussion. The individual in question prefers to remain anonymous.
[22] See footnote 12.

was refused to trans people, who felt outlawed, criminalized, abjected. It was not until 1998, that, in the USA, Professor Milton Diamond discovered the real outcome of John Money's iconoclastic research. The child who had been reassigned had never been happy in their new gender, had always believed themselves to be a boy, and as soon as they were able to, had reassigned to male. Money's findings were revealed as being grossly overstated at best, but not before a generation of tertiary specialists had been misled, a generation of patients mistreated, and a generation of citizens denied civil identity.

Interestingly, though, even before Diamond's discovery, Money's 'nurture' position had shifted towards a multifactorial one, so that in 1994, he stated 'causality with respect to gender identity disorder is subdivisible into genetic, prenatal hormonal, postnatal social, and postpubertal hormonal determinants' and suggested that 'there is no one cause of a gender role . . . Nature alone is not responsible, nor is nurture, alone. They work together, hand in glove.' (Money, 1994). This clinical view of transsexualism as multi-factorial was supported by the tertiary specialists and researchers (including Money) who contributed to the Parliamentary Forum's production, *Transsexualism: the current medical viewpoint* (de Ceglie *et al.*, 1996). That document, which was produced by activists to provide a clear and authoritative overview of transsexualism, for clinical and non-clinical professionals, rapidly became a standard item of evidence in legal cases in this area.

As the pendulum swung further from nurture and closer to nature, so the idea of transsexualism as an intersex condition began to be raised. Part of the activist agenda in the UK was to provide analogies between transsexualism and other medical conditions, which would erode its formal inclusion in the DSM as a mental illness. For example, medical treatment for trans people was described as a process of moving from an already healthy state of being to an even healthier one, and an analogy was made with pregnancy as a similar movement from healthiness to increased health. The long-term medication that trans people require was compared to that required by diabetics, whose physical condition is otherwise stable. A similar analogy was made with what little is known about the etiology of transsexualism, that it is like an intersex condition, where individuals are born with physical characteristics of both sexes (see also Chau and Herring, this volume).

This metaphorical view was concretised in the public mind by popular science as brain-sex, and in the scientific mind by authoritative clinical research (e.g. Zhou *et al.*, 1995; Swaab *et al.*, 2001; discussed by Johnson, this volume). However, at a cultural level, organisations representing intersex people have strongly contested this identification, and in the discussions currently taking place, there is a sense that the literalisation of the metaphorical analogy has been seen as an encroachment by trans people onto the territory of intersex people. One view that has been expressed to me is that this represents a kind of cultural imperialism by trans people, an attempt to justify themselves by intruding on a medical categorisation that belongs to others, which is culturally oppressive.

Another view I have heard expressed is that these objections are simply trans-phobia, that these are medical classifications rather than definitions of people's whole lives and beings, and that intersex people seem to be perpetuating a cycle of abuse rather than seeking a broader social emancipation.

EDUCATION

'The following section shall be inserted after section 2 of the [1986 c. 10.] Local Government Act 1986 (prohibition of political publicity)' Section 28, 1988

Education was used starkly as handmaiden to politics with the introduction of Section 28 to the Local Government Act in 1988. This effectively removed teaching about gay, lesbian and trans issues from schools, and thus provides a major, obvious intersection between the communities. It provided that:

A local authority shall not—

(a) intentionally promote homosexuality or publish material with the intention of promoting homosexuality;
(b) promote the teaching in any maintained school of the acceptability of homosexuality as a pretended family relationship.

This was education at the service of ultra-conservatism, enacting a centralist propagandist agenda, with the purpose of silencing, and removing identity from, particular minority groups in society. The consequences for school-goers who might suffer in the process were of no concern. Whether they were the siblings, children, relatives or friends of people who were gay, lesbian or trans (see below), or were themselves identified as one of those groups, they were to be given no help, support or sympathy by their teachers. By default, homophobia and lesbophobia became state-sanctioned and acceptable to government, since there was no state-sponsored route to teaching that this might be unacceptable behaviour. As far as sexual behaviour is concerned, transphobia was arguably similarly legitimised: if you are physically male but legally female, or vice-versa, any sexual relationship with any partner is a homosexual one. Sex education became heterosexist sex education, with an elision of issues of sexuality or gender. Children might be curious about sex, but that curiosity could be directed in only one, state-sanctioned direction. The parallel here in compulsory education is with religious education of an earlier period, which taught and allowed inquiry only into Anglican Christianity. In a secularised, multi-faith society, an extreme right-wing viewpoint erected 'the family' in place of 'the Church,' and specified what counted as 'the family'—or, more explicitly, what did not.

Where the Department for Education and Science was gagged by the Conservative government, the Department of Health took over. Healthcare education could legitimately deal with issues forbidden to Local Education Authorities, and at least, at some point in their young lives, adolescents had a possibility of accessing information about a way of living that, while not illegal, was strongly sanctioned against. This was, of course, contrary to ruling orthodoxy about what constituted 'the family,' but it seems to have been placed under the same broad umbrella of acceptable male sexual irresponsibility, as was sexually transmitted disease, the kind of hypocrisy made famous by Michael Portillo's coyly sanctimonious confessions. Healthcare education provided a loophole through which young gay and lesbian people had an opportunity to find some limited authentication of themselves, in a relatively supportive environment, and to develop a starting point for a sense of self-worth.

Adequate education in transsexualism at any level is a more recent phenomenon. Standard psychiatric works, such as the *Oxford Textbook of Psychiatry*, tended to replicate outdated descriptions of trans people. It said little about trans men, focusing on trans women, and provided a diagnostic description which includes 'they usually apply for the kind of work that is done by women and enjoy cooking and sewing.' (Gelder *et al.*, 1997). Similarly, a 2001 survey of Medical School and Postgraduate Deanery teaching about transsexualism in the undergraduate and postgraduate medical curriculum showed that a minority provided any teaching on the subject to medical students. Indeed, one Medical School deliberately excluded it from the curriculum as an inappropriately salacious subject (Playdon, 2002). Fortunately, however, both the *Oxford Textbook* and the various teaching agencies for medicine have demonstrated their willingness to take this issue on board. The former has revised its entry after representations were made to it, and several undergraduate and postgraduate agencies have incorporated new material into their curricula, in response to the Survey.

The enforced elision of GLTB issues from education had a further knock-on effect. Gutter-press journalism became the only generally available source of expertise, and thereby the mediating, educational agency for the UK public. Part of the project of reclamation and re-education thus became challenging unacceptable press coverage. In trans lobbying two major strategies were deployed. One was to complain repeatedly to the Press Association about the use of insulting headlines, such as 'No Nobby Bobby', to report on a trans woman in the police service. The other was to provide deliberately low-key, issues-led press conferences, as fringe meetings at the major national party political conferences until, as one campaigner reported, press officers were overheard to say that they weren't going to the conferences 'because there's nothing sensational there.'[23] This work was accompanied by the dissemination of material produced by support groups. Press For Change and GIRES (Gender Identity Research and Education Society: www.gires.org.uk) were and are pre-eminent in the trans communities in this area, as the Albany Trust and the Campaign for Homosexual Equality (CHE) were in 1960s and 1970s campaigning for gay men,

---

[23] Christine Burns, former Vice-President of Press For Change, both led many of these press conferences and reported this success at a meeting of the Parliamentary Forum on Transsexualism.

as Radicalesbians were in the 1970s, and as the Hall-Carpenter archives (renamed *The Lesbian and Gay Newsmedia Archive* in 2001) continues to be.

The need for education is huge, therefore, to open the silenced discussions about lesbian, gay and trans lives, to remediate distorted images such as that of 'predatory homosexuals,' and to end the moral panics that associate, variously and seemingly interchangeably, homosexuality and transsexuality with paedophilia and anti-social behaviour. This continues to be a crucial arena for activism, with voluntary groups appearing to provide much of the impetus and most of the information needed in this educational project. For example, the Gay and Lesbian Association of Doctors and Dentists (GLADD) produced in 2002 a set of *Guidelines on Dignity at Work for Lesbian and Gay Doctors and Dentists (GLADD)*, and lobbied effectively so that, by 2003, their *Guidelines* had been formally adopted by the Department of Health, the General Medical Council and the British Medical Association (GLADD, 2002).

That example also suggests another set of intersections, the hidden discussions and exchanges that take place between different groups of activists, so that each can learn from, and benefit by, the work of others. So, as part of this informal educational agenda, the barrister who spoke at the GLADD workshop through which its *Guidelines* were initiated, Rambi de Mello, was the same barrister who worked with Madeleine Rees to create and carry through *P v S and Another (Sex Discrimination)*[24]. Similarly, on a personal note, while that case was waiting to be heard by the ECJ, Madeleine and I were casting round for ways by which it might inform and be useful to lesbian and gay campaigning, and hit on the Armed Forces as a fertile possibility. A phone call to Stonewall, the gay and lesbian campaigning body, established that they were thinking along the same lines. Consequently, on one hot June evening, a lot of people crammed a small room in St James, Stonewall's then headquarters, including Madeleine, myself, Rank Outsiders and the solicitor who had just won the landmark Armed Services pregnancy case. Out of that first meeting, where different activists were pooling experiences and sharing possibilities, came the successful action to end discrimination against lesbians and gay men in the Armed Services.

In this connection, the Internet has proved invaluable as a source of information and exchange of ideas. For researchers, it provides archived documents that otherwise are difficult to obtain, and ephemera that would be impossible to source. For activists, it provides a network of contacts that is invaluable. Ceri Edwards, the researcher who put together Liberty's Amicus brief for the case of *Horsham & Sheffield*,[25] provided as part of that brief a chart showing the civil liberties enjoyed by trans people across the world (Liberty, 1997). Press For Change, the lobbying organisation that supplied him with the information, did so by trawling the Internet, and where information was not readily available, found someone elsewhere in the world who could provide it.

---

[24] See footnote 2.
[25] *Sheffield and Horsham v United Kingdom* [1998] 2 FLR 928.

ROADS TO FREEDOM

'Freedom at last! Long sought, long prayed for—ages and ages long: The burden to which I continually return . . .' Edward Carpenter (1896: 3)

The roads to freedom for gay men, lesbians and trans people both intersect and diverge, as the communities seek to work together and also pursue their own legitimate interests. This has produced a curious counterpoint, in which trans people first had a civil identity while gay men were criminalized and lesbians narrowly avoided the same fate. Then when gay men were decriminalised, trans people lost their civil status. Now, at a point when government has announced a draft Gender Recognition Bill to allow trans people to gain legal recognition in their real gender,[26] and new legislation has been implemented in December 2003 to provide employment protection for gay men and lesbians, there is a resurgence of opposition to the removal of Clause 28. It is as if society always needs a victim to assuage its (hetero)sexual anxiety.

The most crucial intersection has been the common actions of organising and activism. If the end-point of the social processes of exclusion is education, as a means of disseminating the outsidership of the abjected group, then the starting point for activism against it is also education: tell the story again, but tell it differently. Valorising the standpoint of marginalized individuals, beginning research with their lived, daily experiences, and developing theories out of that—the approach of feminist praxis—became the almost instinctive response of lesbian, gay and trans activists.

In 1967, homosexuality was decriminalised in England and Wales by Parliament's acceptance of 21 as the age of consent, although it took another thirteen years for Scotland to accept that, another fifteen years for Northern Ireland, and the Isle of Man only got there in 1992. The Stonewall Riot, in New York City, in June 1969, heralded a new phase of gay civil rights lobbying and a new sense of 'gay pride', expressed in the UK by the foundation of the Gay Liberation Front in 1970. This phase found expression in a 'we're here, we're queer, get used to it' approach to public campaigning. In 1973, the Campaign for Homosexual Equality (CHE) was started, working with the National Council for Civil Liberties (now Liberty). In cooperation with other agencies, it established the counselling service, FRIEND. In the same year, the National Union of Students annual conference included 'gay civil rights' on its agenda. Following the punitive introduction of Section 28 of the Local Government Act in 1988, Stonewall was founded in 1989, and is now the most prominent contemporary UK lobbying organisation for gay and lesbian civil liberties. By 1996, a case against the UK government had been brought in the European Court of Human Rights, alleging that the different ages of consent for gay and hetero-

---

[26] Cm 5875, announced by Department of Constitutional Affairs, 11 July 2003.

sexual people breached human rights. This case was suspended in 1997 after the then Home Secretary, Jack Straw, said that the government would do everything possible to change the law. In 2000, the age of consent for gay men and lesbians was set at 16, in England, Wales and Scotland.

The issues of the gay male community were not necessarily those of the lesbian community. After all, lesbianism had never been illegal, and lesbians were not distinguished from other Victorian women in being badly treated—all were disenfranchised, barred from the universities, forbidden the professions, emphatically second-class citizens who should know their place. First-wave feminism was concerned with women in general, therefore, not lesbians in particular. Invisibility was and is an issue for lesbian activists, however. The automatic assumption that all women wish to have a husband and children, and the social invalidation of those who do not, which comprises 'compulsory heterosexuality', is one cause of lesbians being unacknowledged in society. Another facet is the interpretation of the lives of distinguished women in patriarchal terms, so that marriage or absence of marriage is presented as the defining feature of their lives; these are areas investigated by Lynne Segal (this volume). Second wave feminism, in the 1960s and 1970s, presented a robust challenge to these mores, with ideas such as 'until all women are lesbians there will be no revolution' (Johnston, 1973: 166), and the notion of a 'lesbian continuum' (Rich, 1980) of relationality between women, from close affectionate friendship to committed lifelong sexual partnership. As the women's movement developed, so it took different directions in the USA and in Europe. In the USA, the emphasis tended to be on a homogenizing view of 'Women' as being somehow a single, collective group. Politically, US feminism was criticized as 'limited reformism, improving the lot of an already relatively empowered selection of White, middle-class, heterosexual, female individuals' (Munt, 1994: 35). By contrast, European feminism was more open to European social and political critiques, which led it to embrace diverse countercultural projects; to adopt a particular approach of welfare radicalism; and to understand women as occupying a series of intersecting oppressions in society, which could be understood only by an analysis of the lived, everyday experience of individuals. While recognising the differences in these approaches, all were invaluable, in raising consciousness, producing debate, developing written accounts and discussions of lesbian lives and issues, and thereby contributing to the construction of a multiplicity of lesbian identities. Lesbian 'invisibility' had not prevented individuals being treated harshly, and perhaps had contributed to it, since there was less possibility of organised resistance to oppression. The debates produced by, and in response to, second wave feminism were crucial in facilitating organised activism, such as the Lesbian Avengers, the lesbian women at Greenham Common, or the Dykes on Strike who marched against the war in Iraq on International Women's Day 2003 in seventy different countries.[27]

---

[27] International Wages Due Lesbians (2003) *Dykes on Strike* [flyer]. http://womenstrike8m.server101.com.

Trans activism came relatively late to the party. Crushed by the law in 1970, the entry of transsexualism in DSM in 1980 at least provided a rallying point for a sense of shared identity for trans people, as well as providing diagnostic criteria for the first time, and thus ushering in a possibility of more effective healthcare for trans people. Trans issues had been taken on to some degree by Gay Liberation, so that, for example, one of the founding members of the Gay Liberation Front, Roz Kaveney, was later a representative for trans issues at Liberty and at the Parliamentary Forum. However, many of the issues were different from those of gay men and lesbians since, for example, all people treated for transsexualism require a degree of clinical intervention which gay men and lesbians do not, and in the process of gaining that healthcare, they necessarily 'out' themselves: staying 'in the closet' is not an option. In 1978 the Self-Help Association for Transsexuals (SHAFT) was founded, with a strong awareness that the community had previously had full civil liberties. A first political focus was on that issue through contact with trans people who had had their birth certificates corrected in the past, while at the same time providing support to individuals who were in the processes of transitioning. In 1986, the first attempt to gain correction of the Birth Certificate in the European Court of Human Rights failed, as did the second in 1990, the third [in the High Court] in 1998 and the fourth in 2000. But in the early 1990s, the various self-help groups into which SHAFT had developed, collaborated to form an over-arching lobbying group, Press For Change,[28] and shortly afterwards, the Parliamentary Forum on Transsexualism was established. These two bodies brought together legal, medical, and other experts, and sympathetic Parliamentarians, and between them produced a strong pressure for change. The first victory came in 1996, when a case in the European Court of Justice meant that trans people had employment rights.[29] In 1996, Kate More of Gender and Sexuality Alliance produced Guidelines for the Prison Service on the treatment of trans prisoners (More, 1996), which were subsequently used by the Prison Service as the basis for its own draft Guidelines (HM Prison Service Directorate of Healthcare, 1999). In 1998, a High Court case decided that Health Authorities had to make appropriate provision for treatment for transsexualism on the NHS: until then, the norm was for people to pay privately for treatment, something made particularly difficult by their generally unemployed status.[30]

Soon afterwards, in 2002, the decision of the European Court of Human Rights in the cases of *Goodwin* and *I v United Kingdom*, held that the government's failure to alter the birth certificates of transsexual people or to allow them to marry in their new gender role was a breach of the European Convention on Human Rights[31]. Accordingly, the UK government has put into

---

[28] www.pfc.org.uk
[29] See footnote 2.
[30] *R v North West Lancashire H A ex p A, D and G* [2000] 1 WLR 977, QBD.
[31] *Goodwin v United Kingdom* [2002] 2 FLR 487; *I v United Kingdom* [2002] 2 FLR 518.

motion machinery to provide full civil status for trans people, for the first time since 1970. Although a late arrival in the field, and with slender resources at its disposal, trans activism and lobbying has proved to be highly successful.

At the time of writing, then, all three groups are engaged in the project of reclaiming their community for dignity, not abjection, and in rewriting a history, which has systematically excluded or humiliated them. All are now articulate, professional, legally experienced and well-organised, capable of resisting exclusion, committed to working for equality and nothing less. And increasingly, all three are gaining a European identity which is separating them from the USA's fragmented legal system, moralistic medicine, and aggressively conservative politics.

NO FINAL DESTINATION?

My highly selective narrative may have given an impression of cohesion in a series of fields, which are, in reality, fragmented and debated. I have pursued this course of action for five reasons. First, because the areas of commonality between lesbian, gay and trans issues are less frequently considered. Second, because in the practice of activism, it is usual for each group to seek to avoid actions which might have negative repercussions for the others. Third, because the legal teams, which work to advance lesbian, gay and trans issues, are often made up of the same people and certainly cross-consult to use each other's arguments and law. Fourth, because the areas of medical interest, which deal with gay and lesbian issues, intersect with those which deal with trans issues, often informing and supporting each other in a similar way to that of legal teams. Fifth and finally, because there is a growing theoretical literature on queer theory and trans studies, to which this approach may make a contribution.

However, I cannot conclude without turning to a final intersection. As society starts to become, in some degree, less repressive for gay men, lesbians and trans people, in terms of legal sanction and medical punitiveness, so there is an increasing possibility for individuals and groups to understand, debate and assert their own views of their identities. This has been a constant undercurrent in, and backdrop to, all of the activism in the UK for a generation, and from time to time, the divergences of interests have been at least as evident as the intersections. Some second wave feminism rejected lesbians as not really having access to 'women's life-experience'. Gay men were initially consigned to the patriarchy by lesbian feminism, with a return to shared interests only occurring with the AIDS epidemic. Some lesbians—the so-called 'lesbian police'—rejected other lesbians who had formerly been married, as not really having access to 'lesbian life-experience'. Gay politics polarised along the propriety of forcibly 'outing' closeted gay men in prominent public positions. Some feminists rejected trans women as having formerly enjoyed 'the fruits of the patriarchy'. Lesbian politics polarised along the propriety of S & M. There are ongoing debates about, for example, 'ownership' of figures such as Billy Tipton and Brandon Teena/Teena Brandon (passing women or trans men?), about gay and lesbian monogamy or not monogamy, about the arguable oppressive misogyny of drag queens, about loud and proud or quiet assimilation, and about the suitability of lesbians, gay men and trans people as parents, to name a few late-night dinner-party discussions.

Stretching over all this demotic discussion is the post-modern debate, tantalising, exciting, and refusing completion: are lesbian/gay/trans identities based in some kind of biological essentialism or are they purely socially constructed? Or is it possible that there is a kind of self-determined personal essentialism, from which one negotiates the variety of identities available in a socially constructed society? The pragmatic activist might note the power that essentialism has in the courtroom and the public mind, and might wonder whether gay activism would have progressed further if it had not dropped the 'gay gene' argument in favour of a 'gay pride' stance. Such an activist might also acknowledge that their long-term goal was a society in which such arguments had no influence, where people were allowed to construct their lives and identities in freedom. Interrogating the balance between pragmatism and utopianism, judging where only a short term benefit is available but nevertheless acting with long-term objectives in mind, is part of the necessary contradiction through which activism is carried out.

So, what do these alternatives and possibilities mean about the agency of individuals? How do we create difference to denote separate people and groups, while maintaining communality and group identity? Is the idea of gender liberating or oppressive? What would a gender-free society look like? Are such ideas deterministic utopias or achievable socio-political realities? Must political action always be at the reductionist expense of intellectual debate? Is postmodern narrative potentially oppressive in its general inaccessibility and its neglect of the literal difficulty of everyday existence of ordinary people? Isn't it essentially at odds with feminist research? And does post-feminism really open up new possibilities? . . . to name a few post-dinner-party feverish anxieties.

I am pleased to say that I have no answers. Activism, by its nature, is full of questions and neat answers are invitations to scepticism. At the moment, it appears that some significant gains are about to be made in this particular field. But in the same breath, it is necessary to ask how these concessions might be diluted in their administration, how far, for example, Genuine Occupational Qualifications will be used to protect bastions of homophobic bigotry, such as the Anglican Church, from participating in social change? What measures will be taken by employers to implement new legislation, apart from a surface cosmetic change to their Equal Opportunities Policies, if we are lucky? Will government allow the painfully tiny number of trans people—perhaps less than a handful—who still remain in marriages they entered before they transitioned to maintain that marital status or will they be obliged to divorce in order to take up their full civil status, out of the establishment's fear of condoning gay marriages? What pieces of case law will still be vulnerable to challenge and how will we be able to protect them? What interpretations will courts put on cases and how can we second-guess them? Questions. That is the activist's legacy. Questions.

REFERENCES

ALTMAN, D, *Homosexual Oppression and Liberation* (New York, New York University Press, 1971).

AMERICAN MEDICAL ASSOCIATION, *Index Medicus* (AMA, Chicago, 1968).

AMERICAN PSYCHIATRIC ASSOCIATION, *Diagnostic and Statistical Manual of Registered Mental Disorders,* third edition, revised (New York, APA, 1980).

ANDERMAHR, S, LOVELL, ST and WOLKOWITZ, C, *A Concise Glossary of Feminist Theory* (London, Arnold, 1997).

CARPENTER, E, *Towards Democracy* (London, Swann Sonnenschein, 1896).

DE CEGLIE D, DALRYMPLE JL, GOOREN, L, GREEN, R, MONEY, J, REID, R and PLAYDON, ZJ, *Transsexualism: The Current Medical Viewpoint* (London, Press For Change, 1996).

COLAPINTO, J, 'The True Story of John Joan' (1997) *The Rolling Stone*, 11 December, 54.

DALLY, A, *Women Under the Knife* (London, Hutchinson Radius, 1991).

DENZIN, NK and LINCOLN, YS, *Handbook of Qualitative Research* (London, Sage, 1994).

DOAN, L, *Fashioning Sapphism: the Origins of a Modern English Lesbian Culture* (New York, Columbia University Press, 2001).

ELLMANN, R, *Oscar Wilde* (London, Hamish Hamilton, 1987).

FORSTER, EM, *Maurice* (London, Arnold, 1971).

GARDINER, J, *From the Closet to the Screen* (London, Pandora, 2003).

GELDER, M, GATH, D, MAYOU, R and COWEN, P (eds), *Oxford Textbook of Psychiatry* third edition (Oxford, Oxford University Press, 1997).

GLADD *Guidelines on Dignity at Work for Lesbian and Gay Doctors and Dentists* (London, Gay and Lesbian Association of Doctors and Dentists, 2002) http://www.gladd.dircon.co.uk.

HM PRISON SERVICE DIRECTORATE OF HEALTHCARE, *Draft Prison Service Guidelines on the Care, Management and Treatment of Prisoners with Gender Dysphoria* (London, HMPS, 1999).

HODGES, A, *Alan Turing: the Enigma* (London, Random House, 1992).

JOHNSTON, J, *Lesbian Nation: the Feminist Solution* (New York: Simon & Schuster, 1973).

KING, D, *The Transvestite and the Transsexual: Public Categories and Private Identities* (Aldershot, Avebury, 1993).

LIBERTY *Integrating Transsexual and Transgendered People: a Comparative Study of European, Commonwealth and International Law* (London, Liberty, 1997).

MONEY, J, 'The Concept of Gender Identity Disorder in Childhood and Adolescence After 39 Years' (1994) 20 *Journal of Sex and Marital Therapy* 163.

MORE, K, *Proposals for HMPS Review of Guidelines Relating to Transsexual Prisoners* (Middlesborough, Gender & Sexuality Alliance, 1996).

MUNT, SR, *Murder by the Book: Feminism and the Crime Novel* (London, Routledge, 1994).

ORAM, A and TURNBULL, A, *The Lesbian History Sourcebook: Love and Sex Between Women in Britain from 1780–1970* (London, Routledge, 2001).

PAGELS, E, *The Gnostic Gospels* (New York, Random House, 1979).

PLAYDON, ZJ, (1996) *The Case of Ewan Forbes* http://www.pfc.org.uk/legal/forbes.htm (6 March 2003).

—— *Transsexualism in the Medical Curriculum* (Westminster, Parliamentary Forum on Transsexualism, 2002).

PURKISS, D, *The Witch in History* (London, Routledge, 1996).

RAYMOND, J, *The Transsexual Empire: the Making of the She-Male* (Boston, Beacon, 1979).

RICH, A, 'Compulsory Heterosexuality and Lesbian Existence' (1980) 5 *Signs* 631.

SCHOLINSKI, D and ADAMS, JM, *The Last Time I Wore a Dress* (New York, Putnam Riverhead, 1997).

SIMMS, M, 'The Australian Feminist Experience' in N Grieve and P Grimshaw (eds), *Australian Women: Feminist Perspectives* (Melbourne, Oxford University Press, 1981).

SOUHAMI, D, *The Trials of Radclyffe Hall* (London, Weidenfield and Nicholson, 1998).

STONE, S, *The Empire Strikes Back: a Posttranssexual Manifesto* (Austin, University of Texas, 1987).

SWAAB, DF, CHUNG, WCJ, KRUIJVER, FPM, HOFMAN, MA and ISHUNINA, TA, 'Structural & Functional Sex Differences in the Human Hypothalamus' (2001) 40 *Hormones and Behavior* 93.

WHITTLE, S, *Respect and Equality: Transsexual and Transgender Rights* (London, Cavendish, 2002).

ZHOU, JN, SWAAB, DF, GOOREN, LJ and HOFMAN, MA, 'A Sex Difference in the Human Brain and its Relation to Transsexuality' (1995) 378 *Nature* 68.

Part 2

The Development of Sexuality: Contemporary Debates

8

A Biological Perspective on Human Sexuality

MARTIN H. JOHNSON

IN THIS PAPER, I explore how human sexuality has been studied by biomedical scientists. A central conclusion from this exploration is that scientific approaches to its study have been strongly influenced not only by extant biological and evolutionary ideas, but also by social attitudes within and beyond science itself. For example, many biologists see sexuality largely in the context of reproduction and its evolutionary role, and are less inclined to emphasise its social and political context. Gender thus features heavily in 'explanations' of human sexuality and in its classification as 'normal' or otherwise. The current strong emphasis, both socially and scientifically, on the 'New Genetics' has made genetic approaches to the study of human sexuality appealing, and this line of enquiry has further embedded it in an evolutionary context. I conclude from the currently available evidence that it is far from clear that these biomedical frameworks for the study of sexuality are adequate intellectually or practically for tackling the subject. However, biomedical research uses whatever tools and ideas are at hand to address difficult biological questions; whether or not they are adequate to the task. There is a belief that such an approach asserts 'provisional' truths in the form of hypotheses, and these stimulate production of better tools or more appropriate frameworks. I hope to give a flavour of the limitations and possibilities of biomedical approaches to human sexuality in this chapter.

I use the term 'sexuality' in its narrow sense to mean that part of our behaviour (and the underlying mental processes mediating it) concerned with the erotic (Johnson and Everitt, 2000). In fact, almost all the work I will discuss relates to same or opposite sex gender sexualities, which narrows the sense even further. The question of what 'causes' sexuality has vexed scientists and non-scientists alike. Often this question is expressed more narrowly as what causes 'aberrant sexuality' (homosexuality, bisexuality, paraphilias, paedophilia etc, etc) as though heterosexuality is not caused at all and as though 'abnormality' is self-evident. This approach is strongly culturally influenced. Its methodology does, however, reflect a familiar scientific paradigm: that understanding the mechanisms underlying the 'normal' can often best be achieved by studying 'extremes'. In taking this approach, we cannot ignore the fact that often issues of control, of justification, of validation have operated, either as motives for, or outcomes of, research studies. Indeed, the results from biomedical study have often been claimed by non-scientists as much as by scientists as justifications for treating 'abnormal sexualities' as illness, deformity, deviance or sin. Attempts at cure, punishment or elimination have followed, as have pleas for the acceptance of diversity and a better understanding of the concept of natural variation in the context of norms and abnorms (extremes) (see chapter by Playdon, this volume). A better understanding of the process and limitations of biomedical scientific approaches to human sexuality is therefore badly needed.

My starting point will be a general look at the possible forces thought by biomedical scientists to have shaped human behaviour and the processes underlying it. Three main forces have been proposed.

1. NATURAL SELECTION

Natural selection must have exerted a powerful influence on human behaviour and its underlying mental processes. As an evolved species, subject to the same sorts of selection forces as any other species, we have evolved behaviours that benefited survival. Natural selection concerns adaptive survival in a varied environment. The genes from 'unfit' individuals will be diluted out relative to those genes influencing, directly or otherwise, behaviours that improve survival. A key feature of natural selection is that the genes selected for on the basis of their behavioural impact will be common to most members of the species (Buss, 1994), in much the same way that most of us have hands and feet with five digits. For example, acute stress elicits a combined physiological, psychological, and behavioural response entirely characteristic for all *Homo sapiens*. Likewise, Masters and Johnson suggested that the physiology and subjective experience of sexual arousal is qualitatively similar in all individuals regardless of gender. These evoked mental responses and behavioural manifestations may vary in intensity and in culturally dependent expression styles, but their basic features are shared and largely seem to be a product of our biological infrastructure, namely brain structure, wiring patterns and neurochemistry, which are also broadly similar in all individuals. This basic infrastructure is genetically encoded, and chromosomal anomalies and genetic mutations can have profound effects on both brain infrastructure and expressed behaviour. Thus the brain mediates between the genes and the behavioural outcomes through which natural selection operates.

In describing these shared structural and expressive properties, it is important to make three qualifying comments. First, these are shared but not identical properties. Within the population, there are differences. Where these differences have a genetic basis, then it is on this variation that natural selection operates (Bateson, 2001). Of course, not all differences are genetically based, and it is argued from cultural studies that variations in sexual behaviour are largely cultural rather than genetic. Whatever the basis of variation, an enduring problem for medicine and society has been to determine just how far from the norm a person has to be before a psychological or behavioural condition is described as pathological, and is ripe for diagnosis and treatment. Some psychiatric conditions have the appearance of being tails on a normal distribution curve rather than qualitatively different conditions (NCB, 2002). This dilemma is unresolved, and probably unresolvable by science alone. Historically, there has been a tension between 'treating' the person for 'their own' good and treating them for 'society's' good, the balance swinging one way or another depending on current social attitudes. Arguably, the present emphasis on an individual consumer oriented society places more emphasis on individual welfare than 'social good'. For example, the major change over the past 30 years in attitudes of the medical profession towards the 'pathology' of homosexuality (Bancroft, 1989) is reflected in changes to disease classification systems (see Playdon, this volume). Second, the brain, and the psychological states and behaviours that it mediates, are complex. They involve many genes in their developmental elaboration (Bateson and Martin, 1999; Michael and Moore, 1995). The polygenic nature of behaviour explains some of the normal variation in its expression. It also means that individual genes 'for a behaviour', so often claimed in popular reportage, are highly unlikely. Individual genes, when mutated, may well affect a particular behaviour, but that does not imply that the gene 'causes' the behaviour (Bateson and Martin, 1999; Wilkie, 2001). Polygenic phenotypes, in which a large number of genes affect the phenotype, each gene with relatively low impact, also makes the identification of the genes very difficult (Risch, 2000). Third, the fact that behaviours and psychological states depend on brain structure, which in turn is influenced by genes, does not mean that genes 'determine' behaviour or psychological states. Built into our brain development is the capacity for modulation by a whole range of environmental factors operating from conception (or earlier) to adult life (see later) (Johnson, 2001a; NCB, 2002). This responsiveness of brain structural and functional development to non- or epigenetic stimuli does not detract from an underlying genetic basis for human behaviour and psychology. Indeed, this responsive adaptability may be one evolved, and therefore selected, feature that has presumably aided our survival (Oyama, 1985). Thus, the fact that genes do not determine behaviour does not mean that the effects of genes cannot be selected for or against naturally through their impact on behavioural phenotype.

2. SEXUAL SELECTION

Survival is a basic requirement for evolutionary selection, but in itself is insufficient. Unless reproduction occurs, genes cannot be transmitted to future generations and so will be selected against. Reproduction in mammals, including

Homo sapiens, is and remains sexual, notwithstanding advances in assisted reproductive technologies (Johnson, 1999, 2001b). Obligate sexual reproduction requires a male and a female to come together and mate successfully to produce and nurture an embryo through to sexual maturity. In mammals, this sexual congress is usually selective rather than random. Sexual selection of mates has the potential to influence which of the genes mediating survival are transmitted to future generations with higher frequency. Sexual selection is therefore of central relevance to the theme of this volume, since it involves consideration of what is sexually attractive (Gould and Gould, 1997). The problem of sexual selection, in the form of the peacock's tail, greatly vexed Charles Darwin. How could a tail as cumbersome and visible as this be anything other than a liability to survival? Its bulk slows a male down and its brightness increases his visibility to predators. It seems fundamentally disadvantageous. The answer to its evolutionary survival came with his understanding that females liked it and so female mate choice drove the positive selection of the genes encoding its complex structure. Males grew bigger and brighter tails driven by female choice. The marked and very varied sexually dimorphic features of many birds and animals is taken as evidence of the widespread occurrence of sexual selection of males by females as a driving force in evolution. This conclusion is only partially correct, because other forms of sexual selection can exist. For example, some sexually dimorphic features may have been selected indirectly by inter-male competition for access to females rather than by female choice *per se*—for example, widow birds, in which the male feature mediating inter-male competition for territory differs from the feature mediating attractiveness to females (Gould and Gould, 1997). In addition, there may also be sexual selection through inter-female competition for access to males (especially to genetically fit males) as well as selection for male features attractive to females. Sexual selection is complex and shows species-specific differences in emphasis on the selection mechanisms involved. However, what unites all of these types of sexual selection is the capacity to drive the development of features, which might seem at first sight to be liabilities in terms of natural selection.

There appears a potential for tension between the two selection processes. However, natural and sexual selection operate together, of course, and so, across many species, it seems that sexual 'attractiveness' may have evolved such that the feature(s) selected for as 'attractive' indicate a high overall fitness to survive. Thus, symmetry, complexity and size (of anatomical features and/or their use in display) are features that seem to be 'attractive' across many species. Complex, large and symmetrically patterned growth requires the successful actions of many genes. It is thus very sensitive to genetic defects. Those sexually mature males and females which do not achieve symmetric growth are probably therefore genetically 'less fit' than those that do, either because of a direct effect of deficient genes or indirectly through less effective foraging for food or lower parenting skills etc. Thus, elaborate sexual display features can act as surrogate markers for genetic health. In humans, for example, symmetry of sexual features has been shown in several studies to be more attractive (Manning, 1995; Manning, Koukourakis and Brodie, 1997).

However, not all species are strongly sexually dimorphic. Specifically, men and women show only a relatively mild sexual dimorphism (Martin, Wilner and Dettling, 1994). Thus, when populations of human males and females are compared for the spread of a range of phenotypes such as body weights or heights, body shapes, brain sizes, IQs, spatial skills, language skills etc, the distribution curves overlap substantially and the differences between means are usually small even when significant. In general, sex differences (apart from reproductive organs) are not reliably predictive of sex. For humans, therefore, there is little evidence for *strong* selection of male features by females. This could mean that sexual selection has not occurred in the evolution of humans, or only weakly so, or for only a limited period of our evolution. It could also mean that sexual selection has occurred but mutually, males selecting females and females selecting males, and that many of the features selected for are reciprocated. Indeed, it has been argued that sexual selection drove the development of the complex neocortical brain function observed uniquely in humans with our capacity not only for intelligence but also for creative, social, artistic, intellectual and recreational endeavours (Miller, 2000). Our complex brain organisation and function has been likened to the peacock's tail in its complexity, extravagance, size and polygenic basis, and thus in its high survival cost, making it a sensitive indicator of genetic health. The difference between humans and the peacock is that the high level of brain organisation and function is common to both sexes. If indeed mutual sexual selection for brain development has been a part of our evolution, then presumably the features being selected must have been very similar for both sexes? There is indeed evidence that men and women do look for similar or overlapping features when scoring faces for their attractiveness. Thus, computerised and symmetrical facial images of men and women were modified to look more or less masculine, and their attractiveness rating examined in two cultures (Scotland and Japan). It was found that the more feminised face type in **both** men and women was favoured by **both** sexes (Perrett, Lee, Penton-Voak, Rowland, Yoshikawa *et al.*, 1998). Quantitative assessments of the features associated with more feminised male faces emphasised qualities of warmth, honesty, intelligence, emotionality, cooperativeness and quality as a parent. It is unclear to what extent the preference for a feminised male facial phenotype is culturally conditioned or inherent, but the fact that such a preference can be detected may have interesting implications for the evolution of our sexuality (see Discussion). It should certainly caution us against taking an unduly simplistic 'reproductive' view of human sexuality.

Finally, it is important to note that sexual selection depends not only on attractiveness, but also the capacity to exercise free choice on the basis of attraction. For most human societies, this choice simply does not exist. Power, wealth, gender, kinship patterns, age, religion, are all social variables which affect the available social pool of possible mates and the freedom to select from within it.

Such constraints need not eliminate attractiveness as an influence on mate choice, but may well reduce its importance. However, it is unclear whether these constraints operated as we evolved as a species or are recent developments on the evolutionary time scale.

3. EPIGENETIC INFLUENCES

Natural and sexual selection operate to influence genetic transmission. Genotypes are selected for survival and reproduction on the basis of their phenotypic expression in the environment experienced. The genes are perpetuated selectively and there is a consequential evolution of phenotype. However, in addition humans, if not exclusively at least pre-eminently, have culture which can also be transmitted from generation to generation. For example, cultural aspects of diet, whether driven by food provision strategies (gatherers, hunters or growers), fashion, or religion, may impact upon the life of the embryo and fetus in the womb and the individual post-natally with enduring effects (Johnson, 1999, 2001a). Sensory stimulation *in utero* or post-natally can set hormonal and neural circuitry for life. Blood flow and fetal position *in utero* can impact on phenotype. Social learning quite clearly imposes cultural and emotional values and establishes cultural and personal norms that shape individual identity and social relationships early in life and thereby the pattern of life's reactions with or against this early learning (Bateson and Martin, 1999; Hinde, 1997; Johnson, 2001a; Rose, 1997). This non- or epi-genetic information is clearly very important for humans; it distinguishes different cultures, classes and sexes, and although transmitted inter-generationally may also change with time and changing circumstances. Some have argued that sexuality lies at the extreme of socially constructed behaviour.

4. ENVIRONMENTAL AND GENETIC INTERACTIONS

So how can we bring these three influences together? The traditional view of genetics holds that a gene (made of DNA, the base sequence of which encodes information) is faithfully replicated as a messenger (called RNA), which then, through the agency of a protein synthesising machinery translates the code into a protein. Proteins are critical components of our bodies, comprising structural molecules, catalysts and regulators, which basically determine our appearance and behaviour. This is the 'one gene, one protein' model for converting the genotype (our genetic make up) into our phenotype (what we look like and how we behave). However, now that we know the sequence of the whole genome and know more about how it is used, the simplistic nature of that model is very clear. For example, the total number of genes identified in the human genome is around 30–35,000. This number is not much greater than the number of genes in many simpler organisms. It also is far too few to account for the numbers of proteins in our bodies. A more sophisticated and contemporary model for thinking about the relationship between genotype and phenotype understands that there are many steps between DNA sequence and protein function, each susceptible to modulations which influence the final phenotype achieved. Thus, it is clear that whether, when and by how much a gene is activated to make RNA can depend on a variety of contextual factors outside of the genetic code itself. Moreover, even when activated, one gene can actually generate a great variety of different (although related) mRNAs and proteins, which differ in their times and places of expression and in their functional properties. Once produced, proteins can be modified in various ways that further alter their properties. This great variability in the relationship between activation of a gene and production of a functional protein gives scope for the modulating action of non-genetic regulatory factors, including environmental ones. The genotype:phenotype relationship becomes complex. When the phenotype under study involves many genes (is polygenic) because it is itself complex (as behaviour is), the task of unravelling mechanistic relationships becomes even more difficult, not least because each of the multiple gene loci involved may be complexly regulated, often in interactive networks. Indeed, many believe that unravelling the genotype:phenotype relationship for behavioural characteristics such as sexuality may be simply impossible. This, of course, has not stopped scientists from trying, and there are encouraging outcomes that seem to describe how environmental influences might interact with genetic influences to affect behavioural outcomes.

For example, a recent study from birth to adulthood of males who were maltreated as children, some of whom grew up to develop antisocial violent behaviour, reported that a distinctive genetic sequence (called a functional polymorphism) was associated preferentially with those males showing a lower incidence of antisocial behaviour. This polymorphism was located in a gene encoding an enzyme, which controls the destruction of a brain neurotransmitter (monoamine oxidase A or MAOA). One interpretation of these results is that an interaction occurs between childhood abuse (an environmental factor) and MAOA activity (a genetic factor) to influence the likelihood of expression of a particular behavioural phenotype (Caspi, McClay, Moffitt, Mill, Martin *et al.*, 2002). A recent study from the same group (Caspi, Sugden, Moffitt, Taylor, Craig *et al.*, 2003) has suggested that a person's depressive reaction to stress is influenced by a polymorphism in the promoter region of the serotonin transporter (5-HTT), again implicating gene-environment interactions to explain variable behavioural outcomes. If these observations are substantiated, and the association shown to be causal, these examples offer opportunity to study further the molecular and cellular mechanisms by which genes interact with environmental signals to produce behavioural outcomes that are not simply determinative, as the one gene, one protein model tends to imply. So the take home message is that there is nothing determinative about genes that influence behaviour. Complex genetic and epigenetic interactions will affect the ultimate behaviour that develops. This level of complexity presents the scientific method with a great challenge, which it has not yet succeeded in meeting in the context of human sexuality.

5. HUMAN SEXUALITY

Where does human sexuality fit into this analysis? Sexuality is usually considered as divisible (for research methodology purposes if for no other) into two components. Sexual identity is the internal mental state of what you feel yourself to be sexually, and sexual role is the external behavioural manifestation of your sexuality, whether or not it is congruent with your sexual identity (Golombok and Fivush, 1994). A consideration of the scientific methodologies of study of human sexuality is important, because implicit in informative scientific studies is a clearly identifiable phenotype.

Sexual role may be studied observationally or through history-taking or self-reporting of sexual activities in diaries (what have you done sexually, with whom, and how often etc). Sexual identity is usually and most readily studied by questionnaires or interviews (what are your sexual beliefs, feelings, fantasies, self-identity etc). Clearly, the validity of such studies relies on the truthfulness of the responses, and so in the best studies efforts are made to control for distortion or lying. For example, ensuring confidentiality and/or anonymity, looking for convergence in answers to different questions addressing the same sexuality, planting questions to detect inconsistencies in responses etc. A more attractive approach to scientists, because of its apparent objectivity, might be physiological responses to erotic material. For example, phallometric assessment of comparative sexual arousal or aversiveness in response to different sexual stimuli (e.g. naked men versus naked women) uses plethysmography to measure relative changes in genital blood flow (Harris and Rice, 1996). Carefully controlled use of this approach in connection with sex offenders (rapists and child sexual abusers) has been claimed as useful in sentencing and treatment (see Brooks-Gordon, Bilby and Kenworthy, this volume). However, there remain concerns about its inappropriate or improper use, lack of standardisation and validation, that it may be susceptible to undetected voluntary control (both suppression and false excitation) or habituation, and about its personal invasiveness, which may bring its own problems of sensitisation and false positive arousal (Launay, 1999; Lumiere and Harris, 1998; Marshall and Fernandez, 2000). Despite these concerns, the phallometric approach has been claimed as useful in research studies of homo-/hetero-sexual preference (Adams, Motsinger, McAnulty and Moore, 1992; Adams, Wright and Lohr, 1996). Less physically invasive, objective methods that might be used alternatively or additionally are the monitoring of response to sexual imagery in skin conductance and heart rate, pupillography (McGraph, 1991), relative attention by eye movement patterns (Abel, Huffman, Warberg and Holland, 1998; Abel, Lawry, Karlstrom, Osborn and Gillespie, 1994; Harris Rice, Quinsey and Chaplin, 1996; Wright and Adams, 1994), or localised brain blood flow by thermal imaging (as already applied to erotic arousal differences in men and women (Beauregard, Levesque and Bourgouin, 2001; Karama, Lecours, Leroux, Bourgouin, Beaudoin *et al.*, 2002), but not, as far as I can ascertain, to homo-/hetero-sexual preference). It is interesting to note that the use of physiological testing methodologies, as for questionnaires, has indicated that human sexual responses are complex and both context and individual specific. Overall, these studies raise real concerns about the validity of assessment techniques. Are they capable of measuring what we think they are measuring?

For studies to be valid, there must be a clearly defined and measurable phenotype. Some published studies are unclear on the sexuality phenotype under study, using general descriptive terms that may have different meanings to different people. For example, is it satisfactory to ask someone to categorise themself as homosexual or heterosexual? Do persons who have experimented sexually across and within gender, or been forced into particular sexual activities through social pressure or circumstance, or lived in different societies in which sexuality is organised differently all respond in a consistent way? It is unlikely. More discriminating surveys have established, for example, that in a sample of young males, there were more who self-described as heterosexual and had some homosexual feelings than there were self defined homosexual males, that is most homosexual feelings were found in the heterosexual subgroup (Buhrich, Armstrong and McConaghy, 1982; McConaghy, Buhrich and Silove, 1994). Questions may need to be specific when undertaking surveys or recruiting to groups. For example, have you kissed/had penetrative sexual intercourse with a man/woman ever/in the last year/more than 5 times in the last year/when you were under 20 years of age, and/or have you fantasised about doing so etc etc. Clearly some balance between 'lumping' and 'splitting' has to be achieved for practicable studies to be undertaken, but we do need to know where this balance point should be (Weinrich, Snyder, Pillard, Grant, Jacobson *et al.*, 1993). The problem with many scientific studies of human sexuality is that the complexity of our sexuality is not really acknowledged and the appropriate level of discrimination does not occur. Scientists may complain that the more refined the sexuality classification, the smaller each cohort size becomes, and less the power of the analysis. That is an understandable but unreasonable complaint! Perhaps the very variety of sexuality may be telling us something important!

Even if we could achieve valid measures of human sexuality, the measures must also be reliable. Given that different types of sexual roles and identities have different emotional and social values, one must be alert to bias. Negatively viewed sexuality will tend to be under-represented and socially accepted sexuality over-represented in research. Moreover, within each category of sexuality used in the study, there may be a tendency by those who do respond to exaggerate aspects of their sexual activity or identity. This may occur even when studies are anonymised, since self-affirmation as main-stream or oppressed can be an important element of sexual identity. Most importantly, how different individuals are recruited for study can introduce bias, since self-selection out or in may not be random across different sexualities (Purdie, Dunne, Boyle, Cook and Najman, 2002). Finally, researchers (scientific and social) are sexual beings and bring their own values and prejudices to their studies. Unless studies are well controlled and blind and free from censorship, they will be compromised. Many if not most of those published do not escape this criticism. After all, when social reactions to sexuality research can be so extreme, a degree of sub-conscious or conscious manipulation of results and/or their presentation to favour the scientists' own social views is highly likely.

Against this methodological background, is there anything that can usefully be concluded from available published information?

6. THE SEARCH FOR A BIOLOGICAL BASIS FOR SEXUALITY

Most studies have focussed on the heterosexual-bisexual-homosexual axis of sexuality, some based on the Kinsey classification system (Kinsey, Pomeroy and Martin, 1948). This system uses sets of scales rating people as 0-6 (hetero- to homo-sexual) for fantasies, identity and past and current behaviour. Broadly, studies can be divided into those that look for genetic influences, and those that look for brain/hormonal influences.

Genetic studies

Two sorts of genetic study have been undertaken: twin studies in an attempt to gain a measure of the heritability of sexuality, and family studies, which try to identify chromosomal regions that influence sexuality.

Twin studies

In twin studies, monozygotic and dizygotic twins (and in some cases natural or adoptive non-twin siblings) are compared for sexuality concordance. Usually the question has been: are both heterosexual (Kinsey 0 or 0-1) or non-heterosexual (Kinsey scale 1-6 or 2-6)? A measure of heritability is produced, which is simply a quantitative description of that part of the phenotypic varia-tion within the study population that can, under the specific circumstances of the study, be ascribed to a genetic influence. The heritability in most studies of complex behaviours tends to be less than 50% (Plomin, DeFries, McClearn and Rutter, 1997), which means that non-genetic factors account for more of the variability in phenotype. It will be clear from the discussion in Section 4, that attempts to separate out genes and environment into discrete components may be conceptually misleading—the two are closely interwoven during development. Thus, when the heritability of a trait is described as being 45%, it does not explain how the genes contribute 45% of the trait or at what level or through what sorts of interactive processes. Neither does it mean that the answers to each of these questions are the same for different individuals or different populations under different conditions: it is an averaging statement about a particular population within which variety exists. It is also important to note in the context of twin studies that, although the uterine environment is now recognised as important for a number of post-natal phenotypic attributes, simply sharing a uterus need not expose you to identical environments. For example, the haemodynamics of co-twin circulations may differ, and lead to marked differences in nutrition, birth weight and appearance, despite genetic identity. For example, monozygotic twins, despite their genetic identity, may differ in their facial symmetry and this has been shown to affect their relative attractiveness (Mealey, Bridgestock and Townsend, 1999). Likewise, the uterine environment may be very important for behavioural development. Comparative modelling studies on IQ, in mono- and dizygotic twins (which share the same uterine environment) and in siblings from different gestations (which do not), have suggested a large maternal (uterine) effect of around 20% for twins and 5% for siblings of IQ covariance (Devlin, Daniels and Roeder, 1997).

Results from some of the larger twin studies are summarised in Table 1. Overall, there is a trend for rates of concordance for sexuality to be higher in monozygotic than dizygotic twins, and for twins to show higher values than non-twin siblings. Concerns about these studies include: (i) potentially biased recruitment of samples (studies 1–5), (ii) use of unsophisticated instruments to assess sexuality (and in some cases failure to check reported sexuality of co-twin) (studies 1, 3, 8), (iii) pooling of men and women, which is not likely to be legitimate (Bailey, Dunne and Martin, 2000) (studies 3, 6, 8), and (iv) assumptions made in calculating heritabilities, which account for the wide ranges listed. Although most studies suggest that there is a heritable component to non-heterosexuality in both men and women, the most rigorous study (Bailey, Dunne and Martin, 2000) provides the lowest estimate for heritability. This study recruited from a twin data-base and did not specify homosexuality as the main aspect of the study when recruiting, leading perhaps to less selecting out of the least confident homo- and bi-sexual respondents. Interestingly, this study also had many more Kinsey category 1 respondents (mildest bisexuality). Kirk, Bailey, Dunne and Martin (2000) also recruited 4901 participants in a similar way from the same Australian twin data-base and used a more complex analytic instrument to explore multiple dimensions of sexuality. They then used multivariate structural equation modelling to estimate a heritability of 50–60% for women and 30% for men.

Table 1. Summary of sexuality concordance rates from twin studies in which one twin or sibling was the index case against whom their co-twin or sibling was compared.

MZ=monozygotic; DZ=dizygotic; NT=non-twin natural sibling; Adop=adopted sibling; W=women; M=men

Study (sex)	% MZ twins (nos.)	% DZ twins (nos.)	% NT siblings (nos.)	% Adop siblings (nos.)	Recruitment of subjects	Assessment instrument	Authors' conclusions
1.	100 (37/37)	15 (4/26)			Psychiatric patients, correctional inmates & recruits from the clandestine homosexual world'	A version of Kinsey (unspecified)	
2. (M)	52 (29/56) (P<.005)	22 (12/54)	9 (13/142)	11 (6/57)	Homophilic press	Kinsey ratings (adult fantasy & behaviour) from interview & questionnaire; homo- & bi-sexual = non-heterosexual	Heritability for non-heterosexuality 0.3–0.7; assumes sexuality is polygenic and multi-factorial in origin.
3. (M+W)	M+W 25 (5/20)	12 (3/25)			Homophilic press	Questioned about sexuality; self identification as gay	

4. (M & W)	M 65 (22/34) W 75 (3/4)	M 30 (4/14)		Homophilic press & personal referral	Kinsey rating from questionnaire + interview for some	Heritability 0.4–0.7 (same assumption)
5. (W)	48 (34/71)	16 (6/37)	6 (2/35)	Homophilic press	Kinsey ratings for adult fantasy & behaviour; interview questionnaire; lumped homo- & bi-sexual as non-heterosexual	
6. (M+W)	M47 W 48					
7. (M & W)	M 20 (9/39) W 24 (14/79)	M 3 (1/31) W 18 (8/45)		Australian voluntary twin registry	Questionnaire only used to rate on Kinsey scale	Heritability 0.0–0.7 for both (same assumption)
8. (M & W)	M+W 32 (6/19)	13 (2/15)	27 (10/41)	US National survey random sample	Single question: are you hetero-, homo- or bi-sexual (last two grouped as non-heterosexual)	Calculates heritability for non-heterosexuality of between .28 and .65.

Family Studies

Family studies take a different approach, which potentially allows larger cohorts since they do not rely on finding twins. Such studies have searched for evidence of higher rates of homosexuality among relatives of the index homosexual person (e.g. Bailey and Bell, 1993; Pillard and Weinrich, 1986). Pillard and Bailey (1998) reviewed these family studies, and listed ranges of same-sex sibling rates of homosexuality of 9–22% for men (controls 0–4%) and 6–25% for women (controls 1–11%). There was a non-significant trend towards the opposite-sex sibling homosexuality rate also being higher. Reliable data on vertical familial transmission, for example from father to sons, seem hard to come by. These figures are interesting, but, unlike twin studies, do not allow calculations of proportionate genetic influence, as the confounding effects of environment are difficult to control. They are potentially valuable, however, for pedigree analysis. Pedigree analysis involves the identification of DNA coding variations between the same regions of a chromosome in different individuals and the determination of whether the possession of a particular coding variant associates with a particular feature, such as homosexuality. In essence, one is trying to relate the possession a particular genetic variant to expression of a particular behaviour. This is called a genetic 'linkage' study (Wilkie, 2001).

Two studies used pedigree analysis to claim a genetic linkage of homosexuality in some males to a marker on the long arm of the X chromosome (at a location called Xq28). Hamer, Hu, Magnuson, Hu and Pattatucci (1993) recruited index cases from HIV clinics, gay mental health clinics and homophile publications and used Kinsey scale assessments. By asking about relatives' known sexuality (some of which were checked by interview), an excess of maternal male relatives was found, at a frequency of up to 6 times the control level, suggesting possible maternal X chromosome involvement. Molecular analysis of the X chromosome suggested an excess of a particular genetic sequence (called an allele) at the Xq28 region in some, but not all (33/40 = 82%), families of 40 gay brother pairs. Note that 20/40 (50%) would be random (in the simplest case), so deviations from this suggest genetic linkage. A further study by this group on families of selected index cases (33 men and 36 women) confirmed the above study for men (22/33 = 66%), but found no evidence for linkage of female homosexuality to Xq28 (Hu, Pattatucci, Patterson, Lin, Fulker *et al.*, 1995). It is important to stress that these analyses were undertaken on a highly selected group of families. For inclusion, homosexual index cases had to score Kinsey 5/6, not have a homosexual father, and have at least one gay male sibling. The familial *heterosexual* Xq28 typing was performed only in those families in which both gay siblings were Xq28 concordant. Despite this high criterion selectivity, the Xq28 region was not found to be associated with all male homosexuals, even in these families. An attempt to replicate independently these findings on 48 families, using similar inclusion criteria to those of Hamer, failed to detect any linkage to Xq28 (20/46 shared = 42%) (Rice, Anderson,

Risch and Ebers, 1999). It is unclear why this attempt at replication failed. However, it should be noted that many linkage studies on complex traits are not reproducible (Risch, 2000). One must be suspicious that inclusion/exclusion by either subject or experimenter played a role. This possibility was tested in a study of three family cohorts for which index subjects were recruited in different ways (Bailey, Pillard, Dawood, Miller, Farrer *et al.*, 1999). Despite a larger total of index subjects (517), no evidence of linkage to the X chromosome was found, regardless of recruitment method. If X-linked genes can influence male homosexuality, they seem to account for few cases in the general population.

Conclusions

Taken together, results from these twin and family studies are consistent with genes influencing the variation in sexual attraction to the same sex among both men and women. The studies do not allow a secure quantification of the genetic effect(s) nor identify genes or genetic regions responsible. Such conclusions are unremarkable. One would be surprised if genes did not influence the variety of sexual expression. The data certainly provide no support for a gene or genes specifically encoding a particular sexuality. Indeed, they argue against strong selection pressures during evolution for such a genetic mechanism.

Endocrine influences

Analysis at quite a different level probes the influence of developmental hormones on sexuality. The general hypothesis here is that some feature of the endocrine pattern in fetal and/or neonatal life causes structural changes to the developing brain that affect the subsequent expression of sexuality. A large body of experimental data from animals supports the idea that levels of sex steroids (notably androgenic steroids) can affect brain structure and/or local neuro-endocrinology (hormone receptors or modifying enzyme activities) during a critical developmental window to 'fix' them in a male rather than female pattern of *sexual responsiveness*. In the absence of androgens, a female-type responsiveness is the 'default' state. When these animals reach adulthood, the *expression* of the appropriate sex behaviours may then require a second exposure to the appropriate hormone to elicit sex typed behaviour (see review by Swaab, Chung, Kruijer, Hofman and Ishunina, 2001). Most animal studies examine sex-stereotypic behaviours to see whether addition or absence of androgens at critical times leads to more or less masculine or feminine behaviour respectively. Clear effects are observed, although they are usually quantitative rather than absolute. The effects can also be complex, for example loss or gain of male-type behaviour is rarely balanced by the reciprocal gain or loss of female-type behaviour; mixed patterns of behaviour occur. A key site of sex hormone sensitivity in animals is the anterior region of the hypothalamus, a small region at the base of the brain. At this site, clusters of nerve cells (neurons) called nuclei bind and metabolise sex steroids, show male:female differences in size, composition and/or activity, and, when stimulated or inhibited locally, elicit or affect sex-typed behaviours. The traditional animal model has been the rat, which shows opportunistic mating rather than long-term pairing as part of a larger social group, like humans. The sex-typed behaviours analysed have mainly been copulatory, and most studies were done after experimental manipulations involving hormone injections, castration and other assaults on bodily integrity. In applying this sex-difference animal model to humans, there is an implicit assumption that our sexuality is a sex-specific trait and that there is a natural concordance for maleness, masculinity and sexual selection for females and for femaleness, femininity and male sexual selection. It is arguable that this model is highly inappropriate for humans. Recently, however, different animal models have been developed.

First, there has been a realisation that both heterosexuality and homosexuality occur naturally among animal populations. There has been some reluctance to equate animal same-sex partner selection with human sexual preference, suggesting that it only occurs *in extremis* (no opposite sex available) or is social rather than sexual (for example, part of dominance hierarchies or alliance formation)—as though neither of those situations ever apply in human society! Whilst some same sex sexual interactions in animals may have these functions, others do not seem to be readily explained this way. For example, some 6-10% of rams (domestic and wild) are found to court or mount only rams, but never ewes. They show no female-like behaviours as adults (for example, they do not solicit other males or allow themselves to be mounted). No effect of social hierarchy or rearing has been shown to be associated with their behaviour (Roselli, Resko and Stormshak, 2002). This male sexual partner preference is correlated with distinctive patterns of oestrogen binding and androgen metabolism (by a process called aromatisation) in nuclei in the medial preoptic area of the anterior hypothalamus, the homosexual rams resembling ewes more than heteterosexual rams in this regard (Perkins, Fitzgerald and Moss, 1995; Pickard, Stellflug, Resko, Roselli and Stormshak, 2000; Resko, Perkins, Roselli, Fitzgerald, Choate *et al.*, 1996). This area of the hypothalmus has been implicated in sexual partner preference in experimental studies in other species such as the rat (Paredes, Nakagawa and Nakach, 1998) and ferret (Paredes and Baum, 1995). So these studies seem to identify homosexual behaviour distinct from other disturbances of sex-specific behaviours in a non-manipulated animal model, in which hypothalamic involvement in altered sexual preference is detected.

Second, a quite different model has been developed in zebra finches (Adkins-Regan, 2002). Zebra finches are social birds, which pair for life, largely monogamously but with occasional extra-pair matings. The pairs form close physical and behavioural bonds, share parental care (including egg incubation and chick feeding), and spend time together in non-copulatory tasks. In one series of experiments, newly hatched female birds were treated immediately after hatching with masculinising hormones and then kept either in mixed-sex or female only groups until maturity. Treated females reared with other females preferentially (and atypically) selected other females over males for pair bonding.

This expansion of animal models of same sex attraction and activity beyond the surgically operated rodent is certainly welcome. Whether these models are adequate for humans is another matter, given that social structures are very species specific. However, they may provide clues for novel methodological and/or theoretical approaches to the study of human sexuality. What about studies on humans?

Androgens, Homosexual Brains and Behaviour

In general, human studies have followed a gender-based approach to homosexuality, comparing homosexual men (but rarely women) with heterosexual men and women to see which they most resemble. This approach conflates sexuality with gender and views sexual behaviour as a gender attribute—a direct transposition from animal studies. In studies on post-mortem brain samples, LeVay (1991) examined four nuclei in the anterior hypothalamus (called Interstitial Nuclei or INAH 1–4). INAH3 was found to be twice the volume in heterosexual men than in women and homosexual men. In contrast, another study has shown recently that whilst both nuclear volume and cell number were higher in men than women, neither was significantly reduced in homosexual men (Byne, Tobet, Mattiace, Lasco, Kemether *et al.*, 2001). Allen & Gorski (1992) reported that the anterior commissure (which connects the two halves of the brain) was larger in homosexual men than heterosexual men, and that it was also larger in women. However, several studies have failed to find any effect of sex on this region of the brain, and the only one which examined brains from homosexual men also failed to find an effect (Lasco, Jordan, Edgar, Petito and Byne, 2002). Other studies have examined not size differences but the numbers of neurons within a nucleus that express particular neurotransmitters or hormones, and found no difference in VIP-containing neurones (Zhou, Hofman and Swaab, 1995).

Thus, the number of reports of brain structures in humans correlating with sexual orientation is very small, with relatively few brains examined, and all claims for difference are contested. A much larger literature exists for differences comparing brains from men, women and transexual persons (both trans men and women: Kruijver, Zhou, Pool, Hofman, Gooren *et al.*, 2000), in particular suggesting that the structure of the bed nucleus of the stria terminalis in the anterior hypothalamus correlates with gender identity (but *not* with sexual orientation). However, even these more extensive studies on men:women differences are the subject of some disagreement (Byne, Tobet, Mattiace, Lasco, Kemerher *et al.*, 2001). Recent studies have shown that gender differences in human brain nuclei size and chemistry can vary markedly with adult age, brain pathology and adult endocrine state (Swaab, Chung, Kruijver, Hofman and Ishunina, 2002; Swaab, Chung, Kruijver, Hofman and Ishnina, 2001). This means that inter-group comparisons need to be well controlled. Thus, until a more complete and independently replicated data set is available to compare homosexual and heterosexual brains, we should be very cautious. If brains themselves are not yet informative about sexual orientation, what about surrogate measures of brain activity such as behaviour?

Some studies have examined behavioural features, again comparing (mostly) homosexual men with heterosexual men and women for supposedly gender specific traits. This approach also rests on the assumption that male:female differences can be measured reliably. Unfortunately, there is considerable disagreement as to whether differences are consistently observed (Caplan, Crawford, Hyde and Richardson, 1997; Sanders, Sjodin and de Chastelaine, 2002). Where differences are observed, they are often small, with considerable variation within sex and overlap between sexes. The differences are not predictive of sex. Often it is not clear whether any differences found result from structural organisation due to past hormonal and/or genetic influences during development or depend on ambient hormone levels. The latter show circadian, monthly (in women) and seasonal variation and do influence performance in behavioural tasks (Sanders, Sjodin and de Chastelaine, 2002). Finally, sex differences seem to be very task specific, for example different tests of spatial or verbal ability giving sex differences in opposite directions. Thus, although in only about a third of reported tests of spatial ability and laterality were differences between women and men found, even in these the differences were not always in the same direction (Halpern, 1992; Hyde and Linn, 1988). The outcome of test results will also be influenced by motivation, expectation and practice, all of which may differ through social expectations and experiences. With these considerable caveats in mind, when the same sorts of tests are used to compare heterosexual men, homosexual men and women, some do show the latter two to be more similar to each other than to the first. Thus, heterosexual men are more lateralised and spatially adept as a group than women and homosexual men, but less good on tests of verbal ability (Reite, Sheeder, Richardson and Teale, 1995; Sanders and Wright, 1997; Wegesin, 1998). For some tasks, the performance of homosexual and heterosexual men is reported as being similar but differing from women (see, for example, Sanders and Wright, 1997), which has led to the suggestion that sexuality differences comprise only a subset of gender differences. However, as for the sexes, differences are often small, overlap is large, and results not predictive. The clearest results that distinguish homo- and hetero-sexual men come in tests where the biggest between-sex differences are evident (Sanders and Wright, 1997).

There have been very few studies on the brains of female homosexuals. Indirect studies on the possible role of fetal and neonatal androgens on female homosexuality have been reported. Studies of women, who experienced elevated androgens due to congenital adrenogenital hyperplasia (CAH) *in utero*, suggested that they showed a significantly elevated incidence of male gender role play as girls within girl groups and, in some cases, also increased cross gender association with boys (Berenbaum and Snyder, 1995). As these girls move into adulthood, they persist in rating more masculine activities and interests compared to non-CAH girls (Berenbaum, 1999), suggesting an enduring influence of the fetal androgens. This influence may of course be indirect rather than direct, since it could just reflect the pattern of socialisation in childhood. There are reports of the prevalence of lesbian fantasies in some CAH girls as adults, and a weak suggestion that cross-gender association with boys might be more predictive of this. However, the incidence of lesbianism is not confirmed as particularly high.

Overall, these studies of brains and behaviours are inconclusive. It is simply not yet possible to be sure that those differences which are observed between people of different sexes and different sexualities are based on real sustained differences in brain organisation resulting from fetal/neonatal hormonal effects. The overlap between groups suggests (i) small differences, (ii) subgroups within the major sex and sexuality classification systems, which affect means and increase variance (Sanders, Sjodin and de Chastelaine, 2002), and/or (iii) operation of multiple influences, particularly social factors. It is also a problem that many measures used are influenced by *ambient* as well as *historical* hormonal exposure, which complicates the clean separation of early and late effects. Before leaving this subject, tests of early hormone actions considered less likely to be moderated by environment or experience subsequently will be considered.

Surrogate Markers of Early Androgenisation in Women

Surrogate markers of early androgen levels are features laid down early in life and thereafter thought to be relatively fixed. One such measure is the ratio of the length of the second digit (index finger) to the fourth digit (ring finger). This ratio is stabilised by 2 years of age. It is significantly greater in women than men, is reduced in women exposed to androgens *in utero* due to CAH, and is even smaller in men exposed to the same condition (Brown, Hines, Fane and Breedlove, 2002), suggesting that it might function as a measure of fetal/neonatal androgen dosage. Volunteer lesbian women have a significantly reduced ratio compared to heterosexual women (Williams, Pepitone, Christensen, Cooke, Huberman *et al.*, 2000), and lesbians who self-identified as 'butch' showed a more significant reduction than did self-identified 'femmes' (Brown, Finn, Cooke and Breedlove, 2002). Homo- and hetero-sexual women have also been compared using measures of auditory sensory perception and processing called otoacoustic emissions (OAE) and auditory evoked potentials (AEP) (McFadden, 2002). OAEs are weak but measurable sounds produced by the inner ear. AEPs are 'brain waves' elicited in response to click stimuli. Both are present from birth, stable through life, and characteristic for the individual. There is evidence of sex differences for both measures. Females, potentially exposed to androgens *in utero* from a male co-twin, have OAEs more like males (McFadden, Loehlin and Pasanen, 1996), although whether they show more masculine behaviour patterns is controversial (Loehlin and Martin, 1998; Resnick, Gottesman and McGue, 1993). Volunteer bisexual and lesbian women also have OAEs intermediate between heterosexual women and heterosexual men (McFadden and Pasanen, 1998).

These studies have been taken to suggest a correlation between early androgen exposure and female homosexuality (in at least some women). However, it is unclear what this association means, as the effects may not be clean mechanistically. Thus, the very basis of these surrogate measures is that early elevated androgens affect a number of features in women, including physical features such as bone growth, genitalia and body hair patterns, as well as behavioural play patterns, as we saw earlier. So a clear and direct effect on sexuality cannot be assumed, since both the girls themselves and their parents may pick up on their relatively masculinised phenotype, thereby leading to differences in the way that they are treated. Indeed, social conditioning models for sexuality emphasise the sex-stereotypic aspects of homosexuality, so it is possible to argue that homosexuality may seem like a socially acceptable choice for some masculinised girls/women. These data illustrate the difficulty of isolating cleanly one direct biological 'cause' of sexuality from other aspects of sexual and social development.

Androgens and Male Homosexuality

The digit ratio study has also been applied in a comparison of homosexual and heterosexual men (Williams, Pepitone, Christensen, Cooke, Huberman *et al.*, 2000), and no differences were found. However, men with two or more older brothers were found to have a significantly lower digit ratio (indicating higher androgens) than men with no older brothers (no effects of older sisters were observed). This observation might suggest that successive male pregnancies result in fetuses with either *higher* androgen levels or *increased sensitivity* to androgens. This fraternal birth order effect on digit ratio was similar for both homo- and hetero-sexual men. Interestingly, however, a number of separate studies has also indicated that homo/bi-sexual men are more likely than heterosexual men to have more than one older brother—but not more older sisters (Bogaert, 1998; Williams, Pepitone, Christensen, Cooke, Huberman *et al.*, 2000; reveiwed in Blanchard, 2001). Calculations from data from various studies suggest that male homosexual prevalence increases from 2% for first born son to 8% for 6th born son, and that ⅐ gay men 'owe their sexuality' to fraternal birth order effects (Cantor, Blanchard, Peterson and Bogaert, 2002). The effect of increased maternal or paternal age or of post-natal factors, rather than fraternal birth order *per se*, has been excluded as responsible for this increase. There is a rather tenuous, if intriguing, argument here implicating fraternal birth order, higher androgens (by inference), and later homosexuality. However, it is unclear how prior male pregnancies might elevate androgen levels or sensitivity (neither of which has been measured directly). Intriguingly, although homosexual men do not differ from heterosexual men for OAPs (McFadden and Pasanen, 1998), they do show relatively *hypermasculinised* AEPs compared to heterosexual men. It has also been claimed that homosexual men have larger external genitalia, which might also reflect higher androgenic stimulation of the genital tubercle developmentally (Bogaert and Hershberger, 1999). It is ironic, and possibly interesting, given the gender based model of sexuality, that gay men might be considered 'more masculine' than heterosexual men!

Fraternal Birth Order, the H-Y Antigen Complex and Homosexuality

The above studies might suggest some memory response residing in the mother of previous male pregnancies. However, it is unclear how such a memory might be mediated through increased androgen production or sensitivity. A completely different sort of explanation for birth order effects has been advanced by Blanchard and his colleagues (Blanchard, 2001; Blanchard and Ellis, 2001; Blanchard and Klassen, 1997). They (and others previously) report that boys with older brothers weighed significantly less at birth. Girls with older brothers did not. Moreover, homo/bi-sexual men with older brothers weighed less than did heterosexual men with older brothers. They hypothesise that a maternal immune response against the male-specific antigen complex on the Y-chromosome (H-Y) (Roopenian, Choi and Brown, 2002) in some way reduces birth weight, increases androgens, and increases the chance of homosexuality. Epitopes of the H-Y antigen complex are expressed on a number of cells, including embryonic cells, spermatozoa and neuronal cells. There is some experimental evidence from mice that prior hyper-immunisation of females to male cells can influence the sex ratio in subsequent pregnancies (but how and in which direction is not agreed: Hings and Billingham, 1984; Singh and Verma, 1987), that mouse pregnancies carrying male fetuses are associated with an immune reaction to H-Y (Hancock and Faruki, 1986) and that active immunisation to male antigens can affect birth weight of male offspring (but whether up or down is not agreed: Blanchard and Ellis, 2001). Ideas as to how androgens and sexuality might be influenced by increasing maternal immune reaction to H-Y are highly speculative (Blanchard, 2001).

Gender and homosexuality

The model of homosexuality implicit in the foregoing discussion is as a gender anomaly. Is this a valid model? Bancroft (1989) has argued that homosexual men and women are not necessarily effeminate or masculine respectively, and often have strong gender identities as men and women. However, empirical data

from Lippa (2000, 2002) has used large-scale collection of data on hobbies, interests, occupational preference, personality traits and self-reported gender-related
identity to produce homosexual-heterosexual diagnostic measures that are
claimed to predict accurately the sexual orientations of most men and women
tested. Developmental analyses have also commented on an apparently strong
association between crossed sex-type *play* in children and non-heterosexuality
in adults (reviewed by Bailey and Zucker, 1995). Two types of study have been
performed. In general, prospective studies have followed (mainly) boys
identified by marked gender atypical play and association patterns, and find
(perhaps unsurprisingly if the boys are identifed as gender atypical?) an elevated
incidence of homosexuality in later life. Retrospective studies on homosexual
men and women also report higher levels of recall of atypical sex play and also
of cross-sex association (of boys with girls rather than in same sex groups) than
for heterosexual recall. Independent recall of childhood gender nonconformity
by both members of a twin or sibling pair also correlated highly with a later concordant non-heterosexual orientation (Bailey, Dunne and Martin, 2000;
Dawood, Pillard, Harvath, Revelle and Bailey, 2000). There may be some
concern that an element of selective recall or suppression might influence these
retrospective studies. However, the data, taken together, do suggest a high predictive value of cross-gender childhood play for adult non-heterosexuality. If
accepted at face value (a big if), it could mean that both childhood gender non-
conformity and later non-heterosexuality are both partly inherited (common
underlying cause) or that one predisposes to or reinforces the other. For example, gender non-conformity might, through social learning in cross-sexed play-
groups and/or through social or parental reactions to cross-sexed play, tip the
balance towards non-heterosexual identity. One problem for establishing
sequence is that there is little agreement on when sexual identity is established,
although it is generally held to follow establishment of gender identity (see chapter by Jessop, this volume). However, it is again important to observe that many
homosexual adults do not report crossed gender infant experiences, nor do all
those infants with cross gender experiences develop into non-heterosexual
adults (Bailey and Zucker, 1995).

7. DISCUSSION

Contemporary biological investigations into human sexuality have been
founded on two basic premises. First, that humans, having evolved as part of the
vertebrate radiation, will share with other vertebrates broadly similar mechanisms for the selection of sexual partners. This view has been reinforced by the
extra-ordinary advances in human biology and medicine that have come from
understanding molecular mechanisms in distant relatives, such as mouse,
amphibians, insects and worms. This premise immediately focuses scientific
attention on genes and evolution, since it is our genetic inheritance that we share

with other organisms to greater or lesser extent. Second, the selection of sexual partners, and thus sexual orientation, has been seen as one component of the differences between the sexes. The premise runs that women and men differ and part of that difference is their attraction to opposite sex individuals. This view is reinforced by the important role of sexual selection in mammalian reproduction, through which it also has the capacity to drive evolutionary genetic change. This model firmly locates homosexuality as 'gender anomalous'. Taken together, these two premises have led to the broad conclusion that the genetic basis for sexual selection will be expressed phenotypically through structures and functions that mediate sex differences, especially brain and behavioural differences. Both these premises seem logically reasonable and at least consistent with what we know in general about animals, but neither is robustly sustained by the evidence currently available.

The many studies seeking a genetic influence on human sexuality, unsurprisingly, find one. The importance of the genetic effect relative to shared and unshared environments is unclear, but seems likely to be no more than 50% and probably less. All studies assume polygenic influences, and no single chromosomal locus has yet been shown unambiguously to be associated with homosexuality. Overall, the finding of a general genetic influence on the variety of human sexuality is not epiphanic. It has not advanced decisively our understanding of *how* genes might influence the development and variety of sexuality. The identification of natural animal models for homosexuality, if validated, may offer opportunities through breeding studies for a more analytical investigation as to whether any particular genetic loci can be identified. Identification of genes involved in animal models might then focus forward genetic analysis in humans. Finally, the large non-genetic component to sexuality variation leaves room for environmental influences of various sorts, the nature of which remains unclear.

The sex difference model of sexuality directs our attention to the brain. The studies of men:women differences in post-mortem brain nuclear volume and/or neuron density are still evolving towards a consensus view, and the evidence for differences between heterosexual and homosexual men is slight and controversial. This may be because differences are not real, or because differences do exist but studies have not always been adequately controlled for the effects of age, pathology, artefacts of post-mortem shrinkage, and pre-mortem drug use and hormonal state. It has also not been established whether sexual behaviour or activity might themselves affect the size or composition of those nuclei for which differences are claimed. Which came first, structural brain difference or behaviour? Developmental studies may be informative in this regard. The hypothalamus shows considerable post-natal development and differentiation between birth and puberty. It is thus potentially a target for modulation by social or other epigenetic influences. Indeed, the bed nucleus of the stria terminalis, a nucleus the properties of which may be correlated with gender identity in trans people, does not show gender-related morphological differences until after puberty, even though trans people are aware of their gender identity before adulthood (Chung, DeVries and Swaab, 2002). However, simply mapping developmental morphology may be misleading. Hormones at fetal/neonatal stages may fix a sex-specific pattern of *sexual responsiveness* unrevealed through morphology, which is then only revealed at puberty, this later *expression* occurring perhaps in response to a second exposure to the appropriate hormone, perhaps influenced by environmental inputs, to elicit morphological differences and sex typed behaviour. More sophisticated neuropharmacological or functional analyses of brain nuclei throughout life may be needed to detect the earliest changes—a difficult task. Perhaps a prospective *functional* study of the hypothalamic nuclei of boys and girls using brain imaging techniques might help (Beauregard, Levesque and Bourgouin, 2001), if such a study could achieve ethical approval?

It remains unclear, however, that the current biomedical model being used to explore and explain sexuality is adequate for the job. Current gene/brain-based ideas replaced an early environmental model, largely derived from behavioural and psycho-analytical research in the 1950s and 60s, which itself was considered to be inadequate. The contemporary model is itself more attuned to the recent emphasis on mapping the human genome. However, science has moved on. There is now an increasing awareness that neither a genetic model nor an environmental model will alone provide an adequate explanation.

First, the idea that the sex-gender-sexuality triplet can come as neat package of two readily defined phenotypes (male-masculine-female attracted and female-feminine-male attracted) is not really sustainable in the light of evidence. Morphological variation within the male and female sex categories occurs, as do intersex conditions, and we know increasing amounts about the genetic and developmental basis of this variation (see chapter by Chau and Herring, this volume). The measurement of gendered behavioural traits has emphasised the similarities between the sexes rather than their differences—we are not a very sexually dimorphic species, and the sexes overlap on most behavioural attributes (see chapter by Ingham, this volume). Sexuality is much more complex and individual than a simpler bipolar classification allows. With each link in this triplet association, the argument for bipolar categorisation weakens, and within-triplet concordance decreases. We need a much more sophisticated view of the range of possible phenotypes.

Second, as the post-genome sequence era develops, and the complexities of the links between gene sequences and the proteins become understood, the ways in which epigenetic factors can modulate genetic expression through to protein and phenotype are emerging. The ways in which these factors influence sexuality development in the context of the genetic sex-difference model need exploring. I offered two examples of how this is happening from animal systems. The zebra finch model implicated early hormonal exposure in the sex of life partner selection. However, in a series of experiments, in which non-hormone-exposed hatchlings of either sex were kept in either mixed or same sex only groups until maturity, birds from the latter all-male or all-female groups did not show the usual preferential selection of opposite over same sex for pair bonding, being equally likely to select either (Adkins-Regan, 2002). Thus, these studies support an early hormonal organisational effect on pair bonding, but also suggest a learning component dependent upon environmental exposure. The ram model of homosexuality described earlier also implicated endocrine effects on anterior hypothalamic nuclei in sexual selection. However, cross-species fostering of lambs to goats and kids to sheep results in the development of adult males, in which the foster mother facial phenotype is found to be more socially and sexually attractive (heterosexually) than the genetic mother's phenotype. This attraction persisted even when the adult offspring had lived exclusively with their own genetic type (i.e. goats with goats etc) for up to three years. In contrast, fostered female offspring showed a weaker attraction to foster mother type and lost it completely within 1–2 years of adult life with their own types (Kendrick, Hinton, Atkins, Haupt and Skinner, 1998). This result suggests a strong learning component to sexual attractiveness, at least in males, in addition to any hypothalamic influences. In a social species like humans, it seems inherently likely that even stronger social influences will operate. It is difficult, for example, to imagine that some sorts of sexuality, such as erotic arousal by clothes or objects, is hard-wired into the human genetic code. Associative learning seems a more plausible explanation. So perhaps we need to be thinking more about how genes might interact developmentally with environment to produce the range of sexuality phenotypes that exist. Although direct genetic effects on brain structure and behaviour may occur, these may then influence, for example, the way parents or peers treat you as a child, your childhood perceptions of risk and novelty, and/or your willingness to act on them, or the timing or intensity of your general sexual responsiveness and/or sensitivity to stimuli as a child and thereby to erotic associations. And might your responses directly affect the development of neuronal networks in your brain? A dialogue between the developing brain and the environmental feedback it receives might then nudge a probability of a particular gender identity or sexuality into a certainty, through a system of reinforcement in certain directions. This idea of the plastic moving to the committed, dependent on experience, is common for many developmental decisions at the morphological level, and especially in the brain.

I end with a final speculation about human sexuality. Humans are not very sexually dimorphic, have an extended immature developmental phase, and are highly social. If Miller (2000) is right, and humans evolved their large frontal cortices through mutual sexual selection to produce this non-dimorphic slowly maturing species, then what we find attractive in the opposite sex may not be too dissimilar to what we find attractive in our own sex. The finding reported earlier that feminised male faces are more attractive to both men and women than masculinised faces (Perrett, Lee, Penton-Voak, Rowland, Yoshikawa *et al.*, 1998) fits with this idea. Perhaps we have evolved gender ambiguity in sexual attraction as part of our evolution as cooperative social beings? Certainly the wide spread occurrence of homosexual interactions across all societies studied argues for a flexible sexuality being an integral part of the human condition (Ortner and Whitehead, 1981).

ACKNOWLEDGEMENTS

I would like to thank the other participants, my fellow editors, and in particular Martin Richards for helpful discussion.

REFERENCES

ABEL, G, HUFFMAN, J, WARBERG, B and HOLLAND, C, 'Visual Reaction Time and Plethysmogrpahy as Measures of Sexual Interest in Child Molesters' (1998) 10 *Sexual Abuse: a Journal of Research and Treatment* 81.
—— LAWRY, S, KARKSTRIN, K, OSBORN, C and GILLESPIE, C, 'Screening Tests for Pedophilia' (1994) 21 *Criminal Justice and Behaviour* 115.
ADAMS, H, MOTSINGER, P, MCANULTY, R and MOORE, A, 'Voluntary Control of Penile Tumescence among Homosexual and Heterosexual Subjects' (1992) 21 *Archives of Sexual Behaviour* 17.
ADAMS, H, WRIGHT, L and LOHR, B, 'Is Homophobia Associated with Homosexual Arousal?' (1996) 105 *Journal of Abnormal Psychology* 440.
ADKINS-REGAN, E, 'Development of Sexual Partner Preference in the Zebra Finch: a Socially Monogamous, Pair-Breeding Animal' (2002) 31 *Archives of Sexual Behaviour* 27.
ALLEN, L and GORSKI, R, 'Sexual Orientation and the Size of the Anterior Commissure in the Human Brain' (1992) 89 *Proc Natl Acad Sci U S A* 199.
BAILEY, J and BELL, A, 'Familiality of Female and Male Homosexuality' (1993) 23 *Behavioural Genetics* 313.
—— DUNNE, M and MARTIN, N, 'Genetic and Environmental Influences on Sexual Orientation and its Correlates in an Australian Twin Sample' (2000) 78 *Journal of Personality and Social Psychology* 524.
—— and PILLARD, R, 'A Genetic Study of Male Sexual Orientation' (1991) 48 *Archives of General Psychiatry* 1089.
—— —— 'Genetics of Human Sexual Orientation' (1995) 6 *An Rev Sex Res* 126.
—— —— NEALE, M and AGYEI, Y, 'Heritable Factors Influence Sexual Orientation in Women' (1993) 50 *Archives of General Psychiatry* 217.
—— and ZUCKER, K, 'Children's Sex-Typed Behaviour and Sexual Orientation: a Conceptual Analysis and Quantitative Review' (1995) 31 *Developmental Psychology* 43.
BAILEY, M, PILLARD, R, DAWOOD, K, MILLER, M, FARRER, L, *et al.*, 'Family History Study of Male Sexual Orientation Using Three Independent Samples' (1999) 29 *Behavioural Genetics* 79.
BANCROFT, J, *Human Sexuality and its Problems* (Edinburgh, Churchill Livingstone, 1989).
BATESON, P, 'Design, Development and Decisions' (2001) 32 *Stud. Hist. Phil. Biol. & Biomed. Sci.* 635.

—— and MARTIN, P, *Design for a Life. How Behaviour Develops* (London, Jonathan Cape, 1999).

BEAUREGARD, M, LEVESQUE, J and BOURGOUIN, P, 'Neural Correlates of Conscious Self-Regulation of Emotion' (2001) 21 *The Journal of Neuroscience* RC165.

BERENBAUM, S, 'Effects of Early Androgens on Sex-Typed Activities and Interests in Adolescents with Congenital Adrenal Hyperplasia' (1999) 35 *Hormones and Behavior* 102.

—— and SNYDER, E, 'Early Hormonal Influences on Childhood Sex-Typed Activity and Playmate Preferences: Implications for the Development of Sexual Orientation' (1995) 31 *Developmetal Psychology* 31.

BLANCHARD, R, 'Fraternal Birth Order and the Maternal Immune Hypothesis of Male Homosexuality' (2001) 40 *Hormones and Behaviour* 105.

—— and ELLIS, L, 'Birth Weight, Sexual Orientation and the Sex of Preceding Siblings' (2001) 33 *Journal of Biosocial Science* 451.

—— and KLASSEN, P, 'H-Y Antigen and Homosexuality in Men' (1997) 185 *Journal of Theoretical Biology* 373.

BOGAERT, A, 'Birth Order and Sibling Sex Ratio in Homosexual and Heterosexual Non-White Men' (1998) 27 *Archives of Sexual Behaviour* 467.

—— and HERSHBERGER, S, The Relation Between Sexual Orientation and Penile Size' (1999) 28 *Archives of Sexual Behaviour* 213.

BROWN, W, FINN, C, COOKE, B and BREEDLOVE, S, 'Difference in Finger Length Ratios Between Self-Identified "Butch" and "Femme" Lesbians' (2002) 31 *Archives of Sexual Behaviour* 123.

—— HINES, M, FANE, B and BREEDLOVE, S, 'Masculinized Finger Length Patterns in Human Males and Females with Congenital Adrenal Hyperplasia' (2002) 42 *Hormones and Behaviour* 380.

BUHRICH, N, ARMSTRONG, M and McCONAGHY, N, 'Bisexual Feelings and Opposite-Sex Behavior in Male Malaysian Medical Students' (1982) 11 *Archives of Sexual Behaviour* 387.

BUSS, DM, *Evolutionary Psychology* (New York, Allyn & Bacon, 1994).

BYNE, W, TOBET, S, MATTIACE, L, LASCO, M, KEMETHER, E, *et al.* 'The Interstitial Nuclei of the Human Anterior Hypothalamus: an Investigation of Variation with Sex, Sexual Orientation, and HIV Status' (2001) 40 *Hormones and Behaviour* 86.

CANTOR, J, BLANCHARD, R, PATERSON, A and BOGAERT, A, 'How Many Gay Men Owe Their Sexual Orientation to Fraternal Birth Order?' (2002) 31 *Archives of Sexual Behaviour* 63.

CAPLAN, PJ, CRAWFORD, M, HYDE, JS and RICHARDSON, JTE, *Gender Differences in Human Cognition* (New York & Oxford, Oxford University Press, 1997).

CASPI, A, McCLAY, J, MOFITT, T, MILL, J, MARTIN, J, *et al.*, 'Role of Genotype in the Cycle of Violence in Maltreated Children' (2002) 297 *Science* 851.

—— SUGDEN, K, MOFFIT, TE, TAYLOR, A, CRAIG, IW *et al.*, ' Influence of Life Stress on Depression: Moderation by a Polymorphism in the 5-HTT Gene' (2003) 301 *Science* 386.

CHUNG, W, DEVRIES, G and SWAAB, D, 'Sexual Differentiation of the Bed Nucleus of the Stria Terminalis in Humans may Extend into Adulthood' (2002) 22 *Journal of Neuroscience* 1027.

DAWOOD, K, PILLARD, R, HARVATH, C, REVELLE, W and BAILEY, J, 'Familial Aspects of Male Homosexuality' (2000) 29 *Archives of Sexual Behaviour* 155.

DEVLIN, B, DANIELS, M and ROEDER, K, The Heritability of IQ' (1997) 388 *Nature* 468.

GOLOMBOK, S and FIVUSH, R, *Gender Development* (Cambridge, Cambridge University Press, 1994).

GOULD, JL and GOULD, CG, *Sexual Selection. Mate Choice and Courtship in Nature* (New York, Scientific American Library, 1997).

HALPERN, D, *Sex Differences in Cognitive Abilities* (Hillsdale, New Jersey, Erlbaum, 1992).

HAMER, D, HU, S, MAGNUSON, V, HU, N and PATTATUCCI, A, 'A Linkage between DNA Markers on the X Chromosome and Male Sexual Orientation' (1993) 261 *Science* 321.

HANCOCK, R and FARUKI, S, 'Assessment of Immune Responses to H-Y Antigen in Naturally Inseminated and Sperm-Injected Mice Using Cell-Mediated Cytotoxicity Assays' (1986) 9 *Journal of Reproductive Immunology* 187.

HARRIS, G and RICE, M, 'The Science in Phallometric Testing of Men's Sexual Preferences' (1996) 5 *Current Directions in Pyschological Science* 156.

—— —— QUINSEY, V and CHAPLIN, T, 'Viewing Time as a Measure of Sexual Interest Among Child Molesters and Normal Heterosexual Men' (1996) 34 *Behaviour Research and Therapy* 389.

HINDE, RA, (1997) *Relationships* (London, Psychology Press).

HINGS, I and BILLINGHAM, R, 'H-Y Antigen and Immunity: A Means for Controlling the Secondary Sex Ratio?' (1984) 6 *Journal of Reproductive Immunology* 345.

HU, S, PATTATUCCI, A, PATTERSON, C, LIN, L, FULKER, D, *et al.*, 'Linkage between Sexual Orientation and Chromosome Xq28 in Males but Not in Females' (1995) 11 *Nature Genetics* 248.

HYDE, J and LINN, M, 'Gender Differences in Verbal Ability: a Meta-Analysis' (1988) 104 *Psychological Bulletin* 53.

JOHNSON, M and EVERITT, B, *Essential Reproduction* (Oxford, Blackwell Science, 2000).

JOHNSON, MH, 'A Biomedical Perspective on Parenthood' in A Bainham, S Day Sclater and M Richards (eds), *What is a Parent? A Socio-legal Analysis* (Oxford and Portland, Hart Publishing Ltd, 1999).

—— 'The Developmental Basis of Identity' (2001a) 32 *Studies in History and Philosophy of Biological and Biomedical Sciences* 601.

—— 'Reproduction in the Noughties: Will the Scientists have all the Fun?' (2001b) 198 *Journal of Anatomy* 385.

KALLMANN, F, Twin and Sibship Study of Overt Male Homosexuality' (1952) 4 *American Journal of Human Genetics* 136.

KARAMA, S, LECOURS, A, LEROUX, J-M, BOURGOUIN, P, BEAUDOIN, G *et al.* Areas of Brain Activation in Males and Females during Viewing of Erotic Film Excerpts' (2002)16 *Human Brain Mapping* 1.

KENDLER, K, THORNTON, L, OILMAN, S and KESSLER, R, 'Sexual Orientation in a U.S. National Sample of Twin and Non Twin Sibling Pairs' (2000)157 *American Journal of Psychiatry* 1843.

KENDRICK, K, HINTON, M, ATKINS, K, HAUPT, M and SKINNER, J, 'Mothers Determine Sexual Preference' (1998) 395 *Nature* 229.

KING, M and McDONALD, E, 'Homosexuals who are Twins: a Study of 46 Probands' (1992) 160 *British Journal of Psychiatry* 407.

KINSEY, A, POMEROY, W and MARTIN, C, *Sexual Behavior in the Human Male* (Philadelphia, Sanders, 1948).

KIRK, K, BAILEY, J, DUNNE, M and MARTIN, N, 'Measurement Models for Sexual Orientation; a Community Twin Sample' (2000) 30 *Behavioural Genetics* 345.

KRUIJVER, FP, ZHOU, JN, POOL, CW, HOFMAN, MA, GOOREN, LJ, SWAAB, Dr Foster 'Male-to-Female Transsexuals Have Female Neuron Numbers in a Limbic Nucleus' (2000) 85 *The Journal of Clinical Endocrinology & Metabolism* 2034.

LASCO, M, JORDAN, T, EDGAR, M, PETITO, C and BYNE, W, 'A Lack of Dimorphism of Sex or Sexual Orientation in the Human Anterior Commissure' (2002) 936 *Brain Research* 95.

LAUNAY, G, 'The Phallometric Assessment of Sex Offenders: An Update' (1999) 9 *Criminal Behaviour and Mental Health* 254.

LEVAY, S, 'A Difference in Hypothalamic Structure between Heterosexual and Homosexual Men' (1991) 253 *Science* 1034.

LIPPA, R, 'Gender-Related Traits in Gay Men, Lesbian Women, and Heterosexual Men and Women: the Virtual Identity of Homosexual-Heterosexual Diagnosticity and Gender Diagnosticity' (2000) 68 *Journal of Personality* 899.

—— 'Gender-Related Traits of Heterosexual and Homosexual Men and Women' (2002) 31 *Archives of Sexual Behaviour* 83.

LOEHLIN, J and MARTIN, N, 'A Comparison of Adult Female Twins from Opposite-Sex and Same-Sex Pairs on Variables Related to Reproduction' (1998) 28 *Behavioural Genetics* 21.

LUMIERE, M and HARRIS, G, 'Common Questions Regarding the Use of Phallometric Testing with Sexual Offenders' (1998) 10 *Sexual Abuse: a Journal of Research and Treatment* 227.

MANNING, J, 'Fluctuating Asymmetry and Body Weight in Men and Women: Implications for Sexual Selection' (1995) 16 *Ethology and Sociobiology* 145.

—— KOUKOURAKIS, K and BRODIE, D, 'Fluctuating Symmetry, Metabolic Rate and Sexual Selection in Human Males' (1997) 18 *Evolution and Human Behaviour* 15.

MARSHALL, W and FERNANDEZ, Y, 'Phallometric Testing with Sexual offenders: Limits to its Value' (2000) 20 *Clinical Psychology Review* 807.

MARTIN, RD, WILLNER, LA and DETTLING, A, 'The Evolution of Sexual Size and Dimorphism in Primates' in *The Differences Between the Sexes* (Cambridge, Cambridge University Press, 1994).

MASTERS, WH and JOHNSON, VE, *Human Sexual Response* (London, Churchill-Livingstone, 1966).

McCONAGHY, N, BUHRICH, N and SILOVE, D, 'Opposite Sex-Linked Behaviors and Homosexual Feelings in the Predominantly Heterosexual Male Majority' (1994) 23 *Archives of Sexual Behaviour* 565.

McFADDEN, D, 'Masculinization Effects in the Auditory System' (2002) 31 *Archives of Sexual Behaviour* 99.

—— LOEHLIN, J and PASANEN, E, 'Additional Findings on Heritability and Prenatal Masculinization of Cochlear Mechanisms: Click-Evoked Otoacoustic Emissions' (1996) 97 *Hearing Research* 102.

—— and PASANEN, E, 'Comparison of the Auditory Systems of Heterosexuals and Homosexuals: Click-Evoked Otoacoustic Emissions' (1998) 95 *Proc. Natl. Acad. Sci. USA* 2709.

McGRAPH, R, 'Sex-Offender Risk Assessment and Disposition Planning: A Review of Empirical and Clinical Findings' (1991) 35 *International Journal of Law, Offender Therapy and Comparative Criminology* 328.

MEALEY, L, BRIDGESTOCK, R and TOWNSEND, G, 'Symmetry and Perceived Facial Attractiveness: A Monozygotic Co-Twin Comparison' (1999) 76 *Journal of Personality and Social Psychology* 151.

MICHAEL, GF and MOORE, CL, *Developmental Psychobiology* (Boston, MIT Press, 1995).

MILLER, G, *The Mating Mind* (London, William Heinemann, 2000).

NCB *Genetics and Human Behaviour* (Nuffield Council of Bioethics, 2002).

ORTNER, SB and WHITEHEAD, H, *Sexual Meanings: the Cultural Construction of Gender and Sexuality* (Cambridge, Cambridge University Press, 1981).

OYAMA, S, *The Ontogeny of Information* (Cambridge, CUP, 1985).

PAREDES, R and BAUM, M, 'Altered Sexual Partner Preference in Male Ferrets given Excitotoxic Lesions of the Preoptic Area Anterior Hypothalamus' (1995) 15 *Journal of Neuroscience* 6619.

PAREDES, R, NAKAGAWA, Y and NAKACH, N, 'Lesions of the Medial Preoptic Area/Anterior Hypothalamus (MPOA/AH) Modify Partner Preference in Male Rats' (1998) 813 *Brain Research* 1.

PERKINS, A, FITZGERALD, J and MOSS, G, A Comparison of LH Secretion and Brain Estradiol B Receptors in Heterosexual and Homosexual Rams and Female Sheep' (1995) 29 *Horm Behav.* 31.

PERRETT, D, LEE, K, PENTON-VOAK, I, ROWLAND, D, YOSHIKAWA, S, *et al.* 'Effects of Sexual Dimorphism on Facial Attractiveness' (1998) 394 *Nature* 884.

PILLARD, R and BAILEY, J, 'Human Sexual Orientation has a Heritable Component' (1998) 70 *Human Biology* 347.

—— and WEINRICH, J, 'Evidence of Familial Nature of Male Homosexuality' (1986) 43 *Archives of General Psychiatry* 808.

PINCKARD, K, STELLFLUG, J, RESKO, J, ROSELLI, C and STORMSHAK, F, 'Review: Brain Aromatization and other Factors Affecting Male Reproductive Behavior with Emphasis on the Sexual Orientation of Rams' (2000) 18 *Domestic Animal Endocrinology* 83.

PLOMIN, R, DEFRIES, J, MCCLEARN, G and RUTTER, M, *Behavioral Genetics* (New York, W.H. Freeman and Co., 1997).

PURDIE, D, DUNNE, MP, BOYLE, F, COOK, M and NAJMAN, J, 'Health and Demographic Characteristics of Respondents in an Australian National Sexuality Survey: Comparison with Population Norms' (2002) 56 *Journal of Epidemiology and Community Health* 748.

REITE, M, SHEEDER, J, RICHARDSON, D and TEALE, P, 'Cerebral Laterality in Homosexual Males: Preliminary Communication using Magnetoencephalography' (1995) 24 *Arch Sex Behav.* 585.

RESKO, J, PERKINS, A, ROSELLI, C, FITZGERALD, J, CHOATE, J, 'Endocrine Correlates of Partner Preference Behavior in Rams' (1996) 120 *Biology of Reproduction* 55.

RESNICK, S, GOTTESMAN, I and MCGUE, M, 'Sensation Seeking in Opposite-Sex Twins: an Effect of Prenatal Hormones?' (1993) 23 *Behavioural Genetics* 323.

RICE, G, ANDERSON, C, RISCH, N and EBERS, G 'Male Homosexuality: Absence of Linkage to Microsatellite Markers at Xq28' (1999) 284 *Science* 665.

RISCH, NJ, 'Searching for Genetic Determinants in the New Millennium' (2000) 405 *Nature* 847.

ROOPENIAN, D, CHOI, E and BROWN, A 'The Immunogenomics of Minor Histocompatibility Antigens' (2002) 190 *Immunological Reviews* 86.

ROSE, S, *Lifelines* (London, Allen Lane, 1997).

ROSELLI, C, RESKO, J and STORMSHAK, F, 'Hormonal Influences on Sexual Partner Preference in JJ Rams' (2002) 31 *Archives of Sexual Behaviour* 43.

SANDERS, G, SJODIN, M and DECHASTELAINE, M, 'On the Elusive Nature of Sex Differences in Cognition: Hormonal Influences Contributing to Within-Sex Variation' (2002) 31 *Archives of Sexual Behaviour* 145.

SANDERS, G and WRIGHT, M, 'Sexual Orientation Differences in Cerebral Asymmetry and in the Performance of Sexually Dimorphic Cognitive and Motor Tasks' (1997) 26 *Archives of Sexual Behaviour* 463.

SINGH, J and VERMA, I, (1987) 'Influence of Major Histo(in)Compatibility Complex on Reproduction' (1987) 15 *American Journal of Reproductive Immunology and Microbiology* 150.

SWAAB, D, CHUN, W, KRUIJVER, F, HOFMAN, M and ISHUNINA, T, 'Sexual Differentiation the Human Hypothalamus' (2002) 511 *Adv Exp Med Biol* 75.

—— —— —— —— —— 'Structural and Functional Sex Differences in the Human Hypothalamus' (2001) 40 *Hormones and Behaviour* 93.

WEGESIN, D, 'Event-Related Potentials in Homosexual and Heterosexual Men and Women: Sex-Dimorphic Patterns in Verbal Asymmetries and Mental Rotation' (1998) 36 *Brain Cognition* 73.

WEINRICH, J, SNYDER, P, PILLARD, R, GRANT, I, JACOBSON, D, *et al.*, 'A Factor Analysis of the Klein Sexual Orientation Grid in Two Disparate Samples' (1993) 22 *Archives of Sexual Behaviour* 157.

WHITAM, F, DIAMOND, M and MARTIN, J, 'Homosexual Orientation in Twins: a Report on 61 Pairs and Three Triplet Sets' (1993) 22 *Archives of Sexual Behaviour* 187.

WILKIE, AOM, 'Genetic Prediction: What Are the Limits?' (2001) 32 *Stud. Hist. Phil. Biol. & Biomed. Sci* 619.

WILLIAMS, T, PEPITONE, M, CHIRSTENSEN, S, COOKE, B, HUBERMAN, A *et al.*, 'Finger Length Ratio and Sexual Orientation' (2000) 404 *Nature* 455.

WRIGHT, L and ADAMS, H, 'Assessment of Sexual Preference Using a Choice Reaction Time Task' (1994) 16 *Journal of Psychopathology and Behavioural Assessment* 221.

ZHOU, J, HOFMAN, M and SWAAB, D, 'No Changes in the Number of Vasoactive Intestinal Polypeptide (VIP)-Expressing Neurons in the Suprachiasmatic Nucleus of Homosexual Men; Comparison with Vasopressin-Expressing Neurons.' (1995) 672 *Brain Research* 285.

9

Men, Women, People:
The Definition of Sex

PAK-LEE CHAU
JONATHAN HERRING

INTRODUCTION

BE IT DECIDING which toilet cubicle to enter or applying for a grocery store's
loyalty card you are required to indicate whether you are male or female.
Commonly, the first question asked on receiving news of a new birth is 'is it a
boy or a girl'? At the very start of life the law requires parents to register the
birth of the child and declare the child's sex.[1] The child's classification as a boy
or a girl can have hugely important consequences: from what clothes they[2] will
be expected to wear to what kinds of behaviour are thought to be appropriate
(Butler, 1993).

Much of the academic discussion surrounding the legal definition of sex has
focussed on the position of transsexual people (or trans people—see Playdon,
this volume). However, this chapter focuses on the intersex state (sometimes
also referred to in the medical literature as the pseudohermaphroditic state) and
argues that it poses a radical challenge to the long standing social and legal
assumption that everyone can be classified as either male or female.[3]

The state of intersex is far from uncommon. The exact rate of intersexual
states cannot be stated with certainty because there is no accepted definition of
intersexual states and because some doctors believe that the intersex state of a
baby should be kept secret.[4] One recent study has estimated 'conservatively'
that between 1 and 2 newborn babies per thousand require 'corrective genital

---

[1] Section 2, Births and Deaths Registration Act 1953 requires registration of birth within 42 days.
On registration parents are required to declare the sex of the child.

[2] The dominance of the assumption that a person must be either male or female is revealed in the
difficulty in finding a pronoun, which describes someone without indicating whether they are male
or female (See further Rothblatt, 1995: 127–29, 149–53). In this paper we use 'they'. See also
Playdon, this volume, on the use of trans terminology for transsexual individuals.

[3] The leading works on intersexuals from a social science viewpoint are Fausto-Sterling (2000)
and Herd (1996).

[4] It should also be noted that the rate of some intersex conditions varies in different parts of the
world (Dreger, 2000).

surgery' as a result of intersex states (Blackless *et al.*, 2000). The same study suggested that 17 babies per thousand born could be labelled intersex, even if not to such an extent as to require surgery.[5]

Given the prevalence of the intersex state, we argue that the law must recognise a diverse range of sexual identities, rather than the two presently recognised. The chapter will start by clarifying the difference between gender and sex. It will then summarise the biological evidence on the nature of intersexual states and consider the medical approach to the treatment of intersex children. We will then turn to the legal approach to the definition of sex. We will argue that the present law is unsupportable in the light of a proper understanding of intersex states and the current medical approach to such intersex individuals. The chapter will conclude by considering ways by which the law could approach definition by sex.

DISTINGUISHING GENDER AND SEX

Before discussing the legal and medical responses to intersex states, it is necessary to analyse the distinction drawn between sex and gender.[6] The traditional response is that one's sex (whether one is male or female) is essentially a 'fact', a scientific question, whereas gender (masculinity or femininity—the behaviour expected of persons of that sex[7]) is a social construction (Valdes, 1994). However, the distinction between sex and gender is not so straight-forward (Chanter, 1999). Some commentators have argued that the 'biological fact' of sex is only a 'fact' of interest, because societies attach significance to it (Delphy, 1984: 144). Further, gender (the social roles expected of men and women) may in part reflect the assumed differences between their bodies. For example, in the past women's bodies were perceived as weaker and therefore women were thought unsuitable for 'hard manual labour'. This means that the definition of sex (what makes a male or female body) is intertwined with gender (what behaviour is expected of that body; Gatens, 1996; Herd, 1996; Cealey Harrison and Hood Williams, 2002; Jackson and Scott, 2001). Indeed it is society, rather than nature, which has created the expectation that there are only two sexes (see also Johnson, this volume). For example, it is interesting to note that some societies around the world do not restrict their understanding of sex to only two sexes: men and women. They have accepted terms for intersex people who are regarded as neither male nor female (Edgerton, 1964; Williams, 1986; Herd, 1996). To understand further how intersex states challenge traditional under-

---

[5] Other studies have suggested higher and lower rates (see Greenberg, 2002 and Herd, 1996).

[6] For a stimulating discussion on whether it is possible to define what is a woman without reference to gender or sex see Moi (2001).

[7] There is much debate over the extent to which sexual identity, the sex which a person regards himself or herself as having is an aspect of gender (see Cealey Harrison and Hood-Williams, 2002: Chapter 11).

standing of sex, a medical exploration of the origins of intersex states is required.

DEFINING INTERSEX STATES

The development of a fertilised ovum into a sexed individual is a complex process and many factors are involved. Three separate processes can be observed:

1. **Sex determination.** This refers to the genetic events that bring about male or female gonadal development (i.e. the development of testes or ovaries).
2. **Sex differentiation.** This refers to all subsequent morphogenetic and physiological events that establish functional sexuality, sexual dimorphism and secondary sexual characteristics. Morphogenesis refers to the embryological processes that lead to the formation of tissues, organs and other structures. Sexual dimorphism means the differences in anatomy and physiology of individuals of the two sexes.
3. **Establishment of fertility.** This refers to the survival and development of the germ cells in the ovary and testis. If germ cells fail to survive and develop, even when a testis or ovary is clearly present, eggs and spermatozoa will not form and the individual will not be fertile.

In a typical embryo (or more properly zygote) the sex of the individual is primarily determined by the genes, which reside almost exclusively on the chromosomes. Sex determination of a typical fertile female individual depends on:

  (i)   the absence of the Y-chromosome;
 (ii)   two intact X-chromosomes; and
(iii)   certain non-sex chromosomes (called autosomes).

The determination of a typical fertile male individual depends on:

  (i)   the presence of the Y-chromosome (in particular, the SRY gene);
 (ii)   a single X chromosome, and
(iii)   a number of other genes residing on the X-chromosome and the autosomes.

Genes on chromosomes dictate gonadal development and thereafter the expected sex differentiation. Research has been able to document the effect of specific genes on sex determination (Vaiman and Pailhoux, 2000). Having established the correct gonads, the embryo proceeds to elaborate the primary sexual organs such as the penis or the vagina, depending on the sex of the individual.

In the case of intersex individuals this complex process can be disrupted, leading to incomplete sex determination and/or differentiation. Some of the ways these processes can be disrupted will be briefly outlined:

Genetic Abnormalities in Sex Determination

Three particular kinds of genetic abnormality in sex determination are as follows:

Cellular Mosaicism

This is a very rare state, where the cells of an individual are derived from two distinct fertilised ova. For example, some individuals (known as 45XO/46XY karyotype) would have cells some of which had XY chromosomes and other cells only one X chromosome (Yordam *et al.*, 2001).[8]

Disruptions Caused by Gene Translocations

When normal genes are translocated to the wrong chromosome, sexual determination can become abnormal. For example, if a gene for female sex determination on the X-chromosome is translocated to the Y-chromosome, or vice versa, this can lead to sex-reversed states with XY-females and XX-males (Schiebel *et al.*, 1997). Some of these XX-males are true hermaphrodites, possessing both testicular and ovarian tissue (Kusz *et al.*, 1999; Sarafogolou and Ostrer, 2000). Some of these gene translocations are compounded by other disorders.[9]

Gene Mutation in Sex Determination

This term describes the situation where the genes are on the correct chromosome, but the gene sequence has undergone either spontaneous or inherited mutation. This can cause an intersex state. The following provide examples of these:

(a) A large number of males with *SRY* gene mutations have been documented. This can lead to XY-males, but with complete or partial gonadal dysgenesis (development) (McElreavey and Fellous, 1999).

(b) In the female, gene deletions on the X-chromosome have been documented to cause ovarian failure (Simpson and Rajkovic, 1999).

---

[8] The karyotype is the configuration of the chromosomes of the body. It is denoted by the number of chromosomes and the configuration of the sex chromosomes, so 45XO/46XY means both clones of cells of the subject possess the normal autosomes, or non-sex chromosomes, but whilst one clone has the normal male karyotype, the other clone has only one X-chromosome.

[9] Cases of the 45XO/46X,idic(Yq) karyotype have been documented (Teraoka *et al.*, 1998). 45XO/46X,idic(Yq) mosaic possess a clone of 45XO cells, and another clone of 46XY cells, where the Y-chromosome is a mutant with two centromeres, the q-arm of the chromosome is repeated but the p-arm of the chromosome is missing (normal chromosomes have one centromere, flanked on two sides by the p-arm and the q-arm). This is a case of mosaicism combined with gene translocations.

(c) The mutation of the *DAX-1* gene that resides on the X-chromosome can lead to atypical development of gonads (Muscatelli *et al.*, 1994) or even sex reversal (Bardoni *et al.*, 1994).

(d) Autosomal genes are also essential in sex determination. In particular the *WT1* gene is implicated in early gonadal development. Mutations of this gene can also lead to complete or partial gonadal dysgenesis (Davies *et al.*, 1999).[10] The *Wnt-4* gene, which resides on chromosome 1, can lead to sex reversal if over-expressed (Jordan *et al.*, 2001).

(e) Another important gene lies on chromosome 15. This gene ensures the production of an enzyme (cytochrome P-450 aromatase) which causes the conversion of androgens to oestrogens. Mutation of this gene can lead to non-functional ovaries (Ito *et al.*, 1993).

Sex Differentiation

Having established the correct gonads, the embryo proceeds to elaborate the secondary sexual organs (in males penis, scrotum, prostate and other secondary sex glands, epididymus, vas deferens etc; in females vagina, uterus, oviduct). It does this in the male through the secretion of hormones from the testis, notably androgens and a hormone called Müllerian Inhibitory Hormone (MIH). In the absence of these hormones, female genitalia develop. The course of sex differentiation sometimes does not yield male and female genitalia, but leads to 'secondary intersex states', in which there is ambiguity about genitalia or reversed genitalia, inappropriate to the gonads and/or sex chromosome constitution.

Many of these intersex states result from genetic mutations. For example, in XY males a genetic condition known as androgen insensitivity can result in the presence of a short vagina and development of a female external appearance including breast development. However, internally there is a testis, but no other male internal structures and also no uterus, cervix and fallopian tubes. This condition arises because, even though androgen secretion is normal, the androgen receptor through which it works is abnormal (Gottlieb *et al.*, 1998, 1999a). The individual's tissues are 'blind' to the androgens. The condition is of varying severity. The extreme form is described above (complete testicular feminisation), while the milder forms show varying degrees of external genital intersex states (incomplete testicular feminisation).[11] Another form of sex differentiation

---

[10] Mutation of the SOX9 gene can lead to sex reversal in XY-individuals (Wagner *et al.*, 1994). Other autosomal genes involved in male sex determination are the SF-1 (Achermann *et al.*, 1999). For discussion of the DAX-1 see Goodfellow and Camerino, 1999 and for SOX9 see Wagner *et al.*, 1994. In females mutations in the follicle-stimulating hormone receptor gene on chromosome 2 can lead to gonadal dysgenesis (Aittomaki *et al.*, 1996).

[11] The use of this terminology although used by doctors is (unsurprisingly) not favoured by many intersex people themselves.

abnormality is the persistence in XY males with testes of those embryonic rudiments, which would give rise to elements of the female reproductive tract such as the cervix, uterus and oviduct (Belville *et al.*, 1999). This condition arises because of genetic defects in the Müllerian Inhibitory Hormone system.

Secondary intersex states involving XX females with ovaries can also occur genetically. For example, in congenital adrenal hyperplasia, one of the enzymes for the production of the stress hormone cortisone by the adrenal is defective. This leads to increased levels of androgen production by the adrenal gland. The high androgens can lead to varying degrees to characteristics traditionally seen as male, such as increased clitoral size and, in extreme states to full penile development (Collett-Solberg, 2001). Other types of secondary intersex states have been observed in XX individuals with ovaries, such as septa in the vagina, an absent vagina, fused labia, cervical absence, and abnormally shaped, septated or duplicated uteri (Simpson, 1999). Some of these states have been mapped to a specific genetic mutation, for example, deletion of part of chromosome 4 is correlated with absent uterus (Wilcox *et al.*, 1970).

Establishment of Fertility

Many of the above primary and secondary intersex states compromise fertility. Thus, abnormal or missing external or internal genitalia may prevent coition and/or the successful establishment of pregnancy. Wherever a gonad contains germ cells that are not genetically concordant (i.e. XX sperm precursors in a testis or XY egg precursors in an ovary), the individual will be infertile. This is because eggs require two X chromosomes for their development, whereas two X chromosomes are lethal for sperm development.

Such a situation also means that a subgroup of people who suffer from a discrete form of atypical sexual development involving the gain or loss of entire sex chromosomes are also infertile. Thus, in the presence of only one X-chromosome (XO) an ovary does develop, as do the secondary sex organs, so technically this person would not be classed medically as intersex. However, all the eggs die and so the ovary becomes secondarily abnormal ('gonadal dysgenesis') and infertile (Ohno, 1967; Speed, 1986).

Summary

An individual with any of the states described above may then be classed as intersex.[12] It is important to appreciate that the label 'intersex' in fact covers a wide range of medical states in which, in different ways, sex differentiation or

---

[12] There is much debate over whether trans people should be regarded as intersex (see Playdon, this volume, Chau and Herring, 2002; Raymond, 1994; Sharpe, 2002; Whittle, 2002).

sex determination has not taken place as expected. What links intersex individuals is that they cannot be categorised unequivocally as either male or female, using the traditional definitions of these terms.

It should be noted that intersex states are not unique to humans. The phenomenon has been observed in fish (Kinnison *et al.*, 2000) and in non-human mammals (Markandeya *et al.*, 1998; Watson *et al.*, 1997; Pailhoux *et al.*, 1997; Cole *et al.*, 1997; Robinson *et al.*, 1996). In fact, intersex states can be seen as playing an important role in the evolutionary process or natural selection (Darwin, 1859). In all species, there is random variation of the configuration and characteristics of the genes (the genotype) leading to variation in observed characteristics (the phenotype) of the individual. This variation means that, if there is a change in the external environment, although some individuals in the species may not be able to survive, others may be able to survive and reproduce, thanks to a slightly different genotype and phenotype. If there were no variation at all, then when the external environment changes, the species could become very vulnerable to extinction. The variation in the genotype and hence phenotype is largely random, so whilst some variations may confer survival and reproductive advantages in a changed external environment, other variations may be harmful to the survival of the individual. Seen from the perspective of the species, this phenomenon of random variation in sexual structures, though sometimes deleterious to particular individuals, is essential to the survival of the species. Whether intersex states may confer some survival advantage to humans under certain states is still unclear, though in some species, it has already been demonstrated that intersex states are linked to the environment (Dunn *et al.*, 1996). Thus intersex states in humans, being a variation that may or may not have survival advantages, could be viewed in the same light as variations in hair colour or body height.

From this discussion three crucial points should be emphasised. First, it is not possible to classify everyone as clearly male or female (Dreger, 1998a: Ch 1). It is not that it is hard to find out whether an intersex person is male or female, but rather that even knowing everything there is to know about them they do not fall into the accepted description of male or female.

Second, saying that there are three sexes:[13] male, female and intersex is oversimplistic. The range of intersex states is too large and diverse for them sensibly to be lumped together in one classification simply on the basis of not clearly falling into the category of male or female. It would even be a simplification to suggest that people can be placed on a scale of maleness and femaleness, because in some respects a person may be classified as male and in other aspects female. A person may, for example, be at one point in such a scale in respect of chromosomes and at another point in relation to breast development.

---

[13] Or even five sexes as suggested by Fausto-Sterling (1993). She has since rejected her own analysis in Fausto-Sterling (2000).

Third, intersex states should not be seen as an illness.[14] They should be regarded as a natural aspect of humanity and indeed in other animals have proved essential to survival. We will be returning to these points later in this chapter.

MEDICAL PRACTICE IN RESPONSE TO INTERSEX STATES

For almost four decades, the medical response to intersex states was dominated by the work of John Money (Money, 1968, 1998; Money and Ehrhardt, 1972).[15] He advocated that a doctor should decide the best sex for an intersex child as early as possible (and by 24 months at the very latest). Having assigned the sex, surgery should be carried out so that the child's outward appearance matched the assigned sex and that the child be raised in accordance with that sex. It was crucial, he argued, to ensure that doubts over the child's sexual identity did not persist, to avoid severe psychological harm. In fact, he recommended that the individual should never be told their medical history (Beh and Diamond, 2000). Parents should be told that the child's sexual organs were 'unfinished' and that any surgery was just completing their natural development (Money, 1968: 62). As will be appreciated from our description of intersex states above this was untrue, as Money appreciated, but it was seen as a way of helping the parents raise the child in line with assigned sex. For decades Money's approach to intersex children was regarded as the standard approach. As late as 1996, Money's approach was still followed by the American Academy of Paediatrics (American Academy of Pediatrics, 1996: 590).

Money's views have come under increasing challenge.[16] Not least because his approach was substantially built on a study of one patient, widely known as the Joan/John case. John's penis was accidentally removed during a circumcision and Money, in consultation with the parents, advised that the baby be brought up as a girl, Joan (Money, 1968). Surgery was performed so that the baby appeared to be female. Money argued that as long as the child was raised as a girl and not told about her medical history she would successfully live as a woman. He reported that this indeed occurred and Joan had grown up as a normal girl. Further research, however, revealed that this claim was inaccurate (Diamond and Sigmundson, 1997b). Later in life Joan had rejected her sex and lived as a man, and was married with an adopted child (Colapinto, 2000). Further, John was profoundly distressed by the way he had been treated during his childhood and adolescence.

---

[14] Kessler (1998) documents how intersex conditions have been seen as deformities.

[15] The reception to his work is discussed in Kipnis and Diamond (1998). Beh and Diamond (2000), Diamond and Sigmundson (1997a,b), and Hird and Germon (2000) provide summaries of the development of medical practice in this area.

[16] Summarised in Martin (2002), although as Creighteon *et al.* (2001) discuss there is no consistent practice in the UK at present. For arguments that Money's approach is contrary to many versions of children's rights theories see Chau and Herring (2002).

Money's approach has also been challenged by studies of intersex people who did not receive surgery, but would have done had the normal procedures been followed (Reilly and Woodhouse, 1989; Diamond and Sigmundson, 1997a, b; Lee, 2001; Slijper *et al.*, 1998).[17] All of these individuals were found to be happy with their sexual identities and did not suffer psychological harm from not having the surgery. In contrast pressure has grown from intersex adults objecting to the procedures performed upon them as babies or young children.[18] Such groups argue that they should have been able to decide for themselves what surgery, if any, they wished to have carried out. In other words that cosmetic surgery should not be carried out on them as babies born with ambiguous genitalia and instead any surgery should have been delayed until they were old enough to be able to decide for themselves what surgery should be performed. Some intersex people suggest that they were assigned the wrong sex, but many of those involved in political campaigning are happy to regard themselves as not falling into either of the traditional categories of male or female, and would prefer the description intersex (Fausto-Sterling, 2000). Others complain that the surgery performed, while giving what the doctors regarded a normal appearance, failed to provide sexual satisfaction.[19] The surgery is used not for the intersex person's own benefit but to deal with society's problem of coping with intersex people, by seeking to ensure that they appear to be either male or female.

A further difficulty with the Money approach is revealed in the detailed guidance to doctors. There are concerns that the basis on which doctors assigned sex is unduly focussed on the size of the child's penis or clitoris (Griffin and Wilson, 1992). In a sense, this is understandable because it is the size of genitals that is likely to be the first indication to a paediatrician that there are question marks over the sex assignment of a child.[20] The traditional approach to deciding the assignation of sex was summarised by Money—' "Too small now, too small later" is a useful working rule with regard to construction or reconstruction of a penis.' (Money, 1968: 66). The accepted approach was that a penis of less than 2 cm should be removed, as should a clitoris greater than 1cm.[21] It was felt that boys with such short penises would suffer from low self-esteem (Hird and Germon, 2000) and that girls with a large clitoris would feel unfeminine (Meyers-Seifer and Charest, 1992).[22]

This emphasis on the size of penis or clitoris, rather than, for example, sexual satisfaction or fertility, is controversial. It used to be assumed that if there was

---

[17] A useful summary of this research is found in Colapinto (2000). Later research found similar results (Bin-Abbas *et al.*, 1999).

[18] Most notably the Intersexual Society of North America (ISNA). See Chase (1998).

[19] Indeed one study has found that surgery is often unsuccessful, if judged by the ability to engage in sexual intercourse (see Mulaikal *et al.*, 1987).

[20] It would be extremely expensive to carry out an ultrasonography on every child, which would be necessary if we wanted to detect every child with an intersex condition.

[21] Eg Catlin and Crawford (1994); McGillivray (1991: 366); Newman *et al.* (1992: 651).

[22] There is much doubt over the medical benefits of such an operation (Kipnis and Diamond, 1998).

any doubt over the correct assignation of sex, it was better to choose female than male.[23] In other words an 'inadequate' penis would lead to classification as a woman. Typical of the traditional approach is the following suggestion in a medical textbook: 'If the subject has an inadequate phallus, the individual should be reared as female, regardless of the results of diagnostic tests.' (Griffin and Wilson, 1992). It is not surprising that feminist scholars have been quick to point to this as an example of women being the 'other'—'the non-male'—and of the close identification of the male with the penis (Dreger, 1998b; Naffine, 1997: 77).

Such criticism has led many doctors to adopt a new approach towards intersex states.[24] Their approach is based on a perspective which does not see intersex people as abnormal or 'ill' and in need of 'mending' by surgery so that they can live as male or female. Rather, intersex states are seen as a variation from the standard (just as an unusual hair colour may be; Dreger, 1998a). This shift in medical practice and attitude has led to the setting up of the North American Task Force on Intersexuality which first convened on October 1999[25] in the United States and to the British Association of Paediatric Surgeons' Working Party on the Surgical Management of Children Born with Ambiguous Genitalia.[26] Their aim is to move away from the Money approach and develop a more sensitive response to intersex babies.

There is general acceptance that some intersex states require immediate surgery to ensure the medical well-being of the baby (for example, to repair any defects in the genito-urinary system so that physiological functions can be carried out normally).[27] What is disputed is the use of operations, which are essentially cosmetic: performed just so that the child will appear to accord with one sex or the other. Increasingly, it is accepted that cosmetic surgery should normally be avoided at birth and delayed until later, although there is no agreement on when that should be (Diamond and Sigmundson, 1997a). Some argue that the doctors should wait until the children are sufficiently mature to decide for themselves what surgery, if any, should be performed (Phornphutkul *et al.*, 2000; Creighton *et al.*, 2001). Others argue that surgery should be delayed until the child exhibits clear behaviour in line with one sex, even if at that point the child is not yet mature enough to make a reasoned decision about their sexual identity (Slijper *et al.*, 1998). Adherents of this latter view fear that waiting until the

---

[23] Although the approach still has its supporters: Krstic *et al.* (2000) stress the difficulties facing men who were unable to achieve erections or ejaculate. Greer (2000) strongly objects to female being presumed the appropriate sex in cases of ambiguity as it perpetuates the view that female is defined as those without an adequate penis.

[24] For an argument that Money's approach infringes the basic human right to bodily integrity see Beh and Diamond (2000), Ford (2001), Greenberg (2000) and Chau and Herring (2002).

[25] Information is provided at www.natfi.org.

[26] British Association of Paediatric Surgeons (2001).

[27] This is not to say that there are not medical conditions connected with intersexuality that may require treatment; for example, hypospadias in some forms of congenital adrenal hyperplasia.

child's teenage years, when they will be competent to make the decision themself, will involve surgery at an age particularly traumatic for sexual development.[28]

Were it shown that children who do not have surgery for ambiguous genitalia suffer permanent psychological harm or social difficulties, then genital surgery, at an early stage could perhaps be justified.[29] However most research does not suggest such harm.[30] Indeed as the ISNA has argued:

> 'Surgeons argue that genital surgeries must be performed on intersex children in order to save them from feeling different from other children, or being marginalized by society. But many children grow up with physical differences, which may cause them to be marginalized by society, yet we do not advocate using plastic surgery to eliminate all physical differences. For instance, children of racial minorities are often marginalized, teased, and even subject to violence. Yet few would condone using non-consensual plastic surgery during infancy to eliminate racial characteristics.' (ISNA, 1998)

If surgery is to be delayed, there is some dispute over how intersex children should be raised.[31] Some argue that parents should raise the child as either a boy or girl (while being open to the possibility of the child choosing a different sex when older; Diamond and Sigmundson, 1997a); while others argue that the child should be raised as neither male nor female, but as intersex, thereby giving them the maximum opportunity to decide once they are older whether they wish to live as male, female or neither of these (Warne, 1998).

Whatever the ideal for the child, the position of the parents must be emphasised (Hermer, 2002; Ford, 2001; Daaboul and Frader, 2001). There is some evidence that parents would find it difficult to raise a child as intersex (Glassberg, 1998, 1999). Some parents may insist on the child being raised as a boy or a girl. If the parents are adamant about this, their wishes will have to be respected, unless the drastic step of taking the child into care is taken.

Those who maintain the Money approach argue that the child (and even their parents) should not be told about the intersex state (Natarajan, 1996; Williams, 2002). This is very much a minority view. Not least because it is likely that the child will discover their intersex status at some point during their life and it would be extremely harmful for the child to discover this, say, in their early teens (Groveman, 1996). Further, some intersex states can be linked with medical problems, which may require early treatment to be effective.[32]

Whatever point in time the surgery is proposed we suggest that a strong case can be made for intervention to follow two key principles:

---

[28] Hermer (2002) arguing for a flexible approach to be taken.

[29] However Creighton *et al.*'s (2001) survey found that further surgery had to be carried out at adolescence in 98% of cases where surgery on intersex children was performed so that they would appear to be female shortly after birth.

[30] Colapinto (2000) provides a useful summary of the evidence to date and suggests that providing 'psycho-sexual counselling' provides a more appropriate point response than surgery.

[31] There is an interesting analogy here with children's rights to know their genetic origins.

[32] There is evidence that osteoporosis is linked to some intersex conditions (Vanderschueren and Vandenput, 2000).

1. The surgery should be the minimal thought necessary for the well-being of the child or the patient.
2. Where possible the surgery should be reversible. This would facilitate reversal of the decision made during their childhood, should the individual wish it later in life. Alternatively, if better reconstruction methods were available in the future, the old reconstruction could be undone, and the new methods applied.

Having considered the changing medical response to intersex individuals we now turn to the legal definition of sex.

THE LEGAL DEFINITION OF SEX

As the law has sought to equalise the position of men and women, there are now relatively few situations in which it is necessary for a court to determine someone's sex and so rarely have the courts had to address the definition of male and female.[33] One of the most significant areas where it is necessary to distinguish male and female is the law on marriage and it is in this area that most of the detailed discussion on the legal definition of sex has taken place.[34]

The Legal Definition of Sex in England and Wales

Section 11(c) of the Matrimonial Causes Act 1973 states that a marriage will be void if the parties to it are not male and female. The statute does not provide any definition of who is male or female and the question has been left to the courts to answer.

W v W (Nullity: Gender)

The legal position of intersex people has recently been reconsidered by Charles J in *W v W (Nullity: Gender)*[35] who was required to consider the validity of a marriage between a male applicant and the respondent.[36] The respondent had been born intersex, but by the time of the hearing lived as a woman. This key question for the court was whether the respondent was male or female?

Charles J focussed his attention on the leading case on the definition of sex: *Corbett v Corbett (otherwise Ashley)*,[37] in which Ormrod J had had to decide

---

[33] For an excellent discussion of the legal definition of sex see Grenfell (2003).
[34] The issue is also relevant in certain sexual offences, which can only be committed by or against a man or a woman.
[35] [2001] Fam 111, [2001] 1 FLR 324. The case is discussed in Herring and Chau (2001).
[36] His judgment has since been approved by the House of Lords in *Bellinger v Bellinger* [2003] 2 FCR 1.
[37] [1971] P 83.

the sex of a trans person. In *Corbett* the applicant had been born a man, but as an adult underwent a surgical operation removing her 'male organs' and creating the 'female organs'. The issue was whether the applicant could be regarded as a man or a woman. Key to Ormrod J's reasoning were four points:

1. That sex is 'fixed at birth (at the latest) and cannot be changed, either by the natural development of organs of the opposite sex, or by medical or surgical means'.[38]
2. Gonadal, chromosomal and genital tests at birth determined the sex (these terms are defined later). He explicitly rejected an argument that psychological sex was relevant for the law's definition of sex.[39]
3. In determining a person's sex for the purpose of marriage, the capacity for heterosexual intercourse with their partner was crucial.[40] This was because he saw heterosexual intercourse as key to the understanding of marriage.
4. Certainty as to sex was crucial for the law. The law should not permit people to flit between one sex and the other; nor should there be people about whom the law cannot produce a clear answer whether they are male or female. By denying the relevance of psychological attachment to a sex and focussing on the biological 'facts' at birth he was able to ensure a legal definition of sex that was certain and fixed.

Corbett has become regarded as the leading case on the legal definition of sex, not only in England and Wales, but in many other countries.[41] Its persistence is in part due to the expertise brought to the case by Ormrod J himself (he was medically qualified), but also the certainty, so beloved of lawyers that the test appeared to provide.

Charles J in *W v W* started by applying *Corbett* test. He found that the respondent's sex was not resolved by considering her chromosomal, gonadal and genital factors. The respondent had 'partial androgen insensitivity syndrome'[42] and Charles J concluded that the respondent was chromosomally male, gonadally intersex, genitally intersex, and psychologically female. This meant that Charles J was left with the task of determining how to define sex in a case where the *Corbett* test did not produce a clear answer. Ormrod J in

---

[38] [1971] P 83 at 104.

[39] In *Re Kevin (Validity of Marriage)* [2001] FamCA 1074 Chisholm J powerfully criticises Ormrod J's assumption that psychological sex is not relevant to the legal definition of sex.

[40] This did not require the couple to be fertile (*Baxter v Baxter* [1948] AC 274).

[41] Eg *In Re Ladrach* 513 NE 2d 828 (Ohio Prob Ct 1987); *B v B* 355 NYS 2d 712 in USA; *Lim Ying v Hiok Kian Ming Eric* [1991] SLR 184 in Singapore; *W v W* [1976] 2 SALR 308 in South Africa.

[42] Androgen is a hormone and, like most hormones, needs to bind to a receptor to exert its effect on target cells in the body. If the androgen receptor has undergone a mutation and its functioning is changed, androgen will no longer be able to exert its effects. Those individuals with this syndrome are XY-males chromosomally, but their primary sexual organs and secondary sexual characteristics have female elements. For example, depending on the degree of severity, individuals suffering from partial androgen insensitivity may not be able to carry out spermatogenesis (i.e. produce sperm), they may develop breasts and have female hair-growth pattern. See for further information Gottlieb (1999a, b).

Corbett had acknowledged that his test would not provide an assignation of sex for some intersex people and left such cases to another day, although he hinted that the genital factor should be the determining criterion in a case of doubt. Charles J did not take up this suggestion. He proposed that in cases where the Corbett factors did not all point in one direction, all of the following factors should be considered:

'(i)   chromosomal factors,
 (ii) gonadal factors (i.e. presence or absence of testes or ovaries),
(iii) genital factors (including internal sex organs),
(iv)   psychological factors,
 (v)   hormonal factors, and
(vi)   secondary sexual characteristics (such as distribution of hair, breast development, physique etc).'[43]

This list was approved by Lord Nicholls in the House of Lords in *Bellinger v Bellinger*, although he also added the style of upbringing and living. These factors require some elaboration:

(i)   Chromosomal sex is the presence of the XY chromosomes in males and the presence of XX chromosomes in females, although XX males and XY females do exist.

(ii) By gonadal sex is meant the state of the gonads: the testes in the case of men and the ovaries in the case of women.

(iii) The genital sex is defined by the state of the primary sexual organs, namely the penis, the scrotum, and the tubular system linked to the testes in the male; or the vagina, the cervix, the uterus and the fallopian tubes in the female.

(iv) Psychological 'sex' is much more difficult to define; it encompasses what the individual feels himself/herself to be. To what extent these feelings are the result of structures in the brain or the result of social/cultural factors is a matter of debate (see Johnson, this volume).

(v)   The hormonal factors, as explained earlier, are ultimately an expression of the chromosomal factors, because almost all genes for hormones are found on the chromosomes. The hormonal factors are important in sex determination and in sex differentiation; they influence how genes are expressed to give rise to gonads, primary sexual organs and secondary sexual characteristics. In fact it could be argued that as hormonal factors are so dependent on chromosomal factors there is little point in adding them as a separate criterion.

(vi) By secondary sexual characteristics are meant those characteristics not directly related to reproduction, but which are commonly different in males and females, for example, breast development, hair growth patterns or fat deposition patterns. The secondary sexual characteristics are ultimately effects of hormone action.

---

[43] At 363.

Charles J gave no indication of how to weigh the six factors when they point in different directions. It seems it is not simply a case of seeing whether the majority of these factors lie on one side of the line or another. Rather it is a matter for the judge's discretion, considering all of these factors. Although he does not say so explicitly, we suggest that where these factors point in conflicting directions the individual's psychological attachment to one sex or the other is likely to be regarded as the crucial factor. On the facts of *W v W*, Charles J found that the respondent was female.

The Impact of the European Convention on Human Rights

The European Court of Human Rights in *Goodwin v UK* and *I v UK*[44] heard applications by trans individuals claiming that the refusal of the United Kingdom to recognise their sex infringed their human rights. The European Court held that post-operative trans people have the right under article 8 and 12 of the Convention to be recognised by the law as being of the sex they claim to be and that sex was not necessarily defined at birth.

The Government's response to the decisions of the European Court of Human Rights in *Goodwin* and *I* has been to propose that a trans person be permitted to apply to be recognised in their present sex, rather than the sex recorded in the birth certificate (see Lord Chancellor's Department (2003) and the Gender Recognition Bill of 2003).[45] However, these proposals are inadequate for intersex persons[46] since the judgement upholds the principle of there being only two sexes and so does not provide for the right of a person to be recognised as intersex.[47] The government proposals perpetuate the assumption that a person is either male or female.

CRITICISM OF THE LEGAL DEFINITION OF SEX

We now seek to criticise the present law's approach to the definition of sex, with particular focus on intersex people.

Corbett is not Consistent with W v W

In our view the *W v W* test developed by Charles J to deal with intersex people is, in fact, inconsistent with the points that form the cornerstones of the

[44] [2002] 2 FCR 577; [2002] 2 FCR 613.
[45] The House of Lords in *Bellinger* [2003] 2 FCR 1 held that it was not for the courts to change the English law to permit trans people to marry in their sex.
[46] Of course, they are better than doing nothing.
[47] Home Office, (2000) at para. 3.6.3 indicates a willingness to delay issuing an intersex baby's birth certificate until the sex is clear, but the assumption still appears to be that the baby must be either male or female.

approach in *Corbett* described above. Following W *v* W three key tenets in the Corbett judgement are open to challenge.

Sex Cannot be Determined at Birth

By permitting secondary sexual characteristics and psychological factors to be taken into account, Charles J accepted that factors not apparent at birth could determine the sex of an adult. He therefore rejects the view that sex is fixed at birth and cannot subsequently be changed. But why should the law insist that sex is fixed at birth for some people but not for others? Once it is accepted that sex is not necessarily fixed at birth and can change over time, the concept of sexual identity becomes a more fluid one.

The Ability to Engage in Sexual Intercourse should not be Key to Determining Sex

Ormrod J in *Corbett* saw the ability to have sexual intercourse as a key element in defining sex for the purposes of marriage. So in *Corbett,* deciding whether the respondent was a woman for the purpose of marriage, a crucial question was whether she was capable of naturally 'performing the essential role of a women in marriage.'[48] He found she was not.

Charles J in W *v* W rejected this emphasis on sexual intercourse. He argued that the fact a couple may or may not be able to consummate the marriage will not necessarily determine whether the parties are male and female. As he pointed out, there is much more to marriage and to individual identity than sexual intercourse. Once the fundamental importance attached to the capacity to engage in sexual intercourse is denied, it becomes harder to justify the fundamental importance attached to genitals in the *Corbett* definition of sex.

We submit that Charles J was correct to depart from the centrality of sexual intercourse to marriage. Three reasons in particular are offered:

(i)   First, that sexual intercourse is not key to marriage (see Lind, this volume). Companionship, intimacy and mutual support are of far more importance. This point is in fact, recognised in section 11 of the Matrimonial Causes Act 1973, which states that non-consummation of marriage renders a marriage voidable, rather than void. Therefore the lack of consummation of a marriage will only invalidate a marriage if either party to the marriage complains about it to the court. If both parties are happy with the absence of sexual intercourse, the marriage is valid at law.

(ii)   When considering the definition of sex generally for the law, the *Corbett* test is openly based on an assumption that heterosexual intercourse ('ordinary and complete intercourse'[49]) is key to determining a person's

---

[48] At 48.
[49] At 49.

sexual identity. The objection to this approach is not just that a homo-sexual person would not regard heterosexual intercourse as key to sexual fulfilment, but also many people find sexual fulfilment with non-penetrative sexual activities. If the law or medicine wishes to place import-ance on the ability of an individual to engage in sexual activity, the issue should be about an individual's capacity to find sexual fulfilment, not limiting that to any one particular form of sexual activity.

(iii) The emphasis on sexual intercourse too easily leads to unacceptable assumptions about the sexual roles expected of men and women. For example, some doctors working in the field have defined adequate inter-course for the women as 'successful genital penetration' (Kupfer *et al.*, 1992: 328). This can be seen as regarding the vagina as nothing more than a hole into which a penis can be placed. Whether or not the sexual activity was potentially pleasurable or fulfilling is not regarded as a relevant con-sideration. Indeed, as mentioned above, intersex people who have not been operated upon have given evidence of sexual satisfaction despite the 'abnormality of the genitals' (Diamond and Sigmundson, 1997a: 1049), even when penetrative sex has not been possible (Fausto-Sterling, 2000: 95).

It is Wrong to Limit Sexual Identity to Physical Characteristics

Thorpe LJ in *Bellinger* has criticised the Corbett test in these terms:

> 'In my opinion the test that is confined to physiological factors, whilst attractive for its simplicity and apparent certainty of outcome, is manifestly incomplete. There is no logic or principle in excluding one vital component of the personality, the psyche.'

In other words the *Corbett* approach to defining sex focuses wrongly on physi-cal factors and downplays the person's psychological factors. Indeed it is inter-esting that in other areas of the law the House of Lords have been unwilling to accept that a clear demarcation between the body and the mind can be drawn.[50] Yet this is precisely what the Corbett test does. Stephen Whittle makes the point eloquently: 'what makes a person is what takes place between the ears and not between the legs' (Whittle, 2002: 72). The significance of emphasising psycho-logical factors would be that if an intersex person regards themselves as neither male nor female, but intersex (or some other designation) then the law should respect that. After all, in claiming to be intersex, they are making a true state-ment.

---

[50] For example, in *R v Ireland and R v Burstow* [1998] AC 147 the House of Lords was willing to define the statutory terms actual bodily harm and grievous bodily harm as including psychological harms.

Both *Corbett* and W *v* W demonstrate a reluctance to depart from the assumption that everyone is either male or female (Weiss, 2001). As discussed above, this 'binary sex paradigm' (Greenberg, 1999) has decreasing support amongst medical experts in the field of intersexuals (see also Johnson, this volume). First, as already mentioned, up to one percent of people cannot at birth be labelled male or female. For many intersex people it is only by performing surgery that they can clearly fall into the category of male and female. Second, there is increasing acceptance of the view among medical practitioners that surgery should not be performed at the birth of an intersex child and be delayed until a later point. The significance of this is that much medical practice now accepts that in the early years the child will be of 'unknown' sex or intersex. Many experts are happy to accept that the child and adult may legitimately decide to live as an intersex person, rather than male or female (Schober, 2001). The legal insistence that everyone must be male or female is no longer consistent with medical practice.

So if we are not rigidly to require every person to be placed in the male or female box what alternatives are there?

Recognising a Third (or Fourth or Fifth) Sex?

One possibility would be for the law and society to recognise that there are three sexes: male, female and intersex. This is a solution adopted widely already in communities in which surgical reassignment was simply impossible.[51] The only legal reform that would then be required would be to state how the law on marriage, sexual offences, and other areas apply to intersex people. In our view it would not be satisfactory simply to recognise three sexes. As noted above the term 'intersex' in fact covers a wide range of states, and it would be quite misleading to group all of these into one heading. Indeed support groups have been set up by individuals showing particular intersex states.[52] An individual may indeed deny any classification based on sex, claiming to be transgendered or androgynous. Once one accepts the argument that the male-female dyad is a social construction, which unreasonably restricts people's sexual identity into one of two sexes (see Johnson, this volume), it becomes hard to deny that restricting people to three identities is open to identical objections.

---

[51] Kogan (1997) emphasises that some cultures (eg Native American, Indian, and Sambian cultures) have recognised a third sex.
[52] Eg Androgen Insensitivity Syndrome Support Group; Congenital Adrenal Hyperplasia Group.

Recognising a Scale of Sexual Identity

Rather than requiring people to be classified as male or female, we suggest that it would be preferable to utilise a scale of sexual identity with individuals being placed at a point somewhere along the scale (see for example, Dobac, 1999; Storrow, 1997). This has been described by Rothblatt as 'sexual continuism' (Rothblatt, 1995). This vision 'posits that humanity is composed of a continuous blend of sexual identity, far beyond any simplistic male or female categorization.'[53] She states:

> 'Labelling people as male or female, upon birth, exalts biology over sociology. Instead, the new feminist principles inspire us to permit all people to self-identify their sexual status along a broad continuum of possibilities and to create such cultures of gender as human ingenuity may develop.'[54]

Some argue that this approach is misguided. Allen writes:

> '[T]he majority of the population is also heterosexual, and what is heterosexuality but a sexual attraction toward the opposite sex? Male and female are inescapable biological and sexual referents. To expect the mainstream to radically reinterpret itself for the sake of transgenderist ideology is the sort of conceit typical of a member of any minority.'[55]

We do not find Allen's opposition convincing for two main reasons. First, the suggestion that male and female are 'inescapable sexual referents' is untrue. As shown above it is not possible to point to any one biological factor as inevitably consistent with being male or female and notions of what is inherently male or female have changed over time and between societies. It is important to remember that, despite a few differences, men and women have very similar bodies (see also chapter by Johnson, this volume, and Fausto-Sterling, 2000). Those differences that are often stressed are not as crucial as often supposed: only some women have the capacity to become pregnant, some women do not have ovaries; some women do not menstruate, some men lactate (Jaggar, 1983), not all men produce sperm. According to David Munday (2001/2002), the distinction between male and female lies at the heart of a Judeo-Christian world view,[56] which underpins the law (see MacDowell, this volume). However, it is hard to see how the legal abandonment of the significance of sex would plunge the legal system into crisis, there being so few cases where it matters.

Second, we find as unconvincing the argument that the 'mainstream' (the majority of whom would clearly identify themselves as male or female; Smith, 1971) should not be required radically to reinterpret itself. The acceptance of a continuum approach does not require an individual to reject their own sexual

---

[53] At 102.
[54] At 13.
[55] Allen (1996: 133).
[56] There is not space to explain why we disagree with him about this.

identity. It is likely that many will stick to the traditional definition of clearly male or female (Frye, 2000). In any event, around one per cent of people can be described as intersex. This is not a tiny minority who are seeking to challenge important social categories, but a significant section of the population. Similarly, those who suggest that calls to remove the bi-polar classification are unrealistic (Nye, 1998: 255) overlook the point that for intersex people a sexual continuism is the daily reality, not some form of utopia.

Kogan opposes the sexual continuum approach on different grounds:

> 'Rothblatt's vision purports to offer an alternative to a dimorphic vision of sex/ gender. But does it really? Although she adopts the conceptual structure of a contin- uum to describe sex, her theory reinforces a dimorphic view of sex by placing the categories "male" and "female" at the endpoints of the continuum. Under such a view, individuals are inevitably defined as more or less male, or more or less female. The determining concepts remain bipolar.' (Kogan, 1997: 1250)

He prefers the recognition of a third sex to the continuum approach. There is force in his argument, but it would not be difficult to express the continuum approach in a way which would overcome his concerns. If we accept that the male and female sexes are not fixed boxes but fluid categories, then it is possible to accept that individuals could have different forms of sexual identity (or indeed none) for different purposes. Kogan's point about maleness and female- ness remaining the key reference points is a good one, but that is only likely to be so until different ways of expressing sexual identity are developed. [57]

There is still a major concern with the continuum approach here. Around the world most governments and legal systems claim to seek to promote equality between the sexes. Debates within the feminist movement have revealed that the promotion of equality does not necessarily require the law to ignore or dimin- ish the differences between men and women (see eg Herring, 2001b: 11–13). But rather the law should seek to ensure that inequality should not result from the differences. If male and femaleness were abolished as legal categories this might be thought to inhibit such policies (Colker, 1996: 6–8). We suggest not. Moves to ensure that the care for children is afforded proper social, economic and polit- ical recognition; that pregnant workers are protected; that those doing the same jobs are granted equal pay can, of course, be taken without the need to refer explicitly to definitions of sex. Policies could be directed to prevent discrimina- tion against groups of people engaging in activities traditionally understood to be performed by women (eg child care), without the need for a reference to sex.

If the sexual continuum approach is adopted, there would be wider implica- tions for the legal system than simply accepting the existence of a third sex. In practice it would become impossible for the law to place any legal significance on sexual differences, because it would recognise that people may have a wide

---

[57] Scales-Trent (1990) discusses the benefits of social classification (in for example providing a sense of belonging), as well as the disadvantages (for example, that they can be used as tools of oppression).

range of sexual identities, indeed perhaps having different identities for different purposes.[58] Instead of talking of men and women the law will treat each individual as a person (Coombs, 1998).

CONCLUSION

Sigmund Freud, no less, stated 'When you meet a human being, the first distinction you make is "male" or "female"? and you are accustomed to make the distinction with unhesitating certainty' (Freud, 1964). We have sought to challenge the assumption that every person can be placed in the category of either male or female. Around one percent of children born can be classified as intersex. The traditional medical response to intersex babies: that they must be assigned as male or female as quickly as possible and then surgery used to design their bodies to conform to the outward appearance expected of that sex; is nowadays accepted by only a few doctors. Until recently the law has followed the traditional medical approach in assuming that a person's sex must be either male or female. This can be seen as an aspect of what Foucault has described as 'a society of normalization' (Foucault, 1980: 107); that everyone should be required to fit into a norm. However, both these legal and medical assumptions have been challenged.

This chapter has outlined the research and pressures, which have led to a change in medical practice amongst many of the experts in the field. It is no longer assumed that an intersex person can be correctly assigned to one sex or the other. Indeed many advocate not performing surgery until the child is old enough to decide their sexual identity for themselves. Further, it is becoming increasingly acceptable and common for an individual to choose to live as an intersex individual. We suggest that with increasing understanding and acceptance of intersex individuals the sharp distinction between male and female can no longer be sustained. It is no longer possible to define all people as male or female and the law must cease to use sex as a legal category. The law should instead recognise a wide range of sexual identities. Of course, before people can break free from the shackles[59] that gender can impose, major changes in society are required, but the law can lead the way by accepting that people should not be restricted to being either male or female.[60]

REFERENCES

ACHERMANN, JC, ITO, M, HINDMARCH, PC, and JAMESON, JL, 'A Mutation in the Gene Encoding Steroidogenic Factor-1 Causes XY Sex Reversal and Adrenal Failure in Humans' (1999) 22 *Nature Genetics* 125.

---

[58] Cruz (2002).
[59] Albright (2002) talks of transliberation.
[60] We are grateful for the very helpful comments of the editors on earlier drafts of this chapter.

AITTOMAKI, K, HERVA, R, STENMAN, UH, JUNTUNEN, K, YLOSTALO, P, HOVATTA, O, DE LA CHAPELLE, A, 'Clinical Features of Primary Ovarian Failure Caused by a Point Mutation in the Follicle-Stimulating Hormone Receptor Gene' (1996) 81 *Journal of Clinical Endocrinology and Metabolism* 3722.

ALBRIGHT, JM, 'Gender Assessment: A Legal Approach to Transsexuality' (2002) 55 *Southern Methodist University Law Review* 593.

ALLEN, JJ, *The Man in the Red Velvet Dress* (New York, Carol Publishing, 1966).

AMERICAN ACADEMY OF PEDIATRICS, 'Timing of Elective Surgery on the Genitalia of Male Children with Particular Reference to the Risks, Benefits, and Psychological Effects of Surgery and Anesthesia' (1996) 97 *Pediatrics* 590.

BARDONI, B, ZANARIA, E, GUIOLI, S, FLORIDIA, G, WORLEY, K, TONINI, G, FERRANTE, E, CHIUMELLO, G, McCABE, ERB, FRACCARO, M, ZUFFARDI, O and CAMERINI, G, 'A Dosage Sensitive Locus at Chromosome Xp21 is Involved in Male to Female Sex Reversal' (1994) 7 *Nature Genetics* 497.

BEH, H and DIAMOND, M 'An Emerging Ethical and Medical Dilemma: Should Physicians Perform Sex Assignment Surgery on Infants with Ambiguous Genitalia?' (2000) 7 *Michigan Journal of Gender & Law* 1.

BELVILLE, C, JOSSO, N, and PICARD, JY, 'Persistence of Muellerian Derivatives in Males' (1999) 89 *American Journal of Medical Genetics* 218.

BIN-ABBAS, B, CONTE, F, GRUMBACK, MM, KAPLAN, SL, 'CongenitalHypogonadotropic Hypogonadism and Micropenis: Effect of Testosterone Treatment on Adult Penile Size—Why Sex Reversal is Not Indicated' (1999) 134 *Journal of Pediatrics* 579.

BLACKLESS, M, CHARUVASTRA, A, DERRYCK, A, FAUSTO-STERLING, A, LAUZANNE, K and LEE, E, 'How Sexually Dimorphic are We?' (2000) 12 *American Journal of Human Biology* 151.

BRITISH ASSOCIATION OF PAEDIATRIC SURGEONS, *Statement of the British Association of Paediatric Surgeons Working Party on the Surgical Management of Children Born with Ambiguous Genitalia* (London, British Association of Paediatric Surgeons, 2001).

BUTLER, J *Bodies that Matter* (London: Routledge, 1993).

CATLIN, E and CRAWFORD, J, 'Neonatal Endocinology' in F Oski *et al.* (eds), *Principles and Practice of Paediatrics* (2nd ed) (New York, Lippincott Company, 1994).

CEALEY HARRISON, E and Hood-Williams, J, *Beyond Sex and Gender* (London, Sage, 2002).

CHANTER, T, 'Beyond Sex and Gender: On Luce Irigaray's this Sex which is Not One' in D Welton (ed.), *The Body* (Oxford: Blackwell, 1999).

CHASE, C, 'Hermaphradites with Attitude: Mapping the Emergence of Intersex Political Activism' 4 *Gay and Lesbian Quarterly* 189.

CHAU P-L and HERRING J, (2002) 'Defining, Assigning and Designing Sex' (1998) 16 *International Journal of Law Policy and Family* 327.

COLAPINTO, J, *As Nature Made Him: The Boy Who Was Raised As A Girl* (New York: Quartet Books, 2000).

COLE, J, BROADWELL, M, and ROGERS, G, 'Intersexuality in a Charolais Heifer' (1997) 141 *Veterinary Record* 656.

COLKER, R, *Hybrid: Bisexuals, Multi-racials, and Other Misfits under American Law* (New York, New York University Press, 1996).

COLLETT-SOLBERG, PF, 'Congenital Adrenal Hyperplasia: from Genetics and Biochemistry to Clinical Practice' (2001) 40 *Clinical Pediatrics*, 1 and 125.

CREIGHTON, SM, MINTO, CL, and STEELE, SJ, 'Objective Cosmetic and Anatomical Outcomes at Adolescence of Feminising Surgery for Ambiguous Genitalia done in Childhood' (2001) 358 *The Lancet* 124.

CRUZ, DB, 'Disestablishing Sex and Gender' (2002) 90 *California Law Review* 997.

DAABOUL, J and FRADER, J, 'Ethics and the Management of the Patient with Intersex: a Middle Way' (2001) 14 (9) *Journal of Pediatric Endocrinol Metab* 1575.

DARWIN, C, *On the Origin of Species by Means of Natural Selection* (London: John Murray, 1859).

DAVIES, R, MOORE, A, SCHEDL, A, BRATT, E, MIYAHAWA, K, LADOMERY, M, MILES, C, MENKE, A, VAN HEYNINGEN, V, and HASTIE, N, 'Multiple Roles for the Wilms' Tumor Suppressor, WT1' (1999) 59 *Cancer Research* (supplement), 1747s.

DELPHY, C, *Close to Home: A Materialist Analysis of Women's Oppression* (London: Hutchinson, 1984).

DIAMOND, M and SIGMUNDSON, HK, 'Management of Intersexuality: Guidelines for Dealing with Persons with Ambiguous Genitalia' (1997a) 151 *Archives Pediatric Adolescent Medicine* 1046.

—— 'Sex Reassignment at Birth: Long Term Review and Clinical Implication' (1997b) 151 *Archives of Pediatrics and Adolescent Medicine* 298–304.

DOBAC, J. 'Pansexuality and the Law' (1999) 5 *William & Mary Journal of Women & Law* 297.

DREGER, A, *Hermaphrodites and the Medical Invention of Sex* (Cambridge, Harvard University Press, 1998a).

—— 'Ambiguous Sex or Ambivalent Medicine? Ethical Issues in the Medical Treatment of Intersexuality' (1998b) 28(3) *Hastings Center Reporter* 24.

—— 'Doubtful Sex', in L Schiebinger (ed), *Feminisim and The Body* (Oxford, Oxford University Press, 2000).

DUNN, AM, MCCABE, J and ADAMS, J, 'Intersexuality in *Gammarus duebenii* (*Amphipoda*), a Cost Incurred in Populations with Environmental Sex Determination?' (1996) 69 *Crustaceana* 313.

EDGERTON, R, 'Poket Intersexuality: An East African Example of the Resolution of Sexual Incongruity' (1964) 66 *American Anthropologist* 1288.

FAUSTO-STERLING, A, 'The Five Sexes' (1993) March/April *The Sciences* 1.

—— *Sexing the Body* (New York: Basic Books, 2000).

FREUD, S, 'Femininity' in New Introductory Lectures on Psycho-Analysis' in J Strachey (ed), *The Standard Edition of the Complete Psychological Works of Sigmund Freud* (London, Hogarth Press and the Institute for Psycho-Analysis, 1964).

FORD, K-K, 'First, Do No Harm—The Fiction of Legal Parental Consent to Genital-Normalizing Surgery on Intersexed Infants' (2001) 19 *Yale Law & Policy Review* 469.

FOUCALT, M, 'Two Lectures' in C Gordon (ed), *Power/knowledge: Selected interviews and other Writings 1972–1977 by Michael Foucault*(New York, Pantheon, 1980).

FRYE, PR, 'The International Bill of Gender Rights vs. the Cider House rules' (2000) 7 *William & Mary Journal of Women &* Law 133–216.

GATENS, M, *Imaginary Bodies,*(New York, Routledge, 1996).

GLASSBERG, K, 'The Intersex Infant: Early Gender Assignment and Surgical Reconstruction' (1998) 11 *Journal of Paediatric & Adolescent Gynaecology* 151.

GLASSBERG, K, 'Editorial: Gender Assignment and the Pediatric Urologist' (1999) 161 *Journal of Urology* 1308.

GOODFELLOW, PN and CAMERINO, G, 'DAX-1, an 'Antitestis' Gene' (1999) 55 *Cellular and Molecular Life Sciences* 857.

GOTTLIEB, B, LEHVASLAIHO, H, BEITEL, LK, LUMBROSO, R, PINSKY, L and TRIFIRO, M, 'The Androgen Receptor Gene Mutations Database' (1998) 26 *Nucleic Acids Research* 234.

—— —— —— —— 'Androgen Insensitivity' (1999a) 89 *American Journal of Medical Genetics* 210.

—— —— —— —— 'Update of the Androgen Receptor Gene Mutations Database' (1999b) 14 *Human Mutation* 103.

GRENFELL, L, 'Making Sex: Law's Narratives of Sex, Gender and Identity' (2003) 23 *Legal Studies* 66.

GREENBERG, J, 'Defining Male and Female: Intersexuality and the Collision between Law and Biology' (1999) 41 *Arizona Law Review* 265.

—— 'When is a Man a Man, and When is a Woman a Woman?' (2000) 52 *Florida Law Review* 745.

—— 'Deconstructing Binary Race and Sex Categories: A Comparison of the Multiracial and Transgendered Experience' (2002) 39 *San Diego Law Review* 917.

GREER, G, *The Whole Woman* (London, Anchor, 2000).

GRIFFIN, J and WILSON, J, 'Disorders of Sexual Differentiation' in P Walsh, A Retik, T Stamey and E Vaughan (eds), *Campbell's Urology* (New York, Saunders, 1992).

GROVEMAN, S, 'Letter to the Editor' (1996) 154 *Canadian Medical Association Journal* 1829.

HERMER, L, 'Paradigms Revised: Intersex Children, Bioethics & The Law' (2002) 11 *Annals of Health Law* 195.

HERD, G, (ed), *Third Sex, Third Gender: Beyond Sexual Dimorphism in Culture and History* (New York, Zone Books, 1996).

HERRING, J, *Family Law* (Harlow, Longman, 2001).

—— and CHAU, P-L, 'Assigning Sex for Intersexuals' (2001) 31 *Family Law* 762.

HIRD, M and GERMON, J, 'The Intersexual Body and the Medical Regulation of Gender', in K Backett-Milburn and L McKie (eds), *Constructing Gendered Bodies* (Harlow, Palgrave, 2000).

HOME OFFICE *Report Of The Interdepartmental Working Group On Transsexual People* (London, Home Office, 2000).

ISNA *Amicus Brief on Intersex Genital Surgery to the Columbian High Court*, (1998) 7 February 1.

ITO, Y, FISHER, CR, CONTE, FA, GRUMBACH, MM and SIMPSON, ER, 'Molecular Basis of Aromatase Deficiency in an Adult Female with Sexual Infantilism and Polycystic Ovaries' (1993) 90 *Proceedings of the National Academy of Sciences USA*, 11673.

JACKSON, S and SCOTT, S, 'Putting the Body's Feet on the Ground: Towards a Sociological Reconceptualization of Gendered and Sexual Embodiment' in K Backett-Milburn and L McKie (eds), *Constucting Gendered Bodies* (Harlow, Palgrave, 2001).

JAGGAR, A, *Feminist Politics and Human Nature* (New York, Rowman & Allanheld, 1983).

JORDAN, BK, MOHAMMED, M, CHING, ST, DELOT, E, CHEN, X-N, DEWING, P, SWAIN, A, RAO, PN, ELEGALDE, BR and VILAIN 'Up-Regulation of WNT-4 Signalling and Dosage-Sensitive Sex Reversal in Humans' (2001) 68 *American Journal of Human Genetics* 1102.

KESSLER, S, *Lessons from the Intersexed* (New Brunswick:, Rutgers University Press, 1998).

KINNISON, MT, UNWIN, MJ and JARA, F, 'Macroscopic Intersexuality in Salmonid Fishes' (2000) 34 *New Zealand Journal of Marine and Freshwater Research* 125.

KIPNIS, K and DIAMOND, M, 'Paediatric Ethics and the Surgical Assignment of Sex' (1998) 9(4) *Journal of Clinical Ethics* 398.

KOGAN, T, 'Intersections of Race, Ethnicity, Class, Gender and Sexual Orientation: Transsexuals and Critical Gender Theory: the Possibility of a Restroom Labelled "Other"' (1997) 48 *Hastings Law Journal* 1223.

KRSTIC, ZD, SMOLJANIC, Z, VUKANIC, D, VARINAC, D and JANJIC, G, 'True Hermaphroditism: 10 Years' Experience' (2000) 16 *Pediatric Surgery International* 580.

KUPFER, S, QUIGLEY, C and FRENCH, F, 'Male Pseuodhermaphroditism' (1992) 16 *Seminars in Perinatology* 319.

KUSZ, K., KOTECKI, M, WOJDA, A, SZARRAS-CZAPNIK, M, LATOS-BIELENSKA, A, WARENIK-SZMANKIEWICZ, A, RUSZCYNSKA-WOLSKA, A and JARUZELSKA, J, 'Incomplete Masculinisation of XX Subjects Carrying the SRY Gene on an Active X Chromosome' (1999) 36 *Journal of Medical Genetics* 452.

LEE, PA, 'Should we Change our Approach to Ambiguous Genitalia?' (2001) *The Endocrinologist* 118.

LORD CHANCELLOR'S DEPARTMENT, *Government Policy Concerning Transsexual People* (London, LCD, 2003).

MARLAMDEUA, NM, DHOBLE, RL, KULKARNI, GB, and DHUMAL, MV, 'Studies on Intersexuality in Osmanabadi Goats' (1998) 75 *Indian Veterinary Journal* 35.

MARTIN, PL, 'Moving Toward an International Standard in Informed Consent: The Impact of Intersexuality and the Internet on the Standard of Care' (2002) 9 *Duke Journal Gender Law & Policy* 135.

McELREAVEY, K and FELLOUS, M, 'Sex Determination and the Y-chromosome' (1999) 89 *American Journal of Medical Genetics* 176.

McGILLIVRAY, B, 'The Newborn with Ambiguous Genitalia' (1991) 16 *Seminars in Perinatology* 365.

MEYERS-SEIFER, C and CHAREST, N, 'Diagnosis and Management of Patients with Ambiguous Genitalia (1992) 16 *Seminars in Perinatology* 332.

MOI, T, *What is a Woman?* (Oxford, Oxford University Press, 2001).

MONEY, J, *Sex Errors of the Body* (Baltimore, John Hopkins University Press, 1968).

—— *Sin, Science, and the Sex Police: Essays On Sexology And Sexosophy* (Baltimore, Prometheus Books, 1998).

MONEY, J and EHRHARDT, A, *Man & Woman/Boy & Girl: The Differentiation and Dimorphism of Gender Identity From Conception to Maturity* (Baltimore, John Hopkins University Press, 1973).

MULAIKAL, R, MULAIKAL, M, MIGEON, CJ and ROCK, JA, 'Fertility Rates in Female Patients with Congenital Adrenal Hyperplasia due to 21-Hydroxylase Deficiency' (1987) 316 *New England Journal of Medicine* 178.

MUNDY, LL, 'Hitting Below The Belt: Sex-Ploitive Ideology & The Disaggregation Of Sex And Gender' (2001/2002) 14 *Regent University Law Review* 215.

MUSCATELLI, F, STROM, TM, WALKER, AP, ZANARIA, E, RECAMS, D, MEINDL, A, BARDONI, B, GUICLI, S, ZEHETNER, G, RABI, W, SCHWARTZ, HP, KAPLANS, J-C, CAMERINI, G, MEITINGER, T and MONACO, AP, 'Mutations in the DAX-1 Gene give Rise to both X-linked Adrenal Hypoplasia Congenita and Hypogonadotrophic Hypogonadism' (1994) 372 *Nature* 672.

NAFFINE, N, 'The Body Bag' in N Naffine and RJ Owens (eds), *Sexing the Subject of Law*

(Sydney, LBC, 1997).

NATARAJAN, A, 'Medical Ethics and Truth Telling in the Case of Androgen Insensitivity Syndrome' (1996) 154 *Canadian Medical Association Journal* 568.

NEWMAN, K, RANDOLPH, J, and ANDERSON, K, 'The Surgical Management of Infants and Children with Ambiguous Genitalia' (1992) 215 *Annals of Surgery* 644.

NYE, JL, 'The Gender Box' (1998) 13 *Berkeley Women's Law Journal* 226.

OHNO, S, *Sex-Chromosome and Sex-linked Genes* (Berlin, Springer-Verlag, 1967).

PAILHOUX, E, PELLINIEMI, L, BARBOSA, A, PARMA, P, KUOPIO, T and COTINOT, C, 'Relevance of Intersexuality to Breeding and Reproductive Biotechnology Programs; XX Sex Reversal in Pigs' (1997) 47 *Theriogenology* 93.

PHORNPHUTKUL, C, FAUSTO-STERLING, A, and GRUPPUSE, P, 'Gender Self-Reassignment in an XY Adolescent Male Born with Ambiguous Genitalia' (2000) 106 *Pediatrics* 1.

RAYMOND, JG, *The Transsexual Empire: The Making of the She-Male* (New York: Teachers College Press, 1994).

REILLY, J and WOODHOUSE, C, 'Small Penis and the Male Sexual Role' (1989) 142 *The Journal of Urology* 569.

ROBINSON, ES, VAN DE BERG, JL, WATSPM, CM and DOOLEY, TP, 'Intersexual Phenotypes and Sex Chromosome Complements of Five South American Opossums *(Monodelphis domestica)*' (1996) 46 *Laboratory Animal Science* 555.

ROTHBLATT, M, *The Apartheid of Sex: A Manifesto on the Freedom of Gender* (New York, Crown, 1995).

SARAFOGOLOU, K and OSTRER, H, 'Familial Sex Reversal: A Review' (2000) 85 *Journal of Clinical Endrocrinology and Matabolism* 483.

SCALES-TRENT, J, 'Commonalities: On Being Black and White, Different, and the Same' (1990) 2 *Yale Journal of Law and Feminism* 305.

SCHIEBEL, K, WINKELMANN, M, MERTZ, A, XU, X, PAGE, D, PETIT, C and RAPPOLD, G, 'Abnormal XY Interchange between a Novel Isolated Protein Kinase Gene, PRKY, and its Homologue PRKX, Accounts for One Third of All (Y+) XX Males and (Y−) XY Females' (1997) 6 *Human Molecular Genetics* 1985.

SCHOBER, J, 'Sexual Behaviors, Sexual Orientation and Gender Identity in Adult Intersexuals: A Pilot Study' (2001) 165 (6, part 2) *Journal of Urology* 2350.

SHARPE, A, *Transgender Jurisprudence* (London, Cavendish Press, 2002).

SIMPSON, JL, 'Genetics of the Female Reproductive Ducts' (1999) 89 *American Journal of Medical Genetics* 224.

—— and RAJKOVIC, A, 'Ovarian Differentiation and Gonadal Failure' (1999) 89 *American Journal of Medical Genetics* 186.

SLIJPER, FME, DROP, SLS, MOLENAAR, JC and DE MUNICK KEIZER-SCHAMA, SMPF, 'Long-Term Psychological Evaluation of Intersex Children' (1998) 27 *Archives of Sexual Behaviour* 125.

SMITH, DK, 'Transsexualism, Sex Reassignment Surgery and the Law' (1971) 56 *Cornell Law Review* 963.

SPEED, RM, 'Oocyte Development in XO Fetuses of Man and Mouse: the Possible Role of Heterologous X-Chromosome Pairing in Germ Cell Survival' (1986) 94 *Chromosoma* 115.

STORROW, RF, 'Naming the Grotesque Body in the "Nascent Jurisprudence of Transsexualism" ' (1997) 4 *Michigan Journal of Gender and Law* 275.

VAIMAN, D and PAILHOUX, E, 'Mammalian Sex Reversal and Intersexuality: Deciphering the Sex Determination Cascade' (2000) 16 *Trends in Genetics* 488.

VALDES, F, 'Queers, Sissies, Dykes, and Tomboys: Deconstructing the Conflation of "Sex," "Gender," and "Sexual Orientation" in Euro-American Law and Society' (1994) 83 *California Law Review* 3.

VANDERSCHUEREN, D and VANDENPUT, L, 'Androgens and Osteoporosis' (2000) 32 *Andrologia* 125.

WAGNER, T, WIRTH, J, MEYER, J, ZABEL, B, HELD, M, ZIMMER, JJP, BRICARELLII, FD, KEUTAL, J, HUSTERT, F, WOLF, U, TOMMERUP, N, SSHEMPP, W and SCHERER, G, 'Autosomal Sex Reversal and Campomelic Dysplasia are Caused by Mutations In and Around the SRY-Related Gene SOX' (1994) 79 *Cell* 1111.

WARNE, GL, 'Advances and Challenges with Intersex Disorders' (1998) 10 *Reproduction, Fertility and Development* 79.

WATSON, CM, JOHNSTON, PG, RODGER, KA, MCKENZIE, LM, O'NEILL, RJW and COOPER, DW, 'SRY and Karyotypic Status of One Abnormal and Two Intersexual Marsupials' (1997) 9 *Reproduction, Fertility and Development* 233.

WEISS, JT, 'The Gender Caste System: Identity, Privacy, and Heteronormativity' (2001) 10 *Law & Sexuality* 123.

WHITTLE, S, *Respect and Equality: Transsexual and Transgender Rights* (London, Cavendish, 2002).

WILCOX, AR, ADAMS, FG, COOKE, P and GORDON, RR, 'Deletion of Short Arm of No.4 (4p): A Detailed Case Report' (1970) 7 *Journal of Medical Genetics* 171.

WILLIAMS, N, 'The Imposition of Gender: Psychoanalytic Encounters with Genital Atypicality' (2002) 19 *Psychoanalytic Psychology* 455.

WILLIAMS, W, *The Spirit and the Flesh: Sexual Diversity in Indian American Culture* (New York: Beacon Press, 1986).

YORDAM, N, ALIKASIFOGLU, A, KANDEMIR, N, CAGLAR, M and BALCI, S, 'True Hermaphroditism: Clinical Features, Genetic Variants and Gonadal Histology' (2001) 14 *Journal of Paediatric Endocrinology and Metabolism* 421.

10

The Development of Sexuality

JULIE A. JESSOP

CONTEMPORARY SOCIETY IS increasingly characterised as a 'sexualised' world (Hawkes, 1996), and yet what constitutes 'normal' sexuality is a source of constant debate and controversy. Although we now know more than ever about the physiological processes which result in sexual arousal (cf. Masters and Johnson, 1966), and the propensity towards 'deviant' sexual behaviours (cf. Kinsey *et al*, 1953), the issue of how sexuality 'normally' develops remains relatively unexplored.

Historically, the way in which people became sexual was generally seen to be unproblematic, based on the 'natural' biological processes of human development and the need to procreate. Hormonal changes and the resultant development of secondary sexual characteristics associated with puberty were seen to herald the beginning of sexual interest and be the pre-cursor to sexual activity. Although during the last few decades such a biological-determinist view has been strongly criticised for ignoring the social context within which sexual relationships take place and sexual identities are developed, there is still little understanding of exactly how sexuality develops. Even developmental psychology, aiming to uncover universal patterns of development, has little to say about sexuality, with the implicit assumption being that, once gender identity has been established, the biological changes associated with puberty will automatically lead to sexual behaviour (Richards, 1996).

One of the reasons for the lack of understanding can be seen to be the inherent difficulty/ambivalence associated with studying sexuality, especially with respect to children and young people. As Treas (2003: 399) points out 'Although premarital sex is increasingly accepted, teen sex is still seen as problematic'; and the linking of children with sexuality is even more culturally taboo (Jackson, 1982). As such, although research into adolescent sexuality is deemed legitimate due to the on-set of puberty, there is still very little documentation or research into pre-adolescent sexuality. This is the case even though Udry and Campbell's (1994) review of the research points to the fact that many males, especially those from African-American backgrounds, begin sexual activity before they reach puberty. And it also ignores the anecdotal evidence of sexual exploration and experimentation between young siblings and peers.

Sexology, initially concerned with the 'scientific' classification of sexual behaviour and responses, has become more and more focused on sex as a medical matter; and one which equates good sex with a 'healthy life' (Tiefer, 1995). As Jackson and Scott (1997: 557) point out '. . . increasingly sexuality is talked of in the idiom of health promotion and life-style choices', leading to the observation that:

> Currently, within discourses of consumption and social marketing, 'healthy sex' ranks along with high fibre low fat diets as part of the personal management of bodily vitality (1997: 558).

Such an emphasis, however, highlights the tension between wider cultural frameworks of understanding, between the pursuit of sexual pleasure as a rational healthy life goal, part of the 'project of the self' (cf. Giddens, 1992), and the view of sex as unruly, intractable and resistant to rational management. This tension is evidenced in sex manuals that are set out like cook-books, and in which we are 'taught' how 'natural' sex should be done, and how to 'arrange' for it to be 'spontaneous' (Jackson and Scott, 1997).

So what constitutes 'normal' sex? How does 'normal' sexuality develop? And how do we know what we know?

Survey data, apart from a few exceptions (e.g. Kinsey), has generally focused on teenage sexuality rather than that of older adults. The British survey research into adolescent sexual behaviours carried out by Schofield in the 1960s and 1970s was an attempt to document the prevalence of sexual intercourse and the use of contraception. This research was based within a 'problem orientated' discourse, and although useful in documenting frequencies and behaviours, did not look at the subjective experiences of the individuals involved. The AIDS crisis of the 1980s, however, whilst still problem orientated, prompted a new awareness of how little was known about sexuality and the social contexts in which it took place. Although tackling the issue of who, what, where, when, how (e.g. Johnson *et al*, 1994) such research has tended to treat the study of sexuality independently from that of relationships. And, as Herold and Marshall (1996: 71) point out, in survey data 'the strong emotional responses that adolescents can experience in relationships are often minimised in importance'. Whilst behaviour patterns are useful in analysing trends, more qualitative research is needed to understand how such trends are experienced by individuals themselves. On this basis there is now a growing body of research which documents how teenagers themselves experience their emerging sexuality.

This chapter focuses primarily on the growing number of empirical studies which take a more qualitative approach to the subject of sexuality, and at how biological, psychological and social processes interact in its development. Although work on gay/lesbian sexuality has in fact been pivotal in providing a 'space' to unpack the socially determined nature of heterosexuality in our culture (Lees, 1993), because the majority of work has been conducted on the emergence of heterosexuality rather than gay/lesbian sexuality (an issue which is discussed further below), we concentrate on this aspect of 'normal' development. The theoretical and methodological limitations of studying sexuality are addressed, together with the reasoning behind focusing specifically on adolescence as the main site for the development of sexuality. The principal issues that have been identified through the research to be of particular importance to adolescents themselves are also discussed.

Theorising about the development of sexuality has, to a large extent, been constrained through both the emphasis on biological processes and functions, and the influence of religious and medical doctrines. Once these historical and cultural mores are taken into consideration, however, the 'naturalness' of what we consider appropriate sexual behaviour, and how it develops, becomes open to question (cf. Tiefer, 1995; and Gagnon and Simon, 1973 for discussion on the social construction of sexuality).

Psychological theories of development, based on universal trajectories culminating in 'adulthood', also limit the way in which sexuality is researched and how it is thought to develop. The focus on adolescence as the main site of sexual development is based on the assumption that puberty marks the onset of adult sexuality. This focus is strengthened through research which tracks life-course events and can be seen to link behaviour such as early sexual debut with more sexual partners etc, leading to a belief that 'Formative sexual experiences resonate across the life-course' (Treas, 2003:400). However, such a focus, as with many developmental theories, tends not only to presuppose that once 'adulthood' is reached development stops, but also fails to take into account earlier developmental processes and experiences which may effect sexual development (Richards, 1996).

Sexuality, seen as a disruptive force, has been the focus of regulation and control throughout history (cf Foucault, 1972), and in this context it is not surprising that the majority of research which has been conducted into adolescent sexuality has adopted a perspective which highlights the negative consequences and adopts a 'problem orientated' view which tends to focus specifically on teenage pregnancy and the proliferation of sexually transmitted diseases (STDs). As Moore and Rosenthal (1993: x–xii) point out, whilst 'All theories of adolescent development give sexuality a central place in negotiating the transition from child to adult', most problematicise it rather than seeing it as a 'normative' event/stage which can have both positive and negative consequences.

Herold and Marshall (1996) in a 20 year review of sex research in America, found that from a theoretical perspective studies generally fell into two overarching paradigms: sexuality as a biological imperative, and sexuality as socially shaped and learned. However, they argue that 'it is at the interface between these two paradigms that advances in theory and research should be focused' (p 69). The shift in emphasis to look at how adolescents themselves experience their emerging sexuality explores this interface.

In the UK, the Women Risk and AIDS Project (WRAP) and Men Risk and AIDS Project (MRAP) explored the sexual practices, beliefs and understandings of young men and women aged between 16 and 21 in London and Manchester. These studies were based on a qualitative approach which included both in-depth interviews and focus groups which have led to a greater understanding of teenage sexuality and have worked to highlight the ways in which individual sexuality is socially constructed (Thomson and Scott, 1991; Holland et al., 1993 etc.).

Although first sexual experience, especially for boys, is generally masturbation, most research into adolescent sexuality has been framed within the context of sexual intercourse and contraception use. Brooks-Gunn and Paikoff (1997), however, argue that

> the study of sexuality must be reframed in order to take into account behaviours *and* feelings, to promote a more multi-dimensional approach, and to explore sexual transitions other than age of first intercourse and of first contraceptive usage (1997: 213).

Alongside this is a growing ecological approach which documents how environmental factors affect the sexual behaviour of young people, e.g.

> If adolescents are living in economically disadvantaged communities where adult-status behaviours, such as employment, are difficult to attain, sexual activity may be highly valued as a symbol of adult status (Herold and Marshall, 1996: 72).

Such factors are also linked to educational achievement, with girls early sexual debut being negatively associated with attainment .

CHILDHOOD SEXUALITY

One of the reasons for the lack of research into childhood sexuality, as Jackson (1982: 1) points out, is that :

> To write about children and sex is to bring together two sets of issues that are highly emotive, that readily provoke moral outrage and righteous indignation.

At the same time, however, whilst we perceive sexuality to be an adult (or at least adolescent) activity from which children need to be protected, we are often guilty of simultaneously attaching inappropriate sexual significance to children's desires and actions.

From a Freudian psychoanalytic perspective, childhood is highly correlated with the development of the libido and mature adult sexuality, to the extent that almost any form of sensual pleasure, from thumb sucking to defecating, can be seen as having a sexual context. However, Jackson (1982: 77) argues that such an approach can be criticised for 'over-estimating children's sexual capacities and attaching too much sexual significance to their desires and activities'.

Whilst the capacity for sexual arousal may be present from birth, and many young children may masturbate to orgasm, these experiences and sensations do not hold the same sexual connotations as they do for adults. Not until children learn the societal mores associated with adult sexuality can their behaviour be deemed to be sexual in the adult sense, and in attaching sexual significance to childhood activities adults can be seen to be projecting their own motivations on to those of children.

Paradoxically, however, through emphasising adolescence as the main period in which sexuality develops, sexuality as a whole life-course phenomenon is ignored and the role of early childhood experiences are often deemed extraneous. The fact that babies and young children indulge in behaviour which is labelled 'sexual' is discounted as irrelevant, and the influences of infant and early childhood development and exploration are minimised and de-sexualised (Reibstein and Richards, 1992). Whilst the early years of childhood may not constitute overt sexuality in the adult sense, it is in this period that children become conscious of both culturally specific gender identities and societal conventions and morality regarding sexual activity. To this extent innocent sensual pleasure seeking can come to be seen as wrong or 'dirty' and guilt inducing as children are told not to touch themselves, linking into socially proscribed attitudes towards genitals as 'rude', and becoming the basis of later sexual experience (Jackson, 1982).

ADOLESCENT SEXUALITY

As previously mentioned, adolescence, rather than early childhood or adulthood, has been the main focus for the majority of the research into the development of sexuality. Adolescence is seen as the transition phase from childhood to adulthood and, as Brooks-Gunn and Paikoff (1997) point out,

> No matter how much adults might like to ignore it, sex has great meaning in the lives of youth, whether they have had any sexual experience or not. A sexual identity or identities have to be formed; sexual exploration . . . will occur during adolescent years; and the negotiation of autonomy and intimacy will take place within sexual situations (1997: 193).

Such increasing sexual exploration during adolescence takes into account demographic changes which have seen the postponement of marriage together with earlier onset of sexual intercourse, leading to a situation in which 'Greater sexual experimentation and experience are expected now before making serious relationship commitments' (Miller and Benson, 1999).

Research into adolescence has, however, also generally been based within a male biased paradigm which emphasises autonomy over intimacy. As Lees (1993: 12) points out, 'In youth research . . . maturity has been defined as the development of autonomy rather than of responsibility for others or inter-dependence'. Although feminist research is beginning to redress this balance (cf. Gilligan, 1982), this emphasis has marginalised research which focuses on relational development in favour of that of the individual. And it has often worked to obscure the gendered nature of sexuality.

(a) Biological Determinants and Puberty

Although puberty represents a process of biological development that culminates in the maturation of sexual genitalia, this process and the consequences it has for sexual development, is heavily influenced by the social context in which it takes place and the specific experiences of the individual. The work of Brooks-Gunn *et al.,* (1997) highlights the ways in which the timing of puberty can affect adolescent well-being, with early pubertal onset being associated negatively for girls and positively for boys. Such an influence, however, is as much to do with the social consequences of such changes as to the physiology itself (Miller and Benson, 1999).

Because testosterone has been found to be necessary for maintaining adult sexual interest, in both males and females, Udry and Campbell (1994) looked at the effects of testosterone and other hormonal fluctuations during puberty. They conducted extensive testing of boys and girls over a three-year period, including taking samples of hormone levels and conducting interviews. Their conclusion was that although hormones can have an indirect causation through the 'attractiveness effect',

> The lack of significant hormone-behaviour relationships among our findings precludes the possibility that the role of pubertal development represents hormone effects on behaviour (1994: 165).

However they believe that the lack of significance may indicate the need for more sophisticated research tests rather than a lack of direct causation and advocate that prenatal hormone levels may need to be studied in order to uncover individual predispositions to sexual behaviour (1994: 203).

(b) The Gendered Embodiment of Sexuality

Jackson (1982) argues that 'In order to become fully sexual young people have to develop an awareness of their bodies as a source of sensual pleasure' (1982: 118). Such an awareness is necessarily gendered and conditional on prevalent socio-historical mores as much as physical development. As Moore and Rosenthal (1993: 49) point out, although recent research shows us that young people are not mere slaves to hormonal changes, there is no doubt that these changes can have complex emotional and behavioural effects, with 'one of the most compelling examples of the biological-social nexus com[ing] from teenagers' concerns about their bodies' (1993: 51). Traditionally, especially within feminist theory, research into body image has been more concerned with female representations/control and the effects these can have on adolescent development with respect to issues such as anorexia nervosa (although increasing depiction of male bodies is leading to a growing awareness of the effects on young males). Even within this research, however, body image is generally associated with outside appearance with little or no attention being focused on how women (or adolescents) feel about their genitals.

Hillier *et al.* (1999) in their research into the 'meanings of sex' for adolescents (as outlined below) highlight the fact that whilst boys' main descriptions of sex related to the physical act itself, often with the partner 'disembodied' and reduced to her sexual parts, there were no

> responses written by young women which described their bodies or their genitals as a site of sexual pleasure. Instead, love and relationships were more often than not given as the reasons for having sex (1999: 82).

Whilst they believe that part of the reason for this was the 'rurality' of the sample and the increased surveillance which prescribes young people to act in socially acceptable ways, these findings are not unique.

Holland *et al.* (1993) in their study of adolescent boys argue that the dominant Western version of masculinity is based on competition and aggression and is thus always based in relation to others: 'The idealised conception of 'real men' pressures young men to differentiate themselves from gay men, women and failures' (1993: 1). This leads to peer group competition to lose their virginity and for their first sexual experiences to be something that they do in order to be able to boast to their friends. Group talk for these young men rendered sex as an act devoid of emotion, and although many admitted that the reality was not necessarily like this, the lack of emotion worked as a defence against vulnerability.

Research with adolescent girls highlights the lack of scope for developing alternative feminine identities. Thomson and Scott (1991) found that although girls were critical of the sexist messages portrayed in teen magazines and in the media in general, that very often these were still subscribed to, and that:

> Given the lack of other positive messages about their sexuality available to young women, romantic ideology and sexual knowledge inevitably become linked in the cultural framework within which information is available to them (1991: 33).

This cultural framework tends to ignore female sexual pleasure, and Thomson and Scott found that:

> Most of the young women we spoke to had little experience of exploring their own bodies, their understanding of sex being rooted either in romantic or protective discourses (1991: 35).

Placing sexual experiences in such a romantic idealised context, however, leads the majority of girls to be extremely disappointed with their first sexual encounters.

In semi-structured interviews conducted by Martin (1996) with 55 young people aged between 14–19, strong gender differences were found with respect to views about their bodies and the embodiment of sex:

> ... girls still feel shame about their adult bodies, particularly breast development and menstruation. Girls still 'do it' to keep their boyfriends, and boys often 'do it' so they can 'go tell their friends, 'yeah, yeah!'.

Martin believes that the 'pubertal ambivalence' that girls often feel is in part based on their lack of knowledge about their own bodies, particularly their genitals, and the lack of exploration that girls engage in. As such she found that even when girls were sexually active 'Their boyfriends were allowed more access to their bodies than they allowed themselves' (1996: 22).

The work of Holland *et al.* (1994), as part of the WRAP research, found that in interviews with 150 young women aged between 16 and 21 'reference to and discussion of the body is almost absent' (1994: 23). This, in part, is felt to be due to the pressure of conforming to feminine stereotypes and the fact that girls who reveal sexual knowledge or express physical desire risk gaining a 'reputation'. Holland *et al* believe that part of the problem girls have in changing the status quo is that many are actually unaware that they are indeed 'living a disembodied femininity', and that things will only begin to change once women begin to 'reclaim their own experience and claim their bodies as the site of their own desires' (1994: 35).

Boys' bodies tend to be much more integrated into their sense of self and they are often less concerned, when asked, about their general appearance. However, whilst boys are more inclined to be open about their engagement with masturbation, there is still little known about wet-dreams and, even though they may be looking forward to it, first sexual encounters are not necessarily unproblematic (Martin, 1996).

Sex is now a large selling point for adolescent magazines, especially those aimed at young women (e.g. Just 17, Young Cosmo) and although they quite often emphasise active female sexuality, these issues are generally dealt with under the rubric of 'how to satisfy your man' or how not to be too emotional or possessive (Jackson and Scott, 1997). Martin (1996) found that the boys included in her study seemed to be looking for a blend of friendship and sex, rather than 'ideal love' (but see methodological limitations discussed below, e.g. only certain types of boys come forward to participate).

The emphasis on heterosexuality militates against safe sex practices through placing the female as passive, and also reinforces homophobic attitudes through marginalising gay and lesbian sexual relationships as 'deviant'. In the majority of studies conducted with adolescents this issue was never raised by adolescents themselves and was not something mentioned in any formal sex education that they had received (West, 1999; Buston *et al.*, 2002).

Such a gendered embodiment of sexuality is reflected in the 'double standards' for male and female sexual behaviour. Whilst some researchers believe that the 'double standard' of sexual behaviour for boys and girls is diminishing (Miller and Benson, 1999), others argue that it is in fact 'alive and well' (Holland *et al.*, 1993; Lees, 1993; Fromme and Emihovich, 1998). In a recent New Zealand study based on focus group work with 16–18 year old girls, Jackson and Cram (2003) found that although some young women were able to disrupt the double standard by challenging sexist language and positioning the self within alternate discourses, the voices of resistance tended to be individual rather than collective. They also found that 'young women's talk did not reveal a language of sexual desire grounded in bodily sensation or experience' (2003: 123) but one that relied more on sexuality as constructed through cognitive processes.

These findings echo those of Lees (1993) in her work with inner-city girls in England, which emphasises the socio-economic conditions that work to perpetuate gender stereotypes. Lees found that sexual reputation was a big issue for girls and highlights the fact that 'The only terms for active female sexuality are derogatory' (1993: 63). Whilst boys often levelled sexual insults at girls as a form of 'male bonding' and 'camaraderie', such insults were also used by girls themselves towards any who failed to conform to the norms of behaviour, whether they were actually 'sleeping around' or not.

(c) Romance and Desire

The majority of research studies point to strong gender differences in both the reasons for first intercourse and the circumstances surrounding it. Girls are much more likely than boys to say first intercourse was within a steady relationship, and much more likely to say they were 'in love' with their partner (Miller and Benson, 1999). But why do girls see sex in terms of 'love' and boys as 'physical desire', and what does it mean to the adolescents themselves?

Romance is still central to adolescent popular culture in most Western countries and

> cultural norms and proscriptions most clearly shape the development of romantic notions by defining who is perceived to be an eligible partner and what characteristics make particular persons more or less attractive (Miller and Benson, 1999: 103).

Previous studies of 'mate-selection'/'pair-bonding', generally see romance as an evolutionary adaptation aimed at maximising reproductive success (Miller and Benson, 1999; see also Johnson, this volume). However such research does not include adolescents because, as their relationships are not necessarily about long-term commitments, such theories are not applicable. Nevertheless, as Brown, Feiring and Furman (1999: 11) point out,

> If we are to understand why and when adolescents engage in different forms of sexual behaviour, it seems essential to consider their partner in sexual activity and the nature of their relationship.

Thompson (1994) conducted a narrative analysis of 400 adolescent (aged 13–20) girls' 'stories', based on interviews carried out between 1978–1986, in order to explore how they dealt with emerging relationships. The collective stories heard most often fell into two distinct categories; those of romance-melodrama, which were generally told by working-class white girls, and those of the romantic-comedy put forward by white middle-class participants. The melodramatic stories centred on 'love' as the main reason for life, work was not a priority, 'and sex was the foundation of adult love, as they understood it' (1994: 213). This emphasis on 'love' reflected the romantic ideals put forward in teen magazines and romance books, and the worse thing that could happen was being 'dumped', especially after having intercourse.

Thompson argues that because sex was so strongly equated with love, these girls were particularly pre-occupied with the how, where and when of the event *but* did not take contraceptive precautions because in the end it had to be 'a spontaneous thing' (1994: 214) (see also Jackson, 1982; Moore and Rosenthal, 1993). The reliance of these girls on romantic notions of love and sex meant that although they were often devastated when relationships failed to continue, the fault was eventually seen to be resultant on the choice of partner, and the pattern repeated until the 'right' man was found, or the girl became pregnant (although failed relationships did make girls more likely to take contraceptive precautions in subsequent relationships).

Those girls who subscribed to the 'romantic-comedy' outlook took a more strategic view of sex and relationships 'positioning themselves as active, able, optimistic . . . rather than passive and anxious victims' (1994: 221). In these narratives girls did not expect romance to give meaning to their lives and were aware of career choices and other things they wanted to do before settling down. Their stories were often humorous and emphasised the pragmatic nature of relationships. As such, when relationships failed, they were able to take a more reasoned view, were not 'devastated', and more likely to see the breakdown as a measure of lack of compatibility rather than the sole fault of the other. Also, in contrast to the 'broken-hearted narrators', they tended to take a pro-active stance with respect to contraception and 'put contraception just under desire . . . [in] a list of coital preconditions' (1994: 225). These girls were able consciously to refuse the melodramatic romantic script found in the majority of teen fiction and media portrayals through adopting a pragmatic stance. This stance, however, was often seen to be dependent on the girls having high economic and vocational expectations of their own, and having mothers who themselves had professional careers.

Class differences were also found by Martin (1996) in the extent to which girls felt pressured into having intercourse. She found that for many working-class girls the pressure, whether knowingly exerted by boys or not, often led to sex 'just happening' to them rather than it being a conscious decision. Whilst the same pressure could be felt by middle-class girls, they were more able to resist.

The emphasis on romantic relationships, based on mutuality, often obscures the fact that coercive relationships are more common than recognised. In a national (US) survey of 18–25 year olds, 25% said that they had at some time been forced into unwanted sexual encounters, and more than half of pregnant teenagers had been sexually abused in some way (Miller and Benson, 1999: 112). And, because the majority of studies of adolescent sexuality are focused on adolescents themselves, the issue of coercion and abuse of teenagers by adults is often not looked at.

(d) Heterosexuality—What is Sex?

Many researchers have commented on the continuing equation of 'sex' not only with heterosexuality, but with vaginal penetration. Auto-erotic or solitary sexual behaviour is not generally studied, and socio-sexual behaviour is seen to be a matter of progression from kissing to coitus, with little acknowledgement of historical/cultural specificity (Moore and Rosenthal, 1993; West, 1999; Jackson and Cram, 2003). What, however, do adolescents themselves think of as sex?

As part of a large-scale survey of 'small-town' Australian youth conducted by Hillier *et al.*, (1999), 511 15–17 year olds were asked specifically about the 'meanings of sex'. The results showed a marked reliance on heterosexual gender specific stereotypes both in behaviour and attitudes, with only nine (2 boys and 7 girls) mentioning, in response to the question 'what is sex?', anything other than penetration. This 'single-faceted construction of sex' not only silences any same-sex relationships but perpetuates the dominant meaning of sex as something that is active for men and passive for women.

Since the Clinton/Lewinski debacle, the issue of whether or not oral sex constitutes sex has become a topic of some debate, especially with respect to adolescents. Remez (2000) relates US media articles which posit the view that oral sex is not only becoming more popular amongst American teenagers but that it is likely to start at considerably earlier ages than full intercourse. The evidence for this comes from a small but growing number of young people who have contracted STDs that have been transmitted orally. Remez believes that part of the reason for the increase in oral sex (which is generally fellatio rather than cunnilingus and further reinforces women as pleasure givers rather than receivers) is to do with oral sex being equated with 'safe sex' or even with abstinence. In a survey of 600 Midwest university students, 59% did not believe that oral sex counted as sex. Remez also argues that the earlier age of those who engage in oral sex is partly due to the fact that 'For the teens, oral sex appears to be much less intimate or serious than vaginal intercourse' (2000: 300), which is somewhat the opposite of oral sex for adults which may be associated with higher levels of intimacy. Moore and Rosenthal (1993), based on Australian research, also found that oral sex is becoming more common, and happening at a younger age. Although they stress that this could be due to the fact that it is now more likely to be reported rather than an increase in actual incidence, or being engaged in as an alternative 'safe sex' strategy.

So, how do adolescents find out about sex and how to negotiate their emerging sexuality?

(e) Sexuality and the School

Treas (2003: 398) argues that 'Cultural ideologies promoting self-determination and individual fulfilment have undermined popular support for the family control of marriage and sexuality', and that the increase in STDs and the advent of AIDS has meant that 'Schools and communities have stepped up their efforts to augment family responsibility for teen sexuality' (2003: 399). As far as school sex education is concerned, however, the majority of research indicates its total lack of relevance for the teenagers that it is aimed to inform. Whilst Epstein and Johnson (1998) point out that school is where the majority of children gain sexual knowledge, either formally or informally, society's discomfort with the thought of children as being (or becoming) sexual prohibits open discussion:

> the idea of childhood sexual innocence inhibits attempts to alter, in more hopeful and progressive ways, the terrible and oppressive tangles which form part of child-adult relations in our culture (1998: 2).

Through linking sex with reproduction the emphasis is placed on vaginal intercourse, which reinforces masculine priorities and ejaculation as central. This biologically based focus works to divorce sex from relationships, emphasises conception rather than emotions, and is both sexist and heterosexist (Jackson, 1982).

In the US, sex education is currently undergoing an ideological shift to the right with the emphasis being placed on abstinence. Whether the reasoning behind the promotion of abstinence is on moral or health reasons, however, the continuing increase in teen pregnancy and STDs shows that such a focus does not work (Treas, 2003). One of the reasons for this, as in the discussion of oral sex outlined above, is that a lack of clear definitions as to what counts as 'sex' makes it difficult: you need to know exactly what it is you are supposed to be abstaining from. Fromme and Emihovich (1998) also argue that through promoting abstinence rather than giving adolescents relevant sex education, the problems of teenage pregnancy and STD transmission may actually be increased as 'Many adolescents will deny responsibility for contraception if they believe sexual involvement is wrong' (1998: 184).

Thomson and Scott (1991) as part of the WRAP studies asked girls about school sex education, and although they found that there was a wide variety in how different schools handled the subject, 82% of those asked thought that it had been inadequate. The main criticism levelled at it was that it had little or no relationship to the real chores and pressure around sexuality that affected the young women in question (1991: 6).

This is, in part, seen to be due to the focus on biological processes which 'reinforces a passive and negative view of female sexuality' (1991: 8). It was also noted that even within a biological paradigm, mention of female anatomy was generally restricted to the reproductive organs with no discussion of the clitoris, and when masturbation was mentioned (which was rarely) it was only in relation to men.

As part of a large-scale study of youth in the Avon area, West (1999) interviewed 147 young people aged between 14–21 about sex education and health clinics. The main finding of this study was that both the young women and men wanted more opportunity to talk about feelings and relationships connected with sexuality rather than the school focus on biological processes. One recurrent theme in these interviews was that of 'embarrassment', both on the part of the adolescents and the perceived embarrassment of the teachers. West links such situations to generational dynamics and the fact that sex, as mentioned previously, is not something many adults want to think or talk about in relation to adolescents. It was also found that 'young people are frustrated by the restricted agenda of most sex education, by the separation of sex from general relationships' (1999: 541). What these young people said they would like was a more progressive sex education format which was interactive, allowed debate, involved role play to practice sexual encounters, and gave adolescents time to talk about feelings and emotions. However, given limited resources and competing moral agendas there is very little progressive sex education available to youth in the UK (and USA).

Buston *et al.* (2002), based on 66 in-depth interviews and focus group work with adolescents aged 14–16, found that most were uncomfortable in sex education lessons because of both the sensitive nature of the topic and also the gender dynamics within the classroom. They believe that boys' generally disruptive behaviour is an attempt to subvert embarrassment through the use of humour, and girls are unlikely to ask questions for fear of being labelled as too knowledgeable or interested. The issue of teacher embarrassment was also seen as an important factor, and discomfort for the adolescents was heightened if it was perceived that the teacher was uncomfortable with the topic and/or unable to control the classroom situation. They argue that there is a need for much more progressive forms of sex education in which adolescents are encouraged to participate in a non-threatening environment, and which lessens embarrassment. They also make the point that whilst

> discussing sexual issues with the opposite sex should in principle develop a greater understanding of, and respect for, gendered perspectives and develop young people's ability to talk about sexual issues with the opposite sex (2002: 332),

this can only happen if the young people are comfortable and engaged, which is not generally the case. Given the inadequacy of school sex education in preparing adolescents for their emerging sexuality, where else do teenagers get their information from?

(f) Peers and Family

Peer influence becomes more dominant in adolescence, and Miller and Benson (1999: 105) link 'the strengthening of peer ties to a lessening of dependency on parental and family relationships during adolescence'. Romantic ties lessen family ties even further and fulfil adolescents' needs for independence, identity and intimacy.

Whilst sexuality is generally seen as part of the 'private' rather than 'public' domain, the majority of research shows that adolescents very rarely talk to their parents about it. And that when it is discussed, it is usually between mothers and daughters and within the context of avoiding pregnancy and problems, rather than as a source of pleasure or an aspect of human relationships. Jackson writing in 1982 posits the view that 'In coming to terms with their own sexuality and learning to manage sexual relationships, young people are very much alone' (1982: 116). This leads many teenagers to rely on the (often mis-) information provided by peers.

The study by West (1999), outlined above, highlighted the fact that most teenagers do not talk to their parents about sex even if they felt they had a good rapport with them. West found that to the adolescents interviewed, 'fathers were almost universally marginal' as far as discussing sex was concerned, and even with mothers most conversations centred on risk avoidance as opposed to relationships or the possibility of pleasure. Martin's (1996) study of adolescents, based on interviews with both boys and girls, found that:

> when fathers do talk to boys about sex, it is often in the vein of joking or boasting about sex and women or warning them to use condoms (1996: 6).

The research carried out by Wight (1994) with working-class adolescent boys, based on in-depth interviews with 58 14–16 year olds, also found that parents were not the primary source of information, with friends and television being stronger influences. For these boys, the construction of masculinity was conventional and homophobic, with male peers being the main reference point for behaviour such that 'for the 14–16 year olds studied, relationships with girls were largely subordinated to male company' (1994: 712), and primarily valued as a way of gaining esteem from their peers. Girls were objectified to the extent that 'the language the boys use for talk about sex implies that sexual intercourse is not a joint activity but something males do to females' (1994: 722). However, this is in part due to a male culture based on humour, bragging and teasing (bonding through competition and 'joking' insults) and in which to express any strong emotions is to become open to ridicule and derision.

The work of Fromme and Emihovich (1998) in the USA, based on retrospective interviews with university students, also highlighted the ways in which boys objectified women. They found that these young men generally described their experiences in terms of 'a body-centred sexuality, in which sexual relations are casual and pleasure centred' (1998: 175). They also found that these young men, through lack of more realistic relationships with women, subscribed to views received through TV, and make the point that 'that males in our study perceive television portrayals as a reflection of reality is particularly troubling' (1998: 177).

The fact that parents are unlikely to talk to their children about sexuality, in part due to embarrassment (on both sides), does not mean that adolescents are not picking up cues from them as to the nature of sex and relationships. Schalet (2000), in a small-scale study of parental behaviour and attitudes, conducted in-depth qualitative interviews with 14 American and 17 Dutch white middle-class parents who had 16-year-old children, in order to see how different cultural ideas affect adolescent attitudes and behaviours.[1] Schalet found that ' Dutch and American parents differ sharply in their definition of adolescent sexuality and the strategies they prefer for its management' (2000: 76). US parents emphasised the biological basis of sexuality, and reflected the view that teenagers were unable to control their impulses and had to be protected from themselves and their urges. The Dutch parents, however, were more likely to see sexuality as part of the 'normal' process of growing up, and to place it within relational contexts.

Schalet believes that

> The notion that teenagers possess the ability to restrain themselves and to commit to others enables Dutch parents to normalise adolescent sexuality, to treat it, in other words, as something that neither is nor should be a problem (2000: 86).

This reflects different attitudes towards adolescents in general as well as sexuality, and places the emphasis on adolescent/adult relationships in terms of 'negotiation' rather than 'control'.

The emphasis on vertical respect rather than mutual consideration, on control rather than negotiation, can be seen to lead to the one thing happening that Americans are most trying to avoid, with the irony being

> that while Dutch parents regard the sexual development of teenagers as beyond the control of parents and the use of parental authority to regulate sexuality as inappropriate, they may, in fact, influence the sexual behaviour of teenagers to a very large extent (2000: 95) (see also Ingham, this volume).

Although this study is small and homogenous, Schalet argues that it represents the dominant cultural values of the particular societies and also shows clearly the need to question research which refers in general terms to trends or attitudes across 'Western' society.

---

[1] Given that the USA has a much higher teenage birth rate than the Netherlands.

The problems associated with studying sexuality are manifold. The private and controversial nature of the topic predisposes it to issues of authenticity and political rhetoric. Obtaining funding is difficult and tends to mean that research that is carried out continues under the rubric of health outcomes and deviance. And the linking of children, adolescents and sexuality further compounds difficulties due to the existence of social taboos. Also, as Martin (1996) found with respect to adolescent boys, difficulties in recruitment invariably leads to problems of bias and representativeness; something which is often compounded by the fact that, because of ethical requirements, the obtaining of consent can be an intimidating process.

The work of Wight and West (1999) clearly highlights some of the difficulties associated with asking young people about their sex lives. They conducted research with 58 adolescent boys at age 19, all of whom had taken part in a large general survey one year earlier which had included questions about sexual attitudes and behaviour. They found 'considerable discrepancies' between responses at the two time points, even with respect to relatively straight-forward 'facts' such as age at first sex; with 44% of those who were sexually active giving different ages. Wight and West believe part of the reason for such discrepancies lies in variations as to how respondents wanted to be perceived in the different research settings, along with embarrassment (either through not wanting to seem too experienced or, conversely, too inexperienced) and inadequate understanding of the survey questions. The more in-depth interviews allowed for probing or clarification and also helped with recall. The age and gender of the interviewers was also seen to be an issue, although they believe that 'the more important variable is whether the interviewer was unabashed by talking about sex explicitly' (1999: 68). Ten of the adolescents who gave different responses were asked about the discrepancies, and all stuck by the responses given in the in-depth interview blaming the earlier answers on poor recall, not understanding the question and embarrassment.

DISCUSSION

Hill, writing in 1973, argued that:

> the development of sexual behaviour must be understood in terms of a complex, but patterned, series of learning experiences super-imposed upon and in interaction with some biological givens (quoted in Herold and Marshall, 1996: 69).

Thirty years later and although we are beginning to understand more about the development of sexuality and how it is experienced by individuals, there is still a long way to go.

The qualitative research on adolescents' subjective experiences highlights the complexities associated with the development of sexuality and the cultural influences that mould its formation. In showing how adolescents themselves experience becoming sexual, the gendered nature of sexuality and the cultural stereotypes which continue to be adhered to, emphasise the 'learnt' nature of the biological act manifested as social relationship. And language and the differences in communication styles between boys and girls can be seen to be one of the main ways that structure adolescents' emerging sexuality. The difficulties of communication between men and women (boys and girls) has been highlighted through the work of Tannen (1992) who argues that whilst women use language to connect/reinforce intimacy, for men its use is in preserving independence and negotiating status. As such, the 'separate worlds' that each gender inhabits traps them into clearly delineated sexual roles, and Moore and Rosenthal (1993: 101) point out that 'Understanding more fully the nature of sexual communication may help young people to explain to each other their point of view'.

Emphasising communication could not only help adolescents to understand their own bodies and emotions and those of their partner, but could also lead to a reduction in unwanted (or misperceived) sexual advances and to an increase in contraception use. Fromme and Emihovich (1998) found that 'young men who discussed contraception with their partners prior to sexual activity were more likely to report condom use' (1998: 182). However, the cultural prohibitions that continue to be associated with open sexual discussion between adults, leaves adolescents at a distinct disadvantage in this respect.

Alongside the need for the study of sexuality to be placed within a more relational context is the need for a broadening of scope to encompass a life-span approach to its development. Although an ageing population has lead to an increased interest in what happens both socially and sexually to those in later years (Doyle, 2002), adolescence continues to be the main focus of research into sexuality and there is very little knowledge of middle adult experience, with the development of sexuality often seen to be over by the age of 20 (Moore and Rosenthal, 1993). Gagnon and Parker (1995) point out the ways in which sexuality is socially constructed and, likewise, it has to be remembered that the research into sexuality itself is framed by culturally and historically specific interests and agendas.

REFERENCES

ADAMS, GR, MONTEMAYOR, R and GULLOTTA, TP, *Psychosocial Development During Adolescence* (Thousand Oaks, Sage, 1996).

BROOKS-GUNN, J and PAIKOFF, R, 'Sexuality and Developmental Transitions During Adolescence', in J Schulenberg, JR Maggs and K Hurrelmann (eds), *Health Risks and Developmental Transitions During Adolescence* (New York, Cambridge University Press, 1997).

BROWN, BB, FEIRING, C and FURMAN, W, 'Missing the Love Boat: Why Researchers have Shied away from Adolescent Romance' in W Furman, BB Brown and C Feiring (eds), *The Development of Romantic Relationships in Adolescence* (New York, Cambridge University Press, 1999).

BUSTON, K, WIGHT, D and HART, G, 'Inside the Sex Education Classroom: the Importance of Context in Engaging Pupils', (2002) *Culture, Health and Sexuality,* 4;3: 317–35.

DOYLE DRIEDGER, S, 'Old Flames', (2002) *Maclean's,* 22–8.

EPSTEIN, D and JOHNSON, R, *Schooling Sexualities* (Buckingham, Open University Press, 1998).

FOUCAULT, M, *The History of Sexuality, Volume 1* (Harmondsworth, Penguin, 1972).

FROMME, RE and EMITIOVICH, C, 'Boys Will be Boys: Young Males' Perceptions of Women, Sexuality, and Prevention' (1998) *Education and Urban Society,* 30; 2: 172–88.

GAGNON, JH and PARKER, RG, 'Conceiving Sexuality' in RG Parker and JH Gagnon (eds) *Conceiving Sexuality: Approaches to Sex Research in a Postmodern World* (Routledge, New York, 1995).

GAGNON, JH and SIMON, W, *Sexual Conduct: The Social Sources of Human Sexuality* (Chicago, Aldine, 1973).

GIDDENS, A, *The Transformation of Intimacy: Sexuality, Love and Eroticism in Modern Societies* (Cambridge, Polity Press, 1992).

GILLIGAN, C, *In a Different Voice: Psychological Theory and Women's Development* (Cambridge, MA: Harvard University Press, 1982).

HAWKES, G, *A Sociology of Sex and Sexuality* (Buckingham, Open University Press, 1996).

HEROLD, ES and MARSHALL, SK, 'Adolescent Sexual Development' in GR Adams, R Montemayor and TP Gullotta, (eds), *Psychosocial Development During Adolescence* (Thousand Oaks, Sage, 1996).

HILLIER, L, HARRISON, L, and BOWDITCH, K, ' "Never-Ending Love" and "Blowing Your Load": The Meanings of Sex to Rural Youth', (1999) *Sexualities,* 2; 1: 69–88.

HOLLAND, J, RAMAZANOGLU, C, and SHARPE, S, *Wimp or Gladiator: Contradictions in Acquiring Masculine Sexuality* (London, Tufnell Press, 1993).

—— —— —— *et al,* 'Power and Desire: The Embodiment of Female Sexuality', (1994) *Feminist Review,* 46: 21–38.

JACKSON, S, *Childhood and Sexuality* (Oxford, Basil Blackwell, 1982).

JACKSON, SM and CRAM, F, 'Disrupting the Sexual Double Standard: Young Women's Talk about Heterosexuality' (2003) *Journal of Social Psychology,* 42: 113–27.

JACKSON, S and SCOTT, S, 'Gut Reactions to Matters of the Heart: Reflections on Rationality, Irrationality and Sexuality', (1997) *The Sociological Review,* 45; 1: 551–75.

JOHNSON, AM, WADSWORTH, J, WELLINGS, R *et al, Sexual Attitude and Life Styles* (London, Blackwell Scientific Publications, 1994).

KINSEY, AC, POMEROY, WB, MARTIN, C *et al, Sexual Behaviour in the Human Female* (Philadelphia, Saunders, 1953).

LAMANNA, MA, 'Living the Postmodern Dream: Adolescent Women's Discourse on Relationships, Sexuality, and Reproduction', (1999) *Journal of Family Issues,* 20; 2: 181–217.

LEES, S, *Sugar and Spice: Sexuality and Adolescent Girls* (London, Penguin, 1993).

MARTIN, KA, *Puberty, Sexuality and the Self: Boys and Girls at Adolescence* (New York, Routledge, 1996).

MASTERS, W and JOHNSON, V, *Human Sexual Response* (London, Churchill, 1966).

MILLER, BC and BENSON, B, 'Romantic and Sexual Relationship Development During Adolescence' in W Furman, BB Brown, and C Feiring, (eds), *The Development of Romantic Relationships in Adolescence* (New York, Cambridge University Press, 1999).

MOORE, S and ROSENTHAL, D, *Sexuality in Adolescence* (London, Routledge, 1993).

MORAN, JP, *Teaching Sex: The Shaping of Adolescence in the 20th Century* (Cambridge, M.A., Harvard University Press, 2000).

REIBSTEIN, J and RICHARDS, M, *Sexual Arrangements: Marriage and Affairs* (London: Heinemann, 1992).

REMEZ, L., 'Oral Sex Among Adolescents: Is it Sex or is it Abstinence?' (2000) *Family Planning Perspectives,* 32; 6: 298–304.

RICHARDS, M, 'The Childhood Environment and the Development of Sexuality' in CJK Horny and S J Ulijaszek, (eds), *Long-Term Consequences of Early Environment, Growth, Development and the Life-Span* (Developmental Perspective. Society for the Study of Human Biology. Symposium 37. Cambridge University Press, 1996).

SCHALET, AT, 'Raging Hormones, Regulated Love: Adolescent Sexuality and the Construction of the Modern Individual in the United States and the Netherlands' (2000) *Body and Society,* 6; 1: 75–105.

SCHOFIELD, M, *The Sexual Behaviour of Young People* (London, Harmondsworth, 1968).

—— *The Sexual Behaviour of Young Adults* (London, Allen Lane, 1973).

TANNEN, D, *You Just Don't Understand: Women and Men in Conversation* (London, Virago, 1990).

THOMPSON, S, 'Changing Lives, Changing Genres: Teenage Girls' Narratives about Sex and Romance', in AS Rossi (ed), *Sexuality Across the Life-Course* (Chicago, The University of Chicago Press, 1994).

THOMSON, R and SCOTT, S, *Learning About Sex: Young Women and the Social Construction of Sexual Identity* (London, Tufnell Press, 1991).

TIEFER, L, *Sex is Not a Natural Act: And Other Essays* (Colorado, Westview Press Inc., 1995).

TREAS, J, 'Sex and Family: Changes and Challenges' in J Scott, J Treas and M Richards (eds), *Companion to the Sociology of the Family* (Oxford, Blackwell, 2003).

UDRY, JR and CAMPBELL, BC, (1994) 'Getting Started on Sexual Behaviour' in AS Rossi (ed), *Sexuality Across the Life-Course* (Chicago, The University of Chicago Press, 1994).

WEST, J, '(Not) Talking about Sex: Youth, Identity and Sexuality' (1999) *Sociology,* 47; 3: 525–47.

WIGHT, D, 'Boys' Thoughts and Talk about Sex in a Working Class Locality of Glasgow' (1994) *The Sociological Review,* 42; 4: 703–37.

—— and WEST, P, 'Poor Recall, Misunderstandings and Embarrassment: Interpreting Discrepancies in Young Men's Reported Heterosexual Behaviour' (1999) *Sexuality,* 1; 1: 55–78.

11

Sexual Health and Young People: the Contribution and Role of Psychology

ROGER INGHAM

INTRODUCTION

THIS CHAPTER ADDRESSES some issues relevant to young people's sexual health, and reflects on the contribution that psychological research has made—and should be making—to the understanding of sexual activity and risk-taking. The concept of good *sexual health* is regarded as involving not only the avoidance of obvious negative physical aspects (unintended conceptions and sexually transmitted infections including HIV) but also positive psychological aspects such as mutuality and respect, the avoidance of negative impacts on self-esteem, and the reduction of regret. Further, acceptance of preferred sexual lifestyles by others is taken as an indication of a healthy sexual society. *Pleasure* is shown in small font to reflect the attention it has been afforded in both theoretical and policy related approaches. The chapter attempts to illustrate how wider legal and policy contexts in this area have important implications for individuals' sexual health, and how psychology as a discipline has revealed a tendency to avoid becoming embroiled in such aspects.

Many of the issues covered here are relevant to both richer and poorer countries, even though concerns about the manifestations of poor sexual health vary in extent between countries. In some countries, the emphasis is on unplanned and early pregnancies, in other, HIV and AIDS are priority concerns and, in others still, early marriage, unsafe abortions and childbearing are related to relatively high levels of mortality. Generally, work in poorer countries has hitherto been primarily dominated by the use of descriptive population surveys to ascertain the extent of sexual activity and correlates of risk amongst young people, variously defined (see, for example, Cleland and Ferry, 1995). In richer countries, in addition to the surveys that have provided some very rich and useful information, there has been rather more theoretical work using both quantitative and qualitative methods.

Brief Historical Perspective and Policy Context

All societies have in place fairly rigid rules and regulations regarding who may have sex with whom and when; most of these are based on interpretations of religious writings, cultural traditions, and so on. Generally, sex has been regarded as a God-given gift to be 'enjoyed' (at least for half of the population) within a stable and committed relationship between people of the opposite sex. Anything else was (and still is in many places) regarded as abnormal, deviant, and a justification for censure and punishment.

But all this has changed over the past few decades, at least in many western countries. First came the 'sexual revolution' of the 1960s, during which the contraceptive pill, amongst other innovations, enabled a rather more liberated approach to sexual activity through separating sex from procreation. Perhaps more importantly, drastic changes occurred in the early- to mid-1980s when HIV first made its appearance. Faced with this massive threat, it was realised that behavioural change would be needed, and needed urgently. The problem was, of course, that the dearth of prior research into the area meant that clear answers as to appropriate ways forward were not to be found in the scientific literature. In addition to these changes, many poorer countries are finding their traditional ways of doing things challenged by the impact of globalisation and the westernisation of their younger generations.

The emergence of HIV unleashed a myriad of responses from all quarters. From one direction came the moral brigade and their conviction that this was God's punishment for the immoral lifestyles that had been allowed to creep into Britain and the USA during the 1960s and 1970s. The fact that HIV appeared (in western countries) to be more prevalent amongst men who had sex with men led to public expressions of homophobia by politicians and chief constables, and popular newspapers contained headlines describing the 'Gay Plague'. Many commentaries at the time made distinctions between 'innocent' victims (babies and recipients of infected blood supplies) and others, thereby introducing apparently causal explanations based on moral imperatives. The impact of the introduction of these discursive approaches was profound.

When the 1995 amendments to the Education Act were being considered in the House of Lords, for example, there was a series of debates on the sex education component. One of my Ph D students, Diane Stevens, carried out a detailed thematic analysis of the various speeches. Two clear positions emerged, illustrated by the following examples (taken from *Hansard*, 1995):

Position A

It is no use preaching that the family is the natural unit of society and then doing something to undermine it. The needle, not normal sex, is the major source of AIDS. (The Earl of Halsbury)

. . . information on the kind of sex education that is being given in schools today is not just information; it encourages them to act on it. It affects their moral outlook, their moral behaviour and their conduct in general . . . it is not just information, it is an encouragement to promiscuity. (Baroness Ellis)

I believe that the real answer for dealing with AIDS is for the Government to take their courage in both hands and tell citizens that, if they want to avoid these diseases, they should be chaste before marriage and faithful within it. (Lord Ashbourne)

Position B

In our society everything from coffee to cars is sold through sex appeal. Sexuality is part of our art and culture. We cannot avoid it . . . therefore let us provide the facts . . . I cannot think of any period in history when abstinence has been the norm . . . I suggest that a more realistic approach is to provide information. (Lord Addington)

We have no right . . . to deny children information which it may be essential for them to have to lead happy and healthy lives. Unless they have information and knowledge, they can fall into the trap of temptation which surrounds them. The temptations are far more powerful than the equipment that they have to resist them. (Lord Houghton)

We must be realistic and recognise that however bad the teaching of sex education may be in the classroom, it will probably be better than the murky sex education of the playground. (the right of) withdrawal . . . may lead parents into thinking that their children are unsullied by the grubby half truths of the playground. (The Lord Bishop of Guildford)

I do not know how many of those women became pregnant out of ignorance . . . I am certain, however, that far more of these young people became pregnant out of ignorance than they did out of a desire to obtain a council house. (Earl Russell)

One particular Lord had a very clear view of the answer to all these problems:

the only bright thing on the horizon comes from correspondence I have had from America which says that there is a group there which has become aware of the fact that the kind of sex education that I have just read out is counter-productive. A new movement has sprung up and is gaining momentum, as far as I can see. It is described as the abstinence movement . . . it is said that 'American children are learning the A to V of a new kind of sex education—A for abstinence and V for virginity'. Students are being told to 'just say no'. In California, teenagers following a course called Self Respect chant a chastity pledge—Do the Right Thing, Wait for the Ring!' It emphasises traditional family values, and the benefits of idealism and self-discipline. . . We copy so much that comes from the United States, so would it not be a good idea to copy some of that instead of the stuff that I have read out earlier? (Lord Stallard)

These examples from the House of Lords are mirrored in many school governing bodies when they discuss (as they are legally obliged to do) the sex education curriculum in their schools. All sorts of reasons are put forward to deliver the minimum required—parents will object (despite a number of studies which show quite clearly that parents want more and earlier sex education in schools—see, for example, Stone and Ingham, 1998), they say they do not have time because they are worried about increasing their position in the examination league tables[1], there is a fear about what the local press (or the Daily Mail) might say if they introduce a programme that is seen as being too risky, and so on.

Some people working in the health services also erect a range of barriers to improved sexual health by making access difficult. I recall one young woman telling us how she had to negotiate her way through a receptionist to get to see the doctor for emergency contraception. On the way out, the receptionist said, in a voice loud enough to be heard in the whole street, let alone the waiting room, . . . *and don't let me see you here again* . . . . Needless to say, she didn't.

Such debates are not, of course, restricted to the UK. Let us consider some further examples. Some very vocal and sometimes powerful people argue that their religious, cultural or personal beliefs are much too important to be challenged by impediments like evidence. Successive Presidents of the United States have poured money into abstinence-only education, despite increasing evidence that it simply does not work (Advocates for Youth, 2000; Kirby, 2001; Collins *et al.*, 2002). Not only do many of those who have received abstinence-only education still have sex (albeit a few months later than others) they are much less likely to use contraception since they have not been told about it. A recent study of the impact of the 'virginity pledge' movement found that, although there was a delay in first sex amongst the 'pledgers' (if there were not too many of them in the community), amongst those who did break the pledge contraception use was considerably lower than amongst those who had not signed up (Bearman and Brückner, 2001).

The abstinence-only proponents also tend to be anti-abortion. President Clinton offered states increased federal funding if they could lower their rates of teenage conceptions without increasing abortion rates. There is a website in the US that lists the names of 200 doctors willing to carry out abortions. Six of the names on the list have been crossed out, these doctors having been murdered in the past few years. A legal challenge to the publication of this list on the grounds that it contained a clear invitation to cross out further names was recently dismissed under the Freedom of Information Act.

One of the very first acts of President Bush when he assumed office was to withdraw overseas aid funding from any organisation that supported and enabled abortion, and some of the US charitable international donor organisations have followed suit. This has occurred despite the very clear evidence that in countries where abortion is illegal or very difficult to obtain, the number of maternal deaths (especially amongst young people) is relatively high. An anti-abortion law does not prevent rape and coercion and financial pressures and

---

[1] My suggestion some years ago that schools should publish data on the number of conceptions amongst their pupils as a way of letting parents see how well they're doing in sex education has not yet been taken up.

mistakes from happening, but it seriously impacts on the consequences of these. In Nepal some years ago, a girl of fourteen years was raped. She obtained an illegal abortion, was found out, and was sent to prison for twenty years. The rapist escaped punishment. More recently, a young woman in India who reported to the police that she had been raped was allegedly murdered by the father of the accused (*The Guardian*, 13 March 2003).

In the wider international arena, there are many other examples of barriers to improved sexual health being put in place by the gatekeepers. On a recent visit to Zimbabwe, I saw pages and pages in the national papers of pictures of people who had died. Most people I spoke to take one day a week off work on average to attend a funeral. And yet the government appears to refuse to acknowledge that it has a problem despite one third of young adults being HIV positive. The official line is that abstinence education is the only way, and Zimbabwe is not alone amongst sub-Saharan countries in adopting this stance of denial. Within this climate, some young women can only afford to better themselves through education if they find a sponsor to pay for their schooling and books in return for sexual favours. Some girls in rural areas are pressured into sex by their teachers in return for better grades and a bar of soap. Little appears to be being done officially to acknowledge these abuses.

In many countries of Central and South America, sex education in schools is not encouraged due to the very close links between the Catholic Church and the governments. In many African countries, young women escape from their rural poverty to get work in towns and cities as domestic servants, and boys to find work wherever they can. Alone and often without money, they are highly vulnerable to sexual exploitation. In Sierra Leone, displaced young people— many of them soldiers—live in camps where rape is frequent and services virtually non-existent. In Bangladesh and India, young women are lured into employment in garment factories so that westerners can have cheaper sweat-shirts; again, sexual exploitation is not infrequent.

On the evening before the last International Conference on Population and Development in New York a couple of years ago, the UK's then Secretary of State for Overseas Development, Clare Short, said in an interview '. . . speaking as a Catholic, I have to say that the Catholic Church is responsible for one million deaths a year'. Strong words, and only part of the story. Add on all the other fundamentalist religions and dogmas that can be found all over the world, and we are forced to ask ourselves whether all the signatories to the international agreements, to the UN Convention on the Rights of the Child, the UN Declaration on the Rights of Women to be free from Violence, and so on, are really serious in saying they wish to improve sexual health and to reduce gender inequalities. In the light of all these barriers—from those in some school governing bodies who limit educational initiatives through to national policies (or lack of policies) that facilitate the spread of HIV and are oblivious to high rates of child and maternal deaths, one has to ask 'just who are the risk takers?'

Conflicts involving different religious and cultural viewpoints and rights are not easy to resolve. There are no objective standards by which to evaluate alternative positions, and so ideological battles continue to rage in attempts to win the hearts and discourses of young people and policy-makers. Whilst these battles rage, young people continue to acquire HIV at alarming rates in many poorer countries, teenage conception rates remain high in the USA and the UK, rates of sexually transmitted infections continue to increase in many countries, the extent of sexual coercion remains unabated, many young women continue to die from illegal abortions and many young women and men continue to suffer psychological harm and confusion.

Given this climate, research is clearly needed to attempt to find ways through the debate.

Dominant Approaches Within Mainstream Psychology

Much of the quantitative theoretical work in richer countries has been guided by individual models of health and social behaviour (for example, the Health Belief Model, the Theory of Reasoned Action, the Theory of Planned Behaviour, etcetera). However, there is increasing recognition of their short-comings in terms of both methodological and theoretical issues, as well as with regard to their actual and potential contribution to policy, programme and intervention development. Although the aim of this chapter is not to engage in a detailed critique of such approaches, a few points are worth noting (drawing on Ingham, 1994; Ingham *et al.*, 1992; Kippax and Crawford, 1993):

—generally, these traditional theoretical frameworks are based on an assumption of individual rationality based on health maintenance and preservation.
   In reality, there are many other 'rationalities' that influence young people's
   sexual lives and actions;
—the major outcome variable in such approaches is normally the stated *intention* of the individual towards a particular behaviour (for example, condom
   use) and relatively less consideration has been given to the relationship
   between intentions and actions (but see Sheeran *et al.*, 1999);
—the models generally assume a high level of volition amongst young people.
   This tends to overlook the importance of (a) power dynamics, especially
   gendered, within specific relationships and interactions, (b) the potential
   effects of other immediate situational factors, such as alcohol and drugs (and
   passion?), (c) structural features that deny (or at least place barriers in the
   way of) possibilities for action, and (d) the many others who have a strong
   vested interest in what young people do and don't do—these include parents,
   teachers, church officials, friends, partners, and others;
—the quantitative demands of existing models of risk behaviour and risk
   behaviour change enforce a particular form of data-collection in the form of

self-completion seven-point rating scales. Their use assumes that all the participants understand the terms in the same way, over-simplifies the range of answers by enforcing circles or crosses as responses (for example, there is no place for an 'it all depends' response) and makes invisible other possible dimensions that may be important but that do not fit in to the particular theoretical model being assessed;

—most work has been conducted on convenience samples, with very little work being reported that has considered cross-regional, cross-class or cross-national variations. There is strong evidence regarding variations in sexual health indicators at these levels of analysis, and these traditional models contribute little to explaining such variations;

—the dominant models have been developed in the USA and Europe, and have little relevance, for various reasons, to the situation in poorer countries of the world;

—even where statistical relationships are found between components of the models. these are often quite modest and do not normally permit substantively significant causal relations to be identified, nor an understanding as to how such attitudes and/or knowledge were derived, thereby having little programmatic or policy value.

A Move Towards Contexts

In recent years, some social scientists and programme developers have moved on from understanding risk behaviour as being solely, or even primarily, determined by individual knowledge and attitudes to one that engages more directly with the environmental and social contexts as providing opportunities and/or barriers to the promotion of health.

It would be simple to say that the term *contexts* could be used to capture everything that affects young people over and above their individual personal and cognitive attributes. Thus, for example, we can accept that individual attributes are important (albeit challenging to measure accurately) and that wider contexts interact with these to produce an outcome; indeed, many authors adopt just this view (contexts as 'unexplained variance').

On the other hand, some authors take a more structurally deterministic view, and suggest that individual attributes are of marginal significance in understanding the complexities of behaviour, and that social and material structures are all-important. The relation between individual actors and the environment in which they live has been hotly debated within social sciences for many years now, and will undoubtedly be so for many years to come. In a nutshell, the key issue is the extent to which we regard young people (and indeed all of us) as being primarily 'agents' or as 'victims' largely constrained and/or enabled by their circumstances.

As ever, such simple dichotomies do not assist us much in understanding how to progress in order to improve the health and welfare of young people.

Certainly, emphasising a contextual approach provides a strong warning against the 'inoculation' model of health improvement, whereby it is felt that if only we could inject the right level of knowledge and the right type of attitudes into people, then all would be well.

Of course, the two areas overlap to a very large extent, so much so that it is almost impossible to measure them separately. One promising approach is provided by the increasing interest over recent years in the concept of *discourses* as a means to understand social action (Parker, 1992; Burman and Parker, 1993). Put simply, *discourses* are sets of taken-for-granted *logics*—assumptions that people hold and that guide their actions in particular areas. In some respects, it is felt that there is a range from which we can pick and choose depending on the situation. In other respects, there is a sense in which we are embedded within particular discursive frameworks and cannot stand outside (or escape from) them.

For example, in many western societies, discourses of *love* frame the contexts within which young people (and adults) are encouraged to understand and act upon their sexual desires and needs. In parts of the world less influenced by such discursive frames, *duty* may be the dominant framework for understanding (for example, the *duty* of a wife towards her husband and *vice versa*). A distinction is made in some eastern societies between arranged and love marriages, reflecting changing discourses and norms. In many countries, young men are encouraged to appear knowledgeable about sex and contraception whereas young women are expected to appear ignorant.

The relevance of this approach to the focus of this chapter is as follows: the social contexts will to a large extent determine the views and attitudes (the discursive frameworks) of young people and key adults (policy-makers, parents, service providers, teachers, etc.). In other words, contexts become internalised and any attempt to separate the social from the individual is problematic. Sexual identities themselves are socially determined to a large extent (Plummer, 1995). The extent to which different stakeholders can influence discursive frameworks is affected by the power relations that pertain; in general, young people—and young women in particular—have little relative power. Thus, to make young people the only (or a key) focus of research efforts (by measuring and attempting to change knowledge and other cognitions) is to miss some crucial points.

In a fine example of a discursive approach, Schifter and Madrigal (2000) identified the various sexual discourses existing in Costa Rican society; these include the formal—emanating from *scientific rationality*, *religion* and *the state*—and the informal—rooted in *local feminism* or *romantic love*. The authors illustrate how these are normative, coercive, how they complement and contradict, how they overlap and change, and how they are not politically neutral and can engender resistance. They argue that the power of the state and its close links with religious ideologies ensure that the formal discourses dominate, but that these bear little relation to the informal level more frequently observed amongst young people.

To provide some simple illustrations of the likely impact that alternative discourses may have on practice; a health service for young people may founder if the 'clients' and the staff do not share a common discourse of sexuality. A young client may wish to acquire condoms in order to engage in pre-marital sexual activity with a partner with whom he or she is in love, or may be planning to start earning money through sex work in order to buy food for her baby, or to feed a drug dependency. Should the staff in the service operate within a different discursive framework—perhaps a religious framework promoting the sanctity of sex within marriage—then a meaningful dialogue between client and staff is unlikely to occur. In such an event, the likelihood of a continued relationship between the service and the client is minimal. Similar analyses could be made regarding school-based sex and relationships education (in which a common result of research is that most curricula are too biological and ignore the issues of direct concern to young people), the extent of, and nature of, any discussion between parents/carers and their children, and other domains (see Ingham and Kirkland, 1997). Alternative approaches can also affect the extent to which different local statutory and voluntary agencies can work harmoniously together to improve sexual health (cf. Ingham *et al.*, 1997).

These examples remind us, first, that any approach to assessing contexts must be sensitive to more than just the physical infra-structure and, second, that attempts to separate individual factors from contextual factors is not a simple task.

Having said this, we still need to understand what is meant by the term *context*. As mentioned above, it can be defined in negative terms—that is, what is not *inside* the individual (even if we accept that what is inside heads is contextually determined). In some senses, this definition does capture the way in which the term has been used in the literature; some authors have used a vague notion of context to 'sweep up' anything that is left over after individual factors have been accounted for. Thus, for example, a failure of a particular theoretical model to account for much variance in a study can be explained away by reference to 'other' (ill-defined environmental or contextual) factors.

Others, however, have adopted a more positive definition, recognising the great importance of external environments on individual and group action. The range covered is indeed extensive, from the general policy and legal context right down to the specifics of particular interactions between actual or potential sexual partners, and all stops in between. The ways in which these different levels inter-relate and affect each other is far from fully understood, although important advances have been made in such understanding, particularly within the HIV/AIDS field (Aggleton, 2002). Aggleton points out the difference between 'risk' (the probability that a person may acquire HIV infection through their activities) and 'vulnerability' (the extent to which environmental and societal factors influence risk related activity):

In the context of HIV/AIDS, vulnerability is influenced by interaction between at least three sets of factors: (i) personal factors, (ii) factors pertaining to the quality and coverage of services and programmes, and (iii) societal factors. In combination, these influences enhance or reduce vulnerability to HIV/AIDS (and presumably to other issues affecting sexual and reproductive health) (Aggleton, 2002: 5/6).

He further points to a large range of factors that affect vulnerability at these three levels, including inequalities—in age, gender, poverty and social exclusion.

Some Alternative Research Initiatives

So far, I have suggested (as have others) that the traditional individual model-based approaches to health and social psychology have failed to address the wider contexts that lead to conditions of vulnerability. Qualitative approaches offer greater insight into the ways in which young people's meanings and understandings affect their sexual activity, understandings of risk, the conflicting and contradictory nature of much health promotion, and so on. Valuable as much of this research is, it is still normally carried out on young people themselves (through focus group discussions and individual interviews). And when discourses are identified, little clear evidence is obtained as to their origins, factors that maintain and support them, the dynamics of change, and so on. In other words, there is a large amount of individual, cultural and societal variance that is yet unaccounted for. The challenge for psychologists (and others) is to broaden the theoretical and methodological scope of their research agenda in an effort to develop greater understanding of all the various issues that impinge on sexual activity.

I want to outline some selected examples of research studies that throw light on aspects of sexual health and which have implications for policy development. In some cases, these have been carried out by psychologists; in other cases, other disciplines have guided the work. But, in each case, the work poses challenges for all those involved—including psychologists—in the endeavour of improving sexual health amongst young people. In my view, the results of these studies additionally—and crucially—help to inform the ideological and religious debates mentioned earlier. They also lead to suggestions as to where further research questions might usefully be directed. Cross-national comparisons provide useful data on the extent of variation in sexual health outcomes, and may also suggest places to explore as to where the sources of such variation may lie; some recent examples are presented.

The UNICEF Innocenti Research Centre considered the teenage birth rate in 28 OECD countries. The latest available rates per thousand women aged between 15 and 19 years range from 2.9 in Korea and 4.6 in Japan through to 52.1 in the USA; the UK achieves second place with a rate of 30.8. Such data, apart from anything else, reveal just how important social contexts are; if early sexual activity were biologically driven (as some commentators would have us believe) one might expect the rates to be rather more similar. After detailed analyses of various economic and social indicators, the authors conclude that,

> This commentary has stressed throughout that success in lowering teenage birth rates is a matter of both motivation and means . . .
>
> means—availability of contraception and education to enable informed and mutually respectful choices
>
> motivation— . . . a stake in the future, a sense of hope, and an expectation of inclusion in an economically advanced society . . . (UNICEF, 2001)

The highly respected Alan Guttmacher Institute in the USA considered the situation in a number of developed countries; Great Britain, Canada, France and Sweden. After exhaustive consideration of a wide range of factors, the authors conclude that

> Where young people receive social support, full information and positive messages about sexuality and sexual relationships, and have easy access to sexual and reproductive health services, they achieve healthier outcomes and lower rates of pregnancy, birth, abortion and STDs. (Darroch *et al.*, 2001)

Similar conclusions regarding the efficacy of a comprehensive approach were reached by Hosie's (2002) policy review of some other European countries and, in relation to the impact of sex education on knowledge, attitudes and self-reported sexual activity, by the World Health Organization's international reviews (Grunseit and Kippax, 1993; Grunseit, 1997).

A quite different approach was adopted in a study funded under a European Commission programme. The basis of the study was to build on qualitative work that had earlier been carried out in the UK and the Netherlands in an attempt to understand more from young people's perspectives in the two countries.

Our earlier UK-based work (Ingham *et al.*, 1991; Woodcock *et al.*, 1992) had involved carrying out detailed interviews with a couple of hundred young people on their sexual histories and related issues; these were tape-recorded, transcribed, and thematically analysed. Most of the respondents described heterosexual activities.

Amongst the key results were:

—There were many reasons provided by young people to account for their early sexual activity; these include love, the natural progression of the relationship, reputations and status, curiosity, experimentation, peer and partner pressures, alcohol, etcetera. Different levels of risk were associated with the different contexts and reasons given;

—There were misunderstandings of 'official' advice being given by the Health Education Authority and others at the time, such as *get to know your partner, find out about their sexual history* and *always use a condom if you don't know your partner;*

—There was a range of elaborate reasons for perceptions of invulnerability; we identified at least 18 separate reasons; a few of these, but by no means all, were compatible with the rational approach to health promotion adopted in national campaigns, and assessed in most social cognitive approaches to understanding risk;

—The implications and impact of unequal gender power relations were very powerful, revealed by fairly high levels of coercive sexual activity, subsequent regret especially amongst younger women, lowered self-esteem, etc.;

An unexpected result was that many respondents thanked the interviewers for their time and for the opportunity it provided to talk about these issues, revealing just how little attention had previously been paid by others to this most important component of their lives and identities.

The key conclusions of this research were:

—. . . that early sexual activity is very complex . . .

—. . . and mystified (by parents, schools, media, etc.) . . .

—. . . and we became even more convinced than we had been before that it was extremely unlikely that relevant aspects could be adequately captured by the existing traditional models using seven-point scales.

Many aspects of this work were supported, from a different ideological perspective, by the results of the Women's Risk and AIDS Project (Holland *et al.*, 1991, 1992a, 1992b, 1998).

Work in the Netherlands at that time tended to use one of two approaches. First, there was a dedicated group of social cognitive researchers who refined the scales and dimensions to improve the amount of variance accounted for (Richard and van der Pligt, 1991). At the same time, another group, based at NISSO (Netherlands Institute of Socio-Sexological Research) were using qualitative methods to explore sexual histories with a particular focus on their impact on actual interactional processes (Rademakers *et al.*, 1992; van Zessen, 1995; van Zessen and Zijlmans, 1993).

During a seminar on comparisons of data drawn from large European national surveys (Hubert *et al.*, 1998) it became increasingly apparent that, whilst such data were extremely valuable in identifying differences between countries in levels of sexual activity and risk taking, they could go little further than pure description. The prior UK and Netherlands qualitative research had used somewhat different protocols, and so Gertjan van Zessen, Ine Vanwesenbeeck and I applied for EC funding to enable a closer working relationship. The application was successful, and researchers from ten countries were involved in the development of new qualitative research tools. The aim was to supplement the data being collected in the various national surveys that were being carried out by producing a protocol that could be used cross-nationally; of relevance in this context are the results obtained in the two main countries involved.

The UK and the Netherlands make for an interesting comparison in terms of sexual health; the former has the highest rate of teenage conception in Western Europe, whilst the latter has one of the lowest. Amongst all teenagers, the rate in the Netherlands is around one-seventh of the rate in the UK, and it is doubtful whether there is any other health outcome for which there is such a large difference between two well-developed countries.

Detailed interviews were carried out with matched samples of about 100 young people in each country, thematically analysed, coded and compared on a large number of variables. In summary, the key results were:

In the Netherlands, compared with the UK,

—there is greater discussion of, and more openness about, sex by parents;
—there are lower levels of reported gender stereotypical behaviour by parents;
—there is earlier and more relationship oriented sex education in schools;
—young people report more opposite sex close friends during early teenage years;
—young people report greater feelings of ease with opposite sex.

In terms of actual sexual activity, in the Netherlands:

—the age of first penetrative intercourse is later;
—there is less stigma attached to using sexual health services;
—there is more discussion of contraception between partners before first intercourse;
—there is higher reported use of contraception;
—young men are much more likely to report *love/commitment* as a major reason for first ever intercourse (60 percent as against 15 percent in the UK), with corresponding lower levels of *curiosity*, *experimentation*, and *physical attraction* (amongst women, the percentages who report *love/commitment* are around 60 percent in both countries). This pattern of reported reasons suggests that higher levels of mutuality exist. This interpretation was strongly supported in the focus group discussions that were held in each country;
—there is lower reported regret amongst women after their first ever intercourse, suggesting lower levels of coercive sex and greater control.

What this pattern suggests is that more open acceptance of teenage sexuality— not encouragement or condoning, but acceptance—is protective, leading to higher levels of sexual and interactional competence. Where possible, data from large national surveys were used to confirm the general patterns found in the comparisons of the qualitative samples (Johnson *et al.*, 1994; Brugman *et al.*, 1995).

Of course, countries vary in many other respects other than just levels of sex education in schools and at home; there are variations in distribution of wealth, in the religious composition, in educational structures, and in other areas. We cannot easily just copy one or two aspects of one culture and assume that they will work elsewhere.

It is extremely difficult to pin down precisely what it is about Netherlands culture that leads to these seemingly large differences in sexual attitudes and meanings, as well as the pattern of activities. Indeed, it is unlikely that it would be possible to identify one specific factor; an issue, by the way, that has important implications for the value of random control trials that seek to explore change in just one form of service provision at a time.

On the basis of this and other work, we developed what we called a dynamic processual framework (Ingham and van Zessen, 1997; Vanwesenbeeck *et al.*, 1999). The starting point is that the key focus should be on what actually occurs (or could potentially occur) during the sexual interaction itself; that is, whether, and what form of, sexual activity takes place, whether contraception is used effectively, and so on. The framework attempted to incorporate the various factors that appear to impinge on the outcomes of this event. It includes a range of factors as shown below.

---

antecedent factors
socio-economic background, emotional climate in family, sexual and physical abuse, social integration, normative social influence, sex education/information

intermediate context
socio-cultural context, interpersonal context, sexual meanings and motivations, risk related cognitions, gender/sex related attitudes, interactional skills

immediate context
situational and temporal factors, activation of attitudes, opportunities and access, specific events and stimuli, subjective appraisals

sexual interaction
interaction skills/strategies/tactics, communicative and interaction patterns, issues of power and control

consequent factors and feedback
sex, interaction and risk, intentions for the future

Each person in the interaction brings their own set of antecedent factors that influence their meanings and understandings and assumptions, and each encounter takes place within intermediate and immediate contexts which together combine to determine the outcome of the interaction. No attempt is made to allocate relative 'scores' or 'values' to each of these other factors.

As psychologists, we could think in terms of an individual trait called *interactional competence*, which would reflect the individual's ability to express their wishes, to negotiate successfully if and when faced with opposition, and so on. One task of improving sexual health then becomes one of improving levels of competence through skills training. Indeed, such an approach has, for some years, been incorporated into some sex and relationships education through, for example, role-plays and other similar activities (although it is of great interest to note that in the SHARE project—a large random controlled trial in Scotland—role-plays were the part that teachers found most difficult to implement, and they were often omitted from the carefully designed curriculum, Wight *et al.*, 2002).

The WRAP project identified a range of levels of competence (termed *empowerment* by the authors) amongst the young women that they interviewed. Whilst most reported feeling low levels of empowerment in their heterosexual interactions, some seemed to manage well. Of particular interest were a group who were described as being *intellectually* empowered, but not *experientially* empowered. In other words, they knew what they *should* do, but found it difficult in practice to implement their intentions (Holland *et al.*, 1992b). They point out that increasing an individual woman's level of competence (or interactional skill) is of little value unless there are also changes in the underlying power dynamics between the genders.

Although there are indeed researchers in the Netherlands who draw attention to gendered power differentials, the interactional patterns we observed during our analyses suggested that these were substantially lower there than in the UK. Not only did many of the women appear to be more able to express, and act upon, their wishes, there was clear evidence of these being less contested than in the UK. Data from a series of focus group discussions carried out in each country supported the conclusion that Dutch men are generally more 'sensitive', mutual and respecting of women.

On the basis of these data, we developed the notion of *cultural competence*; that is, the extent to which various different sectors within society appear to accept aspects of young people's sexuality and interest, the level of cultural acceptance of differing forms of sexual expression, the extent to which important gatekeepers—such as policy-makers, health service staff, parents and teachers—appear to be in a perpetual conflict-ridden relationship with young people, and so on. At this stage, it is difficult to define *precisely* what it is about the Netherlands that has led to the somewhat higher levels of cultural competence but, whatever it is, it appears to provide a safer and more enabling environment for young people to develop in sexually healthy ways rather more successfully than is the case in the UK and many other countries.

The analyses summarised so far were what we call *horizontal* analysis; this involved coding all the interview transcripts to identify the range of categories that arose within the selected themes. Over 500 codes resulted, and the patterning of these enabled the comparisons between the UK and the Netherlands summarised above. Additionally, we carried out some *vertical* analyses; these involve using the derived codes to explore individual patterns and continuities. This case study approach was carried out on all of the transcripts.

In both countries, it appeared that some of the factors that appeared to char-acterise differences *between* the countries also appeared to be related to varia-tion *within* countries. Key amongst these was the way that the reported level of openness between the young people and their parents, both in general terms and in relation to specific discussion of sexual and relationship issues, was related to more competent styles of interaction. In other words, young people who reported that one or both of their parents were more available and open to dis-cussion of intimate issues were more able to delay intercourse if they wished to and to use contraception effectively.

Clearly, the numbers involved in cross-national qualitative research are necessarily fairly small due to budget constraints (restricting the time for data collection as well as transcribing, translation and coding). Accordingly, a survey using a sample of almost 1000 young people in the UK was designed and carried out; this involved a self-completion questionnaire, designed to explore some of the relationships found within the national samples (the survey was sponsored by Channel 4 television to introduce their series called *Generation Sex*). The questionnaire covered aspects of early development (including atmosphere within the family, relationship with parent(s), openness of discussions of sex, perceived positivity or negativity of the ways in which their parent(s) talked about sexual matters); early teenage development (including friendship patterns, ease with same and opposite sex, sex education received) and sexual activity histories (including age at first kiss, light and heavy 'petting', oral sex, vaginal sex, reasons for first ever intercourse, reactions before and after first ever intercourse, relationship with partners, contraceptive use). Those who had not yet had penetrative intercourse were asked a series of questions about why or how they had managed to resist. Collection of postcodes permitted allocation to wards, and hence to an index of the social deprivation of the areas in which they lived. This latter variable was considered important in the light of the vast variations in rates of teenage conceptions between areas differing in levels of deprivation (Clements *et al.*, 1998; Diamond *et al.*, 1999).

Analysis of the data from this relatively large UK sample did indeed support the general patterns identified earlier (Stone and Ingham, 2002). Using multiple regressions, effective contraceptive use at first intercourse was powerfully asso-ciated with the extent of discussion with the partner in advance of intercourse. Amongst men, what we termed *intimate* reasons for having sex were associated with the likelihood of prior discussion. In turn, amongst the whole sample, the likelihood of discussion with partners was predicted by the reported relation-ship with parents in terms of general accessibility, as well as openness regarding sexual issues.

Rates of Teenage Conception and Social Deprivation

It has long been established that rates of teenage conceptions are higher in areas with greater levels of social deprivation (Smith, 1993; Singh *et al.*, 2001). Clements *et al.* (1998) obtained the postcodes of all teenage conceptors in the former Wessex Health Authority region over a five year period. Converting these to rates enabled us to identify which electoral wards had the highest and lowest rates. Census data on these wards were obtained, involving over 20 separate indices of deprivation, the numbers of students, service provision, ethnic composition, presence of armed services personnel, density, and a range of other measures. Multilevel modelling enabled the explanation of a high proportion of the variance, the key predictor variables being four specific measures of deprivation, the numbers of students in the locality and the proximity to specialist young people's sexual health services (not general practitioners or generic family planning clinics).

Although a great deal of the variation in conception rates between geographical areas is accounted for by these few indices, such an analysis does of course raise more questions than it answers, a key one being why are rates of conception higher in deprived areas than in others? One popular explanation in the media (or at least in certain sections of the media) is that young deprived women choose to have babies early on so that they can obtain council flats and other benefits, although there is no evidence that this is the case. Certainly, there will be some who have chosen to start their child bearing early, possibly to escape from a dysfunctional family, possibly to be able to express and receive love, possibly because they just don't want to go to university or they see their employment opportunities limited, some because it is the accepted thing to do in their communities, possibly because they are in a close and committed relationship, and so on.

But, recall that these data refer to conceptions, rather than births. Although the proportions of conceptions that are terminated are also predicted by similar variables to those that explain conceptions (albeit in the opposite direction), this proportion amongst the under-16 age group is around 50 percent. This indicates that a large number of these conceptions are not planned or intended; indeed, the termination proportion would arguably be higher if access to abortion services in some areas were better.

So, there must be other factors at work here. Basically, differences can be explained by either different levels of sexual activity, or different levels of contraception, or a combination of the two. Results from the second UK national survey (NATSAL2) indicate that both of these are the case. Younger ages at first intercourse are associated (after controlling for other variables) with lower level of educational qualifications, disrupted family structure and low communication with parents (Wellings *et al.*, 2001). Lower probability of contraception use at first intercourse is associated with lower educational levels, reporting 'friends and others' as being the major sources of information about sex and, amongst men, lower levels of reported communication about sex with their parents(s).

A notion of 'competence' at first intercourse was also explored in the second national survey in the UK (NATSAL2); using a composite measure derived from reported willingness, autonomy of reason, subsequent regret, and contraceptive use, a strong relationship with age at first intercourse amongst both men and women was obtained (Wellings *et al.*, 2001). Further, lower competence was associated with earlier age at leaving school and lower communication about sex with parents for both men and women.

Level of deprivation, as such, is not an explanatory variable in a psychological sense. However, through consideration of the results from the modelling of rates study, and the Channel 4 and NATSAL2 surveys, the associations between geographical deprivation, poor education and teenage conception rates within the UK become clearer. It appears that the relationship may be mediated through the same sorts of variables that appear to account for cross-national variations—these being ease of cross-sex communication, gender relations and parental openness. Whereas aspirations may well differ between young women living in different social contexts—which may reflect a more direct effect of deprivation—there is clearly a lot else going on.

If we allow ourselves to be a little more speculative, we can take this line of thinking further. A major difference between the UK and the Netherlands related to the reported reasons for first intercourse amongst men. In the former country, just about 15 percent reported love or commitment as a major reason, compared with around 60 percent in the Netherlands. Main reasons in the UK were concerned with curiosity and experimentation, peer pressure and the opportunity having arisen. In other words, any body would suffice.

Reputations amongst friends featured strongly; additional support for this comes from Frosh *et al.*'s (2002; Phoenix *et al.*, 2003) analysis of working class young men, in which they argue that a major reason for early heterosexual experiences is a desire (or a need) to prove to one's friends that one is not homosexual. Further, having close friends of the opposite sex during early teenage years (not at all unusual in the Netherlands) laid young men open to the accusation of showing feminine characteristics, and was therefore to be avoided (or carefully concealed). Wight's analysis of working class young men in Glasgow, building on Hollway's earlier classic work (1984) on the discourses of heterosexual relations, revealed that there was a realisation that love and marriage would eventually seem appropriate, but not just yet (Wight, 1994). Others have written extensively on the difficulties faced by young women in negotiating their way through the minefield of reputation (Lees, 1993).

Just as an aside here, naturally some of the respondents in the Channel 4 survey had not yet experienced intercourse. In traditional approaches, such people might be regarded as 'low risk-takers', with the right knowledge, attitudes, behavioural control, self-efficacy, or whatever, to be able to have resisted pressures to engage. These respondents were asked why they thought this was so. Of course, some reported strong religious beliefs and/or the failure yet to meet the 'right' person. But there was a not-insignificant minority who clearly had no moral or empowered objection to being sexually active but had simply not had the opportunity; one young woman wrote, rather plaintively, on her open-ended response, '. . . because no one has loved me back yet'.

Integrating Levels of Explanation

What is appealing about this approach is that we can see continuities between 'real' data (in the sense of actual teenage conception data), cross national patterns, variations between geographical areas within this country, large sample survey data and those derived from qualitative approaches, inter-familial variations and interpersonal communication. Of course, there is still a great deal to do to complete the picture, but what seems to be clear is that the whole issue is rather more complex than is captured by some of the social cognition model driven approaches within social and health psychology, or, to be quite fair and balanced, some of the more extreme positions within discursive and/or sociological approaches.

So, we have tried to argue that contexts are crucial in understanding sexual activity and vulnerability; contexts that range from the interpersonal (potential) sexual interaction through to early family environments, social background, levels of understanding of gender relations, and so on. Clearly, focussing just on young people themselves in our research endeavours (no matter which health / social psychological model is used to guide such research) is missing some pretty crucial aspects of the whole picture.

In terms of the policy implications of the approach outlined, they are fairly clear, and include

—encouraging parents to be more open;
—encouraging earlier and more open sex education in schools;
—teaching interaction skills to young people;
—providing improved services for young people (more accessible, available and welcoming);
—addressing gender issues;
—removing homophobia.

Clearly, further research is needed into exactly how to achieve these aims. This would be a reasonable and not at all unusual place to end a chapter, but there are some outstanding issues to address.

Some Remaining Dilemmas

The reality is that there are a lot of people who have a vested interest in what young people do and don't do, and there are many barriers to effecting these suggested changes. I have already referred to the UK parliamentary debates on school based sex education, and some other examples.

Let us consider some specific ramifications of the argument that cultural change is required before we can hope to see progress. The first concerns how we assess change. If we use a discourse that says that the problem lies in young people's deficits, then we are led to intervene by 'correcting' these deficits. We identify them, measure them, inject suitable knowledge or attitudes or skills (through, say, a school based sex education programme), and then measure again to see if the programme of interventions has worked. These deficits are, of course, often defined by adults on the basis of what they believe young people should think and do, rather than through consultation with young people themselves. Having identified these deficits, we then introduce an intervention to see what will 'work'.

The 'ideal' way of doing this, according to some scientists (see, for example, Oakley *et al.*, 1995), is the randomised control trial. Much attention is paid to the results of these, and a recent example in the UK has led to mixed outcomes. The MRC-funded SHARE project in Scotland—in which a newly designed sex education course, based on best psychological and sociological principles, was introduced into a number of schools and compared with the usual programme in matched control schools—showed no differences in age at first intercourse or levels of condom use (it did, however, lead to lower reported regret amongst women and more positive evaluations of the teaching sessions) (Wight *et al.*, 2002). Given the importance of the former two outcome measures, some commentators claimed that this provides evidence that school based sex education does not work. This could have a devastating impact on the many people in different parts of the country (and world) who are struggling in their own ways to improve matters for young people. We must acknowledge that the sheer complexities of sexual discourses, and the many factors that affect sexual practice, are unlikely to be altered by one intervention lasting between 15 and 20 lessons. However, I think what the approach tells us beyond the implications for how psychologists should go about their work is rather more challenging. For psychologists to focus primarily on young people—and just to try to explain why some are more or less risky than others—is missing some crucial aspects, and raises a further important ramification.

There is not space to go into the implications of the various terms used in psychology to describe young people: *adolescents* (with its association with 'storm and stress'), *youth* (with its association with drugs and other problems), and *young adults*, for instance, but no matter which term we prefer to use, we need to question the basic approach we take to the issues. Do we consider young people to be a 'walking bunch of deficits', to be controlled and into whom (when the time is right, but not before) we need to inject some knowledge and skills, or do we see them as a resource for the future whom we need to foster, support and encourage to develop in healthy and respectful ways? How we answer this question will determine, to a large extent, the policy directions that are taken, and the sorts of research in which we engage.

I see a great deal of research within psychology on the shortcomings of young people themselves—and, of course, this is essential—but I see a lot less on the attitudinal structures of otherwise intelligent people who refuse to acknowledge evidence, or on those who turn a blind eye to sexual exploitation across the world, or on the many gatekeepers who, wittingly or unwittingly, contribute to denying the information and services that young people need, and the cultural change that will enable healthy sexual development.

Those who support and maintain these cultural and societal barriers are, of course, not just paying insufficient heed to the emerging research evidence, but they are also disregarding the demands of a human rights approach. For example, the UN Convention on the Rights of the Child is quite clear in calling for the entitlement of all children (defined as under 18 years old) to education and services that will enable them to protect their health and be free from all forms of exploitation. The agreements reached at the International Conference on Population and Development (ICPD) and ICPD+5[2] similarly called for young people to be regarded as a priority group for focus in relation to reproductive rights. In some countries, good progress has been made towards these aims, but there remains a massive amount to be done. It is, of course, pertinent to note that the USA is one of just two countries in the world that have not signed up to the UN Convention on the Rights of the Child.

Of course, a rights approach does pose real dilemmas for policy-makers and others. By respecting young people's rights, we are affording a level of autonomy that some would argue is potentially dangerous. For example, we argue for greater openness amongst parents in relation to their children's emerging sexuality, and yet we wish to respect the right of confidential access to services (indeed, one of the major barriers to young people accessing services in the UK and the USA is a fear that their parents will be informed (*cf* Stone and Ingham, 2003). Research findings can help us through this dilemma; the data linking parental openness to more responsible sexual activity should provide comfort for those who fear a breakdown of the moral fabric of our society, as should the results that demonstrate clearly that earlier provision of sex and relationships

---

[2] The International Conference on Population and Development took place in Cairo in 1994. More than 180 countries endorsed a comprehensive programme of action with regard to development issues for the next twenty years. These included: the protection and promotion of the rights of adolescents to reproductive health education, information and care; a reduction in STIs and pregnancy among adolescents; government and non-government organisations to meet the special needs of adolescents and establish appropriate programmes to respond to those needs. A follow-up session to review progress was held at the UN General Assembly in New York in 1999 (ICPD+5). Further details can be found at www.unfpa.org/icpd/icdp/

education in schools does not lead to earlier sexual experimentation. The data that show that more egalitarian gender relations are associated with lower levels of early coercive and regretted sexual activity suggest that interventions directed at a wider level may be more effective in the longer term than specifically targeted sex education programmes.

The introduction of the new Sexual Offences Act 2003 in the UK could be a risky manoeuvre in these respects. Whereas there should be widespread support for the need to prevent adult abuse of young people, the potential criminalisation of (the vaguely defined) mutually agreed sexual activity between young people could have the effect of reducing service use by young people for fear of being prosecuted (see Bainham and Brooks-Gordon, this volume). Similarly, well-intentioned and responsible adults could become fearful about providing advice and support lest they be regarded as 'grooming' young people for sexual activity. The Fraser Guidelines[3] provide some level of protection and reassurance for medical staff, and it is important that decisions in the area of support and respect for confidentiality continue to be made on child protection grounds rather than on moralistic grounds. The new law will not prevent young people from wishing to express their love and passion for their chosen partners through sexual and bodily means, but how a wide range of adults interpret and act upon the law will have an important impact on the physical and psychological outcomes of these desires.

So, to conclude, what is, or what should be, the relation between psychology and policy in the field of young people's sexual health? The emerging research evidence is pointing in quite clear directions in terms of the benefits of cultural change towards greater openness and the need for values to be encouraged that are based on mutuality and respect rather than on religious and cultural dogma. The line between research and advocacy does sometimes become somewhat blurred, and we need to remember what our role as psychologists should be. But by placing emphasis on the individual deficits of young people, there is a risk that we make invisible and divert attention away from the very real structural and attitudinal barriers to improved sexual health.

REFERENCES

ADVOCATES FOR YOUTH, *Toward a Sexually Healthy America; Roadblocks Imposed by the Federal Government's Abstinence-Only-Until-Marriage Education Programme* (2000), www.advocatesforyouth.org/publications/abstinenceonly.pdf

AGGLETON, P, 'Sexuality, HIV Prevention, Vulnerability and Risk', Lecture Delivered at 'Challenges in Sexual and Reproductive Health: Technical Consultation on Sexual Health', World Health Organisation, January 2002.

---

[3] The Fraser Guidelines were introduced by the Lords Fraser and Scarman in the 1985 House of Lords ruling in the case of *Gillick v West Norfolk and Wisbech Health Authority* [1986] 1 AC 112. They state that a doctor can prescribe contraceptives to women aged under 16 without parental consent, subject to certain specified criteria, including the fact that the woman must be judged to be competent.

BEARMAN, P and BRÜCKNER, H, 'Promising the Future; Virginity Pledges and First Intercourse' (2001) 106 *American Journal of Sociology*, 859–912.

BRUGMAN, E, GOEDHART, H, VOGELS, T *et al, Jeugd en Seks* (Utrecht, SWP, 1995).

BURMAN, E and PARKER, I, (eds), *Discourse Analytic Research; Repertoires and Readings of Texts in Action* (London, Routledge, 1993).

CLELAND, J and FERRY, B, (eds), *Sexual Behaviour and AIDS in the Developing* World (London, Taylor and Francis, 1995).

CLEMENTS, S, DIAMOND, I, STONE, N *et al.*, 'Modelling the Spatial Distribution of Teenage Conception Rates within Wessex' (1998) 24 *British Journal of Family Planning*, 61–71.

COLLINS, C, ALAGIRI, P, SUMMERS, T *et al, Abstinence Only vs. Comprehensive Sex Education; What are the Arguments, What is the Evidence?* (University of California, San Francisco, AIDS Research Institute, 2002).

DARROCH, JE, SINGH, S, FROST, JJ and the study team, 'Differences in Teenage Pregnancy Rates Among Five Developed Countries; The Roles of Sexual Activity and Contraceptive Use' (2001) 33 *Family Planning Perspectives*, 244–50 and 281.

DIAMOND, I, CLEMENTS, S, STONE, N *et al*, 'Spatial Variation in Teenage Conceptions in South and West England' (1999) 162 *J. R. Statist. Soc. A*, 273–89.

FROSH, S, PHOENIX, A and PATTMAN, R., *Young Masculinities* (London, Palgrave, 2002).

GRUNSEIT, A, *Impact of HIV and Sexual Health Education on the Sexual Behaviour of Young People; A Review Update* (Geneva, UNAIDS, 1997).

GRUNSEIT, A and KIPPAX, S, *Effects of Sex Education on Young People's Sexual Behaviour* (Geneva, WHO/GPA, 1993).

HANSARD, HOUSE OF LORDS, 10 May, 21 June, 6 July, (London; HMSO, 1993).

HOLLAND, J, RAMAZANOGLU, C, SCOTT, S *et al.*, 'Between Embarrassment and Trust: Young Women and the Diversity of Condom Use' in P Aggleton, G Hart and P Davies (eds), *AIDS: Responses, Interventions and Care* (London, The Falmer Press, 1991).

HOLLAND, J, RAMAZANOGLU, C, SHARPE, S *et al.*, 'Pressured Pleasure: Young Women and the Negotiation of Sexual Boundaries'(1992) 40 *The Sociological Review*, 645–74.

HOLLAND, J, RAMAZANOGLU, C, SCOTT, S *et al.*, 'Pressure, Resistance, Empowerment: Young Women and the Negotiation of Safer Sex' in P Aggleton, P Davies, and G Hart, (eds), *AIDS: Rights, Risk and Reason* (London, The Falmer Press, 1992).

HOLLAND, J, RAMAZANOGLU, C, SHARPE, S *et al, The Male in the Head; Young People, Heterosexuality and Power* (London, The Tufnell Press, 1998).

HOLLWAY, W, 'Gender Difference and the Production of Subjectivity' in J Henriques, W Hollway, C Urwin, *et al* (eds), *Changing the Subject; Psychology, Social Regulation and Subjectivity* (London, Methuen, 1984).

HOSIE, A, *Sexual Health Policy Analysis in Selected European Countries* (Edinburgh, Health Education Board for Scotland, 2002).

HUBERT, M, BAJOS, N and SANDFORT, T, *Sexual Behaviour and HIV/AIDS in Europe* (London, Taylor and Francis, 1998).

INGHAM, R, 'Some Speculations on the Concept of Rationality' in G Albrecht (ed), *Advances in Medical Sociology, Vol. IV: A Reconsideration of Models of Health Behavior Change* (Greenwich, CN, JAI Press, 1994).

—— and KIRKLAND, D, 'Discourses and Sexual Health; Providing for Young People' in L Yardley (ed), *Material Discourses of Health and Illness* (London, Routledge, 1997).

—— and ZESSEN, G VAN, 'From Individual Properties to Interactional Processes' in L Van Campenhoudt, M Cohen, G Guizzardi *et al* (eds), *Sexual Interactions and HIV Risk;*

New Conceptual Perspectives in European Research (London, Taylor and Francis, 1997).

INGHAM, R, JARAMAZOVIC, E and STEVENS, D, 'Constraints in the Development of Sexual Health Alliances' in P Aggleton, P Davies, and G Hart (eds), *AIDS; Activism and Alliances* (London, Taylor and Francis, 1997).

—— WOODCOCK, A and STENNER, K, 'Getting to Know You . . . Young People's Knowledge of Partners at First Intercourse' (1991) 2 *Journal of Community and Applied Social Psychology*, 117–32.

INGHAM, R, WOODCOCK, A and STENNER, K, 'The Limitations of Rational Decision Making Models as Applied to Young People's Sexual Behaviour' in P Aggleton, P Davies and G Hart (eds), *AIDS: Rights, Risk and Reason* (London, The Falmer Press. 1992).

JOHNSON, A, WADSWORTH, J, WELLINGS, K et al., *Sexual Attitudes and Lifestyles* (Oxford, Blackwell Scientific Publishing, 1994).

KIPPAX, S and CRAWFORD, J, 'Flaws in the Theory of Reasoned Action' in D Terry, C Gallois, and M McCamish (eds), *The Theory of Reasoned Action; its application to AIDS-preventive behaviour* (Oxford, Pergamon Press, 1993).

KIRBY, D, *Emerging Answers: Research Findings on Programs to Reduce Teen Pregnancy* (Washington DC, National Campaign to Prevent Teen Pregnancy, 2001).

LEES, S, *Sugar and Spice; Sexuality and Adolescent Girls* (London, Penguin Books, 1993).

OAKLEY, A, FULLERTON, D, HOLLAND, J et al., 'Sexual Health Education Interventions for Young People: A Methodological Review' (1995) 310 *British Medical Journal*, 158–62.

PARKER, I, *Discourse Dynamics: Critical Analysis for Social and Individual Psychology* (London, Routledge, 1992).

PHOENIX, A, FROSH, S and PATTMAN, R, 'Producing Contradictory Masculine Subject Positions: Narratives of Threat, Homophobia and Bullying in 11–14 Year Old Boys' (2003) 59 *Journal of Social Issues*.

PLUMMER, K, *Telling Sexual Stories: Power, Change and Social Worlds* (London, Routledge, 1995).

RADEMAKERS, J, LUIJKX, JB, ZESSEN, G VAN et al, *AIDS-Preventie in Heteroseksuele Contacten. (AIDS-Prevention in Heterosexual Contacts)* (Amsterdam, Swets and Zeitlinger, 1992).

RICHARD, R and VAN DER PLIGT, J, 'Factors Affecting Condom Use Amongst Adolescents' (1991) 1 *J. Community and Applied Social Psychology,* 105–16.

SCHIFTER, J and MADRIGAL, J, *The Sexual Construction of Latino Youth: Implications for the Spread of AIDS* (New York, The Haworth Press, 2000).

SHEERAN, P, ABRAHAM, C and ORBELL, S, 'Psychosocial Correlates of Heterosexual Condom Use: A Meta-Analysis' (1999) 125(1) *Psychological Bulletin*, 90–132.

SINGH, S, DARROCH, JE, FROST, JJ and the study team, 'Socioeconomic Disadvantage and Adolescent Women's Sexual and Reproductive Behaviour; the Case of Five Developed Countries' (2001) 33 *Family Planning Perspectives*, 251–58 and 289.

SMITH, T, 'The Influence of Socio-Economic Factors on Attaining Targets for Reducing Teenage Pregnancies' (1993) 306 *British Medical Journal*, 1232–5.

STONE, N and INGHAM R, 'Factors Affecting British Teenagers Contraceptive Use at First Intercourse: The Importance of Partner Communication' (2002) 34 *Perspectives on Sexual and Reproductive Health*, 191–7.

—— and INGHAM, R, *Exploration of the Factors that Affect the Delivery of Sex and Sexuality Education and Support in Schools*, Report prepared by the Centre for Sexual

Health Research, University of Southampton for the Wessex NHS Research and Development Sexual Health Taskforce (1998) available at (http://www.socstats.soton.ac.uk/cshr/Publications.htm#Centre).

—— and—— 'When do Young People in the UK First Access Sexual Health Services for Contraceptive Help and Advice?' (2003) 35 *Perspectives on Sexual and Reproductive Health*, 114–20.

UNICEF, *A League Table of Teenage Births in Rich Nations*, Innocenti Report Card No. 3 (Florence, Unicef Innocenti Research Centre, 2001).

VAN WESENBEECK, I, ZESSEN, G VAN, INGHAM, R *et al.*, 'Factors and Processes in Heterosexual Competence and Risk; an Integrated Review of the Evidence' (1999) 14 *Psychology and Health*, 25–50.

WELLINGS, K, NANCHAHAL, K, MACDOWELL, W *et al.*, 'Sexual Behaviour in Britain; Early Heterosexual Experiences' (2001) 358 *The Lancet*, 1843–50.

WIGHT, D. 'Boys' Thoughts and Talk about Sex in a Working Class Locality of Glasgow' (1994) 42 *Sociological Review*, 703–37.

—— RAAB, G, HENDERSON, M *et al.*, 'Limits of Teacher Delivered Sex Education; Interim Behavioural Outcomes from a Randomised Trial '(2002) 324 *British Medical Journal*, 1430–3.

WOODCOCK, A, STENNER, K and INGHAM, R, 'Young People Talking about HIV and AIDS; Interpretations of Personal Risk of Infection' (1992) 7 *Health Education Research: Theory and Practice*, 229–47.

ZESSEN, G VAN, *Wisselend Contact; Seksuele Levensverhalen van Mensen met Veel Partners* (Leiden, DSWO Press, 1995).

ZESSEN, G VAN and ZIJLMANS, W, *Contactgerichten en Casanova's. Levensloop, identiteit en veilig vrijen* (Utrecht, NISSO, 1993).

Part 3

'Problematic' and Prohibited Sexuality

12

Reforming the Law on Sexual Offences

ANDREW BAINHAM and BELINDA BROOKS-GORDON

'I want you to listen to me', he said from the podium in the Roosevelt Room, wagging his finger at the American public. ' I'm going to say this again: I did not have sexual relations with that woman, Miss Lewinsky' (Isikoff, 1999).

Bill Clinton's much publicised difficulty with what does or does not constitute sexual relations is not one apparently shared by the Government, either in its White Paper, *Protecting the Public* (Home Office, 2002) or in the Sexual Offences Act 2003. That which is 'sexual' is defined in section 78 to be essentially what 'a reasonable person' would consider to be sexual. The provision is just one of many in the Act which presuppose the existence of a 'normal view' of sex and sexual activity, to which the majority of us subscribe and which can be recognized by reasonable people. This, in the criminal law, means either the magistrates or a jury. Those who do not conform to this supposed normality are a deviant minority deserving of criminalization. So much is clear from the Home Secretary's Foreword to the White Paper in which he refers to 'our common values' which 'can be undermined by the behaviour of a minority'.

Even if the assumption in the White Paper is right that there exists such a thing as 'normality' in sexual behaviour (a point which we would strongly contest) this would not begin to provide a justification for the criminalization of behaviour merely because it departed from any such norm. The ultimate sanction of the criminal law should be used sparingly and reserved for the more serious forms of wrongdoing. We acknowledge in this respect the seriousness of the problem of the sexual abuse of children (see Freeman, this volume; Pearl, this volume). Nevertheless, in this paper we attempt to demonstrate that the Act offends, in a fundamental way, a number of the key precepts of the criminal law including the principles of minimum criminalization, maximum certainty and fair warning (Ashworth, 2003). The Act represents, we argue, a dangerous departure from the usual requirements of subjective mental culpability for serious offences, and brings about an unwarranted proliferation of criminal liability where no identifiable harm has yet occurred. It is these aspects of the legislation with which this chapter is concerned. The legislative opportunity for a much needed rationalisation of the haphazard and sometimes antiquated laws governing sexual behaviour is being used, at least in part, as an occasion to slip through a significantly more punitive approach towards, as opposed to tolerance of, sexual diversity. This approach is manifested both by the considerable expansion of the range of sexual conduct caught by the criminal law and by a major escalation in the accompanying penalties for offences.

The Sexual Offences Act 2003 follows two reviews, the *Review of Part 1 of the Sex Offenders Act 1997* (2001) and *Setting the Boundaries* (Home Office, 2000). Contextually, the Act and the review which preceded it, should be located in the contemporary pattern of Home Office policy making; policy made in response to media outrage and paedophilia-panic in successive Acts which have increased police powers and increased penalties for sexual offences generally and also policy made in response to what the Home Office perceives as 'anti-social' or 'unacceptable' behaviour.

It has been argued that the public clamour and hysterical outbursts which resulted in disorder in Aberdeen, Stirling and Swindon, when mobs gathered outside the homes of convicted sex offenders who had served their sentences and been released from prison, has impacted upon policy, not least the Sex Offenders Act 1997 (Lawton, 1997) and its subsequent manifestations. The Criminal Justice and Courts Services Act 2000 gave police and probation services a new statutory duty to make joint arrangements for assessing and managing high-risk offenders, including people convicted of sexual or violent crimes. And in July 2001 a review of Part 1 of the Sex Offenders Act 1997, which had been started in June 2000 by Charles Clarke to identify areas of 'weakness' in the legislation, was produced. The Government website declared: 'Just a few weeks later, following the death of Sarah Payne, widespread public concern was expressed about the dangers posed by sex offenders. *In response*,[1] the Government introduced in autumn 2000, a number of amendments to the then Criminal Justice and Courts Services Bill to strengthen the Sex Offenders Act'.[2]

The Home Office website explicitly mentioned the events at Soham in which two young girls had been killed and, as the Sex Offenders Act was published, media outrage continued but this time around *Operation Ore*, the largest police investigation of internet child pornography to date. Later, during the passage of the Act through Parliament, a twelve year old girl, Shevaun Pennington, went missing in July 2003 and travelled to France with an ex-army soldier who was found to have befriended her over the internet.

At the same time anti-social behaviour became a dominant policy issue. The Crime and Disorder Act 1998 introduced antisocial behaviour orders (ASBOs) to protect the public from behaviour which causes or is likely to cause harassment, alarm or distress. These are civil orders issued by magistrates to address low level nuisance. The Criminal Justice and Police Act 2001 added new powers of arrest for many offences, involving kerb crawling and the placing of

---

[1] Our emphasis.
[2] http://www.sexualoffencesbill.homeoffice.gov.uk/consult.htm

prostitutes' advertisement cards. The Police Reform Act 2002 extended the geographical area that an ASBO could cover to any defined part or whole of England or Wales. The Home Secretary appointed a Head to the new Anti-Social Behaviour Unit in November 2002, illustrating that low level nuisance became worthy of a Government department (Home Office Press Release 305/2002).[3] The White Paper *Respect and Responsibility: Taking a Stand Against Anti-Social Behaviour* [Cmnd 5778] was published on 13th March 2003 followed by the Criminal Justice Act 2003 and Anti-Social Behaviour Act 2003. It was alongside these two phenomena of anti-social nuisance and paedophilia panic that the Sexual Offences Act 2003 started its passage through the House of Lords.

We would broadly agree with Francis Bennion's characterisation of the Sexual Offences Bill (as it then was) as 'sex negative' in that, in failing to acknowledge sexual diversity, it reinforces the position where 'the happy acceptance of human sexuality, seeking its fulfilment, is largely absent from our society-even though it is essential for human happiness' (Bennion, 2003; Bennion, 1991). This theme was taken up by Lord Thomas of Gresford in his speech at the second reading of the Bill where he said:

> . . . it is important to set out a principle at the beginning: that sex between two consenting adults and, in our culture, in private is a healthy, life-enhancing, pleasurable activity. That should be recognised as in my view a great amount of deviant behaviour takes place because it is not recognised due to guilt, inadequacy and immaturity. (Hansard, 13 Feb, 2003, col 779)

Bennion's principal criticism of the Bill was that, while it proposed fundamental changes to the criminal law on sexual behaviour, it did not do so on the basis of any officially acknowledged set of morals or values. Both the Bill and the White Paper which preceded it, he said, were strangely silent on an 'agreed common morality'. We would approach this same issue from a slightly different angle. It is our view that in one sense the opposite is true. While it is certainly the case that there is no official articulation of a common morality, we would argue that the Act rests on the erroneous assumption that such a common morality does indeed exist and is identifiable by reference to what the 'reasonable person' believes it to be. While such a consensus clearly exists in relation to the most serious sexual violations, such as rape and forced penetration, no such consensus is likely to exist with regard to the plethora of sexual activities falling short of this. In very many instances there is scope for a good deal of disagreement about what is normal and that should be, if anything, a matter for celebration not censure. There is a clear duty on the legislature to give fair warning of potential liability arising from social interaction and to leave such matters to the magistrates or a jury is an abdication of responsibility which is likely to lead to breaches of human rights.

Article 8 of the European Convention on Human Rights guarantees the right to respect for private life. The European Court has held that this convention

---

[3] http://www.policereform.gov.uk/docs/press_release_305.pdf

right extends to 'the right to establish and develop relationships with other human beings'[4] and that sexual life is the most intimate aspect of private life.[5] Any interference with this right must be 'necessary' and 'proportionate' to a legitimate state aim. In our view the major extension of criminal liability in the sexual arena, which the Sexual Offences Act represents, is neither necessary nor proportionate to the government's stated aims of modifying and rationalizing the law of sexual offences and offering sufficient public protection, especially to children and the vulnerable. In attempting to strike a balance between necessary protection and individual autonomy it is in danger of badly skewing it.

We begin by giving a brief overview of the new offences which the Act introduces (the Act's contents are listed in the Appendix to this chapter), high-lighting the changes which these represent and drawing attention at the same time to what in our view were some of the more needed reforms. In the follow-ing section we look at the way in which the Act shifts the foundations of liability in many instances from the mental culpability represented by intention and recklessness to *negligence*-the normal standard for civil liability and not one usually thought appropriate for serious criminal offences. This is followed by consideration of those provisions in the Act which again demonstrate the prob-lem of vagueness and uncertainty, especially with regard to the lack of definition of the concept of 'exploitation' in dealing with prostitution. This piecemeal approach to the laws governing prostitution, so typical of English law, falls well short of the comprehensive review which is required. It can only serve to undermine what is supposed to be a comprehensive new code governing sexual offences. In the following section we draw attention to a cluster of other offences, including the new offence of voyeurism, for which we argue there is an insufficiently reasoned justification and insufficient empirical evidence support-ing criminalization.

WHAT IS THE SEXUAL OFFENCES ACT TRYING TO DO?

Part II of the Act re-enacts with modifications measures designed to protect the public from sexual offending. Most notably it introduces two new kinds of order for dealing with sex offenders, the Sexual Offences Prevention Order and the Risk of Sexual Harm Order. The latter is specifically designed for the pro-tection of children. We focus here, however, on Part I which deals with the reform of sexual offences and seeks to give effect to many of the recommenda-tions in *Setting the Boundaries*.

Setting the Boundaries attempted to identify the proper policy objectives of a sexual offences code. The key principles were that 'the criminal law should not intrude unnecessarily into the private lives of adults' and that 'most consensual

---

[4] *Niemietz v Germany* (1993) 16 EHRR 97.
[5] *Dudgeon v United Kingdom* (1981) 4 EHRR 149.

activity between adults in private should be their own affair'. Conversely, the criminal law, it was said,

> has a vital role to play where sexual activity is not consensual or where society decides that children and other very vulnerable people require protection and should not be able to consent.

The Review took the position that what was right or wrong in sexual relationships depended crucially on the principle of *harm* and an assessment of harm done to the individual. A coherent and fair code, which paid proper regard to human rights, would also be gender-neutral and ought not to discriminate between men and women, boys and girls, whether as victims or perpetrators of sexual offences, unless there was a good reason for departing from this principle. The law should also reflect 'the looser structure of modern families.' And, of course, a primary objective would be to replace the archaic and outdated rag-bag of offences with a clear and coherent code fit for the twenty-first century.

In a number of respects the Act goes some way towards meeting these objectives. The new offences are gender-neutral with the noteworthy exception of rape. This may still only be perpetrated by a male since it remains a concept confined to *penile* penetration (S1(1)). Forced fellatio will for the first time be brought within the definition since penetration of the mouth is thought as abhorrent as penetration of the vagina or anus (S1(1)(a)). The gravity of non-consensual penetrations is reflected in a new offence of assault by penetration which, like rape, carries a maximum sentence of life imprisonment (S2). The distinction is therefore between penile penetration and penetration with other parts of the body or objects and this offence also extends to penetration of the vagina, anus or mouth. The offence would be committed, for example, by the non-consensual insertion of a finger or bottle. Its introduction is welcome recognition that the existing offence of indecent assault was expected to embrace far too many gradations of behaviour, from the mildest touch or stolen kiss, through 'groping', to the grosser violations involving penetration. The latter, it was thought, should be taken as seriously as rape.

This is not to say that the new offence of *sexual* assault, which is intended to replace *indecent* assault, does not suffer from the problem of being over-inclusive and, indeed, we argue below that it does in the sense that it may lead to the criminalization of trivial and unexceptionable behaviour. The problem is compounded by the apparent assumption that wrongs previously encompassed by the concept of 'indecency' may be readily transferable into the new concept of what is 'sexual'. Yet, the point should be made that there is surely a distinction between the two ideas. 'Indecent' is a pejorative term which implies moral (and legal) wrongdoing, whereas 'sexual' is a morally neutral word which has no such connotation. Is there not a legitimate concern, therefore, that a jury might be tempted to include within their idea of 'sexual' conduct that which they might not have accepted as 'indecent'? Indeed, depending on the context, 'sexual' can and should have a very positive implication.

Gender-neutrality is achieved by the abolition of certain gender-specific offences, notably the offence of gross indecency which could only be committed by men and which was held to breach the European Convention on Human Rights in *ADT v United Kingdom*[6] and what remained of the offence of buggery is also abolished. The Act also extends the principle of gender-neutrality to those offences of prostitution which were previously gender-specific in that they were capable of being committed only by women (selling sexual services) or men (buying sexual services) (S56).

The seriousness with which the protection of children and other vulnerable people is taken cannot be doubted. It is reflected in the Act in a whole raft of new offences and in conclusive presumptions that a child below the age of 13, together with those having a mental disorder or learning disability, lack the capacity to provide a valid consent to sexual activity.[7] Child sex offences include sexual activity with a child (S9), causing or inciting a child to engage in sexual activity (S10), engaging in sexual activity in the presence of a child (S11), or causing a child to watch a sexual act (S12), child sexual offences committed by children or young persons themselves (S13), a new offence of 'meeting a child following sexual grooming' (S15), and the substantial re-enactment of various offences relating to abuse of positions of trust which were introduced by the Sexual Offences (Amendment) Act 2000 (SS16–24). In relation to these child sex offences, and the analogous offences applying to persons with a mental disorder or learning disability (SS30–44), we would argue that the Act goes too far—both in potentially criminalizing innocent experimentation by children and adolescents (contrary to the gathering autonomy which the law allows to them in other areas),[8] and in denying to those with learning disabilities any possibility of sexual fulfilment which may be seen as an aspect of their human rights.

The Act also takes account of 'the looser structure of modern families' in the formulation of 'familial' child sex offences (SS25–9) which replace the crime of incest. The offences will apply to sexual activity between 'family members' which are defined to include, as well as blood relations, adoptive, step and foster relationships and also relationships with those who live, or have lived, in the same household as the child concerned and been regularly involved in caring for, training, supervising or being in sole charge of that child. The common denominator here is again perhaps the abuse of a position of trust or a dominant position within the family analogous to abuses in the institutional settings in which the abuse of trust offences take place. And abuse of trust is further dealt

---

[6] [2000] 2 FLR 697.

[7] There is effectively strict liability in relation to sexual activity involving children under the age of 13 since it need only be proved that the accused intended to engage in the conduct in question. Any belief, or absence of belief, about the child's age is irrelevant for these most serious sexual offences against children.

[8] Principally following the landmark decision of the House of Lords in *Gillick v West Norfolk and Wisbech Area Health Authority* [1986] 1 AC 112 and many provisions reflecting respect for the views of children in the Children Act 1989. See also Spencer (2003).

with in great detail with regard to offences against persons with a mental disorder or learning disability.

The media-popular topic of indecent photographs of children is covered (SS45 and 46), and here the Act redefines a 'child' for the purposes of the Protection of Children Act 1978 as a person under 18 years, rather than 16 years of age. Thus, there will be offences of taking, making, distributing or showing, or possessing with intent to distribute, indecent photographs or pseudo-photographs where they are or *appear* to be of 'children' aged 16 or 17 years. 'Making' a picture includes downloading one from the internet. The exceptions are where the child has consented to this, and the marriage/relationship exception applies unless the photographs were taken before the start of the relationship, or where pictures were 'made' in order to prevent crimes.

The Act however fails to discriminate properly between children and adults in the sections on prostitution and child pornography (SS47–57) and trafficking (SS57–60). There are the offences of paying for sex with a child (S47), causing or inciting child prostitution or pornography (S48), controlling a child prostitute or child pornography (S49), arranging or facilitating child prostitution or pornography (S50). There are offences of causing or inciting (adult) prostitution for gain (S52), controlling prostitution for gain (S53), and penalties for keeping a brothel.[9] Offences also include trafficking into, within and out of the UK for sexual exploitation (SS57–9). The Act provides a statutory definition of prostitution, gain and payment (S51). We will argue that these offences define, without a logical or evidentiary basis, adult prostitution (which is not illegal) as inherently exploitative. These provisions are also discriminatory and questionable in terms of civil liberties. In characterising prostitutes as different from ordinary citizens the Act does not comply with the legitimate aims of public safety, or long-term health benefits. Proportionality requires the sanction of the criminal law only where there is *real* harm to others and by not defining difference.

Preparatory offences based on intent are contained in the Act such as administering a substance (S61), of committing an offence with intent to commit a sexual offence (S62), or trespass with intent to commit a sexual offence (S63). The existing offence of incest is replaced by two new offences. Adult sexual relations are criminalized if these take place with an adult relative who is a blood relative (S64), although these offences define these consensual sexual relations so as to include only those activities involving penetration. A sexual relationship between two people will therefore be lawful where there is no penetration. It is at least questionable whether this offence is consistent with the general objective of respecting consensual sexual activity between adults.

A final section of the Act (SS66–71) contains a diverse collection of offences including sexual activity in a public lavatory (S71), exposure (S66), voyeurism (SS67–8), intercourse with an animal (S69) and sexual penetration of a corpse

---

[9] S 55. This extends S 33 of the Sexual Offences Act 1956 (c 69).

(S70). It also extends the jurisdiction beyond the United Kingdom for all the offences to include countries where the offence is already an offence, or would constitute an offence if carried out in the UK (S72). General provisions relating to interpretation and the definition of offences are set out in the Act (SS73–9) and these include a definition of consent (S74) and the definition of 'sexual' mentioned earlier (S78).

It is in relation to the core principle of harm, and the need to establish harm to the individual before criminalization, that we have our principal misgivings. In our view the Act has lost sight of this essential requirement. It casts the net so wide that it would criminalize many actions that are not overtly or uncontroversially harmful and many others where the harm postulated is insufficiently proximate to the actions of the accused. It would, moreover, criminalize many of those who will lack any subjective appreciation that they are acting unlawfully or even unwisely. In short, the new offences are capable of trapping many types of conduct which ought not to be the business of the criminal law at all.

THE RETREAT FROM MENTAL CULPABILITY: NEGLIGENCE AS THE BASIS OF SEXUAL OFFENDING

Generally speaking the criminal law demands that before there can be liability for serious crime, the accused should not only have performed the prohibited act but should also have acted with mental awareness or *mens rea*. This subjective requirement of mental culpability is generally satisfied where it is shown that the accused intended to perform the prohibited act or was at least *subjectively* aware of the risk of some harm (albeit not necessarily harm of the same gravity) which has resulted from his or her actions. This latter mental state came to be known as *Cunningham*[10] recklessness. It was distinguishable from another species of recklessness, *Caldwell*[11] recklessness, which controversially applied an objective test of failing to have regard to an obvious risk; obvious, that is, to the reasonable person. Yet this latter test of recklessness was heavily criticised because it blurred the distinction between recklessness and negligence. It had been all but confined to the single offence of criminal damage. In October 2003 the House of Lords, in *R v G and Another*[12] revisited *Caldwell* and unceremoniously overruled it on the basis that it was plainly wrong when it was decided. In so doing the House reasserted subjective recklessness as the baseline requirement for serious criminal offences. For virtually all serious offences against the person therefore, including all assaults, it is the *Cunningham*, subjective version which has hitherto applied. A rare exception is manslaughter, one species of which may be established by gross negligence; but it should be noted that this is an extreme version of negligence and not negligence *per se*.

[10] [1957] 2 QB 396.
[11] [1982] AC 341.
[12] [2003] UKHL 50 on appeal from [2002] EWCA Crim 1992.

There is a strong presumption of the requirement of *mens rea* which may be displaced only where Parliament has evinced a clear intention to the contrary (*Sweet v Parsley*,[13] B,[14] K[15]). The more serious the offence, the stronger the presumption will be. Two cases involving sexual activity with teenage girls went to the House of Lords on the question of whether an honest mistake about the ages of the respective girls could operate as a defence. In the first, *B (A Minor) v DPP*[16] B, a boy of 15, was sitting next to a 13 year old girl on a bus. He asked her several times for a 'shiner', not in this context a black eye but an act of oral sex. He was charged with committing an act of gross indecency with a girl under 14 contrary to the Indecency with Children Act 1960. In the second case, *R v K*[17], a 26 year old man was charged with an offence of indecent assault on a 14 year old girl. His defence was that the activity was consensual, that she told him that she was 16 and that he had no reason to disbelieve her. He was described as a man of good character.

Neither in the Indecency with Children Act 1960, nor in the Sexual Offences Act 1956 did Parliament expressly stipulate that *mens rea* was required as to the age of the girl in relation to these two separate offences. The prosecution in each case argued that the nineteenth century authority of *Prince*[18] should apply. *Prince* was a case of child abduction, not sexual assault, where it had been held that there was strict liability as to the age of the victim. In other words, an honest mistake, even if a reasonable one, as to the girl's age could not be a defence. In the House of Lords *Prince* was comprehensively discredited. The House held in each of the two cases before it that the normal presumption of *mens rea* applied. An honest or genuine belief as to the age of the girl would be a defence *and it was not necessary that this should be a reasonable belief*, provided that it was genuine. The Sexual Offences Act 2003 immediately overrules these two decisions by requiring that any such mistake as to age must be *reasonably* held in relation to the new child sex offences and familial child sex offences. In relation to child sex offences[19] it must be proved that B (the child) was under 16 and that A (the accused) did not reasonably believe B to be 16 or over (SS9–12). In the case of familial child sex offences the relevant age is 18 and it must be proved that A did not reasonably believe B to be 18 or over (SS25, 26). Where the child is under 13, there will be strict liability as noted above.

The new offences therefore depend on proof of *negligence*, a departure from an objective standard, rather than on recklessness, which requires subjective awareness of a risk. The very fact that Parliament has almost immediately overruled two recent decisions of the House of Lords is controversial enough. But

---

[13] *Sweet v Parsley* [1970] AC 132.
[14] [2000] 2 AC 428.
[15] *R v K 'Age of Consent: Reasonable Belief)* [2002] 1 AC 462.
[16] [2000] 2 AC 428.
[17] *R v K 'Age of Consent: Reasonable Belief)* [2002] 1 AC 462.
[18] (1875) LR 2 CCR 154.
[19] The exception here is child prostitution and pornography for which the age is 18 years.

the Act goes very much further than this. In relation to *most* of the new offences it is *negligence* and not recklessness which will represent the minimum requirement of culpability. In our view this represents a dangerous development, though we recognise that there is an argument for importing elements of liability based on negligence into the special cases of rape and assault by penetration. Before looking at these special cases, we should consider in what ways negligence will, under the Act, become the baseline requirement of liability. The point should of course be made that in many cases of sexual violation, perhaps most, the accused *will* have acted intentionally or recklessly. Our concern is with the *minimum* basis for liability since this determines where the line is drawn between liability under the civil law, or no liability at all, and those actions which should attract the full weight of public condemnation through criminalization.

One of the principal ways in which negligence is imported into the proposed code is through the definition of what is 'sexual' in section 78 to which we alluded earlier. The full definition, which applies to a wide range of offences in the Act, is as follows:

> For the purposes of this Part (except section 71),[20] penetration, touching or any other activity is sexual if a reasonable person would consider that—
>
> a) whatever its circumstances or any person's purpose in relation to it, it is because of its nature sexual, or
>
> b) because of its nature it may be sexual and because of its circumstances or the purpose of any person in relation to it (or both) it is sexual.

The purpose of sub-section (a) is to exclude from the definition of what is 'sexual' objectively innocuous activities which the vast majority of people would not regard as sexual, but from which a small minority of people might derive sexual gratification, such as the 'shoe fetish' in *George*.[21] But, subject to that, what is sexual is left entirely at large for the jury to assess as 'reasonable people'. This, fundamentally, is to be the key component in what is required for sexual offending under the Act and it makes insufficient allowance for the subjective views of the accused. It is predominantly a matter of negligence; of failing to appreciate what reasonable people supposedly appreciate and of acting as reasonable people supposedly act. Under the previous law, where what occurred was ambiguous—in the sense that it was not objectively clearly decent or indecent—the jury was *obliged* to have regard to the accused's motives.[22] The Act waters down this requirement in that although the jury *may* have regard to the accused's motives, they are not *necessarily* required to do so. It is open to them to decide that, because of the circumstances alone, it should be regarded

---

[20] Sexual activity in a public lavatory. See below.
[21] [1956] Crim LR 52.
[22] *Court* (1988) 87 Cr App R 144.

as sexual even though objectively it *may* only be sexual.[23] Quite apart from the objection to liability for serious offences without *mens rea*, it is the sheer range of conduct which may be caught by this definition which compounds the issue. We discuss below why we would accept the case for imposing liability at least in part on the basis of negligence in the case of penetration, but this definition also extends to 'touching or any other activity'. This is staggeringly wide. Take touching. This is defined in the Act to include

touching–

a) with any part of the body,
b) with anything else,
c) through anything

and in particular includes touching amounting to penetration (S79 (8)).

And this is before we even get on to 'other activities'. Yet it will be entirely left to the discretion of the magistrates or jury to determine what kinds of touchings are 'sexual' and the accused's beliefs about this may or may not be taken into consideration or given weight. The Act, however, seeks to introduce another crucial element of negligence. This is that throughout the range of offences in the Act, A will no longer be able to rely on the defence that he held an honest belief that B was consenting to the conduct in question. For liability will now arise not simply in those cases where A does not honestly believe there was consent, or was reckless in giving no thought to whether B was consenting, but also to those cases in which 'A does not *reasonably* believe that B consents'.[24] Whether or not a belief is to be considered reasonable is to be determined 'having regard to all the circumstances, including any steps A has taken to ascertain whether B consents'.[25]

A is at the office Christmas party. He fancies B, a younger colleague, and decides to chance a kiss under the mistletoe. He thinks that B will enter into the spirit of things but B has no intention of doing so. A could now face criminal prosecution. The fact that he genuinely believed that that B would not take exception to a Christmas kiss will not save him if the magistrates or jury take the view that it is was doubtful whether B would have consented and that a reasonable person would have inquired whether B consented before making the approach. For this indiscretion, A risks conviction for sexual assault and, if tried on indictment, a maximum punishment of ten years imprisonment.

What about social interaction between adults and children? A, a man aged say 30, encounters B, a girl aged 13 on a crowded beach. They are both in swimsuits. They enjoy some friendly banter and 'horseplay' during which A puts his

---

[23] This is all the more unsatisfactory taken alongside the argument above, that the concept of what is 'sexual' may be wider and catch more conduct than the narrower notion of what is 'indecent'.

[24] See especially S 1 (1) (c) (rape); S 2 (1) (d) (assault by penetration); and S 3 (1) (d) (sexual assault). Our emphasis.

[25] See S 1 (2), S 2 (2) and S 3 (2).

arm around B and helps her climb the rocks by supporting her bottom. Her father sees this and informs the police. Whether or not it entered A's head that these might be 'sexual' touchings, or that B might not have agreed to them, will be irrelevant if the magistrates or jury take a different view. It is true that in the circumstances a jury might well conclude that they were not, but A will still have to run this particular gauntlet and the consequential damage to his reputation whatever the verdict. Neither is it sufficient to leave such matters to prosecutorial discretion, since it is the very labelling of such conduct as criminal which is the chief matter of concern.

We agree with Bennion that provisions such as this, along with the new offence of meeting a child following sexual grooming (S15) stand a good chance of 'inhibiting, even destroying, that wide social intercourse between adults and children, that hitherto has been a constant feature of human life' (Bennion, 2003). The situation regarding the most serious offences of penetration is, we think somewhat different and that, solely in this context, the arguments may be more evenly balanced (Temkin, 2002). There has, for many years, been debate about the appropriate *mens rea* for rape and concern at the extremely low conviction rate. For example, prevalence estimates from the British Crime Survey on the rape and sexual assault of women, showed that 61,000 women had been raped in the year preceding 2000, and approximately one in twenty women said they had been raped since age 16 years; an estimated 754,000 victims. Approximately one in ten women (9.7 per cent of the population) said they had experienced some form of sexual victimisation (including rape) since the age of 16 years (Myhill and Allen, 2002). The Home Office thus perceived a need to raise the number of rape convictions. This aim was made explicit by the Home Office in a press release during the drafting of the Bill: 'Government determined to turn around worryingly low reporting and conviction rates for rape'.[26] It was not however universally accepted in the House of Lords that this problem would be resolved by changing the *mens rea* requirement. Indeed, new problems would arise and Lord Lloyd of Berwick argued:

> if the Government think they will get even one extra conviction by relying on the new definition in subsection (3), in my opinion they are gravely mistaken. The only result of subsection (3) will be not more convictions but more appeals (Hansard 13 Feb 2003, col 860).

The lowest mental requirement for rape before the 2003 Act was something of a hybrid form of recklessness. It had to be proved that the accused had sexual intercourse (whether vaginal or anal) with a person who at the time did not consent to it and that at the time he knew that the person did not consent to it or was reckless as to consent. This species of recklessness has been held to cover those who do not believe the other person is consenting as well as those who 'couldn't care less'.[27] This was interpreted by most commentators to require at

---

[26] (Home Office Press Release, ref 203/2002, 23/7/2002).
[27] *Satnam* (1983) 78 Crim App R 149.

least some subjective awareness that someone *may* not be consenting or, put another way, *Cunningham* recklessness. This state of mind clearly does not exist where the accused genuinely, though unreasonably, believes that the other person has consented.[28] It is this which has caused all the controversy, especially since the evidence in many rape trials will come down to one person's word against the other. The Act abolishes this requirement of subjective awareness and replaces it with an objective test of negligence. Under the Act, rape will be committed where 'B does not consent to the penetration, and A does not reasonably believe that B consents' (S1 (1)).

This imports negligence into the law of rape by requiring that the accused measure up to an objective standard of behaviour in that only a reasonable belief will count. The Act goes on to create presumptions about the absence of a belief in consent (S75) and conclusive presumptions about what amounts to consent itself (S76). These presumptions apply not only to rape but to the offences of assault by penetration, sexual assault and causing a person to engage in sexual activity without consent (S77). The presumptions about an absence of belief in consent, which will apply unless sufficient evidence is adduced to raise an issue as to whether the accused reasonably believed that there was consent, will arise in cases where there was violence or the threat of violence, unlawful detention of the complainant, where the complainant was asleep or unconscious and in cases of physical disability. The conclusive presumptions that the complainant did not consent apply where the defendant intentionally deceived the complainant as to the nature or purpose of the relevant act or induced consent by impersonating a person known personally to the complainant.

What are the arguments for and against this substantial relaxation in the mental requirement for rape? In favour, it is said that the potential violation of personal integrity is so great in rape, that the offence is in the scale of things so serious, that there should be a duty to take relatively straightforward steps to ascertain the simple fact which makes all the difference—whether the other party was consenting or not. This is an argument located fundamentally in the 'proportionality' principle. What is required of the accused is something which can easily be ascertained and this requirement should exist because of the dire consequences of getting things wrong. Against the change, it can be pointed out that what is at stake is a serious matter not just for the victim but also for the accused. Thus, to require only negligence as to consent will produce a single class of defendants which

> would contain not only those with subjective fault but also all those who merely failed to take proper care, all of whom would be convicted of a grave offence carrying a maximum of life imprisonment (Ashworth, 2003).

Further, it is argued that the law already indirectly required the accused to behave reasonably because reasonableness goes to credibility. This was given

[28] *DPP v Morgan* [1976] AC 182.

explicit statutory recognition in S1(2) of the Sexual Offences (Amendment) Act 1976 which provided that:

> if at a trial for rape the jury has to consider whether a man believed that a woman or man was consenting to sexual intercourse, the presence or absence of reasonable grounds for such a belief is a matter to which the jury is to have regard, in conjunction with other relevant matters, in considering whether he so believed.

In other words, if the defendant was behaving unreasonably, in the jury's view, they were not likely to believe him when he said that he honestly believed the other party was consenting and they would convict.

While we acknowledge the force of both arguments, we are inclined to think that some change to the mental requirement for rape (which would extend to the equally serious assault by penetration) and which may have the effect of imposing a specific duty to ascertain whether or not there is consent,[29] is justified. At the same time, we would argue that elsewhere in the law of sexual offences there is no place for liability based on negligence alone. In relation to rape, we are unconvinced that the law currently demands enough of those who risk non-consensual intercourse. Where the circumstances clearly involve violence we believe it likely that the jury, looking at the situation, will convict because they will not believe that the accused could have had a genuine belief in consent in that kind of scenario. This appears to be borne out by the experience of those practising in the field. As Baroness Mallalieu put it:

> there is no difficulty in obtaining convictions in the kind of rape that has been referred to as 'towpath' rape—the burglar who enters through a window, the stranger in the street or the rape committed at knife point or so after a beating. In my experience in most cases juries convict and readily do so (Hansard, 13 Feb 2003, col 850).

Where, on the other hand, there is little or no available evidence of force or violence it may well be a case of one person's word against another about the extent to which, for example, a person was prepared to go along with sexual involvement. Here, we do not think that the requirement in the 1976 Act provided a sufficient safeguard since the accused's statement, that he believed there was consent, would be more credible in these circumstances.

We consider that the more general extension of negligence as a basis for liability for sexual offending is liable to breach the proportionality principle and lead to human rights violations. Where what is at stake is much less serious, even perhaps trivial conduct, we can see no case for criminalization on the basis of a mere failure to act as a jury might think reasonable. In these instances the risk of serious harm is not well known and there is considerable scope for ambiguity in the range of activities which may take place. The risks of importing negligence into the whole area of lesser sexual assaults are disproportionate to the

---

[29] In order to demonstrate reasonableness it is likely that the accused would have had to take reasonable steps to address the issue of consent. The Act, as we have seen, visualises this by allowing the jury to have regard, inter alia, to 'any steps A has taken to ascertain whether B consents'.

legitimate objective of protecting from harm. These dangers very much influenced the House of Lords in the decision that there should be a presumption of *mens rea* in relation to indecency with children and indecent assault on a child. As Lord Nicholls of Birkenhead put it in relation to the former offence in *B (A Minor) v DPP*:

> The more serious the offence, the greater is the weight to be attached to the presumption, because the more severe is the punishment and the greater the stigma which accompany a conviction. . . . Further, in addition to being a serious offence, the offence is drawn broadly ('an act of gross indecency'). It can embrace conduct ranging from predatory approaches by a much older paedophile to consensual sexual experimentation between precocious teenagers of whom the offender may be the younger of the two. The conduct may be depraved by any acceptable standard, or it may be relatively innocuous behaviour in private between two young people. These factors reinforce, rather than negate, the application of the presumption in this case.

We would share these concerns, not simply in relation to the child sex offences in the Act but also to many of the other offences which would, as currently drawn, be capable of embracing much 'relatively innocuous behaviour' whether between adults, two young people or an adult and a young person. In such cases, we would argue, there is no place for negligence alone as the basis of liability.

PUNISHMENT WITHOUT HARM:
CRIMINALIZING ADULT COMMERCIAL SEXUAL ACTIVITY

The aim in the Act to criminalize commercial sexual activity, in the sections on prostitution, is significant for a number of reasons. First it is theoretically significant that adult prostitution is defined in this Act, without any analysis of 'exploitation', as inherently exploitative. If the ability to consent to such activities is removed from women and men then they are denied any agency, and their lives are interfered with, despite the claims by Hilary Benn (then Parliamentary Under Secretary) that 'this Bill is not about interfering with the lives of consenting adults. We have no interest in that whatsoever' (Evidence to Home Affairs Committee, 29 April 2003).

Second, the sections on prostitution, when taken with the widely drawn definitions of 'prostitution' 'payment', 'gain', and 'sexual' and sections on voyeurism, along with other creeping inroads into the lives of sex workers and their clients, are discriminatory. Finally, the proposals not only depart from the government's own policies in related areas, such as those relating to social exclusion, but also conflict with wider policies of the EU and the UN in this area. All of this has taken place without any systematic evidence of 'harm' done by sex workers or their clients.

We want to focus on sections 52–60 in relation to which a 'prostitute' is defined as a person:

who, on at least one occasion and whether or not compelled to do so, offers or provides sexual services to another person in return for payment or a promise of payment to A or a third person; and 'prostitution' is to be interpreted accordingly (S51(2)).

The definition of prostitute/prostitution along with the undefined and vague 'sexual' (S78) could mean that sexual 'services' or performances such as stripping, pole-dancing, and chat-lines, could all be regarded as a prostitution, as could selling kisses for charity (Kinnell, 2003).

Within the Act, 'payment' is defined as 'any financial advantage, including the discharge of an obligation to pay or the provision of goods or services (including sexual services) gratuitously or at a discount' (S51(3)). The Act does not define sexual exploitation nor differentiate it from consensual adult prostitution. The Act makes the assumption that all sex work is exploitation. This is difficult territory, not least, as Nicola Lacey (2001) has pointed out that, in *Setting the Boundaries* the key question whether selling sex always involves abuse or exploitation, was sidestepped in the discussion of prostitution-related offences. Such an analysis would have to include broad socio-cultural investigation that would also render vast tracts of the labour market inherently exploitative (Bindman, 1997).

The offence of causing or inciting prostitution for gain (S52) is aimed at adult women and for these purposes 'gain' is defined as:

a) 'any financial advantage including the discharge of an obligation to pay or the provision of goods or services (including sexual services) gratuitously or at a discount; or

b) the goodwill of any person which is or appears likely, in time, to bring financial advantage'(S54(1)).

Yet there is no clear definition of 'cause' or 'incite' and as it stands the section, taken with the interpretation of 'prostitution', is overarching in such a way that it would cause more problems than it would solve. It could for example be used to criminalize the benign relationships of those involved in sex work in the same way that 'living off immoral earnings' (Sexual Offences Act 1956 s32 (1)) has been in the past.

The existing offence of 'living off immoral earnings' under s32 (1) of the Sexual Offences Act 1956 is repealed by the Act; a law under which longstanding husbands, and even sons over 16 yrs were criminalized in practice. The new offences carry the penalty of six months imprisonment on summary conviction or up to seven years in prison on conviction on indictment.

Defining prostitution, which is not illegal under current law, in this way would mean that every person who ever had any sexual activity for any sort of material or abstract gain or goodwill, at any time or in the future, would be criminalized. By logical application this could criminalize every woman or man who has slept with their boss or head of department, accepted a job, or merely expected some sort of gain from a sexual relationship in practice; it could criminalize a gift from a lover or friend.

Furthermore, 'controlling' in the section 'controlling prostitution for gain' (S53) could be applied to 'maids' who are employed by sex working women to see clients in and out and offer company to sex working women. The term could also apply to a receptionist in a massage parlour. The penalties for keeping a brothel used for prostitution are increased by amending The Sexual Offences Act 1969 as follows:

It is an offence for a person to keep, or to manage, or act or assist in the management of, a brothel to which people resort for practices involving prostitution (whether or not also for other practices) (S55).

Given that off-street work is the safer option for women working in prostitution, it is possible that this section could limit the options for off-street work for women, leaving only the more dangerous and harmful option of street work (Barnard, Hart, and Church, 2002). When this was challenged in the House of Lords, the Minister of State was ambiguous about the protection sex workers would be afforded.[30]

Despite commendable attempts by the government[31] to try and separate the sections on child prostitution and adult prostitution from each other a conceptual confusion still exists. One Commons' debate was held under the heading of clause 51 'controlling a child prostitute'[32] yet the debate slides in and out of adult and child prostitution, illustrating the confusion that exists. The general interpretation of prostitution as it applies to adult men and women in sections 53-55 is given in a section entitled 'Abuse of *children* through prostitution and pornography'.[33] This places the adult sex working man or woman alongside children which, whilst giving the impression of protecting children, at the same time removes consent which sex working male or female adults may give as to how they use their bodies.[34] There is no rational basis for this given the lack of definition of exploitation. The logic on which these laws have been proposed is thus flawed.

There is no safeguard in the Act to protect NGOs or outreach workers from charges of 'incitement'. In this respect, the law *does* differentiate between adults and children as section 14 of the Act defines the concept of acting for the protection of a child from pregnancy or sexually transmitted infections, to protect

---

[30] Hansard, col 270.

[31] Amendments were made after effective intervention by Baroness Noakes, Lord Faulkner, Baroness Walmesly and Lord Lucas in the House of Lords (col Hansard, 13 May 2003).

[32] This is now S 49. Hansard col 270.

[33] Neither is the conceptual distinction between adults and children apparent in House of Commons debates: for example, Hilton Dawson MP stated: 'The Government are worthy of enormous praise for the introduction of clauses 49 to 53. For the first time, the range of offences related to the abuse of children through prostitution and pornography are properly laid out in law'. (Commons Hansard, 18th September, 2003).

[34] There was further evidence of this in parliament when Sandra Gidley MP stated: 'consent often should not be a factor in such cases because prostitution and child pornography are both coercive in nature and not something that 16 or 17-year-olds, or anyone of any age, indulge in if they have any choice' (col 263, House of Commons Hansard, 18th September, 2003). To this Dominic Grieve MP adds: 'prostitution is undesirable in relation to those of any age' (column 263, op cit.).

their physical safety or to promote emotional well-being by the giving of advice. Adult sex workers are not given this protection and NGOs or outreach workers who provide advice or condoms to promote the safety of sex workers from infection or pregnancy are not protected from charges of 'incitement' in the Act.

Before we proceed with further anomalies created by the Act, it is necessary to discuss the preceding review and the parliamentary process of the Act. The government review *Setting the Boundaries* began with a noble aim of a safe, just and tolerant society. It also aimed to reflect the principles of the ECHR. In the process it tried hard to be open and inclusive, and to include the best evidence available. However, it is clear that there was little evidence available to the writers of the report on consensual adult sex work, at that time, within the time frame within which they were working. Nor did the Review seek to fill gaps in knowledge by commissioning research into this specific area.

The Review took a rather idiosyncratic comparative approach to the law and explored the laws on prostitution elsewhere in the Commonwealth but not Europe (except the Republic of Ireland).[35] It is thus necessary to have a review that explores all the policy elements of the member countries in Europe. The membership of the Review did not include any sex worker groups, nor was there any representative from the sex worker branch of GMB union. Under such circumstances the Review Group could not really be expected to take a holistic approach to prostitution policy. To their credit, they highlighted this in the subsequent report. 'Nor were we charged with considering whether, and if so, how, prostitution should be regulated by law, that is a major subject in its own right' (p 3). Indeed it is, and a very necessary one to pursue. It seems inappropriate to be tinkering with the law on prostitution now with a full review on prostitution on-going. In this respect the government has departed from the recommendations of its own review. Moreover, it is also acting against the evidence submitted to the Home Affairs Committee (Ev 21, Ev 34, Ev 70).

As regards the scientific basis of *Setting the Boundaries*, there was no independent systematic review of the literature on prostitutes, their clients, nor residents. Neither was there any independent systematic research review carried out on interventions to address prostitution. The type and validity of the research on prostitution used by the Review team was sparse. Some of the methods used, such as telephone surveys, have been shown to be inadequate data collection methods for this type of information. This is not to criticise the researchers, for when concerns were raised with them about the methods of research it was clear that the funds allocated limited the scope of the research. The review team stated that prostitution and kerb crawling issues were complex and beyond the remit of the review. Yet at the same time parliament introduced the power of arrest for kerb crawling in the Criminal Justice and Police Act 2001 (S71), along with broad provisions enabling speculative searches of DNA data-

---

[35] A nation state in which the Governmental response to sexual activity might be regarded as pre Vatican II.

bases (S81). These offences can only serve to criminalize a vast number of men about whom the government has little knowledge, especially as the number of men who are clients has doubled over the past decade and is increasing.[36] It certainly seemed precipitous of the government to have made changes even before its own Home Office evaluation of crime reduction programmes on prostitution was completed.

Notwithstanding the lack of methodological rigour, it has been argued that sectional interests were represented as universal interests in the review, and that many voices were silenced. For example the Law Society's published response stated:

> The Criminal Law Committee are extremely concerned that proposed amendments to the law on prostitution are brought piecemeal into the remit of this Review. The Committee considers that the law on exploitation in prostitution requires urgent review, and root and branch reform. Members of the Committee were personally discouraged from commenting on the law on prostitution during the initial consultation on the grounds that a review on prostitution was to commence in the near future (Law Society response to *Review* para 58).[37]

The medical association GLADD[38] reported:

> these recommendations [48–52] relate to prostitution. Given that Recommendation 53 recommends a review of prostitution it seems inappropriate to make these changes in isolation.

If female prostitution and kerb crawling were considered too complex and to be considered beyond the remit of the Review team, then male prostitution was not even mentioned in the Review: yet the Act will criminalize male prostitution. There was no discussion with stakeholders and no groups representing the male sex work industry were identifiable from the consultation lists. Further limitations are apparent when in the evidence from all those concerned about appropriate consultation with sex worker groups is examined, it is stated in much evidence to the Home Affairs committee that these bodies felt excluded from the consultation process. Such exclusion is borne out by the process, in that none of those who provided written evidence to the Home Affairs Committee (Ev 21, Ev 34, Ev 70, Ev 101, Ev 104) on this issue were called as witnesses, and the Government's response to the Home Affairs Committee report omits to respond to this large body of evidence.

The subject matter was an emotive one for the authors of *Setting the Boundaries* and they state that they were moved by what they found:

---

[36] Throughout the last decade, according to the National Sexual Attitudes and Lifestyles Survey (2001), the number of men who reported paying for sex increased from 1 in 48 men to 1 in 23. The figure rises to 1 in 11 in London (Wellings *et al.*, 2001).

[37] http://www.lawsoc.org.uk/dcs/fourth_tier.asp?section_id=5399&Caller_ID=NS490

[38] The Gay and Lesbian Association of Doctors and Dentists. It has 350 members.

The extent and nature of abuse that can take place within families, within institutions and within communities is only now coming to be realised in all its complexity and horror (p 3, para 1.1.9)

and 'we were profoundly moved by the extent of sexual abuse against vulnerable people' (p vi, para 0.17). The review placed more emphasis on 'protection' than its other aims of 'fairness' or 'justice' in respect of those too young or too vulnerable to be in prostitution. This is all highly appropriate when the aims of fairness and justice are going to be pursued later to balance the equation for those who are not young or vulnerable.

Adult prostitution offences differ from child prostitution offences in that they have to be 'for gain'. All work is for gain, and there is an inherent flaw here in the drafting. The offences should be drafted in terms of fear, force or fraud if they are to capture true exploitation. Unfortunately, sensible amendments tabled to insert 'fear, force or fraud' into the clauses on prostitution[39] or 'using force, coercion, deception', or the insertion of 'abuse of power or of a position of vulnerability'[40] into the trafficking offences were, curiously, rejected by the government.

Even more strangely, parliamentarians who spoke in the debate appeared to find prostitution offensive in proportion to the amount of money that is made from the activity: 'prostitution offences run the whole gamut from deeply offensive in terms of public nuisance and the degree to which vast sums are earned, to less offensive'.[41] There seems to be a view among policymakers that if someone (a brothel owner) is making a lot of money, then exploitation must be taking place. The debate all too easily reads as if the police target people *because* they are making a lot of money out of prostitution. Such confusion in a debate would be inconceivable if any other business was being debated.

Within the parliamentary debates the confusion between children and adults, and exploitation and money-making, coalesce. For example, with regard to the controlling of child prostitution, Sandra Gidley MP states:

I admit to having tabled the amendments after reading the Metropolitan police's comment that prostitution and pornography were big business and that, although the police had no problem prosecuting the small guys, often, at the bigger businesses end of the market, particularly in prostitution, there was a human firewall between the pimp and the enterprise. (House of Commons, Hansard, 18 Sept 2003, col 270).

It is striking how often ministers and MPs mention the police, and submissions and presentations from the Metropolitan Police in particular, are mentioned during the parliamentary debates. In addition, the police were highly proactive in coaching MPs in various policing initiatives such as Operation Sapphire (on rape). During the passage of the Sexual Offences Bill through parliament many MPs had the opportunity to go on the 'parliamentary police scheme'; a scheme

---

[39] Hansard 13 May 2003, col 181.
[40] Hansard 13 May 2003, col 202.
[41] Hansard 13 May 2003, col 199.

in which MPs are drilled in the mechanics of policing sexual offences from a police perspective.[42] The Paedophile Unit at Scotland Yard provided a 'teach-in' and from the debates it is clear that a number of MPs had enrolled on the scheme(s) and were moved, even traumatised, by it. One male MP stated: 'I was scarred by the day I visited the paedophile unit'.[43] Sandra Gidley MP stated ' I drafted the amendment after the briefing from the Paedophile Unit, when I assumed that everyone was out to do terrible things'.[44] Did such intense police involvement limit the possibility for an even-handed debate?

We seriously question whether there has been over use of police and police involvement in the parliamentary process—not least because it occurred at a time when the Metropolitan police were seeking a seven figure sum (tens of millions of pounds) from the Home Office and they would not have any vested interest in 'talking down' the crimes they advised upon.[45]

Questions about the human and civil rights of sex workers and their clients also have to be asked as there are many aspects of the Act that are liable to make things more dangerous for sex working men and women. This is part of a steady flow of legislation being applied to prostitutes and their clients[46] without systematic evaluation of sex work in all its various forms. For example, the amendments in s 46 and s 47 of The Criminal Justice and Police Act 2001 were enacted before any intervention had been trialled or evaluated.[47] This legislation, the product of a campaign against sex workers by Westminster Council, banned prostitutes' advertisements from public telephone boxes. It has not cleared the telephone boxes, but it has had the net-widening effect of criminalizing a further group of people. The penalties imposed have received legal criticism in the context of the Human Rights Act (Wasik, 2001). In addition, the use of ASBOs under s1 of the Crime and Disorder Act 1998 against sex working women, has re-introduced imprisonment for prostitute women (which had been removed in s 71 of Criminal Justice Act 1982), and has been considered to be a retrograde step (for example, Jones and Sagar, 2001). Anti-Social Behaviour Orders (ASBOs) are increasingly being used against women, even though this is a corruption of their purpose, which was to target noisy neighbours.[48]

Whether the Act met human rights requirements was a matter for the Joint Committee on Human Rights to determine. However, at the Committee stage of the Criminal Justice Bill 2003, the provision to extend police powers was

---

[42] House of Commons Hansard, Standing Committee B, 16 September 2003, col 206.

[43] House of Commons Hansard, Standing Committee B, 16 September 2003, col 10.

[44] House of Commons Hansard, Standing Committee B, 16 September 2003, col 224.

[45] http://www.met.police.uk/sapphire/press_articles/reopen.htm

[46] For example, kerb crawling only became a recordable, as opposed to summary, offence when all 'sexual offences' were up-tariffed in 1997.

[47] See Brooks-Gordon and Gelsthorpe for a socio-legal history of this.

[48] Lord Bassam sought to justify the use of ASBOs and imprisonment thus: 'It is worth reflecting on precisely what surrounds the act of prostitution, including noise disturbance, such as the banging of car doors, and more general disruption for parts of our communities' (Hansard 13 May 2003, col 199).

found wanting by the Joint Committee on Human Rights. The Committee drew attention to

> the compatibility of provisions for admitting evidence of bad character and hearsay evidence (clauses 81 to 102) with the right to a fair hearing, drawing attention to the risk of incompatibility in a number of respects.

It is interesting to note that these flawed provisions[49] would be liable to produce results not dissimilar to the way sex working women are treated already when ASBOs are served on them. But more importantly, the broad definition of a person as a 'prostitute' in statute is of the same questionable compatibility with the right under ECHR to a fair hearing. These issues were not put to the Committee on Human Rights when considering this Act, as the wider issues in prostitution were deemed to be beyond the remit of the Sexual Offences Act.

The Sexual Offences Act 2003 will extend the laws on prostitution, paradoxically, by making them gender neutral (S56). While Sections 48 to 55 replace existing legislation on prostitution, these sections do not replace *all* existing prostitution legislation and the provisions relating to loitering or soliciting for the purposes of prostitution,[50] application to the court following a caution for loitering or soliciting,[51] permitting premises to be used for the purposes of prostitution,[52] kerb crawling,[53] among others, remain on the statute book and have been strengthened by making them 'gender-neutral'. In the past, owing to the gender-specific nature of the law, a prostitute was defined as a woman, and a kerb crawler as a man. Such gender specificity provided a number of loopholes through which women sex workers who worked from their own cars for better safety and comfort would evade the kerb crawling laws. Likewise, many male sex workers avoided being prosecuted for soliciting and their partners avoided being prosecuted for 'living off a immoral earnings'. However, the new proposals on prostitution, added like an afterthought, half-way through the Bill's passage through Parliament[54] will mean that male sex workers will be criminalized to the degree that women sex workers are, and female clients (of which there are an increasing number if the advertisements of male sex workers servicing women are an indication) will be criminalized alongside male clients if they look on the street for sexual services.

---

[49] This is especially the case with hearsay evidence, which contravenes ECHR Article 6 which protects the right to a fair hearing. As the Joint Committee on Human Rights states: "there is as yet no case in which the European Court of Human Rights has held a trial to be fair in which a conviction was based wholly on oral hearsay testimony which the defendant had no adequate opportunity to test. Nevertheless, we consider that there is potential for a violation of rights under Article 6, and we consider that the matter deserves to be drawn to the attention of each House." (Joint Committee on Human Rights Second Report, 31 January, 2003) (http://www.parliament.the-stationery-office. co.uk/pa/jt200203/jtselect/jtrights/40/4003.htm#a4)

[50] S 1 (1) Street Offences Act 1959.

[51] S 2 Street Offences Act 1959.

[52] S 36 Street Offences Act 1956.

[53] S 4 (1) Sexual Offences Act 1985.

[54] Hansard 13 May 2003, col 197.

These proposals are in conflict with Government policy on social exclusion.[55] Such proposals, with the further penalties they place on sex workers, will make it likely that workers will work in more, and not less, dangerous ways. It will also make sex workers less likely to report the violence they suffer, or access wider services for them as they risk, or put their families and partners at risk of, legal penalties for their engagement in prostitution. The extension of gender specific offences to encompass both men and women is counter to the spirit of the gender discrimination legislation which would aim to bring the status of marginalized groups up to that of dominant groups rather than extending discrimination to wider groups. Whilst we would otherwise support gender neutrality in the Act we would argue that the Act offers gender negativity rather than gender neutrality in respect of its current approach to sex work.

Conflicts with European Policy

The proposals in the Act conflict with wider European policy. They leave England and Wales with the most punitive laws on sex work at a time when the rest of Europe is beginning to address the vulnerability of sex working women in more positive way. For example, in April 2000 the Parliamentary Assembly adopted recommendation [1450 (2000)] on the subject of violence against women in Council of Europe member states. This aims to:

—Introduce training programmes for officers dealing with sex worker victims of violence
—Run information and awareness-raising campaigns to educate the public of unacceptability of violence against sex working women
—Make funding available
—Step up collaboration between state institutions and NGOs to improve protection of women
—Trial tolerance zones (safety parks)

The Act's provisions also conflict with UN policy which stresses that:

Criminal law in the area of prostitution impedes the provision of HIV/AIDS prevention and care by driving people engaged in the industry underground. Such laws should be reviewed with the aim to decriminalize sex work where no victimisation is involved, and regulate occupational health and safety conditions to protect sex workers and their clients. (UN Handbook for Legislators on HIV/AIDS, Law and Human Rights, p 56).

By creating a more punitive environment for sex work, the Act takes British policy in a totally different direction to policy in similar jurisdictions to our

---

[55] It is ironic that the same day the Bill was debated questions were put to government concerning sentencing policy and the inequitable sentencing of women which has resulted in the recent increase of women in prison (*Hansard*, 13 February, 2003, col 819).

own. For example, a Private Member's Bill, which was supported by all parties in Ottawa Canada, has just been passed and the Canadian Parliament has instructed the Standing Committee on Justice and Human Rights to review federal law around solicitation. Their task will be to recommend changes that would reduce the dangers facing sex workers. At least 60 missing women and 15 murder charges focussed the Canadian Government on the need to reduce the violence against sex workers. In New Zealand, laws have been passed to legalize brothels: the principal aim of these laws, which were given great consideration, has been the safety of the women working within the industry.

The Act also goes against some key views of the public, which have, by and large, sympathy for sex working women. In Soho, a petition with over 10,000 names was signed following the eviction of sex working women onto the streets by Westminster Council. The local Rector, the Soho society, and other community groups protested following the killing of a young mother, whose body was found in bin bags in Camden, and who was one of three sex working women killed in recent years following eviction.[56] That there are problems with street prostitution cannot be denied. The problems can include noise, litter, and nuisance but these problems, such as they are, should not lead to criminal offences being applied to an already vulnerable group.

THE ACT'S CONCEPTION OF CRIMINAL LAW

The Act's conception of the social role of the criminal law is, in our view, flawed. In the protectionist rush, adult sex working women (and now men) are infantilised by the law, have their right to choose removed, and are criminalized as a result. This is extended in the Act's clauses on trafficking. The sections which cover the trafficking of adults into the UK (ss57–60), and within the UK, for 'sexual exploitation' suffer the same lack of definition of 'sexual exploitation' as do the sections on prostitution. The sections are not age-specific but relate to 'persons' who could be men, women, or children. They imply that the issues for adult women are the same as for children, which is not the case. The assumption is made within these sections that *all* trafficking is exploitative and this could be used to criminalize anyone who facilitates the movement of sex workers within the UK, including someone merely offering a lift. It appears that the conceptual confusion between adults and children in the trafficking provisions may be purposeful for a veiled up-scaling of punishment. For example, the Home Secretary has suggested that:

> when trafficking offences that apply to adults as well as children are combined with offences involving children—to which certain penalties would apply independently— the penalties are sufficient . . . if . . . combining the offences is not enough we need to decide whether aggravation of the offence should carry additional penalties (House of Commons Hansard 15 July 2003, col 187).

[56] Press release from press conference held on 10 February 2003.

As drafted, these sections could cover the movement of all adults who work in the sex industry as they travel across borders. Given the other definitions in the Act they could, for example, criminalize a trade unionist sex worker from Holland who comes to the UK to talk to the sex workers' trade union in this country. This discriminates against sex working women who travel across boundaries, and thus interferes with their civil liberties. For many in the sex industry their motive is poverty—the desire to obtain goods that others in modern society take for granted, such as heating or housing. As regards the wider political context, definitions around prostitution are often made in relation to migration. The Review team stated that they had not looked at 'brothel keeping' . . . 'kerb crawling' or the Street Offences Act 1957 except insofar as they link to the sexual exploitation of others. This area is a substantial one and worthy of consideration. Trafficking is too often discussed with little critical debate, for example trafficking is described as a 'problem' when in fact what emerges is either migration or morality that is the problem.

It is acknowledged in *Setting the Boundaries* that the majority of women who migrate to work in the sex industry know they will be working in the sex industry. What they may be deceived about are the conditions in which they may end up working. However, such conditions only abound because of the status of illegal immigrants and the penalties placed on those working in the sex industry. Many years ago, Lord Tebbit said that to get on one's bike to find work was an admirable thing to do. Yet it is suggested within the debates in parliament that when people migrate from one area to another with the same motive—that of feeding the family—it is either condemned or assumed that they are hapless victims of rogue gangs. The sex industry needs to be reviewed without the emotive discourses surrounding 'illegal' immigration and 'trafficking' clouding these issues.

More recently one argument that has been levelled against sex work and the movement of sex workers is the human rights abuses that take place within certain parts of the sex industry. Yet when similar abuses are found in other industries, the whole industry is not closed down. Rather, the bad factories, or the bad employers are held to account so that the industry, and by extension society, is healthier. Yet criminal charges, levied by ASBOs, deprive sex workers of their basic human rights. From this perspective, the United Nations Rights Treaties guaranteeing the right to free choice of work and to just and favourable work conditions are clearly violated with the placing of criminal laws as legal obstacles to engagement in sex work (Bindman, 1997). The lack of human rights protection for sex workers in general leaves them vulnerable to exploitation. These conditions preclude the application of existing labour laws to employer-employee relationships, thus increasing the opportunity for harassment and extortion by police and authorities.

The UK has some of the most punitive laws in Europe against sex working women. The law against carding has made it harder for women to work off-street. Our laws at present create the space for the pimp to enter. In Denmark,

Danish-born sex workers can work legally especially indoors but are not allowed to pay third parties such as pimps. In the Federal Republic of Germany there are areas where women can work (Thorbeck and Pattanaik, 2002).

English law now sits uneasily between the *sexköpslag* (sex buying law) in Sweden which criminalises clients who buy sex but allows women to sell it, and the relative freedom enjoyed by women in Holland since the legalisation of brothels there in 2000. There, voluntary sex work is legal and women can pay their taxes, take out health insurance, and receive social welfare benefits. This Dutch law has made businesses more professional and they can be inspected at any time, just like other businesses, to make sure they are complying with labour law. Their premises have strict rules about hygiene and condom use. The law has created opportunities and conditions in which sex working women have rights for the first time. Any form of forced prostitution, pimping, or forced trafficking is illegal. Women who wish to work outside may work in allocated sites (safety parks) outside cities.

We welcome the amendments which have separated child prostitution from consensual adult sex work. Yet other anomalies in sex work that have been created to criminalize aspects of consensual adult sex work over the years, which is not in itself illegal, (qv Self, 2003) have not been addressed, and we have commented above where this has happened. The law creates the vulnerability of sex workers and then criminalizes them for it.

The only argument against sex workers being able to work legally, pay taxes and have access to social security and pensions etc, can be a moral one—but this fails on a number of counts:

1) Morality is not the business of the law. As the human rights organisation, Liberty puts it: 'It is not for the state to determine the morality of prostitution in terms of criminality' (Liberty, ev 21, Home Affairs Committee HC 639).
2) It rests on the assumption that paying for a sexual service is worse than gaining one by some other means (Kuo, 2002).
3) It implies that in all other respects 'morality' is high, when in fact the National Sexual Attitudes and Lifestyle (NATSAL) survey shows people have more partners than ever before, and more one-night partners than ever before (compare, for example, Wellings *et al.*, 1994 to Wellings *et al.*, 2001, and also Johnson *et al.*, 2001).[57]

The sex industry is so steeped in myths and notions that we need to re-examine even the most common assumptions. Policy recommendations need to be based on an analysis of *all* the laws which relate to prostitution. *Setting the Boundaries* presented a good opportunity to do this but the review held that many of the laws relating to prostitution were beyond its remit. Evidence put to

---

[57] For an outline of major findings of NATSAL 2000: http://www.mrc.ac.uk/prn/index/public-interest/public-press_office/public-press_releases_2001/public-30_november_2001.htm

the Home Affairs Committee recommended that 'abuse of children ought to be in a separate Act which does not confuse their needs with those of adults' (ev. 101). This was echoed in some of the debates.[58] There are many influences which affect the trafficking of children but which do not affect adults. There are many issues which affect adult trafficking and do not affect children, such as the economic migration of adult sex workers.

Combined with the broad and overarching definition of 'sexual' in section 78 which suggests that something is sexual because of 'its nature; its circumstances or the purposes of any person in relation to it' then any person who is known to sell sex could be penalized just on that basis. The addition of '*any* other activity that is sexual' could be used to include a sex working woman holding hands with a client if their purpose is to find a hotel room in which to have sex. It therefore discriminates against sex working women and will cause disproportionate harm to these women and their clients. Such penalties do not sit well with a so-called tolerant and diverse society. These sections would worsen the situation rather than promote social justice. The penalties imposed would hamper the challenge to end social exclusion, with which the government is trying to deal, and would have serious consequences for social exclusion and net-widening as they will sweep even more women and men into the criminal justice system.

THE SOCIAL ROLE OF CRIMINAL LAW: HARM VERSUS MORALITY

In this section we explore the rag-bag of offences in sections 66 to 71 which complete Part 1 of the Act and we question the conception underlying this part of the Act of the social role of the criminal law. We argue that this should turn on harm rather than vague notions of morality. The Act makes it an offence for a person to observe for sexual gratification another person committing a 'private act' where the person being watched does not know they are being watched (SS67–8). The aim of this offence is to capture so-called 'voyeurs', people who get some sexual pleasure out of watching others semi-clad or engaged in sexual activity. Psychologically it has long been argued that, in itself, interest in viewing naked women or men should not be considered deviant as it is an important component in normative sexual response. For example, in a review of studies it was found that over 50 per cent of a community of men reported having sexual fantasy of a 'scene where you witness the sexual performance of other persons' (Hanson and Harris, 1997). Freud ([1905] 1962) only considered 'normal' voyeurism a perversion if, instead of being preparatory to the 'normal' sexual aim, it supplants it. Nowadays we would only consider it a perversion clinically if it occurs over a long period of time *and* causes marked distress to the person who does it.[59]

---

[58] Hansard 13 May 2003, col 207.

[59] The diagnostic criteria for voyeurism is 'a) Over a period of at least 6 months, recurrent, intense sexually arousing fantasies, sexual urges, or behaviours involving the act of observing an

Pure voyeuristic behaviour is rare and research in the area suggests it is of low clinical priority, curious, but not important by psychiatric or psychological standards, and that it is seen as 'a pathetic attempt to steal sexual pleasure' (Hanson and Harris, 1997, p 328) by members of the public, and as a curious, but not particularly important sexual variation by the psychological/psychiatric community. And classic ethnographic studies on voyeurism or 'watching windows' have shown it to be related to an occupational pastime (for example, Feigelman, 1974), a shared group activity by those who happen to work in places that afford the opportunity, such as high-rise building sites overlooking hotels (and that there is a hierarchy of activities watched, of which the highest is a heterosexual couple engaged in coitus). This has nothing to do with wanting a relationship with the 'victim', which is, anyway covered by the Protection from Harassment Act 1997.

Much criticism was made of this section in the House of Lords and in the press. But one thing which has not been mentioned in the context of voyeurism is that it could also relate to those involved in street prostitution as it could be applied to cruisers who drive through red light districts just looking at the women. This, in the present policy context shown in *Respect & Responsibility* could be used to criminalise kerb crawlers further as the provision allows for a class of persons to which it is possible the voyeur will belong. People who are caught 'peeping' already have social disapprobation heaped upon them and are shamed by the media. For example, erstwhile Chair of Manchester United, Martin Edwards, made front page news when he was reported to have been peering under a cubicle door at a health club.[60] The explanatory notes in the Act make it clear that the offence of voyeurism is 'not designed to apply to journalists where they are pursuing legitimate journalistic activity' on the grounds that 'in these circumstances the observing or taking of images will not be done for sexual gratification'. Quite. Not only has 'legitimate journalistic activity' been shown in a number of cases to be a problematic concept but this illustrates a serious lack of internal consistency in the Act. Commercial activity is criminalized on the one hand in the adult prostitution clauses, but on the other hand commercial activity is exonerated in the voyeurism provision. It has to be questioned which might do more harm to a subject, peering under a cubicle door or revealing the peccadilloes of those who do for the titillation of the masses? Notwithstanding the Act's inconsistency, should voyeurism be within the remit of the criminal law? The human rights group Liberty, whilst welcoming the recognition of privacy in Art 8. of the European Convention, thinks not.

Sexual intercourse with a living animal is criminalized in the Act, or sexual intercourse where one is 'reckless' as to whether it is with a living animal (S69), apparently on the grounds that 'sexual activity with animals is generally recog-

---

unsuspecting person who is naked, in the process of disrobing, or engaging in sexual activity. b) The person has acted on these urges, or the sexual urges or fantasies cause marked distress or interpersonal difficulty.' DSM-IV-TR (302.82).

[60] *Daily Mirror*, August 29, 2002.

nised to be profoundly disturbed behaviour' (*Protecting the Public*). It cannot be said that individual 'disturbance' provides a basis for criminal liability. In the first place a behaviour can only be said to be profoundly disturbed if it is causing the individual distress, for example, excessive hand-washing, or door-locking. In the second place there are many profoundly disturbed behaviours which *do* cause the individual distress, but which are not a justification for criminalization. The principle upon which the law should be based is harm rather than morality. In this case, harm to the animal would need to be demonstrated, rather than disturbance of the individual perpetrator, and this is in any case covered by animal cruelty legislation.

The introduction of the offence of sexual penetration of a corpse (S70) is interesting for two reasons. The reasoning behind its inclusion is explained in the White Paper. Such an offence 'will ensure that a defendant who is found guilty on both charges is sentenced accordingly and is *treated and monitored as a sex offender both in prison and after release*' (*Protecting the Public*, Chapt 6.80). Thus treatment issues have been taken into consideration in the drafting of the law. This however makes the assumption that treatment works; indeed in an exchange between Mr Hilton Dawson MP and the Home Secretary David Blunkett, Mr Dawson stated: 'Well-developed models now exist for addressing the dangerous and abusive offending behaviour of adults. If we provide the means for people to be treated, we can protect children.' This is an assumption founded on little or no evidence available to date (see Brooks-Gordon et al., this volume).

Secondly, the offence of sexual interference is framed in terms of penetration only and not to other types of sexual activity on a dead body. It would not, for example provide for a case where the offender had beheaded the victim and masturbated over the head. Thus the law is unlikely to meet its intended aim of including offences, of which there are many, which are non-penetrative but which have a sexual purpose or release. The White Paper shows the Government's thinking: 'We believe that this behaviour is so deviant as to warrant the intervention of the criminal law'. This relies on a concept of deviance based on the assumption of a normal sexuality, a concept which we find problematic.

CONCLUSION

This is a blunderbuss Bill[61]

The Sexual Offences Act 2003 pretends to be a comprehensive modernisation of the law relating to sexual offences. There is no doubt that reform was necessary and we applaud certain aspects of the legislation. The shift away from the exclusive concentration on penile penetration, and the concomitant recognition of

[61]   Dominic Grieve MP, House of Commons Standing Committee B, 18th September 2003.

the seriousness of other forms of non-consensual penetration, is welcome and overdue. Likewise the shift towards gender-neutrality in the law's approach to sexual offending is a desirable and necessary development in the light of human rights obligations.

On the other hand, the Act may be criticised both for being *under-inclusive* and for being *over-inclusive*. It is under-inclusive in a number of key respects. The addition to the law of several new offences relating to prostitution is unhelpful and only serves to highlight the pressing need for a thorough and wide-ranging review of the whole of the law relating to prostitution which has been promised, but not delivered, by the government. It is under-inclusive too in failing to deal at all with sado-masochistic practices which, despite their obvious sexual content, remain within the concept of *non-sexual* assault offences. The current legal position whereby an offence will be committed wherever actual bodily harm results from such practices, and despite the fact that the activities were consensual,[62] is untenable in an era of human rights and is inconsistent with the objectives of the new law to respect activities between consenting adults in private. Those provisions in the Act which continue to criminalize consensual sexual relations between adult relatives may be criticised for much the same reason. And those which prohibit all sexual activity between children have the potential for causing much damage to harmless experimentation as an aspect of growing up. It is more than possible that there will be ongoing challenges to the new law under the European Convention in such cases. The Law Commission provisionally put forward the sensible suggestion that those consensual sado-masochistic practices which did not reach the severity of causing a 'serious disabling injury' should be decriminalised. The sort of transient pain or discomfort resulting from activities such as spanking or caning would, under such a reform, be taken outside the criminal law (Law Commission, 1995). This was surely the occasion for the matter to be addressed, but the legislative opportunity has been allowed to pass.

In other respects, this is a strikingly illiberal piece of legislation which is far too over-inclusive in its attempt to regulate sexual conduct which, in our view, should be no business of the law. We have questioned aspects of the parliamentary process which we believe may have contributed to such over-inclusion. It is at least a matter of some relief that some of the more ludicrous provisions in the original Bill, such as that relating to sex in a public place, have not survived parliamentary scrutiny. But the Act has created certain places as strictly off-limits for sexual activity, irrespective of how private the place might be. This includes public lavatories. Neither is it a sufficient reaction to penal legislation which is too widely drawn to say that there is a prosecutorial discretion which may be exercised against prosecution in the more trivial cases. It is the very labelling of these activities as criminal which is the fundamental problem. We have highlighted the way in which it is negligence, rather than conscious wrongdoing,

---

[62] *Brown* [1994] 1 AC 212.

which will be the baseline requirement for sexual offending more or less throughout the Act. As well as being inappropriate in the context of serious criminal offences, this is a development which is patently inconsistent with developments elsewhere in the criminal law. This was demonstrated all too recently by the demise of *Caldwell* and the House of Lords' reassertion of its commitment to subjective recklessness as the minimum requirement for serious criminal offences. We think it is worth bearing in mind what Lord Bingham of Cornhill had to say on this subject almost immediately before the Sexual Offences Act reached the statute book:

> . . . it is a salutary principle that conviction of serious crime should depend on proof not simply that the defendant caused (by act or omission) an injurious result to another but that his state of mind when so acting was culpable . . . It is clearly blameworthy to take an obvious and significant risk of causing injury to another. But it is not clearly blameworthy to do something involving a risk of injury to another if (for reasons other than self-induced intoxication . . .) one genuinely does not perceive the risk. Such a person may fairly be accused of stupidity or a lack of imagination, but neither of those failings should expose him to conviction of serious crime or the risk of punishment.[63]

We would entirely endorse those sentiments in the context of sexual behaviour.

REFERENCES

ASHWORTH, A, *Principles of Criminal Law* (4th edition, Oxford, Oxford University Press, 2003).

BARNARD, M, HART, G. and CHURCH, S, 'Client Violence Against Prostitute Women From Street and Off-Street Locations: A Three City Comparison' *The Economic and Social Research Council Violence Research Programme Research Findings* (2002).

BENNION, F, *The Sex Code: Morals for Moderns* (London, Weidenfeld & Nicolson, 1991).

—— *Sexual Ethics and the Criminal Law: A Critique of the Sexual Offences Bill 2003* (Oxford, Lester Publishing, 2003).

BINDMAN, J, (with participation of DOEZEMA, J), '*Redefining Prostitution as Sex Work on the International Agenda*'. (London, Anti-Slavery International, 1997).

BROOKS-GORDON, B, Memorandum of Evidence to Home Affairs Committee, Ev. 34, Appendix 5, House of Commons Home Affairs Committee, Sexual Offences Bill, Fifth Report of Session 2002–2003, HC 639, 2003.

—— and GELSTHORPE, L., 'Hiring Bodies' in A Bainham, S Day Sclater and M Richards (eds), *Body Lore and Laws,* pp 193–210 (Hart, Oxford, 2002).

FEIGELMAN, W, 'The Pattern of Voyeurism Among Construction Workers', (1974) *Urban Life and Culture*, April, pp35-49.

FREUD, S, *Three Essays on the Theory of Sexuality* (J Strachey trans) (London, Hogarth 1965). Originally pub. 1905.

---

[63] *R v G and Another* [2003] UKHL 50 at para 32.

HANSON, RK and HARRIS, AJR, 'Voyeurism: Assessment and Treatment' in RD Laws and W O'Donohue (eds), *Sexual Deviance* (London, New York, Guilford Press, 1997).

HOME OFFICE, *Setting the Boundaries : Reforming the Law on Sexual Offences,* July (2000).

—— *Protecting the Public: Strengthening Protection Against Sex Offenders and Reforming the Law on Sexual Offences* (CM 5668, 2002).

—— *Respect and Responsibility: Taking a Stand Against Anti-Social Behaviour* (CM 5778, 2003).

—— /SCOTTISH EXECUTIVE, *Consultation Paper on the Review of Part 1 of the Sex Offenders Act 1997,* (July 2001).

—— *The Government Reply to the Fifth Report from the Home Affairs Committee Session 2002–2003 HC 639 Sexual Offences Bill* (CM 5986).

HOUSE OF COMMONS HOME AFFAIRS COMMITTEE, *Sexual Offences Bill, Fifth Report of Session 2002–03,* HC 639.

ISIKOFF, M, *Uncovering Clinton: A Reporter's Story* (New York, Crown Publishers, 1999).

JOHNSON, AM, MERCER, CH, ERENS, B, COPAS, AJ, McMANUS, S, WELLINGS, K, FENTON, KA, KOROVESSIS, C, MACDOWELL, W, NANCHAHAL, K, PURDON, S, and FIELD, J, 'Sexual Behaviour in Britain: Partnerships, Practices and HIV Risk Behaviours' (2001) 358 *The Lancet* 1835–42.

JONES, H, and SAGAR, T, 'Crime and Disorder Act 1998: Prostitution and the Anti-Social Behaviour Order' (2001) *Criminal Law Review* 873.

KINNELL H, (Personal correspondence, February 2003).

KUO, L, *Prostitution Policy: Revolutionizing Practice Through a Gendered Perspective* (New York, New York University Press, 2002).

LACEY, N, 'Beset by Boundaries: The Home Office Review of Sex Offences' (2001) *Criminal Law Review* 3.

LAW COMMISSION, Consultation Paper No. 139 on *Consent in the Criminal Law* (London, HMSO, 1995).

LAWTON, F, 'The Abuse of Child Abuse', *The Spectator,* (1997) 1 November, available at: http://www.ipce.info/ipceweb/Library/99-131_abuse_of_abuse.htm

MYHILL, A, and ALLEN, J, *Rape and Sexual Assault of Women: Findings from the British Crime Survey* (Home Office Research, Development and Statistics Directorate, 159, 2002).

SELF, H, *Prostitution, Women and Misuse of the Law* (London, Frank Cass, 2003).

SPENCER, J, 'The Shameful Sex Crimes of Adrian Mole aged 13¾' *The Times,* October 7th, 2003.

TEMKIN, J, *Rape and the Legal Process* (2nd edition, Oxford, Oxford University Press, 2002).

THORBEK, S, and PATTANAIK, B, *Transnational Prostitution: Changing Global Patterns* (London, Zed Books, 2002).

WASIK, M, 'Legislating in the Shadow of the Human Rights Act: The Criminal Justice and Police Act 2001' (2001) *Criminal Law Review* 931.

WELLINGS, K, National Sexual Attitudes and Lifestyle Survey (NATSAL) UK National Survey of Sexual Attitudes and Lifestyles (Natsal, 2000) 358 *Lancet* 2001; 1835–42.

—— FIELD, J, JOHNSON, AM, and WADSWORTH, J, *Sexual Behaviour in Britain* (Penguin, London, 1994).

—— Nanchahal, K, Macdowall, W, McManus, S, Erens, B, Mercer, CH, Johnson, AM, Copas, AJ, Korovessis, C, Fenton, KA and Field, J, 'Sexual behaviour in Britain: early heterosexual experience' (2001). 358 *Lancet* (9296): 1843–1850.

APPENDIX

SEXUAL OFFENCES ACT 2003

Rape

1. Rape

Assault

2. Assault by penetration
3. Sexual assault

Causing sexual activity without consent

4. Causing a person to engage in sexual activity without consent

Rape and other offences against children under 13

5. Rape of a child under 13
6. Assault of a child under 13 by penetration
7. Sexual assault of a child under 13
8. Causing or inciting a child under 13 to engage in sexual activity

Child sex offences

9. Sexual activity with a child
10. Causing or inciting a child to engage in sexual activity
11. Engaging in sexual activity in the presence of a child
12. Causing a child to watch a sexual act
13. Child sex offences committed by children or young persons
14. Arranging or facilitating commission of a child sex offence
15. Meeting a child following sexual grooming

Abuse of position of trust

16. Abuse of position of trust: sexual activity with a child
17. Abuse of position of trust: causing or inciting a child to engage in sexual activity

18. Abuse of position of trust: sexual activity in the presence of a child
19. Abuse of position of trust: causing a child to watch a sexual act
20. Abuse of position of trust: acts done in Scotland
21. Positions of trust
22. Positions of trust: interpretation
23. Sections 16 to 19: marriage exception
24. Sections 16 to 19: sexual relationships which pre-date position of trust

Familial child sex offences

25. Sexual activity with a child family member
26. Inciting a child family member to engage in sexual activity
27. Family relationships
28. Sections 25 and 26: marriage exception
29. Sections 25 and 26: sexual relationships which pre-date family relationships

Offences against persons with a mental disorder impeding choice

30. Sexual activity with a person with a mental disorder impeding choice
31. Causing or inciting a person, with a mental disorder impeding choice, to engage in sexual activity
32. Engaging in sexual activity in the presence of a person with a mental disorder impeding choice
33. Causing a person, with a mental disorder impeding choice, to watch a sexual act

Inducements etc. to persons with a mental disorder

34. Inducement, threat or deception to procure sexual activity with a person with a mental disorder
35. Causing a person with a mental disorder to engage in or agree to engage in sexual activity by inducement, threat or deception
36. Engaging in sexual activity in the presence, procured by inducement, threat or deception, of a person with a mental disorder
37. Causing a person with a mental disorder to watch a sexual act by inducement, threat or deception

Care workers for persons with a mental disorder

38. Care workers: sexual activity with a person with a mental disorder
39. Care workers: causing or inciting sexual activity
40. Care workers: sexual activity in the presence of a person with a mental disorder
41. Care workers: causing a person with a mental disorder to watch a sexual act
42. Care workers: interpretation
43. Sections 38 to 41: marriage exception
44. Sections 38 to 41: sexual relationships which pre-date care relationships

Indecent photographs of children

45. Indecent photographs of persons aged 16 or 17
46. Criminal proceedings, investigations etc.,

Abuse of children through prostitution and pornography

47. Paying for sexual services of a child
48. Causing or inciting child prostitution or pornography
49. Controlling a child prostitute or a child involved in pornography
50. Arranging or facilitating child prostitution or pornography
51. Sections 48 to 50: interpretation

Exploitation of prostitution

52. Causing or inciting prostitution for gain
53. Controlling prostitution for gain.
54. Sections 52 and 53: interpretation

Amendments relating to prostitution

55. Penalties for keeping a brothel used for prostitution
56. Extension of gender-specific prostitution offences

Trafficking

57. Trafficking into the UK for sexual exploitation
58. Trafficking within the UK for sexual exploitation
59. Trafficking out of the UK for sexual exploitation
60. Sections 57 to 59: interpretation and jurisdiction

Preparatory offences

61. Administering a substance with intent
62. Committing an offence with intent to commit a sexual offence
63. Trespass with intent to commit a sexual offence

Sex with an adult relative

64. Sex with an adult relative: penetration
65. Sex with an adult relative: consenting to penetration

Other offences

66. Exposure
67. Voyeurism
68. Voyeurism: interpretation
69. Intercourse with an animal
70. Sexual penetration of a corpse
71. Sexual activity in a public lavatory

Offences outside the United Kingdom

72. Offences outside the United Kingdom

Supplementary and General

73. Exceptions to aiding, abetting and counselling
74. 'Consent'
75. Evidential presumptions about consent
76. Conclusive presumptions about consent
77. Sections 75 and 76: relevant acts
78. 'Sexual'
79. Part 1: general interpretation

13

Unnatural Acts: Sexuality, Film, and the Law

ANDREW WEBBER

THIS ESSAY WILL consider the triangular relations between sexuality, film, and the law, as exemplified by selected cinematic performances of homosexuality. It will ask questions about how the law regulates representations of sexuality in film, and about how film represents the regulation of sexuality by the law. As a medium of performance, at a remove from routine social reality but also involved with it, cinema projects a heightened form of the types of performance that characterise the construction of sexuality in culture at large. The essay will argue that film provides a prime example both of the legislative constraints which society puts upon sexuality and of the loopholes and blind spots in its system. The performance of 'unnatural' acts in film tests the viability of the category of naturalness as a basis for law making, exposing it as a social construct in need of constant revision.

From the start, film, as a medium of bodily projection, has had a special relationship to sexuality. It emerges from the cultural context of the attraction, the framed spectacle of the variety act, with a powerful appeal to voyeurism. Seen under cover of darkness, at the intersection of public and private spheres, film thus provides opportunities for illicit thrill, with an intrinsic relation to the peepshow. The corollary of this licentiousness is the social control of the licence, as exercised through systems of censorship, and part of the concern of the paper will be to explore the operations of censorship in the domain of film. The material to be discussed here was produced in Germany and France between the 1920s and the 1980s, a period which saw an, albeit intermittent, development towards more liberal censorship regimes in the West. Each of the examples to be discussed arises in different historical and cultural circumstances, creates a different form of scandal, and elicits different modes of control or retribution. What they have in common, however, is their contestation of the boundaries between public and private spheres, licit and illicit acts, social reality and representation. They show how complicated and compromised the legislative management of representations of sexuality has been and continues to be. Current debates over obscenity and censorship, not least around paedophilia, show that these issues are still acutely active in what might appear to be a post-taboo age.

Official certification by the censor is only one element in a network of controlling agencies imposing voluntary or involuntary codes on the production of desire in film. Sexual pleasure is clearly not single or simple, but polymorphous and subject to hierarchical ordering. The regulation of this order, the laws that desire follows or is made to follow, will be illustrated here through a particular attention to sexualities that are constructed as marginal, abject,[1] or outlaw. I will be guided by recent gender and queer theory in suggesting that such sexualities have a particular role to play in revealing the workings of the orders of gender and sexuality at large. Sexuality is understood here as a function of performativity, in the sense developed in particular by the leading feminist and queer theorist Judith Butler. Butler radicalises the constructionist view of sexual identity discussed by Jeffrey Weeks (this volume). For her, sexuality is indeed in the naming, a function of social discourse rather than a natural given, a performance insistently scripted and regulated by cultural codes (contrast the standard biomedical view, Johnson, this volume). In her discussions of social and cultural acts (including acts of filmic representation), she shows both the stringency of the performance codes that govern them and the possibilities they create, in spite of themselves, for forms of counter-performance. If she calls her pioneering book on the subject *Gender Trouble* (Butler, 1990), this is because the regulation in question is both troubling for the desiring subjects who are called upon to perform the laws and, reciprocally, for the legal acts which are invested with the power to govern their performance. To adopt and adapt the terms used by Lynne Segal (this volume), Butler sees sexuality as both battleground and playground: a site of political contest and trouble making that is also one of pleasurably subversive performance.

Homosexuality plays a privileged role in revealing the sexual trouble with the law. In his *History of Sexuality*, Foucault highlights homosexuality as a paradigm for the operation of the law in particular and the dialectical functions of discourse in general. The 'unnatural act', where law stakes its authority as the law of nature, is at once a key focus for instrumental correction and a model form of the sort of 'stumbling-block' that provides 'a point of resistance and a starting point for an opposing strategy.' (Foucault, 1990: 101). Before the emergence of new psychiatric and other discourses in the nineteenth century, homosexuality is at once subject to drastic punishment and yet, because unspeakable, tolerated in peculiar ways, not least within military and legal institutions. When it comes to be more speakable for the law, it is at once subject to more extensive control and yet also provided with a discourse that can be mobilised against that control. The trial and imprisonment of Oscar Wilde establishes a model for this dialectical working of the law in a heightened mode of performance. The film

---

[1] The term abject is used here in the sense developed by Kristeva (1982) to denote the unpalatable excess that is at once the cause and the subversive effect of systems of law.

material to be considered here follows Wilde's example in being divided between the melancholia of punishment and loss of agency and the theatre of resistance.

In order to investigate the legislation of desire as performed in film, I will consider three films which focus in different ways on a particularly acute clinch between sex and the law, a place where law appears to conspire in the production of the illicit or outlaw: gay sex in prison. Prison is at once designed, as part of its punitive regime, to enforce sexual abstinence (following the normative assumption that sex is heterosexual) and yet creates a potentially promiscuous environment for sexual adventure and experiment of another kind. The law is constantly twisted in its dealings with this transgression of its own making. The recent debates in the UK over condom provision in prison expose this legal paradox only too clearly. Attention has been drawn, in particular, to the difficulty produced by a law that allows homosexuality between consenting adults in private when transposed into an environment that isolates offenders from the public, but one without normal standards of privacy, always under the potential 'public' eye of the warder, with or without the consent of the internee.[2]

As a more or less hidden site of law that is also under acute surveillance, prison provides a place for public punishment and more private desires to become confused, a place for open secrets. It thus qualifies as a heterotopian site, in Foucault's sense, a place at once located outside the normative domain, defined as other to it, and yet representing, and so contesting, its structures in inverted fashion (Foucault, 1986). Prisons are designed to imitate the controls of the social order, but in an absolute, panoptical form. In fact, they are sites of secret disorder with implications for the world outside, as is evident not least in the possibility that the transgression of homosexuality might be something approaching the rule in them. In the structure of the cell, closed off and yet fitted with a peephole, the prison environment converges with two models of public-private viewing: the peep-show booth and the closet. As we will see, prison films have a tendency to exploit the exhibitionist and secretive potentials of these two models, often in ambiguous combination.

The alluring threat which gay sex represents for the homosocial order and its institutions might be illustrated by a whole range of filmic examples, from the soap-dropping cliché of prison showers to more complex and challenging representations. My examples, taken from the more sexually dissident end of the spectrum, are: the 1928 silent melodrama *Geschlecht in Fesseln* (Sex in Chains), by Wilhelm, later William, Dieterle; the wilfully anachronistic black-and-white silent of 1950 *Un Chant d'amour* (A Song of Love) by cult queer author Jean Genet; and the technicolored but noirish *Querelle* of 1982, Fassbinder's last film, based on a novel by Genet. What I aim to show is how these films find ways of

---

[2] See Baroness Walmsley's contention in the second reading of the Sexual Offences Bill in the House of Lords (Lords Hansard 13 February 2003, Column 868) that a prison cell should be deemed 'a private place' for the purposes of the Bill.

considering the law from a deviant perspective. If the term queer is, as Alice Kuzniar has pointed out, etymologically related to the German 'quer' (Kuzniar, 2000: 6), suggesting a skewed or transverse angle on things, then the three films can be said to look more or less queerly at the authority of legal acts in the control of sexual ones.

1. SEXUALITY IN CHAINS: *GESCHLECHT IN FESSELN*

While the films by Genet and Fassbinder represent the taboo subject of sex between men in prison in provocatively explicit ways, *Geschlecht in Fesseln*, notwithstanding its graphic title (suggesting the capture of genital physicality as well as sex in a more conceptual sense) is cast in the constraining and obscuring chains of the censorship of its time. Its queer look at imprisonment is necessarily more oblique than that of the later two films. In order to trace its engagement with the law, I will rely as much on the screenplay,[3] with its amendments and erasures, and the documents of the film's censorship history, as on the relatively sanitised finished form that it came to take.

The plot of *Geschlecht in Fesseln* follows a standard melodramatic pattern of the breakdown of the domestic framework. It tells the story of an unemployed man named Sommer who is imprisoned when he challenges and accidentally kills a man who has been molesting his wife. In prison, the inmates are tormented by enforced sexual abstinence, which expresses itself in a series of 'perverse' forms, including homosexuality. The protagonist becomes involved with a young prisoner. Meanwhile his wife, no less tormented by their separation, enters into an affair with her husband's ex-cellmate, who, after his release, campaigns for penal reform and in particular conjugal rights for prisoners. The film ends with the husband's release and the exposure of the two affairs; unable to resume their relationship, husband and wife commit suicide together.

The film belongs to the genre of the sexual education film (in German, the 'Aufklärungsfilm'), which became well established internationally in the 1920s, not least as part of the libertarian tendency in the culture of the Weimar Republic. The new genre enabled a potent combination of two of the cinema's distinguishing appeals: voyeuristic attraction and enlightened demonstration.[4] Many of these films, dealing with subjects like STIs, birth control, abortion, and homosexuality, became objects of censorship. The vehicle of cinematic melodrama that they generally adopted was designed to achieve full emotional effect for the reformist message, as well as giving the films a more amenable guise for the legal authorities. Combining perceived sexual obscenity with challenges to a range of articles of socio-sexual law, they represented a dual threat, and a

---

[3] The director's copy of the screenplay is held in the archive of the Berlin Filmmuseum.
[4] For an account of the phenomenon in Weimar Germany, see Hagener (2001). Dyer (1990) discusses perhaps the most famous German example of the genre, Oswald's film about homosexuality, *Anders als die andern* (1919).

slippery one, for the censors: in the educational context, framed by discourses of medicine and social welfare, the boundaries of the obscene resist the conventional definitions.

As Annette Kuhn has shown in her Foucauldian study of the regulation of early 'health propaganda' films in Britain, works in the genre of *Geschlecht in Fesseln* expose in a particularly acute way 'the institutional practices, powers and knowledges which organise the sexual within and beyond these films, and which are involved in their construction as objects of censorship.' (Kuhn, 1988: 10). The censorship history of *Geschlecht in Fesseln* certainly illustrates the ideological organisation of sexual knowledge and, in particular, its importance for the *Kulturkampf* between liberal and reactionary interests that was conducted over film censorship in the Weimar Republic. The first level of intervention is self-censorship. The fairly explicit treatment of homosexual relations in the original text of the screenplay is toned down by a series of alterations;[5] thus, where in a bathroom scene in the original conception the naked chests of the protagonist and his lover rubbed against each other, the former remains fully dressed in the corrected version and only gets to stroke the young man's head. Whatever the grounds for a series of corrections of this type written into the script, they certainly anticipate the official acts of censorship. While the film was released in 1928 in more or less unadulterated form, it met with forceful demands for censorship. The journal *Filmtechnik* (24 November 1928) reports an official complaint by a Nationalist Member of the Prussian State Parliament that the filmmakers had been allowed to shoot this 'deeply offensive' and tendentious film in state institutions. In fact, only external shots of a Berlin penitentiary were used. When the Bavarian Ministry of Justice, acting on local complaints, made representations that the film should be banned, the more liberally inclined 'Filmoberprüfstelle' (Principal Film Classification Office) in Berlin responded in January 1930 by requiring that certain sections of the film, including the scene in which the young prisoner climbs onto Sommer's bed and embraces him, should be cut before a new certificate could be issued.[6] The judgement stresses that film dramas cannot be expected to conform absolutely to the paragraphs of the penal code; that is, it recognises the ability of film to achieve a degree of free play in its performance of the law. The charge that the

---

[5] Dieterle's copy of the script, with annotations, is held in the collection of the Filmmuseum Berlin.

[6] The 'Filmoberprüfstelle' is still guided by Weimar liberal tendencies. It acknowledges the 'tact' (for which read self-censorship) with which the potentially offensive topics of the film have been handled. The Bavarian authorities later complained that the text of the judgement had been released for verbatim publication in the journal *Filmkurier*, suggesting that the 'Filmoberprüfstelle' was thereby colluding with anti-government tendencies. Much of the press coverage of the film (e.g. the review in *Welt am Montag* (29 October 1928) or that in *Kinematograph* (27 February 1929)) welcomed its challenge to established ideas. The formulation of the film's 'unspeakable' homosexual content, ranging from the time-honoured epithet of the unnatural to more euphemistic descriptions, provides a barometer of ideological judgement in this pivotal period in German history. The documents are included on the website of the Deutsches Filminstitut Frankfurt as part of their series on censorship.

film might have been shot in a real prison indicates something of the ability of a hybrid work like *Geschlecht in Fesseln*, mixing documentary campaigning with fiction, to perform an act that transgresses and thereby exposes the law, not least Paragraph 175 of the German penal code, which forbids any 'unnatural sex act committed between persons of male sex'.[7]

This relative performative freedom is, however, only acquired in a contract with censorship (both internal and external to the film's production), and its licence is provisional. The application from the Bavarian Ministry of the Interior illustrates how questions of sexual decency become embroiled with broader ideological issues, most notably here the representation of the law as brutal and counter-productive and of religion and politics as complicit in this brutality. This also anticipates the grounds for the banning of the film by the Bavarian National Socialist authorities in 1933, when it appears in a list of films of 'sexual tendency' that are subsumed under the heading of films with 'Communist, Marxist, and pacifist content'. The fact that amongst the list of mainly sexual educational films there is also Pabst's version of Brecht and Weill's *Threepenny Opera*, and that the list appears alongside films like Eisenstein's *Battleship Potemkin* and Dudow's *Kuhle Wampe* in the list of those 'of Communist tendency', shows that sexual and revolutionary political tendencies are bracketed for the purposes of National Socialist ideology. Films about STIs, fertility, or naturism are all seen as posing a political threat to the 'natural' rule of law.

As well as attracting the full force of the law, the socio-sexual propaganda film found subversive ways of exposing the weakness of its logic at these points of excessive legislation. The principal mode for this exposure in *Geschlecht in Fesseln* is the implicit representation of incarceration as a type of second-order closeting. As Alice Kuzniar has suggested, the film follows a visual code whereby 'the opening and closing of doors and (prison) gates suggest the closet and its misery.' (Kuzniar, 2000: 41).[8] It seems likely that some of the prisoners in the shared cell have fallen foul of Paragraph 175. And the protagonist comes to join them in that transgression at the centre of the legal system of surveillance and correction, in the blind spot that it creates for itself through the regime of incarceration. What is unclear here is whether the representation of homosexuality is an intrinsic part of a more general reform agenda or whether it is instrumentalised, along with representations of suicidal despair, nymphomania, and fetishism, to show the sort of unnatural disorder that enforced sexual abstinence can lead to. The prison serves as a suitably ambivalent site for the film's performance of a challenge to the law: the film takes its enactment of transgression into the very institution of law, but thereby also signals the constraint that the performance is under.

---

[7] Paragraph 175 was introduced in 1871, came under pressure for reform in the Weimar Republic, and was brutally imposed under the Nazi regime.

[8] One case of the opening of doors is, literally, that of Sommer's closet, where his wife finds his clothes to fondle in his absence, rather than the secret of his homosexuality.

The film's representation of the prison as closet is focused on an architecture of confinement at once real and symbolic, one which proves however to be permeable. The prison is constructed on the panoptical model, as emphasised by the scene in the parade ground where the prisoners circulate beneath the tower under the watchful gaze of the guards. However, one young prisoner almost succeeds in mutilating himself in that scene, and kills himself with a gun grabbed from a guard in a later scene. The panopticon has blind spots.

Acts 2–5 all open with an establishing shot of the prison walls, the repetition emphasising the immured condition of the prisoners and the law which controls them. Bars function as a leitmotif, casting their shadows over the *mise-en-scène* both within the prison and in the world outside. At the same time, this architecture corresponds to what the *Filmkurier* brochure for the film calls the 'wall of disgust' which intervenes between Sommer and his wife, but is also internalised by him: the 'disgust' he experiences at the young prisoner's advances turns into self-abjection ('disgusted by himself') when he comes under the sway of homosexual desire and is unable to touch his wife.[9] Abjection works here as contagion (compared elsewhere in the screenplay to poison) and introduces a system of boundaries which are figured through a sort of touch-taboo. It is telling that the washroom is a key site for the film's development of the homosexual relationship, a place that enacts the cleansing logic of the prison but, through the physical exposure between men that is necessary for ablution, also provokes a return of the abject in the form of homoerotic desire. This primal scene for prisons and their fantasy life returns with the same slippery logic in the two other films.[10] And the logic extends to the walls. While the prison walls and bars are designed to mark the secure boundaries of the abject for the social order, abjection is shown to be a more invasive and uncontrollable condition. The prison walls act on the one hand as a sort of screen for heterosexual film fantasy, a place to pin images of starlets and for Sommer to graffiti a picture of his wife that is then animated by his imagination. The wall sustains the mind-screen images of the characters, and thus contributes to a pervasive structural effect of *mise-en-abyme*, of reflection upon film-making and -viewing, within the film.[11] But the heterosexual projections become confused with the homosexual, which in turn involves a queering of gender difference. In the screenplay, the young prisoner sees his own, homoerotic fantasies projected onto the ceiling, captured amongst the shadows of the window-bars.[12] And the naked female figure conjured up by Sommer in Act 5 is superimposed upon his own body. What this relay of scenes reveals is a performative logic controlling the orders of

---

[9] Screenplay, 34 & 57.

[10] In *Un Chant d'amour*, one of the paraded prisoners masturbates as he soaps himself, and in *Querelle* Vic washes himself provocatively in front of Querelle as foreplay to his murder.

[11] This is signalled at the start when Sommer is employed as a street-photographer, and one shot has the camera pointed at the spectator. The publicity card handed to passers-by, telling them that they have just been filmed, thus also interpellates the spectator into the conditions of the film.

[12] Screenplay, 54.

gender and sexuality. Much of the sexual interaction between the inmates is figured as theatrical impersonation, with performances of femininity (Sommer's wife's handkerchief adopted as a fetish), and Sommer coming to mimic in spite of himself the lascivious expression of the older prisoner marked as a sexual degenerate. If the young prisoner who is driven to suicide is diagnosed as a 'Simulant' by the prison doctor, this suggests a perverse theatre of sexual frustration and imitation, where the performance—as in the case of the suicide—is enacted as real.

If the prison cell is indeed understandable as a second order closet, then its function is profoundly ambivalent: the turning queer of the fantasy film-theatre projected within it seems to want to be read as a negative effect of the unnatural state of the law—a perverse and unreal performance, but it might also be readable as the release of a repressed sexuality, an underlying natural reality, which could only emerge in the intensely homosocial condition of imprisonment. This fundamental ambivalence of the screening space provided by internment is a feature that, as we shall see, recurs in the other two films.

2. CAUGHT IN THE ACT: *UN CHANT D'AMOUR*

Un Chant d'amour was made as an underground film, shot in 16mm, what Jane Giles calls 'the experimental, porn and home movie format of that time' (Giles, 1991: 18). The interests of the avant-gardist, of the pornographer, and of the home viewer are thus combined here. As with the 'Aufklärungsfilm', this generic hybridity, cast between art-house and pornography, cinema as public and private medium, renders the film a challenging object for the censors. The film was intended for select audiences, with special aesthetic and sexual interests, in private viewings. It has never had general release, and its limited distribution history is marked by acts of ad hoc censorship, with drastic interventions by authorities ranging from the NYPD to Hull City Council. The uncertified screening of 1964 in New York is particularly telling in its exposure of the business of censorship. The police raided the premises, brutalised and imprisoned the organiser, and informed him 'that he deserved to be shot in front of the cinema screen for "dirtying America"' (Giles, 1991: 25). Censorship here follows the circular logic of abjection: dirt is to be excluded not only by being locked away but also by being subjected to a dirty act of public violence. The punishment for the moral pollutant is to be turned into another kind of cinematic spectacle to be paraded before the screen, one motivated by the desire for obscene violence. The censorship fantasy imitates its object in a specific and profoundly ironic way. In the scenario of the film, the prison warder, excited by the teasing sexual displays of the prisoners in their cells, beats one of them with his belt and puts a revolver in his mouth. Not for nothing is the warder recurrently caught under the sign 'murder' as he spies on the inmates. In the manner of many a queer hate crime, the punishment shooting, given orally, is thus a violent reworking of the scenario of 'obscenity'. I have no record of what members of Hull Council might have had in mind when they banned the screening in the city's Film Theatre, this in the context of Clause 28.

Un Chant d'amour is a variation on scenarios familiar from Genet's novels and dramas. The prison provides a suitable setting for his obsessive interest in the sexual act, specifically the homosexual one, as an enactment of power relations through fantasies of subordination. He developed several other film scripts on the same basis, one titled *Le Bagne* (The Penal Colony), what he calls a 'pederast drama' set in a version of Devil's Island, and another *Le Langage de la muraille: cent ans jour après jour* (The Language of the Wall: Day after Day for a Hundred Years), based on his own experiences of punishment and erotic community in the Mettray borstal.[13] As the title of the borstal film suggests, imprisonment has two key features for Genet: the wall as at once separating the prisoners and holding them in together, and coming thereby to be invested with sadomasochistic libido; and a structure of extreme repetition over time, an iterative regime which is reflected in Genet's obsessive return to prison in his works, the structure of serial crime being transferred into a more general seriality of punishment and of desire. With *Un Chant d'amour*, this involves a logic which follows that of the proto-cinematic apparatus of the peep-show, as the warder moves from one cell key-hole to the next,[14] from attraction to attraction, with the prisoners performing their exhibitionistic sex acts. The panoptical regime of prison surveillance is turned to more illicit viewing here. In a trick shot, when the warder's eye is first seen looking through the spy-hole it is turned upside down, figured as inverted by a visual pun. The inversion of the surveillant eye stands for a more general exposure of the prison as *ordo inversus*. This deviant viewing might itself be subject to punishment, as indeed it was in the scripts of both *Le Bagne* and *Le Langage de la muraille*, where the voyeuristic warder is caught in the act by the prisoner, who pushes a needle through the peep-hole into his eye.

The wall comes to have a language, following the title of the borstal film, in various ways. As Jane Giles has noted, it works dialectically: designed to withhold desire, it in fact elicits it (Giles, 1991: 11). In a more developed fashion than in *Geschlecht in Fesseln*, the walled enclosure can be understood as a counter-construct to the closet. It combines claustrophobia with the perverse possibility of claustrophilia. In his discussion of Genet and film, Richard Dyer has suggested that it represents a fundamental ambivalence:

---

[13]   As the borstal establishes the prison for Genet as a cultic site, a place of perverse, ritual attachment and martyric sainthood, so Foucault describes a scene which he sees as the sacramental inauguration of the modern mode of 'carceral' discipline, the making of the 'first penitentiary saint', when the last words of a child who dies at Mettray are a lament at having to leave it so soon (Foucault, 1991: 293).

[14]   If Genet doubtless derived this perspective from his own experience, the peephole is also an interfilmic quotation from Cocteau's *Le Sang d'un poète* (1930).

> 'Yoking together desire and confinement (in a literal prison or the prison of masculinity and taboo sexuality) may be seen to make a point about the repression of homosexuality or else to make confinement one of the conditions making homosexual pleasure possible' (Dyer, 1990: 99).

Certainly this version of the closet has, following Eve Sedgwick (1991), its own epistemology. On the one hand it is a site of inscription: graffiti (especially phallic and floral) features here, as in so many of Genet's narratives, as an investment of the wall with the desires and aggressions of the imprisoned. The prison's version of the closet produces primitive acts of writing and drawing as notes towards the song of the film's title and so towards Genet's project of writing and film-making in the tradition of Wilde's *Ballad of Reading Gaol*. The graffitied symbols from the pack of cards represent the idea of a game of chance within a system of apparently total control, and the arrow through the heart symbolises the eroticisation of imprisonment. It also establishes a correspondence with the tattoo which a young prisoner fondles: the fetishistic marking of the skin implies a metonymic construction of the wall, with its pictures and inscriptions, as a second skin. The wall is yearningly embraced by the prisoners, a penis is played against it, the prisoners signal through it by knocking and smoke is ardently exchanged through a hole in the wall between two neighbouring cells. Yet it is in the character of such communication of smoke and other signals to be ambiguous. There are codes that govern the exchange of such signs: the language of walls and the body, graffiti and tattoos, is regulated, but also open to misconstrual. The oral exchange of smoke between the two prisoners is suddenly curtailed and provokes the intervention of the warder who has been spying for us through another hole. The lyrical exchange of secret bodily communications leads to a violent punishment. Genet recognises in his *Miracle de la rose* that the codes can easily be jumbled and so produce contrary effects. As Giles notes, when he engraved the words 'tattooed Jean' in the cell wall they read instead as 'tortured Jean' (Giles, 1991: 59); the erotic display achieved by a controlled, aesthetic piercing of the skin is turned into a more irredeemable suffering of violence.

The eroticisation of the prison walls and the incorporation of the warder into the homoerotic network of those he guards also allows the film to free itself, in fantasy, from its containment.[15] Two fantasy sequences are released, one apparently belonging to the warder, who becomes a protagonist in a series of erotic clinches between two naked male bodies, the second to the two neighbouring prisoners who are liberated into a woodland romance. The film thus appears to become the song of love it purports to be. In fact, though, it remains an ambiguous combination of different forms of fantasy: lyrical and murderous. As it moves between and combines fantasies which apparently belong to the guard

---

[15] As Dyer has pointed out, this containment also works on the level of shot construction. Until its final shot, the cinematic 'song of love' follows a tightly symmetrical patterning that could be compared to poetic composition (Dyer, 1990: 50–4).

and the prisoners, it fundamentally questions the position open to, or imprisoning, the viewer. In the figure of the warder as outlaw, the film creates a provocative representation of the ambivalence which attaches to such cinematic sex acts: how do we as viewers legislate in the act of viewing which is primarily aligned with that voyeuristic figure's masturbatory and ultimately sadistic pleasure-seeking? It is a film that, in its confusion of sex and violence, the legal and the criminal, the private and the public, involves its most liberal viewer in uncomfortable questions of the ethics of censorship. In that sense, it works performatively on the viewer, asking for us to pronounce it and our viewing of it acceptable or not.

Just as censorship can only work by constitutionally breaking its own laws (censors always have to see what will be deemed unfit to be seen) so the viewer is caught here in acts of self-censorship that can only be based upon a licensed act of transgression. Genet himself performs a mirror image of this legal double bind in his response to the awarding of a prize to pay for the film to be restored for exhibition. Seeing this as a ruse by the legislators to lure him into acknowledging their power to apply censorship, the outlaw auteur insists upon his own legal rights of ownership and the power to perform an act of total self-censorship by refusing to allow the film to be certified for release. In his *Journal du voleur*, Genet famously defines his dissidence as arising from a form of discipline, in complicity with the false charges made against him. The criminal becomes criminal, outlaw or abject, when acknowledging that he is being named as such by the law.[16] That is, following Butler's Althusserian theory of performativity, the legal interpellation of the subject demands recognition and thereby achieves its performative effect. When Genet refuses to be interpellated by the law precisely by calling upon its authority ('it's the law'),[17] he nicely shows the room for relative freedom which can be achieved by the canny outlaw. He cannot rewrite the law as such, but he can undertake acts of what Dollimore has called 'transgressive reinscription' of his licence as subject to it (Dollimore, 1991: 318–19). By maintaining the legal status of the film as private property,[18] Genet seeks to hold on to the subversive power of exposing the law as fundamentally compromised, rendered perverse and violent in response to the queerness and the violence that it would seek to contain.

---

[16] 'I felt within me the need to become what I had been accused of being [. . .] the coward, traitor, thief, fairy they saw in me.' (Genet, 1967: 145).

[17] See Giles (1991: 28) for an account of this appeal to the law.

[18] In *The Thief's Journal*, Genet described how in acts of theft he also performs the presence of the absent proprietor: 'I am steeped in an idea of property while I loot property' (Genet, 1967: 129).

3. BEHIND BARS, AGAINST THE WALL: *QUERELLE*

Fassbinder's *Querelle*, based on the Genet novel *Querelle de Brest*, also has a clear interfilmic relationship to *Un Chant d'amour*.[19] No less than Genet's film, *Querelle* is what Thomas Elsaesser calls 'very private but international art cinema' (Elsaesser, 1989: 311), establishing a particular form of art-house aesthetics for the representation of a sexual fantasy plot designed for a special interest audience. Like *Un Chant d'amour*, *Querelle* is enclosed in the symbolic fantasy space of the prison as counter-closet, and here too, as Elsaesser notes, the 'closed sets' also create the effect of 'peep-show cubicles' (Elsaesser, 1996: 297). The film thus heightens the sense of entrapment that characterises Fassbinder's cinematic aesthetics, a 'way of seeing' which, as Dyer argues, 'pins characters down in static takes, traps them between compositional bars' (Dyer, 1980: 58). Specifically, in *Querelle*, Fassbinder seeks what he calls a 'surrealisation' of Genet's landscape, one organised around the defining figure of the wall, used here as a kind of screen, at once enclosing the filmic space and providing a site for projection (Fassbinder, 1992: 169–70). While the novel and the screenplay both feature Genet's home ground of the prison as a key location, the film disperses the idea of imprisonment across the whole *mise-en-scène*. The ubiquitous obscene graffiti is a signature for this and establishes a particular intertextual connection to Genet's film.[20] And if the phallus and the wall are brought into contact, in both bodily and pictorial form, in *Un Chant d'amour*, here the eroticisation of enclosure, a recurrent feature of the Genet novel, is marked more drastically in the protuberant phallic shaping of the town wall.

The navy boat docked in Brest is figured as a sort of prison ship or slave galley,[21] attached to a penal colony, both under constant surveillance by officers and policemen. The boat travelling from colony to colony, brothel to brothel, is for Foucault the heterotopia *par excellence*, a counter-cultural site which relates to the order of culture, its laws and rites 'in such a way as to suspect, neutralise, or invert the set of relations that they happen to designate, mirror, or reflect.' (Foucault, 1986: 27, 24). The prison ship at once reflects and inverts the social institution of law, a place of hyper-surveillance and of hyper-transgression. Not for nothing does Monika Treut (1994) describe this at once closely watched and marshalled and violently transgressive homosocial regime as 'a claustrophobic, frozen environment of male paranoia'. Many of the key scenes are shot underground in the abandoned bagnio, a place of performance with the trappings of

---

[19] In an interview for the journal *Filmfaust* (quoted in the publicity brochure from Scotia Filmverleih), Fassbinder is somewhat coy about the degree of the influence.

[20] The film is recurrently shot through panes of glass, those of the brothel etched with floral designs and others with phallic graffiti. Thus Genet's configuration of the phallus and the flower is iconographically displayed in Fassbinder's reading of his work.

[21] In Genet's novel, Lieutenant Seblon, who commands the *Vengeur*, fantasises himself in the role of captain of a convict ship (Genet, 1953: 235).

Behind bars: Querelle and Mario in the bagnio. Photograph courtesy of bfi Collections and the Fassbinder Foundation.

an S/M dungeon. The film follows Genet's novel in incorporating the penal institution into the stylised, theatrical architecture of its set.[22] The location indicates something of the paradox that regulates the criminological system of *Querelle*: the fugitive hides out in the law's site of confinement. This form of open enclosure, shot either through bars from outside or from inside with the shadows of the bars prominent, is projected onto other focal spaces of the film, the ship, the glass-walled brothel, and the pissoir. The paradox of open confinement, resting on a confusion of the public and the private, is constitutive for the film. While Querelle eludes the law after murdering an accomplice in his opium dealing, he is marked out, as the screenplay has it, as under arrest.[23] And, as in *Un Chant d'amour*, the agents of the law are also on the side of the criminal, with the policeman Mario and the brothel-keeper Nono playing double roles. Nono, who has a history as a legionnaire in a prison academy, is also present at police interrogations and acts as an intermediary when Querelle turns informer. Mario, dressed in a leather mock-up of a police uniform, is twice

[22] The bagnio is an archetypal homoerotic fantasy location with a pedigree stretching from Mirbeau and Kafka to the book and film *Papillon*. In Genet/Fassbinder's version of the bagnio the fantasy scenes of the penal colony, the gaol, the brothel, and the bathhouse are combined.

[23] Screenplay, 60. The screenplay is held in the archive of the Berlin Filmmuseum.

described as 'part of the furniture' in the brothel. In this leather scene uniform,[24] he seduces the criminal Querelle, whilst in his detective garb in the police station he conducts interrogation by performing linguistically the obscene acts attributed to the criminal. Like Genet's warder, or Lieutenant Seblon, who furtively leaves his sexual graffiti in the public toilets of Brest, the cop is both the authorised surveillant and, through complicity in transgression, a figure of what Genet calls 'abjection' (Genet, 1953: 230).

Just as Genet, the auteur, subjects the band of criminal acquaintances he assembles to play the parts in his film to his direction and claims the ownership of the resulting work, the fantasies of domination and subjection which feature in Fassbinder's film also extend to his auteurist performance of authority. The actors record the extraordinary control that he imposed upon them, on occasion to the point of violence.[25] In the publicity brochure, the director claims that he never makes them do anything they would not wish to do, but the consensual character of the acts is open to question. If Fassbinder subtitles his film 'A Pact with the Devil', this might be construed as extending to the authorial pact he undertakes with respect to Genet, signing the film off with an autographed letter of Genet's. This is Genet as novelist and director *maudit*, whose cult of sexual violence is that of the perverse anti-saint and who controls the Sadean fantasies that are played out in his works. Querelle, described by one intertitle as artist and author, and figured as a sublime criminal, is, it seems, the embodiment of the pact of queer desire against conventional morality that Fassbinder enters into with Genet.

The two directors, both men of the theatre, share an attachment to the performative as the mode of film-making. On the one hand this involves the authority invested in the director as auteur, the legislator on the film-set, pronouncing what has to be done. The filmic acts that are thus prescribed are always marked as acts in a double sense. They have the drastically physical character of the real act as well as the theatrical character of pure performance. The stylisation of the film's *mise-en-scène*, with costumes in the style of stage acts from Zarah Leander or Marlene Dietrich to The Village People,[26] the extreme shaping of the set and the insistent framing, mirroring, screening, and colouring of shots, constantly exposes the physical clinches and penetrations of the figures as performance. Fighting to the death and sexual coupling are precisely choreographed,

---

[24] That the uniform also plays on the performance of the costumes of fascism in the leather scene is revealed when Querelle greets Mario with a Nazi salute. Al LaValley describes this 'theater of sex' as an enactment of leather bars which Fassbinder knew like the Anvil in New York (LaValley, 1994: 136). The fascistic character of the display also echoes Genet's preoccupation with Nazism, as when a concentration camp commandant is included in his gallery of criminals in *Querelle de Brest* (Genet: 1953: 16–17). At the same time, it signals Fassbinder's recognition that his film of the Genet text would have to achieve a difficult ethical navigation between fascism and kitsch (Fassbinder, 1986: 191).

[25] Burkhard Driest, who plays Mario and co-wrote the screenplay with Fassbinder, describes this in the publicity brochure.

[26] Dietrich is invoked in *Querelle de Brest* (Genet, 1953: 192).

with the balletic duel between Querelle and his brother played off against the ritual display of the bleeding body of Christ in the Passion procession. The choreographic logic of the film is, like the omnipresent graffiti and the page-like intertitles, evidence of Fassbinder's desire here, as elsewhere, to have his cinema understood as a form of writing.[27] The film, as he says in the publicity brochure, is designed to be read like a book. Cinematography, choreography, and iconography are all carefully designed to create a form of visual text and thereby to elicit a more readerly and ideologically aware form of viewing. Like Genet, he seeks to rewrite the laws of conventional morality through his queer travesty of them and thereby to make the viewer read them critically.

The performative logic applies, in particular, to the film's questioning of gender identities and sexual acts: whether to perform a given sexual act or gender role is to be the identity that it is taken to represent. The action is organised around polarised identity labels like stallion, queen, and fairy that seem to mark a hypostatic binary order of gender and sexual identities, but these are pervasively undermined or queered in performance. Not for nothing does the *mise-en-scène* of *Querelle* recurrently focus on the cabaret act as travesty. Gil is said to sing in the style of a 'little girl', while Jeanne Moreau, in the role of Lysiane, performs a song with lyrics from *The Ballad of Reading Gaol* in the manner of a drag artist, as a second order gender impersonation.[28] As Alice Kuzniar has argued, the film's performance of genders and sexualities is profoundly ambiguous (Kuzniar, 2000: 74–9). And the relationships of power that are enacted in them follow a slippery, dialectical logic. As in Judith Butler's reading of the film *Paris is Burning*, drag cabaret provides a model for the questioning of acts of gender for their constructedness, but one which is also tightly bound to the constructions in question as well as to other forms of social category, like class and race (Butler, 1993: 121–40). What emerges is a complex interplay of what Butler calls the appropriation and the subversion of the dominant ideology.

Both *Un Chant d'amour* and *Querelle* cross their fantasy performances of sexuality with those of race, and both work at once to appropriate the dominant ideological configuration of those categories (the black man as heterosexually hyper-virile) and to subvert it. In Genet's film, the author's obsession with negritude as a corollary of queer transgression is reflected in the incorporation of a dancing black prisoner in the sequence of exhibitions.[29] The sequence appeals to the idea of the primal physicality of the black man, but the penis he exposes swings detumescent in the dance, in a film that is not otherwise coy about showing erections. And after subjecting himself to penetration by Nono, Querelle emerges blacked up in soot, in imitation of the black man, married but only

---

[27] For further discussion of Fassbinder's idea of film as text to be read, see Webber (2000).

[28] For second order we should in fact read third. As Butler has shown, drag is the copy of what is already a copy: the routine heteronormative performance of gender (Butler, 1990).

[29] Gayatri Spivak has suggested that this figure represents an image of sexuality 'outside of the fantasy of coupling' and thus the power relations of the film (cited by Dyer, 1990: 88).

interested in gay sex, who has mastered him.[30] Querelle adopts a subaltern appearance, doing dirty work he does not have to do, but then proceeds to engage in a dialectical power game with Lieutenant Seblon, a master-slave exchange following a rhythm of what might be called subalternation, implying both subordination and succession by turn. The slave masters the master by blacking up as slave and insisting on returning to his fellow-slaves, rather than consorting with him. Black here stands for a crossing of submission with domination in the combined relations of power and desire. Race and rank are at once established orders which are replayed in the sexual performances of the film and also laid open to queer disordering.

Like the prisoners on exhibition in Genet's film, the apparently submissive part in the act—the exhibitionist, the masochist, or the penetrated—can be figured as having control of the performance. Fassbinder provocatively lists amongst the *dramatis personae* of his film a set of photographs, pornographic shots of a female figure—Paulette—who never appears as a live presence in the film, but is represented as a transgender impersonation by her brother Robert. The performer of the Paulette figure is thus actively credited for that performance, but only through the photographs. The performance is purely virtual and is fixed in subjection to the gaze of those that handle the photos, supposedly as criminal evidence, in the course of the film.[31] By the interpolation of these images, Fassbinder strategically elides the boundaries between art and pornography as modes of performance, confusing the aesthetic scene with the 'ob-scene'. But the agency that is given to the pornographic performance artist in this process is clearly a limited one.

Performance is always liable to be reduced to imprisonment in set-piece acts. In one scene, which is included in the screenplay for *Querelle* but not incorporated in the final form of the film, a group of construction workers perform one of the most hackneyed of homophobic routines by appealing to the prison fantasy of the danger of dropping the soap in the showers. By referring to this as a 'number',[32] they suggest that it is an act that can be instigated and controlled in its performance by its ostensible victim. What they fail to acknowledge is what drives their own 'number', their linguistic performance of the act. This logic of disavowal is exposed when, in a scene not eventually included in the film, the homophobic performer Theo *plays* Gil as an effeminate, submissive gay who takes too long in the showers.[33] All of the characters in the film are in this sense performing 'numbers'.[34]

---

[30] In *Querelle de Brest*, the protagonist is explicitly cast in the mask of the 'nègre sauvage', the 'wild negro', at this point (Genet, 1953: 78).

[31] This sequence may well quote Welles's *The Trial* and thus the scene in Kafka's novel where the law books turn out to be dirty in more ways than one.

[32] Screenplay, 11.

[33] Ibid., 47–8.

[34] Querelle is also described by Nono as a 'hot little number'.

In the context of this queer fantasy film, identity is at once brutally enforced and radically relativised as a construct of performance. The film follows Genet's novel in interrogating the ideas of sameness and difference through structures of replication. Separate identities are subject to confusion through doubling. Thus, Lysiane desperately tries to find the difference between Querelle and his brother so that she can assert her own identity in relation to their impenetrable narcissistic dyad. The complicity between woman and man, active and passive partner in sex acts, brother and brother or sister, criminal and policeman, officer and marine, raises fundamental questions about ontological status and ethical responsibility. One of the many doubled relationships in this film of mirrors can illustrate this. The screenplay describes how Gil, who has been betrayed to the police by Querelle, goes in chains to his execution, his awkward gait reminiscent of 'Querelle's sailor's walk'.[35] That is, he comes to perform the performance that is Querelle's identity, one which is based upon self-impersonation (Querelle wears his cap 'in the style of Querelle').[36] Does an ethos of performativity give licence for the enactment of any form of fantasy scenario and so allow the mock-execution of anal sex to be judged in the same way as acts of murder or of capital punishment? In particular, does the performance of anal sex as killing serve to expose the inversion in the laws of decency that has allowed murder to be represented more-or-less freely in film while subjecting this abjected act to extreme censorship?

The case of Querelle, a provocation to normal moral laws, is thus also designed to raise fundamental ethical questions about the rule of law. It sustains Genet's critique of the law as unable to incorporate singularity. The sublimation of the criminal as perpetrator of an art form which follows 'singular laws' is designed, as an allegory of the radically queer, to expose the universalist assumptions of systems of law.[37] Fassbinder takes up this theme of the 'singular laws', which he sees as 'in service of an astonishing mythology' in Genet's texts (Fassbinder, 1992: 169). On this level of mythological fantasy, Fassbinder can be said to look in Genet for the sort of alternative system of laws that would be the basis of a queer nation. The play of sameness and otherness in the enclosed criminal society of Brest explores the paradoxical possibility of queer singularity finding community, following a counter-universal system of perverse laws. It lays down a challenge to the judgement of the viewer, censor or otherwise. To quote the voice of Querelle, objectivity is a necessary condition for 'total moral authority', and the film dismantles any possibility of objective response by incorporating all figures of authority into the subjective regime of fantasy. Not for nothing does Fassbinder see the 'discrepancy between objective plot and subjective fantasy' as the distinguishing feature of the Genet novel (Fassbinder, 1992: 169). The film's insistence upon the logic of performativity at once

[35] Screenplay, 173.

[36] Ibid., p. 6.

[37] Genet writes of the superintendent, that he could not know that each murder obeys 'singular laws' that make of it a work of art (Genet, 1953: 129).

interpellates the viewer, via fantasy, into acts of judgement and suggests that those performative pronouncements are intrinsically compromised.

Inevitably, *Querelle* has provoked strong judgements from mainstream and alternative critics alike. Both feminists and gay activists have, in their different ways, been troubled by the film's appeal to structures of pornography and criminality in a regime between men and dominated by the male gaze. Does the film get beyond the political melancholia which Dyer diagnoses in Fassbinder (Dyer, 1980: 55), the 'vicious circles' which Elsaesser (1980) tracks in his films, or the 'arrestation at the site of suffering' which for Silverman characterises Fassbinder's resistance from the margins to the hegemonic system of male subjectivity (Silverman, 1992: 286)? LaValley (1994) has argued that the film in fact transcends the idea of masochistic-melancholic arrest with a more poly-morphous and anarchic challenge to convention. Ultimately, it is tempting to suggest that these contradictory positions are both right, and therefore wrong, about the film. Like *Paris is Burning*, as read by Butler, this film of drag performances at once repeatedly enacts the coercive power of patriarchal law, showing that it acts to recuperate all that seeks to challenge it, and yet also shows the possibility for the performative dissident to 'outlaw' that law, however provisionally.

This is, indeed, the sort of paradox that applies to all three films considered here, in spite of their evident cultural historical and other differences. They chal-lenge the confinement, both physical and ideological, which is exacted by acts of law, with 'unnatural' acts of their own that follow more 'singular' or queer rules. But they also show, not least in their susceptibility to self-censorship,[38] that to perform an outing of the law, whether in the more assimilatory manner of *Geschlecht in Fesseln* or the more resistant mode of the other two films, is not simply to achieve gay liberation or queer nationhood. Their relationship to the law, its powers and its deficiencies, remains fundamentally ambivalent, and in this they have a telling way of performing the ambivalence that is inherent in the legislation of sexuality, from Paragraph 175 of the Weimar German penal code to the Sexual Offences Act of 2003.

REFERENCES

BUTLER, J, *Gender Trouble: Feminism and the Subversion of Identity* (London/New York, Routledge, 1990).
—— *Bodies that Matter: On the Discursive Limits of 'Sex'* (London/New York, Routledge, 1993).
DOLLIMORE, J, *Sexual Dissidence: Augustine to Wilde, Freud to Foucault* (Oxford, Clarendon Press, 1991).

[38] Though the precise details are uncertain, Fassbinder made substantial cuts in the more provocative sequences of *Querelle*.

DYER, R, 'Reading Fassbinder's Sexual Politics' in T Rayns (ed.), *Fassbinder* (London, BFI, 1980).

—— *Now you See It: Studies on Lesbian and Gay Film* (London/New York, Routledge, 1990).

ELSAESSER, T, 'A Cinema of Vicious Circles', in T Rayns (ed.), *Fassbinder* (London, BFI, 1980).

—— *New German Cinema: A History* (Basingstoke, MacMillan, 1989).

—— *Fassbinder's Germany: History Identity Subject* (Amsterdam, Amsterdam University Press, 1996).

FASSBINDER, RW, *Die Anarchie der Phantasie: Gespräche und Interviews*, ed. Michael Töteberg (Frankfurt a. M., Fischer, 1986).

—— *The Anarchy of the Imagination: Interviews, Essays, Notes* (Baltimore/London, John Hopkins University Press, 1992).

FOUCAULT, M, 'Of Other Spaces' (1986) 16 *Diacritics* 22.

—— *The History of Sexuality: An Introduction*, trans. R Hurley (Harmondsworth, Penguin, 1990).

—— *Discipline and Punish: The Birth of the Prison*, trans. A Sheridan (Harmondsworth, Penguin, 1991).

GENET, J, *Querelle de Brest* (Paris, Gallimard, 1953).

—— *The Thief's Journal*, trans. B Frechtman (Harmondsworth, Penguin, 1967).

GILES, J, *The Cinema of Jean Genet: Un Chant d'amour* (London, BFI, 1991).

HAGEMER, M (ed.), *Geschlecht in Fesseln: Sexualität zwischen Aufklärung und Ausbeutung im Weimarer Kino 1918–1933* (Munich, text und kritik, 2001).

KRISTEVA, J, *Powers of Horror: An Essay on Abjection* (New York, Columbia University Press, 1982).

KUHN, A, *Cinema, Censorship and Sexuality* (London/New York, Routledge, 1988).

KUZNIAR, AA, *The Queer German Cinema* (Stanford, Stanford University Press, 2000).

LAVALLEY, A, 'The Gay Liberation of Rainer Werner Fassbinder: Male Subjectivity, Male Bodies, Male Lovers' (1994) 63 *New German Critique* 109.

SEDGWICK, E, KOSOFSKY, *Epistemology of the Closet* (New York/London, Harvester Wheatsheaf, 1991).

SILVERMAN, K, *Male Subjectivity at the Margins* (New York/London, Routledge, 1992).

TREUT, M, 'Man to Man' (1994) 4 *Sight and Sound* 69.

WEBBER, A, 'Narcissism and Alienation: Mirror-Images in the New German Cinema', in M Brady and H Hughes (eds), *Deutschland im Spiegel seiner Filme* (London, CILT, 2000).

14

The Sexual Abuse of Children

MICHAEL FREEMAN

I FIRST WROTE about the sexual abuse of children 25 years ago (Freeman, 1978). Almost no one else was, certainly in this country. The article was to have formed a chapter of a book, a socio-legal study entitled *Violence In The Home* (Freeman, 1979), but the book was deemed too long, and I readily acceded to excisions: the removal of a chapter on sexual abuse seemed an obvious place to start. Few thought it was a serious problem, even a problem.

It could have been recognised but for too long a discreet veil was drawn over it, a veil that became all the thicker as Freud's explanations/rationalisations took root (Freud, 1933). Its existence was hardly acknowledged. So even when nascent child protection bodies investigated abuse and called for legislation, little or no attention was directed to sexual abuse. Thus, a report of the London SPCC in 1884 referred to 12 cases which concerned 'an evil which is altogether too unmentionable' (London SPCC, 1884, 5–6). A year later, the public was sensitised to the problem of child prostitution, and the age of lawful consent to sexual intercourse for girls was increased from 13 to 16 (Criminal Law (Amendment) Act 1885), but child sexual abuse within the family was not discussed publicly. It was thought to be exclusively a vice of the poor, linked to low intelligence and a product of overcrowded sleeping conditions (Wohl, 1978). Incest did not become a crime until 1908 (Bailey and McCabe, 1979), and when it did there were few prosecutions.

A Royal Commission on Venereal Diseases in 1916 took childhood infection for granted. When gonorrhoea was noticed to be prevalent amongst girls in institutions, a *Lancet* editorial offered a simplistic explanation and simple advice: 'No towels, baths or bedroom chambers should ever be shared by girl children in institutions' (*The Lancet*, 1925). There was not the hint of a suspicion that these girls might have been sexually abused. But, as Carol Smart (1999) has shown, though the orthodoxy may have been innocent transmission 'there were counter-discourses available from within the medical profession itself', mainly from prominent female doctors. She draws attention to the chilling belief, 'reported as "fact" ' in the Report of the Royal Commission, that sex with a virgin could cure a man of venereal disease (a myth that has reappeared in South Africa in the even more frightening context of HIV-infection). As such, of course, it was neither abuse and certainly not rape, but rather 'misdirected medical effort' (Smart, 1999: 397–8).

There were calls for legal reforms in the 1920s and the 1930s. It was the 1990s before these reforms were implemented (Criminal Justice Act 1991). The legal response at the time—and for decades thereafter—was to blame the victim. A remarkable report in 1925 recommended radical reforms, but these met legal resistance (Departmental Committee, 1925). Had it been implemented, it would have put this country in the forefront of the fight against sexual abuse, but it outraged the legal establishment which, Smart rightly characterises, saw childhood as a phase of both resilience and insignificance.

> Children did not matter in this scheme of things, at least the working class girls they were likely to see did not matter. On the other hand men . . . did matter; they were recognised as legal subjects (Smart, 1999: 403).

When, more than 60 years later, the Butler-Sloss report looked forward to a time when children would be persons in their own right, not merely objects of concern (Cleveland Inquiry, 1988: 245), what may have been overlooked was that in relation to sexual abuse they had hardly become even objects of concern until the events which triggered the inquiry.

WHAT IS SEXUAL ABUSE?

Child sexual abuse takes many forms (Faller, 1988: 12–16). There is non-contact sexual abuse ('sexy-talk', exposure and voyeurism). There is sexual contact, which includes any touching of the intimate body parts and frottage. There is oral-genital sex (most commonly fellatio). There is sexual penetration, which may be digital (sometimes as a prelude to sexual intercourse), use objects or involve the penis entering the vagina or anus. There is also inter-femoral intercourse, in which the perpetrator's penis is placed between the child victim's thighs (where the vaginal opening is too small or to avoid pregnancy). It is usual now to include forms of sexual exploitation within the abuse concept (child pornography and child prostitution). From the perspective of the perpetrator these may be different—the motive is financial gain rather than sexual gratification—but as far as the victim is concerned the activities may be at least as invasive and destructive.

The official definition of sexual abuse (Department of Health, *Working Together*, 2000: 6) is

> forcing or enticing a child or young person to take part in sexual activities, whether or not the child is aware of what is happening. The activities may involve physical contact, including penetrative (e.g. rape or buggery) and non-penetrative acts. They may include non-contact activities, such as involving children in looking at, or in the production of, pornographic material or watching sexual activities or encouraging children to behave in sexually inappropriate ways.

This is more comprehensive than that produced in the same publication in 1991: 'Actual or likely sexual exploitation of a child or adolescent. The child may be dependant or emotionally immature' (*Working Together*, 1991: 49). And previous Guidance, dating from 1980, had not included sexual abuse at all. But the latest Guidelines still have gaps: they do not distinguish abuse within and outside the family and they say nothing about the age of the perpetrator or about age difference or relationship. Finkelhor (1984) addresses age and age difference, the latter rather unconvincingly. He defines 'sexual victimisation' as 'sexual encounters' of children under 13 with persons at least 5 years older, and encounters of children between 13 and 16 with persons at least 10 years older. This may be thought to be somewhat rigid. Neither the Guidance nor Finkelhor emphasise intention, but this can also be important. An act may be rightly labelled as sexual abuse even if it is not so seen by the child. Not every child will identify the same acts as sexual, and very young children will not be capable of labelling in this way even the most overt of sexual acts. For these reasons the intention of the abuser is crucial, and the inclusion within the definition of anything that gives him sexual gratification is meaningful. It is crucial to stress this element for two reasons: first, there are actions (voyeurism is an example) of which the child is unaware, and secondly, by emphasising what it does for the perpetrator, child sexual abuse can be seen as a wrong that reduces the child to a sexual object—her person is not the subject of 'equal respect and concern' (Dworkin, 1977: 180; see also Freeman, 1988).

Age difference may be important but, as it is postulated by Finkelhor for example, it may miss the point. He clearly wishes to suggest coercion or undue influence. More significant is the ability to fend off advances, and this is heavily dependant on development. Schechter and Roberge, in a much-quoted definition, approved in the Butler-Sloss report into Cleveland, take account of this. They define sexual abuse as:

> the involvement of dependant, developmentally immature children and adolescents in sexual activities that they do not fully comprehend and to which they are unable to give informed consent or that violate the social taboos of family roles (1976: 60).

The concept of 'informed consent' is crucial. Victims of sexual abuse often do not object to participating in sexual activities but either lack knowledge of their social meanings and the psychological impact of sexual encounters, or, because of the powerless and dependant position they occupy, lack the autonomy.

What is surprising is that neither official Guidance nor other authoritative literature on the definition of sexual abuse (e.g. Glaser and Frosh, 1988) engages with corporal punishment (but see McGillivray, 1997). Green, Butt and King, in an important recent article 'Taking the Chaste out of Chastisement' (2002) (and see also King, Green and Butt, 2003), have addressed the relationship. They observe:

> . . . it is possible not only that some adults may use corporal punishment to sexually abuse children or as a form of sexual abuse, but that some children may perceive such

punishment sexually, even if there is no adult sexual intention and the motive is purely juridical [they mean 'judicial'], that is disciplinary (2002: 216).

It is interesting, even insightful, that Tony Blair should defend corporal punishment in a classic oxymoron as a 'loving smack'. For Blair this was to counter the association of corporal punishment and physical abuse. There was surprisingly little discussion of sexual abuse at the time of the so-called 'consultation' after *A v United Kingdom* (1998). But the association has been clear to writers since Rousseau (1782), at the latest (see his *Confessions*). In one recent study of sexuality in children's homes, corporal punishment was a strategy used by some adult sexual abusers both to groom children for further abuse and also to abuse them (Green, 1998). Can we really allow 'smacking' to continue if we want to rid ourselves of child sexual abuse? It is, perhaps, because abuse is seen as 'deviant', associated with paedophiles rather than family members, rather than as 'normal', that physical punishment has not been problematised in this way.

HOW MUCH CHILD SEXUAL ABUSE IS THERE?

The question is always asked how much is there? How prevalent is it? And, because it now gets so much exposure, there is added 'and has it increased or is it that it is more readily identified, reported, investigated or responded to?'. Of course, we do not know the answer to the first question. Much depends on definition. La Fontaine (1990: 68) is surely right to conclude that

> There has been enough research to show that the sexual abuse of children is not a negligible issue or a question of public hysteria but a serious social problem. Even the lowest estimate of its prevalence indicates a large number of children are involved.

The earliest work (e.g. Mrazek *et al*, 1983) found a rate of 0.3 percent and, it is accepted, grossly underestimated the size of the problem. Nash and West (1985) studied young women and students in Cambridge and found 48 percent had experienced some form of abuse (but 82 per cent of this number were abused in the first instance by non-family abusers). Kelly *et al.*, (1991), in a similar study, found 59 percent of women and 27 percent of men reported at least one experience of sexual abuse. Baker and Duncan (1985), using a broad definition and a large (2,019 women and men aged 15 and over) representative sample, found 10 percent with experiences of sexual abuse before the age of 16. Cawson *et al.*, (2000) found the incidence of sexual abuse to be 16 percent (21 percent girls and 11 percent boys). They found, as Kelly *et al* had, brothers and stepbrothers to be equally if not more implicated than parents (including stepfathers). Both Kelly *et al.*, and Cawson *et al.*, found that 1 percent of respondents reported sexual abuse by parents (virtually all fathers or stepfathers). The suspicion that it may have increased following the sexual revolution of the 1960s and 1970s is not supported by evidence, though there is U.S. evidence suggesting higher rates of abuse among women born in the period 1936–1945 who experienced the disruption of war and its aftermath, including fathers who left and then returned after a long absence (Russell, 1984; Finkelhor *et al.*, 1990).

It is significant that prevalence studies in the UK (and most other countries) found girls to be significantly more vulnerable to sexual abuse than boys—the risk is between 1.5 and 3 times as high for girls. But would the uplift be quite as steep if we acknowledged the sexual component of corporal chastisement?

HOW IS CHILD SEXUAL ABUSE TO BE EXPLAINED?

Do we know why it occurs? There is a large corpus of writing on the aetiology of physical abuse, and different models of explanation are postulated. One—the earliest to emerge—emphasises that abusers are 'sick' (the so-called medical or psycho-pathological model). A second, that abuse is located in stress produced by socio-environmental factors such as the multi-faceted correlates of poverty (and see Pelton, 1978). A third, that abuse is to be explained in cultural terms, as a consequence of the fact that children have been treated as property rather than persons, as social problems rather than as participants in the social process (Freeman, 1980). Physical abuse is easier to comprehend and explain than sexual abuse. Nevertheless, the three models may be used and, I would argue, that in both physical and sexual abuse it is the third which is the most convincing.

It is, of course, a particular feature of the third model because one factor in sexual abuse stands out and separates the phenomena of physical and sexual abuse. Most perpetrators of child sexual abuse, as with sexual abuse generally, are men (Finkelhor, 1986; Glaser and Frosh, 1988; Bendixen *et al.*, 1994; Freel, 2003) and most victims are female. Banning (1989) thought sexual abuse by females to be on the increase and attributed this to the blurring of roles between men and women. It may be but, as Finkelhor points out (1984: 184)

> to take the appearance of some forms of sexual abuse by females to mean that sexual abuse is not primarily committed by men is also wrong and has no support in any of the data.

The general source of sexual abuse must therefore be located in male sexuality. A male sexual interest in children is relatively common (Briere and Runtz, 1989; Hayashino *et al.*, 1995). It is surprising—or perhaps it is not—that the gender of the perpetrator for too long was rarely made explicit. Thus, discussion relating to the events in Cleveland was invariably about 'parents'. The Baker-Duncan study, in the mid 1980s, distinguished 'intra-familial', 'extra-familial' and stranger abuse, but did not refer to the perpetrator's gender. It is noteworthy that many of the early studies included women in the figures for perpetrators, not only when they had abused a child, but also when they had allowed sexual abuse to occur. It is common to find mother-blaming in the orthodox literature on child sexual abuse (e.g. Justice and Justice, 1980; Forward and Buck, 1981; Kempe and Kempe, 1978). Nelson (1987: 108) noted that 'professionals cling to the collusive wife theory like drowning men grasping at flotsam'. 'Could it be', she asks, 'because it is such a powerful defence against admitting the male abuse of power?'

The feminist perspective on child sexual abuse is now widely espoused (Rush, 1980; Dominelli, 1986; Macleod and Saraga, 1988; Driver and Droisen, 1989; Cowburn and Dominelli, 2001; Itzin, 2001) and within feminism there is consensus on why it happens and the form it takes. Thus, Macleod and Saraga state:

> Generally boys and men learn to experience their sexuality as an overwhelming and uncontrollable force; they learn to focus their sexual feelings on submissive objects, and they learn the assertion of their sexual desires, the expectation of having them serviced (1988: 41)

Similarly, Campbell, writing at the same time, saw abuse as 'an expression of a patriarchal sexual culture' (Campbell, 1988: 62).

Feminism offers greater insight into child sexual abuse than other theories because it makes us ask questions about culture and power (and these are relevant also to an understanding of other forms of abuse). Feminism not only offers a different interpretation of child sexual abuse, but also challenges the responses of orthodoxy, which new English 'official' thinking and practices now encode. Feminist insights remain marginalised. Dominant discourses—in particular those constructed by the media—fail to problematise masculinity and, therefore, feminists' concerns

> with the broader issues of hegemonic masculinity and its validation of sexual violence against less powerful groups of women and children have become less publicly visible (Cowburn and Dominelli, 2001: 403).

Family systems theory asks what is the wrong with the functioning of the family, and how its fragmented pieces can be successfully reconstructed. But it refuses to indict or to blame: instead, it prefers to share responsibility. Thus the Department of Health in its direction-setting 'Messages from Research' (1995: 32) thought 'unnecessary distress caused to family members who may then be unwilling to co-operate with subsequent plans' was 'of particular concern'. The reason is that 'professionals . . . may have to rebuild a sense of trust with family members to enable them to participate'. One feminist critic (Wattenberg, 1985: 206) responds to policies rooted in this ideology: 'The father rapes, abuses, brutalises and assaults the children and the mother, but somehow it is the mother's or child's fault'. An understanding of abuse requires an understanding of power. Sex, dominance and abuse do not have to be linked; there is no biological inevitability. But in our culture they are, and they produce the conditions in which the sexual abuse of children is perpetrated, and in which excuses are offered.

It would be wrong to use the feminist explanation in a reductionist way. Child sexual abuse cannot be explained exclusively in terms of patriarchy (and see Featherstone and Lancaster, 1997), any more than domestic violence or rape can. So we must look for other explanatory accounts, even if we conclude, as I do, that the dominant cause is so located.

When one turns to 'non-feminist' literature, what does one find? As with the physical abuse of children, often it is individual factors in the abuser which are stressed. And findings can contradict. Thus, for example studies have found abusers to be below average intelligence (Bender and Blau, 1937), of average intelligence (Meiselman, 1978), and of above average intelligence (Mayer, 1985). And they have been defined as aggressive (Groth and Birnbaum, 1979), and as passive (Gottlieb, 1980). There may be some explanation for these variations—different factors may be important in different cases, but it should concern those who subscribe to a pathological model that the variations can be so great (they are also in relation to physical abuse). Rarely does the literature which hypothesises individual pathology use control groups. It points to such factors as a harsh or deprived childhood (Groth and Birnbaum, 1979), to such matters as parental marital discord (Gruber and Jones, 1983), multiple caretakers (Justice and Justice, 1979), the experience of physical (De Young, 1982, 1983) or sexual abuse (Parker and Parker, 1986). But why does this lead to these men becoming sexual abusers? If experiencing sexual victimisation predisposed people to perpetrate sexual abuse in their turn, we would expect to find many more women committing sexual abuse. Those who work within this paradigm do not explain why this does not happen: they content themselves with asserting that they marry abusing men and become pathological 'colluding' mothers. There is, so far as I know, no research on men who were abused as children and do not abuse their own children, probably because such men do not come to the attention of clinicians. If there were a significant link between being victimised as a child and becoming an abuser, we would find many more boy victims than we do; those who explain child sexual abuse in individualistic terms do not account for this shortfall.

Not all of those who work within an individual personality framework present such a crude analysis. Araji and Finkelhor (1986), for example, link the individual psychological and the socio-cultural in an attempt to construct a multi-dimensional explanation. They build a theory of sexual abuse on a cluster of factors: emotional congruence ('sexual abusers choose children for sexual partners because children have some especially compelling emotional meaning for them' (1986: 94)); sexual arousal to children, possibly produced by the effects of victimisation, blockage of alternative avenues of gratification ('a timid inability to make contact with contemporaries' according to Storr (1965)); and disinhibitions of conventional social constraints, which includes explaining social and cultural elements that encourage or condone sexual behaviour directed toward children and thus weaken inhibitions (anything that reinforces excuses for sexual abuse . . . acts to reduce inhibitions (1986: 113)). Finkelhor, then, is not attributing abuse to personality traits alone, but is combining these and experiences, such as being abused in childhood, with internal characteristics such as a lack of relationship skills, situating the whole within a socio-cultural context which makes some attempt to explain the effect of social-isation on men, the role of patriarchy in the denigration of women and children, the effect of pornography, and other disinhibiting factors. Of course, the femi-nist theories concentrate on the disinhibition factors. Finkelhor, by contrast, argues that these do not really offer full explanations of sexual abuse for they 'take for granted some prior motive in the abuser to interact sexually with a child' (1986: 114). For Finkelhor these disinhibiting factors are a necessary, but not a sufficient, condition for abuse to occur. However, since the motive to indulge in a sexual relationship with a child hinges on man's sexuality or on social or cultural values, Finkelhor's thesis can be reconciled with a feminist interpretation of child sexual abuse (on Finkelhor and other models see Ward and Siegert, 2002).

Again, as with physical abuse, the then dominant theory locates the source of sexual abuse in socio-environmental factors. Although this interpretation (or complex of interpretations) has less relevance than the individualistic/psycho-pathological explanations—it is not directly related to responses—some account must be given of it, if only to show its inadequacy. It is noteworthy that the earliest writers on sexual abuse saw it in socio-economic class terms (Flugel, 1926; Sonder, 1936; Guttmacher, 1951). These studies can be readily dismissed; the cases were limited to deviants already successfully prosecuted or to victims hospitalised in mental institutions. The evidence is, in other words, grossly dis-torted by sampling biases (and see Wiener, 1964). Similar criticisms can be made about any conclusions based on cases of sexual abuse which come to the atten-tion of child protection agencies and the police: these involve the poor dispro-portionately, but their behaviour is more likely to come under professional scrutiny. With sexual abuse, the evidence is overwhelming that it crosses social class barriers (Cawson *et al.*, 2000; Gillham *et al.*, 1998). This is supported by American evidence as well (Russell, 1986). It could be that the middle classes are more open about abuse experienced when questioned by middle class inter-viewers, and so report more abuse, but there is no evidence or inferential sup-port for this conclusion.

Even if poverty were linked with sexual abuse, it would still be necessary to demonstrate a causal relationship. What in poverty could be said to lead to sexual abuse? Unemployment leading to greater access to the child? If so, why do not more women abuse children? Overcrowding and lack of privacy? But this may give the other parent greater opportunity to observe the abuse and to 'col-lude' or report it to the authorities, so that it would show up in the statistics. Social isolation? This is commonly cited as a cause of sexual abuse. Thus, the Kempes in *The Common Secret* assert that 'there are isolated communities or sub-cultures in which incest is accepted readily' (Kempe and Kempe, 1984: 51). Is there any evidence for this? Or does it just find its source in racist myths and class stereotypes? How much credence can be placed on evidence, some of it lit-tle more than anecdotal, that sexual abuse (or at least incest) is more common in rural areas? Until recently too little attention was paid to what is meant by social isolation (Did parents isolate themselves to prevent discovery of their abuse or become isolated because they abused their children?). Some attention is now being paid to this (see Seagull, 1987; Coohey, 1996). Coohey (1996) lists three important variables that should be measured to assess the impact of isolation: the number of network contacts, the amount of received support, and the parents' perception of that support. Both Coohey and Seagull (1987) found there to be a higher correlation between social isolation and neglect than for any other form of abuse.

Other socio-environmental factors do correlate with abuse. A number of studies have found higher vulnerability to sexual abuse among women who have lived without their biological fathers at some time during childhood (Finkelhor, 1984). There may also be a link between parental unavailability and abuse: girls who are victimised are more likely to have mothers who were disabled or ill (Herman and Hirschman, 1981; also Finkelhor, 1984) (but since the illnesses associated are alcoholism, depression and psychosis, one wonders which came first—the illness or the abuse?); they are more likely to witness conflict between their parents, and to report a poor relationship with one of their parents (Gruber and Jones, 1983). Again, with these last two factors, there must be some doubt as to whether they are genuine risk factors rather than findings which result from abuse: a girl being abused by her father is likely to perceive there is a conflict between her parents and/or perceive a poor relationship with her mother. These socio-environmental factors cannot be discounted: on the other hand, it is not always easy to disentangle them from issues of power.

And an understanding of sexual abuse requires, I reiterate, an understanding of power. We have come to accept that rape is not so much a crime of sex, but a power trip (Schwendinger and Schwendinger, 1974). In part, sexual abuse has to be similarly understood. Herman (1981), for example, documents the way in which fathers of incest victims appear to those victims, when interviewed as adults, to have been dominating and authoritarian. These men exercise rigid and authoritarian control over wives and daughters, if necessary using force to impose their domination. And Jackson (1982: 173) notes that

> child molesters and child rapists are almost invariably men who have learnt to express their sexuality through aggression, to seek power over others and to be attracted to the vulnerable.

The question therefore arises as to whether it is possible to understand masculinity without seeing it in terms of aggression and violence. And the answer is sometimes, given—perhaps less so now—that male sexuality is predetermined biologically. So, men cannot help it: their sexuality is uncontrollable. To quote Ruth Porter:

> these men may misunderstand the adolescent's behaviour and be sexually aroused by it; or physical chastisement may send the perpetrator to the excitement that blends into sexual activity (1984: 9).

Incidentally, this is an interesting and rare acknowledgement of the relationship between abuse and chastisement, referred to earlier. There is an element too in Porter's analysis of 'blaming the victim', which, as we know, is an all-too-common phenomenon (Ryan, 1976). But the suggestion is that male sex abusers have not resisted or thrown off those definitions of masculine sexuality which most boys acquire during socialisation. Fortunately, most do; at least most men do not become child sexual abusers.

It becomes important, therefore, to understand the processes by which masculine sexuality is constructed. There is no better account of this than Stephen Frosh's:

> Some theorists . . . draw attention to differential patterns of conscious and unconscious socialisation for boys and girls which, together with wider social images of masculine sexuality, have the effect of constructing men as alienated from intimate relations and from our sexuality. . . The characteristic patterns of masculinity, focusing on independence and 'hardness' and turning away from intimacy and nurture, follow from this. In particular, it produces a severely narrowed rendering of sexuality, operating primarily in two convergent ways. First, sex is one of the few means by which men aspire to closeness with others, and as such it becomes the carrier of all the unexpressed desire that men's emotional illiteracy produces. However, this same process makes sex dangerous to men whose identity is built on the denial of emotion; sex then becomes split off, limited to the activity of the penis, an act rather than an encounter. At the same time, sex becomes tied up with competition, separation and power—something used to bolster a man's sense of masculinity rather than to create a bond with another. The link between such a form of masculinity and sexual abuse is apparent; it is not just present, but inherent in a mode of personality organisation that rejects intimacy. Sex as defence and sex as triumph slides naturally into sex as rejection and degradation of the other (Frosh, 1987; see also Glaser and Frosh, 1988: 24).

Frosh acknowledges, too, that there are also important questions relating to the process whereby most men learn not to abuse children. (And this, I would add, applies to all forms of abuse, and not just sexual abuse). Frosh sees these as connected with the

> quality of their relationships in early life, internalisation of moral constraints, and the development of capacities to form positive sexual and emotional relationships with adults.

But he adds,

> if there are systematic factors that make men more likely to sexually abuse children, then these factors will be present more or less strongly in all men.

Sex, dominance and abuse do not have to be linked. But in our culture they are, and they produce the conditions in which sexual abuse of children is perpetrated, and excuses and rationalisations, which are rarely convincing, are proffered. It is the cultural explanation of child sexual abuse which is the most convincing. Armed with this, would we not look at orthodox solutions differently? The remainder of this paper looks at these 'orthodox' solutions critically, and then asks how we may set out towards eliminating child sexual abuse.

THE FAMILY SUPPORT MODEL

We made little or no attempt to recognise the existence of child sexual abuse until the Cleveland panic of 1987. What happened in Cleveland was important in that sexual abuse was seriously addressed for the first time. It is unlikely that the true facts of Cleveland will ever be known and few emerged from it with any credit. The Butler-Sloss report (1988) was rightly critical of everyone involved (though the magistracy without whom the children could not have been removed and who granted every application for a place of safety order got off 'scot-free'). This is not the place for a critical overview of the events of Cleveland or the Inquiry report (but see Freeman, 1989, or 1997 for a revised version).

At the time of Cleveland the orthodox approach to child abuse, including sexual abuse, was the child protection model. But this was thought to focus attention on securing the safety of a small number of children at risk of 'serious' abuse, whilst at the same time drawing into the bureaucratic net many more cases for which it was not appropriate. The model came under attack after Cleveland—in part because of Cleveland—and the Children Act of 1989 reflected concern with its emphasis. If the family was the building block of democratic society, if children had the right to 'autonomous parents', as influential American commentators urged (Goldstein, Freud and Solnit, 1979), then there was a need for minimum coercive intervention by the state, and this is what the 1989 Act gave us (Freeman, 1992a and 1992b). But writing at the time I feared the Act might 'situate the welfare of the child in the shadow of the welfare of the family' (1992a). And the shift to a family support model has done just this.

Of course, by adopting the family support model, the English approach to child abuse has moved closer to the dominant strategy found in other parts of Europe. The Netherlands were the first to emphasise support (Freeman, 1977). Others followed. Thus, in Germany, 'the intervention of a third party only takes place with the agreement of the family and as a rule with the family itself present' (Wustendorfer, 1995). In Austria, child protection centres are said to operate 'without the threat of punishment' (Planicka, 1995: 68). The family group conference emerged in New Zealand—in part a response to cultural pluralism—and has spread.

The child protection model may be thought to reify child abuse and to separate it from issues of child care generally. But it is possible to promote positive child care—the discouragement of corporal and the inappropriate forms of punishment is a case in point—whilst acknowledging that child abuse is a thing apart and has to be tackled separately. The danger is that an emphasis on family support can conflate the interests of parents—and they may not be identical—with that of the child, whose interest may well conflict with those of the parents or, at least, one of them. The system of family support can reaffirm and perpetuate power differentials within the family, those of age and, in the context of sexual abuse but also elsewhere, of gender. There is a real danger too that the child's voice will be suppressed. Both the Children Act and the United Nations Convention on the Rights of the Child emphasise the importance of the child's participation in the decision making process. But what space does the family support system afford the child victim?

It is significant that the system is being questioned within those countries in which it is most firmly entrenched. Thus, there is concern in France that the child's perspective is often unheard by the *juge des enfants* (Armstrong and Hollows, 1991), and of the Netherlands, Van Montfoort has commented that the welfare approach risks 'overlooking power relationships within the family' (1993: 62).

Different approaches adopted in different countries at different times reflect different interpretations of abuse, its aetiology and its implications. If abuse is interpreted as a symptom of family dysfunction, then solutions will be sought which aim to rehabilitate the family as a functioning unit. Thus, Cooper *et al.*, (1995: 6), writing of child 'protection' work in France can describe it as 'first and foremost a family affair'. And they add:

> It is not the individual child who is the primary focus of concern and intervention but the child-as-part-of-the-family, and the whole thrust of the French system is towards maintaining children as part of their families of origin.

But does a family systems explanation satisfactorily account for child abuse? Whilst conceding that there is no one explanation, that the causes of sexual abuse are multi-layered, the family systems model woefully underplays the agency and responsibility of the abuser, disempowers the non-abusing parent and glosses over the power issues related to masculinity which are now increasingly agreed to be central to our understanding.

One of the ironies of the English move towards tackling abuse through family support is that our understanding of the causes of abuse is more advanced than it is in the countries we have copied. Certainly, we were, also, aware of the problem and of its prevalence before our continental counterparts. This is in part why the Dutroux case in Belgium, the Roum affair in Denmark, the scandals in Ireland, all relatively recent, provoked such concern and media attention in those countries. Pringle and Harder (1997: 168) have, rightly I believe, pointed to the 'real tragedy of the situation in England and Wales' that 'the enormity of the problem has been more realised here than elsewhere in Western Europe but the system designed to deal with it is wholly inadequate'. That abuse, particularly sexual abuse but also sexual violence against women generally, is better known about in Britain is in large part because the problem has been politicised by feminists and others who have challenged the very cosy arrangements which (unintentionally) family systems theorists and practitioners endorse.

It is worth emphasising too that there is another reason why it was wrong to embrace the continental approach. Doing so presupposes that solutions can be isolated from ideologies and from structures. But we have a different context, a different view of society and the individual (we tend to be more individualistic), a different vision of the role of state and community. As Hetherington *et al.*, (1997: 34) note:

> when services for children are enshrined by the principles of social solidarity, sub-sidiarity and citizenship, one consequence is that institutions which organise, deliver and shape local responses to child protection are structures into, and derive their authority from, a total conception of society

These principles, they argue, are absent from a Britain which has not recovered from 18 years of Conservatism (or is it now 25?), 'a period which witnessed a consolidation of ideologies of individual rights . . . and a general decline in ideas of collective responsibility' (1997: 85). In fact, the roots of this go even deeper, grounded as they are on a set of assumptions about the relationship of the individual to society and to government.

The child protection model did not work as well as it should have done. But that is only part of the reason why we came to reject it. The family systems model does not work either. There is evidence of that from countries where, given their assumptions about society, it was more likely to work. Given the enormity of the problem it cannot be expected to work in Britain any more than elsewhere. Nor is it just a question of resources. Both approaches over-rely on professionals. This is not to downplay the pivotal role of professional expertise: the emergence of the family group conference alarms me because it vests the family, and potentially therefore the abuser, with too much decision-making power.

We must find a role for the family, but it must be a role in prevention, not one assigned to decision-making. It is important that we find ways of empowering non-abusing family members. And there are ways in which the law can assist this process: an example is by the use of residence orders in favour of relatives where this is appropriate and can avoid the need for a care order to be made. But, where the opportunity arose for the House of Lords to take the lead and endorse such a practice, it inexplicably and inexcusably failed to do so (*Re M*[1]; Masson, 1994; Hayes and Williams, 1999).

Preventing Abuse

A role in prevention must also be found for non-family members. There are many lessons to be learnt from the James Bulger case eleven years ago, but one that can all too easily be overlooked is that he would not have died had one of

---

[1] [1994] 2 AC 424.

the 38 (or more) adults who witnessed his fateful walk intervened (Morrison, 1997). What has been called 'a protected environment' (Smith, 1996) needs investigation. Smith argues that

> our prevention programmes should be aimed first at the adults who surround children in their day-to-day lives: parents, extended family members, childminders, nursery workers, and teachers among others.

And, writing of the Bulger case, she observes that it demonstrates that

> we, as a community of adults, are reluctant to take responsibility for protecting other people's children. Hence protectiveness has become increasingly professionalised and more removed from the natural networks that surround children where it would be most effective.

Whether such networks are effective depends on a number of things. It depends on whistle-blowers—the law protects such people rather better than it did. Nevertheless, it 'goes against the grain' to speak out of turn. It is inconceivable that there were not 'non-abusing' care workers, for example, able to expose abusers in children's homes. It depends also on children 'telling'. They cannot tell if they do not know, and they will not tell if they have no confidence that they will be believed. For knowledge and understanding, children need education. They need to be given insight into coping strategies. This may not be easy: there is a lot of evidence suggesting it does not work (Melton, 1987). But is there an alternative? To speak out they must have confidence that they will be taken seriously. In this lies the importance of children's rights officers, of a children's ombudsman (or commissioner), of a network of people committed to the ideals of the United Nations Convention on the Rights of the Child, in particular Article 12 of this. We are so far from recognising this that the recent Climbié Inquiry addressed none of these issues: nor did it advocate an anti-spanking law (Laming, 2003). The Children's Bill of 2004 does at least and at last offer us a Children's Commissioner.

Children must be encouraged to 'tell'. And here also the 'protected environment' becomes significant. It is much more likely that children will tell persons known to them than statutory agencies. We must give children the confidence to do so. Much then depends upon how these people, other family members, neighbours, friends' parents, teachers respond, and this will depend upon how they perceive children and how they perceive abuse.

Twenty-six years ago pioneer researches into child abuse Kempe and Kempe wrote that 'before [child abuse] could be acknowledged as a social ill, changes had to occur to the sensibilities and outlook of our [in their case American] culture' (Kempe and Kempe, 1978: 17). If child abuse is to be extinguished numerous changes in sensibilities and outlook are required. We must ask why children's bodies are still exploited, sexually molested and subjected to physical and psychological violence. The answer is complex, but can partly be explained in the way childhood has come to be constructed (Jenks, 1996). If we are to eradicate the abuse of children, we must learn to take children's rights seriously, we must accept that children are not property or pretty playthings or (literally) 'whipping boys', but individuals whose physical, sexual and psychological integrity is as important, if not more important, than that of the adult population. Even where there is intervention to protect children, it is all too easy to concentrate on adult services and outcomes, and children can get 'lost in the process'.

Smith's concept of a 'protected environment' is important but it needs more content. We must learn to take abuse more seriously. Far too many children are left in, or indeed put into, abusive environments. The abuse legislation (the Children Act 1989) needs to be interpreted in a purposive way to protect children's integrity rather than their parents' privacy. It is a pity that when we came to enact human rights legislation in 1998 we merely took on board a convention that was nearly 50 years old, and which, of course, said nothing about children as such (Fortin, 2003). We could—though I doubt if we would—have done better.

If we are to create a 'protected environment' we must make it unlawful to hit children. There is a concern that this would lead to greater intervention into the family, more prosecution of parents and more care proceedings. But this is not the experience of countries which have passed such legislation (Freeman, 1999). Other measures are also required such as policies to target domestic violence, child pornography, child prostitution, sex tourism. Of course, there have been measures aimed at each of these evils, but much more can be done. And abuse itself must be taken more seriously. Legislation should spell out parental responsibilities—it does so in Scotland—there should be greater guidance on good parenting practices. We should be less reluctant to intervene. Care orders should be easier to obtain. But the direction is the other way. Were the House of Lords right in *Re H*[2] to accept a simple balance of probabilities test? Lord Nicholls— and he would be the first to admit that child law was not his subject—reasoned that a court, when assessing probabilities, should have in mind that

> the more serious the allegation the less likely it is that the event occurred and, hence, the stronger should be the evidence before the court concludes that the allegation is established on the balance of probabilities.

Is it not bizarre that the more serious the anticipated injury, the more difficult it becomes for an authority to satisfy the initial burden of proof, and thereby secure protection for the child?

A good illustration of what this reasoning can lead to occurred in *Re M and R*.[3] The first instance judge found 'a real possibility that [sexual] abuse' had been perpetrated, but he held, following *Re H*, that 'such a possibility cannot justify a conclusion that the threshold criteria are satisfied'. On appeal it was argued that the judge, having found that there was a real possibility of sexual abuse, had erred in not taking into account the allegation of sexual abuse in his

---

[2] [1996] AC 563.
[3] [1996] 2 FLR 195.

assessment of the children's welfare at the discretionary stage (an order cannot be made even if these threshold criteria are met unless it would be in the best interests of the child). The balance of psychiatric evidence was unanimously to the effect that sexual abuse had probably occurred. Butler-Sloss LJ rejected these arguments. She said:

> They amount to the assertion that under s 1 (which lays down the paramountcy principle) the welfare of the child dictates the court should act on suspicion or doubts, rather than facts.

But, she argued, 'the welfare of the child dictates the exact opposite'. She concluded:

> If . . . the court concludes that the evidence is insufficient to prove sexual abuse in the past, and if the fact of sexual abuse in the past is the only basis for asserting a risk of sexual abuse in the future, then it follows that there is nothing (except suspicion or mere doubts) to show a risk of future sexual abuse.

I am sure the House of Lords, and subsequently the Court of Appeal, failed to find the best answer to the evidentiary problem. Whether they found the answer which Parliament expected of them is another matter. The decisions may well be in line with the dominant ideology of the Children Act. Local authorities are under a duty to provide services for children who would otherwise be at risk of sustaining impaired health or development, and such services must be directed to preventing the need to take coercive measures. The aspiration is liberal: it is family-oriented. The reality is that many of these children continue to be abused or neglected (or both) by parents who lack and are unlikely to develop acceptable child-rearing skills. Children are allowed to drift: 'children who wait' has taken on a new meaning. We as a society are failing these children. Our consciences are pricked when we read of a Victoria Climbié (Laming, 2003), but less dramatic cases are a daily occurrence. Even when proceedings are initiated to protect children, they meander through the courts. A Protocol, introduced in November 2003, has set a target of 40 weeks for the completion of cases (Department for Constitutional Affairs, 2003; Saunders, 2003; Sale, 2003). I doubt whether it will be met: the will is not there; nor are the skills or the resources.

We are failing children. And we do less about children who are victims than children who victimise others. This has always been so—delinquency which affects us has always concerned us more than child abuse which only impacts upon a child population—but is strikingly illustrated by modern developments such as the parenting order (introduced in the Crime and Disorder Act 1998). This may be made in a number of circumstances, including where a child safety order has been made. The purpose of the order is to require parents to attend courses which will assist them to prevent their children offending. The child safety order is a flawed concept, and it is not working, but where one is made a parenting order may also be made. A parent can be required to attend counselling or guidance sessions where *inter alia* his/her child has acted in a manner that caused or is likely to cause harassment, alarm or distress to someone outside his household, but not where that parent is rearing his/her child in a dysfunctional environment. And this is despite evidence that such children are more likely to commit the delinquent acts targeted by the child safety order. Parenting orders could be lifted from this inappropriate context, and invoked as a weapon in the war on child abuse. We already accept the value of similar management techniques in the not dissimilar context of domestic violence: in both there is the need to inculcate appropriate behaviour.

Ultimately, the eradication of the sexual abuse of children requires a reexamination of why it happens. There is no one cause, and no two cases are the same. But what I think is clear is that the source is to be found in male sexuality and in the position which children occupy in society.

To address each of these issues requires more space than is available, and both are the subject of fuller treatment elsewhere, in the latter case by this author. In pinpointing male sexuality I will be accused of essentialism: of course, it is true that there is not a single maleness. But we cannot overlook what too often emerges as 'narrowed rendering of sexuality' (Frosh, 1987), the ways in which sex is used as a power trip, as a way of degrading others, as a characteristic of far too many men. In drawing attention to the status of children, I light upon the 'nightmare' that childhood has been (De Mause, 1974). The corner may have been turned: the United Nations Convention on the Rights of the Child in 1989 was a great achievement (Van Bueren, 1995), but we have a long way to go (Freeman, 2000). We will not see the end to sexual abuse of children until we take children and their rights seriously.

REFERENCES

ARAJI, SK and FINKELHOR, D, 'A Review of the Research' in D Finkelhor (ed.), *A Sourcebook of Child Sexual Abuse* (Beverley Hills, California, Sage, 1986).

ARMSTRONG, H and HALLOWS, A, 'Responses to Child Abuse in the EC' in M Hill (ed.), *Social Work and the European Community* (London, Jessica Kingsley, 1991).

BAILEY, V and McCABE, S, 'The Punishment of Incest Act 1908: A Case Study of Law Creation' (1979) *Criminal Law Review* 708.

BAKER, A and DUNCAN, S, 'Child Sexual Abuse: A Study of its Prevalence in Great Britain' (1985) 9 *Child Abuse and Neglect* 457.

BANNING, A, 'Mother-Son Incest: Confronting a Prejudice' (1989) 13 *Child Abuse and Neglect* 563.

BENDER, L and BLAU, A, 'The Reaction of Children to Sexual Relations with Adults' (1937) 7 *American Journal of Orthopsychiatry* 500.

BENDIXSEN, M, MUUS, K and SCHEI, B, 'The Impact of Child Sexual Abuse. A Study of A Random Sample of Norwegian Students' (1994) 18 *Child Abuse and Neglect* 837.

BRIERE, J and RUNTZ, M, 'University Males' Sexual Interest in Children: Predicting Potential Indices of 'Pedophilia' in a Nonforensic Sample' (1989) 13 *Child Abuse and Neglect* 65.

BUTLER-SLOSS, E, *Report of the Inquiry into Child Abuse in Cleveland 1987* (London, H.M.S.O., 1988).

CAMPBELL, B, *Unofficial Secrets—The Cleveland Case* (London, Virago, 1988).

CAWSON, P, WATTAM, C, BROOKER, S and KELLY, C, *Child Maltreatment in the United Kingdom: A Study of the Prevalence of Child Abuse and Neglect* (London, NSPCC, 2000).

COOHEY, C, 'Child Maltreatment: Testing The Social Isolation Hypothesis' (1996) 20 *Child Abuse and Neglect* 241.

COOHEY, C, and BRAUN, N, 'Toward An Integrated Framework for Understanding Child Physical Abuse' (1997) 21 *Child Abuse and Neglect* 1081–94.

COOPER, D, HETHERINGTON, R, BAISTOW, K, PITTS, J, and SPRIGGS, A, *Positive Child Protection: A View From Abroad* (Lyme Regis, Russell House Publishing, 1995).

COWBURN, M, and DOMINELLI, L, 'Masking Hegemonic Masculinity: Reconstructing the Paedophile as a Dangerous Stranger' (2001) 31 *British Journal of Social Work* 399.

DE MAUSE, L, *The History of Childhood* (London, Souvenir Press, 1976).

DEPARTMENT FOR CONSTITUTIONAL AFFAIRS, *Protocol for Judicial Case Management in Public Law Children Act Cases* (London, Dept for Constitutional Affairs, 2003).

DEPARTMENT OF HEALTH, *Working Together To Safeguard Children* (London, Stationery Office, 2000).

DOMINELLI, L, 'Father-Daughter Incest: Patriarchy's Shameful Secret' (1986) 16 *Critical Social Policy* 8.

DRIVER, E and DROISEN, A, (eds.), *Child Sexual Abuse: Feminist Perspectives* (London, Macmillan, 1989).

DWORKIN, R, *Taking Rights Seriously* (London, Duckworth, 1977).

FALLER, K, *Child Sexual Abuse: An Interdisciplinary manual for Diagnosis, Case Management and Treatment* (New York, Columbia University Press, 1988).

FEATHERSTONE, B, and LANCASTER, E, 'Contemplating The Unthinkable: Men Who Sexually Abuse Children' (1997) 17 *Critical Social Policy* 51.

FINKELHOR, D, *Child Sexual Abuse* (New York, Free Press, 1984).

—— *A Sourcebook on Child Sexual Abuse* (Beverley Hills, California, Sage, 1986).

—— HOTALING, G, LEWIS, I. and SMITH, C, 'Sexual Abuse in a National Survey of Adult Men and Women: Prevalence Characteristics and Risk Factors' (1990) 14 *Child Abuse and Neglect* 19.

FLUGEL, JC, *The Psychoanalytic Study of the Family* (London, Woolf, 1926).

FORWARD, S, and BUCK, C, *Betrayal of Innocence: Incest and Its Devastation* (Harmondsworth, Penguin, 1981).

FREEL, M, 'Child Sexual Abuse and the Male Monopoly: An Empirical Exploration of Gender and a Sexual Interest in Children' (2003) 33 *British Journal of Social Work* 481.

FREEMAN, M., 'Towards The Prevention of Child Battering—The Dutch Approach' (1977) 7 *Family Law* 53.

—— 'Sexual Abuse of Children' (1978) 8 *Family Law* 222.

—— *Violence In The Home: A Socio-Legal Study* (Aldershot, Saxon House, 1979).

—— 'The Rights of the Child in the International Year of the Child' (1980) 33 *Current Legal Problems* 1.

—— 'Taking Children's Rights Seriously' (1988) 1 *Children and Society* 299.

—— 'Cleveland, Butler-Sloss and Beyond—How Are We To React to the Sexual Abuse of Children?' (1989) 42 *Current Legal Problems* 85.

—— *Children, Their Families and the Law* (Basingstoke, Macmillan, 1992(a)).

—— 'In The Child's Best Interests? Reading The Children Act Critically' (1992(b)) 45 *Current Legal Problems* 173.

—— *The Moral Status of Children* (The Hague, Martinus Nijhoff, 1997).

—— 'Children Are Unbeatable' (1999) 13 *Children and Society* 130.

—— 'The End of The Century of The Child?' (2000) 53 *Current Legal Problems* 505.

FREUD, S, *The Complete Introductory Lecture on Psycho-Analysis* (ed. and transl. by J Strachey) (New York, Norton, 1933).

FROSH, S, 'Issues For Men Working With Sexually Abused Children' (1987) 3 *British Journal of Psychotherapy* 332.

FORTIN, J, *Children's Rights and The Developing Law* (2nd edn, London, Butterworths, 2003).

GILLHAM, B, *et al* 'Unemployment Rates, Single Parent Density and Indices of Child Poverty: Their Relationship to Different Categories of Child Abuse and Neglect' (1998) 22 *Child Abuse and Neglect* 79.

GLASER, D and FROSH, S, *Child Sexual Abuse* (London, Macmillan, 1988).

GOLDSTEIN, J, FREUD, A and SOLNIT, A, *Before The Best Interests of The Child* (New York, Free Press, 1979).

GREEN, L, 'Caged By Force, Entrapped By Discourse: A Study of the Construction and Control of Children and their Sexualities in Residential Children's Homes' Ph.D Thesis, University of Huddersfield, 1998 (Unpublished).

GREEN, L, BUTT, T, and KING, N, 'Taking the Chaste Out of Chastisement: An Analysis of the Sexual Implications of the Corporal Punishment of Children' (2002) 9 *Childhood* 205.

GOTTLIEB, B, 'Incest: Therapeutic Intervention In a Unique Form of Sexual Abuse' in CC Warner (ed), *Rape and Sexual Assault: Management and Intervention* (Germantown, Maryland, Aspen Publications, 1980).

GROTH, A and BIRNBAUM, H, *Men Who Rape: The Psychology of the Offender* (New York, Plenum Press, 1979).

GRUBER, K and JONES, R, 'Identifying Determinants of Risk of Sexual Victimization of Youth' (1983) 7 *Child Abuse and Neglect* 17.

GUTTMACHER, M, *Sexual Offenses* (New York, Norton, 1951).

HAYASHINO, D, WURTELE, S and KLEBE, J, 'Child Molesters: An Examination of Cognitive Factors' (1995) 10 *Journal of Interpersonal Violence* 106.

HAYES, M and WILLIAMS, C, *Family Law* (2nd edition, London, Butterworths, 1999).

HERMAN, J, *Father-Daughter Incest* (Cambridge, Mass, Harvard University Press, 1981).

—— and HIRSCHMAN, L, 'Families At Risk for Father-Daughter Incest' (1981) 138 *American Journal of Psychiatry* 967.

HETHERINGTON, R, COOPER, A, SMITH, P and WILFORD, G, *Protecting Children: Messages from Europe* (Lyme Regis, Russell House Publishing, 1997).

ITZIN, C, 'Incest, Paedophilia, Pornography and Prostitution: Making Familial Males More Familiar as Abusers' (2001) 10 *Child Abuse Review* 35.

JACKSON, S, *Childhood and Sexuality* (Oxford, Blackwell, 1982).

JENKS, C, *Childhood* (London, Routledge, 1996).

JUSTICE, B, and JUSTICE, R, *The Broken Taboo* (New York, Human Sciences Press, 1979).

KELLY, L, REGAN, L, and BURTON, S, *An Exploratory Study of Sexual Abuse in a Sample of 16–21 Year Olds* (London, ESRC, 1991).

KEMPE, CH and KEMPE, R, *The Common Secret: Sexual Abuse of Children and Adolescents* (New York, Freeman, 1984).

KING, N, BUTT, T and GREEN, L, 'Spanking and the Corporal Punishment of Children: The Sexual Story' (2003) 11 *International Journal of Children's Rights* 199.

LA FONTAINE, J, *Child Sexual Abuse* (Cambridge, Polity Press, 1990).

LAMING, LORD, *The Victoria Climbié Inquiry,* (London, Stationery Office, 2003).

MACLEOD, M and SARAGA, E, 'Challenging The Orthodoxy: Towards a Feminist Theory and Practice' (1988) 28 *Feminist Review* 15.

McGILLIVRAY, A, 'He'll Learn It on His Body: Disciplinary Childhood in Canadian Law' (1997) 5 *International Journal of Children's Rights* 193.

MASSON, J, 'Social Engineering in the House of Lords' (1994) 6 *Journal of Child Law* 170.

MAYER, A, *Sexual Abuse* (Holmes Beach, Florida, Learning Publications, 1985).

MEISELMAN, K, *Incest: A Psychological Study of Causes and Effects With Treatment Recommendations* (San Francisco, California, Jossey-Bass, 1978).

MELTON, G, *Reforming the Law: The Impact of Child Development Research* (New York: Guilford Press, 1987).

MORRISON, B, *As If* (London, Granta Books, 1997).

MRAZEK, P, LYNCH, M and BENTOVIM, A, 'Sexual Abuse of Children In the United Kingdom' (1983) 7 *Child Abuse and Neglect* 147.

NASH, C and WEST, D, 'Sexual Molestation of Young Girls' in D West (ed), *Sexual Victimisation* (Aldershot, Gower, 1985).

NELSON, S, *Incest: Myth and Fact* (Edinburgh, Stratmullion, 1987).

PALLER, H, and PARKER, S, 'Father–Daughter Sexual Abuse: An Emerging Perspective' (1986) 56 *American Journal of Orthopsychiatry* 531.

PELTON, L, 'Child Abuse and Neglect: The Myth of Classlessness' (1978) 48 *American Journal of Orthopsychiatry* 608.

PLANICKA, H, 'Child Abuse in Austria' in C Birks (ed.), *Child Abuse in Europe,* vol 1 (Nurnberg, Emwe Verlag, 1995).

PORTER, R, *Child Sexual Abuse Within The Family* (London, Tavistock, 1984).

PRINGLE, K, and HARDER, M, 'Conclusion: Transnational Comparisons and Future Trajectories' in M Harder and K Pringle, *Protecting Children in Europe: Towards A New Millennium* (Aalborg, Aalborg University Press, 1997).

RUSH, F, *The Best Kept Secret* (Englewood Cliffs, New Jersey, Prentice-Hall, 1980).

ROUSSEAU, J-J, *Confessions* (London, Everyman Library, 1981, originally 1782).

RUSSELL, D, *Sexual Exploitation: Rape, Child Sexual Abuse and Workplace Harassment* (Beverley Hills, California, Sage, 1984).

—— *The Secret Trauma: Incest In The Lives of Girls and Women* (New York, Basic Books, 1986).

RYAN, W, *Blaming The Victim* (New York, Vintage Books, 1976).

SALE A, 'Delay Reactions' (31 July–6 August 2003) *Community Care,* Issue 1483, 26.

SAUNDERS, E, 'Conducting Care Cases' (2003) 153 *New Law Journal* 1070.

SCHECHTER, M and ROBERGE, L, 'Child Sexual Abuse' in R Helfer and C Kempe (eds), *Child Abuse and Neglect: The Family and The Community* (Cambridge, Mass, Ballinger, 1976).

SCHWENDINGER, J and SCHWENDINGER, H, 'Rape Myths' (1974) 1 *Crime and Social Justice* 18.

SEAGULL, E, 'Social Support and Child Maltreatment: A Review of the Evidence' (1987) 11 *Child Abuse and Neglect* 41.

SMART, C, 'A History of Ambivalence and Conflict in the Discursive Construction of the "Child Victim" of Sexual Abuse' (1999) 8 *Social and Legal Studies* 391.

Smith, G, 'Reassessing Protectiveness' in Batty, D and Cullen, D (eds), *Child Protection: The Therapeutic Option* (London, BAAF, 1996).

Sonder, T, 'Incest Crimes in Sweden and their Causes' (1936) 2 *Acta Psychiatrica at Neurologica* 379.

Storr, A, *Sexual Deviation* (London, Heinemann, 1965).

Van Beuren, G, *The International Law On The Rights of The Child* (The Hague, Martinus Nijhoff, 1995).

Van Montfoort, A, 'The Protection of Children in the Netherlands: Between Justice and Welfare' in H Ferguson, R Gilligan and R Torode (eds), *Surviving Childhood Adversity* (Dublin, Social Studies Press, 1993).

Ward, T, and Siegert, R, 'Toward a Comprehensive Theory of Child Sexual Abuse: A Theory Knitting Perspective' (2002) 8 *Psychology, Crime and Law* 319.

Wattenberg, E, 'In A Different Light: A Feminist Perspective on the Role of Mother in Father-Daughter Incest' (1985) 64 *Child Welfare* 203.

Weiner, I, 'On Incest: A Survey' (1964) 4 *Excerpta Criminologica* 37.

Wohl, A, 'Sex and the Single Room: Incest among the Victorian Working Classes' in A Wohl (ed), *The Victorian Family* (London, Croom Helm, 1978).

Wustendorfer, W, 'Violence Against Children in Germany' in C Birks (ed), *Child Abuse in Europe* vol 1 (Nurnberg, Emwe Verlag, 1995).

15

The Care Standards Tribunal:
The Correct Balance

DAVID PEARL

INTRODUCTION

T HE PROTECTION OF Children Act 1999 established a specialist Tribunal to
hear appeals brought by individuals who were placed on the statutory lists
regulating those people deemed unsuitable to work with children. The jurisdiction of the Tribunal (referred to as the Care Standards Tribunal) has been
widened by the Care Standards Act 2000, the Education Act 2002, the Tax
Credits Act 2002, and the Criminal Justice and Court Services Act 2000. The
Tribunal has a legal Chairman, and two lay members with appropriate experience as set out in Regulation 3 of the Protection of Children and Vulnerable
Adults and Care Standards Tribunal Regulations 2002. The Lord Chancellor
appoints all the members. It is not the purpose of this chapter to deal in detail
with the various strands of this ever-widening jurisdiction. Many of the cases
that have come before the Tribunal in the first eighteen months of its existence
have involved issues that are not related to the subject matter of this book, for
example the difficult questions of demarcating the exact line between a care
home and an independent hospital. But a not insubstantial number of cases have
concerned the difficult question of whether a person is unsuitable to work with
children and a significant proportion of these have involved allegations of sexual misconduct (on the sexual abuse of children more generally, see Freeman
this volume).

I concentrate in this chapter on the issues that arise when the Tribunal struggles with the important and complex responsibility of balancing the protection
of children and assessment of risk as against the human rights of the individual
to work with children (even on an unpaid basis) in his chosen field.

The Department of Education and Skills is responsible for maintaining two
statutory lists of persons who are prevented from working with children. One
list is known as the Protection of Children Act list (or the PoCA list) prohibiting
social workers from working with children[1]. The other list prohibits or restricts

---

[1] S 4 Protection of Children Act 1999.

employment in schools on grounds of misconduct or health (sometimes referred to as 'List 99').[2] There is a right of appeal to the Care Standards Tribunal when a person is placed on one of these lists. In addition, when a person is convicted of one of the specified offences, the sentencing judge must impose a ban on him working with children (Criminal Justice and Court Services Act 2000). There is a right to seek from the Tribunal a revocation of this disqualification, but only ten years subsequent to being sentenced (five years for those who are under 18 at the time of sentence). In the social worker cases, the Tribunal has two tasks set down by s 4(3) of the Protection of Children Act 1999. It has a fact-finding function: was the individual guilty of misconduct that harmed a child or placed a child at risk of harm? The second function is a risk assessment exercise: is the individual unsuitable to work with children? There is a similar fact finding exercise in the teacher cases. The risk assessment is expressed in the Guidance to Education Staff in a slightly different way. Certain behaviour can be seen as presenting an unacceptable example, and the emphasis is placed on the necessity to uphold high standards of behaviour in members of the teaching profession. A person's behaviour may well have a bearing on his or her suitability to work with children and such a person will be considered not to be a fit and proper person.

Inevitably, there are major and sometimes conflicting policy issues. For example, should safeguarding children extend to protecting them from the private behaviour of an adult whose example may be 'unacceptable'? We are talking here of draconian powers. The implementation of the Human Rights Act 1998, bringing European Convention standards into direct application in domestic law, has highlighted the tension that has always existed between children's welfare and the right to work as a professional or a volunteer in a chosen child-centred profession. Principles of proportionality, so important in any consideration of the European Convention on Human Rights, must now play the critical role in these difficult and sensitive decisions, for there are two conflicting arguments, both clearly understandable, that can be persuasive.

First, it could be argued that the creation of a system that bars a person from working with children in certain situations is necessary so as to instil confidence in the provision both of public child care and the education services. The ultimate justification is the protection of children from the risk of harm; thus balance and proportionality *in an individual case* are not the only factors. There may be a trump card. Secondly, and in contrast, some may argue that in the context of these essentially individual decisions taken by Government departments is the sometimes overriding need of Government to ensure that the crisis in teacher and social work numbers is not unduly accentuated. These are matters that cannot be wholly ignored by decision makers, either at first instance or on appeal. In weighing these policy issues, it is argued here that proportionality and

---

[2] Education (Prohibition from Teaching or Working with Children) Regulations 2003 SI 1184 made under the Education Act 2002.

balance must be a key link to ensure that the correct approach is taken and that possibly conflicting policy considerations are placed in the appropriate balance. The cases that have been argued before us so far have tended to involve 'front-line' staff; classroom teachers and social workers. However, as a result of the very powerful findings in the Laming Report on the Victoria Climbié Inquiry (Laming, 2003), it is possible that the statutory regulatory net may begin to encompass those in senior positions as well. If so, appeals can be foreseen from such people. The defence 'no one ever told me' (Laming, 2003: 5) did not appeal to Lord Laming. Whether it would appeal to those responsible for the two statutory lists maintained by the Department of Education is problematic. Is the Director of Social Services of a local authority where a child has been killed by those who are looking after him or her (Victoria Climbié) guilty of misconduct which harmed a child or placed a child at risk of harm to the extent that the individual is unsuitable to work with children? It would be a brave civil servant who would recommend to the Minister that such a person be placed on the statutory list. But what of a headmaster, or a senior manager of a children's home, where abuse has taken place (Waterhouse, 1999)? These are matters that could well exercise the Tribunal in the years to come.

STANDARD OF PROOF WHEN FACT FINDING

The issues relating to the standard of proof facing the Tribunal arose in a stark form in the case of 'C', considered by the Court of Appeal on 22nd January 2003.[3] It is perhaps relevant to note at the outset that in that case, as in a number of others, the problem facing the Tribunal was exacerbated because it did not hear any live evidence either from the appellant or from the alleged victim of the sexual abuse.

The statutory provision places the burden of proof on the Secretary of State. What is more of an issue however is the *standard* of proof that is required to discharge this burden. This basic legal question masks complex policy matters relating to the need to assess risk, the importance of protecting children, and the human rights of the individual to work in his chosen field and to ensure that his name is not included incorrectly on a list that prevents him from so doing. It is important to observe that the Tribunal has no power to place a person on the sex offenders' register, this being a matter solely for the criminal process. What is clear is that the standard of proof is not the criminal standard. Attempts to argue that it should be a criminal standard by analogy with proceedings before disciplinary panels such as the Solicitors' Disciplinary Committee[4] and the General Medical Council[5], have always failed. It is lower than that. But what is it?

[3] [2003] EWCA Civ 10.
[4] *Re a Solicitor* [1992] 2 All E.R. 335.
[5] *McAllister v GMC* [1993] 1 All E.R. 982.

It is generally assumed that the standard of proof is to satisfy the Tribunal on the balance of probability that the appellant is guilty of misconduct that harmed a child and is thus unsuitable to work with children. The question was a highly significant one in the case of 'C'. As we have already said, neither the appellant nor the alleged victim of sexual assault gave live evidence. The Tribunal held in 'C' that the fact that no evidence was called live by the Respondent in effect meant that it had not come up to proof. Scott Baker J did not interfere with this decision, but the Court of Appeal remitted the matter to the Tribunal for a rehearing, taking the view that the failure to consider whether to draw an adverse inference of the appellant's decision not to give evidence himself was an error of law.

In the context of this case, both Latham LJ and Thorpe LJ refer to the general principles underlying the legislation. Thorpe LJ says that he recognises that his approach as a family lawyer:

> inclines me to favour the submission that the primary purpose of the statutory scheme is child protection, albeit balanced by a proper reflection of the rights of individuals to pursue careers in childcare and education.

Latham LJ adopted similar reasoning when he said

> The interests of the individual are safeguarded by the fact that the burden of proof is on the appellant. The overall objective, however, is preventative, that is the protection of children from exposure to the risk of abuse. The means employed seem to me to be proportionate to that purpose.

In another case that came before the Court of Appeal prior to its being heard by the Tribunal, R (on the application of M) v London Borough of Bromley[6], Judge LJ speaks of the

> statutory scheme [that] seeks to balance the interests of the vulnerable and avoid the risk of harm to them from contact with an unsuitable adult, while . . . protecting an innocent individual from wrongful inclusion on the list.

In this discussion on standard of proof, it is essential to remember that the Tribunal has two questions to consider. Firstly, has the applicant been guilty of misconduct, whether or not in the course of his duties, which harmed a child or placed a child at risk of harm? The second issue is whether the individual is unsuitable to work with children. The first matter inevitably raises findings of fact; the second, assessments of suitability. Both issues, of course, deal with complex risk assessments. If the Tribunal decides that the appellant has not been guilty of misconduct, the issue of unsuitability does not arise. If the Tribunal decides that the appellant *has* been guilty of misconduct, then it will turn its attention to the separate, yet interlocked question, of unsuitability. The Tribunal has held in *Cunningham*[7] that one aspect of suitability to work with

---

[6] [2002] EWCA Civ 1113.
[7] [2002] 2 PC.

children is an assessment of risk, and that inevitably involves issues of balance and proportionality

So what is the appropriate standard to apply when making findings of fact? Scott Baker J said the following when the matter in 'C' came before him[8]:

> At the heart of the case lie the allegations that C raped and indecently assaulted S1. If true, the test in s 4(3) has plainly been satisfied. C was guilty of conduct which harmed a child and is unsuitable to work with children. The section makes it plain that the burden of proof before a tribunal lies on the Secretary of State. The standard of proof is the balance of probability. The more serious the allegation, the stronger should be the evidence before the court is satisfied that the event occurred. See Lord Nicholls in *Re H and others* [1996] 1 All ER1 and Lord Hoffman in *Secretary of State v Rehman* [2001] 1 All ER 122 at 144.

Latham LJ returned to the full dictum of Lord Nicholls in *Re H and others* and said that Lord Nicholls approached the question in two stages. First, the more serious the allegation the less likely the event occurred. Secondly, the less likely the event the stronger the evidence to support it must be. Latham LJ stated in terms that this approach remained an important protection for the individual.

Not all commentators are happy with the approach of Lord Nicholls in *Re H*. For example, when commenting on the Tribunal decision in 'C',[9] Professor Gillian Douglas hints that the balance may well have gone too far in the wrong direction. The individual now has a superior means of challenge than was previously the case via judicial review alone, but she hints that the protection of children may not be adequately safeguarded. She suggests that proof on the balance of probability may perhaps not be the appropriate test to apply in these types of case (See also Freeman, this volume). One could add, although she does not say so, that this would inevitably be the situation when bearing in mind the fact that the allegations are by definition always serious and thus will always require stronger evidence.

AN ALTERNATIVE APPROACH

An alternative approach could be expressed as follows. If assessment of risk is the issue in these cases, then the more serious the allegation the greater the risk, and the less need there should be for powerful evidence. The approach that has been urged on the Tribunal, so far without success, is the approach that would govern a local authority when conducting investigations. The issue came before Scott Baker J in *Re S (Sexual abuse allegations: A response)*.[10] In this case, the claimant formed a relationship with the mother of a 12-year-old girl. A couple of years later he was arrested and charged with having indecently assaulted the

---

[8] [2002] EWHC 1381 (Admin).
[9] [2002] *Family Law* 516.
[10] [2001] 2 FLR 776.

girl over the previous 18 months. He was acquitted. The claimant formed a relationship with another woman who had daughters of 11 and 7 and the couple
wished to set up house together with their respective children.

Both the local authority in whose area they wished to reside and the former
local authority began investigating the risks involved, under their powers laid
down in s 47 of the Children Act 1989. This section states:

> Where a local authority (b) have reasonable cause to suspect that a child who lives, or
> is found, in their area is suffering, or is likely to suffer, significant harm, the authority
> shall make, or cause to be made, such inquiries as they consider necessary to enable
> them to decide whether they should take any action to safeguard or promote the
> child's welfare.

And by s 47(8), where a local authority conclude that they should take action to
safeguard or promote the child's welfare they shall take that action so far as it
is both within their power and reasonably practicable for them to do so.

Both local authorities in this case made adverse findings. Indeed, the new
local authority formed the view that there was a medium to high risk of sexual
abuse to children unrelated to him and who lived in the same house. It concluded therefore that the new partner's former husband should be informed of
the risk analysis. Not unsurprisingly, the claimant sought judicial review of the
decisions of the local authorities.

Scott Baker J decided in this case that a local authority was entitled to proceed on the basis that there might be truth in allegations of sexual abuse, even
though there had been an acquittal at a criminal trial. All that was needed to
enable a local authority to proceed, was sufficient evidence to justify a finding of
reasonable cause to suspect a likelihood of significant harm. In effect they were
not required to make a finding on the balance of probability as to past conduct
before assessing risk and taking any necessary protective steps. The local
authority had to make a decision on risk.

There is of course a very significant difference between a test which talks
about 'balance of probability' (especially with the 'upward' gloss on that
approach as set down by Lord Nicholls), and 'reasonable cause to suspect' as
applied by Scott Baker J in *Re S (Sexual Abuse Allegations: Local Authority
Response)*. It could be argued that using the first test in the context of regulatory and prohibitory lists, emphasises, in a way that Parliament did not intend,
the individual's right to work with children, whilst the second test reflects the
protective nature of the legislation. However, the second approach, it could be
said, undermines the right of the individual to have an appeal on the merits of
the decision of the regulatory body and thereby undermines also Article 6 of
the European Convention on Human Rights (which protects the individual's
right to a fair hearing) now of course part of UK law. In addition, the application of the second test ignores the statutory basis of the Protection of
Children Act where the Tribunal is engaged in fact finding as well as risk
assessment.

All the cases so far have resulted in the application of Lord Nicholls' approach. This is almost certainly a reflection of the lawyers' reluctance to depart from the normal rules of the civil standard of proof, unless expressly directed so to do by Statute. Fact finding by its nature requires evidence, and it is therefore inevitable that the Tribunal will apply readily ascertainable evidential tools.

CARE STANDARD TRIBUNAL CASES

Let us look at a number of the decided cases, most dealing with issues of sexuality although others with abuse allegations generally. All the cases appear as files on the Care Standards Tribunal website (www.carestandardstribunal. gov.uk). The cases selected for discussion are of course only examples, but they do represent the beginnings of a developing jurisprudence in this sensitive area of the law and social policy.

An interesting case, already mentioned, is *Cunningham*[11]. It was common ground in this case that Mr Cunningham's name was included on the statutory Protection of Children Act (1999) list of those unsuitable to work with children, because he was named in the Waterhouse Report (Waterhouse, 1999). There were two incidents that formed the basis of the listing. The first took place whilst he was employed as a temporary child care officer and the second when he was a night care officer. They go back to dates in 1983 and 1984. In the first incident he is alleged to have head butted a child in the face causing the child's nose to bleed. The Waterhouse Inquiry concluded that he had used excessive force against this boy in provocative circumstances. The Tribunal looked at all the evidence. Mr Cunningham continued to deny that this particular event occurred. The Secretary of State did not produce any witness in support of the allegation and relied on documentary evidence taken in the form of a statement by another boy (who admitted that he had been sniffing glue at that time) made in 1992 and the transcript of his evidence before the Waterhouse Inquiry in 1997. The Tribunal decided on the basis of the evidence presented before it that the Secretary of State had not come up to proof on that first allegation and that in consequence Mr Cunningham was not guilty of misconduct as alleged. Thus, unsuitability as an assessment of risk exercise was not an issue.

So far as the second incident was concerned, an allegation of assault, Mr Cunningham had admitted all along that he had caused injury. The issue before the Tribunal therefore was whether he was unsuitable to work with children, the allegation of misconduct being proved. The Tribunal said:

> We are under a duty to assess the risk to children if Mr C were to return to work with children. He has no training in social care. We believe that the (second) incident is an illustration of his vulnerability within the environment in which he was working in

[11] [2002] 2 PC.

1983/84. There is nothing that we have read or heard which persuades us that the situation has changed since then. We feel that if Mr C were to be placed in such a provocative situation again, he would not be able to handle the situation in any way that would be different from how he dealt with the situation in 1984.

A successful appeal was brought by Dewi Black.[12] In 1998, the local authority were notified by a clinical psychologist that 'A' had disclosed to her that he had been sexually abused by Mr Black while residing in a Children's Home. There was an investigation. He was never prosecuted; however a Disciplinary Panel decided that three allegations of gross misconduct were found to be proved dating back to the early 1980s and he was dismissed. The Tribunal did hear evidence in this case, stretching indeed over four days. The Tribunal concluded that the evidence of the complainant was unreliable. The Tribunal therefore was not satisfied on the balance of probability that Mr Black was guilty of misconduct which harmed a child or placed a child at risk of harm. Assessment as to suitability to work with children was therefore not an issue.

A similar result occurred in M[13], involving allegations of sexual assault on children with severe learning difficulties. This case occupied the Tribunal for eight days. There were four charges against the applicant but no criminal proceedings were ever taken. The charges were as follows:

—That on an unspecified date, at a flat occupied by B, he instructed A (then a child) to take a shower and then watched and did nothing to intervene while another, unidentified man had sexual intercourse with A in the shower
—That on another unspecified date, also at the flat occupied by B, he kissed, stroked and cuddled R (then a child) during an episode when B had oral sex, and . . .
—That on another unspecified date he was present at the flat occupied by B when B had sexual intercourse with S and X (both of whom were then children) and he himself had sexual intercourse with S and X and then also had sexual relations with B in the presence of S and X and others
—That on many unspecified dates, in the bedroom of [the home] and/or at his own home, he repeatedly indecently assaulted and raped Y, both vaginally and anally, and subsequently threatened to kill Y, members of her family and/or her pet dog if she revealed what had happened to her.

The case against the appellant in M depended entirely upon interviews with A, R, S and Y. There were no video tapes or audio tapes of these interviews and the Tribunal could not properly judge the extent to which answers were spontaneous or given in response to leading questions. They were also unclear about the way the interviewees responded to the photographs and dolls. The Tribunal concluded on this evidence: '[It] was generally unable to give weight to the answers reportedly obtained or to attach significance to the reported non-verbal responses.'

---

[12] 0087.
[13] [2002] 7 PC.

These cases can be contrasted with *Woodcock*[14] and *M*[15], two schoolteacher cases. In *Woodcock*, the Tribunal said that it was satisfied 'to a very high standard' that Mr W kissed a number of pupils and that this kissing was misconduct within the meaning of the Act. The Tribunal said:

> We are supported in our view by the limited admission made by Mr W in this respect when he was first interviewed by the police and by the evidence of the other young children who were interviewed in connection with this matter, the majority of whom gave clear evidence, in an entirely consistent way, of Mr W kissing them and other boys in the class. We take the view that this evidence is probative as to dispel any reasonable doubt that these two matters are proved.

They made other findings that some acts occurred 'to a high level of probability' whereas they could not be satisfied 'given the high level of proof, which is required' that those other allegations were made out by the Department. The Tribunal applied the test in *Re H*, and indeed expressly rejected the criminal standard. It then turned to consider the question of suitability, and concluded that, given the seriousness of the allegations which it found proved, there was no doubt as to his unsuitability to work with children. The Tribunal said:

> We have reached this conclusion both because of the seriousness of the misconduct and the fact that Mr W has consistently denied that misconduct and has hence had no opportunity for treatment which might have led us to a different conclusion.

M was another case involving a teacher, who was alleged to have downloaded child pornography on to his home computer. He had been prosecuted for these matters, and the Crown Court had overturned a conviction in the Magistrates' Court. He denied any knowledge of having this material on his computer, and insisted that friends of his with access to his home computer must have downloaded it. This case turned solely on fact finding, because Mr M himself, whilst denying that he was responsible for the material on his computer, accepted categorically in his evidence that anyone who did download such material should not be allowed to teach.

Paragraph 25 of the Guidance for Education Staff states that certain behaviour may present an unacceptable example, and that it is necessary to uphold the high standards of behaviour expected of members of the teaching profession. There will therefore be cases where the facts are proved, and suitability becomes the primary issue.

One such case is *H*[16]. In 1996, Mr H was arrested and interviewed in connection with offences relating to magazines and other material found in his possession. He was convicted of five offences under s 42 of the Customs Consolidation Act 1867 relating to the importation of magazines of an indecent and obscene nature. The material was mainly collections of photographs of boys aged seven

14 [2002] 4 PC.
15 [2002] 11 PC.
16 [2002] 10 PC.

to eighteen. It included pictures of young boys and teenagers actually mastur-
bating or simulating masturbation. He was fined £150 on each conviction and
ordered to pay costs amounting to £1000. His work as a schoolteacher was
restricted by the Department of Education, which in effect said that he could
only be employed at a school that did not admit male pupils. He appealed to the
Tribunal, in effect saying that his 'interest in the physical development of children is purely academic and had never involved any risk to children.'

The Tribunal in this case assessed the risk. Mr H had urged upon the
Tribunal the view that the material that led to his conviction was not obscene.
He said that this material is legitimately available in Germany and it contained
material of general naturist interest. He is an active naturist and attends naturist events, such as weekends and holidays and sporting activities, such as swim-
ming. The Tribunal took a contrary view. It accepted that the possession of the
material indicated an interest in young males that was inappropriate. The
Tribunal was concerned to explore whether there might be a 'break through'
into actual activity with a pupil, such as touching. They decided that the risk,
although small, was real not least because Mr H did not appear to recognise the
boundaries of acceptable behaviour. They dismissed the appeal and maintained
the restriction on Mr H's teaching in schools with male pupils.

In an early case, *Ovens*[17], the allegations were all of excessive discipline. The
appellant had been dismissed as a result of these allegations being proved before
a disciplinary hearing. She then attended a full-time Advanced Diploma in
therapeutic counselling and as part of this course she was required to undergo
regular personal therapy and group therapy. She told the Tribunal that this had
enabled her to learn a great deal about herself, where her skills lay and the extent
of her limitations. The Tribunal assessed the risk of allowing her to resume
work with children now. It said:

> In determining the applicant's suitability to work with children now, account needed
> to be taken of the fact that the applicant had taken stock of the situation and had taken
> positive steps to find a position and career which she enjoyed and was good at. As part
> of a counselling course she had undergone personal therapy which had made her
> aware of her strengths and weaknesses.

The Tribunal was not satisfied that the applicant was now unsuitable to work
with children, and the appeal was allowed.

CONCLUSION

All the above cases have necessarily been decided on their own facts. It is always
difficult to find facts proved or not in this area, especially bearing in mind that
there will be cases where the allegations go back many years. The knowledge

---

[17] 0017.

that successful negligence actions have been launched forms the backdrop to some of these 'legacy' cases, and standards and acceptable practices have changed over the years. Social policy in social work and education has shifted over time. The Tribunal is tasked with achieving the correct balance; a responsibility that it has been happy to accept. Only experience will provide the information as to whether the decisions have provided the clarity and guidance that is so important in this field.

REFERENCES

LAMING, LORD, (Chair), *Report of the Victoria Climbie Inquiry* (Cm 5730, 2003).

WATERHCURSE, R, (Chair), *Lost in Care : Report of the Tribunal of Inquiry into the Abuse of Children in Care in the former County Council Areas of Gwynedd and Clwyd since 1974* (The Stationery Office, London, 2000).

16

The Sexual Zone between Childhood and the Age of Majority: Claims to Sexual Freedoms Versus Protectionist Policies

KERRY PETERSEN

1. INTRODUCTION[1]

In general, laws regulating sexuality are based on social constructs about moral values, cultural assumptions and gender issues. However, in the case of young people, these laws are also shaped by claims to personal autonomy, parental responsibilities and the state's duties and powers. It is well established that parents today no longer have absolute rights over their children. Rather, during the 18 years from the time of birth until the age of majority, laws and policies recognise that 'children can exercise rights only to the extent of their evolving capacities' (Heinz, 2000). This is acknowledged in article 5 of the international blueprint on children's rights, the Convention of the Rights of Child, which requires Parties to:

> [R]espect the responsibilities, rights and duties of parents [or guardians] to provide in a manner consistent with the *evolving capacities of the child*, appropriate directions and guidance in the exercise of the rights recognised in the present Convention.[2]

Even though liberal democracies wrestle with perceptions of children's sexuality, it is also well recognised that the evolving capacities of children require appropriate direction and guidance from parents or guardians and respect for children's rights. Children do not become sexual beings suddenly on the day of the 18th birthday! In any case, children learn about sex from an early age

---

[1] I would like to acknowledge and thank Tessa Hanscombe for her assistance with the research for this paper and for her generosity, humour and diligence.

[2] Emphasis added.

through the media, books, the internet and advertising. Many have sexual experience by the time they reach 18 years (Rissel *et al.*, 2003).

In this chapter I address the criminal regulation of consensual adolescent sex and explore tensions between autonomy rights and the state's duty to protect children from harm through an examination of common law developments in family and medical law. The statutes governing 'under age' sex offences in the Australian States and Territories will be used to illustrate how the state regulates adolescent sexuality. It is important to emphasise at the outset that the primary focus of this chapter is on young people engaging voluntarily in consensual sexual activity, rather than *non*-consensual sexual activity. The formal legal terms for children under 18 years are child and minor; however, words such as adolescent, teenager or young person are also used to describe a person who is enjoying the years between childhood and the age of majority. Sometimes, the word children is more convenient, particularly when referring to all persons under 18 years—as a broad cohort.

It is regarded as common ground that the regulation of consensual sexuality between adolescent peers can be problematic because of the diversity of social and moral values which form the basis of liberal democracies. In addition, approaches to adolescent sexuality are influenced by the interconnection of:

—parental rights and duties
—children's rights to personal inviolability and agency
—state rights and duties

As parental rights have dwindled, the autonomy rights of children have expanded in various areas of law including family law, medical law and disability law. Nevertheless, and in the face of these developments, the criminal law continues to restrict adolescent sexual activity ostensibly on protection grounds.

Criminal law is a powerful social instrument which is presumed to reflect and reinforce ideas of sexual normality including gender, sex roles and stereotypes. It structures moral thinking and defines social assumptions about limits and legitimacy (Lacey, 2001). It also performs a vital role 'in setting standards of acceptable and unacceptable conduct' (Home Office, 2000 para 3.1.2). However, it is a very blunt tool for restricting the sexual autonomy of competent and consenting adolescents to engage in sexual activity. Moreover, as the role of the criminal law is to prohibit heinous and abhorrent behaviour and to protect individuals and the community from harm, there is real concern about the potentially harmful impact of criminal legislation on adolescents who are not engaging in genuinely criminal behaviour.

It is contended here that consensual adolescent sexuality is neither heinous nor abhorrent and that using criminal laws to prohibit adolescents from engaging in sex in private, may be more harmful than not. A better approach to respecting autonomy rights and protecting adolescents from harm can be gleaned from medical law principles governing competence and consent to medical treatment. The application of these principles would also enhance reproductive choice and health interests, which are an extension of the right to sexual autonomy. After all, there is no real choice unless adolescents are provided with information about sex and the potential health consequences of sexual activity through schools based sex-health education programmes and access to counselling, contraception and abortion.

The developments in medical refusal cases are also relevant to ideas about sexual autonomy because they make it clear that being medically or sexually competent is not the same as having full agency and that the state retains residual power to protect the interests of all minors. On this basis, it is acknowledged that it may be appropriate to use the criminal law to protect competent young people from their peers when sex is not strictly consensual because of a power imbalance—even between legally competent minors. This is referred to as 'coercive peer sex' because consent would *not* be a free and genuine agreement to the act. The lack of agreement could be express or implied from the context. For example, where there is bullying or coercive behaviour, but where the nature of coercion would not satisfy the criminal elements required to establish a lack of consent for an assault or rape charge.

2. CHILDREN'S RIGHTS: BACKGROUND

A snapshot of the family law and medical law background in Australia and England provides insights into early developments affecting the legal and social status of children. In the contemporary world of individualism and rights where words are regarded as an important form of ideological expression, the phrase 'married women, infants and lunatics' previously found in statutes would be offensive to many. This phrase was inherited from the ancient common law *parens patriae* jurisdiction and it encapsulated the *traditional* western family— a social unit dominated by a patriarchal husband/father and a wife who at common law, with infants and lunatics, had no legal capacity.

The gradual emancipation of married women from the legal restrictions of *coverture* began in the late nineteenth century.[3] However, the recognition of children's rights and interests only began to emerge in the second half of the twentieth century (Eekelaar, 1992). In the much-cited case *Re Agar-Ellis*,[4] the Court of Appeal held that a father continued to have control over the person, education and conduct of his children until they reach 21 years. However, nearly a century later, in *Hewer v Bryant*[5] Lord Denning took the view that parental custody rights started with the right to control and dwindled to little more than

---

[3] For an overview of the legal consequences of marriage for women and the Married Women's Property Acts in Britain and the Australian States in the late 19th and early 20th centuries, see Graycar and Morgan (2002): 90–6.

[4] (1883) 24 Ch. D. 317.

[5] [1970] 1 QB 357.

the right to advise—as the child grew older. Nevertheless, in the 1913 medical consent case *Schloendorff v Society of New York,* Justice Cardozo specifically excluded children from the right to self determination when he stated that 'every human being of adult years and sound mind has the right to determine what shall be done with his own body.'[6]

(a) England: Consent and Refusal to Medical Treatment

In England and Wales, minors who attained the age of 16 years were permitted to give an effective consent to medical and dental treatment by the Family Law Reform Act in 1969. However, common law rights for those under 16 years continued to be unclear until *Gillick v West Norfolk and Wisbech Area Health Authority*[7] was decided. *Gillick's case* concerned the right of children under 16 to obtain contraception advice and treatment from a doctor without parental consent. The age of 16 was particularly relevant because of the Family Law Reform Act and also because of the possibility that a doctor who prescribed contraceptives to a young girl could be charged with aiding and abetting an offence of unlawful sexual intercourse under section 6 of the Sexual Offences Act 1956. The plaintiff, Victoria Gillick, sought to determine the primacy of parental rights over her children. The central issue was whether parents could veto medical treatment by failing or refusing to give consent to treatment to which the child might consent.

The majority of the House of Lords rejected any rule of absolute parental authority until a fixed age. It held that a doctor could lawfully give contraceptive advice or treatment to a girl under 16 without parental knowledge or consent, providing she had sufficient understanding and intelligence to enable her to understand fully what was being proposed. A young person who passed this test became known as a 'mature minor' and is referred to as '*Gillick*-competent'. The House of Lords also held that parental rights stem from the duty to protect and as children become increasingly independent parental authority dwindles accordingly.[8] *Gillick's case* is widely acclaimed throughout common law jurisdictions as a benchmark decision in the area of children's rights. However, the speeches of the Lords reveal an underlying 'conflict between competing views of childhood' which also lies at the core of debates about laws and policies (Heinz, 2000: 19).[9]

These common law and statutory developments regarding '*Gillick*-competence' have had a significant impact on sexual autonomy and reproductive choice. The exercise of personal autonomy is dependent on adolescents

---

[6] (1914) 105 NE 92, 93.
[7] [1986] AC 112.
[8] For recent legal and policy developments see Bridge (2002).
[9] For an analysis of the judicial attitudes towards children's rights see Pilcher (1997).

being sufficiently informed about the consequences of engaging in sexual activity—so that they can make choices and protect themselves from harmful consequences. However, the access to sexual and reproductive choice in this context depends to a large extent on the provision of information and the support of health professionals. As legal gatekeepers, health professionals have considerable influence over access to the means of exercising choice in terms of physical health and reproduction. This responsibility covers respect for confidentiality and privacy issues as well as public health concerns.

In the early post-*Gillick* phase, it was accepted by many that the right to consent to treatment was accompanied by the parallel right to refuse treatment. However, as time went by the complexities of the ruling began to unfold in refusal cases. Mason argues that while consent and refusal are both aspects of personal autonomy, it seems that the test of '*Gillick*-competence' 'requires a different quality of understanding in respect of refusal of treatment than is needed for a valid consent' (Mason, 1998: 57). His view that the level required of understanding may be higher for refusal than consent has been borne out by the English courts in a number of refusal cases (Mason, 1998). The courts have retained control over a minor's refusal to consent to medical treatment by establishing that the *parens patriae* jurisdiction applies to competent minors.

In the following cases, where the potential for serious medical outcomes was imminent, the courts overrode the wishes of competent adolescents on the basis of the 'best interests' test. In *Re R (A Minor) (Wardship): (Consent to Treatment)*[10] a 15 year old minor with a sad family history in the care of the local authority consented to go to an adult psychiatric unit and take antipsychotic drugs. She became increasingly psychotic but also had rational periods during which she objected to taking medication. The local authority began wardship proceedings and applied to the court for leave to administer the medication without her consent. According to the medical evidence, R would return to a psychotic state without the drugs, but between episodes she understood the nature of her illness and treatment. During intermission periods she was sufficiently competent to give or refuse consent. The Court of Appeal granted an order overriding *R's* decision to refuse treatment irrespective of her competence. The girl in this case was below the age of 16, but in any event, the court found R was not sufficiently competent to refuse consent because of the fluctuating nature of her mental illness.

In *Re W (A Minor) (Medical Treatment)*[11] a minor aged 16 years was suffering from anorexia nervosa and in the care of a local authority. She was in imminent danger of becoming infertile and eventually dying of starvation. Although the trial judge found that W had sufficient understanding to make an informed decision and was legally competent, he made an order permitting the authority

---

[10] [1991] 3 WLR 592.
[11] [1992] 3 WLR 758.

to move her to another unit against her wishes and to administer treatment without her consent. The Court of Appeal, without disturbing the trial judge's finding, ordered that W should be fed artificially and transferred to the specialist unit holding that the Court retained a residual power to order treatment and against the minor's wishes. Lord Donaldson queried her competence to make a decision on the basis that anorexia nervosa is a disease which is capable of destroying the ability to make an informed choice. The Court of Appeal ruled that competency which satisfies the 'mature minor' test does not give minors the power of veto. Lord Donaldson outlined the legal position as follows:

> There is ample authority for the proposition that the inherent powers of the court under its *parens patriae* jurisdiction is theoretically limitless and they certainly extend beyond the powers of a natural parent. There can therefore be no doubt that it has the power to override the refusal of a minor, whether over the age of 16 or under that age but '*Gillick* competent'.[12]

In *Re M (Child: Refusal of Medical treatment)*[13] a minor aged 15 and a half had suffered heart failure and according to medical advice her only chance of surviving was to receive a heart transplantation. M's mother gave her consent to the transplantation but the girl refused. The issue of competency was fudged but there was no finding of incompetence. The case differed from *Re R* and *Re W* in so far as she was not a ward of the court but living with her mother. Citing Lord Donaldson's speech in *Re W* with approval, Johnson J drew in the inherent powers of the court in its *parens patriae* jurisdiction and overrode M's wishes on the basis that the heart transplantation was in her best interest.

The final case in this section on refusal cases concerned a competent 15-year-old minor who was not facing death or a serious medical outcome but was being forced to leave her home. In *South Glamorgan County Council v B and W*[14] the court decided that the minor could be sent to an adolescent unit for assessment and treatment against her wishes, on the grounds that the court's jurisdiction over minors is unlimited and the decision was in her best interests.

These cases illustrate how the English courts have re-established the primacy of state interests over minors since *Gillick* was decided. These developments have occurred mainly in the refusal cases where there was severe danger to life and health and where the courts increased the level of understanding required, but the *Glamorgan County Council* case signals how far the courts are prepared to intrude on children's autonomy rights.

---

[12] [1992] 3 WLR, 769.
[13] [1998] Fam.Law 753.
[14] (1992) 11 BMLR 162.

(b) Australia: Consent and Refusal to Medical Treatment

The recognition of children's autonomy rights in the field of medical law also emerged in the Australian parliaments and courts later in the twentieth century. Similar statutes to the English Family Law Reform Act 1969 were enacted in the Australian states of New South Wales and South Australia clarifying the rights of older children to consent to medical treatment.[15] In the other states and territories, common law rights regarding consent and refusal for children under 16 years were unclear prior to the decision in *Secretary, Dept of Health and Community Services v JWB and SMB (Marion's Case)*.[16] In *Marions's case*, the majority of the High Court of Australia upheld the principle of personal inviolability and confirmed that the court's consent is required for invasive procedures such as sterilisation. The High Court adopted the 'mature minor' principle developed in *Gillick* and decided that the capacity of a child to give an informed consent to medical treatment depends upon the rate of development of each individual child. The '*Gillick*-competence' test is now part of the Australian common law.[17] The High Court also decided that 1983 amendments to the Family Law Act 1975 (Cth) conferred jurisdiction on the Family Court similar to the *parens patriae* jurisdiction. The '*Gillick*-competence' test has been applied in subsequent Family Court cases where consent has been sought.[18]

Guidelines are now available for medical practitioners, when assessing a minor's competence and maturity to consent to medical treatment. For example, guidelines published by the Medical Practitioners Board of Victoria (MPBV) specifically advise medical practitioners that:

> the doctor is entitled to accept consent from the minor without parental consent provided that:
>
> —The child refuses to inform parents or legal guardians of intended treatment
> —The treatment is in the child's best interests
> —The proposed treatment or outcome are not so grave and complex as to be difficult for a minor to fully understand (MPBV (2002)).

Medical practitioners are also advised to document the assessment of maturity in the medical record together with the factors taken into consideration.

However, the question of whether or not the Family Court of Australia would override the refusal of a '*Gillick*-competent' minor and follow the English

---

[15] Minors (Property and Contracts) Act 1970 (NSW) s 49; Consent to Medical treatment and Palliative Care Act 1995 (SA) ss 6, 13. See also Morgan (1986).

[16] (1992) 175 CLR 218.

[17] Australian courts are no longer bound by English precedents but they may be regarded as having persuasive authority. In *Marion's case*, the High Court of Australia went a little further and probably took this step to clarify and unify consent law for minors in all the Australian jurisdictions.

[18] See: *Re A* [1993] FLC 92–402; *Re Michael* [1994] FLC 92–471.

authorities has yet to be tested. Much would depend upon the requirement of understanding and the nature of the proposed procedure. Nicholson *et al.*, have suggested that the Family Court of Australia would be likely to adopt a similar approach to the Court of Appeal if circumstances such as the ones in *Re R* and *Re W* arose (Nicholson *et al.*, 2001: 239).

The MPVB Guidelines advise that parents cannot override the consent of a competent minor but the Family Court may do so if the Court decided this would be in the minor's best interests (MPBV (2002)).

3. AUSTRALIAN CRIMINAL LAWS REGULATING SEX: PERSONS UNDER 18

Australia is a federation of six States and two Territories. Parliaments have jurisdiction over offences such as the 'age of consent' laws which were inherited from England in the nineteenth century.[19] Today, it is said that the purpose of these laws is to protect children from harm (Home Office, 2000: para 3.1.4). As Lancaster says:

> The protection is provided by the law until the young are sufficiently mature and physically, mentally and emotionally to understand all the implications that attach to sexual relationships and the consent they give to them (Lancaster, 2001: 34).

In common with other countries, the Australian jurisdictions structure legislation according to the chronological age of the child. The following Tables compare the laws in each state and territory. At one end of the age scale, there is the age of sexual majority, commonly referred to as the 'age of consent'. Once they reach this statutory age, young people have full agency over their sexual behaviour (Table 1). At the other end of the age scale, a line of statutory prohibition has been created by statute under which sex with children below a certain age is forbidden (Table 2). In between is a grey area in which there are zones of qualified prohibitions which permit, via statutory defences, some consensual sex and which are based on age (Table 3). Finally, some states have passed 'Special Care' offences whereby it is an offence for persons in position of care or authority to have sex with a young person—even when they have reached the age of consent but are not yet 18 years old (Table 4).

---

[19] English 'sexual ravishment' laws goes back to the thirteenth century commencing with the Statute of Westminster I, 1275 which made it an offence to ravish 'any maiden without age' whether or not she gave her consent. Later, the Statute of Westminster II, 1285, upgraded the offence to a felony punishable by death. Initially the age was considered to be under 12 years but later it was not treated as the felony of rape if the girl was between 10–12 years and gave her consent. In England, the current age of consent is 16 years (Bevan, 1973).

(a) **Age of Sexual Majority:**

Table 1. Age of sexual majority

State/ Territory	NSW	QLD	SA	Tas	Vic	WA	ACT	NT
Age	16	Female: 16 Male: no limit	17	17	16	16	16	Female: 16 Male: no limit

The age of sexual majority is the age when people are regarded as possessing full capacity to consent to sexual relationships.[20] The age of sexual majority ranges from 16 to 17 years in each Australian jurisdiction, except in Queensland and the Northern Territory where there are no limits placed on the age at which males can have heterosexual sex: see Table 1 above. For example, in Queensland, a 14-year-old male can have sex lawfully with a woman who is 16 or over. However, a 14-year-old male cannot have homosexual sex until he reaches the age of majority.

In NSW, unequal and discriminatory provisions were recently removed by the Crimes Amendment (Sexual Offences) Bill 2003. Now the law provides for the equal treatment of sexual offences irrespective of whether the victim or the perpetrator is male or female. The new provisions have also established the same age of consent for heterosexual and homosexual intercourse, bringing NSW into line with all other Australian jurisdictions except the Northern Territory and Queensland.

Table 2. Prohibitions: penetrative sex

State/ Territory	NSW	QLD	SA	Tas	Vic	WA	ACT	NT
Age	< 10	Female: <12 Male: no limit	< 12	<12	<10	<13	<10	Female: <12 Male: no limit

[20] In 'special care' relationships, the age of sexual minority has been extended by a year or two in all jurisdictions except Tasmania and the ACT. See Table 4.

Below the age of majority, the laws prohibit penetrative sex with a child who is under a certain age. Once again, there is variation throughout the Australian jurisdictions ranging from under 10 to under 13. No limits are placed on the age when males in Queensland and the Northern Territory can have penetrative sex. The rationale underlying these prohibitions is that children under these ages are unable to give a true consent to engage in sex because they are physically and emotionally dependent and not yet fully mature.

In addition, it is worth pointing out that crimes can only be committed by children above a certain age and therefore any form of sexual activity between two children under this statutory age is not criminal.[21] This means sexual games between children such as 'doctors and nurses' are not prohibited.

(c) Consensual Penetrative Sex: Statutory Defences:

The law permits some sexual activity before a young person reaches the age of sexual majority in most jurisdictions through the creation of specific legislative defences.[22] Each State and Territory except NSW classifies consensual sexual penetration under the age of sexual majority as a criminal offence, but qualifies the offence with the defences of similar age, mistaken age and marriage.

Defence of Similar Age

In Victoria,[23] Tasmania,[24] South Australia, Western Australia and the ACT[25], a statutory defence is provided for consensual sexual activity where the young persons are similarly aged. However, this defence is not available to young people in NSW,[26] the Northern Territory and Queensland. In South Australia, the defence only applies where both parties are aged 16.

---

[21] For example, in NSW, SA and Victoria, the age of criminal liability is 10. Children (Criminal Proceedings) Act 1987 (NSW), s 5; Young Offenders Act 1993 (SA) s 5; Children and Young Persons Act 1989 (Vic) s127.

[22] There are also provisions dealing with indecent acts not involving penetration with children which also include legislative defences; however, these offences go beyond the discussion in this chapter on sex between consenting young people.

[23] In Victoria the defence applies if the child is 10 or older and the accused is no more than 2 years older. Crimes Act s 45 (4) (b).

[24] Tasmanian legislation proscribes two different age cohorts: where the young person is aged 15 or 16, a defence applies where the accused is not more than 5 years older than the young person: *s 124(3)(a)*. When the young person is aged 12, 13 or 14, a defence applies where the accused is not more than 3 years older: *s 124(3)(b)*. However, these similar age defences do not apply to heterosexual or homosexual anal intercourse: *s 124(5)*.

[25] In ACT, a defence arises where the young person is 10 or older, and consents to sexual intercourse with the accused who is not more than 2 years older than the young person.

[26] The recent amendments to the NSW Act abolished the defence previously available to people aged between 14 and 16 engaging in consensual sexual activity and the situation is now subject by prosecutorial discretion.

Table 3. Legislative defences

	NSW Criminal Law Act 1900	QLD Criminal Code 1989	SA Criminal Law Consolidation Act 1935	Tas Criminal Code Act 1924	Vic Crimes Act 1958	WA Criminal Code Act 1913	ACT Crimes Act 1900	NT Criminal Law Consolidation Act 1935
Consensual penetrative sex where partner is a similar age	No defence	Female: No defence / Male: All ages	16 s 49(4)	12–16 124(3)	10–15 s 45(4)(b)	13–15	10–15 s 92E(3)(b)	Female: No defence / Male: All ages
Consensual homosexual penetrative sex with partner of similar age	No defence	18 208(1)	16 s 49(4)	No defence 124(5)	10–15 s 45(4)(b)	13–15	10–15 s 92E(3)(b)	18 s 128
Consensual sexual activity where offender is mistaken of the child's true age	No defence	Female: 12–15 / Male: All ages	16 s 49(4)(b)(ii)	12–16 s 124(2)	10–15 s 45(4)(a)	13–15 s 321(9)	10–15 s 92E(3)(a)	Female: 12–16 s 129(3) / Male: All ages
Consensual sexual activity where both parties are married to each other	16 s 73(5)	No defence	12–16 s 49(8)	No defence	10–15 s 45(4)(c)	13–15 s 321(10)	No defence	No defence

Consensual penetrative sex between young people is an offence but legislative defences apply in various circumstances. Relatively, this can be described as a flexible form of regulation but the law continues to label consensual sex between teenagers as a criminal act. The rationale underlying these provisions is that *not all* adolescents in this age group have sufficient maturity to understand the consequences of engaging in sexual activity.

In most jurisdictions, the same prohibitions and defences apply to both heterosexual and homosexual penetrative sex. This means young people are permitted to have either anal or vaginal intercourse at the same age. However, in Tasmania and Queensland anal sex ('sodomy' in Queensland) is prohibited for all young people under 18 years old. This means a young person reaches the age of sexual majority for heterosexual sex before they are permitted to engage in homosexual or heterosexual anal sex. In the Northern Territory, females but not males are permitted to engage in anal sex and anal sex involving males under 18 is prohibited as 'sexual intercourse or gross indecency between males.' Yet, in the Northern Territory and Queensland the minimum age for heterosexual activity is not limited for boys. Homosexual sex between males is subject to more regulation with heavier penalties than all other forms of sexual acts in those jurisdictions.

Defence of Reasonable Mistake

In all jurisdictions except NSW, the accused can plead a defence of reasonable mistake regarding the age of the victim and the criminal onus is on the prosecution to prove that the accused lacked an honest belief. In NSW, this defence of reasonable mistake was removed by the Crimes Amendment (Sexual Offences) Bill 2003. In South Australia, the defence only applies where the accused believed on reasonable grounds that the minor was of or over the age of 16 *and* the accused was not more than three years older than the minor.[27] This defence does not apply to young males in the Northern Territory or Queensland because there are no limitations on women having sex with them.[28]

Defence of Marriage

As an expression of cultural tolerance, some Australian jurisdictions have refrained from criminalising consensual sex between married spouses who are under the statutory 'age of consent'. In Australia, the marriageable age is 18

---

[27] However, in SA, the defence of reasonable mistake does not apply where the accused is the guardian, schoolmaster, schoolmistress or teacher of a young person under 18: Criminal Law Consolidation Act SA (1935) s 49(5). WA similarly restricts the defence of reasonable mistake to situations where the accused is not more than 3 years older than the child (*s 321(9a)*, and does not apply where a similarly aged accused is in a position of care, supervision or authority over the child (*s 321(9)*).

[28] However, in Queensland, the crime of sodomy with a person under 18 is subject to the defence of reasonable mistake where the offender reasonably believed the young person was aged over 18: *s 208(3)*.

years. However, in exceptional and unusual circumstances, it may be lowered by the court for a person who has attained the age of 16.[29]

(d) Indecent Acts

The laws in Table 3 do not cover non-penetrative sex such as touching or exhibitionism. These sexual activities may come under statutory provisions dealing with indecency. For example, in the State of Victoria, it is an offence for a person to commit willingly an indecent act with or in the presence of a child under 16 years to whom he or she is not married. Consent is not a defence but legislative defences such as similar age, reasonable mistake as to age, and marriage are available to the accused.[30]

(e) 'Special Care' Offences: Table 4

	NSW	QLD	SA	Tas	Vic	WA	ACT	NT
Consensual penetrative sex with adult in position of 'special care'	18 s 73	Female 16 ——— Male[31] All ages	18 s 49(5)	–	18 s 45(2)(b)	18 s 322	–	Female 16 ——— Male No

These offences come under the scope of the state's protective duty even though they can apply even where the young person has reached the age of sexual majority. In these jurisdictions, an irrebuttable presumption has been imposed on sexual relationships where there is an imbalance of power between a young person and a person in a position of care, authority or supervision. In some States, the legislature has adopted an inclusive approach and refers to people in care, supervision and authority, such as teachers and guardians. On the other hand, NSW has adopted an exclusive definition, and specifically refers to certain categories of people, such as heath professionals, religious instructors and step-parents. These provisions also cover the situation where a minor has authority over younger children, for example in a school situation where an older student is supervising a younger one. Tasmania and ACT have no specific special care provisions in the criminal law.

[29] Marriage Act 1961 (Cth) ss 11, 12.
[30] Crimes Act 1958 (Vic) s 47.
[31] No person in any position can commit sodomy with any male person under 18 (*s 208, 229B(10)*). Where the child is in the guardianship or care of the offender, a penalty of life imprisonment applies for sodomy (*s 208(2)(b)(ii)*).

(f) Discussion

In international terms, the age of consent varies from country to country; however, there is a trend towards standardisation between 15 and 17. Spain has the lowest age of consent at 12. In Italy the age of consent is 14. Canada permits consensual sex from the age of 14 and throughout the United States the age of consent varies from 14 to 18. In France, Sweden, Denmark, Poland and the Czech Republic, the age of consent is 15. Germany, the Netherlands, Switzerland, New Zealand and Portugal set the age limit at 16. In England, Wales and Scotland it is 16 but Northern Ireland and the Republic of Ireland have an age of 17 for heterosexual sex (Home Office, 2002: para 3.5.4). Australia and the UK both have an age of sexual majority which is tends to be on the higher part of the age scale.

Laws governing the statutory line of prohibition vary from 10 to 13 in Australia In addition, there are considerable variations throughout the Australian jurisdictions in the grey areas where teenagers under the age of sexual majority can engage in consensual sex with their peers. As Australia is generally a homogenous country, and leaving aside minority ethnic and indigenous factors, it seems unlikely that the sexual behaviour of teenagers varies greatly. Yet why are male teenagers in Queensland considered competent to consent to sex at all ages, while males and females in South Australia and Tasmania must wait until they turn 17? It seems more likely that different laws in each jurisdiction are driven by political and other interests rather than a genuine protection based policy. Possibly, these legislative frameworks represent a world that powerful 'elders' regard as morally appropriate, rather than the world we live in, which imposes 'constant pressure of sexualised images in Western countries [creating] pressures on adolescents to have sexual relationships' (Skinner and Hickey 2003: 159). Another way of addressing consensual teenage sex under the age of sexual majority is to substitute a *Gillick*-style test of competence for the indiscriminate system of defences currently available. The recent UK Law Commission Report includes some discussion on the benefits of introducing a statutory test for capacity to engage in sexual relationships which is based on the *Gillick* test and in line with post *Gillick* case developments. This test could be adapted to the Australian legal schema. Essentially, it would provide that a person has capacity to consent to sex if he or she has the maturity to make a decision about engaging in sexual activity; and has sufficient understanding or intelligence to understand the information relevant to the decision, including information about the reasonably foreseeable consequences of deciding one way or another or of failing to make the decision. In determining whether a minor has sufficient understanding and intelligence for these purposes, account would need to be taken of the seriousness and implications of the decision to engage in sexual activity (Law Commission, 2000: 3.7).

4. ADOLESCENT SEXUAL ACTIVITY

The following studies on teenagers and sexual activity are discussed briefly in order to place the criminal laws on under-age sex in the context of the adolescent experience. The major focus of the published research has been on heterosexual activity, but more information is becoming available about same sex adolescent activity.[32] Moreover, a recent Australian study found that 8.6% of women and 5.9% of men reported some homosexual experience in their lives. And 25% of the men who reported homosexual experience were 15 years or younger; whereas only 14.6% of women were the same age (Grulich *et al.*, 2003: 155). The following information refers mainly to heterosexual adolescents, but issues concerned with health and education are equally applicable to same sex adolescents.

There are three main points to be made about adolescent sexual activity. First, it is well established that there has been a steady decline in the age of first experience of vaginal intercourse in Australia and the UK, and this is consistent with international trends. Second, the health and well being interests of adolescents are best served by delaying sexual activity until they are mature enough to understand the consequences and this is best achieved through school based sex-health education programmes designed to assist adolescents to make informed decisions about engaging in sexual activity. Third, clearly a proportion of adolescents will inevitably engage in sexual activity before they are sufficiently mature, legally and individually or personally, to understand the consequences of sexual activity.

(a) Age of Sexual Debut

In the mid 1990s, it was reported that the majority of Australian students had experienced some sexual activity such as kissing and sexual touching, and 68% of those who reached the final year of secondary school had experienced sexual intercourse.[33] By 2003, it was reported that the median age for sexual touching was 15 years or less, and the median age for sexual intercourse was approximately 17 years for secondary school students. However, in technical schools, the median age of first intercourse was reported to be 16 years.

Rissel *et al.*, observe that:

The majority of high school students think it is acceptable to engage in genital touching, oral sex and vaginal intercourse before the age of 17 years (Rissel *et al.*, 2003).

---

[32] See Hillier *et al.*, 1998).

[33] 'The majority of the young people have experienced some sexual activity such as kissing or sexual touching. Also, 20% of year 10 students (15 years old) and 48% of year 12 students (17 years old) has experienced sexual intercourse' see Lindsay *et al.*, (1997).

The incidence of teenage pregnancy is another way of gauging sexual activity in that age group. In 2003 it was reported that a substantial proportion of Australian teenagers are sexually active and Australia has the sixth highest teenage pregnancy rate and one of the highest teenage abortion rates among selected OECD countries (Skinner and Hickey, 2003: 159). More specifically the evidence shows that legally induced abortions were the second most common hospital procedure and reason for hospital admission in young women aged 12–24 in Australia in 1997–1998.[34] In addition, the average national abortion rate is estimated to be 22 abortions per 1000 teenagers per year, compared with 19 live births (Moon *et al.*, 1999).

At the start of the 1990s, heterosexual teenagers in the UK were becoming sexually active some four years earlier than those making their sexual debut in the early 1950s (Wellings *et al.*, 1995: 418). It was reported in a 1990–1991 UK study that, 'of women aged 16–19, 18.7% had sexual intercourse before the age of 16 . . . for men the equivalent proportions are 27.6% of men' aged 16–19 (Wellings *et al.*, 1995: 418). A later study of a probability sample survey taken between 1999 and 2001, found that although young women were more sexually active in the 1990s than those in earlier decades, there has been 'a stabilisation of the proportion having first heterosexual intercourse before age 16 years among young women'. In addition, the median age at first intercourse was lower for men than women (Wellings *et al.*, 2001). Finally, the 2000 NATSAL (National Survey of Sexual Attitudes and Lifestyles) Survey found that the average age at first intercourse had fallen for women and men from 17 years to 16 years (cited in House of Commons Health Committee (2003): para 70).

Once again, teenage pregnancy rates are an important indicator of sexual activity amongst young people. More recent information based on data for 1998 reveals that the UK today has the highest rate of teenage pregnancy in Europe (almost five times higher than the Netherlands) and is second only to the United States in the developed world (House of Commons Health Committee (2003): para 64). Furthermore, in the year 2000 there were 8000 conceptions among girls under 16 years, and this constituted less than a tenth of the total number of teenage conceptions. Of these conceptions, 400 were to girls under the age of 14, and 160 of them led to maternity (para 65).[35]

Statistics show that the abortion rates in England and Wales have almost quadrupled since therapeutic abortion was made legal by the Abortion Act 1967 (UK). However, although the incidence is relatively high compared with the Netherlands, it is stabilising at the rate of 16.9/1000 women aged 15–44 (House of Commons Committee (2003) para. 69).

---

[34] For an overview of Australian abortion laws see Petersen (1999).
[35] This represents a fall of 4.5% for conceptions under 16 between 2000–01 ie since the launch of the Government's teenage pregnancy strategy.

These findings strongly support the view that criminal 'age of consent' laws bear little relationship to the day to day lives of many teenagers in both Australia and the UK.

Health Policy Issues

In terms of health policy, the major concerns are unplanned pregnancies and associated physical and psychological problems; and sexually transmitted diseases (STDs) including Chlamydia and HIV/AIDS which pose an increasingly high health threat for young people. As the figures above indicate, the rate of teenage pregnancies is a continuing cause for concern in Australia and the UK. In Australia the most common notifiable STD is Chlamydia genital infection which can lead to pelvic inflammatory disease—a major cause of infertility which is often asymptomatic until a woman is in her 20s (Skinner and Hickey, 2003). In addition, STDs and HIV present a particular problem for this age group as some have a high number of partners.

Another approach to reducing these problems is to discourage early sexual activity. It has been found that 'Teenagers having sexual intercourse before age 16 are more likely to take risks,' and 'postponement of first intercourse would be likely to have medical and social benefit' (Mellanby *et al.*, 1995: 414). According to Wellings *et al.*, research also shows that the decision to defer sexual activity has further individual and social benefits:

> [E]arly experience of sexual intercourse is more likely to be accompanied by feelings of regret; it is associated with larger numbers of sexual partners, both in the recent past and over a lifetime; and—of greatest importance in terms of health consequences—it is less likely to be protected from unplanned pregnancy (Wellings *et al.*, 1995: 417).[36]

Confidentiality

Health professionals have a very important role to play in counselling and advice regarding contraception, pregnancy, abortion and health. Confidentiality is a critical part of this health strategy and adolescents need to be informed that, as patients, they have a right to expect that doctors will not disclose any information involving a third party without their consent. In spite of the 'age of consent' statutes it is lawful for medical practitioners to assist sexually active adolescents under the age of 16. The duty to maintain confidentiality and the duty of care in this case overrides the criminal law. The BMA reports that in the Netherlands 'assurance of confidentiality in all contraceptive services has been a key factor in reducing the teenage pregnancy rate to the lowest of all developed countries' (BMA, 1994).

---

[36] See also Mellanby *et al.*, 414.

The duty of confidentiality can only be breached in most exceptional circumstances or where there are statutory exemptions. Examples in the area of abortion law are judicial by-pass statutes which encroach on the duty of confidentiality. Western Australia is the only Australian jurisdiction which requires a dependant minor under 16 years, who is being supported by a custodial parent or legal guardian, to meet an additional consent requirement if seeking a termination of pregnancy. Her consent will not be lawful unless the custodial parent(s) have been informed and given the opportunity to participate in counselling with the medical practitioner. In exceptional cases applications can be made to the Children's Court for an exemption from the requirement.[37]

School Based Sex Education Policies

Adults need to accept that young people are sexual beings, and young people should be encouraged to accept their sexuality and sexual feelings and desires. Social and health policies are most beneficial if they are directed at supporting young people to:

> . . . make informed choices about whether or not to engage in sexual activity [which] means for some young people delaying intercourse until they are emotionally, socially and developmentally ready or as it accords with the values of the communities in which they live. For others, it will mean helping them accept their sexual feelings and activity and to develop skills to protect themselves (Talking Sexual Health, 1999: 28).

The same study also found that:

> Young people's ability to participate in safe-sex behaviours, including the decision not to have sexual intercourse, needs to be supported by a climate that affirms their sexuality as a significant component of their identity (Talking Sexual Health 1999: 28).

School-based education programmes have been a most controversial issue. The resistance of, or antipathy to school based health-sex education illustrates the tension between sexual autonomy and protectionism in relation to adolescent sexual activity. The evidence strongly suggests that school-based policies, guidelines and programmes assist adolescents to accept their sexuality and to develop informed decision-making skills. The evidence also suggests that sex education is the best way of protecting adolescents from health risks and unplanned pregnancies.[38] Pointing to the overwhelming evidence supporting school-based sex education, the Australian study 'Talking Sexual Health' emphasises the advantages of delaying sexual activity and taking responsibility for safe-sex behaviour.

---

[37] Health Act 1911 (WA) s 334.

[38] In the US, it has been reported that an 'abstinence policy' prior to marriage is the best way of achieving these goals. Evidence of the effectiveness of this policy seems to be disputed, however, by different groups: see Overington (2003): 3.

Research indicates that if young people are involved in comprehensive sexuality pro-grams they are far more likely to delay the onset of sexual activity and, if already sex-ually active, to increase safe-sex behaviours (Talking Sexual Health, 1999: 28).

The UK research has reported similar findings. Mellanby *et al.*, observe that:

Sex education using an effective methodology can be associated with postponement of first intercourse . . . students appreciate a broad-based sex education programme which includes learning negotiation skills (Mellanby *et al.*, 1995: 416).

This observation is supported by Wellings *et al.*, and the comments about the differences between young men and women is interesting:

men who reported learning most about sex from school sex education lessons were less likely to have had intercourse before the age of 16, than others who reported learn-ing about sex from friends, girlfriends, family or other. The correlation was weaker for women (Wellings *et al.*, 1995: 419).

In spite of this persuasive evidence about the efficacy of sexual health pro-grammes, neither Australia nor the UK have implemented effective sex-health programmes to assist young people to cope with external pressures to have sexual relationships and to learn how to protect themselves from harm. Unfortunately, resistance to supporting such programmes 'is based on the ill-founded but powerful sentiment that the education of children and young adolescents about conception and safe sex will promote earlier sexual activity' (Skinner and Hickey, 2003: 159).

5. CONCLUSIONS

Under the guise of protectionism, political agendas are being used to criminalise consensual teenage sex and to propagate a traditional view of the 'innocent child'. This approach denies that children and young people are sexual beings and is more likely than not to be harmful. In effect, the 'age of consent' laws are about the prioritisation of moral standards over autonomy rights. To some extent the setting of moral standards may be appropriate, but society should also recognise that adolescent sexuality is neither heinous nor abhorrent behav-iour, that consensual teenage sex ought not to be labelled as criminal; and that these laws offend human rights. The majority in *Gillick* recognised that the state rights over children are annexed to the duty of protection and most importantly that children have evolving capacities. Nevertheless, the English courts have made it abundantly clear that minors do not have full agency and that state rights co-exist with individual autonomy rights until the age of majority is reached.

Research on adolescent sexual activity strongly suggests that the interests of adolescents are served by not engaging in consensual sex too early in their lives. However, 'age of consent' laws do not achieve this objective and most likely hinder, rather than enhance, the right of teenagers to health and physical and mental well being as contained in Article 24 of the CROC (Jones and Basser Marks, 2001). Adolescents need to know that being sexual is natural and appropriate, and they also need information as well as skills to handle sexuality, be it heterosexual or same-sex. Furthermore, it should be recognised that the sexual health needs of teenagers differ from those of adults and that more research and policies are needed for the reproductive and sexual health needs of adolescents (Skinner and Hickey, 2003). Conveying these life skills to adolescents and implementing adolescent sex-health policies should be a significant part of the state's protective role in this area.

Apart from human rights considerations, a major flaw underlying the 'age of consent' laws is that the evolving capacities of individuals are not sufficiently taken into consideration. This occurs because the legislation is based on the chronological age of the child, a legal fiction, which discounts the developmental concepts recognised more than two decades ago in *Gillick*. It is a truism to observe that age limits are not concerned with capacity to consent. The statutory test outlined in the UK Law Commission Report is based on the *Gillick* test and in line with post *Gillick* developments. In a legal sense, one way of balancing all the relevant interests would be through a hybrid legal model which recognises the duty of the state to protect and respect the interests of minors by penalising 'coercive peer sex' *and* permitting competent minors to engage in consensual sex. As noted earlier in this chapter, 'coercive peer sex' refers to behaviour that is non consensual but would fail to satisfy the elements required for an assault or rape conviction. Penalisation would have the advantage of giving police and child welfare officials the authority to take action in these difficult cases. A hybrid legal model, along the lines of Western Australia abortion legislation, could be followed. This approach links criminal legislation with non-criminal or health legislation. Specifically it provides that section 199 of the Criminal Code Act 1913 (WA) states that an abortion is unlawful unless it is performed by a qualified medical practitioner *and* is justified under section 334 of the Health Act 1911 (WA). Moreover, an abortion is justified if the woman gives an 'informed consent', meaning that her consent is freely given once she has complied with the counselling requirements specified in section 334 (5) of the Health Act 1911 (WA). This model could be drawn upon and applied to teenage sex. It is particularly apposite in this context because of the similarities between criminal abortion laws and the 'age of consent' laws. In both cases, criminal laws have been ignored and rarely enforced; and moreover, in both cases, criminalisation can be linked to serious health consequences. Most importantly, however, developing a legal framework based on these principles enables the state to perform its protective duties in cases of 'coercive peer sex' and also provide a blue print for respecting adolescent autonomy.

REFERENCES

BMA, Confidentiality and People Under 16: Guidance issued jointly by the BMA, GMSC, HEA, Brook Advisory Centres, FPA and RCGP (1994) http://www.bma.org.uk. (accessed 27.02.03)

BEVAN, HK, *The Law Relating to Children* (London, Butterworths, 1973).

BRIDGE, C, 'Religion, Culture and the Body of the Child' in A. Bainham, S Day Sclater and M Richards (eds), *Body Lore and Laws* (Oxford, Hart Publishing, 2002) 265–87.

EEKELAAR, J 'The Importance of Thinking that Children have Rights' in P Alston, S Parker, J Seymour (eds) *Children Rights and the Law* (Oxford, Clarendon Press, 1992) 221.

GRAYCAR, R and MORGAN, J, *The Hidden Gender of the Law* (Sydney, Federation Press, 2002).

GRILICH AE, DE VISSER, RO, SMITH, AMA, RISSEL, CE and RICHTERS, J, 'Homosexual Experience and Recent Homosexual Encounters' (2003) 27 *Australian and New Zealand Journal of Public Health* 155.

HEINZ, E., 'The Universal Child' in E. Heinz (ed), *Of Innocence and Autonomy* (Ashgate, Dartmouth, 2000).

HILLIER, L *et al.,* 'Writing Themselves In: A National Report on the Sexuality, Health and Well-being of Same-Sex Attracted Young People' Melbourne: La Trobe University, Australian Research Centre in Sex, Health and Society, 1998 [reprint 2002] Monograph Series No 7.

HOME OFFICE, *Setting the Boundaries: Reforming the Law on Sex Offences* Vol 1 (London, Home Office Communication Directorate, 2000).

HOUSE OF COMMONS HEALTH COMMITTEE, *Sexual Health*, Vol 1 Third Report of Session 2002–03 (London, House of Commons 2003).

JONES, M and BASSER MARKS, L A 'United Nations Convention on the Rights of the Child: A Blueprint for Australia's Children in Medical Procedure Cases' in M Jones and Basser Marks, L A (eds), *Children on the Agenda* (NSW, Prospect Press, 2001) 1.

LACEY, N, 'Beset by Boundaries: The Home Office Review of Sex Offences' (2001) 3 *Criminal Law Review* 10–13.

LANCASTER, J, 'Who Benefits from the Equalising of the Age of Consent Provisions?' (2001) 26 *Children Australia* 34.

LAW COMMISSION, *Consent in Sex Offences: A Report to the Home Office Sex Offences Review* (London, HMSO, 2000).

LINDSAY, J. SMITH, AMA and ROSENTHAL, DA, *Secondary Students, HIV/AIDS and Sexual Health 1997,* (Melbourne, Centre for the Study of Sexually Transmissible Diseases, Faculty of Health Science, La Trobe University, 1997) Monograph Series No 3.

MASON, JK *Medico-Legal Aspects of Reproduction and Parenthood* (2nd ed, Ashgate, Aldershot, 1998) 57.

MELLANBY, AR, PHELPS, FA, CREIGHTON, NJ and TRIPP, JH, 'School Sex Education: An Experimental Program with Education and Medical Benefit' (1995) 311 *BMJ* 414.

MOON, L, MEYER, P, GRAU, J, 'Australia's Young People: their Health and Wellbeing' (Canberra, Institute of Heath and Welfare, 1999) cited in Skinner and Hickey (2003).

MORGAN, J, 'Controlling Minors' Fertility' (1986) 12 *Monash University Law Review* 161.

MPBV Guidelines 'Minors' Right to Consent to Medical Treatment' (2002) accessed at http://medicalboardvic.gov.au. (12.09.02).

NICHOLSON, A, HARRISON, M and SANDOR, D, 'The Role of the Family Court in Medical Procedure Cases' in M Jones, and LA Basser Marks (eds), *Children on the Agenda* (NSW, Prospect Press, 2001) 239.

OVERINGTON, C, 'No Sex Please, We're Teens' *The Age* March 1, 2003, Insight 3.

PETERSEN, K, 'Criminal Abortion Laws: An Impediment to Reproductive Health' in I Freckelton and K Petersen (eds), *Controversies in Health Law* (Sydney, Federation Press, 1999).

PILCHER, J, 'Contrary to *Gillick*: British Children and Sexual Rights since 1985'(1997) 5 *International Journal of Children's Rights* 299.

RISSEL, CE, *et al.*, 'First Experiences of Vaginal Intercourse and Oral Sex among a Representative Sample of Adults' (2003) 27 (2) *Australian and New Zealand Journal of Public Health*, 131–7.

SKINNER, SR and HICKEY, M, 'Current Priorities for Adolescent Sexual and Reproductive Health in Australia (2003) 179 *Medical Journal of Australia* 158.

Talking Sexual Health, National Framework for Education about STIs, HIV/AIDS and blood-borne viruses in secondary schools (Canberra, Australian National Council on AIDS, Hepatitis C and Related Diseases, 1999).

WELLINGS, NANCHAHAL, *et al.*, 'Sexual Behaviour in Britain: Early Heterosexual Experience' (2001) 358, *The Lancet*, 1843.

WELLINGS, WADSWORTH, *et al.*, 'Provision of Sex Education and Early Sexual Experience: the Relation Examined' (1995) 311 *British Medical Journal* 417.

17

Regulating Sex: Young People, Prostitution and Policy Reform

JOANNA PHOENIX

'When I use a word' Humpty Dumpty said, in rather a scornful tone, 'it means just what I choose it to mean. Neither more or less.'
'The question is' said Alice, 'whether you can make words mean so many different things'.
'The question is', said Humpty Dumpty, 'who is the master. That is all'.

–Lewis Carroll, *Alice in Wonderland*

AFTER SEVERAL YEARS of political struggle and campaign, policy innovations were introduced in Britain that saw a complete change in the way in which young people in prostitution were to be understood and treated. This chapter offers an analysis of those innovations in policies regarding young people in prostitution and the paradoxes and ambiguities therein. It argues that the policy reforms are limited and contradictory. It further argues that shifting modes of youth governance and discourses on children and sex condition those limitations and the ways that those contradictions are made meaningful. In particular, I argue that contemporary constructions of 'childhood' and 'sex' render silent the paradox of using child protection methods for young people in prostitution who are at (or near) the age of sexual consent. In this respect, the object of analysis in this chapter is not the outcomes of the policy, nor is it the success or failure of specific interventions in particular young people's lives. Rather, the object of analysis is the policy, itself, and the conditions of possibility that shape the policy. This chapter is divided into three sections. In the first section, I chart the innovations and reforms that have lead to Britain's youth prostitution policy. In the second section, I outline the ambiguity and partiality of this new policy field and argue that there are significant discontinuities between the reforms and the lived realities of those young people who are subject to them. Following on from this, the final section investigates the conditions of possibility for the introduction of this policy.

The last five years have seen the emergence and formalisation of a new policy field—childhood and youth prostitution policy.[1] By this I do not mean the creation of a new field of policy akin to housing or education policy that is delimited by the broad remit of a specific governmental department or departments. Rather, there has been a formal re-organisation of already existing policies, laws and institutions in a way that focuses attention on dealing with young people in prostitution. There has been no comparable re-organisation or reform of policy in relation to adult prostitution. The 1990s saw, arguably for the first time in British history, the demarcation of childhood and youth prostitution from adult prostitution and the differentiation of it from juvenile lawbreaking. In this section, I describe Britain's youth prostitution policy, the binary construction of youth prostitution it formalised and the new interventions it conditioned.

The Formalisation of Youth Prostitution Policy: New Guidance in Old Structures

In March 2000, the Department of Health and Home Office jointly issued a new appendix to *Working Together to Safeguard Children* (which informs all Local Authorities and other agencies working with children how the Children Act 1989 should be implemented). Entitled *Safeguarding Children Involved in Prostitution (SCIP)*, this appendix advised that the involvement of children in prostitution should be seen in the first instance as an act of abuse and that there exists a statutory obligation to (i) treat these children as victims of abuse (and not offenders); (ii) safeguard and promote their welfare; (iii) work together to create 'exit strategies'; and, (iv) use the full force of the criminal law against those who would exploit, coerce, induce, or compel young people in the course of their involvement in prostitution.[2] *SCIP* neither created new law nor did it

---

[1] This has not occurred because the 'problem' of childhood and youth prostitution was 'discovered' in the 1990s. There have been concerns about young people in prostitution in Britain for at least the last 150 years. Indeed, many such concerns provided the impetus and backdrop against which the age of consent was raised in the Criminal Law Amendment Act 1885. Moreover, the emergence of this policy field has not come about because new organisations or institutions were developed to deal with an old problem rediscovered. The institutional structure underpinning this new policy field remains that which had dealt with troublesome and troubling young people for many decades—specifically social services, police, child welfare voluntary organisations and sexual or public health outreach programmes.

[2] *Safeguarding Children in Prostitution* uses the statutory definition of 'children' as 'a person under the age of eighteen' (Children Act 1989 S105). However, in the analysis of these reforms that follows, I have bracketed off the under 10 year olds completely and only occasionally refer to the 14 and under age group for reasons that will become clear as the argument progresses.

decriminalise prostitution for the under 18s. It merely sought to re-focus the energies and attentions of those who already come into contact with young people in prostitution in order that the criminal law was not used against them in the first instance, and to change the direction of what was perceived to be common practice (i.e. the arrest, caution or prosecution and punishment of young people for prostitution-related offences).

Elsewhere I have discussed the problematic understandings of young people's involvement in prostitution that shaped *SCIP* and for the purposes of this chapter only a brief summary of this is needed (Phoenix, 2002a). *SCIP* transposes the problem of young people's involvement in prostitution into a 'problem' of child (sexual) abuse. It does this by re-defining what the 'real' problem of youth prostitution is and who the 'real' criminals are. The real problem, we are informed, is not the social and material privations or the devastated financial and emotional lives that makes involvement in prostitution not only possible but also plausible and at times 'attractive' for some young people. It is, instead, that involvement in prostitution is a manifestation of young people's victimisation at the hands of unscrupulous men. The 'real' criminals, thus, are not the young people who may be breaking the law by soliciting or loitering, but the men who target homeless, vulnerable, damaged young lives for their own pecuniary gain. *SCIP* tells Local Authorities and police that traditional criminal justice intervention in young people's lives should, thus, be re-directed to arresting and prosecuting the 'real' criminals who commit the 'real' crimes. One impact of constructing the problem of youth prostitution in this fashion, however, is that the social and economic actualities of many of these young people's lives are simply erased: young people whose economic and social realities are circumscribed with anti-youth, anti-social policies are symbolically transformed into victims of abuse. More than this, however, the guidance is very specific in asserting that not all young people in prostitution are victims of coercion; that some are involved in prostitution voluntarily. For these young people, who are constituted as also being 'real' offenders, criminal justice intervention is deemed appropriate (this is an issue to which I will return later).

Youth prostitution policy in Britain has been formalised by the adoption of what can only be described as a *de facto* model of intervention (Phoenix, 2002c). *SCIP* constituted the problem of youth and child prostitution as being a problem of child abuse by claiming two things: young people's experience in prostitution is marked by exploitation and violence and young people do not consent to their involvement in prostitution (despite the overwhelming evidence and years of academic debate about the complicated nature of consent and the inability to conceptualise consent in this case as the ability to have acted otherwise). *SCIP* does go to some length to ensure that whilst each local authority is obliged to act on young people's involvement in prostitution, it should not necessarily adopt this view and that each locality should investigate the nature of youth prostitution in its specific context. Notwithstanding this, recent research indicates that most authorities adopted the construction of youth prostitution as being a problem of child abuse (Phoenix, 2003). This created the conditions in which a framework for and method of intervention suggested itself. In the process of implementing *SCIP*, most local authorities simply 'grafted' the issue of youth prostitution onto their already established protocols and procedures for child protection work. Thus, almost without exception and despite the possibility of being otherwise, a *de facto* national protocol and method was developed and with that youth prostitution policy was formalised. Youth prostitution was dealt with as though it was 'just' another child protection issue in which young people are exploited or abused by the adults in their lives.

And still the story does not end there because despite the introduction of a child protection model of intervention, *SCIP* did not challenge or displace older understandings of young people's involvement in prostitution. Instead, a 'persistent' and 'voluntary-returner' clause was introduced which enables local authorities to take criminal justice action against young people in prostitution if it can be shown that they have not been coerced into prostitution and that they engage in it of their own free will. By doing so, *SCIP* made official a binary construction of young people in prostitution as either victims or offenders. Victims are those who are coerced, abused and exploited; offenders are those who could have made other choices. With that, two interlocking but different formal modes of intervention and regulation were made possible: victims are offered protection and offenders are given punishment.

THE QUESTION OF PARADOX: RE-CONTEXTUALISING SCIP

In what follows, I argue that the policy reforms at the heart of current youth prostitution policy are paradoxical and partial. To wit, youth prostitution policy is marked by specific paradoxes and ambiguities. How and in what ways such a paradoxical policy is rendered coherent is the subject of the final section. This middle section, however, will examine the question of coherence by: (i) showing that the evidence base drawn upon as justification for the policy reform is questionable; (ii) detailing the profound discontinuities between what the policy aims to do and the lived realities of the young people that are its subject; and, (iii) sketching how the *de facto* model of intervention that has been developed is at best irrelevant and at worse perverse and punitive in its outcomes.

The Misuse and Selective Use of Evidence

SCIP was put forward (although not explicitly so) as a piece of 'evidence-based' policy. And, as is often the case with such policies, the 'evidence' that it draws upon and the way in which it is used is selective. Absent from the guidance is twenty and more years of empirical, qualitative research which argues that one of the key factors in young people's involvement in prostitution is the limited social and material conditions that they inhabit. Specifically, in a context where young people have limited (or no) choices available to them in terms of housing, employment, living arrangements and so on, prostitution becomes a form of survivalism (Phoenix, 2001; Carlen, 1996; O'Neill *et al.*, 1995). This is not to say that young people do not suffer terrible abuse and exploitation in the course of their involvement in prostitution. Rather, it is to emphasise that much of the empirical research has shown time and again that in a context marked by the aggregate effects of poverty and limited choices, prostitution becomes a 'low-cost' means of survival: it does not involve the young people in the same risks of punishment and imprisonment as, for example, burglary, theft, dealing drugs or shoplifting. However, in ignoring this research, *SCIP* ends up conflating the experience of victimisation that many young people have with the 'causes' or conditions that impel them into prostitution.

Moreover, throughout *SCIP* there is the assertion that children 'as young as 10' have been criminalised for their involvement in prostitution. It is repeatedly claimed that one of the main aims of the guidance is 'to ensure that criminal justice action against children is taken only when it is necessary to do so' (DOH, 2000:13); that 'the priority for criminal justice action must be to investigate and prosecute those who abuse a child' (*ibid* 27); and that 'the entire emphasis of the Guidance is on diversion using a welfare based approach to children and that it should be adopted *in all cases*' (*ibid*, emphasis in the original). In addition, the guidance makes frequent reference to a series of British research reports generated in the late 1990s. The key focus of these reports was to highlight the perversity of criminalising young people who are often abused in prostitution when, according to the Children Act 1989, the state has an obligation to protect them from 'harm'. Collectively, the reports referred to, and injunctions within the guidance, create an imperative to action by giving the impression that there are significant numbers of young people and children being criminalised. However, just how problematic this assumption is can be seen in a brief examination of the official criminal statistics for prosecutions and convictions for soliciting and loitering for the purposes of prostitution.

Most social scientists understand that official criminal statistics tell us little, or nothing, about the 'true' extent of crime; that statistics often tell the informed reader much more about the priorities, procedures and organisation of the police and the criminal justice system. Thus, prosecution and convictions figures under the Street Offences Act 1959 S1 (1) are not a measure of the *actual* numbers of individuals soliciting or loitering for prostitution. Analysis of them does, however, provide an indication of whether and to what extent the police have focused on using their powers of arrest *vis-à-vis* women working from the street. When examining the official statistics for prosecutions and convictions for soliciting and loitering, there is evidence to suggest that the ways in which the police had been dealing with prostitute women and young adults had fundamentally altered in the 10 years prior to the introduction of *SCIP*. As Figures 1 and 2 demonstrate, there has been a dramatic decline in both prosecutions and convictions of all age groups for soliciting and loitering in the years since 1990.[3] Overall there was a 71% decrease in prosecutions and a 72% decrease in convictions.

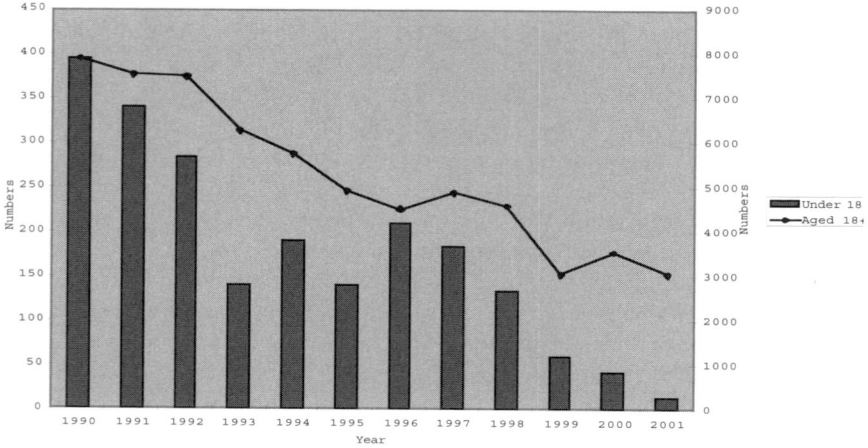

Fig. 1. Prosecutions for Loitering and Soliciting in England and Wales

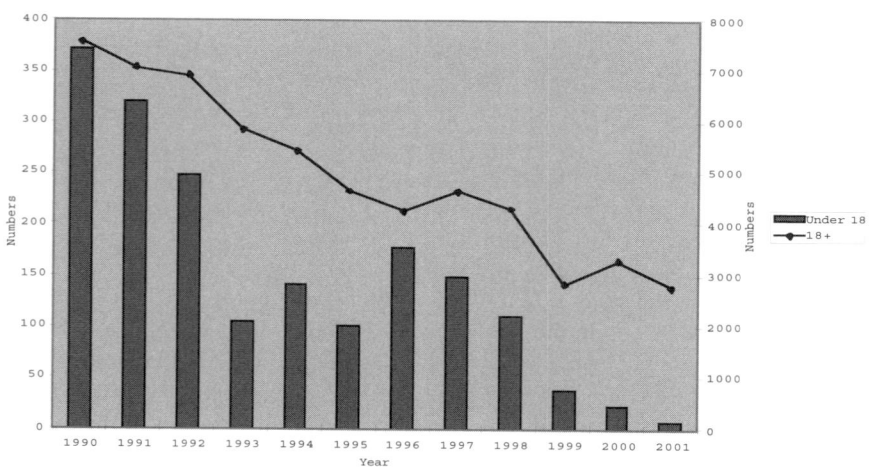

Fig. 2. Convictions for Loitering and Soliciting in England and Wales

[3] Figures One and Two were compiled from information provided by the Offending and Criminal Justice Group of the Home Office and on a principal offence basis.

Table 1. Prosecutions for Soliciting and Loitering for the Purposes of Prostitution: England and Wales

	Under 18	Age 10–14	Age 15–17	Age 18–20	Aged 18+	All Ages
1990	396	1	395	2165	7898	10459
1991	340	3	337	2290	7535	10165
1992	284	2	282	1726	7493	9449
1993	139	1	138	1496	6269	7904
1994	190	9	181	1082	5757	7029
1995	140	1	139	806	4917	5863
1996	210	0	210	940	4510	5660
1997	183	1	182	774	4879	5836
1998	133	0	133	754	4589	5476
1999	60	0	60	475	3044	3579
2000	43	1	42	437	3540	3583
2001	14	0	14	324	3051	3065

Table 2. Convictions for Soliciting and Loitering for the Purposes of Prostitution: England and Wales

	Under 18	Age 10–14	Age 15–17	Age 18–20	Age 18+	All Ages
1990	371	1	370	2075	7574	10020
1991	321	3	318	2175	7063	9559
1992	247	1	247	1616	6914	8778
1993	105	0	105	1375	5868	7348
1994	141	4	137	994	5439	6574
1995	101	0	101	758	4653	5512
1996	177	0	177	884	4251	5312
1997	148	1	147	728	4633	5509
1998	110	0	110	698	4310	5118
1999	38	0	38	418	2832	3288
2000	23	1	22	324	3294	3317
2001	7	0	7	270	2774	2781

Source: Offending and Criminal Justice Group, Home Office, 2003
NB: All figures in Tables 1 & 2 are on a principal offence basis.

These percentages do, however, mask the marked differences between age groups. For instance (and rather surprisingly) the most dramatic decline does *not* occur in the 10–14 year old age group, as this was an age group over which the police rarely exercised their powers of arrest. The largest decline is in the 15–17 year old age group. As Tables 1 and 2 demonstrate, in 1990, 395 girls aged 15–17 were prosecuted and 370 were convicted. By 2001, these numbers had fallen to 14 and 7 respectively. This is a decrease of 94% and 98%.

In comparison, there was an 85% decrease in prosecutions and 87% decrease in convictions for the 18+ age group. As a point of contrast, the way in which the police dealt with other prostitution related offences does not show the same dramatic decrease in numbers. As Table 3 details, prosecutions and convictions from 1990–1999 under the Sexual Offences Act 1985 Sections 1 and 2 (kerb-crawling and persistent solicitation of women) declined, although at nowhere near the rate evident in the figures for loitering and soliciting. As Table 4 indicates, prosecutions and convictions under the Sexual Offences Act 1967, Section 5(1) (living wholly or in part on the earnings of a prostitute, or as more commonly known 'pimping' or 'poncing') are extremely rare.

Table 3. Prosecutions and Convictions for Kerb-Crawling and Persistent Solicitation of Women: England and Wales

| | Kerb-crawling | | Persistent Solicitation | |
	Prosecution	Conviction	Prosecution	Conviction
1990	1360	1215	89	70
1991	1314	1132	71	51
1992	1003	827	69	50
1993	772	636	68	48
1994	1112	919	46	30
1995	1262	1095	58	34
1996	1239	1092	79	55
1997	947	811	86	68
1998	808	700	94	65
1999	689	599	67	51

Table 4. Prosecutions and Convictions for Living on the Earnings of a Prostitute

	Prosecutions	Convictions
1990	1	2
1991	1	0
1992	0	0
1993	0	0
1994	1	1
1995	1	1
1996	2	3
1997	1	2
1998	1	1
1999	1	0

Source: Offending and Criminal Justice Group, Home Office, 2003.
NB: All figures in Tables 3 & 4 are on a principal offence basis.

These statistics raise a number of issues. These figures certainly reconfirm the sexual double standard that exists in the policing and official treatment of women and men in prostitution. They also indicate that the policing of street prostitution changed at least seven years in advance of the introduction of *SCIP*. This was as much the case for adult women as for young girls. It is possible to speculate about the role that Sexual Health Outreach Programmes might have had in diverting police practice from arrest, prosecution and conviction. One of the key 'informal' roles that many of these organisations perform is liaison work between the women and the police, both helping to educate the police about the issues, factors and processes that often drive women into prostitution as well as those that make it difficult for them to leave. It is also possible to speculate about the impact new technologies such as the mobile telephone, computer chat rooms and telephone sex lines may have had in providing different avenues from which women can work without the threat of arrest, prosecution and conviction.

Two further questions are raised by these official statistics. Firstly, why the reforms were introduced when they were? As shown above, the active criminalisation of the under 18 year olds in prostitution was already well in decline. Secondly, why was 'the problem' of young people's involvement in prostitution constructed as a child abuse problem when, as the statistics would indicate, the bulk of young people who were criminalised (and thus in need of **different** welfare-based treatment) were 15–17 year olds?

The Appropriateness of Child Protection Methods

It is quite possible to argue that youth prostitution policy reforms were introduced after practice had already changed, if only to ensure that there could be no return to previous bad practice. However, when questions about the evidence base of *SCIP* are added to questions about the discontinuities, limitations and ambiguities inherent in the implementation of the policy, it is possible to argue that the policy is, indeed, paradoxical. I now go on to address the question of the coherence of introducing a child protection model of intervention for, largely, 15–17 year old girls in prostitution.

Recent research into national provision and services for young people in prostitution found that one of the central limitations of current youth prostitution policy is that the child protection model of intervention does little to facilitate agencies and individuals who work with young people in prostitution.[4] Specifically, a child protection response with its methods geared to investigating and working with children who are being abused within families is not always appropriate for older young people who: often live outside their families, experience abuse from boyfriends, pimps or clients and have usually had long

---

[4] Unless otherwise stated the data drawn on in this section comes from Youth Prostitution: A Database, ESRC grant no: R000223916. The final report detailing the findings from this research project is freely available on the Regard website (http://www.regard.ac.uk).

histories of involvement with social services. Child protection methods of work are not necessarily capable of accommodating the subtlety and complexity of the problems of young people's involvement in prostitution and are not structured to recognise both the victimisation of young people and their desires and abilities to fashion their own lives (as will be discussed in the section below). One respondent, who worked in a voluntary agency, commented 'people who are clued up know that social services are a waste of time'. Other respondents recounted incidents wherein young people aged 16 & 17 years of age, who had been living independently for several years (through prostitution or other criminogenic lifestyles) were placed within Children's Homes or offered foster placements. In many such cases, the girls would abscond and in some cases, they have not been heard of since. Comments such as these were not made to denigrate the work of social services, but rather to highlight the difficulties encountered when using the same methods of intervention for 15, 16 and 17 year olds in prostitution as for younger children abused within families.

There are, however, other ways in which child protection models of intervention are not always suitable. In a context where local authority social services struggle with increasingly strained resources, 15–17 year old young people in prostitution were occasionally not seen as the same sort of priority as younger children. Those working with young people in prostitution often experience their work as tiring and frustrating. Respondents discussed the intransigent nature of involvement in prostitution and how this made interventions of any kind very difficult particularly where there are no additional resources available to help the young person economically survive without recourse to prostitution. In 2003, there were only 43 projects in Britain that catered specifically for young people in prostitution and most of these were concentrated in 13 cities in Scotland and England (Phoenix, 2003).

In addition, the techniques and strategies used both to campaign for a change to the practice of criminalising young people in prostitution and implement *SCIP* acted to limit welfare-based interventions. As indicated earlier, a 'renaming game' took place that privileged a newly emerging ideology of youth prostitution victimhood that marginalised and sidelined the material and social conditions and realities of young people's involvement in prostitution. The key point of *SCIP* was to change the way that agencies thought about young people in prostitution. But, as commented on previously, *SCIP* did not challenge the understanding of young people as offenders—it merely overlaid this understanding with a different possibility—that they could be victims. Moreover, youth prostitution was rendered epiphenomenal to child abuse and in so doing, the key focus for intervention becomes the lifestyles and relationships that the girls have. In other words, the guidance takes one moment in the girls' lives (the exchange of sex for money) and elevates it in such a way as to wipe out the girls' history or wider social context. More than this, the translation of youth prostitution as a problem of child abuse focuses the agencies' energies on 'risk assessment' and especially in adjudicating the motivation of the young person (so as to assess voluntarism, consent or coercion) and the risk to the agency (so as to ensure that liabilities to the agency are militated.) And, such a process creates the very conditions in which more young women (rather than fewer) will end up incarcerated not for prostitution-related offences, but for their own protection. As agencies come to define more and more aspects of young prostitutes' lives as toxic and harmful, as they struggle with having only individual solutions to much broader socio-economic problems, the provision of safety for these young people through the mechanism of secure containment becomes more and more plausible, possible and warranted. Thus, on one level, the way in which youth prostitution policy reforms were implemented created the very conditions that justify and allow a greater level of incarceration through the unintended consequences of focusing on consent and coercion (Phoenix, 2002c).

The Trouble with Consent

Issues of consent and by extension coercion, exploitation and abuse in relation to young people's involvement in prostitution are complex. There are two different frameworks of understanding about consent that are relevant in any discussion of young people's involvement in prostitution; legal frameworks and in particular the legislation which determines 'age of consent'; and, sociological frameworks which underpin the analysis of young people's sexual activity. In this section, I describe some of the manner in which these two different frameworks are present within *SCIP* and the impact this has on both practitioners and the analysis that follows in this chapter.

Underpinning *SCIP* and the actions of the professionals charged with its implementation are the laws pertaining to the age at which it is legal to engage in sex. As discussed in Petersen's contribution to this volume, age of consent legislation is shaped by cultural assumptions, moral values and constructions of gender. Britain's 'age of sexual consent' legislation is prohibitive in that sexual activity under the age of 16 years old is illegal, as those under this age are not deemed to be sufficiently emotionally or physically mature enough to engage in sex. Such a framework creates an imperative to action: those under the age of sexual consent must be protected by official agencies.

In contrast, sociological and criminological understandings of the notion of consent (sexual or otherwise) draw on philosophical arguments about free will and the manner in which social structures shape and determine an individual's action. Within these constructions, consent is constituted as the capacity an individual has to make choices. This capacity can be either circumscribed or enabled by the context that the individual occupies. Thus, in relation to analyses of the causes of crime, individuals have been constituted as though they are impelled to particular forms of action because they possess particular, usually pathological, biological or psychological characteristics or because they are located within specific social contexts that make such actions inevitable. For example, writing at the beginning of the twentieth century, S. and E. Glueck claimed that prostitutes were different from ordinary women: their involvement in prostitution was caused by psychological pathology. This pathology acts in a way that, when poverty is encountered, the women's psychological 'inhibitions' and 'constraints' against prostitution are reduced (Glueck and Glueck, 1934). Such a 'hard' conception of determinism was critiqued in the 1960s (Matza, 1969), and what has largely taken its place is an understanding of freewill being constrained by external circumstances. In this way, individuals are understood as making choices about how and in what ways to act, but in conditions not of their own choosing (Box, 1996). Such a framework structures an analysis which focuses on both the individual and how they make sense of the world around them and the ways that the social context shapes or structures the range of the individual's choices and capacity to choose.

Contained within *SCIP* are both conceptions of 'consent' and, to some extent, they conflict with each other. The section detailing the legal framework for the guidance makes clear that 'anyone engaging in sexual activity (whether for money or not) with a girl or boy under 16 (whether male or female) . . . is committing an offence' (DOH, 2000:12). As stated above, the sexual age of consent legislation prohibits adults from engaging in sexual activities with the under 16 year olds. The focus of practitioners and police is on both criminalising the adults and protecting the young people. For these young people, questions of whether and to what extent they consented to the sexual exchange are deemed irrelevant. Those under the age of 16 years old simply do not have the legal capacity to consent. Here a contradiction between the 'spirit' of *SCIP* and the letter of the law emerges. *SCIP* instructs all agencies to view anyone under the age of 18 years old as 'children in need, who may be suffering, or may be likely to suffer, significant harm' (DOH, 2000: 9). The rationale for this is that 'the majority of children do not voluntarily enter prostitution: they are coerced, enticed or are utterly desperate' (DOH, 2000: 15). At this point, *SCIP* invokes a notion of coercion that is based on a lack of voluntarism, a lack of 'consent' as in the capacity to make other choices. Such an understanding is based on a simple notion of free will as opposed to the more sociologically informed understanding which situates individuals within particular social contexts. But, the sex that clients are purchasing from 16 and 17 year olds, is lawful sex. The conflict then arises between a young person's formal legal ability to engage in sexual activity (however inappropriate that activity may be deemed) and the obligations of social services and the police to 'protect' these older, young people.

Although the law differentiates those below 16 years old and those 16 years and older, the analysis that follows does not. Instead, the differentiation is drawn at 15 years old. This is for two principal reasons. Firstly, as evident in interviews with practitioners, there is a blurring of the age boundary when making decisions about intervention. Practitioners, and in particular social workers and the police, regularly commented that 'for all intents and purposes, 15 is 16 years old'. This decision was driven as much by a context of limited resources (and the way that context structures practitioners' priorities, time and energies) as it was any specific understanding of the young person's capacity to make choices. In other words, a differentiation is drawn: not in accordance with the age of sexual consent but through the routine practice of 'second guessing' what would 'stand up in court' and the assumption that 15 year olds, whilst not legally defined as such, do make choices about sex. Such a practice has a profound impact: as the statistics have shown, it is precisely the 15–17 year olds who are most regularly criminalized for their engagement in prostitution (i.e. deemed to have consented, voluntarily, to it). Secondly, research into the lives of young prostitutes provides evidence that the social context in which young people become engaged in prostitution differs markedly for those older, young people (i.e. 15–17 years old). In circumstances where their abilities to live independent lives are severely curtailed by poverty, involvement in prostitution becomes a form of economic and financial survival. In this respect, they do make choices, albeit harmful and socially disapproved ones (Phoenix, 2001; Pearce *et al.*, 2002). It is worth noting that it is not my intention to suggest that 15 year olds should be understood as having the 'right' to engage in prostitution in the same legal manner that those 16 years old and above do. Instead, I merely point out that in practice, the legal framework matters less than the professionals' judgment about whether child protection interventions and the resources needed to secure a successful intervention could (or should) be allocated to a young person on the cusp of being able to offer consent.

A cursory examination of youth prostitution policy reform and implementation shows that far from being understandable and meaningful, Britain's youth prostitution policy is paradoxical, limited and partial. It was introduced after dramatic declines in the practice of arresting, prosecuting and convicting young people in prostitution. The form that the policy innovation has taken is one which arguably will do little for young people in prostitution apart from increase the likelihood of their (protective) incarceration. Underpinning it is a blurring of the boundaries around the age of sexual consent. It does little or nothing to address material poverty and limited opportunities that structured their involvement in prostitution. Yet, when talking to agencies, organisations and workers, *SCIP* was hailed as an achievement and innovation. It is to this paradox that the next section turns.

Safeguarding the Innocent and Punishing the Guilty: The Paradox of Sex and the Governance of Youth

In this section, I argue that discourses on childhood sexual innocence provide the context in which young people's involvement in prostitution is understood as being the sort of threat that necessitates the intervention of state agencies. I further argue that shifting modes of governing youth in contemporary Britain provide the conditions that shaped the specific limitations and ambiguities of Britain's youth prostitution policy.

There is nothing new in the recognition that both childhood and sexuality are socially constructed or that 'children' and 'sex' are both socially constructed and symbolically separated. Analysis of the constitutive discourses of childhood and sex have shown how this discursive separation has conditioned particular forms of regulation and intervention into the lives of children, parents, families and neighbourhoods (Donzelot, 1979; Rose, 1989; Evans, 1993). Specifically, children have been constituted as 'corruptible innocents'; as non-adults and outside the realm of sexuality but prey to 'perverse' adult proclivities. As Evans (1993) argues, such discursive positioning created the conditions for the introduction of state sponsored regulatory systems to police the boundaries between adults and children. So, for instance the nineteenth century saw the introduction of legislation which gradually removed children from the adult world of production, enclosed them in the world of education and constituted their dependency on their families. And, as Donzelot and Rose demonstrate, social services and such regulatory structures, institutions and agencies were created specifically to provide protection for innocent, corruptible children.

More recently, perceived greater sexual demands in modern culture combined with an increasing attention paid to 'dangerous male sexualities' have cast doubt on the private family's ability to protect fully their charges (Evans, 1993). The key modes of regulating and policing the sexual boundaries between children and adults have been portrayed as being in crisis through widespread media panics about child sexual abuse, paedophilia, sexual exploitation and abuse on the internet, the abuse of trust by professionals, child pornography and trafficking in children. Such a charged symbolic context can, arguably, provide the framework that explains *SCIP's* focus on the sexual predation, abuse and exploitation of children through prostitution. For, in constituting children as corruptible innocents who are increasingly 'at risk' from dangerous male sexuality, an imperative of protection is generated in which children are protected from the harm to their innocence and the damage to their development that involvement in prostitution is seen to bring.[5]

What an informed examination of the links between *SCIP* and discourses on children and sex cannot address, however, is the way in which Britain's youth prostitution policy focuses regulatory (as in formal penal) attention, not on the aberrant male sexual predator (although he is not without notice), but on the lives of the young people and why it should be that policies have been constituted such that some young people are positioned as being responsible for their own victimisation. In short, what remains at question is why the 'protection' that is offered in current youth prostitution policy is encompassed within a

---

[5] I am not arguing that involvement in prostitution does not damage children or that children in prostitution are not victims of abuse and exploitation. I am simply trying to trace the symbolic backdrop that created the conditions in which the involvement of the under 18 year olds is seen as always and already a child protection issue.

broader, more punitive regulation of young lives that has all but erased the specificity of prostitution and the realities of poverty and destitution faced by many of Britain's older, young people in prostitution.

It might be appealing to understand *SCIP* as little more than a retelling of the sexual panics *vis-à-vis* children that have periodically marked the nineteenth and twentieth century. But, such an understanding is inadequate. Instead, I argue that *SCIP* and current youth prostitution policy can be more adequately explained as part of the broader shifts in the way that young people are governed in contemporary Britain. For as noted earlier, the paradox that is accommodated within the policy is that the children who are involved in prostitution are, generally speaking, over the age of sexual consent (or very near to it) and often engage in prostitution in order to survive. In other words, these children are not 'children'—they are youths.

Governing Youths: Shifting Boundaries of Dependency, Responsibility and Blame

Just as it is now common practice to acknowledge that childhood is socially constructed, so too is it conventional to recognise that there is nothing essential about 'youth'. 'Youth' is constituted as an interstitial phase in the life course, as a time between the full dependency of childhood and the independence of adulthood, and as a phase in which the boundaries at both ends are in a constant state of flux (Jones and Wallace, 1992). Fundamental to the negotiation of these boundaries is the way in which the semi-dependency and semi-independence of 'youth' is constituted, regulated, policed and maintained. Children are unable to enter into legal contracts and do not bear the burden of the responsibility of their actions. They are understood as being dependent within the household and family who are assumed to take responsibility for that child until they negotiate the phased transition to adulthood. Where those families fail, the state offers children surrogate families (i.e. foster care, children's homes, adoption). Conversely, adults are all that children are not—independent, able to enter into work and contracts, full citizens with rights and duties and, ultimately, responsible for their own actions. But symbolically and in policy terms, young people occupy an in-between ground. They are neither children nor adults; they are both independent and dependent. Thus, in practice and policy this line is seldom clearly drawn and is always contingent upon wider socio-economic factors. For instance, the ability of young people to live independently is contingent on young people having access to resources (i.e. grants, benefits or income) and a particular state of the housing market whereby there is material provision of accommodation for students, trainees, etc.

Recently, there have been changes to the modes of youth governance in Britain which impact directly on the construction and implementation of youth prostitution policy. It is to these that I now turn.

Education, Education, Education: Elongating and Deepening Dependency

The last twenty years has seen a profound shift in the way in which young people are expected to make the transition to adulthood and, consequently, how 'normal youth' is understood. It is now assumed, for instance, that young people need a longer and more staged 'transition' into adulthood. Such a construction of 'youth' underpins policies that have prolonged and broadened the dependency of young people on their family. This constructed dependency is seen most clearly in how successive governments shaped the school-to-work transition in the contexts of mass (youth) unemployment and restructuring of the labour market. Until the mid 1970s, most young people went straight from school into employment. This 'one-step' transition meant that by the age of 16 many young people were financially independent, or at least well on their way (Coles, 1995: 35). However, the simplicity of this movement was disrupted with the mass unemployment of the 1970s and 1980s and the resulting 'vanishing youth labour market'. This wider economic backdrop provided the justification for year on year growth of training schemes geared to making specific young people more employable by developing their marketable skills and by the massive expansion of post-16 year old education. So, for instance, the Youth Opportunity Programmes offered to 16 year olds were originally designed as six month long programmes largely comprised of work experience courses. By 1982, these programmes were replaced with twelve month long Youth Training Schemes that were eventually extended to two years in 1985. By 1991, the then discredited YTS was replaced with Youth Training which was intended to focus more on the achievement of qualifications. At the same time as these training schemes were developed, and more so recently, there has been an expansion of post-16 education through the development of, *inter alia*, City Technology Colleges, financial incentives to schools to keep more of their 16+ year olds, the proliferation of post-16 qualifications (i.e. NVQs, ONDs, HNDs, Btechs and so on) and now governmental targets for 50% of all young people to attend Universities. More recently, the current Labour government is concerned with ensuring that the transition of young people to adulthood is a seamless movement from full-time education into training programmes or apprenticeships and into full-time employment (or continuing their full-time education through their early twenties by attendance at University) (Social Exclusion Unit, 1999).

Combined with this more complex and staged transition from school to work has been the almost wholesale removal of entitlement to welfare benefits. In 1982, young people 16 years and older could claim supplementary benefit, housing benefit and a host of other non-means tested benefits. However, the Social Security Acts of 1986 and 1988 removed the entitlement to income support (the replacement of supplementary benefit), any social fund grants, housing benefit and so on. The argument ran that no young person needed to be unemployed because, if they were out of work, they should be in post-16 education or the expanding training programmes.

The impact of extending young people's transition from school to work whilst at the same time removing the 'safety net' of welfare benefits is profound. At a stroke, young people's dependency on their families or other institutions was deepened in nature and prolonged in time. Grants for full time education have all but disappeared, income from Youth Training is notoriously low and what work is available for the 16–18 years olds is usually temporary, low paid, insecure, unstable and does not form the basis for sound financial independence.

Hence, it is possible to argue that the main modes of governing young lives have shifted in the last twenty years (Muncie and Hughes, 2002). Whereas once young people were governed by employment and welfare, now greater and greater emphasis is placed on the regulations and disciplines of education, training and family life whilst lesser and lesser energies are given to ensuring a 'safety net'. For, so the assumption goes, there is no reason for a young person to be outside school, college, work or the family.

Responsibilising Young People: Culpability and Punishment

In this section, I argue that in addition to prolonging the dependency of youth, there has been a shift in the citizenship obligations and duties of young people (Carlen, 1996). Fundamental to these shifts are the *responsibilising strategies* of successive governments. In the context of crime control, Garland described *responsibilising strategies* as being the strategies that involve 'central government seeking to act upon crime not in a direct fashion through state agencies (police, courts, prisons, social work etc.) but instead acting indirectly, seeking to activate action on the part of non-state agencies and organisations' (Garland, 2000: 452). The key to these strategies, claims Garland, is that central government is 'seeking to renegotiate the question of what is properly a state function and what is not' (*ibid*). It is my contention that this process extends far beyond the remit of renegotiating the boundaries of responsibility *vis-à-vis* crime: it also extends to renegotiating the boundaries for the responsibility of troubled young lives (i.e. young people who are outwith education, family, employment or training). There are numerable shifts in policy which coalesce in ways that symbolically denude 'troubling' young people of the social, material and economic conditions they exist within and in so doing, locate them as being responsible (and thus blameworthy) for their own 'troubles'. Here I focus on two aspects that support my argument *vis-à-vis* youth prostitution.

Recent changes in criminal justice policy are underpinned by a growing emphasis on the 'blameworthiness' and 'responsibility' that young people have for their less than law-abiding behaviour (Goldson, 2002; Muncie, 1999). So, for instance, the Crime and Disorder Act 1998 made provision to abolish the presumption of *doli incapax* which acted as a legal 'safeguard'. In accordance with *doli incapax,* it had to be established in legal proceedings that children between the ages of 10 and 13 years old knew that what they did was 'seriously wrong' and not just naughty. The explicit governmental rationale for doing so was that such proceedings served to 'clog' the system and thereby produce inefficiency and unwarranted delays. It should also be noted however, that from the late 1970s onwards there was a rise in 'popular punitivism'. This reached its zenith in the early to mid 1990s with public and media outrage at the treatment of two boys aged 10 and 11 accused of killing the toddler James Bulger. Whatever the cause, the abolition of *doli incapax* signified a fundamental change in the understanding of young lawbreakers: children as young as 10 are seen as fully understanding the gravity of what they do.

A further consequence of the growing popular punitivism and responsibilisation of young people has been a new climate of penal practice. There has been a year on year increase and expansion in the use of custodial sentences of young people throughout the decade of the 1990s and into the new millennium. The Criminal Justice and Public Act 1994 Section 1 created a new penal sentence— a secure training order—for 12 to 14 year olds (previously incarceration was only used for the older age groups). And, with the introduction of the secure training order, an 80 year long decarceration trend was reversed and the custodial net was cast further down the age range. Although the secure training order was abolished in April 2000, it was replaced by a detention and training order which extended the courts' power to incarcerate children as young as 10 years old; directly remand into custody children aged 12 and above and imprison those aged 12 and above for non-grave offences. Of particular relevance to young girls in prostitution, there is currently no specialist provision for the incarceration of young girls outside secure accommodation. Thus those punished with custodial sentences often find themselves placed in adult women's prisons, of which only four in the country are able to take young girls. These penal changes are combined with the development of new community penalties (such as Anti-social Behaviour Orders, Anti-social Behaviour Contracts, Intensive Supervision and Surveillance Programmes and so on) and the almost wholesale abandonment of rehabilitation programmes of intervention. Indeed, in March 2003, it was announced that the Labour government would seek to criminalise begging and make it punishable by 'on-the-spot' fines for children as young as 10 years old—despite the plethora of empirical evidence about the social and material privations that the young homeless face.

As Muncie, Goldson and others have argued, underpinning these (and other similar) developments in policy is the shift to a 'decontextualised' and 'dematerialised' understanding and acting upon young people's lawbreaking. In other words, there is an almost complete foreclosure in current policy directions of the social, political and economic conditions faced by young people. And, with that, the conditions are created that permit increased blame (and thus increased responsibility) to be placed on either the young people themselves, or their parents and families.

Accommodating the Paradox: Shifting Modes of Youth Governance

In the preceding discussion, I have briefly sketched some of the important shifts in the last twenty years in the way in which youth is both constituted and governed. It is my argument that the limitations, partiality and ambiguities of Britain's youth prostitution policy are partly attributable to paradoxical constructions of children and sex and the way in which these constructions render silent the specificities of young people's involvement in prostitution (especially in relation to the contradiction of invoking child protection intervention for young people at or near the age of sexual consent). But its introduction at the turn of the millennium and the specific shape and form it took (i.e. the lack of challenge to constructions of young people in prostitution as offenders or the need to use the criminal justice route to deal with them and the almost complete erasure of the social and economic specificities and context of prostitution) were only made possible by the ways in which youth governance has shifted in the last two decades. For, these shifts have created the social, political and ideological climate in which it makes sense to punish young people for their attempts to survive the poverty that is foisted upon them when they are outwith family, education or training at the same time as denying them the rights and entitlements to protection against the abuses and crimes committed against them.

Conclusion

Two dangers of taking a critical perspective on innovations in the area of youth prostitution policy are that: firstly, in challenging the dominance of young people's status as victims in prostitution, the energies, efforts and commitment of voluntary and statutory agency workers are minimised or called into question; and, secondly, that unless carefully explicated, critique of child protection methods of intervention elides into a critique of recognising the victimisation of young people in prostitution. The objective of this chapter has been neither to dismiss or denigrate the work of professionals, nor to call into question the strategy of recognising the abuses perpetrated against young people in prostitution. Instead, this chapter has provided a brief history of the development of youth prostitution policy in Britain, raised questions about partiality and limitations of the ways in which this policy has been implemented and lastly has addressed the wider conditions of possibility that shaped youth prostitution policy and practice.

One of the more interesting features of examining Britain's youth prostitution policy is that any analysis quickly moves away from an investigation of the governance of sex and rapidly develops into an study of both youth governance and the conditions of existence for many of Britain's young people outwith the disciplines of family, education or training. As previously said, *SCIP* deploys the discourses of childhood and sex, but the mode of regulation it invokes is part of the broader mode of youth governance. Young people are rewarded for conformity to the disciplines and regulations of dependency within families, education and training or low paid work. Those that, for a variety of reasons, are not committed and are outwith these disciplines are punished in two ways. Firstly, via rejecting the economic deal offered them within families and education and low level work, young people are exposed to poverty and destitution if only because successive governments have removed welfare benefits entitlement. Secondly, various responsibilising strategies and a discursive sleight of hand that position young people as both responsible and blameworthy, young people are then blamed for the poverty they experience and criminalised for the activities that they engaged in to survive that poverty. Within this context, we see that what appears on the surface as progressive policy innovation, protecting the vulnerable from abuse and exploitation ends up as both a means of policing the boundaries of separation between sex and children and part of a much wider strategy and technology of governing young non-conforming lives.

Acknowledgements

I would like to thank both the Nuffield Foundation (SGS00049/a) and the Economic and Social Research Council (no: R000223916) for their grants permitting me to conduct the two research projects that generated the data that informs this chapter. I would also like to express my deep gratitude to Jenny Pearce for her always insightful and stimulating input that manages to combine academic excellence, political astuteness and practice pragmatics. More specifically, I am grateful for her comments on drafts of this paper.

REFERENCES

Box, S, 'Crime, Power and Ideological Mystification' in J Muncie, E McLaughlin and M Langan (eds), *Criminological Perspectives: A Reader* (London, Sage, 1996).
Carlen, P, *Jigsaw: a Political Criminology of Homelessness* (Buckingham, The Open University Press, 1996).
Coles, B, *Young People and Social Policy: Youth Citizenship and Young Careers* (London, Routledge, 1995).
Department of Health and Home Office, *Safeguarding Children Involved in Prostitution* (HMSO, London, 2000).
Donzelot, J, *The Policing of Families* (London, John Hopkins, 1979).
Evans, D, *Sexual Citizenship* (London, Routledge, 1993).
Garland, D, 'The Limits of the Sovereign State' (2000) 36 *British Journal of Criminology* 4.
Glueck, S and Glueck, E, *Five Hundred Women Delinquents* (New York, Knopf, 1934).
Goldson, B, 'New Punitiveness: the Politics of Child Incarceration' in J Muncie, G Hughes and E McLaughlin *Youth Justice: Critical Readings* (London, Sage in association with The Open University, 2002).

JONES, G and WALLACE, C, *Youth, Family and Citizenship* (Buckingham, The Open University Press, 1992).

MATZA, D, *Becoming Delinquent* (Englewoods NJ, Prentice Hall, 1969).

MUNCIE, J and HUGHES, G 'Modes of Youth Governance: Political Rationalities, Criminalisation and Resistance' in J Muncie, G Hughes and E McLaughlin *Youth Justice: Critical Readings* (London, Sage in association with The Open University, 2002).

MUNCIE, J, *Youth and Crime: A Critical Introduction* (London, Sage, 1999).

O'NEILL, M, GOODE, N and HOPKINS, K, 'Juvenile Prostitution: The Experience of Young Women in Residential Care' (1995) 113 *Childright*.

PEARCE, J with WILLIAMS, M and GALVIN, C, *It's Someone Taking a Part of You* (London, National Children's Bureau, 2003).

PHOENIX, J, *Making Sense of Prostitution* (London, Palgrave, 2001).

—— 'In the Name of Protection: Youth Prostitution Policy in England and Wales', (2002a) 22 *Critical Social Policy* 2.

—— 'Youth Prostitution Policy Reforms: New Discourse, Same Old Story' in P Carlen (ed), *Women and Punishment: The struggle for justice* (Collumpton: Willan Publishing, 2002b).

—— 'Youth Prostitution Policy: A Final Report to the Nuffield Foundation' (Bath, University of Bath, 2002c).

—— 'Working with Youth Prostitution: A Database. A Final Report to the Economic and Social Research Council' (Regard Database: www.regard.ac.uk, 2003).

ROSE, N, *Governing the Soul* (London, Routledge, 1989).

SOCIAL EXCLUSION UNIT, *Bridging the Gap: New Opportunities for 16 to 18 Year Olds Not in Education, Employment or Training (Cm 4405)* (London, The Stationary Office, 1999).

18

Sexual Offenders:
A Systematic Review of
Psychological Treatment
Interventions

BELINDA BROOKS-GORDON, CHARLOTTE BILBY
and TRACEY KENWORTHY

> *. . . it is better, and safer for the public, to treat someone than to leave that person
> untreated and unsupported on a register . . . Treatment has to be the right approach.*

The Rt. Hon. Mr David Blunkett, Home Secretary[1]

S EXUAL OFFENDING HAS become one of the major public policy issues in
debates on sexuality. Victim surveys illustrate higher incidence and prevalence levels than are reported and it is generally accepted that there is a high proportion of hidden sexual victimization (Hood *et al.*, 2002). The human and
financial cost of sexual offending to victims and the social and health services is
inestimably large, as is the public investment in policing, prosecuting and incar-
cerating offenders. In 1996, Megan's Law was passed in the state of New Jersey
to allow private and personal information, on those registered as sex offenders
against children, to be made available to the community. Today, people who
have committed a sexual offence represent nearly one quarter of the total population in state prisons in the United States (McGrath, 2003) and sixteen states
have enacted sexual predator laws. Such statutes specify which offences are
sexually violent and permit life-course civil commitment of dangerous mentally
disordered sexual offenders who exceed the permitted level of risk of committing sexually violent crimes.

In the UK, provisions in the Sexual Offences Act 2003 greatly increase the
number of sexual offences (see Bainham and Brooks-Gordon, this volume). The
Act also brings substantial increases in sentence length, along with increased
state control, in terms of notification requirements and supervision, for up to 10
years after a sentence has been spent, for many sexual offences.

---

[1] Hansard, House of Commons, 15 July 2003, column 189.

Exaggerating the danger that sexual offenders pose is problematic and may increase public fear, stigmatise and hinder rehabilitation of offenders who have changed their lifestyles, while wasting valuable resources on unnecessary surveillance (Soothill, 2000). Psychological interventions which reduce re-offending are clearly not only socially desirable but also cost-effective.

TREATMENT PROVISION

Responsibility for the psychological assessment and treatment of sexual offenders falls on a number of different services: the prison service, the national probation service[2] and psychiatric services. In the USA, the cost of treatment may have to be borne by the offender, and in such cases there may be an element of choice as to which services are used. In the UK the majority of treatment is borne by the state. Sexual offenders may be treated in prison, in hospital, or the community. The majority of people have treatment following contact with the criminal justice system, but a minority of people may seek treatment voluntarily for behaviours which may make them feel, or seem to be, at risk of offending.[3]

Early theories of treatment, following psychoanalytic thinking, rested upon developmental failures (Wood *et al.*, 2000). More recently developmental theories have been put forward based on attachment theory (e.g., Ward, Hudson and Marshall, 1996). Most common is cognitive behavioural treatment which has been broadly divided by Perkins *et al.* (1998) into: 1) helping the offender to gain insight into his/her acquisition of offending behaviour/personality, 2) helping to control or remove those influences which maintain the offending pattern, and 3) helping to prevent relapse into re-offending when under stress/in high risk situations in the community. There is a consensus amongst therapist-researchers that all three are important. Cognitive behavioural interventions are the basis of sex offender treatment in prison systems and community programmes in England, Canada, New Zealand, and the US. In the UK National Health Service, however, psychodynamic approaches are common (Grubin, 2002).

Treatment for sexual offenders is carried out either in group work or in individual settings. Group work is widely reported as the most effective context for treatment with adult sexual offenders. These settings have the obvious advantage of being cheaper in terms of time and money. There are clinical reasons for the dominance of group work in the field: the interaction with other people can be harnessed to facilitate change; group work reduces the likelihood of a therapist entering into a collusive relationship with a client, as offenders challenge each others' thinking and behaviours. Group process may help the offender to

---

[2] This may change when the proposed merger between the prison and probation services takes effect in June 2004.

[3] Risk of offending, as used within this review, incorporates those seeking treatment voluntarily for behaviours which would be classified as illegal in whichever jurisdiction they are reported.

be less secretive, begin to deal with unresolved guilt, anger or anxiety, and move towards more socially acceptable behaviour. The group provides a safe environment to practice new skills and ways of thinking, and motivation can be enhanced in a group.

There are a number of large-scale treatment programmes in Canada, Australia, the United States, and England. Following a number of serious prison riots, the Woolf report (1991) published recommendations for the management of imprisoned sexual offenders. The national Sex Offender Treatment Programme (SOTP) was established in England in 1992 and provides a good example of a large-scale multi-site treatment programme. It was centrally designed, and adopted a cognitive behavioural approach based on evidence of treatment efficacy at the time (see Mann and Thornton, 1998 for further details); this programme still exists, though in a more developed form.

The programme revolves around a central course of treatment called the 'Core Programme'.[4] This is primarily for offenders serving a prison sentence of four years or more and it comprises 70 to 75 two-hour sessions. Offenders with an IQ of less than 80 are excluded from this programme. Offenders are also excluded from these main programmes if they totally deny their offence. Offenders selected for treatment have tended to be those who are highly motivated to change and eager to enter into the treatment process (Friendship, Mann, and Beech, 2003). There is a variety of programmes for various types of offenders: the Extended Programme is an additional programme for longer term, higher risk offenders and is based on schema theory; the Rolling Programme is based on attachment theory and deals with attachment styles as, uniquely, group members 'roll' on and off the cyclical programme as they complete it in rotation. Additionally, the Adapted Programme is for sexual offenders with special learning needs.

In order to be deemed suitable for treatment within this framework the prisoner must admit to the offence, and be serving in prison for long enough to complete treatment. The facilitators or therapists are drawn from a variety of professional disciplines, principally psychologists, probation officers, and prison officers. All facilitators are trained centrally through a large-scale two-week training programme. One aspect that has been noted about the treatment delivery by the English and Welsh prison and probation services is that it lacks sophistication, and has little or no emphasis on therapeutic style or group process (Desautels, 2003) compared with other psychotherapy models (for example, those based on object relations theory). When the programmes were first implemented, facilitators worked with no formal supervision or monitoring of practice—although this has since changed and there is now some formal supervision in place.

---

[4] This was subsequently amended and re-launched as 'Core 2000'.

EVALUATION CONTROVERSY

Opinion is divided about the lack of relevant evaluative research on the effectiveness of psychological treatments for sexual offenders despite the growth in literature on the merits of treatment (Quinsey, 1998). Randomised controlled trials in this field are often complex and difficult. There is controversy regarding denial of treatment to this participant group. Given the belief that treatment works, despite weak evidence, there are human rights and ethical implications should a potentially helpful treatment be withheld within a controlled trial. This controversy hampers researchers wishing to undertake evaluative studies and randomised controlled trials are rarely undertaken in criminal justice settings. It is arguable that randomised treatment studies could deny a prisoner an effective treatment and may also affect the security classification of that prisoner and decisions regarding parole (Friendship, 2002). As a result, prisoners allocated to non-treatment groups could be denied an intervention package that could affect the chances of early release or re-categorisation to a lower security level (Hood, 2002).

To date, no positive treatment effects have been found in quasi-experimental institutional treatment programmes (Quinsey, 1998). One meta-analysis using matched longitudinal follow up studies found 'failure to complete treatment' to be a moderate predictor of sexual recidivism, but concluded this was more likely to be due to the monitoring of risk rather than treatment efficacy (Hanson and Bussiere, 1998). One empirical review identified three random assignment studies, too few to draw meaningful conclusions (Hanson *et al.*, 2002) and found no difference in sexual recidivism between offenders who explicitly refused treatment and those who volunteered. A Cochrane review[5] of randomised trials identified only two relevant studies (total n = 286) and no clear effects of group therapy/relapse prevention (White *et al.*, 1998).

Since these reviews, further evidence of the efficacy of psychological intervention has begun to emerge (Beech *et al.*, 1998) and the theoretical sophistication with which sexual offending is explained has advanced (Ward and Siegart, 2002). Analysis of treatment outcomes for almost 11,000 sexual offenders from 79 sex offender treatment studies found that people who participated in relapse prevention programmes had a 7.2% re-arrest rate compared with 13.2% for all treated offenders, and 17.6% for untreated offenders (Alexander, 1999). Small treatment effects, measured by reconviction, have been found in low and medium risk offenders (Friendship, 2003b) although many years of follow up are necessary before any intervention is deemed to be fully evaluated (Wood *et al.*, 2000). As a considerable number of offenders have multiple victims, a small treatment effect is important due to the significant reduction in harm to society (Hanson and

---

[5] A Cochrane Review is a review which contains a synthesis of all the best available evidence about the efficacy of a particular health care or medical treatment.

Harris, 2000) and proponents of treatment suggest greater effects might be detected using more sensitive psychometric measurement than reconviction data (Friendship *et al.*, 2003). Research has come to light regarding no treatment effects (i.e., no significant reduction in sexual, violent, nor general recidivism, Hanson and Broom, 2003), and the lack of treatment effect is argued to be a function of a lack of sensitivity in the way in which treatment effects are measured, that is by reconviction, reoffending and recidivism (Falshaw *et al.*, 2003).

What is not in doubt, however, is that treatment *should* be evaluated, and one of the most rigorous ways of doing this is by systematic review of treatment studies; necessarily one which evaluates both randomised control trials (RCTs) and also qualitative research. The term 'systematic' refers to a type of review that is designed and carried out with strategies to avoid bias. For example, only a small percentage of the research ever carried out finds its way into publication. Research written up in the English language, or research reporting positive treatment effects, is more likely to be published. Systematic reviews aim to overcome such bias and provide the best evidence available on the risks and benefits of interventions. These reviews exist to inform the decision-making of practitioners and policy makers, to identify areas where further research is needed, and to guide the allocation of resources. They necessarily detail exactly how the material has been gathered which informs the overall conclusion. This chapter presents the methods and evidence available to date from one such review. It offers a breakdown of the studies gathered, the search strategies developed and the outcomes identified. We also discuss the process of developing an extraction tool for the qualitative research papers.

The aim of the review upon which this chapter is based was to evaluate a range of psychological interventions on adults who have been convicted of, or cautioned for, sexual offences or who sought treatment or were considered to be at risk of sexual offending. This includes participants who have been treated in institutional or community settings for either sexual behaviours which have resulted in conviction or caution for sexual offences or offences with a sexual element (for example incest or rape); violent behaviours with a sexual element (for example, murder where there is a sexual element), or who were perceived to be at risk of offending.

METHOD

The criteria for considering studies for the review included all relevant randomised control trials, quasi-randomised trials, and qualitative studies. The authors worked with the Cochrane Schizophrenia Group (CSG) to develop the RCT search strategy. Forty-five specific search terms were used for the identification of studies.[6] Thirty-three electronic databases were searched for

---

[6] For details of specific search terms see the Cochrane International Collaboration website: http://www.cochrane.org/index0.htm.

randomised control trials. The qualitative search terms were developed by the research team, with the support of members of the Cochrane Qualitative Research Methods groups and other colleagues. A specified selection of qualitative search terms was used as the initial search filter along with a specified set of sex offender search terms. Using these search terms, six selected databases were searched. These particular databases were selected based on the 'high hit' nature of the databases. In respect of the qualitative search terms, as the systematic reviewing of qualitative research studies is still in its infancy, we developed a set of thirty search terms that will act as a starting point for future research in this area.

In order to address publication bias of studies in English, the literature published in languages other than English was explored. Hand searches were conducted of journals in which literature reviews have found database searches to be poor. To explore the grey literature, a call for information went out to academics and those involved in sex offender treatment programmes through the International Association for the Treatment of Sexual Offenders (IATSO), the Association for the Treatment of Abusers (ATSA), and the National Organisation for the Treatment of Abusers (NOTA).

Assessment of quality was carried out to allocate randomised control trials to three quality categories, as described in the Cochrane Collaboration Handbook (Clarke and Oxman, 2001). The qualitative criteria were based on the process used in the Critical Appraisal Skills Programme (CASP) pioneered by the Cochrane Qualitative Methods Group and used by the Campbell Process Implementation Group. This appraisal programme asks specific questions of the study revolving around whether an explicit account of the theoretical framework and/or the inclusion of a literature review are given and a clear statement of the aims of the research is provided. Further issues concern the appropriateness of qualitative methodology, the sampling strategy, data collection, data analysis, research partnership relations, exposition of the findings and the interpretation of those findings, the transferability of findings, and the relevance and usefulness of these.

Assessment of the methodological quality of process evaluations remains an exploratory exercise. Taken together, the above criteria represent one of the first steps to generate a way of assessing the validity and reliability of the research results and conclusions of a number of process evaluations. Essentially they provide a framework to review whether enough information has been provided in order to judge whether the evaluation, context, sample, methodology, data analysis and data interpretation used in the process evaluations take into account, or make explicit, any possible alternative explanation for the findings shown and/or conclusions drawn (see Popay *et al.*, 2003).

In this respect, such assessment differs from the methodological assessment of outcome evaluations. These criteria were not used to generate a sub-set of evaluations from which 'reliable' evidence could be drawn. Rather, the aim was to provide a synthesis, within an explicit framework of methodological quality, of the findings of process evaluations and their implications for developing and implementing psychological interventions for sexual offenders.

An important feature of these is in the critical appraisal of studies describing processes involved in implementing interventions, as well as those designed to assess their impact on the target population.[7] The searches were carried out and stored in ProCite software. All titles and abstracts were inspected (by TK) and re- inspected by a second reviewer (BB-G or CB) in order to ensure reliable selection. Once the full articles were obtained, the three reviewers determined whether they met the criteria for inclusion.

RANGE AND DEFINITION OF PSYCHOLOGICAL INTERVENTIONS

The range of psychological interventions included behavioural interventions, cognitive-behavioural treatments (CBT), psychodynamic therapy, and psychoanalysis.

Behavioural Interventions

Styles of intervention associated with traditional classical and operant learning theory are generally referred to as behaviour modification or behaviour therapy. The hallmark of these interventions is an explicit focus on changes in behaviour by administering a stimulus and measuring its effect upon overt behaviour. Within sex offender treatment this is often used to address deviant sexual interest alongside penile plesmograph for 'objective' measurement. Examples include aversion therapy (exposure to deviant material followed by aversive stimulus), covert sensitization (a deviant sexual experience is imagined until arousal and then a powerful negative experience imagined), olfactory conditioning (unpleasant odour with high risk sexual situation) and masturbation satiation/orgasmic reconditioning (masturbation to an appropriate sexual fantasy).

Cognitive-Behavioural Interventions

A range of interventions has fallen under the rubric of cognitive-behavioural treatment. McGuire (2000) has characterised this range of interventions as a continuum. In the middle of the continuum are interventions that seek to change the individual's internal (cognitive and emotional) functioning as well as their overt behaviour; this best represents cognitive-behavioural treatment in the

---

[7] The analysis reported here was also inspired by the reviews carried out at the EPPI-Centre (The Evidence for Policy and Practice Information and Co-ordinating Centre) at the University of London Department of Education—an important feature of which is the exploration of barriers and facilitators to effective intervention.

sense in which it flows from social learning theory. Finally, there are cognitive therapies in which the focus is exclusively on changing some aspect of the individual's cognition. This approach is more likely to have a base in some variant of cognitive theory, such as information processing, than in learning theory.

Cognitive-behavioural treatment should at least involve attempts to change internal processes—thoughts, beliefs, emotions, physiological arousal—alongside changing overt behaviour, such as social skills or coping behaviours. However, as the label cognitive behavioural therapy has been applied to a variety of interventions, it is difficult to provide a single, unambiguous definition. Recognising this, we constructed criteria that were felt to be both workable and to capture elements of good practice in cognitive behavioural therapy. In order to be classified as 'well defined' the intervention must clearly demonstrate the following components: i) the intervention involves the recipient establishing links between their thoughts, feelings and actions with respect to the target symptom, and ii) the intervention involves the correction of the person's misperceptions, irrational beliefs and reasoning biases related to the target symptom). The intervention should involve either or both of the following: a) the recipient monitoring his or her own thoughts, feelings and behaviours with respect to the target symptom, and b) the promotion of alternative ways of coping with the target symptom. In addition, all therapies that do not meet these criteria (or that provide insufficient information) but are labelled as 'CBT' or 'Cognitive Therapy' were included as 'less well defined' CBT.

Psychodynamic Interventions

As there could be as many definitions of psychodynamic or psychoanalytic therapy as there are studies, we constructed criteria that were felt to be both workable and to capture elements of good practice in psychodynamic or psychoanalytic therapy. All interventions that did not meet these criteria but are labelled as 'psychodynamic/analytic therapy' or 'psychoanalysis', were included as 'less well defined' therapies.

Psychodynamic psychotherapy was defined as regular individual therapy sessions with a trained psychotherapist, or a therapist under supervision. Therapy sessions were to be based on a psychodynamic or psychoanalytic model. Sessions could rely on a variety of strategies, including explorative insight-oriented, supportive or directive activity, and applied flexibly. However, therapists should use a less strict technique than in psychoanalysis. To be considered well-defined psychodynamic psychotherapy, trialists needed to include working with transference.

Psychoanalysis was defined as regular individual sessions with a trained psychoanalyst, lasting a minimum of 30 minutes, three to five times a week. Psychoanalysis was required to continue for at least one year. Analysts were required to adhere to a strict definition of psychoanalytic technique. To be considered well-defined psychoanalysis, trialists needed to report working at the infantile sexual relations level of psychoanalytic theory.

RESULTS

Randomised Control Trials

We identified nine studies for inclusion in this part of the review. All of the studies except Romero (1983) took place in some type of hospital, often in a secure setting. Some studies did not stipulate that leaving treatment was an option so the acceptability of the treatment (i.e., to the recipient) cannot be judged. Romero (1983) remains the largest study (231 participants) in this area, although Marques (1994) also randomised considerable numbers of men (n = 155). At the other end of the scale is Ryan (1997) with an exploratory study involving only eight people. The duration of studies varied, and at one extreme, a crossover study by Rooth (1974), only reported usable data at the point of crossover (1 week). Other trials present data only at the point where the 6–8 week intervention ends (Anderson-Varney 1991; McAnaney 1981). Marques (1994), McConaghy (1985) and McConaghy (1988) followed people up for one year, and Romero (1983) for up to a decade.

Participants

Of 567 adults included in the eight studies, 283 (52%) had committed sex offences against children. McAnaney's (1981) participants were 25 rapists not stipulated to be paedophiles. Hopkins (1991) involved rapists, paedophiles and incest offenders. McConaghy (1985) included five 'compulsive homosexuals' and one clothes fetishist who do not fit within the criteria of this review.[8] McConaghy (1988) involved 31 people with 'anomalous sexual urges', 19 of whom had been convicted of an offence of a sexual nature. It is unclear what was the seriousness of these people's problems and their danger to others. The large Romero study (1983) (n = 231), however, clearly involved dangerous people, 177 of whom had past convictions relating to paedophilia, exhibitionism, or sexual assault.[9] Finally, Rooth (1974) included 12 persistent exhibitionists and Ryan (1997) comprised eight men who had committed a sexual act not permitted by the Federal law of Texas, USA. It is not clear what these acts were. All participants in the studies were men.

---

[8] Their data were not possible to separate from the 14 exhibitionists, paedophiles and voyeurs, but data from this study are included as the group we do not consider to be sexual offenders constitute a minority.

[9] 'Dangerousness' is of course a highly contentious concept, see The Law Society (1999) and Nigel Walker's explorations of dangerousness (1996).

Outcomes

The longer studies used re-offending or recidivism as an outcome. Marques (1994) measured reoffending by automated records (rapsheets) and reports from the parole system. The participants were deemed to have re-offended if either data source recorded a new sex crime or non-sex violent crime. Romero (1983) measured recidivism by reconviction. Both McConaghy (1985) and McConaghy (1988) recorded the simple outcome of 'no change in target behaviour'. McAnaney (1981) used a scale to record 'heterosocial' skills and social avoidance. Both McConaghy (1985) and McConaghy (1988) recorded simple binary outcomes relevant to 'desire' for target behaviour. Rooth (1974), McConaghy (1988) and McAnaney (1981) all seemed to offer the possibility of leaving the study early. Other studies did not make clear that this was an option. McConaghy (1985) specifically recorded attitudes to treatment. McAnaney (1981), Anderson-Varney (1991) and Hopkins (1991) all used different rating scales to try to measure self-esteem. Anderson-Varney (1991) used a scale to measure cognitive distortions relating to paedophilic behaviour. Ryan (1997) also rated cognitive distortions and immaturity. Anderson-Varney (1991) rated knowledge and beliefs using a continuous scale. Ryan (1997), however, reported a binary outcome of 'poor knowledge of sex'. Ryan (1997) was the only study to rate sexual obsessions and reported these in binary form. McAnaney (1981), Anderson-Varney (1991), and Hopkins (1991) all used different rating scales to try to measure anxiety. Ryan (1997) reported on participants' level of interest in sexual activity. In addition, a variety of psychometric outcome scales were used in the included studies that reported usable data (see Table 2 for psychometric scales used).

Missing Outcomes

There are few data on mental state and almost none on engagement with services. The therapy studies are almost free of measures of adverse effects, except for lack of effect. There are no prison service outcomes and we are left unsure if some of the measures really relate to satisfaction with treatment. Quality of life and economic outcomes are absent. With the exception of Romero (1983) with a follow-up of one decade and Marques (1994), with a follow-up of one year, most outcomes are over such limited duration as to render them of little relevance to many working with offenders over extended periods of time.

Intervention Trial Results

Rooth (1974) examined aversion therapy. Participants self-administered shocks from a standard battery operated shock box during electrical aversion sessions where problematic situations are rehearsed and also during fantasy. Rooth (1974) compared the behavioural electrical aversion with standard relaxation sessions as would be run by many mental health care professionals. One group of people worked with playbacks of situations whilst having exposure in a mirror paired at times with a noxious image.

Rooth (1974), in a small (n = 12) crossover study, compared electrical aversion with self-regulation and with relaxation treatment. It was only possible to extract follow-up data before the first crossover, and as no one left this study within the first week, despite this being a possibility, relative risk is impossible to calculate.[10] In the comparison between relaxation treatment and self-regulation, here too only the Rooth (1974) study can be included and no person left by the end of the first week.

McConaghy (1985) and McConaghy (1988) employed imaginal desensitisation techniques. These involve relaxation training followed by visualising being in situations where they have carried out the anomalous sexual behaviour in the past but visualise not completing the behaviour, while remaining relaxed. McConaghy (1985) carried out covert sensitisation. The study compared the imaginal desensitisation with a covert technique in which, after visualising the situation where they have carried out the anomalous sexual behaviour in the past, participants were then asked to visualise an aversive scene. Imaginal desensitisation was also compared with covert sensitisation. This comparison includes only McConaghy (1985) where 20 exhibitionists, 'compulsive homosexuals' (n = 5), paedophiles, and a clothes fetishist (n = 1) were randomised to an imaginal desensitisation or covert sensitisation programme. The imaginal desensitisation involved imagining target sexual experience and then avoiding arousal by substitution of non-target conclusion. The covert sensitisation involved imagining the target sexual experience until arousal, then imagining a powerful negative experience. Three outcomes were reported: behaviour, desire, and attitude to treatment.[11] Most people in both groups had a change in the target behaviour. Everyone was rated as positively changed by one month, and 75 per cent by one year.[12] For desire, again 80–90 per cent of people improved with no difference between the groups. By one year, only one person, allocated covert sensitisation, was thought to have had a deleterious effect on desire.[13] Attitudes to treatment were measured for whether participants requested further treatment. One person in the imaginal desensitation group

---

[10] For binary outcomes a standard estimation of the fixed effects risk ratio (RR) and its 95% confidence interval (CI) was calculated. Where possible, the weighted number needed to treat/harm statistic (NNT/NNH) and its 95% confidence interval (CI) was also calculated. The number needed to treat means the number required to treat in order to get the effect. For example, if a drug does not work on everyone, the number needed to treat should be calculated in order to get the treated (or harmful) effect.

[11] The options were 'no change' or 'increase in target behaviour'.

[12] RR no change or increase in target behaviour by one year 0.67, CI 0.14 to 3.17.

[13] RR no change or increased desire for target behaviour by 1 year 0.33, CI 0.02 to 7.32.

requested further treatment by one year compared with two of those allocated to covert sensitisation.[14]

Only in McConaghy (1988) is imaginal desensitisation compared with a testosterone-lowering drug for 31 men with anomalous sexual urges and behaviours. Meproxyprogesterone should lower sex drive in men by increasing the levels of female sex hormones. In the McConaghy (1998) study it was given as 150mg intramuscular injections every two weeks for two months followed by the same dose every month. Three outcomes were reported: behaviour, desire, and leaving the study early. By one month all but one man had experienced a change in their target behaviour.[15] Everyone was rated as having had a positive change in behaviour at one year. McConaghy (1988) reports similar results for desires. Most men seemed to experience a positive decline in desire for the problematic behaviour.[16] Despite there being an option to leave the study no one discontinued treatment by one year.

Marques (1994)[17] randomised men undergoing cognitive behavioural therapy. All were men who had molested children and who were volunteers to the Sex Offender Treatment and Evaluation Project (SOTEP), California. They were matched in pairs by age, type of offence and previous criminal history. Pair members were then randomly allocated to treatment/no treatment condition. All in the treatment group received a relapse prevention programme that included cognitive behavioural training, decision matrices, relaxation training and stress and anger management, attendance at therapeutic community meetings and leisure/recreational activity. Participants could also receive treatment for drug or alcohol problems and behaviour therapy for sexual deviation (olfactory aversion, masturbatory satiation or orgasmic reconditioning). All those in the treatment group also attended an aftercare programme for one year after release and recidivism after one year was measured. Overall, in this important study, re-offence declined in the cognitive behavioural group.[18] Marques (1994) reported different types of re-offence and suggested that the cognitive behavioural group therapy did not seem to have much effect on sex crimes.[19] If the re-offending was purely violent, then cognitive behavioural therapy seemed to have an effect.[20]

Cognitive, social and educational therapy was used by Anderson-Varney (1991). A cognitive restructuring model was employed where they challenged irrational beliefs, increased beliefs of control, helped develop interpersonal social skills and provided sex education. McAnaney (1981) employed an eclec-

---

[14] RR 0.5, CI 0.05 to 4.67.

[15] RR no change 0.33, CI 0.02 to 7.32.

[16] RR no change 0.33, CI 0.02 to 7.32.

[17] Although there are many accounts of this programme, only the larger Marques (1994) study (n = 155) is included in this comparison.

[18] RR any sexual or violent crime 0.41, CI 0.2 to 0.82, NNT 5, CI 3 to 20.

[19] n = 155, RR re-offending by a crime of a sexual nature not involving violence 0.78, CI 0.28 to 2.14; RR re-offending by a crime of a sexual nature also involving violence 0.12, CI 0.01 to 2.11.

[20] RR re-offending by a crime of a violent nature 0.28, CI 0.08 to 0.98.

tic mix of social skills training, as used with shy and socially anxious college males, cognitive behaviour modification, sex education and clinical skills from experience. Hopkins' (1991) intervention involved rule setting, listening and verbal skills training, perspective talking/relationships skills, victim awareness, anxiety and aggression management, and group communications and team work. Taken in combination, 115 child sex offenders, paedophiles and rapists were allocated to either programmes involving cognitive restructuring (challenging irrational beliefs, increasing beliefs of control, developing interpersonal effectiveness), social skills training (developed for sex offenders, didactic and experimental, teaching as regards appearance and interaction) and sex education (factual information on sexuality and opinions and attitudes) or standard cares not involving the additional programme. Studies were of relatively short duration (six weeks to six months) with an emphasis on the use of scales as outcome measures. Unfortunately these similar studies did not share outcome scales.

McAnaney (1981) measured 'heterosocial skills' using the Heterosocial Skills Behaviour Checklist in which the mean difference in scores was significantly in favour of the cognitive, social, educational intervention,[21] but the meaning of this finding is unclear. Anderson-Varney (1991) recorded social avoidance and distress using the Social Avoidance and Distress Scale. These skewed data were analysed by the trialists and they found no difference in the average end point scores. For self-esteem, again the three studies employed three different scales. Anderson-Varney (1991), using the Interpersonal Reactivity Index recorded almost identical scores between the two groups. McAnaney (1981) used the Social Self-Esteem Inventory and also found no significant difference between groups. Finally Hopkins (1991), using the Rosenburg's Self Esteem Scale reported similarly equivocal findings at six months. In the measurement of cognitive distortions, Anderson-Varney (1991) found a significant difference for the outcome cognitive distortions as recorded by the Abel and Becker Cognition Scale.[22] This group also used a sub-score of the Multiphasic Sex Inventory to investigate the same parameter. This means of measurement found no difference between groups. Again using the Multiphasic Sex Inventory, Anderson-Varney (1991) measured sexual knowledge but the intervention did not appreciably affect this aspect of knowledge. McAnaney (1981) used the S-R Inventory of Anxiousness to measure men's anxiety and found no clear difference afforded by the intervention.[23] Anderson-Varney (1991) again used the Multiphasic Sex Inventory as a measure of inadequacy and also found no clear difference between standard care and the cognitive, social and educational intervention. Hopkins (1991) measured anxiety using the Fear of Negative

[21] MD 7 7, CI 1.45 to 13.95.
[22] n = 60, MD 13.43, CI 6.81 to 20.05.
[23] We are aware that inadequacy is not the same as anxiety, but have presented them together as we feel they may be related in the context of this review.

Evaluation Scale and found little difference at six months. In McAnaney (1981) participants were free to leave the study early. The great majority did not choose to do so.[24]

Ryan (1997) used a psychotherapeutic technique that cut across various schools of psychotherapy. The transtheoretical counselling group therapy involved stages of pre-contemplation, preparation, action and maintenance (Prochaska, 1984). The aims were to assess at what stage a person is in their need to address their problems and to assist at each stage in order to facilitate change and maintenance. Ryan (1997) used a therapy that involved a combination of relapse prevention model and cognitive behavioural strategies but full descriptions are not reported in the dissertation.[25] Significantly more men allocated to the cognitive group therapy group had poor attitudes to treatment at 24 weeks when compared with those given the counselling approach.[26] Neither intervention showed any effect on cognitive distortions, as measured by the Multiphasic Sex Inventory.[27] Again using the Multiphasic Sex Inventory Ryan (1997) measured sexual knowledge and, at 24 weeks, found it unchanged by the intervention.[28] High levels of sexual obsessions were found after 24 weeks of treatment in both groups.[29] Finally, still employing the Multiphasic Sex Inventory, Ryan (1997) measured levels of interest in sex. This did not seem to be affected by the interventions.[30]

Only Romero (1983) examined the effects of psychodynamic group therapy compared with no group therapy, and reports a randomised control trial of intensive probation plus group therapy versus intensive probation alone. The group therapy was grounded in psychodynamic theory and involved 'redirection of the aggressive drive' to permit expression of the sex needs in a less impulsive, more socially acceptable manner which is promoted in the first place by a sense of social and peer acceptance. Basically, the individual learns to deal with his sexual and other impulses in such a way as to avoid conflict with authority. This study, spanning a decade, reports on a single but relevant outcome—rearrest for offending within 10 years. Eleven percent of the 48 paedophiles, 39 exhibitionists and 144 men guilty of sexual assault reoffended within the ten year follow up and the group therapy did not have a clear effect on this rate.[31]

---

[24] n = 40, RR 2.0, CI 0.2 to 20.33.

[25] Only Ryan (1997) compared cognitive group therapy with a counselling approach not affiliated to any particular school of therapy. This cluster-randomised study is difficult to analyse. The intra-cluster correlation coefficient (ICC) is not reported and the paper analysed as if a standard individual randomised study. With this in mind, we wanted to ensure that this study was presented but that the data were not ascribed more weight than they merit (see Brooks-Gordon *et al.*, 2004 for full details of how the design effect was calculated).

[26] Corrected n = 38, RR poor attitude to treatment 2.8, CI 1.26 to 6.22, NNH 2, CI 1 to 5.

[27] Corrected n = 38, RR cognitive distortions and immaturity 1.0, CI 0.76 to 1.32.

[28] Corrected n = 38, RR poor knowledge of sex 1.10, CI 0.62 to 1.95.

[29] Corrected n = 38, RR high levels of obsessions 1.50, CI 0.80 to 2.81.

[30] Corrected n = 38, RR of denying interest in sex to the point of promoting an asexual image 1.83, CI 0.85 to 3.94.

[31] n = 231, RR re-arrest for sex offending 1.87, CI 0.78 to 4.47.

Five studies used a 'standard care' group (Anderson-Varney, 1991; Hopkins, 1991; Marques, 1994; McAnaney, 1981; Romero, 1983). Most of these studies described standard care as 'no additional treatment' but Romero (1983) described standard care as probation, with the need to report to probation once per month plus one home visit per month.

Methodological Quality of Included Studies

All reports stated that the studies were randomised, but how this was achieved was not described. The trials were therefore regarded as having moderate risk to the introduction of bias.[32] McConaghy (1988), for example, involved three groups with equal numbers (10). A description of how this was achieved would have been instructive. Ryan (1997) randomised groups. It is not clear how this allocation was achieved and if it was concealed from therapists. Most studies were stated not to be blind (McAnaney, 1981; McConaghy, 1988; Romero, 1983; Ryan, 1997), or blinding was not mentioned (Anderson-Varney, 1991; Hopkins, 1991; Marques, 1994; Rooth, 1974). McConaghy (1985), however, attempted a single blind technique with the interviewer being unaware of the participants' allocated intervention but did not test whether the technique had been successful. Three years later the same authors undertook a similar study but did not attempt blinding (McConaghy, 1988).

Overall very few people left these studies before completion. We report on this for the studies only where leaving early was an option (McAnaney, 1981; McConaghy, 1988; Rooth, 1974; Ryan, 1997), and reasons are stipulated. For example, McConaghy (1988) initially involved 31 participants. One man allocated to combined treatment dropped out when he discovered he had low testosterone. He was then treated with imaginal desensitisation alone and was excluded from the analysis within the paper. Of the 20 people receiving injections of meproxyprogesterone (with or without imaginal desensitisation), five dropped out of the treatment; four stopped after 3–5 injections, due to side effects, but continued to report to the study, and one stopped after five injections and was lost to follow-up. It is not clear, however, how this was dealt with in the analysis. For dichotomous data we assume that all those who left the study early did so because they did not improve. Ryan (1997) did not report people leaving early clearly and data could not be used in the analysis, but McAnaney (1981) and Rooth (1974) clearly reported the low number of drop outs.

---

[32] As studies have shown that poor reporting of randomisation increases the estimate of effect (Chalmers 1983) it has to be assumed that all studies in this review may have reported results prone to favour the experimental interventions.

Types of Studies

Two types of study were included: a) qualitative outcome studies or process evaluation studies of interventions; b) qualitative non-intervention research; studies examining the views of people (either facilitators or offenders) about their treatment experience. Prioritising offenders' or therapists' views to examine directly what these people thought might impede or facilitate sexual offender intervention treatment programmes may greatly inform the factors affecting both intervention delivery drop-out rates.

Four studies were found which complied with the criteria for soundness stated above. These include three process evaluations and one exploratory study. In the first process evaluation, Houston *et al.*, (1995) explore the processes and dynamics that occur in a prison CBT programme in the UK (see Appendix). This study is explicit about group structure and composition. It also has a strong and explicit theoretical base but there is no discussion of how data were collected, recorded, or analysed. They do not report how the themes found emerged from the data.

In the second study Lea, Auburn and Kibblewhite (1999) explore the views of professionals and paraprofessionals working with sexual offenders in treatment programmes in the UK. The interviews in this study were transcribed verbatim and the data were triangulated. Two main issues emerged from the findings: training and support. Training influenced the attitudes and understandings and the ability to negotiate the professional-personal dialect. The participants reported a lack of support, such as on-going supervision, further knowledge, or skills training and informal peer meetings available to professionals. The authors discuss these findings in terms of how professional perceptions of sex offenders and sex offences affect their professional practice.

The final two studies for inclusion were both by Scheela (1992, 2001) and carried out in the United States. The former study is concerned with the experiences of incest offenders, and the latter focuses on therapists' experiences and perceptions (both negative and positive) of working with offenders. In both studies the setting is an intervention called the Sexual Abuse Treatment programme (SAT); a two year multi-faceted treatment programme which involves individual, group, family and couple therapy. In addition, there are support groups, educational groups and aftercare after completion of the programme. Scheela (1992) uses the concept of 'remodelling' as a metaphor for treatment process: dynamic, non-linear, simultaneous remodelling process involves offenders' worlds 'falling apart', the offenders 'taking on'—taking responsibility for the offence and also the project of remodelling selves, 'tearing out' damaged parts, 'rebuilding' themselves, their relationships, environments, 'doing the upkeep' to maintain the remodelling accomplished and, eventually, 'moving on' to new remodelling projects.

Scheela (2001) built on the previous study to answer research questions relating to therapists' experiences and perceptions of working with offenders. The aims of the research are clear and the findings illustrate a complex process for therapists during the delivery of a psychological intervention for sexual offenders; the process commonly begins with apprehension, antipathy, and fear. This changes as the therapists begin to see abuse as separate from the person, consider treatment more realistically, and start to enjoy working with offenders, although they report being desensitised to hearing about abuse. Therapists reported the development of stricter personal boundaries. The impacts of carrying out treatment were also analysed and include both negative and positive aspects to the work. The negative impacts included frustration with mandated reporting as the 'antithesis of therapeutic relationship', the impact of worrying about offender recidivism, concern about being sued, transference, counter-transference, safety precautions, and suspicion. The positive impacts included the challenge of the work, working as a team, witnessing offender growth and change, and one's contribution to safety of community. Coping strategies developed by the therapists were also explored. These included developing 'calluses' to abuse stories, processing issues with colleagues, humour to counteract other feelings the work brought, and diversifying therapeutic work. Scheela (2001) documents the difficulties and hazards encountered by therapists working with sexual offenders in order to prevent and 'detoxify' these. Despite these difficulties, the study reports that work with sexual offenders can be satisfying and rewarding. Knowledge of what is positive (even inspiring) about the work may help burnout and enable therapists to view their work with pride.

Both studies by Scheela comply with CASP guidelines of providing explicit detail of the research. In addition, a diagrammatic representation is provided in the first study to show the dynamic relationship between the stages of change. There are a number of original findings in both studies, such as the fear of litigation, which are transferable to the English and Welsh system, and which may also have clinical implications for the delivery of psychological interventions.

CONCLUSION

As a society we simply have to face up to the fact that there are a lot of sex offenders out there and that there are effective ways to deal with their behaviour

(Hilton Dawson, MP, Hansard, col 216, 15 Jul 2003)

Within the analysis of the randomised control trials, the Romero (1983) study is remarkable for its design and follow up. Its eclectic approach to treatment may reflect real world practice and its outcome certainly does. Although other studies do recognise the need to follow people for a substantial period, no other study is able to report on a ten-year follow up. The large number of participants (n=231) highlights the possibilities for such studies in this field. The re-arrest rate is not statistically significantly increased in the therapy group (14%) compared with the no group therapy control (7%), but with only a few more arrests in the intervention group, there would be a suggestion that the therapy was *less* effective than doing nothing for prevention of re-arrest. This finding is likely to be controversial as there is huge investment in sexual offender treatment programmes, and as the quotation above illustrates, many policy makers erroneously and unreservedly assert that sexual offender treatment therapy is effective.

Strengths and Limitations

This review reports the most comprehensive search for controlled clinical trials in the area of sexual offending. Every effort was made to identify and assimilate data in such a way as to minimise the inclusion of bias. The review summarises the results of pioneering studies and highlights that this area of care and management, fraught with difficulties and ethical concerns, can fruitfully employ randomised control trials as an evaluative tool. Many data were lost because of unclear reporting. If the studies we have identified had reported as clearly as is now expected after the CONSORT guidelines (Moher *et al.*, 2001) considerably more would be known on the effects of treatment of sex offenders. Follow up that is too short from trialists is understandable in this difficult area of research but it is not impossible to follow people for years and routinely record outcomes such as re-arrest (Romero, 1983).

Facilitators and Barriers to Treatment

The paucity of studies that met the 'potentially sound' criteria for qualitative studies, despite the large number initially found from the databases, means that facilitators and barriers to treatment outlined here are tentative. The qualitative data, however, suggest some promising areas for future development.

Facilitators to treatment included working in a team, especially a multi-disciplinary team and the level of *esprit de corps* this generated for the therapists. Appropriate levels of de-sensitisation to sexual abuse narratives were also considered to facilitate treatment. The challenge of the work, along with witnessing the growth and change of recipients, was a facilitator to treatment. The feeling that the work was rewarding and the altruistic notion of contributing to community safety were also seen as beneficial. Maintaining diversity in therapeutic caseloads and avoiding being overloaded with sexual offenders was also a facilitator of treatment.

Barriers to treatment included the feeling of frustration with mandatory reporting of previously un-revealed offences. This was seen as anti-therapeutic because elements of these offences could be worked on in treatment and it may have prevented offenders from revealing all of their offences. A lack of institutional support, lack of ongoing supervision, and lack of training or informal peer meetings available to professionals delivering treatment was a further barrier to treatment. In an increasingly litigious age the legitimate concern about being sued raises institutional and legal questions about the protection of staff and liability for treatment. Unresolved counter-transference issues were considered to be a barrier to treatment, particularly where there was insufficient clinical supervision. Inadequate safety precautions and suspicion of the offender were further barriers as were worries about offender recidivism. Finally, therapist burnout was also considered to be barrier to treatment.

Remaining Gaps

There are some notable gaps in the literature. There are no prison ethnographies, nor anything written by sex offenders themselves. Despite the plethora of research uncovered from the searches, there is a paucity of sound qualitative research on psychological interventions with sexual offenders. There are no large-scale process evaluations and no large qualitative outcome or process evaluations of adequate sophistication or complexity. Sexual offending is presented as being of grave concern yet this systematic search of the literature reveals that very little research is being carried out to understand the *processes* of treatment, effective group processes, the effectiveness of psychological treatment, the perceptions of those being treated, or the phenomenology of the sexual offender. It is difficult to estimate the effectiveness of sexual offender treatment programmes without the phenomenological accounts of those going through them or process evaluations of what is actually occurring within them.

The main conceptual issue here is that people act with reference to meaning. They do not engage in sexual *behaviours* (e.g. penis-in-vagina), they enact sexual *practices* (for example, make love or have a one-night-stand) and what distinguishes sexual practice from sexual behaviour is *meaning* (Kippax, 2003). Meaning is not to be confused with cognition, in the sense of meaning residing in the mind of individuals. Meanings are essentially social, in that they are formed in relationships to people. There is a limit to the number of behaviours a person (or two or more people) engages in, but sexual practice is fluid and changing (see Weeks, and Plummer, this volume). Sexual practices differ across cultures and across time. They are social and cultural practices, produced within particular historical times and places and embedded in specific social formations. Despite this important conceptual issue, only 15% (222/1497) of evaluative reports for potential inclusion in systematic reviews of effectiveness of sexual health promotion collect *both* outcome and process data (Stephenson *et al.*, 2003).

One strength of this review concerns the setting of the qualitative process evaluations alongside the RCTs. One of the challenges faced, however, was in developing search terms specifically for qualitative studies, as there is little consensus about appropriate search terms that work efficiently with the main databases. In addition, given the comparative youth of the discipline of defining qualitative search strategies, the task of reducing the vast number of studies which matched the search terms down to those for in-depth review presented a further challenge in terms of time and resources. Just as experimental outcome evaluation is in itself of no value in examining process, a process evaluation is of no value in examining whether an intervention is effective. However process evaluation can answer important questions about factors influencing the development, provision, and delivery of an intervention and help explain *why* an intervention works or not. But a key to good evaluation lies in using both designs.

Ethics

As discussed earlier, arguments have been put forward that it is unethical to carry out RCTs on sexual offenders because some participants may be deprived of the intervention. This argument rests on the assumption that the intervention would benefit the participants. However, not all sexual practice interventions are effective, and some may cause significant harm. When a state of equipoise exists, that is, where there is uncertainty as to whether potential trial participants would benefit or be harmed by being in one arm of a proposed trial rather than another, it is ethical to undertake a randomised control trial (Bonnell, Bennett and Oakley, 2003). In conditions of equipoise, randomisation is arguably the *most* ethical means of determining whether participants receive interventions of unknown harm or effectiveness. Our findings show that uncertainty about effectiveness of treatment remains. In addition, without RCTs and controlled experimentation, uncontrolled experimentation will prevail, and an examination of quasi-experimental studies in the larger report of the review illustrated this (see Brooks-Gordon *et al.*, 2004). One way through the ethical quagmire that has beset sexual offender interventions might be to implement an RCT with a preferential fixed randomisation ratio, such as 70:30 (instead of 50:50). Fixed ratio preferential randomisation is uncontroversial, may enhance consent to take part in the RCT and increase the number of people to be randomised. This would assign more people to the experimental treatment group about which there is more to learn. Alternatively, given what we know about sexual offender networks (for example paedophile networks), and because of the social nature of sexual practices and community norms, it is more likely that people will change their sexual practices if there is a general change in norms of behaviour within that community. It therefore might also be suggested that future trials consider cluster randomisation trials (CRT) by using prisons, mental health units or social networks for treatments, and others as controls.

This has the advantage of logistical convenience and might avoid, although not eliminate, contamination (as there will always be some movement and communication between neighbouring populations). This method would have the advantage of capturing the effects on community infectivity when an offender goes back into (or remains in) a community and if the entire cluster is followed up it is possible to measure the impact on an offender's immediate social world. Persons are social beings and distinguishing between the individual, community and society may make little sense in order to produce change. There is growing evidence that sustained individual change is not only part of, but dependant upon, collective change, whether at the level of the community or society. Sustained sexual practices are associated with supportive social norms and community attachment. An additional advantage of a CRT is in its cost effectiveness as it can illustrate how cost effective a programme would be when applied on a large scale. Clusters may be chosen on the basis of information concerning social and sexual networks, or may be specific prisons or mental health units. In these cases it would be more efficient to have a large number of small clusters than a small number of large clusters. With this in mind, tools such as RevMan[33] may have to develop to accommodate this.

While the practicality of undertaking RCTs within a prison and a therapeutic community has already been subject to empirical assessment (Farrington & Jolliffe, 2002; Campbell, 2003) little has been done with regard to process evidence. Process evidence should inform decisions about where, when and with whom an effective intervention might be more generally deployed. Process evaluation is a necessary complement to outcome evaluation. Such a process evaluation should help to assess which of the sessions or key messages have been effective and which have not. Stephenson (2003) suggests that the development of promising intervention has less to do with RCTs than with exploratory research. Adoption of the MRC[34] approach, which develops and evaluates complex interventions, seems a logical and sensible approach to apply to sexual offending. What works now may not work in a few years' time and trials should include an assessment of contextual factors that are likely to limit or enhance the relevance of the trial now or in the future. In a population with low recidivism rates, a very large RCT trial would be needed to show a significant reduction in recidivism. In such cases it is necessary to use a combination of data: this might include not just behavioural and psychometric data as gathered presently but also ethnographic data or that from simulated clients.

Pragmatic RCTs do not explain essential features of the intervention's success or failure, such as the mechanism by which it worked and the context in which this was possible. This might lead to the adoption of an apparently effective intervention in a different setting where it is likely to fail. There are serious problems with evaluation that focuses exclusively on outcomes. Among the problems are:

[33] Cochrane Collaboration's Review Manager Software.
[34] Medical Research Council.

1) Expensive outcome studies sometimes evaluate a poorly designed intervention. If the outcome shows this is not effective then resources are wasted and it might be assumed, erroneously, that any intervention will fail.
2) Conventional RCT intention to treat analysis can lead to false conclusions and a negative outcome would be assumed to be due to inadequate intervention rather than poor delivery or lack of contrast between the different arms of a trial.
3) Outcome evaluations do little to improve our understanding of the mechanism, or social process, by which the intervention is supposed to work—thus fail to inform development of effective interventions.
4) An RCT or a complex programme will not distinguish *which* components are a success or failure.
5) Outcome evaluations do not investigate crucial contextual factors that facilitate the success of an intervention. Unless contextual factors are known it is difficult to ensure their replication in other settings.
6) Investigating the impact of evaluation of an intervention in aggregate, which is often necessary to have sufficient statistical power, does not explore different effects within the target group. Many programmes have heterogeneous effects and aggregation may obscure more than it reveals.

Thus there have been criticisms of RCTs when applied to sexual practices but we suggest that it is possible to combine the strength of RCTs with the approach put forward by Pawson (2002). The essence of this approach is a thorough understanding of the process of the intervention and good collection of process data. Pawson and Tilley's formula Outcomes = Mechanism + Context is thus an appropriate one in the area of psychological intervention for sexual offenders.

Knowledge in the field of psychological interventions for sexual offenders is incremental, and in many situations a single intervention may not be enough to change behaviour. A multi-component package with a long follow-up may be necessary. These are more complex to implement and more expensive. They may need group, individual, as well as societal change in order to change an individual's sexual practices. It may be difficult to separate out the impact of the various components in the intervention package. Thus a detailed evaluation of all the major processes that would need to occur for the intervention to have a good effect is required.

Alongside the high rate of hidden victimization (Hood, Shute, Feilzer, and Wilcox, 2002), exaggeration of the dangers that sexual offenders pose may unnecessarily increase fear in the public and hinder the genuine rehabilitation of those who *have* changed their lifestyles. This review attempts to provide an overview of treatment effectiveness so that the practitioner can draw upon this evidence. It also serves to aid the scrutiny of the effects of policy makers' responses to the social spectre of sexual offending.

Acknowledgements

This study comes from a larger systematic review of psychological interventions for people who have sexually offended or are at risk of sexually offending. We wish to thank the larger research group who comprised Professor Conor Duggan, Professor Clive Adams, Dr Lucy McCarthy, Dr Tracey Lee, and Mr Mark Fenton. The views of the authors do not necessarily represent the views of all those who contributed to the larger review. We wish to thank the NHS R&D in Forensic Mental Health for funding the study. The views of the authors do not necessarily represent the views of the NHS R&D in Forensic Mental Health. Finally, we wish to thank Ms Helene Wells who formatted the final draft.

REFERENCES

ABEL, G, BECKER, JV, CUNNINGHAM-RATHNER, J, *et al., The Treatment of Child Molesters* (New York: SBC-TM (722 West 168th Street, Box 17, New York, NY 10032), 1999).

ALEXANDER, MA, 'Sex Offender Treatment Efficacy Revisited', (1999) 11 *Sexual Abuse: A Journal of Research of Treatment* 101–116.

ANDERSON-VARNEY, TJ, 'An Evaluation of a Treatment Program for Imprisoned Child Sex Offenders: a dissertation submitted to Michigan State University' (Michigan State University, 1991).

ARKOWITZ, H, LICHTENSTEIN, B, McGOVERN, K *et al.*, 'The Behavior Assessment of Social Competence in Males' (1975) 6 *Behaviour Therapy* 3–13.

BARLOW, DH, 'Assessment of Sexual Behavior' in KR Ciminero, KR Calhoun and HE Adams (eds), *Handbook of Behavioral Assessment* (New York: John Wiley and Sons, 1977).

BEECH, A, FISHER, D, and BECKETT, R, '*STEP 3: An evaluation of the prison sex offender treatment programme*', HMSO, 1998.

BONNELL, C, BENNETT, R, and OAKLEY, A 'Sexual Health Interventions Should Be Subject To Experimental Evaluation' in JM Stephenson, J Imrie, and C Bonnell (eds), *Effective Sexual Health Interventions* (Oxford, Oxford University Press, 2003).

BROOKS-GORDON, B, BILBY, C, KENWORTHY, T *et al.*, 'A Systematic Review of Psychosocial Treatments for Adults who have Sexually Offended or are at Risk of Sexually Offending' *National R&D Programme on Forensic Mental Health, UK.* (Unpublished, 2004).

CHALMERS, TC, CELANO, P, SACKS, HS, SMITH H Jr, 'Bias in treatment assignment in controlled clinical trials' (1983) 309 *New England Journal of Medicine* 1358–61.

CLARKE, M and OXMAN, A (eds), *Cochrane Reviewers' Handbook 4.1.4.* The Cochrane Collaboration. [Updated (2001)] (Oxford: Update Software, 2001).

DAVIS, MH, 'A Multidimensional Approach to Individual Difference in Interpersonal Reactivity' (1980). 10 *JSAS Catalog of Selected Documents in Psychology* 1–85.

DESAUTELS, M, *The Therapeutic Relationship in Sex Offender Treatment.* School of Psychology, Forensic Section. University of Leicester, 2003.

ENDLER, NS, HUNT, JM and ROSENSTEIN, AJ, 'An S-R Inventory of Anxiousness' (1962), 76 *Psychological Monographs* (17): 536.

FALSHAW, L, BATES A, PATEL, V, CORBETT, C, and FRIENDSHIP, C, 'Assessing reconviction, re-offending and recidivism in a sample of UK sexual offenders' (2003) 8 *Legal and Criminological Psychology* 207–215.

FARRINGTON, D, and JOLLIFFE, D, 'A Feasibility Study into Using a Randomised Trial to Evaluate Treatment Pilots at HMP Whitemoor' *Home Office Online Report* 14/02, 2002.

FRIENDSHIP, C, BEECH, AR, and BROWNE KD, 'Reconviction as an Outcome Measure in Research. A Methodological Note' (2002) 42 *British Journal of Criminology* 442–4.

—— FALSHAW, L and BEECH, AR, (2003)' Measuring the Real Impact of Accredited Offending Behaviour Programmes' 8 *Legal and Criminological Psychology*, 115–27.

—— MANN, R and BEECH, A, 'The Prison-Based Sex Offender Treatment Programme—an Evaluation'. In: *Home Office Research, Development and Statistics Directorate Research Findings No. 205* (London: Home Office, 2003).

GRUBIN, D, *Expert Paper: Sex OffenderResearch*. NHS Programme on Forensic Mental Health Research and Development, 2002.

HANSARD, House of Commons, 15 July 2003, column 189.

HANSON, RK and BROOM, I, *Evaluating Community Sex Offender Treatment Programs: a 12-year follow-up of 724 Offenders*. (Unpublished manuscript, 2003).

—— and BUSSIERE, MT, 'Predicting Relapse: A Meta-analysis of Sexual Offender Recidivism Studies', (1998) 61 *Journal of Consulting and Clinical Psychology* 646–52.

—— and HARRIS, AJ, 'Where Should We Intervene? Dynamic Predictors of Sexual Offense Recidivism' (2000) 27 *Criminal Justice and Behavior* 6–35.

—— GORDON, A, HARRIS, AJR *et al.*,'First Report of the Collaborative Outcome Data Project on the Effectiveness of Psychological Treatment for Sex Offenders' (2002) 14 *Sexual Abuse: A Journal of Research and Treatment* 169–94.

HOPKINS, R, 'An Evaluation of Communication and Social Skills Groups for Sex Offenders at HMP Frankland' (1991) *Psychology Conference of Prison Service* 77–91.

HOOD, R, SHUTE, S, FEILZER, M *et al.*, 'Sex Offenders Emerging from Long-term Imprisonment: A Study of Their Long-Term Reconviction Rates and of Parole Board Members' Judgements of their Risk' (2002) 42 *British Journal of Criminology* (2): 371–94.

HOUSTON, J, WRENCH, M, and HOSKING, N, (1995) 'Group Processes in the Treatment of Child Sex Offenders' (1995) 6 *Journal of Forensic Psychiatry* (2): 359–68.

KIPPAX, S, 'Sexual Health Interventions are Unsuitable for Experimental Evaluation' In JM Stephenson, J Imrie and C Bonnell (eds), *Effective Sexual Health Interventions* (Oxford: Oxford University Press, 2003).

LAW SOCIETY, Managing Dangerous People With Severe Personality Disorder: Proposals For Policy Development, Response to the Home Office/Department of Health Consultation Paper, December 1999. http//www.lawsoc.org.uk/dcs/ fourth_tier.asp? Section ID 3186&Caller ID=NS92.

LEA, S, AUBURN, T, and KIBBLEWHITE, K, 'Working with Sex Offenders: The Perceptions and Experiences of Professionals and Paraprofessionals' (1999) 43 *International Journal of Offender Therapy and Comparative Criminology* (1): 103–19.

MANN, R, and THORNTON, D, 'The Evolution of a Multisite Sexual Offender Program' in WL Marshall, YM Fernandez, SM Hudson and T Ward (eds), *Sourcebook of Treatment Programs for Sexual Offenders* (47–57). (New York: Plenum Press, 1998).

MARQUES, JK, DAY, DM, NELSON, C, and WEST, MA, 'Effects of Cognitive-Behavioural Treatment on Sex Offender Recidivism' (1994) 21 *Criminal Justice and Behaviour* 28–54.

McANANEY, M, *Heterosocial Skills Training with Sex Offenders: A Dissertation Presented to the Graduate Council of the University of Florida* (University of Florida, 1981).

McCONAGHY, N, BLASZCZYNSKI, A, ARMSTRONG, MS, and KIDSON, W, 'Resistance to Treatment of Adolescent Sex Offenders' (1988) 18 *Archives of Sexual Behavior* 97–107.

McCONAGHY, N, ARMSTRONG, MS, and BLASZCZYNSKI, A, 'Expectancy, Covert Sensitization and Imaginal Desensitization in Compulsive Sexuality' (1985) 72 *Acta Psychiatricia Scandinavicia* 176–87.

McGRATH, RJ, CUMMING, G, LIVINGSTON, J and HOKE, S, 'Outcome of a Treatment Program for Adult Sex Offenders: From Prison to Community' (2003) 18 *Journal of Interpersonal Violence* 3–18.

McGUIRE, J, 'Defining Correctional Programs' (2000) 12 *Forum on Corrections Research* 5–9.

MOHER, D, SCHULZ, KF, and ALTMAN, D, 'The CONSORT Statement: Revised Recommendations for Improving the Quality of Reports of Parallel-group Randomized Trials' (2001) *JAMA* 285(15): 1987–1991.

NICOLAS, HR and MOLINDER, I, *Multiphasic Sex Inventory Manual* (1984). Available from Nicolas and Molinder, 437 Bowes Drive, Tacoms, WA 98466.

PAWSON, R, 'Evidence-Based Policy: The Promise of 'Realist Synthesis'' (2002) 8 *Evaluation* (3): 340–358.

—— and TILLY, N, *Realistic Evaluation* (London: Sage, 1997).

PERKINS, D, HAMMOND, S, COLES, D, and BISHOPP, D, *Review of Sex Offender Treatment Programmes*. Department of Psychology, Broadmoor Hospital. (Prepared for the High Security Psychiatric Services Commissioning Board (HSPSCB), 1998).

POPAY, J, ROGERS, A, and WILLIAMS, G, 'Rationale and Standards for the Systematic Review of Qualitative Literature in Health Services Research' (1998) 8 *Qualitative Health Research* (3): 341–51.

PROCHASKA, JO, *Systems of Psychotherapy* (Homewood, Illinois: The Dorsey Press, 1984).

QUINSEY, VL, KHANNA, A, and MALCOLM, B, 'A Retrospective Evaluation of the Regional Treatment Centre Sex Offender Treatment Program', (1998) 13 *Journal of Interpersonal Violence* 621–44.

ROMERO, JJ and WILLIAMS, LM, 'Group Psychotherapy and Intensive Probation Supervision with Sex Offenders' (1983) *Federal Probation* 47: 36–42.

ROOTH, FG and MARKS, IM, 'Persistent Exhibitionism: Short-Term Response to Aversion, Self-regulation, and Relaxation Treatments' (1974) 3 *Archives of Sexual Behavior* (3): 227–49.

ROSENBERG, MJ, *Society and the Adolescent Self-image* (Princeton, NY: Princeton University Press, 1965).

RYAN, PE, A *Study of the Effect of the Transtheoretical Approach upon Sex Offenders: a Dissertation Submitted to the Faculty of the School of Religious Education, Southwestern Baptist Theological Seminary* (Southwestern Baptist Theological Seminary, 1997).

SCHEELA, RA, 'Sex Offender Treatment: Therapists' Experiences and Perceptions' (2001) 22 *Issues in Mental Health and Nursing* (8): 749–67.

SCHEELA, RA, 'The Remodelling Process: A Grounded Theory Study of Perceptions of Treatment among Adult Male Incest Offenders' (1992) 18 *Journal of Offender Rehabilitation* (3/4): 167–89.

SPENCE, JT and HELMREICH, RL, 'The Attitudes Toward Woman Scale: an Objective Instrument to Measure Attitudes towards the Rights and Roles of Women in Contemporary Society' (1978) 2 *Psychological Documents* 1–153.

SOOTHILL, K, FRANCIS, B, SANDERSON, B, and ACKERLEY, E, 'Sex Offenders: Specialists, Generalists or Both? A 32-year Criminological Study' (2000) 40 *British Journal of Criminology* 56–67.

STEPHENSON, J, IMRIE, J, and BONNELL, C, *Effective Sexual Health Interventions* (Oxford: Oxford University Press, 2003).

WALKER, N (ed), *Dangerous People*, (London, Blackstone Press, 1996).

WARD, T, HUDSON, S and MARSHALL, W, 'Attachment Style in Sex Offenders: A Preliminary Study', (1996) 33 *Sexual Abuse: A Journal of Research and Treatment* 17–26.

WARD, T and SIEGART, RJ, 'Toward a Comprehensive Theory of Child Sexual Abuse: A Theory Knitting Perspective' (2002) *Psychology Crime and the Law*, 319–53.

WATSON, D and FRIEND, R, 'Measurement of Social Evaluative Anxiety' (1969) 33 *Journal of Consulting and Clinical Psychology* 448–57.

WHITE, P, BRADLEY, C, FERRITER, M, and HATZIPETROU, L, 'Managements for People with Disorders of Sexual Preference and for Convicted Sexual Offenders' (1998) *Cochrane Review*, Cochrane Library, Issue 3, Oxford Update Software.

WOOD, RM, GROSSMAN, LS, and FICHTNER, CG, 'Psychological Assessment, Treatment and Outcome with Sex Offenders' (2000) 18 *Behavioral Sciences and the Law* 23–41.

WOOLF, H, (1991) *Prison Disturbances April 1990* Report of an Enquiry by Rt. Hon. Lord Justice Woolf (Parts I and II) and His Honour Judge Steven Tumin (Part II) Cm 1456 (London: HMSO).

APPENDIX CHARACTERISTICS OF INCLUDED RANDOMISED CONTROL STUDIES

Study ID	Methods	Participants	Interventions	Outcomes	Notes
Anderson-Varney (1991)	Allocation: randomised, pre-test post-test two group design Blinding: not mentioned. Duration: 2 months Setting: medium secure prison.	Problem: child sex offenders N=60. Sex: men. Age: mean ~39 years (SD 10). History: convicted of sex offence against children <14 years old, no previous sex offender treatment, IQ >94, not due for parole.	1. Cognitive, social educational programme: cognitive restructuring (challenging irrational beliefs, increasing beliefs of control, developing interpersonal effectiveness), social skills training (developed for sex offenders, didactic and experimental, teaching re appearance and interaction), sex education (factual information re sexuality and opinions and attitudes) 2 × 1.5 hour sessions / week of each component, 15 sessions. N=30. 2. Control: standard care (no treatment programme) N=30.	Behaviour, dysfunction and knowledge: MSI. Cognitions: ABCS. Attitudes: ATWS. Distress, self esteem: IRI. Social avoidance: SADS.	No person left the study early—but this was not an option as none were due for parole.

Study ID	Methods	Participants	Interventions	Outcomes	Notes
Hopkins (1991)	Allocation: by random sampling —no further details. Blindness: not reported. Duration: 6 months follow up. Setting: prison.	Problem: rapists, paedophiles, incest offenders. N=15. Sex: not reported. Age: not reported.	1. Communication, relationship emotional control and decision making groups: 6 sessions 2hours/ week, 8 weeks. N=8. 2. Standard care waiting list. N=7. Self esteem: Rosenburg's Self-Esteem Scale. Social anxiety and distress: FNE, SADS.	Unable to use — Confidence, learning & enjoyment: (no usable data).	
Marques (1994)	Allocation: randomised — matched by age, type of offence & criminal history— no further details. Setting: Psychiatric inpatient, Atascadero State Hospital, USA.	Problem: 96 molesters of female children, 43 of male. Duration: mean 38.4 months. Inclusion criteria: volunteers to Sex Offender Treatment and Evaluation Project, California, within 18–30 months of release,	1. Relapse prevention programme: cognitive behavioural training, decision matrices, relaxation training, stress & anger management, attendance at community meetings & leisure/recreational activity. Two year treatment intervention	Re-offending (measured by new sex crime or non-sex violent interpersonal crime recorded on automated records (rapsheets) and reports from parole system. Unable to use—	Individuals may also have received treatment for drug/ alcohol problems & behaviour therapy for sexual deviation (olfactory aversion, masturbatory satiation or orgasmic

<3 felonies, IQ 80+, spoke English, admitted offence, no psychotic or organic disorder, not medically debilitated, not severe management problem in prison. N=155. Age: between 18–60 years. IQ: 80+ Language; English History: all participants serving sentence for child molestation or rape, have no more than 2 previous felony convictions, no pending holds or warrants, have 18–30 months until release from prison, admit their offence, and have no psychotic / organic mental illness

(range 14–30 months). N=76.* 2. Control. no treatment. N=79.

Personal responsibility (CDI, J scale, MSI—no SD).

reconditioning). All participants also attended an aftercare programme for 1 year after release.

Study ID	Methods	Participants	Interventions	Outcomes	Notes
McAnaney (1981)	Allocation: randomly allocated using a table of random numbers. Blindness: not blind. Duration: 6 weeks. Setting: Forensic hospital inpatient, Florida, USA.	Problem: paedophiles (15), rapists (25) N=40. Sex: men. Age: mean 25.5 (no range provided). History: Convicted of sex offence, has psychosexual disorder, did not attempt murder, has sentence between 1–11 years.	1. Heterosocial skills training module plus standard care: Skills module included conversation skills, self esteem, body image, negative self talk and anxiety and accepts treatment. 8 × 2hour sessions over 6 weeks. N=20. 2. Control (standard care). N=20.	Heterosocial skills: HSB. Anxiety: SRIA. Self esteem: SSI. Leaving the study early.	
McConaghy (1985)	Allocation: randomised, no further details. Blinding: interviewer blinded, not tested. Duration: 1 year follow up. Setting: psychiatric inpatients.	Problem: exhibitionists (8), compulsive homosexuals (5)*, homosexual paedophiles (4), heterosexual paedophile (1), clothes fetishist (1), exhibitionist and voyeur (1) N=20. Sex: men. Age: mean 36 years, range 15–72.	1. Covert sensitisation: imagine target sexual experience until arousal, then imagine powerful negative experience, 2 × 20min sessions day 1, 3 × 20 min sessions day 2–5. N=10. 2. Imaginal desensitisation: imagine target sexual experience avoiding arousal by substitution of non-target conclusion,	Global: requesting further treatment. Mental state: desire for target behaviour. Behaviour: no change or increase of target behaviour. Unable to use— Global: need for further treatment (no data reported). Behaviour:	Not within criteria of this review, not possible to separate results out from others, but 25% of total so included.

		History: 13 convicted, requested behavioural treatment, not overtly psychotic.	2 × 20min sessions day 1, 3 × 20 min sessions day 2–5. N=10.	intercourse, heterosexual desire (impossible to interpret). Expectancy of success of treatment: (unpublished measure, no usable data). Anxiety: STAI— forms X1 (1month), X2 (1 year), (no SD). Leaving the study early (not reported by group).*
McConaghy (1988)	Allocation: randomly allocated, no further details. Blindness: not blind. Duration: treatment drug – 5 days, ID 6 months, follow up 1 year. Setting: Behaviour	Problem: anomalous sexual urges and behaviours (DSM-III), 1+ paraphilia, 2+ low IQ. N=31. Age: mean 30 years; range Sex: male. History: 19 convicted for sex offences, requested treatment, not actively psychotic.	Anomalous desire & behaviour. Unable to use—Mental state (Spielberger State Trait Anxiety—no SD). 10 people also given meproxyprogesterone alone; unclear if randomized to separate group (not included in review as did not receive what is	

Study ID	Methods	Participants	Interventions	Outcomes	Notes
McConaghy (1988) (*Cont.*)	therapy unit, inpatient, Australia. 16–50.	1. Imaginal desensitisation. N=10. 2. Meproxyprogesterone: dose 150mg IM fortnightly × 4 followed by monthly injection × 4. N=10. 3. Meproxyprogesterone: dose 150mg IM fortnightly × 4 followed by monthly injection × 4 and imaginal desensitisation. N=11.	being defined as tension and abnormal sexual urges (visual analogue scales—no usable data). 'standard').		
Romero (1983)	Allocation: randomly allocated, no further details. Blindness: not blind. Duration: follow up 10 years. Setting: community, no further information available.	Problem: paedophiles (48), exhibitionists (39), assaulters(144). N=289,* 231 by 10 years. Sex: men. Age: range 18–50. History: 170 of sample had previous arrests for sex offences.	1. Group therapy plus probation (standard care): 1 hour group therapy per week for 40 weeks, plus 1 probation home visit per month. 2. Probation (standard care):1 report to probation per month plus 1 home visit per month.	Recidivism—as measured by rearrest for a sex offence. Unable to use—Leaving the study (no data by group). Psychiatric interview schedule (no data). Social interview schedule (no data). Projective test battery: Rorschach,	* by 10 years 231 men remain in cohort. We have found no information on the original numbers assigned to groups.

				Thematic Apperception Test, Bender Gestalt, House-Tree-Person, Self drawing, Hand & IES tests, Sentence Completion test (no data). Psychometric tests: Revised Beta IQ test, Cornell Medical Index, Cattell PF-16 Personality Index, Self rating scale (no data).
Rooth (1974)	Allocation: randomised, Latin square, crossover. Blindness: not mentioned. Duration: 1 week before crossover (preceded by 1 week in hospital). Setting: psychiatric inpatient.	Problem: persistent exhibitionists. N=12. Sex: men. Age: mean 32 years, range 18–53. History: mean duration of problem 16 years, range 5–40, 10 convicted indecent exposure, 6 paedophilic behaviour.	1. Electrical aversion to images: when self reported, occurring during rehearsal—increased to additional self-administered shocks during fantasy after patient 6, 15 shocks × 2 daily 45 min sessions 4 days, standard battery operated shock box, semi-sound-proofed	Leaving the study early. Unable to use—Attitude: semantic differential scales, linear scales, situations scores (no usable data before Target problem: linear scales (no usable data before

Study ID	Methods	Participants	Interventions	Outcomes	Notes
Rooth (1974) (*Cont.*)			room. N=4. 2. Self regulation: accounts of typical acts repeated played back during exposure in mirror and person expressed feelings about situation—increased by one private session imagining a scene with noxious image to counteract it after patient 6, 2 daily 45 min sessions for 4 days. N=4. 3. Relaxation treatments: standard relaxation training—increased to additional private session after patient 6, 2 daily 45 min sessions 4 days. N=4.	crossover). Mood: linear scales (no usable data before crossover).	
Ryan (1997)	Allocation: cluster randomised, 'drawing from the pool of groups'.* Blinding: not	Problem: sexual act not permitted by governing state (Texas) or federal statute. N=8 (groups	1. Transtheoretical approach: counselling identifying awareness or desire to change & assists change,	Cognitive distortions and immaturity: MSI. Sexual knowledge & beliefs: MSI.	* Design effect calculated as $1-((m-1)*ICC)$. m=mean size of group—taken as 8.

undertaken. Duration: immediate on treatment cessation. Setting: psychiatric outpatients.	of 7–9 people). Sex: men. Age: 18 years and over. History: convicted of a sex offence and sentenced to probation/on parole from prison.	24 weekly 1.5 hour sessions. N=4 groups. 2. Group therapy: counselling re relapse prevention and cognitive behavioural strategies, 24 weekly 1.5 hour sessions. N=4 groups.	Sexual obsessions: MSI. Social sexual desirability: MSI. Treatment attitudes scale: MSI. Unable to use—Leaving the study early (data impossible to interpret). Lie scale: MSI (unable to account for clustering). Justification scale: MSI (unable to account for clustering).	ICC= Interclass Correlation Co-efficient= taken as 0.1

ABCS—*Abel and Becker Cognition Scale*
ATWS—*Attitudes Towards Women Scale*
FNE—*Fear of Negative Evaluation Scale*
HSB—*Heterosocial Skills Behaviour Checklist*
IRI—*Interpersonal Reactivity Index*
MSI—*Multiphasic Sex Inventory*
SADS—*Social Avoidance and Distress Scale*
SRIA—*S-R Inventory of Anxiousness*
SSI—*Social Self-Esteem Inventory*
STAI—*Spielberger State-Trait Anxiety Inventory*

Index